RUPERT MURDOCH

*Ringmaster of the
Information Circus*

———◆———

WILLIAM
SHAWCROSS

Chatto & Windus
LONDON

Published in 1992 by
Chatto & Windus Ltd
20 Vauxhall Bridge Road
London SW1V 2SA

A CIP catalogue record for this book is
available from the British Library.

ISBN 0 7011 3451 8

Index by David Lee

Phototypeset by Intype, London
from author's discs prepared by
Coral Pepper
Printed in Great Britain by
Mackays of Chatham, Plc, Chatham, Kent

For Olga, with love

Contents

Contents

Contents

List of Illustrations

between pages 114 and 115

1 Rupert Murdoch's maternal grandfather, Rupert Greene.
2 His paternal grandfather, the Reverend Patrick John Murdoch.
3 Keith Murdoch's official farewell from Lord Northcliffe in London.
4 Rupert Murdoch, aged 5, with Sir Keith.
5 Sir Keith and Lady Murdoch in 1942.
6 Rupert Murdoch on his investigation into aboriginal affairs, 1957.
7 On his yacht *Ilina*, 1960.
8 Rupert Murdoch's marriage to Anna Torv, 1967.
9 Rupert and Anna Murdoch arrive in London with their daughter, 1968.
10 Addressing the meeting of *News of the World* shareholders, 1969.
11 The proprietor of *The Australian* defends the *News of the World*, 1970.
12 At the White House with President Kennedy and Zell Rabin in 1962.
13 Graham King.
14 Max Newton.
15 Rupert Murdoch on the front cover of *Time* magazine, 1977.
16 On the purchase of Times Newspapers, 1981, with Harold Evans and William Rees-Mogg.
17 At *The Times* bicentenary with Margaret and Denis Thatcher.

List of Illustrations

between pages 274 and 275

Author's Note

This is an unauthorized biography. When I began the research, I asked Rupert Murdoch to talk to me. He took a year to consider and in that time I spoke with many of his colleagues and former associates around the world. He then agreed to be interviewed.

I was conscious that, like any biographer of a living person with limited access to individuals and documents, I was dealing only with pieces of the mosaic that made up Murdoch's life. Because he was most helpful, and never sought to impose any conditions upon me, I sent him a draft of the manuscript. He chose to make no comment.

Through the story of Murdoch's trajectory – from Adelaide, through Sydney, London, New York and on to Hollywood – I have tried to understand and describe how he and the communications revolution are changing the world.

The Murdoch Empire

MURDOCH FAMILY

CRUDEN INVESTMENTS — 54% → QUEENSLAND PRESS

41%

46%

NEWS CORPORATION

ASSOCIATED COMPANIES	SUBSIDIARIES
South China Morning Post (50%)	News International (100%)
Pacific Magazines (45%)	Harper Collins (100%)
BSkyB (50%)	News Limited (100%)
Ansett (50%)	Fox Inc. (100%)
IML, New Zealand (50%)	News America Publishing (100%)

Prologue

ON THE ROAD

At the end of 1990, as Rupert Murdoch circulated his proposal for an autobiography which, he promised, would reveal "the fundamental reason I've been successful and other people aren't", his company, News Corporation, nearly disintegrated. On several occasions, the empire that, over the last forty years, he had flung from Adelaide to Hollywood, was minutes away from liquidation.

A handful of companies now dominate the market in the most powerful and lucrative commodity in the world. That commodity is information: its trade is changing the face of the globe and delineating the future. Among these companies, only News Corporation stretches right around the earth and was built and controlled by one man, Rupert Keith Murdoch, native of Australia and citizen of the United States.

Murdoch's power is phenomenal, but the way in which he has acquired it makes him peculiarly vulnerable. By 1990 he had finally reached too far. He and his bankers were embroiled in a hideously complex attempt to roll over and reschedule $7.6 billion of debt which he had accumulated in his attempt to create the largest media company in the Western world.

In the preceding months, a banking crisis, a collapse in the advertising market and a recession exacerbated by the prospect of war in the Gulf had led to an unprecedented credit squeeze. Murdoch had suffered the worst months of his life, a constant round of asking help from people to whom he had never before had to talk, begging banks to renew his debt. Until recently he had not known that his principal lenders had resold parcels of his debt so widely that he now had 146 different creditors all over the world. He was nearly sixty years old, and he was exhausted.

On the morning of 6 December 1990, Murdoch was in Zürich, attempting to charm and cajole officials at Crédit Suisse. That afternoon he flew to London. With him was Dave DeVoe, a forty-four-year-old American, recently appointed as his chief financial officer, with instructions to save the company.

The plane landed late – "Everything was delayed," Murdoch recalled afterwards in his clipped, staccato, but soft tone. As soon as they touched down, Murdoch was on the phone. He ran the company by phone.

He talked incessantly from the car as he and DeVoe were driven into London. There had been continual crises for weeks now, but this one was ominous. Murdoch's fate was in the hands of one little-known bank, the Pittsburgh National, which was refusing at the eleventh hour to roll over a loan. It was a small bank with a minute loan – a A$10 million share of a larger facility. "We didn't really know them well," said Murdoch later. "They had come in through some Australian syndication." The Pittsburgh National Bank knew almost nothing about News Corporation.

"We had to call Pittsburgh," said Murdoch. "Didn't want to do it from the car phone. Went to my apartment." Murdoch's London home is an elegant duplex, overlooking St James's Park, with a marble staircase, dazzling Australian paintings and an English butler. Dave DeVoe placed a call to Pittsburgh, while Murdoch listened.

It was not an encouraging moment, Murdoch said subsequently. "The guy there just said we had to give them the money."

"We said, 'We can't. You know what that means. We'd go out of business.'

"He said, 'That's right.'

"We said, 'You're telling us to liquidate our company?' And he said yes."

DeVoe explained, as he had done a hundred times to different bankers, that News had only a liquidity problem. They were meeting with their principal banks. They had a well-structured plan. They had terrific assets. They were going to get out of this hole.

The man in Pittsburgh was sceptical, DeVoe recalled. "He said,

'I'm sorry, I hear what you are saying. We don't think you have the ability to repay us. Let's put it into receivership.' "

It was horrific, said Murdoch later. "*Horrific!* They were saying, 'Liquidate your company.' All for $10 million!"

If this bank refused to roll, News would be on an unstoppable slide into bankruptcy. The company would go into worldwide default, and that would accelerate all of its public debt. Refinancing would probably be impossible. It would also destroy the company's relations with its trade creditors, to whom it owed some US$3 billion worldwide. One of the most significant companies in the history of global industry would unravel. Everything he had battled for would be lost – in a matter of hours.

Rupert Murdoch was born into a powerful, upper-middle-class Melbourne family. As a young man, he was on the left of politics, celebrating (or appearing to celebrate) Vladimir Ilyich Lenin. By 1990 he was proudly, fixedly on the right, a supporter and friend of Ronald Reagan and Margaret Thatcher, contemptuous of communism, loathing liberalism. His latterday political certainties had earned him almost as many enemies as his acquisitiveness. For some, particularly in Britain and Australia, he had acquired a kind of demonic status. "Lucifer-like" or "Satanic" were terms frequently applied to him by his enemies. Yet his friends and many of his associates spoke of him in terms close to adoration.

He did not give a fig for his enemies. He was sure that what he was doing was correct – though he often seemed at a loss to describe just exactly what he *was* doing, let alone *why*.

At almost sixty, Murdoch was a little stooped but slim and lithe. Like his company, he was in perpetual motion, fidgeting, writing with cheap Pentels, doodling, adding up figures, scarcely ever in repose. In recent years his face had become craggy, somewhat careworn. It could look with kindness, or it could snarl. The lines betrayed both expressions. His eyes were often distant, fixed beyond his companion or his audience, on some distant goal or problem.

News Corporation was testimony to his extraordinary, incessant, brilliant, intuitive instinct – and to his belief that he had become invincible. He had built the company himself after inheriting a small Adelaide newspaper from his father, a prominent Australian newspaper man, almost forty years before. His father had been a manager not an owner, and most of his power had died with him. Rupert Murdoch had determined never to work for anyone.

Since the 1950s, Rupert Murdoch's life had been an endless assault upon the world. One tactical or strategic battle followed another, on and on, incessantly moving, questing, searching, striving, fighting, cajoling, bullying, demanding, charming, pushing – always for more. More newspapers, more television, more space, more power. His life appeared to be a series of psychic leaps, in perpetual acceleration and endless acquisition, with no step, however great, being far enough, no new property an adequate reward. "My past," he said, "consists of a series of interlocking wars."

It had always been so. Since taking over the Adelaide *News* in 1953, his skirmishes, engagements, victories and occasional defeats could be traced in bold lines all over the globe, beginning in Adelaide and stretching to Hollywood.

He had reached first across Australia, to Perth and then Sydney. In the mid-1960s he had created *The Australian*, the first major national paper on the continent, and had sustained it ever since, through many years of losses. Then, as he built up television interests in Australia, he stretched out to New Zealand and Hong Kong. At the end of the 1960s, he acquired his first properties in Britain, the tabloid *News of the World* and the *Sun*. In the 1970s he had reached over to America, buying papers in Texas, starting a new supermarket tabloid, the *National Star*, and acquiring the *New York Post*, the *Village Voice* and *New York* magazine. In the early 1980s he bought more television stations in Australia, half of one of Australia's principal airlines, and Britain's most venerable paper, *The Times*, together with its sibling the *Sunday Times*.

The mid-1980s had been the period of greatest expansion. In America he acquired the *Boston Herald*, the *Chicago Sun-Times*, and, most importantly, Twentieth Century-Fox film studios and Metromedia television stations, which he had melded into a fourth national television network, Fox Broadcasting. To establish a foothold in Asia, he bought Hong Kong's principal paper, the *South China Morning Post*. Back in Australia he took over his father's old paper, the Melbourne *Herald*; then he acquired one of America's oldest publishers, Harper & Row, as well as William Collins, the British publishers, and Triangle, the American group which owned *TV Guide*. Those were just some of the most important of his acquisitions; in the 1980s, the company, which he and his family controlled absolutely, fought for and bought at least thirty new and very diverse international properties. In News Corporation's 1990 annual report, Murdoch announced that with the purchase of Triangle, News Corp's revenue had grown 31 per cent in one year, to almost A$8 billion. But Triangle had cost him US$3 billion, which was considerably more than it was worth. In that same year he had launched his British satellite television service, Sky, which he planned as the core of an international television network to be carried by satellite around the world.

His achievements made Murdoch a major player in the information revolution and the vast communications industry which was driving it, and from which his global power now derived. In the early 1990s, communications is the ninth largest industry in the United States, but it is growing at almost 10 per cent per annum – faster than any other sector save health and medicine.

The world is defined by the extent of communications. The pace of communications today and their extent both shrink and expand the world. Every part of the developed world can be instantly in contact with every other. This means shrinkage. But as the world shrinks, so individual horizons are extended. Arnold Toynbee pointed out decades ago that, in the twentieth century, for the first time it is possible for mankind to contemplate the welfare of the entire race. By the beginning of the twenty-first century, the linkages will embrace the globe like a web of immense complexity. Since the end of the 1980s, Marshall McLuhan's predictions have proved correct. Communications continue to lock much of the world into a global village. And in that village, Murdoch is one of the most powerful barons.

But, just as railroads joined some points and not others in the nineteenth century, so modern communications are unevenly spread. The information map of the world is like a weather map. It shows a dense mass of organized information over North America, Europe, and Japan, very little over the Soviet Union, and almost nothing over Africa. The greater the information activity, the greater the wealth.

The pace of technological change in the world today is infinitely faster than anything that the world has ever seen. Printing was developed in the fifteenth century by Gutenberg. The effects of that breakthrough were spread over centuries. Then came the telegraph (1837), the modern typewriter (1867), carbon paper (1872), and the telephone (1876). Our present revolution is driven by microelectronic technology. Economics has become secondary as a force for change. Politics finishes a poor third.

The industrial society is being replaced by the "Information Society", which is transforming the world's economy, its political institutions, the nature of sovereignty and traditional relationships between governments and peoples, between people and power.

One hundred years ago, less than 10 per cent of the labour force was involved in "information" activities. The vast majority was employed in agriculture and industry. Today over half the labour force of the United States works in the information area. Agriculture and industry together account for only about 30 per cent, and are no longer the major engines of social development. They are being replaced by a force which is still undefined. It draws on human resource capital to transfer knowledge into many kinds of physical and social activity, to generate wealth in new ways, and in so doing to alter profoundly goals and values. We are moving towards a world in which information production and distribution will overshadow material production.

Other activities will not disappear. But their importance will diminish. What is now called "software" – the printed word, film, computer disks – will continue to increase in intellectual and commercial value. The new information machines – computers – amplify intelligence dramatically, just as the machines of the Industrial Revolution amplified physical strength.

With the technological revolution has come a financial revolution. The growth of the world financial market in the last twenty years is so vast that it is almost impossible to conceive of. In the 1960s the volume of foreign exchange transactions was about $3 trillion a year – a trillion being a million million. In 1984 it was about $32 trillion. The next year it *doubled* – to $65 trillion. By

6

1987 it was about $87 trillion, which was more than twenty-three times the US Gross National Product, several times the Gross World Product. Nowadays billions of dollars are traded daily on sparkling screens in Tokyo, London and New York. The trade is constant and the profits are vast.

Historically, a characteristic of national sovereignty was that nation states should issue currency and mandate its value. Now, the international "market" weighs and assesses currencies every minute of the day. At first politicians were slow to realize what was happening, but the money traders swiftly drove their trading caravans across the new electronic routes, and thus created a new monetary system governed by the Information Standard.

Every minute of every day detailed information about every major country's political, economic and fiscal policies is transmitted to hundreds of thousands of screens in trading rooms around the globe. There is no place to hide. The new world favours those who pursue policies of which the traders approve.

The questions and the problems raised by these revolutions are stupendous. The information overload, to use Alvin Toffler's phrase, is both back-breaking and mind-breaking. In the post-industrial Information Age, people begin to ask whether full access to all information is desirable even if it were feasible. There is a danger of a new kind of literacy gap stemming from unequal access to the resources of new communications and information technologies.

Democratic societies must consider such issues as unequal access to information. They have to weigh the implications of a literacy gap on concepts such as "the consent of the governed". And if it is true that we neither need nor can cope with it all, what responsibilities does that place upon the so-called gatekeepers, the journalists and publishers whose tasks are to sift, distil, interpret and disseminate information?

On the international scale there is another consequence, unacceptable to many. It is the ineluctable spread of the American Dream. The new communications networks are like a huge megaphone blaring American messages across the world.

Already by the end of the 1970s, "US cultural imperialism" had stirred great resentment and contributed, for example, to the

rise of Shia fundamentalism in the Middle East. It had also embroiled UNESCO in a hopeless and costly debate about the Western
domination of the flow of news.

But the amount of information flowing across the world from
the United States in the 1970s was nothing to what is now being
exported. Half a dozen companies now control a vast proportion
of the world's media. Time-Warner is the largest media organization in history, controlling an unprecedented number of periodic-
als, books, films and television – in all stages of creation, production and dissemination. Following close behind are companies
controlled by Sony, Bertelsmann, Berlusconi, Disney – and Murdoch's News Corporation. Although only two of these companies
are wholly American-controlled, all are inspired and informed by
American values and American products (even Sony has married
itself to Hollywood.)

"Entertainment" is a vast American growth industry. The
volume of global communications traffic is growing at between 10
and 15 per cent a year – which means that it is roughly doubling
every six years. Much of this comes from the United States. Even
as America's political and economic influence is declining, its
cultural influence continues to grow. Euro Disney opened its gates
in 1992 to complaints by French intellectuals that it was a "cultural
Chernobyl" and the ultimate trap set by the mighty American
mouse. Michael Jackson and Madonna or their successors will
continue to be the greatest international stars and, as such, the
worldwide prophets of the American Dream. It is a dream in
which millions of people have believed for over a century, and in
which Rupert Murdoch has much invested. He is an agent of
influence.

Until 1990 Murdoch had seemed unstoppable and invincible –
both in his own eyes and those of his lenders. Since his victory
over the British print unions at his new plant at Wapping in 1986-
7, News Corporation's revenues and profits before interest had
doubled, and assets had quadrupled. But his new debt had also
increased fourfold. Murdoch had always refused to finance expansion by share issues, because he did not wish to dilute his family's
45 per cent share of the company. He was determined never to

relinquish control. Until the end of the 1980s bankers had been on their knees to Murdoch, begging him to take their cash. But by mid-1990, the financial climate had changed.

The crisis had begun to loom early in 1990 as the euphoria of the political revolutions of 1989 was followed by an international recession of unexpected severity. One of the earliest warnings of a liquidity crisis came in the first half of 1990, when the Japanese suddenly withdrew from the short-term money market in Australia. News Corporation had a borrowing programme of up to A$200 million in this market, where it was in the habit of borrowing overnight, seven-day or thirty-day money. Suddenly this facility was gone.

By the middle of 1990, the orderly retreat of the banks had turned into a rout. Never had the lending markets seemed so dry. The banks themselves were under great pressure as a result of their earlier, injudicious sprees. "We were dealing with a very fragile banking system," said Murdoch.

It was not only Murdoch who was suffering. The shares in Maxwell Communications, the media company run by his long-time rival, Robert Maxwell, had also collapsed – again because of concern at the size of the debt that the company had taken on to finance huge acquisitions.

When News Corporation's annual results were published in August 1990, "They showed us with a lot of short-term debt which shocked the market," said Murdoch, $2.3 billion to be precise. Or £1.2 billion. Or A$2.9 billion. Six times that of the previous year. Murdoch had made a serious mistake. He had expected short-term rates to go down and had therefore kept a lot of borrowings in short-term loans ready to be changed into long-term debt when it became cheaper. Instead, all rates had risen sharply.

At the end of September, the company faced unprecedented difficulties in either repaying or rescheduling a $500 million short-term loan. This was the first time that Murdoch had ever found himself in such a position. He had always prided himself – and the banks had always toasted him – for the fact that over almost forty years he had met every single payment on schedule. Worse still, some $2.9 billion of debt was due to mature between September

1990 and the middle of 1991. One banker described News Corporation's situation to the *Financial Times* as "somewhat terminal".

The banks granted the 30 September roll, for one more month, very unhappily. But only on condition that News Corp agree to rearrange its maddening jungle of debt and adopt a sensible business plan. Citibank, as News's largest creditor, was charged with unravelling the mess and restructuring the company. The project, codenamed "Dolphin", was put in the hands of a vice president of the bank, Ann Lane. In the next few months Murdoch came to depend on Lane as he had on no one else in his life.

Lane was a slim, well-dressed young woman with a firm handshake, short dark hair and blue eyes that looked straight at you. Born and brought up in New Jersey, the oldest child in a "crazy family", she attended Berkeley and then spent several years in finance before joining Citibank in 1982.

She had spent the first part of 1990 restructuring Donald Trump. Murdoch was her encore and she found him a welcome change. Like everyone else, she had heard of Murdoch, but she had not been very familiar with his company or what he owned. As she began to understand News, Ann Lane came to admire Murdoch, and to like him. She realized she was faced with a restructuring that was unparalleled in size and scope. In Murdoch's frantic dash to create a worldwide empire, News had borrowed from all over the world – Australia, the UK, Japan, the Netherlands, the United States, Singapore, Hong Kong, India, and many other places besides. There were hundreds of different News Corp companies; each one had different guarantees and different types of loans.

Lane set up a team. First, she made them find out to which News Corp companies money had been lent. Then they had to determine the structure of the companies. Thirdly, they had to arrive at a clear overall picture. Finally, they had to decide where to go from there.

She found that the main banks had sold loans on and on, and that News Corp now owed money to 146 financial institutions. And the money was in ten different currencies. Lane and her team were continually asking themselves, and each other, and News

Corp people, "Where are we? Where are the companies? Where are the lenders? What do we have? What's everyone's relative position? Where are they negotiating from?" News Corp's financial and organizational charts looked like nightmare wiring circuits assembled by a Frankenstein.

As Lane began to compile the information, the share price went into free-fall. The Australian Stock Exchange demanded an explanation. "What's happened to our share price?" repeated Murdoch. "The history of the world over the last three months has happened to our share price." The more complicated it all appeared, the more simple Lane knew the solution had to be. She could not afford to allow any alternatives or choices – there were so many players that they would talk the whole thing into oblivion. What she had to do was to deliver the company, to reduce its debt. Every bank and institution, but *every one*, had to roll over its loans in order to give Murdoch time. And she had also to tie down News and Murdoch himself. That would not be easy. Until now, Murdoch had always run the company like an Australian Red Baron, by the seat of his pants.

By the second half of October, Lane and her team had divided the banks into three tiers. Tier I consisted of nine banks who were major lenders who had made it clear that they would not provide new loans on their own. They wanted any new monies necessary to keep the company functioning to come from a broader group of banks.

In Tier II there were about thirty banks which were to join Tier I as new money lenders. Tier III banks were in for no new money and, because they were the smallest investors, many of them thought that their participation was not vital. Ann Lane would not agree.

As she was trying to corral the banks, Lane had to whip News Corporation into order. She insisted the company come up with a sound business plan based on what it thought its various companies could earn.

To hear members of her team tell it, people at News started to panic. News Corp was a company that had never known serious financial covenants. The whole company's ethos was to wing it. Ann Lane wanted to put a stake through the company's heart.

Almost twenty-four hours a day Lane stormed round her office in an Armani suit and old sneakers, shouting people into line. She demanded a fully developed and defensible business plan that would allow the loans to be extended, would provide enough cash flow to cover both the increased pricing and a $600 million one-year bridge loan – and also the $2.4 billion debt amortization over three years. She warned them they would be held to the plan, so they had better understand its assumptions.

In the end, the summary of the plan was the size of a phone book. As it was written, Lane and her team were still struggling to understand the debt situation. It was all so complex that she decided the only possible solution was a simple override agreement.

This had just two principles:

1. We are where we are.
2. Nobody gets out.

"We are where we are" was hard for the banks to swallow. It meant some would remain better off than others. "Nobody gets out" was equally tough, particularly for some of the smaller banks, who had precious little idea of what they were in. But Lane knew there was no other way. If just one bank got out, the other 145 institutions would swamp the exits.

When Lane and her team went to News with her plan, the first thing they were asked was "What is Plan B?" She looked them in the eye and said, "There is no Plan B." She told the banks the same. She reckoned that if anyone thought there was the remotest chance of a fall-back position, everyone would want to fall back. Lane was playing hardball. If they failed, it would be a catastrophe. She and her team would lose for Citibank, who had a large investment in the company. Murdoch would lose the empire.

In early October Murdoch had flown to Australia. He announced that he was merging four of his principal Australian papers into two. In Sydney the *Mirror* and the *Telegraph* became the *Telegraph-Mirror*, and more poignantly, in Melbourne, his afternoon broadsheet, the Melbourne *Herald*, was merged with the morning tabloid *Sun*, to become the *Herald Sun*. In effect this meant the death of the *Herald*, the paper on which his father, Keith Murdoch, had made his name and on which he had lavished care and attention between the two world wars.

On 15 October he was at Cavan, his grazing property (and favourite home) on the Murrumbidgee river close to Canberra. There he began secret talks with representatives of British Satellite Broadcasting, the rival of his own Sky Television, on the possibility of a merger. Sky had lost £95 million in the previous year, and he now realized that the talks with the banks would founder if he could not convince them that this haemorrhage would soon end.

On 23 October 1990, Murdoch attended News Corporation's annual general meeting in Adelaide, where the company had been founded and was still registered. The room at the Adelaide Hilton was packed with at least 250 people. Most of the company's directors flew in for the occasion to give Murdoch support. Unlike the previous year's AGM, this was an ill-tempered occasion. Television cameras were banned. Reporters were told by an aggressive and harassed News Corp aide that they were not allowed to tape-record Murdoch's speech. Murdoch declined to tell shareholders how he planned to cope with the debt, about a quarter of which would fall due in the next few months. Richard Searby, the chairman and one of Murdoch's oldest friends, said that the company intended to try to replace all or a lot of the short-term debt with long-term debt.

Despite some protest, Murdoch obtained approval for a controversial proposal that he be allowed to raise equity through the issue of a new class of non-voting shares that would not dilute his own and his family's control over the group. Shareholders were given a News Corp grab bag, containing a copy of *TV Guide*, and a T-shirt emblazoned with "The Simpsons", the cartoon family which was proving such a wild success for Fox Broadcasting, in Australia as well as the USA.

Ann Lane took her plan to the Tier I banks in a series of meetings on 31 October and 1 November, and got them to accept it. Citibank told the most senior bankers, in confidence, that one of the most serious problems had been solved. Murdoch had agreed that

Sky Television, the great bloodsucker of the company, should merge with its rival BSB. The news that this killing competition was ended was crucial to getting the banks' co-operation. Bankers did not all share Murdoch's vision of a satellite-based information system. With the agreement of the Tier I banks in their pockets, Lane, DeVoe and Murdoch began a swift series of global "roadshows" for the banks of Tiers II and III. They intended to get the agreement of them all by Thanksgiving, 28 November. It was a whistlestop world tour – Sydney – London – New York – in five days. To start it off, Lane flew with DeVoe from New York to Sydney to join Murdoch in the second week of November.

On all three continents Lane's authority helped swing the bankers. Murdoch spoke with quiet persuasiveness about the businesses he had spent so long building. He admitted his mistakes. He promised that he would have a stronger management team around him and that he would consult with them. He would not fly solo any more. He was very impressive.

The roadshows also included briefings from other major proconsuls in the Murdoch empire, talking about books, films and the newspapers around the world. It was all a matter of presentation and spin. Lane provided the spin. She rehearsed them all, including Murdoch, telling them what the banks would or would not buy.

After the roadshows, Lane concentrated on negotiating term sheets with News Corp; the banks needed to know the details of the deal. They turned out a draft of the override agreement by 30 November. Lane flew to London to negotiate terms with the company line by line. She wanted to get the first drafts of the override on the banks' desks by mid-December. To negotiate an agreement of such complexity and length in five or six business days and nights is unheard of; but they did it. They were driven by the clock and by loan maturities. This would be the only draft that the banks were going to see.

All the lenders had a thousand questions. Those from Tier II were particularly awkward because they were being asked to provide new money to a company which already had fantastic debts. But, of all the institutions, those in Tier III were the most aggrieved and most difficult to please. Night after night, they tried to get News Corp to buy them out. Lane's problem, and Murdoch's, was that if one were bought out, everyone would demand the privilege. They refused them all.

By the end of 1990, there was a roll every two weeks, great waves that Murdoch had to ride. Almost all were difficult, some were almost impossible to stay atop. "We were in some pretty tough conversations at five minutes to midnight," Murdoch told the *Financial Times*. "Real heart-stoppers." None was worse than the Pittsburgh Bank on the night of 6 December.

That afternoon, when Dave DeVoe had been told by the Pittsburgh banker to liquidate News Corp, Murdoch was in a state of considerable alarm. He called Ann Lane, who was at Clifford Chance, the London commercial lawyers who were acting for Citibank. By now, she knew that Murdoch worked harder and more determinedly than anyone she had ever met. She knew that he would never say, "I can't do it any more." But on this particular afternoon, she also realized that he could not see how to make it happen.

Murdoch told her, "I think it's over. I don't think I'm going to get there with this bank. I'm coming over. I can't deal with it on the phone."

Lane knew how he felt. This roll on 7 December was for a total of A$1 billion. But Pittsburgh could turn the roll into a dive. She felt as if they were falling over a cliff in slow motion.

Murdoch and DeVoe drove over from St James's to Clifford Chance. While they were on their way, Ann Lane called Citibank headquarters on Park Avenue in New York. She wanted John Reed, the chairman, to know what was happening.

In any restructuring there are always creditors who do not want to help. Often they have good reasons to get out. Sometimes they are just playing chicken. There came a time, Lane knew, when you had to put pressure on such people. More poetically, as they constantly put it in her office, you had to "launch" on them.

"Launching" on a lender can take many forms. A multitude of vice chairmen could call the bank that was holding out. If that were not enough, the chairman himself could call. Any federal regulator could "launch". If a huge warhead were needed, the chairman of the Federal Reserve could do it, and indeed Murdoch tried to reach him on that day. Japanese regulators could be "launched" on Japanese banks. The Bank of England could "launch" on British banks. So, as a last resort, could the Prime Minister. But Murdoch's great ally and friend, Margaret Thatcher, had just been compelled to resign.

"Launching" is a delicate process. Lane knew that until the last minute, minimum pressure was better. She did not launch lightly. But now she was convinced it was necessary. She asked that John Reed call Pittsburgh, to launch on the chairman and explain the ramifications of forcing News under.

Those ramifications, Lane believed, were enormous. News would have to be sold off bit by bit in a fire sale. There would be repercussions for the whole Western financial system. Murdoch had made News Corporation more than a company – controlling over 70 per cent of the press in Australia, between 30-40 per cent in Britain, and a major television network in America. News was one of the most important media firms in the world, and its destruction would reverberate through the world economy, accelerating the recession.

As Murdoch drove to see her, Lane prepared. She called New York again, to make sure that John Reed had "launched" on Pittsburgh before Murdoch called the bank. She told one of the partners at Clifford Chance to throw out whoever was in their best conference room to make way for Murdoch. She had two objectives: to make sure that Citibank had done all it could to avert disaster, and to calm Murdoch so that he could be effective.

When Murdoch arrived, Lane told him of everything that was being done. Calls between her, the rest of her team here and in New York, and banks in America, London and Australia, where it was now the middle of the night, were constant. They were doing what they could. Everyone was tense. Indeed, said Lane, everyone was sweating bullets.

Murdoch asked to be led quietly through the process. What was happening and what needed to be done. Ann Lane could see the pressure he was under. He knew that he might lose his ship in a matter of hours, and he was sobered by the prospect. He did not lose control. But she knew that he was aware that this could be the end.

Ann Lane also knew that it was not enough for DeVoe to talk to the chief loan officer in Pittsburgh. Murdoch himself had to talk to the president of the bank. That was now the bottom line. Lane's people in New York called London. They talked Murdoch through the psychology of the man. This call could be the most important he had ever made. It could decide whether or not the company he had inherited from his father and built into an empire went down. This call was the only lifeboat, and Murdoch himself must pilot it.

"It's not a pretty sight to see a great man like that," said Lane. "He was so vulnerable. One phone call could mean the end of his whole life's work. And it had been built from real skills, and not just by shifting piles of paper around."

Lane herself was terrified. "But my job was not to show panic. My job was to keep Rupert calm and focused." She was professional, and so, she said, was he. "He didn't wig out. He was visibly shaking, but he didn't go crazy. He wasn't hyperventilating."

"If we can't get them to roll, it's all over," he said. Lane believed that too, but she did not say so. "Nothing is over till it's over," she said. "Keep the artillery moving forward."

About half an hour after Murdoch arrived at the lawyers', he was ready to place the call. It was, for everyone there, a terrifying moment.

The chairman would not take Murdoch's call.

Here was a man who had for decades been able to call presidents and prime ministers almost at whim, and the chairman of a small bank in Pittsburgh would not speak to him.

Instead, Murdoch was put through to the chief loan officer, the man who had chewed up Dave DeVoe a short time before. Before this official in Pittsburgh, "I had to beg," recalled Murdoch. Then, suddenly, and to Murdoch's utter astonishment, it was all over. The chief loan officer, who had just told them to liquidate the company, had discarded his Mutt voice. Now he was Jeff. He could not have been nicer. There was Murdoch, in London, not hyperventilating but close to the edge and "he didn't let me speak.

He said, 'Oh, Mr Murdoch, it's very nice of you to call. I don't know whether he's told you, I had a very good call from Dave DeVoe. We had a good talk, and I've thought a lot about what he said to me. We don't want to be that difficult.' "

In London, two hours or so to midnight, Murdoch felt the tension draining out of him. "I couldn't believe it," he said later.

The man in Pittsburgh, Murdoch recalled, continued, " 'Perhaps we could come to New York and meet and we could know a bit more about the company, and find a way, see how we can work this thing through . . .'

"So I said, 'We'd be happy to see you.' "

He put down the telephone and looked at Lane. "Phew," he said.

Pittsburgh had been successfully "launched" upon.

"I went out and had a strong drink," said Murdoch. "I was just exhausted."

What was especially exhausting was the unprecedented feeling that he had no power, no control. If the bank had refused to roll, there was nothing he could have done about it. "Once the word was out, then all the banks would have run. You just couldn't open any crack."

They were where they were and nobody had got out.

How had he got there? That was the drama of the past.

And could he get out? This was the drama to come.

Chapter 1

CRUDEN

There is a poem about the Australian character, called "They'll Tell You About Me", by Ian Mudie:

> ... yesterday I was rumour,
> today I am legend,
> tomorrow, history.
> If you'd like to know more of me
> inquire at the pub at Tennant Creek,
> or at any drover's camp,
> or shearing-shed,
> or shout any bloke in any bar a drink;
> they'll tell you about me,
> they'll tell you more than I know myself.
> After all, they were the ones that created me,
> even though I'm bigger than any of them now.
> –In fact, I'm all of them rolled into one.

Of the many questions that are asked about Rupert Murdoch, one occurs again and again. Why? Why has he spent forty years, all of his adult life, restlessly flying around the world to build an international empire? Why does he never pause? Is he driven by political ambition or the desire for personal vindication? What makes Rupert run? To borrow from the famous quest in *Citizen Kane* – what, who or where is his Rosebud?

This is not a psycho-history, but the passage of his life and times and the changes through which he progressed will provide some of the answers to these questions. He contains within his character both an extraordinary gambling instinct and a certain dour puritanism. Perhaps that is not so surprising. One of his grandfathers, Rupert Greene, was a roistering, charming half-Irish gambler. The other, Patrick Murdoch, was a stern pillar of the Free Church of Scotland. Traces of each man can be seen in Rupert Murdoch's conflicting nature. From his Scots Free Church ancestors he seems to have inherited a deep and abiding distaste for the English Establishment and its traditions.

The Very Reverend Patrick John Murdoch lived until 1940, when Rupert was nine years old. Born almost a century before and half the world away, in 1850, in the herring fishing port of Pitsligo on the Moray Firth, he came from a strictly religious and nonconformist family.

His father James (Rupert's great-grandfather) was also a clergyman. Born in Stirling in 1817, he was one of the 190 probationers and 470 ministers who broke with the established Church of Scotland in the great Disruption of May 1843.

James Murdoch and his son were therefore at the birth of the Free Church in the latter half of the nineteenth century. With contributions raised by Presbyterian supporters all over the world the dissidents built hundreds of new churches and schools, thus creating an alternative Presbyterian establishment. They challenged the established Church of Scotland and the government in London, and won.

The Disruption of 1843 had almost nothing to do with theology, divinity or religion. It was the culmination of 130 years of a bitter dispute in which the English crown had sought to control the Scottish Church by the appointment of ministers loyal to London.

In the early nineteenth century a new generation of younger, more radical men had emerged in the Church of Scotland; they were known as the "wild party", or the "popular party", or the Evangelicals. Ecclesiastically and theologically conservative, yet socially and politically liberal (and some of them downright radical), they hated the controls imposed by London through the Scottish lairds. Their rebellion was no empty gesture; it meant abandoning their stipends, their homes, their schools, and high social standing. More than one minister died in poverty in some makeshift manse during the winter of 1843/4.

The landowning aristocracy responded harshly. It refused to

give or even to lease or to sell the Free Church any land on which
to build its houses and schools. Free Church congregations were
harried at every turn.

A probationer in 1843, James Murdoch was ordained as a minister at Pitsligo in 1846. He married Helen Nameth in 1848 and
their son Patrick was born in 1850. Patrick attended the University
of Aberdeen and then studied divinity at New College in Edinburgh, the theological college of the Free Church of Scotland.

The anti-English and anti-Establishment teachings of the Free
Church were drummed into Patrick at his mother's knee, from
his father's pulpit and in the lectures at New College. He almost
certainly acquired a deep and abiding distaste for the Anglo-
Scottish gentry (almost all of whom were Episcopalians), the Conservative Party, and the prelatical and hierarchical structures of
the Anglican Church (in all its forms).

This is not to suggest that he was some wild-eyed moorland
fanatic. The Evangelicals of the Free Church refused to be regarded
as dissenters, seeing themselves as the true repository of the established Kirk of Scotland. Free Church ministers and elders like
James Murdoch tended to be active, hard-headed, well-educated,
practical men, who knew how to make money and how to use it
wisely.

In the first three years of its existence, the Free Church raised
more than a million pounds, an enormous sum in the 1840s. The
church relied heavily on its laymen, many of whom were bankers,
merchants, lawyers, advocates, engineers, ship builders and medical men. William Collins the Glasgow publisher (whose publishing
empire Rupert Murdoch would acquire) was a Free Church zealot
and its publisher. Patrick John Murdoch was raised in a culture
which was certainly Calvinist, but also fiercely democratic, socially
enlightened, self-reliant, pragmatic and energetic.

He became an assistant to an influential preacher in London
and in 1878 he was himself ordained as a minister at the village of
Cruden, a small fishing village in Aberdeenshire. According to the
Annals of the Free Church, the congregation had at first to
worship in a barn; then they raised up a temporary timber church
in the space of a day, and finally moved to a stone building a few
years later.

In 1882, after four years as a minister, Patrick married Annie Brown. Her grandson, Rupert, later said, "She was the daughter of the local landholder and rather spoilt. My father always thought she had married my grandfather on the rebound. She never settled easily." Two years later, in 1884, Patrick accepted "a call" and he was "translated" to the Free Church in Melbourne, Australia, at a time when Scottish immigration to the southern continent was gathering pace.

With Patrick and Annie went his parents (James died later that year), and his younger brother Walter. Walter later became a distinguished professor of English; indeed, Perth's second university is named after him. They arrived in Melbourne in October 1884, almost exactly a century after the first convicts were transported from Britain to New South Wales. Their first home was a terraced house off a'Beckett Street.

MELBOURNE

At the end of the nineteenth century, the world was experiencing a new era in communications. Telephone and radio had been invented, though few people appreciated their potential. In 1879, Sir William Preece, the chief engineer of the Post Office, told the House of Commons that the telephone had little future in Britain. "There are conditions in America which necessitate the use of such instruments more than here. Here we have a superabundance of messengers. The absence of servants has compelled America to adopt communications systems."

The relatively newly-settled continent of Australia was not in the forefront of such enquiry and invention. It had only recently been linked by cable to the northern hemisphere. The telegraph had been invented as far back as 1837 but it was several decades before it reached Australia.

In the 1860s the government of one of the colonies, South Australia, had offered £2,000 to any explorer who could make the incredible journey over 2,000 miles of desert to the north coast.

The cable from London had reached Java and was about to be extended to Northern Australia. The South Australian government wanted to stretch it to its capital, Adelaide, so that that town could be the centre of communications in Australia. John McDouall Stuart bravely won the prize, and South Australia then financed and built the overland cable, 2,200 miles of wire which reached across the outback and linked such desolate stations as The Peak, Beltona, and Alice Springs. Communication across the continent and between Australia and the rest of the world had been established.

After that, of course, the maintenance of the line was all-important. Jeannie Gunn, the author of the Australian classic, *We of the Never-Never*, who lived on a cattle station in the Northern Territory, explained how:

> One of the earliest of our guests that year was the telegraph operator who invited us to "ride across to the wire for a shake hands with the Outside" . . .
>
> For a moment we waited spellbound in the brilliant sunshine, then the dogs ran down to the water's edge, the galahs and the cockatoos rose with gorgeous sunrise effect – a floating grey and pink cloud backed by sunlight flashing white. But the operator, being unpoetical, had ridden on to the wire and presently was shinning up one of its slender iron posts as a preliminary to the handshake, for tapping the line being part of the routine of a telegraph operator, shinning up posts is one of his necessary accomplishments.
>
> And as we stood, in touch with the world, in spite of our isolation, a gorgeous butterfly rested for a brief space with gently-swaying purple wings, and away in the great world men were sending telegrams amid clutter and dust, unconscious of that tiny group of bush folk, or that Nature, who does all things well, can beautify even the sending of a telegram.

Until this wilderness wire linked Australia to the world from which the new Australians had come, newspapers in the colony had competed for foreign news by posting lookouts on South Head, at the entrance to Sydney harbour, to watch for ships. Each paper would launch a whaleboat, dash out to the ship and scoop up the mail packets and overseas newspapers. These were rushed back into the city on horseback, where they were rewritten and published as fast as possible.

A printing press had arrived in Australia with the very first fleet in 1788, but it was not used for newspapers. To begin with, news and comment were circulated hand to hand in "pipes" or handwritten sheets. At the turn of the century the authorities created official papers such as the *Sydney Gazette* and *New South Wales Advertiser*; similar papers were created elsewhere in the colony. Unofficial papers began to spring up in the next two decades; the first one in Victoria was handwritten. There were frequent struggles with the government over freedom of the press, but by the middle of the century there were scores of papers. Most had circulations of no more than a few hundred.

One of the great pioneers of Australian journalism was John Fairfax, the founder of a dynasty whose pre-eminence Rupert Murdoch would one day contest. Fairfax was originally a printer and publisher from Warwickshire who emigrated to Sydney in 1838, with ten pounds in his pocket.

The city, which was celebrating its fiftieth anniversary, had five newspapers. The dominant one was the *Sydney Herald*, founded in 1831 as a weekly by three English immigrants. A commercial success from the start, it began with a circulation of 750 and by 1836 was selling 1,600 copies twice a week. At sevenpence initially (increased to ninepence when it was enlarged to seven columns in 1834) it was cheaper than the other papers. In 1840, a new semi-rotary press enabled it to became a daily and produce 3,000 copies sold at sixpence a copy. By this time, Fairfax was doing freelance typesetting at the *Herald* and had founded the *Temperance Advocate*, which he published at the *Herald* office.

Within six years of his arrival in Sydney he had made enough money to take a partner and buy the *Herald* for some £12,000. He then enlarged the paper and changed its name to the *Sydney Morning Herald*, and acquired a new Cowper press and a steam engine to drive it. The following year he bought out his partner and on the last day of 1856 changed the name of the company to John Fairfax and Sons. In 1860, he installed a Hoe six-cylinder rotary press (imported from New York at a cost of about £6,000) which was able to print 12,000 one-sided sheets per hour.

Newspapers came later to Melbourne, the capital of Victoria, which became a separate colony only in 1850. The first issue of the *Melbourne Age* was published on 17 October 1854. Eight broadsheet pages, it sold for sixpence. A later prospectus promised the *Age* would pay attention to "the advocacy of free institutions, diffusion of truth and the advancement of man". The paper's birth coincided with the city's first inter-colonial exhibition. It was also the year when Cobb & Co started their coach run between Melbourne and Bendigo, where gold had recently been discovered.

Melbourne itself was a boom town in those days, rather like San Francisco in the 1840s. "The bars were always full, the tap-rooms always crowded. The women were as numerous as the men. Wedding parties without end drove up and down the streets by way of cutting a flash." Tens of thousands of new immigrants were dashing to Australia to dig for gold. The diggers created their own culture; luck was probably their most important talisman and their abiding belief. The poorest man could be in silks tomorrow, and this bred a suspicion of credentials which endures today. "There are no gentlemen in the colonies now," wrote one critic. "All barriers are broken down. There are only rich men and poor men; and as the latter may be rich men in a week, everyone is 'hail fellow, well met' with everyone else."

The *Melbourne Age* took a radical stand, supporting the rights of diggers against the government. In 1855 a co-operative of its printers and typographers had to rescue the *Melbourne Age* from financial difficulties. Next year the paper's editor, Ebenezer Syme, bought it for £2,000 and was joined by his brother, David, who took over the paper on Ebenezer's death in 1860. David Syme remained the sole proprietor for the next thirty years; its circulation rose from 2,000 to 130,000, as Melbourne became the largest city on the continent.

The gold rush made "Melbourne, marvellous Melbourne" the largest city in the continent, with a population of about half a million. But by the time Patrick Murdoch and his family stepped ashore in 1884 it was in the thrall of both depression and drought;

economic conditions were harsh, hours were long, salaries low, and there were few laws to protect workers or their health. Electric light was only just arriving, district by district, and water supplies were still mainly from rainwater tanks on rooftops.

Patrick Murdoch's bluestone church stood at the corner of William and Lonsdale Streets, where the Australian Broadcasting Corporation later built radio studios. He was an enthusiastic preacher, who disapproved of sermons over an hour long. Three years after his arrival, another minister from Aberdeenshire, the Reverend James Climie, died. Patrick preached so well at his funeral in Trinity Church, Camberwell, a Melbourne suburb, that the parishioners invited him to become their pastor. He was inducted in August 1887 and was minister there until his retirement on 31 December 1928, remaining a senior member of the church until his death twelve years later.

He was a worldly man who busied himself with the politics of his church, and cultivated temporal politicians as well. He loved golf and bowls and was tall, broad-shouldered, straight-backed and "full of Christian fun". He was elected Moderator of the State Assembly of Victoria in 1898, and of the General Assembly of Australia, the church's highest office, in 1905; and served on the Royal Commission on Religious Education in State Schools. After his death one fellow clergyman thought that "he with a few others moulded the mind and shaped the policy of the Presbyterian Church as it is today in Australia".

He was a fine orator, "a prince of preachers", with "ripe scholarship" and "power of lucid expression", whose "luminous expositions made the Bible a living book". It was said that "young and old of both sexes felt the magnetic force of his personality". In 1915 he published a book of sermons, entitled *Laughter and Tears of God and Other War Sermons*.

He also wrote two religious textbooks; in one, there is a passage on fatherhood which suggests the sort of home he ruled.

The father cannot give his strength or his wisdom to his boy, and he would not if he could, for then the boy would no longer be a boy. But he can give his sense of duty. Through his conduct and his words, he teaches his boy the meaning of the word "ought". And he can give something of his love for men and his desire to serve them.

Patrick was a convinced supporter of the freedom of the press. He called it "probably the strongest foe of tyranny", and he argued, "No autocrat can tolerate the widespread dissemination among his people of a free discussion of his conduct." But he was more equivocal about such freedoms as the right to strike. He feared that this could degenerate into licence, of which there was already a surfeit. "There has been too much easy pleasure indulged by our Australian people."

Patrick's principles were strong, and occasionally too strong for his contemporaries. On one occasion they landed him in prison, when in a bizarre libel case he refused to hand over a document which he insisted belonged to the church and not to the state. Mr Justice Hodges pounced.

> *Hodges*: Will you produce it ?
> *Murdoch*: I cannot produce it.
> *Hodges*: Then I had better send for a policeman.
> *Murdoch* (quietly): Very well.
> *Hodges* (sharply): You produce it, Sir, or I will send you to gaol.
> *Murdoch* (quietly): Very well, Sir, I will go to gaol.

The South Melbourne Presbytery commended him for his defence of the freedom of the church. He was also praised by the press. The presbytery then authorized Murdoch to release the document and he was swiftly freed.

Patrick and Annie Murdoch had seven children. Keith was the second son, and third child, born on 12 August 1885. His childhood and youth were made wretched by the curse of an appalling stammer. Not even his parents were aware of how badly this affected him, and the children at school teased him mercilessly. He often fled home in tears. Under stress his speech would collapse totally.

When he left school, he decided that he did not wish to go on to university, and told his father that he had a spiritual calling towards journalism. His father was unenthusiastic, but when Keith failed to secure a job, the Reverend Patrick spoke to David Syme, the owner of the *Melbourne Age*, and a prominent member of his congregation. Syme arranged for the boy to be given a job covering the middle-class suburb of Malvern.

On hot days in Melbourne, the north wind blew baking air heavy with dust and powdered horse dung into the eyes. Steam trains puffed through the new suburbs – open-sided trams were towed through the centre by an underground cable which the gripman grasped with a pincer on the tram. Fivepence would buy two pounds of the best stewing steak. Beer was threepence a pint pot. Australian Rules football was popular among the young and old; at half-time, Aborigines threw boomerangs as entertainment.

Men with long poles rode around the city on bicycles to light the gas lamps. Most houses were lit by gas jets with fragile cotton mantles; a few had electricity, some still had oil lamps. Harry Lauder, Caruso and Nellie Melba were the great entertainers and there were phonographs on which their reedy voices could be heard. People sang a lot, and as one prominent Melbourne journalist recalls, the songs were a chronicle of scientific progress: "Up above the sky so high with my ballooning girl"; Daisy Bell (who looked so sweet upon the seat of a bicycle made for two), and later "Hallo Hawaii" – "I've had to pawn every little thing I own just to talk on the wireless telephone".

Keith did not find his first assignment easy; most of the middle class residents of Malvern read the rival *Argus*. But he worked hard to change that and he found that his stammer helped him – it aroused sympathy in those whom he was trying to interview. He lived a life of frugality, even austerity, denying himself social drinks, even sandwiches at lunchtime. He was intent on saving every possible penny in order to go to London to study at the London School of Economics, and to find a cure for his stammer. By 1908 he had saved £500, enough to pay for a steerage ticket to London and his board and lodging there for a year or so.

Australia had scarcely had time to find its feet. The writer and poet, Henry Lawson, declared, "My advice to any young

Australian writer whose talents have been recognized would be to
go steerage, stow away, swim, and seek London, Yankeeland or
Timbuctoo rather than stay in Australia till his genius turns to
gall or beer. Or, failing this, to study elementary anatomy . . . and
then shoot himself carefully."

Keith Murdoch, however, had every intention of coming home.
He was homesick as soon as the ship set sail, and he wrote letters
to his father which were both touching and illustrative of his
ambition.

At sea, Straits of Bonifacio. I am dreading these first weeks in
London. My stammering has not improved by the trials of the
voyage and I hardly feel fit. But I am determined to make a
name here before I leave the place . . . I know you have never
been keen on my profession . . . But I see the opportunities and
necessities and I shall go ahead and become a power for good.

London was a terrible disappointment to Keith. His introduc-
tions were no help. He found it impossible either to break into
Fleet Street or to find a cure for his stammer. He had very little
money, lived alone in digs where he made himself toast on his
penknife over a gas ring, and felt miserable. He missed his family
more and more.

I long for great work and I so earnestly desire those gifts of
God, bright children, faithful friends, and a comfortable home.
The plain fact is I get fits of beastly depression here which I'm
shaking off, but which din into my ears, "you are of no account;
your faith may not even withstand the common temptations of
the world".

He found London squalid and cold, with "hunger and depravity
too near luxurious culture . . . A shocking feature of London is
the immorality stalking the streets."

On another occasion, he wrote home:

I have hinted before that London upsets me in many ways.
One's faith in humanity goes at once; these people are

savages ... One's faith in the divine love falters. Educated London declares for materialism and the people in the streets show all the traces of the brutish materialistic evolution ... I do not hide from you the fact that I am being daily driven further from the belief in Christ's divinity ...

In a more robust mood, he wrote:

The survival of the fittest principle is good because the fittest become very fit indeed ... I'll be able to learn much here ... and with health I shall become a power in Australia.

Still stammering, he returned to Melbourne in 1910, via the United States, where the conditions of immigrants on Ellis Island horrified him. The *Age* gave him back his job, and by the end of 1911 his salary was raised from four to seven pounds a week. In 1912, he left the *Age* and became Melbourne parliamentary correspondent for the Sydney *Sun*, a lively evening paper.

By now his interest in politics was growing into a passion. He became a great admirer of the views, acumen and philosophies of two Labor Party leaders, Andrew Fisher, a friend of his father, and William Morris Hughes. Fisher was Prime Minister of Australia 1908–9, 1910–13 and 1914–15, Hughes between 1915 and 1923. One critical biographer of Keith argues that these men's belief in Australia's destiny appealed to the young Murdoch, "for he never lacked faith in the land of his birth. His most cynical detractors will not deny that he was imbued with that faith." He had grown up thinking of himself as an Australian, not as the son of Scottish immigrants.

Just before the outbreak of World War I, the Australian Workers' Union decided to publish a daily newspaper in Sydney, and offered Murdoch the post of news editor at £800 a year. But to his disappointment the entire project was abandoned when war was declared.

GALLIPOLI

On 3 March 1990 *The Times* in London carried two long accounts of the Gallipoli landings on the seventy-fifth anniversary of that battle. The second was entitled "The Journalist who Stopped a War" and was a paean to the role which Patrick Murdoch's son Keith played in exposing the nature of the fighting. It claimed he "almost single handedly stopped a war". The article noted that he had gone on to build a newspaper empire in Australia and that his son Rupert had created an even larger one.

Rupert's father Keith is the stuff of legend in Australia. He created the largest newspaper empire the country had ever seen. By the time he died, he controlled – but did not own – newspapers in every state of Australia except New South Wales. He was a man of gravitas, a friend of political leaders and a collector of art. But more importantly he is known as the reporter who "got our boys out of Gallipoli". Rupert grew up knowing that his father was an authentic Australian hero.

On 25 April 1915, two divisions of Australian and New Zealand soldiers splashed ashore at Gallipoli. This event subsequently became as well known to Australian schoolchildren as Trafalgar was to English ones or Washington crossing the Delaware to Americans. In the 1950s the Australian artist Sidney Nolan painted a series of stark pictures and referred to Gallipoli as "the great modern Australian legend, the nearest thing to a deeply felt common, religious experience shared by Australians – even today". In the 1980s, Rupert Murdoch financed a patriotic film, *Gallipoli*, which perpetuated the legend.

When the Anzac troops landed, on a bleakly rocky shore, they were at once cut down by Turkish soldiers under the command of Mustafa Kemal, later known as Ataturk. About 16,000 Australian and New Zealand soldiers were killed or wounded. Who was to blame? The Australian journalist, Murray Sayle, has expressed a popular view: "British generals, monocles screwed into myopic eyes, brass hats jammed firmly down on heads of oak" were safe in the wardrooms of their battleships, drinking pink gins as the Anzac soldiers fell. That was the first part of the legend. A second part was that the only reporter, British or Australian, who actually had the guts or the brains to uncover the sorry truth of the whole matter was Keith Murdoch.

In essence the story has it that the young Keith Murdoch, a courageous young war correspondent, made his way to the hellish beaches of Gallipoli, was appalled by what he saw of the suffering and waste of Australian boys under the incompetent command of the British, defied British censorship, wrote the truth – and achieved spectacular results. The British Commander-in-Chief of the Expeditionary Force on the Dardanelles Peninsula was recalled; the war against Turkey was abandoned; and a Royal Commission into the war was created. It was even sometimes said that Murdoch brought about the fall of the British Government. It is a story that needs to be examined, not only for its intrinsic merit but because Keith Murdoch's influence on his only son Rupert was immeasurable.

In 1914, on Empire Day, Australian schoolchildren still sang the words:

What is the meaning of Empire Day?
Why do the cannons roar?
Why does the cry, God Save the King,
Echo from shore to shore?
Why does the flag of Britannia wave
Proudly o'er port and bay?
Why do our kinsmen proudly hail
This glorious Empire Day?

Australians had fought for Britain in China during the Boxer rebellion, in New Zealand against the native Maoris and in South Africa against the Dutch Boers. The government went side by side with Britain into war in 1914.

The Reverend Patrick Murdoch was among the patriots. In his war sermons, he tried to show that the Germans, warlike and self-assertive, must be defeated for their own sake as well as for that of the Commonwealth: "However unworthy we are to represent the Christian ideal, we are on that side and against anti-Christ." Furthermore, there was nothing like a threat to make people better appreciate "the great sanctities" of family life and Christian faith and the "great liberties" of democratic government and freedom of speech.

In the service of that freedom, Keith Murdoch applied for the post of official war correspondent to accompany the Australian military forces overseas. He was disappointed when C.E.W. Bean, a highly-regarded editorial writer from the *Sydney Morning Herald*, was chosen instead.

None the less, Murdoch remained determined to get into the war. In 1915, he was appointed London editor of the United Cable Service, a minor news agency. His father's old friend, Andrew Fisher, was by then Prime Minister, and Murdoch obtained from him an assignment to stop en route to London to investigate complaints by Australian troops in Egypt about delays in their mail.

Before he left, Murdoch wrote to the Prime Minister, "I want you to know that I have always felt that I could joyfully perform any task you set me in the service of my country." Then he set sail for Egypt.

He was expected to fulfil his commission from Fisher in Egypt. There was certainly no need for him to visit Gallipoli. But from Cairo, he sent copies of his official letters to General Sir Ian Hamilton, the Commander-in-Chief of the Dardanelles Expeditionary Force, and begged to be allowed to visit what he called "the sacred shores of Gallipoli". He assured the commander that "any conditions you impose I shall of course faithfully observe". On condition that Murdoch accept the censorship regulations imposed upon C.E.W. Bean and all other correspondents, Hamilton agreed.

Murdoch agreed, and he arrived on the island of Imbros, where Hamilton had his headquarters, on 2 September 1915, some four months after the allied troops had landed at Gallipoli. He saw Hamilton, who later recalled him as "a sensible, well-spoken man with dark eyes. He said his mind was a blank about soldiers and soldiering and made me feel uncomfortable by an elaborate explanation of why his duty to Australia could be done better with a pen than by a rifle."

Murdoch was no more than a week in the area, and by most accounts he spent much of that time in the press camp. In his first dispatch he wrote of the Anzac troops as being "stoical but not contemptuous". They had an elation that "knew no fear". They had died "charging with the light of battle in their eyes".

Among those with whom Murdoch spent time was Ellis Ashmead-Bartlett, the correspondent of the London *Telegraph*, who was a distinguished war correspondent, but also a soured, depressed alcoholic.

Ashmead-Bartlett poured out to Murdoch all the criticisms that he was prevented from making in print. Murdoch was deeply shocked and agreed to break his word to Hamilton; he would carry back from Ashmead-Bartlett an open and uncensored letter to the British Prime Minister Herbert Asquith protesting about the conduct of the war.

But this plot was reported to Hamilton. The general expelled Ashmead-Bartlett from Imbros and cabled the War Office in London about Murdoch's plan; when Murdoch landed in Marseilles he was met by a British intelligence officer who compelled him to hand over both the Ashmead-Bartlett letter and his own correspondence.

In a fury, Murdoch then composed a tirade to his own Prime Minister, Andrew Fisher. It was a powerful document. It was also bitter, tendentious, poorly sourced, and filled with errors. Thus Murdoch overstated casualties by some 40 per cent and alleged without proof that British officers had shot their own men "without mercy" if they had lagged behind.

Murdoch wrote *inter alia* that "The General Staff of the British army are unchangeably selfish." He asserted that the British troops suffered from "an atrophy of mind and body that is appalling. They are merely a lot of childlike youths without strength to endure or brains to improve their condition." There were, he wrote, "countless high officers and conceited young cubs who are playing at war. What can you expect of men who have never worked seriously, who've lived for their appearance or social distinction?"

How different were the Australians!

I could pour into your ears so much truth about the grandeur of our Australian army, and the wonderful affection of these fine young soldiers for each other and their homeland, that your Australianism would become a more powerful sentiment than before. It is stirring to see them, magnificent manhood, swinging their fine limbs as they walk about Anzac. They have the noble faces of men who have endured. Oh if you could picture Anzac as I have seen it you would find that to be an Australian is the greatest privilege the world has to offer.

Murdoch concluded, "It is not for me to judge Hamilton, but it is plain that when an army has completely lost faith in its General, and he has on numerous occasions proved his weaknesses, only one thing can be done." His letter characterized Hamilton as committing "murder through incapacity".

Murdoch intended this letter only for the Australian Prime Minister. But in London, he told his story to Geoffrey Dawson, editor of *The Times*, whose proprietor, Lord Northcliffe, one of the first great newspaper barons, was opposed to the Dardanelles campaign and saw the letter as a way of putting pressure on the government. Northcliffe was impressed by the young Australian, and encouraged him.

Murdoch sent a copy of his letter to Asquith who, without checking on its reliability, had it printed as a Cabinet paper. Given its unreliable nature, this was extraordinary. After debate within Cabinet, Asquith cabled Fisher to tell him that there were errors in Murdoch's letter and that actions had been taken to improve the situation in the Dardanelles. Lord Kitchener, the Secretary of State for War, was opposed to withdrawal, saying that the abandonment of Gallipoli "would be the most disastrous event in the history of the Empire. We should lose about 25,000 men and many guns." He thought also that Egypt would soon collapse.

None the less, Hamilton was replaced by General Sir Charles Monro and within three months the Australian force was withdrawn from the peninsula. It is hard to evaluate precisely how much influence Murdoch's letter had on the change of policy.

Hamilton himself certainly blamed Murdoch for his own downfall, though he established that much of the letter was inaccurate. Murdoch talked up his own role as best he could. In 1920 he insisted, "I went to London and hit Sir Ian as hard as I possibly could. I thought the vital thing was to get a fresh mind on the spot. The British Cabinet confirmed this view by recalling him within a week of my report being discussed by it."

The episode established Murdoch in both London and Australia as an unusual man. He was lucky that the letter was not published until fifteen years after his death. Neither its tone nor its accuracy reflected well on him. In 1933, he acknowledged to C.E.W. Bean that he had made mistakes, and that he greatly regretted them. His wife said later that, as he grew older, he realized he could have behaved differently, and "he took a more balanced view". She thought his bitterness about Britain arose from his first visit, when he had failed to find a cure for his stammer, or any work in London.

When Rupert Murdoch was asked about his father's letter in 1989, he said, "It depicted a very idealized sense of the Australian soldier being sent to slaughter by the gin-and-tonic-swilling Brits three miles off the shore. Very powerful letter."

"It's a great letter," agreed his interviewer, Gerard Henderson. "You can't really forget it. On the other hand there were a lot of Brits on Gallipoli, too, which these days many of us don't seem to remember."

"Oh, sure, it may not have been fair," replied Rupert Murdoch, "but it changed history, that letter."

FLEET STREET

Keith Murdoch spent the rest of the war in London. It was very unlike his first miserable visit; his Gallipoli letter had made him a man of notoriety if not substance and he exploited his position adroitly. After Billy Hughes succeeded Andrew Fisher as Australian Prime Minister, he appointed Murdoch his and Australia's principal unofficial fixer and publicist in London. When Hughes came to London, Murdoch held private supper parties at his flat which were attended by Lloyd George, Bonar Law and North-cliffe.

Murdoch fell completely under Northcliffe's spell. From him he learned much about the newspaper business which he then went home to apply in Australia, and later taught his son, Rupert.

Before Alfred Harmsworth, Lord Northcliffe, went mad, he was a genius who understood the communications revolution of his age and knew how to exploit it. The foundation of his empire had been a paper called *Answers*, a marvellous vehicle in which to display his love of trivia. The subjects tackled were diverse: "Strange Things that Happen in Tunnels", and "Why Jews Don't Ride Bicycles", "Do Dogs Commit Murder?", "Can a Clergyman Marry Himself?", "Can Fish Speak?" The paper really took off when Harmsworth (as he then was) began to stage competitions such as guessing the number of people who crossed London Bridge every day. His most famous competition offered the winner "£1 a week for life", which a tramp had apparently told Harmsworth was his great dream of wealth. The prize was to go to the person who could guess the value of the gold in the Bank of England on a particular day. The circulation of *Answers* rose to 200,000.

Harmsworth understood that most of the material in *Answers* could be recycled, almost endlessly, to a newly literate working-class market. *Comic Cuts* followed *Answers*, and then *Illustrated Chips*, *Forget Me Not*, *Home Chat* and many other similar papers. By 1894 his journals were selling over two million copies alto-gether, and Harmsworth was becoming rich. He bought the lack-lustre *Evening News* and by applying his populist techniques restored its circulation and its profits. In 1896 he founded the *Daily Mail*, which sold 400,000 on its first day. "We've struck a gold mine," he declared.

The *Daily Mail*, and other popular newspapers, served the new literate public produced by the Education Acts of the late nine-teenth century. As John Carey has pointed out, "the difference between the nineteenth-century mob and the twentieth-century mass is literacy". The emergence of a huge literate public revolutionized every aspect of the printed word. Without it, Alfred Harmsworth could not have reinvented the newspaper.

The slogan Harmsworth devised for the *Daily Mail* was "The Busy Man's Paper". His philosophy was simple – and crucial to the development of the publishing industry. "A newspaper," he declared, "is to be made to pay. Let it deal with what interests the mass of people." He was anxious simply to "give the public what it wants". This was a revolutionary concept and one which failed to find much favour with intellectuals and educationalists who believed they knew better than the public what that public should want. In the late 1930s, T.S. Eliot insisted that the effect of British newspapers on their readers was to affirm them as a "complacent, prejudiced and unthinking mass".

This tension between intellectuals and the idea of a mass public and its enjoyments continued throughout the twentieth century. Writing of "that anonymous monster, the Man in the Street", Virginia Woolf envisaged "a vast, featureless, almost shapeless jelly of human stuff . . . occasionally wobbling this way or that as some instinct of hate, revenge or admiration bubbles up beneath it". Aldous Huxley complained that universal education "has created an immense class of what I may call the New Stupid".

H.G. Wells had a more serious concern. He thought that news-papers were dangerous because the profit motive forced them to appeal to such crude and vulgar passions as patriotism and war fever. This made them prime organs of mass hatred, and thus a popular newspaper really did become "a poison rag".

Northcliffe went on to own the *Observer*, the *Weekly Despatch*, most of *The Times,* and to launch the *Daily Mirror*. He and his brother Harold, who became Lord Rothermere, were crucial fig-ures in the development of the industry. Mass advertising and rapid distribution by trains made it possible to create truly national newspapers. The new department stores were eager to advertise in the pages of the *Daily Mail* and the railway system meant that their displays could be on everyone's breakfast table. He saw, much earlier than most, that education and communications were changing the world with incredible speed. Automobiles, planes, wireless, all would combine to create a fast new world. At the end of 1900 Harmsworth travelled to New York and at the invitation of Joseph Pulitzer, designed the first issue of *The World* for the new century, on 1 January 1901. It was a tabloid of twelve pages and four columns, and it created a sensation in New York. Harmsworth insisted that no article should be longer than 250 words, and the paper was described as "All the News in Sixty Seconds".

Northcliffe inspired people. Edgar Wallace thought him a "visible tangible genius . . . an almost sacred personage. He had an extraordinary personality and could be a marvellous companion, forever enquiring, eliciting and extemporizing. His ego was without equal."

In 1908 he acquired a newspaper to match his ego, *The Times*. The owners had been reluctant to sell it to such a cad, but business was business, and theirs was not paying. No one was more horrified by his arrival than the staff of the paper, who regarded themselves then (and later) as keepers of a Holy Grail and hated his attempts to make the paper more popular, or, as they saw things, to take it downmarket.

Keith Murdoch had seen Harmsworth during his first visit to London at an Empire Press Union conference in 1909. He was unable to meet him socially because, he wrote to his father, he did not possess a frock coat. But he had at once thought him admirable. "He seems to have a great knowledge and to be simple and direct in his purposes. That, I think, is the secret of his success, if he can claim true success. He knows what he wants and goes straight for it."

After Gallipoli, Northcliffe became one of Murdoch's great confidants, and the most important influence on his life. Murdoch was still London editor of the United Cable Service, with a salary of £1,200 a year, and he had a three-year contract. He was doing well and he extended the news service to India and South Africa. C.E.W. Bean has left us a portrait of him at this rather startlingly public opening to his career. "Tall, strongly built but slow of movement, with the dark hair and heavy brows but twinkling eyes of his Highland ancestry, Murdoch, in mind and writings, corresponded curiously with his appearance," wrote Bean, with evident fascination for his subject. "To wield great power was one of his greatest ambitions. He was ardently Australian."

Murdoch worked out of *The Times* offices; his relationship to

Northcliffe seemed to many to be like that of father and son, and Murdoch called him "as good a friend as I have ever had". On another occasion, Murdoch wrote, "My dear Chief, I address you as such as the Chief of All Journalists (of all ages) and on returning to my desk today wish again (as I often have) that I could call you such in another way ... The days with you were complete ..." He was astute enough to know that their friendship would never survive if he actually became an employee of Northcliffe.

In 1920 Northcliffe gave his young friend Murdoch the coveted freelance assignment of covering the Australia and New Zealand tour of the Prince of Wales for *The Times*. Before leaving Murdoch wrote to the Chief to say:

> You have been the biggest influence and the biggest force over me here, largely on account of the many kindnesses you have shown me, but even more largely from the example I have steadily seen in you and the standard you have set me. I am certainly coming back, but if I never met you again I would retain this influence to the end of my life.

By the end of 1920 Murdoch had caught the attention of the directors of the Melbourne Herald and Weekly Times company. They offered Murdoch the editorship of the *Herald*, an evening broadsheet, at £2,000 a year. Northcliffe urged his thirty-three-year-old protégé to accept.

The *Herald* had started as a morning paper. In 1869, when David Syme had bought it, he turned it into an evening paper and then sold it, thus neatly disposing of a rival to his own morning paper, the *Age*. But, as an evening paper, the *Herald* prospered for a century, far more mightily than Syme would ever have guessed.

When Murdoch took over, the *Herald* had a circulation of about 100,000. Its first edition began to print at 2.30 p.m., and there was another at 4 p.m. Stories from outside the city came into the telephone room, where they were taken down in shorthand to save telephone charges and then typed up by the "telephone-roomers". Thence they were sent up to the sub editors' room to be restyled or rewritten as necessary. Then they were folded into cartridges and shot through narrow tubes to the press room, where they were set in hot metal and printed.

The paper had no competition. Its layout was fusty, the reporting solid but boring, the news pages slack. Sometimes the head printer would appear in the subs' room in the afternoon and declare, "Not another line." The printer, not the journalists, ruled.

Until Murdoch's arrival, the journalists were seen by management as feckless, impractical, Bohemian, incapable of anything sensible or businesslike, and vastly overpaid. Murdoch changed that; he considered that journalists should be gentlemen, and he tried to treat them as such.

Immediately he began to wake the paper up. He issued daily bulletins of criticism and praise, making journalists aware that he was paying attention to them. He sent Northcliffe a bundle of back issues of the *Herald* and asked him how best to improve the paper. The Chief's advice is worth quoting at length as a distillation of the art of popular journalism.

Make-up.
Stop press is needed. Should be above the fold to catch the eye at once. Or it might be lateral. Must always contain some late interesting news. Make far more use of pictures, especially SHOWING ACTION. Blocks are badly reproduced and insufficient. Also badly trimmed.
Advertisements.
No advertisement must dominate. It does not pay the advertiser and spoils the balance of the page. In educating the advertiser an enterprising Jew draper will be useful.
Briefs.
These are valuable because they give an impression of fullness. Pack the news in: condense . . .
Sports.
Exploit them. Prizes and competitions. Pigeon racing (for example).
Serial.
Must be good, or useless. *Daily Mail* goes to great trouble to get the right one . . .

Women.
Run a page EVERY day. Dresses, cookery, social gossip.

Murdoch responded, "Your notes are my bible. I go to them every day."

Murdoch promoted himself to managing editor. He strengthened the *Herald*'s business side, and followed the Chief's advice. He ran serials, started a woman's page, set up stunts, introduced competitions. He made the editorials shorter and the paper altogether crisper. To the horror of the Melbourne Establishment he even staged a beauty contest.

Some months after he became editor, a young girl was found naked, raped and murdered in Gun Alley, off Little Collins Street, Melbourne. The *Herald* pulled out all the stops with gaudy coverage, big headlines, blatant innuendo, even a reward for information leading to a conviction. Circulation rocketed. The defendant, Colin Ross, was, according to one of Murdoch's critics, Humphrey McQueen, "tried and convicted . . . in the pages of the *Herald*". He was hanged. There is no doubt that the coverage of the case was sensationalist if not inflammatory.

In Murdoch's hands, the circulation of the *Herald* rose from 95,000 to around 140,000 within a year. Not everybody approved. "Indeed," wrote one critic, "some observers considered Murdoch's influence begot a somewhat callow approach to the important as well as the trivial affairs of the world." Others accused Murdoch of being a "yellow journalist" who had brought "*Daily Mail*-type journalism to Australia". "I wish I had," he wrote to the Chief.

In fact there was a good deal of hypocrisy about accusations of Murdoch's "sensationalism". Australian journalism had always been fairly brutal. However, he did make the *Herald* far more aggressively competitive and this had a knock-on effect in the cut-throat industry. His official biographer, C.E. Sayers, wrote (in a book which was never published): "His sensationalism, as it was branded early in his career, was received with raised eyebrows by his morning-paper confrères, and a smug disinclination to believe those London methods would succeed in Melbourne. Thus he had the field to himself and he roamed through it keenly and vigorously." For any student of Rupert Murdoch, there is here a certain sense of anticipation.

Keith Murdoch found it hard to settle down in Melbourne after the excitement of London. He wrote to Northcliffe, "The tininess of this place and its people seem to choke me."

To his great pleasure, Northcliffe visited him in Melbourne, and praised him highly to members of the *Herald* board. There was only one way to make money in newspapers, he said: "You have to back the man. And this young Murdoch is someone to back." When the Chief left, Murdoch put him on the boat with another bundle of back issues of the paper and Northcliffe sent more comments, which again Murdoch took to heart:

> The first editorial should be the second thing read every day, the first being the main news ... Smiling pictures make people smile ... I, personally, prefer short leading articles ... People like to read about profiteering. Most of them would like to be profiteers themselves and WOULD if they had the chance ... The church notes are good. People who drink, smoke and swear, have no idea of the interest in church matters ... [Sport] can be overdone, I believe, even in Australia ... Every woman in the world would read about artificial pearls ... I still notice in the Herald an absence of "items". Columns of items a day give the reader a great feeling of satisfaction with this three halfpenny worth ... My young men say you don't have enough stockings in the paper. I am afraid I am no longer a judge of that.

In the late 1920s Murdoch began to expand the Herald group's empire. The *Sporting Globe*, the *Australian Home Builder*, the *Listener In*, *Aircraft*, *Australian Home Beautiful*, and *Wild Life* were among the magazines that the group launched or acquired. In 1925 the group bought the *Herald*'s competitor, the *Sun News-Pictorial*, which became its most profitable paper. The directors were delighted, and in 1926, they raised Murdoch to the board. Two years later he was made managing director. In 1929, he had the Herald group acquire Radio Station 3DB, thus becoming the first Australian newspaper publisher to enter broadcasting. He introduced swift printing presses, pioneered picturegram services, and published the first radio picture from overseas. He always loved to be first.

He saw that nationwide chains were beginning to be established in the United States and determined to do the same in Australia. Under his leadership, a Herald-based syndicate took over the *West Australian*, then he went to war in Adelaide. He bought first the small *Register*, and by dint of fierce competition, induced the owners of the morning *Advertiser* and then the afternoon Adelaide *News*, which was only ten years old, to sell out to the Herald group. He became chairman of Advertiser Newspapers and put in a young man named Lloyd Dumas as managing editor. Advertiser Newspapers Ltd and News Ltd remained separate companies with their own stockholders and their own plants. In 1931 Murdoch joined the board of the Adelaide *News*. In 1933 the two Brisbane morning dailies were added to the group and were merged to become the *Courier-Mail*. He also acquired huge tracts of forest in Tasmania and began to create the continent's own newsprint industry. He was no longer merely "one of Northcliffe's young men"; but for Murdoch, Northcliffe and his version of Fleet Street remained the touchstone. So much so that in Australia he was popularly known as "Lord Southcliffe".

MELBOURNE

By the end of the 1920s, it had seemed possible that Keith, now in his forties, would never marry. He was dedicated to his work and lived alone with his servants in a house on Walsh Street, in the well-to-do suburb of South Yarra. One of his biographers, Desmond Zwar, says that, "after a busy day on Flinders Street, he would arrive home to find his clothes laid out by servants for his next appointment, or a dinner party prepared over which he would preside". One issue of a Herald magazine, *Australian Home Beautiful*, celebrated his "Bachelor's House in Melbourne". It was an extraordinary contrast with the frugal parsonage in which he had grown up. The magazine showed his Chinese screens, his

Welsh dresser and other furnishings, all of which demonstrated, according to the writer, a bachelor of unusual taste.

There were fine pieces in the house, carefully chosen: there was Sung pottery, a William and Mary table from the collection of Sir James Horlick, a walnut tallboy from Lord Swaythling's collection, a Tang dynasty horse, pieces by Chippendale, Georgian silver candlesticks, and a Charles II mirror, among many other items. The dining room was described as "severe" and "a dignified, masculine room" bearing "the stamp of the owner's personality"; the mahogany dining table was Georgian and was laid with silver, including the oldest piece of silver in Australia, a rare Elizabethan chalice. Rupert said later that his father had acquired his expensive tastes while moving in Northcliffe's circle in London. "He loved collecting things, bargaining with dealers. I think they would see him coming and put the prices up, to give him the thrill of knocking them down."

One day in 1927 a photograph scheduled for another of his magazines, *Table Talk*, was placed on his desk for approval. It showed the serious, pretty face of Miss Elisabeth Greene, a debutante of eighteen. Murdoch was struck by her looks and subsequently arranged to meet her at a ball. He did not dare to ask her to dance, but called her the next day to invite her for a drive to the beach.

"I said 'Yes'," she recalled, "but I got into terrible hot water over it. My family were fairly old-fashioned and they thought a young girl going out for the day with a man of forty-three in a motor car was absolutely unheard of! But it was the twenties after all ... " There was, she said on another occasion, "a terrific rumpus" when she became engaged to this middle-aged journalist. But her parents acceded, and the couple were married in June 1928 by the Reverend Patrick Murdoch. Dame Nellie Melba was among the guests. Murdoch had chosen wisely; Elisabeth was a determined girl who became a devoted wife, a formidable mother and an eminent figure in Melbourne society.

"My side is pretty Australian," said Dame Elisabeth in interviews for this book. She enjoyed speaking of her family, who were settlers from Scotland, Ireland and England.

Her grandfather, William Henry Greene, was an Irish railway

engineer, who had moved to England and then emigrated to Australia in the 1860s. He was appointed assistant commissioner of railways and designed and built the railway to Kyneton, north of Melbourne. He married Fanny Govett, whose father, George, was born in Somerset in 1798. As a boy George had been delicate and in 1814 his father sent him on a round trip to Australia for the sake of his health. Ten years later, married and with a son, he returned as a settler to Tasmania. In the mid-1830s Govett shipped his wife, his four children, his cattle and his sheep across the Tasman Sea to the little settlement of Melbourne, which had just been founded on the Yarra river. There his daughter Fanny met and married William Henry Greene.

Their son Rupert was born in 1870. As a boy Rupert Greene was a scallywag, and he learned little at school. He became the New Zealand Loan and Mercantile Agency's leading wool expert and was well liked by his colleagues. In his private life he was a dashing character, a gambler and a spendthrift, always verging on the edge of catastrophic debt. He married Marie "Bairnie" De Lancey Forth, a well-read woman, who seemed mild but was strong enough to appreciate him.

Elisabeth was their third daughter and her father's favourite. Now in her eighties, she recalls wistfully, "He was great fun; very gifted, a great sport, and he had a great eye. He was always gambling on horses and cards. He was popular and amusing and had no idea of responsibility. We had a very chequered family life."

Rupert Greene's gambling debts were often so great that his wife had to rent out their home and move the family into digs. Money was never assured and Elisabeth grew up worried about it, though she was taught by her grandmother that "no gentleman ever spoke about money or age". Rupert Greene was official starter to the two leading Melbourne racing clubs for thirty years, which restricted his gambling; but he remained a wild, swashbuckling and delightful character. In every way, he was the antithesis of the righteous parson, Patrick Murdoch, and of the ambitious, serious-minded Keith. But there is at least as much of Rupert Greene as of Patrick Murdoch in their grandson, Rupert.

Throughout the 1930s Keith Murdoch's power and influence in the community grew as he extended the reach of the Herald group. He was knighted in 1933, but that was also a year in which heart problems laid him low for months. When he was fit, he was frequently away from home, travelling by train to Brisbane or Adelaide, expanding the *Herald*'s empire and thinking increasingly of how to nurture his own. By 1935 Murdoch and the Herald had interests in eleven of the country's sixty-five radio stations. As the *Dictionary of National Biography* put it, "Whatever the prime motive – profit, power, or pulpiteering – Murdoch had forged the first national media chain."

He also encouraged the amalgamation of the existing cable services into the Australian Associated Press Ltd, which he then chaired, later making it a partner of Reuters. In 1938, together with the *Sydney Morning Herald*, he established Australian Newsprint Mills Pty Ltd, to produce newsprint for the country.

Politically, he was moving to the right, but he liked to call himself a "revolutionary conservative". (Rupert later used just such a description for himself.) Increasingly he was becoming a political kingmaker. At the end of the 1920s he had broken with his old friend and patron, Billy Hughes, and begun to promote Joseph Lyons, the acting Treasurer of the Labor Party, as a future Prime Minister. The Herald papers started to call Lyons "Honest Joe". Murdoch took another leaf from Northcliffe's book and began to issue instructions to politicians. Very often they obeyed him. After Lyons became the United Australia Party Prime Minister, he frequently went to lunch with Murdoch at the *Herald*'s office. One day, Lyons's secretary asked her boss why he didn't have Murdoch visit him: "After all, you are the Prime Minister." Lyons replied, "Oh, I like Murdoch; it pleases him to see me in his office and it does me no harm to go there." However, Lyons was no puppet and many people felt that Murdoch overstated his own influence.

At the end of the 1930s, Murdoch became convinced of the need to fight fascism; Lyons was an isolationist, and so Murdoch began to seek a suitable replacement. "I put him there and I'll put him out," he allegedly said of Lyons. Years later, Murdoch's motivation was still being examined. Another Labor politician,

J.T. Lang, who was twice premier of New South Wales, wrote in the Sydney paper, *Truth*, in 1957, "Murdoch had one very simple idea. He wanted to be the most powerful man in the Commonwealth [of Australia]. If he could make the Prime Minister and then boss him around, then he was the Big Boss. It was as simple as that."

There was no love lost between Sir Keith and the Fairfax family, who were still considered the aristocracy of the press. On one occasion Murdoch wrote: "I am learning at last how contemptibly mean and selfish SMH [*Sydney Morning Herald*] people can become. We have to remain partners with them in many things but my feelings at present are strained."

The other great newspaper dynasty was that of the Packer family. In 1939, Frank Packer, the head of Consolidated Press, had slid into financial trouble. His *Daily Telegraph* was losing money and the *Australian Women's Weekly* was not yet making it. So Packer started to negotiate with Murdoch to sell out to the Herald and Weekly Times group. There was nothing that the Fairfaxes wanted less than to have Murdoch expand from Melbourne into Sydney. In order to prevent it, they decided to subsidize Packer. What he needed was a 2d rise in the cover price of the *Telegraph*. The *Sydney Morning Herald* had no need for such an increase, but the Fairfaxes agreed to a simultaneous price rise in February 1940, purely to scupper Sir Keith. Rupert said later that one of the things his father taught him was: "Never trust a Sydney newspaper proprietor."

Sir Keith inevitably made many enemies. In summer 1940 he accepted an odd appointment, given the role he had assumed at Gallipoli. He became chief censor, the Director-General for Information in Robert Menzies's wartime government. Murdoch at once appropriated time on all the country's national and commercial radio stations for a dreary news bulletin produced by the department. In the newspapers voluntary censorship already existed. Now Murdoch gazetted a National Security Directive, giving him the power, whenever he deemed it necessary, to compel a newspaper to publish any statement he produced, and as prominently as he demanded.

Almost every newspaper in the land, apart from those controlled by the Herald group, burst into angry protest. They said the government was trying to "out-Goebbels Goebbels" and the *Sydney Morning Herald* accused the Department of Information of dictatorship. As a result, the regulations were amended and a few months later, Murdoch resigned and returned to the *Herald*.

Of more lasting importance, he set up an American division of his department, intended to entice the USA into the war. He also helped found the Australian-American Association, of which he remained president until 1946. After the fall of Singapore, and the entry of the United States into the war, more and more Australians like Murdoch began to look for inspiration to America rather than to Britain. Writing in his own papers, he called upon the "spiritual sources" of the nation in an almost Messianic way.

His enemies paint a picture of Sir Keith as power-obsessed and hypocritical, with an almost slavish admiration for dictators such as Lord Northcliffe, and an inability to relate to others without exploitation. Labor politicians became increasingly critical of the "Murdoch press". *Smith's Weekly* attacked "the would-be press and radio dictator", and the dangers of a chain of newspapers with identical policies.

He could be stern to the point of pomposity, and impatient with others' eccentricities. He insisted on formal dress and appearance from his journalists, and was suspicious of men who wore beards, a prejudice inherited by his son Rupert. He was keen to recruit sons of smart families to the *Herald*, which some journalists mockingly called his "Sons of Famous Fathers" phase. He often called the *Herald* "The House", as if it were a kind of college or even an aristocratic family over which he presided.

None the less he was able to attract some fine journalists; he paid good salaries and as a result the status of all Australian journalists rose. In the 1930s and 1940s there were journalists who were known, or had been known, as Keith Murdoch's Young Men, just as he himself had once been one of Northcliffe's Young Men. Some fell from his favour and grew embittered. However, just as many adored him, and his letters to them show a genial side to the tough manager.

Sir Keith was prominent in the world of art as well as politics. While politically conservative, he was culturally progressive. In

1931 he sponsored an exhibition of Matisse, Modigliani and other paintings from private collections. Two years later he was appointed a trustee of the National Gallery and took on its very conservative establishment. He encouraged young Australian artists such as Russell Drysdale. In 1939, the *Herald* organized an exhibition of French and British modern art which was seen as an important turning point in Australian art appreciation. Murdoch founded the Herald Chair of Fine Arts at the University of Melbourne and became one of the leading figures in the new art establishment. He also collected rather more than he could afford. He was a generous and discerning patron.

Chapter 2

CRUDEN, VICTORIA

In 1932 the Murdochs moved from the town house in South Yarra to a boom-time mansion named Heathfield in the neighbouring suburb of Toorak. They had already acquired a ninety-acre property about thirty miles south of Melbourne, near to the seaside community of Frankston. Keith named it Cruden Farm, after the Aberdeenshire village of his grandparents.

Gradually Cruden Farm was transformed into a commodious country house in the American colonial style, with Georgian porticoes, and big open fireplaces. Outside were sunken gardens, stables with English fittings, a tennis court, rockeries and a driveway lined with eucalyptus. Such was the country home of the four Murdoch children: Helen, born in 1929, Rupert in 1931, then two more sisters, Anne in 1935 and Janet in 1939.

There are two views of the young Rupert Murdoch's relations with his parents. One, which subsequently became conventional wisdom, was that they were both remote and tough with him, preoccupied with their own lives, quick to find fault, slow to praise and even slower to demonstrate affection. Many of Rupert Murdoch's chroniclers and associates have speculated, sometimes even insisted, that his subsequent drive and restlessness owe much to the denial of his father's approval at an early age. There are those who say that all his life Rupert Murdoch has been striving for the approbation his father denied him.

This theory is emphatically repudiated by Dame Elisabeth, by Rupert Murdoch's elder sister, Helen, and by Rupert Murdoch himself. He insists that his father was a very loving parent and a hero to him. He says that his mother was far sterner with the children. "Dad was the indulgent one. He was older and valued his time with us all the more. He indulged my sisters particularly, but me as well. My mother was the severe one, with us all, and the least close to us. She always thought that as young children we needed to be brought down a peg, made to conform more, and that my father was a softie, which he was a bit." His sister Helen agrees: "Dad could not have too much of our company. He had waited till he was forty-three and we were pretty precious to him. Mum thought Dad would ruin us."

With hindsight, Elisabeth Murdoch does not dissent. "Keith was much more indulgent than I was, and I think I was counteracting that."

From an early age, the young Rupert was aware of the power and the glory and the sheer fun which accrued to his father from newspapers. Sir Keith used to take his son around the *Herald*'s office on Flinders Street, and Rupert often said later that the smell of the ink, the noise of the presses and the highly charged atmosphere were irresistible. "The life of a publisher is about the best life in the whole world. When kids are subjected to it there's not much doubt they'll be attracted to it." At weekends he used to love lying on his father's bed and watching while he went through the papers, marking the good and the bad bits.

Still, for all the affection that Rupert and Helen recall, Sir Keith could be stern and aloof, and was not quick with praise. In 1989 Rupert was asked in a television interview if his father had thought he was wonderful or a "chump" – the latter, he said.

Lady Murdoch imposed high standards upon her children. She wanted them to have good, Christian values, feelings of obligation and of duty. She insisted they understand that money – and all other rewards – had to be earned. Nothing should be taken for granted. "I didn't want the children to be spoilt or over-indulged," she said. "Maybe they thought I was an old monster in those days. But I think they all really appreciate it now."

In one sense, the real day-to-day direction came not from their parents but from their nannies, who were at centre stage. Nanny Russell, a gentle person, was there from the start. "She was," said Elisabeth Murdoch later, "a great influence on them." Rupert's second wife Anna later said that she thought that Nanny Russell was "probably the soft woman in his early life. She was the mother figure." She thought that Elisabeth Murdoch had been both very busy and very strict.

In 1935, when Rupert was four, and Helen six, Sir Keith and Lady Murdoch went on a trip to England – "home", as Lady Murdoch would call it. (This affectionate term for England would later infuriate Rupert, who insisted that only Australia was home.) Nanny Russell suggested they bring back an English governess because she could not teach the children herself. Dame Elisabeth said, "She was right. They were ready for more. But of course Nanny Russell was always their first love."

In England she engaged Miss Kimpton, a woman some six feet tall, who seemed to Lady Murdoch to have had a rather sad, hard life. But "Kimpo" had great character. She arrived in 1936, and stayed with the Murdochs for twenty years, remaining a close part of the family thereafter. "They often used to be very irked by Kimpo," said Dame Elisabeth, "but they are devoted to her." In later years Kimpo boasted: "It was me who taught Rupert Murdoch his arithmetic." "Kimpo has always told Rupert exactly what to do," said Dame Elisabeth. "She'll ring him up and tell him she disapproves, you know . . . " In 1989, Helen took her to the United States to visit Rupert.

Lady Murdoch was certainly eager to toughen Rupert. Except in winter, for most of his childhood he was not allowed to sleep in his room at Cruden; she insisted that he spend every night in a tree house in the garden. "I thought it would be good for Rupert to sleep out. It was pretty tough. He was more than halfway up the tree. He had no electric light." Her son considers that this story is part of his mother's "mythology" of his childhood. The summers at Cruden were very hot and his tree house was in fact "a perfectly nice little room. I think it had electric light. It had a bed, and instead of windows, it had fly wire all around it. By the standards of those days, it seemed perfectly OK to me. It never occurred to me that it was a hardship to be there."

His mother none the less thought that such experiences at least made him adaptable. "Perhaps he gets that from my father. Like my father, he can suit himself to any kind of company. He has this sort of flair for adapting himself. In a way, though he's had a lot of material benefits, he's just as happy with simple things. In all those ways he's very well adjusted."

As a child, Rupert's closest friend was Helen. They were almost a self-sufficient unit. "There was a good deal of 'us against them' – the establishment – my mother, nanny and the governess," she recalled.

Rupert had contrasting memories of his two grandfathers. The Reverend Patrick Murdoch seemed to him a benign old man. "He used to sit in his garden in a wicker chair and smoke a pipe. Once a year he'd make a sermon." He remembered being taken to hear it when he was about six years old and then, at Sunday lunch, "I was embarrassingly quizzed by my father on what I had thought of the sermon. Just teasing really, but very difficult."

Rupert Greene – "Pop Greene" to the children – was quite another matter. Despite, or perhaps because of, Keith's disapproval, he was always fooling around with the children, buying them ice cream, encouraging disobedience and helping them get into scrapes. He allowed them to drive his car when they could hardly reach the pedals; Helen drove it right through a neighbour's fence. He was always on the go, up to some wheeze, the sort of older relation that every child dreams of.

Dame Elisabeth said later of her son, "On Keith's side he is all Scottish. That's what makes him good. But he probably gets a bit of colour and zest from my side of the family. Perhaps Rupert inherited his gambling instinct from my father." Rupert Murdoch himself said that his own father dreaded the influence of Rupert Greene. "My father thought he was a wild, drinking, gambling man. They all got on for the sake of family life, but it was one of my father's nightmares that I'd turn out like my grandfather, which I probably did, a bit."

It was a privileged and in many ways an idyllic childhood, filled with tea parties, ponies, dogs and outings. On fine summer days there would be picnics on the beach near Cruden. Sir Keith, whose heart continued to give him trouble, would sit in a deckchair with his hat over his eyes. Sometimes he would go fishing with the children. But when he and Lady Murdoch were around, there was always a touch of formality – that was his style. Out for a ride in the lanes, he was always impeccably dressed in a well-cut tweed jacket, jodhpurs and polished riding boots. It was "a sort of medieval cavalcade of children, servants, outriders, horses and dogs", wrote the writer, Joan Lindsay. "At the head of the gay motley procession rides Sir Keith on a massive charger, an upright, rather heavily-built figure immaculate in English tweed and riding boots, proud and happy, as well he might be, in the company of the lively affectionate brood . . . " Lady Murdoch would be on a half-wild racehorse, liable to bolt at any moment, and the guests and children on a diverse collection of ponies and old police horses and whatever else was in the stables or fields at the time. Rupert's first mount was a Shetland pony called Joy Boy. After the ride, the grown-ups were offered a chilled Rhine wine, and the children barley water; everyone would have to have a shower and change clothes before a traditional English lunch – perhaps roast beef and a good claret. That too was all part of Sir Keith's style.

In the winters there was another thrill. In 1938 Keith bought a sheep station up country, on the Murrumbidgee river near Wagga Wagga. There were a couple of thousand acres of river flats and behind that about 14,000 acres of rolling, rocky hills. It was a classic sheep station with a history to match – fantastic yarns of bush rangers ("All true," said Rupert Murdoch) were spun around camp fires while he and Helen listened enthralled. "I loved it. It gave me an enduring feeling for the Australian countryside."

Rupert and Helen would ride all day, or catch rabbits, and hares and water rats. His commercial skills having developed early, Rupert would sell the animals for their skins. Water rats were the most valuable catch, but they were hardest to get. Rupert recalled: "We would climb out on fallen trees across a river and attach an open rabbit trap on a wire, and put a bit of aniseed on some meat. The smell would attract the rats and the trap would break their necks." Then they had to be pulled out of the water and skinned. If the catching was the most difficult part of the operation, the skinning was the most unpleasant. Rupert used to make Helen do that. He sold the skins for sixpence each. Although Helen had to do the dirty work, and although she was older, he gave her only one penny per skin.

At Cruden, the young Rupert dealt in manure as well as rabbits. He collected it around the paddocks and down on the beach at

Davies Bay, where there was a family boathouse. Again, Helen and his younger sisters, Anne and Janet, were enlisted as peons; he would then take the bags around to all the old ladies, who doted on him. "I always say that Rupert got his start in life from rabbits, and manure. I never saw any of the money. Rupert did. He spent it on gambling at school," said Helen.

Apart from such business flair, Rupert's mother said that she considered Rupert "an ordinary little boy", amenable and thoughtful. His most noticeable characteristic was that he liked real things. He only liked toys that actually worked. "He had no time for imaginary things, fairy tales and so on. He liked links with reality." Helen agreed. "He didn't like pretendy games." There was one other characteristic Dame Elisabeth also noted. He could not bear dissension at home. "He was a very gentle little boy." To Helen, he was "a bit of a cat who walked alone".

In 1941, at the age of ten, Rupert was packed off to boarding school. Sir Keith was against it, but Lady Murdoch insisted. "I thought that boarding school taught you to live with other people and be more unselfish." She felt this was an especially important lesson for children from such a privileged background. "I think Keith worried that Rupert was not very well understood at school. But I was sure I was right." Rupert was sure that she was wrong.

GEELONG

"I hated Geelong Grammar," says Murdoch. "I've said many times that I would never make the mistake of calling my school days the happiest days of my life."

Geelong Grammar was a spartan school on the windswept shore of Corio Bay, to the southwest of Melbourne. In winter it seemed to the boys to be one of the coldest places on earth.

The personality of the school was very much the personality of the headmaster of the time. This was James (later Sir James) Darling, who arrived from England to take over the school in 1930, the year of its seventieth anniversary, and at a time when it had lost direction.

Geelong Grammar was created in the second half of the nineteenth century for the sons of Australian squatters who had grown rich. By the 1930s some of the school's 350 boys were still the sons of the elite of the Western District of Victoria, the wealthiest farming area in Australia. But there were boys there from all over the country. They were sons of Australia's largest landowners or of the captains of industry, heirs to fortunes from sugar or sheep, the new Victorian Establishment. But the school's "tone" remained somewhat "agricultural".

James Darling had been born in England in 1899, had a classical education at Repton and Oriel College, Oxford, and had served with the Royal Field Artillery in France and Germany in the First World War. A tall man, lithe and vigorous, with a sharp mind and a hoarse voice, he was an imposing figure to some of the boys, who knew him as "The Boss". He was a radical who had a wry sense of humour.

Darling was a dedicated headmaster and a convinced Christian. He encouraged pupils from Malaysia, Indonesia and especially Thailand. In some ways his ideals were those of Lady Murdoch. He aimed to turn out Christians with a strong sense of self-discipline and social responsibility. Darling wanted to make rich boys humble. They made their own beds, did the dishes, served in the dining hall, even nurtured their own vegetable patches to supplement the school's stodgy cuisine. Darling also cared deeply about culture; he insisted on the teaching of art, music and the classics.

The ethos of Geelong Grammar was not attractive to Rupert. He disliked Darling, the second strong man in his life. And it was easier for him to defy his headmaster than his father.

Winters were grim at Geelong Grammar. Winds whistled in from the plains of western Victoria; there was nothing to stop them for hundreds of miles and many of the school's verandas were open to the elements. The boys had cold showers in the morning with a hot bath once a week.

Organized games consisted of cricket in summer and in winter Aussie Rules football. A lot of boys trained for cross-country running and there were also rowing and swimming. Murdoch says, "I hated the organized sport. Maybe it was just laziness. I used to row to get out of playing cricket." He did not even shine at tennis, a game he later played with aggression and application.

Sport is more important to the male image and self-image in Australia than in many countries. Without a sporting personality, a boy at Geelong needed some other strong distinguishing feature, whether it was intellectual ability or some splendidly eccentric mode of behaviour. Rupert did not at first shine in anything, but his contemporaries remember him. Rod Carnegie (later Sir Roderick and a prominent Melbourne businessman) recalls him as "aggressive and opinionated but not a bully. I liked him, but he was not very popular. Partly because he didn't play games. Partly because of Sir Keith."

Rupert was not prepared for the dislike of his father that he encountered for the first time at Geelong Grammar. Sir Keith saw himself as a pillar of the Melbourne Establishment, but many of the other pillars that had stood for some forty years longer disagreed. Old Melbourne money (made before the turn of the century) tended to despise the parvenus who had become rich in or since the First World War. Rupert also discovered that the power which newspaper barons wield rarely makes them popular.

"I felt a loner at school," said Rupert Murdoch later. "Probably because of my father's position. Bullied a lot. I'm sure my kids have had much the same. We've never talked about it." He said this ostracism had had a crucial effect on him. "It made me realize that if you're going to do your job as a publisher or a principal in the media, you've got to be your own person and not have close friendships which can compromise you. That philosophy just evolved, I think. It made you realize you were not looked upon as just another successful businessman, farmer etc."

There are some Geelong Grammar alumni who complain that Rupert was a "pest", but Darryl Wardle enjoyed his company. "For no particular reason, I liked him very much. He was always eminently confident." Wardle thought it was clear that "he was always going to be involved in newspapers. I can recall his pointing out to us how much better the layout of one paper was than another. Pretty unusual for a schoolboy, but not all that many schoolkids had fathers in that situation."

Another boy, Daniel Thomas, who became one of Australia's best-known art historians, liked Rupert enormously. "He was fun to be with. Not bumptious. We had picnics with girls from Melbourne. Life was fun with him." Rupert took Daniel to see his parents – Daniel was impressed by both Sir Keith's art collection and his manner. "He seemed a warm, large, friendly person."

At weekends, the Geelong Grammar boys could get a pass that allowed them to leave the confined school premises and head off into the nearby hills, with or without bicycles. Some boys used to row long distances, others visited a café in Geelong itself, a short bus ride away. Rupert, taking a leaf from his grandfather Greene's book, often used to slip off to the racetrack for a bet on the horses. He kept a motorcycle at a shop nearby.

Murdoch says that he had a terrible education at Geelong Grammar, for which he blames the teachers. Perhaps, he says, the war meant that they could not get any decent staff. This is unfair. Darling attracted interesting men. Two masters were eminent historians: Manning Clark and the left-wing historian Russel Ward. There was a fine English teacher, Peter Westcott, and in 1942 Darling plucked from an internment camp Ludwig Hirschfeld-Mack, a former Bauhaus member, and a refugee from Nazi Germany. Hirschfeld-Mack subsequently refused a chair at Harvard in gratitude to Darling. He was said to be a marvellous teacher and had a profound influence on his more receptive pupils.

Another teacher, the young writer Stephen Murray-Smith, said, "I soon palled up with Rupert, who wasn't that much younger, about sixteen, I would say. We used to roam around the school talking of socialism. No doubt what I had to say was exceedingly callow in its way." Rupert was not an intellectual, "but he had an engaging freshness of approach and willingness to listen and perhaps to think which distinguished him from most of his fellow pupils".

Murray-Smith was embarrassed to find himself "telling Rupert how badly the forces of the Left regarded his father. But Rupert was very good-natured about it all and seemed genuinely interested in what I had to say. And if it is true that Rupert was

Left-inclined at Oxford, I guess my fleeting contact with him may have had something to do with it."

In 1947 Rupert completed his studies at Geelong Grammar. But he then stayed on another year and became a newspaper man. He republished a school magazine, *If*, which had flourished a decade before, and produced two issues, under the title *If Revived*. One of them contained an article: "The Case for Socialism". Though unsigned, this was probably his handiwork. One article he did sign was a heavily intellectual piece about the German Bauhaus movement, presumably inspired by Hirschfeld-Mack.

The Debating Society gave him a chance to assert himself and to be aggressive. His name at last began to appear in the school magazine, the *Corian*. From 1947, there was rarely a debate in which he did not take part. The same was true of his friend Richard Searby, the son of a distinguished surgeon, whom Sir James Darling recalled as "very intellectually able".

Boys chose which side of a debate to speak on. Rupert's debut was in a debate that deplored the growing predominance of scientific engineers. His views were not recorded in the magazine, but the reaction to them was. His speech brought forth an accusation that he was to hear more than once in the years to come: "Mr R.K. Murdoch," noted the *Corian*, "found fault with the Hon. proposer who in turn found fault with Mr Murdoch for misrepresentation."

In a debate on private schooling Murdoch was described as having spoken "in his own inimitable racy style". He argued that private schools should give more places to the poor. He did not see "why the chance of birth into a rich family should allow boys an education most of them did not deserve". At one point in the debate, the *Corian* commented: "Here Mr Murdoch tried again but was subdued by the chairman."

In one debate Rupert took up the cause of planning controls against that of free enterprise. In a debate on the American way of life, he laid into America for being racially intolerant, and he castigated US politics, saying that everything in America was dominated by the capitalists. The subject of trade unions became an inflammatory issue on another occasion. Rupert was for them,

Searby against. According to the *Corian* Rupert ended his speech by publicly declaring that he was "not a commo".

In all these debates, his speeches displayed a fairly consistent anti-Establishment line. Darryl Wardle said that this was one of the things that intrigued him about Rupert. "He was left-wing at school, quite strongly so. I don't mean communist, but left-wing. And he appeared to disapprove of the politics of his father's paper. I don't recall the *Herald* being anything but anti-Labor and he would usually be against the *Herald*."

Their mother had tried to instil in the children a sense of *noblesse oblige* and Murdoch recalled that he and his sister Helen were both conscious of their privileged childhood. "We were always rebelling against it a bit and were into all sorts of causes, like other idealistic youngsters." And, "We certainly had a strong consciousness if not shame about the comfort in which we lived [and] trundled off to the poorer parts of Melbourne, just to see what it was like, to open our eyes ... " He and Richard Searby formed a small group to look at Esperanto, and Murdoch also asserted he was a conscientious objector.

He later denied that his left-wing views were anything to do with James Darling's opinions. Indeed he was contemptuous of Darling. "He used to tell us a lot about our duty to God, then he'd go to Melbourne, to dinner parties at the Melbourne Club. He wanted it both ways, I thought. I thought he was a bit of a poseur and still do." This ungenerous assessment was not shared by all Geelong Grammar boys.

Darling himself has always been discreet about all his former pupils. But he has dropped hints that he never much approved of Rupert, whom he felt to be hypocritical. While he constantly flouted the trust system on which Geelong Grammar depended, he would also frequently go to Darling and other masters, ostensibly to ask advice on his future but in reality, thought Darling, "to make me sweet. He wanted all this and heaven too. He wanted to have his own way and at the same time to be respected and promoted."

Asked the perpetual question, "What makes Rupert run?" Sir James replied, decades later, "What makes any of these people run? It's not peculiar to Rupert. It isn't greed. I don't think it's even power because I don't think he uses power. His father used power much more." He thought Murdoch's only god was himself, and he could not understand why he had inherited so little of his mother's rectitude.

In 1991 Sir James, still sprightly in his nineties, commented on Murdoch's newspaper career with a quotation from the novel *Lucinda Brayford*, by the Australian writer Martin Boyd: " 'Sir,' he said, 'your newspapers for two decades have engaged in the degradation of the proper feelings of our people. What is vile they offer to gloating eyes, what is vindictive they applaud. You have done more harm to this country than any of its external enemies . . . I beg you will leave before my butler throws you down the steps.' "

OXFORD

After Geelong Grammar, Sir Keith fixed Rupert up with a short cadetship on the Melbourne *Herald*; he did a few months' work in the police courts with a friend from school. And then, in summer 1950, it was off to Oxford where Darling had helped obtain him a place at Worcester College. Sir Keith and Lady Murdoch were pleased. His father desperately hoped that after Oxford Rupert would embark upon life as a newspaper man.

Sir Keith's own powers, political and physical, were waning. He was sixty-five, he had had a weak heart for almost twenty years, and had recently suffered another heart attack. He no longer exercised the influence he had once enjoyed over national politicians, and his authority even within the Herald group was diminished. The effects of his weak heart were compounded by a painful operation for cancer of the bowel. In 1949 he had retired as a managing director of the Herald group but he remained chairman.

His views were still heard at board meetings, but the younger managers in the organization were beginning to get restless. Conscious of time running out, he concentrated on consolidating his own small newspaper group which he hoped to leave to Rupert.

Starting in the late 1920s, he had acquired control of Queensland Newspapers, whose principal property was the *Brisbane Courier-Mail*. In 1948 he proposed to the Herald board that they relinquish their monopoly of Adelaide newspapers. He wanted to buy those shares of the Adelaide *News* held by the Adelaide *Advertiser*, which itself was controlled by the Herald group. He promised in writing that if his family ever wanted to sell their shares in the Queensland Newspapers company, they would offer them back to the Herald group. His offer was refused.

Sir Keith decided that he and his wife should accompany Rupert to Oxford and show him a bit of the world. He enlisted the help of the Melbourne *Herald*'s London correspondent, Rohan Rivett, a conscientious journalist who had spent three years in a Japanese POW camp. Rivett was a man of some distinction, who would play an important, and ultimately unhappy part in Rupert Murdoch's life throughout the 1950s. The relationships between Sir Keith and Rupert and Rivett are poignantly illustrated by the correspondence between them. The letters also show how Rupert matured, and both the similarities and the difference between the father's and the son's approaches to editors.

Towards the end of his life, Sir Keith was avuncular, almost paternal with journalists he liked. In September 1949 he wrote from Melbourne to Rivett in London:

My dear Rohan,

I read your work with interest. Are you really very Left, Rohan? You seem to be enthusiastically for the Attlee people. I would be, if I could believe that they are not reducing some necessary incentives; playing politics instead of increasing man-hour production and quality; and running an overweening civil service which includes loafers and inquisitive do-nothing self-proud theorists.

At the end of 1949 he asked Rivett to drive with his wife Nan to Italy the following April to meet him, Lady Murdoch and Rupert. Together they would then drive back across Europe to London, doing some cultural sightseeing on the way. He wrote that he had toyed with the idea of a Rolls-Royce and a driver, "but this, I am afraid, would be too crippling", so he was going to get a Rover instead. He wanted Rivett to find a "clean and decent" Paris hotel off the Champs Elysées. "We do not want expensive hotels. My family will feel just as happy with clean beds in cheaper hotels than in lavish ones."

The Murdochs flew from Melbourne, by the long, stopping routes which operated in those days, to Rome. Then they and the Rivetts drove slowly north. The trip went well, though the hotel which Rivett selected in Troyes was a bit too far downmarket for the Murdochs. Rivett wrote later: "I'll never forget Rupert's face when he found his bath slapped down alongside his bed on a floor that listed about fifteen degrees."

From London the Murdochs flew to Canada, where Sir Keith led the Australian delegation to the Empire Press Union. There they met Pat Gibson, director of the Westminster Press, one of the largest provincial newspaper publishers in Britain. For Gibson and for most of the other British delegates this was a trip to savour; it was the first time they had been able to travel outside Britain (except in military service) since 1939. Gibson liked the Murdochs and found Rupert "very charming". When Sir Keith asked him to help Rupert find a summer job in journalism before he took up his place at Oxford, Gibson readily agreed. He sent him to the *Birmingham Gazette*.

Britain five years after the end of the Second World War could seem a gloomy place to a brash, young Australian. The wartime sense of solidarity had long since disappeared. Industrial relations were bitter. The country was still hemmed in by all sorts of rationing and restrictions as it attempted to rebuild and create a new welfare state. Cyril Connolly wrote, after a visit to New York, that now in England, "the ego is at half pressure; most of us are not men or women but members of a vast, seedy over-worked neuter class, with our drab clothes, our ration books and murder stories, our envious, stricken old-world apathies and resentments – a careworn people". All this, and no sun, either.

Newsprint was rationed, a restriction imposed in the interest of the balance of payments. As a result papers were very thin and many of them were not very good. Aneurin Bevan, a leading Labour politician, complained in terms that have since become ever more familiar, that too much space was devoted either to pornography or to the Royal Family. "Indeed the latter has now reached a point where it has become a national disgrace. It must be deeply repugnant to the persons concerned, who are carrying out difficult duties with commendable dignity and restraint. A sort of newspaper Gresham's law appears to be operating where only bad standards of journalism are commercially successful."

In Birmingham, Britain's second city, Rupert found himself a bedsitting room, and had a fine old time on the *Gazette*. "I even got the diary," he said. He went dog racing, the popular sport in Birmingham, and he noticed that the sports pages were the best-read pages in the tabloid papers.

Sir Keith wrote to him, saying, "I do hope, dear boy, that you are not doing too much but using your time usefully and are in good shape and heart . . . You will, I am sure, make a proper exit from Birmingham and say grateful goodbyes to your colleagues, your bosses and your friends."

In fact, after his stint on the *Gazette*, Murdoch wrote to Pat Gibson to tell him that he should get rid of the editor Charles Fenby. Fenby, a mild-mannered man, is well remembered by others, but he worked Murdoch hard and did not lavish praise upon him. Murdoch later said, "It was an outrageously cheeky letter to write. But all the young journalists thought Fenby was very remote from the staff, stuck in a corner writing editorials, not really editing the paper as we thought it should be done."

Pat Gibson was astonished. He thought Fenby an excellent editor, "a bit cynical, perhaps, but I thought I had done very well to get him for the paper". He did not follow Murdoch's advice, but Fenby got to hear of it and thereafter followed Murdoch's career with unconcealed distaste.

In October 1950, Rupert went up to Worcester College. Most of the British undergraduates had either served in the war or had already done two years' national service. They were mature, and to a young Australian, rather stuffy. Rod Carnegie, who followed Rupert Murdoch from Geelong Grammar to Oxford, also thought that most of them were pretty inhospitable to Australians far from home.

Murdoch's principal tutor at Oxford was Asa Briggs, who was

on his way to becoming one of the most doughty members of the British intellectual, academic and broadcasting elite. Short, plump, with eyes that glittered with energy from behind his spectacles, Briggs was a bustling, enthusiastic figure, who had graduated from Cambridge in 1941 with first-class degrees in both history and economics. He had spent much of the war with other intellectuals in the Intelligence Corps. A voracious learner, a prolific writer and a gifted conversationalist, Briggs was to become one of the most brilliant political academics in Britain, an important member of the Establishment, who none the less retained a slightly radical air. When Murdoch met him, he was beginning to establish himself as a serious historian, and he later developed an especial interest in the theory and practice of the media, particularly of broadcasting.

At Sir Keith's request, Briggs spent a lot of time with Murdoch, and taught him to think logically. Murdoch called him "Isa", a term of endearment which Briggs enjoyed. A mutual friend was another young history tutor, Harry Pitt, who very much liked Murdoch. "He had no sense of class nuances. He just had a good time at Oxford." Murdoch agrees. He was reading Politics, Philosophy and Economics – one of the less rigorous degree courses. He was interested in the Politics, as taught by Briggs, unenthusiastic about the Economics, and contemptuous of the Philosophy. Outside of work, "I loved the freedom, the intellectual excitement, going to different clubs, the Union, the little dining clubs. It was a whole new world to me."

Like his father on his own first visit, however, he did not thrill to Britain. "There were a lot of Australians who embraced everything that was English and rejected everything that was Australian." He, by contrast, was idealistic about Australia. "I hugely resented Aussies there who said they'd never go back." He would come close to fisticuffs on the issue of patriotism. "I was very passionate about Australia. It was special, it was different." He also came away with a dislike bordering on contempt for what he saw as "English" characteristics. He found the country complacent and uncompetitive. As for the ruling class, it left him bursting with spleen ever after. "They distrust money," he has asserted. "They despise business. They create the social and psychological currents which have done so much damage to Britain and its willingness to change."

Murdoch had one of the best rooms in college – the De Quincey room. He had a car, which was an almost unheard-of luxury for an undergraduate, yet he also affected to be a socialist, if not a communist. He had a bust of Lenin in pride of place on his mantelpiece. This may have been nothing more than a sign of Rupert's cockiness. Perhaps he wanted only to provoke his father. But it was provocative in other ways. In the early 1950s, Stalinism was at its most aggressive. The Cold War was beginning. The countries of Eastern Europe were being subjected one by one to Marxist-Leninist terror. To be a Leninist at such a time was scarcely a joke.

His Geelong Grammar friend, Richard Searby, who was now a tall, handsome and serious classicist at Corpus Christi College, has been quoted as saying that no one took Rupert's politics very seriously. Asa Briggs agreed. Still, the combination of money, Marxism and arrogance did not endear him to everyone.

Another Australian at Worcester was George Masterman, who was one year ahead of Murdoch. Like Murdoch, he felt alien to many of the British students. "They were so awful and superior. They never talked to us. Rupert was cocky, rich and a communist. They hated that." Masterman ran a cricket team called the Rustics, and proposed Rupert for membership, but he was blackballed.

Outside of Oxford, Rupert's best friend in England was probably Rohan Rivett. Rohan and his wife and their young children, David and Rhyll, lived at Sunbury on Thames, less than an hour's drive from Oxford. Murdoch was a frequent visitor, and they became his Australian family in England. Years later Nan Rivett remembered him as very exuberant and untidy, his shirt tails always hanging out. Rhyll thought he was like a big bouncy dog; she and her brother adored him. Rohan and Nan were always concerned lest his parents find out about his gambling. Nan Rivett thought that Rupert was always trying to convince his mother that he was as good as his father, something Lady Murdoch clearly doubted.

Rivett saw as much of Rupert as he could, and at the end of

1950 he wrote to Sir Keith, "I am inclined to prophesy that he will make his first million with fantastic ease."

Sir Keith replied that Rupert "has a capacity for living well and I trust he will keep this all his life, whilst at the same time putting his service and creative work first".

Rivett's letters show how anxious he always felt about money, and how meticulously he logged his expenses. Sir Keith would write that he was sorry he could not pay Rivett better: "I feel so guilty sometimes that I have not provided for you and others . . . a much more material advantage out of your profession."

After Rupert made a trip to Paris in early 1951, Rivett wrote that "he delighted Nan and me with his exceedingly shrewd and money-saving junketings in Paris, which suggest to me he will probably prove the greatest income maker from an expense account in *Herald* history when he comes back on the payroll".

In the 1951 Easter vacation, the Rivetts took Rupert to Switzerland with them. Rivett wrote to Sir Keith that his development in the last year had been amazing. "His resources and ability to work things out and get things done are first-rate . . . Nancy and I found him a grand travelling companion in every way and from the first moment until the return he was picking up information, asking questions and absorbing new impressions with enthusiasm."

Rupert also stayed for weekends with Sir Christopher Chancellor, the general manager of Reuters, and visited Pat Gibson, who had a house near Banbury. Gibson remembers it very clearly. Murdoch arrived in a spanking new Rolls-Royce, explaining to Gibson, "Well, I thought I had better have a decent car if I was coming to you. So I rang Rolls and told them that if they lent me a Roller for the weekend, I'd review it for one of our papers." Gibson says that this bravado, coming after his advice to fire Charles Fenby, "made me realize that Rupert was out of the ordinary. We liked him very much. He was great fun. Very critical of his elders." Such criticism remained characteristic, whatever the targets' ages.

Sir Keith constantly wrote to Rupert, giving him news about the family newspapers, hoping to draw his firm interest. His overriding concern now was to settle his affairs so as to leave enough money for his wife and daughters and the beginnings of a newspaper empire for Rupert. Indeed, almost every business move he made in the last four years of his life was directed to this end. He was always worried that Rupert was not responding, and was frittering away his time in Oxford. At one stage Rupert was doing so badly in his studies that Sir Keith decided to bring him back to work on the newspapers in Australia. His mother's intervention saved him. Later she explained: "Rupert was not shining academically, and my husband was anxious to spend time with him . . . Although we both hoped that he would live a lot longer, he was anxious about that. But I did feel that Rupert should see it through." But she made it clear to Rupert that if he failed her, he would lose her "last shred of respect". It was said that her warning shook Rupert to the bones.

In the northern summer of 1951, Sir Keith, now quite unwell, made his last circumnavigation. He flew first to the United States, and in Washington he was given two minutes with President Truman. In London, he summoned Rivett to his suite at Claridge's Hotel and offered him a new job as the editor of one of the two papers he owned personally, the evening tabloid Adelaide *News*. Rivett was overjoyed.

Sir Keith bought a new car, a Ford Zephyr, and told Rupert he could drive it through Europe and then ship it back to Melbourne from the Middle East. He would fly in for part of the trip himself. Thus began a fantastic journey, which can be pieced together from the memories of Rupert and the other travellers, and the letters which Rupert wrote to the Rivetts.

Half an hour before Rupert was due to leave, he went to Australia House to pick up his passport, only to find that "the bloody fool Holt protégées in the Immigration Dept had invalidated my visa to Yugoslavia. You can imagine the panic and the goodly Murdoch calling in all the VIPs from their good lunches to swear to my good intentions . . . " When that crisis was resolved he and his friends, who included George Masterman, roared off.

After a night "in a filthy out-of-the-way French village", Murdoch lost the car keys, had new ones made and then found the originals – "very Murdoch style". He was proud to relate that a girl in Munich told him his journey was *une croisade incroyable*.

Then it was on to Zürich, where, as he wrote to the Rivetts, he argued about the price of his room.

After Sir Keith joined them, they drove in a crowded car (with Sir Keith constantly telling Rupert to slow down), through northern Italy and Austria into Yugoslavia. Rupert was delighted that the Yugoslav border guards failed to discover the black-market dinars he had purchased in Zürich.

Despite the wretched appearance of people in Belgrade, Rupert thought that Tito was "certainly a very great man indeed, and the only man capable of doing half what he is doing now. Just to hold that country together is the work of a genius."

They drove on to Greece. Rupert said later he was bored with Masterman by this time, so they parted company for a while. Father and son drove to Delphi and then to Athens, where they stayed at the best hotel, the Grande Bretagne. Murdoch wrote the Rivetts a four-page letter recounting their adventures so far, and saying how wonderful it was to be scorched by the "bloody sun" again.

Yugoslavia had persuaded him that the Russians now had a terrible choice:

Do they wait for the present arms effort of the West to culminate in busting the Western economies and walking in . . . or is the risk of this not taking place and the power of the US becoming so great that they are finally 1) either bullied into peaceful submission (almost impossible, I would say) or 2) exterminated by a war brought on by the Americans taking their present efforts to a logical and historical conclusion – namely war?

At Athens airport he and his father had tried to get a bag through customs. They had to fight for an hour and a half. It was just a mass of shouting Greeks "all trying to smuggle things in with faked-up diplomatic passes". One man in front of them was discovered smuggling an aeroplane speedometer in a caseful of mink coats.

Sir Keith left him in Athens and flew back to Melbourne. "That was the last time I ever saw him. I don't remember any particular parting or anything."

On his own, Rupert went to Crete, which he loved. "I went up to little villages at the end of tiny paths, expecting to find no one would speak a word of English, and it'd be full of retired greengrocers from Melbourne." Then he and Masterman met up again in Athens and were joined by Asa Briggs and Harry Pitt. The four of them drove on into Turkey, where the car was badly smashed. They limped to Beirut, where Rupert desperately tried to find someone to beat the Zephyr back into shape before shipping it home to his father. When it did eventually reach Melbourne, it had to be sold as scrap.

From Beirut they took a boat to Port Said where they jumped aboard a P & O liner returning from Australia. The few passengers were unhappy British migrants going home. Murdoch was contemptuous. "A lot of bloody whingeing Poms who couldn't take Australia," he said later. Murdoch was very bored on the boat and persuaded Harry Pitt to jump ship with him in Marseilles. They took the train to Paris, where although they were penniless, the Australian Ambassador refused to lend them £10. Rupert was furious.

Back in Oxford, Murdoch decided he wanted to live more freely, outside the city's boundaries and away from the supervision of the university proctors. He moved into digs on Headington Hill with another Australian from Geelong Grammar, John Piper. They had a little attic flat at the top of the house. Murdoch promptly took his landlord to court to get the rent reduced. "And I won. Something like £4 a week reduced to £1."

In 1952 Murdoch decided to stand as secretary of the University Labour Club. In those days, and for a long time thereafter, candidates were not permitted to canvas openly, but in a quiet, British way, their friends used to recommend their man to potential voters. Murdoch despised such hypocrisies and ran an energetic campaign. "Rooting for Rupert" was its slogan.

In May 1952, the student paper *Cherwell* declared: "Australian ex-journalist, Rupert Murdoch ... bombarded Club members with so many plaintive appeals that undergraduate canvassing and socialist majorities hit new highs." The paper continued, "Turbulent, travelled and twenty-one, he is known . . . as a brilliant betting man with that individual Billingsgate touch. He manages *Cherwell* publicity in his spare time." A fortnight later, *Cherwell* announced: "Rupert Murdoch, cataclysmic chauffeur from the outback, prototype of Hollywood's peripatetic publicists, has plastered the town and papered the noticeboards."

Complaints were made to Gerald Kaufman, the chairman of the club. Kaufman and Murdoch had different memories as to what happened next. Kaufman's recollection, published years later, was rather more genial than Murdoch's. He recalled that Rupert was popular at Oxford, but under the rules of the Labour Club he, as chairman, had to convene a tribunal to investigate the charges of electioneering. It discovered, according to Kaufman, that a campaign team had indeed been formed on Murdoch's behalf. He was banned from standing again for office.

Murdoch blames Kaufman (subsequently a Labour Party MP and Shadow Foreign Secretary):

> Fucking Kaufman. He was the same then, a greasy know-all. They found a list I had of people I thought would vote for me . . . that was the evidence against me. There was a kangaroo court. They said I had clearly been canvassing for votes. I was expelled for breaking the rules. Everyone canvassed for votes.

Kaufman declined to comment on Murdoch's recollections.

Back home, Sir Keith was becoming iller and more worried. Despite the empire he had built for the Herald group, he had not made enough money to be sure that he could leave his family as secure and comfortable as he wished. He and Elisabeth both felt that the group had failed to reward him adequately. Letters to his banks, his brokers, his accountant, and to Rupert revealed his constant, nagging anxiety to leave the family financially liquid and especially to clear an overdraft, which he had run up partly in order to leave the foundation of a newspaper empire to Rupert.

He was desperate to increase his share of Adelaide *News* stock. At the end of 1951 he sold more of his small parcel of Herald group shares. He wrote to Rupert to say that he was mortgaging what he could to buy more of the *News*. Rupert said later, "He was never trying to create a dynasty, but he knew there would never be a place for me at the *Herald*, on which he held a paltry number of shares. I guess he wanted me to have an opportunity in journalism."

Sir Keith toyed with another very secret plan. It was to leave the *Herald* altogether, to buy the Melbourne *Argus* and run it against the company which he had built. The *Argus* belonged to the London Mirror group and was losing money heavily. After Cecil King, Northcliffe's nephew, became czar of the London *Daily Mirror* in 1951, Murdoch cabled his congratulations and the two men began to correspond. They devised a scheme to merge the Argus and the Adelaide News into one company. The *Mirror* would have to invest heavily but Murdoch's presence would guarantee good management in the fight against the *Herald*. In the end Cecil King backed away from the deal, partly because he thought Murdoch too old and his health too precarious. Perhaps for Murdoch this was fortunate: the task of taking on his own *Herald* would have been neither pleasant nor widely welcomed in Melbourne. It would have been seen as disloyal to the company he had developed, and Sir Keith valued loyalty.

In early 1952, Hugh Cudlipp of the *Mirror* came to Melbourne. Sir Keith put on a cloak "like Northcliffe's cloak and like Northcliffe's nephew's cloak", observed Cudlipp. Cudlipp thought he affected "the style and speech of the cultured English gentleman of standing; the corset of Australia's twentieth-century respectability fitted him perfectly". Swathed in his cloak, he took Cudlipp to see the Melbourne war memorial. He told him he was concerned about Rupert's "alarming left-wing views". Cudlipp did not think he really need worry, but worrying was part of Sir Keith's style.

He wrote to Rivett, "I am very worried about Rupert in that he does not write home enough. When he gets going, he writes well, and wins marks; but he must learn that all human relationships, even those with his family, have always to be kept in repair; and are infinitely worth a lot of trouble and study . . . "

He also asked Rivett not to "inflate" Rupert. "You have talked once or twice in your letters of his 'brilliant prospects'. His prospects depend entirely on himself."

With some prescience Sir Keith wrote:

By the time the Taxation Commissioner has finished with anybody these days, and he doesn't until you have been dead quite
a time, there is not much money for anybody to inherit and I
hope Rupert will earn whatever he gets. He is inclined to look
forward with gusto to his *opportunities*. The *real opportunity* is
that he makes himself a good man. I feel confident he will do
so.

In 1952, Sir Keith had to have a second prostate operation. He
was two months in hospital, and then spent further time recuperating at Cruden and at Surfer's Paradise in Queensland. While he
was there, he bought more shares in Queensland Newspapers, and
despite his financial concerns, he was still on the look-out for
good paintings, especially by Sidney Nolan and other modern
Australian artists. "I have got four good Nolans for nothing
because I sent him to the Northern Territory to illustrate some
cattle articles."

He continued to write long, affectionate directions to Rohan
Rivett, who was now editing the Adelaide *News*. He warned
Rivett against writing in a style which was "staccato or ejaculatory
or perhaps even slightly breathless". His preferred journalistic
style had softened; he had turned against "*Daily Express*-type
sensationalism".

Rivett continued to adore him, and wrote to Rupert, "It would
be difficult to exaggerate how much I've learnt from him in these
past pretty hectic ten months. He has been extraordinarily patient.
He always says he owes a lot to Northcliffe. I can't imagine that
Northcliffe was one tenth as good as him or as wise and helpful
in guidance as he has been to much less promising material."

Rupert had just completed another tour of Europe and wrote a
long and typically ebullient description to the Rivetts – nine pages
in magenta ink. "It's been striking me that perhaps you may be
in need of some big stuff. Wouldn't that dish rag which you
call your front page be vastly improved by some REALLY BIG
WORLD SCOOP STORIES under big and startling new names
in journalism." He proposed himself as special correspondent at
the Labour Party's annual national conference, to counter "the

ridiculous and damaging lies told by the morning warmongers. What about it? Herr Commissar for Truth, Peace and Women?"

His travels had ended in Deauville. At the casino, he lost all his francs the first night, and was left with only unchangeable Italian lire in an expensive French hotel.

So, waiting for the bank to pull its finger out and send money I amassed a colossal bill and studied the wheels to perfect THE system – with one eye on the floor for dropped chips. Once an old lady did drop a 1,000-francs chip and went away without noticing it. I pounced! Soon there was 5,000 francs, which bought a pornographic novel, a shave, a cable to London, some drinks, and a few small 100-franc chips with which to really amass a fortune. But fate was against me. And finally back to Oxford only £50 worse off.

At the end of September Rupert wrote a long and enthusiastic letter to his parents. It arrived on Thursday, 2 October. Sir Keith read it with the greatest pleasure. He was delighted and encouraged. "I think he's got it," he said to his wife. It was a judgement she always remembered with gratitude. That Saturday, he wrote to one of his daughters, "My beautiful and good Anne . . . We had a splendid letter from Rupert and he is forgiven some of his misdemeanours . . . " A few hours later, during the night of Saturday–Sunday 4–5 October 1952 he died in his sleep.

It was Asa Briggs who came out to Headington early on that Sunday morning to give Murdoch the news. "It was a great shock," said Rupert. "I remember more the shock of it than the grief, in a sense. It was unreal, because of the distance."

The Adelaide *News*'s front-page obituary described Sir Keith as "one of the few very great Australians of his age . . . probably the most outstanding newspaper man of the English-speaking world. His was a romantic success story beyond the dreams of fiction . . . " On a more personal note, Rivett wrote to Rupert, "He has been so awfully good to me . . . What a wonderful teacher and guide, friend and philosopher he has been." Amongst his "Young Men", John Hetherington felt differently, writing later that Murdoch was a "calculating, undeviating, insatiable seeker after worldly riches and temporal power". But Douglas Brass, who had got to know him during the war, found "not the slightest tinge of personal spite in his makeup", and another considered him "the most generous and kindliest employer for whom I ever worked".

In Australia, the family and its friends gathered around Lady Murdoch. Rohan Rivett went straight from Adelaide to Melbourne to pay his respects. He told Rupert, "She was really quite splendid. You would have been even more proud of her than you already are. She's got a tremendous, steel-like quality inside all that sweetness and generosity."

The flight home took Rupert three days. He arrived exhausted and upset. His mother had not delayed the funeral for him. Keith had been buried on Tuesday, 7 October.

The funeral had been a considerable Melbourne occasion. There was a large congregation and more than 500 wreaths covered the lawns outside Toorak Presbyterian Church. In his panegyric, the Reverend A.C. Watson described Keith as "an outstanding leader in the business and public life of this nation, a great Australian and a beloved husband and father . . . Thirty years ago he took in hand a relatively small business, but he saw it not only in terms of what had been, not only in a setting of Melbourne and of Australia. He saw it against the background of a new age."

The pallbearers included prominent members of the Melbourne Establishment; the federal and state governments were well represented. Elisabeth Murdoch was of course the principal mourner, along with Helen, Anne and Janet. Only Rupert was missing.

Rohan Rivett sat behind Lady Murdoch and her daughters, with, he wrote to Rupert, a lump in his throat. "When they walked out they were absolutely stoic . . . It was a tremendous family triumph. They would have made your father very happy."

Rupert said later that although some of his family were shocked by the fact that his mother had not delayed the funeral for his return, it had probably simply not occurred to her to do so; there was an Australian tradition of burying people quickly because of the heat. He claimed: "It didn't really matter, except it probably would have made a big impression on me." This was an understandable rationalization. But Rupert's relationship to his parents was then and remained at the core of his being.

While he was in Melbourne, Rupert discussed his father's estate and in particular the future of the Adelaide *News* and the *Brisbane Courier-Mail* with his family and their advisers. In his will, written in 1948, Sir Keith had declared his intention:

> WHEREAS I desire that Queensland Newspapers Pty Ltd of Queen Street Brisbane and another Newspaper Company approved by my trustees should continue to express my ideals of newspaper and broadcasting activities in the service of others and these ideals should be pursued with deep interest AND WHEREAS I desire that my said son Keith Rupert Murdoch should have the great opportunity of spending a useful altruistic and full life in newspaper and broadcasting activities and of ultimately occupying a position of high responsibility in that field with the support of my trustees if they consider him worthy of that support. NOW I HEREBY BEQUEATH . . .

Over the last four years, as Sir Keith's business fortunes had waxed and waned, three codicils had been added to the will. Originally Rupert had been left a package of shares in Queensland Newspapers; eventually he inherited a major part of Cruden Investments, a family company that held both the Brisbane and Adelaide stock.

Rupert was anxious to keep both the Adelaide *News* and the *Brisbane Courier-Mail*. But his mother felt that the family could not afford to do so. Her daughter Helen says that Elisabeth's childhood memories of her father had given her a terror of debt. She was also heavily influenced by the trustees of Keith's estate, in particular by Harold Giddy, the chairman of the trustees. When Rupert had gone back to Oxford, Giddy persuaded her to sell the family's shares in the *Brisbane Courier-Mail* to the Melbourne *Herald*. Since Giddy was also chairman of the *Herald*, there were those who thought he had a conflict of interest, Rupert among them.

After he returned to Oxford Rupert resumed his correspondence with Rivett – but overnight the tone and subject matter had changed, becoming far less frivolous. Suddenly he became interested in the minutest details of the Adelaide *News*'s finances. His letters showed that he had an instinctive feel for money and power, and how to use them both. He was very frustrated. He was sure that if he had been in Australia, he could have persuaded his mother to keep the *Brisbane Courier-Mail* as well as the Adelaide *News*. But far away in Oxford, "I have the feeling I am fighting a one-man battle," he wrote to Rivett. "Oh for the bloody sun! . . . If it weren't for good friends, I'd have shot myself in this bloody place long ago. Rain, wind, sleet, slush, shit, snow, and starch!"

He spent Christmas 1952 with Douglas Brass, a courteous reporter, and his wife, a friend of his mother, who were now in London for the *Herald,* and cheered up a little in the New Year. In January 1953, he wrote to Rivett, "Your letter of the 15th December is especially interesting. I take it that with the reduced price of newsprint beginning to show itself in the balance sheet, and after taxation, the total profit this year should be in the vicinity of £55,000. Is this not right?"

Rupert then turned to politics. Princess Elizabeth had recently succeeded her father, George VI. Rupert thought her first Christmas address both dull and arrogant, and wrote, "I personally entirely deprecate this thoroughly NEW theory that the Monarchy is above criticism. Don't misunderstand me, I'm not advocating a Republic – which I don't believe in, anyway . . . "

He added an extraordinary postscript, written in magenta ink, reaffirming his loyalty to Lenin. "Yesterday was the 29th anniversary of the Great Teacher. We stood to attention for one minute in front of THE BUST on the mantelpiece and drank several toasts – and then settled down to some good reading of adulatory Russian poetry."

He was honing his political instincts in other ways. With an election imminent in South Australia, he wrote to Rivett, "I implore you not to speak out too loudly on either side." He never wanted to be identified with a loser. In February 1953 he recounted a dinner with one of the great Australian newspaper barons, Frank Packer, at the Chancellors' house. "Packer must be the biggest crook in Australian newspapers, but equally he is the cleverest and he may, in the not too distant future, be in a position to give us great help."

In a postscript he asked, "Just how much are we spending on: a) circulation PROMOTION, b) advertising PROMOTION? NO paper can expect to make headway without VERY generous expenditure in these depts." It was already clear that whereas Sir Keith's letters to Rivett had been much concerned with editorial content, Rupert's dealt first with the bottom line.

Through March, April and early May 1953 he continued to worry about the estate, and about how the Adelaide *News* could beat off the rival Adelaide *Advertiser* which, as part of the Melbourne Herald group, had far greater resources. All the while, his final exams were rushing towards him, and he was terrified – with good reason, for he had done hardly any work. "What about a coronation cover?" he wrote in April. The choice seemed to be between taking syndicated articles by either Hannen Swaffer or Godfrey Winn. "I strongly suggest the former. A mad republican is always better than a pansy."

By this time, Asa Briggs was trying to cram him every day for his finals in June. Richard Searby gave him extra help with the philosophy. In mid-May he wrote again to Rivett about the paper. "I am full of ideas and plans and dreams and can't wait to get back and have some very long yarns with you!" He said he wanted to sit at Rivett's feet and learn. It was now only two weeks to the exams. "Little hope of passing!" In fact, he obtained a third-class degree.

After his finals he congratulated Rivett on his recent editorials:

You have my full support. The American situation is very interesting and we ought not to forget the tremendous importance of their defence potential for us. But equally we ought not to let it blind our view or confuse the application of our very clear principles. I hope you realize just how close McCarthy is to the centre of power in America . . . News circulation sounds excellent. We must keep pushing it hard. Will you please let me see some figures about advertising progress, circulation progress and the current profit trends?

When term ended, he did not return at once to Australia. He thought about making a tour of American newsrooms but instead, decided to do a stint on the *Daily Express,* undoubtedly the best school for what its proprietor, Lord Beaverbrook, called the Black Art of journalism.

Murdoch wrote to Rivett about "the Beaverbrook brothel", but he enjoyed it. "The Beaver" was a wicked and in some ways wickedly attractive man. He had fantastic style and an outrageous sense of mischief. The *Express* was nothing if not racy, with brilliant sub editing and snappy headlines. His Lordship was a formidable role-model, and undoubtedly proved to Murdoch that the best way to run a newspaper was to hold enough stock to make one independent. "If you work for me," Beaverbrook said, "you will never become a millionaire, but you will live like one." Murdoch intended to be one – by working for himself.

On the *Express* he was given a place on the sub editor's desk under the eye of Ted Pickering. No berth in Fleet Street could have been better. His months in Beaverbrook's "brothel" left Murdoch with an abiding admiration for the craft of the London sub editor. Later he called Pickering "my first great mentor".

All the time, he was thinking of how to increase the circulation of the Adelaide *News* and how to do down the *Advertiser.* He told Rivett he was definitely coming to work on the *News.* He did not want a proper job or apprenticeship but "please don't get the impression that I will be walking in as a cocky bastard to tell you what's wrong with everything . . . I will of course be treading softly for a considerable time . . . "

In August 1953 the second Kinsey Report, *Sexual Behaviour in the Human Female*, was published. Still at the *Express* in London, the Patrick Murdoch in Rupert reacted with horror, and his telegram to Rivett is worth quoting in full:

LONDON EXPRESS TODAY QUOTE KINSEY BALLY-HOO BURSTS ON WORLD TODAY PROMOTE SALES HUMAN FEMALE SEX LIFE BOOK STOP SUMMARY HERE STOP PREPOSTEROUS DOCUMENT STOP SWEEPING FINDINGS BASED INTERVIEWS FIVE THOUSAND WOMEN EXHIBITIONISTS BOASTERS

LEGPULLERS STOP FORTUNATELY AVERAGE
AMERICAN WOMAN TOTALLY UNLIKE KINSEY
CREATURES STOP EXPRESS DOES NOT INTEND PUB-
LISH SINGLE WORD OF THE STUFF UNQUOTE EYE
TRUST WE DO NOT EITHER STOP FAMILY NEWS-
PAPERS LIKE OURSELVES GAIN GREAT KUDOS
LEAVING THIS MUCK ALONE STOP FORNICATION
MASTURBATION FRUSTRATION UNSUITABLE FOR
ADELAIDE FAMILY FIRESIDE STOP HOPE YOU
AGREE STOP EYE FELT EYE SHOULD EXPRESS THIS
BEST REGARDS ALL MURDOCH.

In a handwritten note a few days later, Rupert related that he
had been to Cornwall for the weekend. "Nearly got married off
but I should get out of the country intact, I think! I trust my
cable about Kinsey didn't offend you. I feel strongly about the
subject. Cunt is not our line – especially when it's phoney – as
this undoubtedly is. We might *warn* our readers of this *without*
publishing the phoney figures. But that's all."

At the beginning of September 1953, he flew home via South
Africa. At the age of twenty-two, Rupert Murdoch arrived in
Adelaide, to take up his inheritance and to begin the first of what
he himself called his lifelong series of battles with others and with
the world.

Chapter 3

ADELAIDE

Adelaide is on the southern coast of Australia, about a quarter of the way from Melbourne to Perth. It was first settled in 1836 by a group of English farmers determined to create a more orderly state than that which was flowering in New South Wales, where deported convicts were the majority. Land prices, for example, were to be strictly regulated. It was an ideal site for a city, on a fertile plain between the sea and the mountains.

Adelaide took its name from the wife of King William IV. North of the colony was a land of desert and salt lakes. But in the 1860s, South Australia was opened up with the help of the explorer, John McDouall Stuart, and in 1874 the 2,200-mile telegraph cable to the north was completed, linking the major cities of Australia to the world up north and west, and to all its news. Eighty-five years later, Adelaide became the home base of Rupert Murdoch, and the foundation of what would become one of the largest communications companies in the world.

Citizens of Adelaide think of themselves as different from those in the rest of the continent. Prim, closeted, almost cloistered, Adelaide, after the first settlement, was colonized mainly by the Presbyterians from whom Keith Murdoch sprang. They made it into a prosperous trading post at the end of the nineteenth century. In Adelaide, there are few folk stories of convicts with hearts of gold, or of Irish revolutionaries who became judges. Instead, judges were born to the purple and died in the Adelaide Club. There was a saying in Adelaide, "We're well laid out because we've been dead so long." By the 1950s the city was still genteel, and it had faded, but it was beginning to grow – like all of Australia.

It was government policy at that time to bring in 200,000 immigrants (unofficially whites only) every year to fill at least some of the continent's vast space and raise the population to 30 million by the end of the century. European ports were thronged with emigrants, taking passages to the southern sun. Around Adelaide, assembly factories and suburbs were springing up. A whole new market, rather more boisterous than the old Adelaide bourgeoisie liked to think suitable, was growing.

Even so, when Rupert Murdoch travelled to Adelaide to take up his inheritance, it was, his mother said, "like going into the wilderness", far from Melbourne. In the 1950s, the Australian press was still dominated by the Fairfax family, with their flagship, the *Sydney Morning Herald*; the Melbourne Herald group and Frank Packer, who published the *Women's Weekly* and the tabloid Sydney *Telegraph*.

When Rupert Murdoch arrived at the *News*'s small white offices opposite the railway marshalling yards, he was greeted by Rohan Rivett. Editor now for almost two years, Rivett had had a difficult time holding the paper's circulation at some 75,000. Rupert's first priority was to confront the much bigger *Advertiser*, behind which stood his father's old company, the Melbourne Herald group.

As Murdoch saw it, Sir Keith's body was hardly cold, and the eulogies were barely set in type, when the *Herald* tried to destroy what little remained of the small empire he had hoped to leave Rupert. The older he became, the more wrong he thought it that his mother had been pressurized by the trustees into selling the *Brisbane Courier-Mail*. "It shouldn't have been too difficult to merge the Queensland papers and the *News* in some way so that we had the majority," he said later.

The *Herald*'s continuing threat was personified by Sir Lloyd Dumas, one of the so-called "white knights" whose wealth and status gave them great influence over Australian society and government. Dumas was the chairman of the Adelaide *Advertiser*, which was 45 per cent owned by the Herald group.

While Rupert was still at Oxford in early 1953, Sir Lloyd had gone to see Lady Murdoch. In Rupert's words, he said, "Hate to do this, but my board of directors insist. We have to start a Sunday newspaper against you" – against the *News*.

The threat was substantial. The *Advertiser* was a far bigger paper and had a larger organization than the *News* and its *Sunday Mail*. It already outsold the *News* by 2:1 during the week. Dumas's purpose was to make the Murdochs sell out. He offered Lady Murdoch £150,000 for the company.

She asked Dumas to put the proposal in writing and she said she would discuss it with Rupert. His reaction was instant and predictable. "It made me angry. I thought they were trying to take advantage of my mother. They certainly wouldn't have dared do it in my father's time. I said to hell with the idea. We'll fight 'em."

He wrote to Rivett at the time: "Dumas turned on the sob stuff very effectively to Mother – as might be expected of the cunning old bastard." Murdoch was enthusiastic about the coming fight:

> We must clear the decks, so to speak, and pretty fast. Have you got comic contracts well tied up? Advertising too. What do you think about the price of the paper? We must come down NOW if Dumas is planning to undersell us . . . Our balance sheet is going to be knocked to hell, for a short time. It is going to be a great fight and I have complete confidence that we will win.

Soon after he arrived back in Adelaide, there were rumours around town that the *Advertiser*'s Sunday edition was about to appear. Murdoch discussed with Rivett how to react. They decided to publish Dumas's threatening letter to Lady Murdoch. "So we put out a poster: BID FOR PRESS etc," Murdoch recalled. "Dumas was outraged that we should have broken the confidence rule. He said he'd only told my mother out of kindness. So we locked horns for a while. Interesting. Good lesson."

Murdoch remembered the battle in the terms he most enjoys – his own David against the established Goliath. "They produced a very handsome broadsheet, very newsworthy. They had every service in the world in it, colour printing of comics, everything. We had this little paper with great loyalty, the Adelaide *Sunday Mail*." Still the *Mail*'s editor, Ron Boland, gave the *Advertiser* more than a run for its money, and Murdoch loved the contest. A nasty circulation war between the two Sunday papers continued for almost two years. It failed to destroy the *Mail* but the struggle cost them both heavily. Murdoch says that various oblique approaches were made to him through the Adelaide Establishment suggesting compromise or merger. "I told them to go to hell."

Eventually, to Murdoch's great satisfaction, Sir Lloyd backed down. In 1955 he and Murdoch agreed to a scheme whereby the two Sunday papers were merged. Each group took a 50 per cent share in the new paper. This was an unusual compromise for Murdoch. But he rationalized it by saying that the *Sunday Advertiser* was not so much merging as being compelled to disappear. "That was the truth. They'd go out of business and take a 50 per cent interest in our paper, which we would control, run, print and get management fees for." The agreement enabled Murdoch to claim his first victory.

Murdoch startled the staff of the *News* with his energy. There was not one phase of the paper's production process that he did not see at first hand. "He was," said Ron Boland, "always up and going." He was a bustling, pudgy figure in those days, rushing around town, puppy fat bulging out of his dark suits, rolling up his sleeves in the newsroom, dirtying his hands with ink, studying typefaces and ad rates, learning all of the trade. The house magazine published a boyish picture of him with wavy hair and full lips and asserted, "With a terrific zest for work, and a breezy personality, he has readily fitted into the office picture."

He took a flat at Glenelg, a seaside resort close to Adelaide. He was always running, always forgetful, always coming over to the Bolands' or the Rivetts' house with shirts needing buttons sewn on. He loved parties and established a tradition of raucous New Year's Eve office parties which often ended in boisterous gambling games. He was known around town, and even out of state, as "the Boy Publisher".

To Rivett's daughter, Rhyll, he was very much larger than life. "He was a lot of fun, but rather rough. He would swing me about but too hard. He was insensitive, verging on dangerous." He liked big American cars and used to pile the Rivett children in the back and roar around town, exhilarating and terrifying them. He was clumsy and would break vases and chairs. He had a Great Dane called Webster, who was famous for eating firecrackers and rushing around the town on his own. "Everything with Rupert was big – unreal," recalled Rhyll Rivett.

At first Murdoch and his editor collaborated well. They had a family history in common. Rivett had called his third child Keith and asked Rupert to be godfather; they even ran a column by Murdoch's great-uncle, Walter, now a distinguished academic in Perth. All the while Murdoch applied himself to learning his trade and badgered everyone in every department for information – finance, production, advertising rates, distribution, newsprint costs, union problems – he wanted to know everything and to change everything.

Thus, praising one issue of the *Sunday Mail*, he wrote a memo:

> However there is still little flair or imagination shown in the layout of many of the inside pages ... There was a flagrant piece of bad subbing with a small but conspicuous story on Page 3 about a share deal. Normally it would be unpardonable ... The women's section is a worry. It is neither a lift-out nor not a lift-out. Couldn't we limit the social muck – all immensely important, I know – into the first five pages, then the spread of pictures, and then five pages of woman's bureau ...

These criticisms and suggestions were constant. Soon after Murdoch's arrival, one of the staff wrote to Rivett to complain about

> the frequency of Rupertorial interruptions ... The point is: Rupert, in his sincere and charming way, has been making life somewhat wearing. He has been critical of layout, subbing, use of pictures, advertisements, typefaces – the whole bloody gamut ... If he acted like a bastard, I'd tell him so. But when you explain why certain changes can't be effected and he retreats with a "Sorry, I shouldn't have mentioned it" sincerity, all you can do is say "Jimmy Britt" and hope the next interruption won't come too soon.

Murdoch insisted on cutting costs. The entire editorial staff consisted of fewer than forty people. The political reporter, Frank

Shaw, said later that he and another reporter, Ken May, might write up to twenty stories a day. They had a first-class sub editor, Arch Bell. "Without an onside chief sub, you're a dead loss," recalled Shaw. Murdoch's energy was prodigious and infected them all. "We produced three editions a day and in the last edition there might be as many as six page changes." The average paper had thirty-six pages; on Fridays, forty-eight pages. The circulation increased.

State politics were fairly dull. The Liberal and Country League, a coalition between the conservative Liberal Party and the Country Party, seemed to be in government for ever, the Labor Party in perpetual opposition. Tom Playford had been State Premier since 1938 and was known as "Playmander"; the strength of the Liberal and Country League lay in the countryside, and Playford had arranged the electoral boundaries so that one rural vote counted for the same as three in the towns. "It was a small farmers' government," said Murdoch, despite the new industry and the new settlers. Playford was immensely powerful and appeared to be immovable; under Rivett and Murdoch, the *News* accepted this.

But Murdoch did not see himself as a natural Liberal and Country Party supporter. The party's leader was Robert Menzies, the man who had allied himself intimately with Churchill and Britain during the war, who adored the royal family and who was therefore much respected in Britain. From the start of his political consciousness, Murdoch loathed him, in an almost visceral way. "I felt that he was denying the growth of Australian nationalism and the physical growth of Australia." He thought that because Menzies was too intelligent to be genuinely so pro-British and pro-monarchy, he must be hamming that line for cynical reasons. "Nevertheless he got away with it, and in getting away with it, I thought he belittled Australia." Rivett was opposed to the Anglo-French intervention at Suez and Murdoch agreed with him. "Eden used Menzies to go and see Nasser. Our attitude was, 'What is he doing, posing as a world statesman , and on the wrong side, too?' "

Much later Murdoch acknowledged that many of his political ideas were still badly thought-out in the 1950s but, he said, "There was a respect for freedom, and a rather romantic acceptance of the Australian ideal of egalitarianism which, I think, was bred into us very early in the Murdoch family."

It was at this stage that Murdoch began a relationship which was to stand him in good stead for years to come – with the Commonwealth Bank. Murdoch understood that one of the great virtues, often overlooked, of the newspaper game is its cash-and-carry nature. Credit hardly exists: readers pay real money every day for the millions of papers they buy, and every day the publisher gets paid. The practice is not always as neat as the theory, but it is usually pretty straightforward none the less. Newspapers, therefore, are good bets.

When Murdoch arrived in Adelaide, the *News*'s bankers were the National Bank of Australia (later the National Australia Bank), who were also bankers to the Melbourne Herald group, including the *Advertiser*. After Murdoch's first attempt to take over the *Advertiser* was rebuffed, he decided to find his own bankers. He established a relationship with Jack Armstrong, the general manager of the Commonwealth Bank in Sydney, which was then a relatively small and conservative bank owned by the federal government. Armstrong quickly realized that "the Boy Publisher" was a young man of unbounded ambition and considerable commercial acumen. He decided to give him all possible support. Within a few years, News had become the Commonwealth Bank's biggest client. As News grew, so did the bank.

On his side, Murdoch understood that what bankers wanted above all was repayment on schedule. Vern Christie, who became managing director of the bank, said later that his relationship with Murdoch was one of the easiest and most confident that he had with any client. "He would call me on a Friday and ask, 'Would you stand by me if I need another A$150 million?' And the relationship was such that I would say, 'Yes.' The reason for such confidence? He has never, ever not performed with his banks as he said he would. He always meets every payment."

In 1956 Rupert Murdoch married. His bride was Patricia Booker, a young woman who had worked as an air hostess and at Myers department store in Adelaide. She was pretty and blonde. His family was worried about the match, and put it down to his loneliness in the "wilderness" of Adelaide. Part of the couple's honeymoon was spent inspecting the properties he had acquired. Marriage did not in any way slow him down – nor did the birth of their daughter Prudence, in 1959. The child was given full rein in the relaxed Murdoch household and went to bed more or less when she chose. They began as a happy family.

By the second half of the 1950s, the *News* was making enough for Murdoch to think of stretching out of small-town Adelaide. When he looked at other newspaper families – Fairfax, Beaverbrook, Northcliffe, Cecil King – he saw empires, or at least chains. First he expanded a minor interest in Southdown Press, a Melbourne-based magazine publisher, into total ownership. Despite opposition from the more cautious members of his board, he secured their agreement to buy *New Idea*, a weekly woman's magazine published in Melbourne, and then his second newspaper, the *Sunday Times* in Perth, capital of Western Australia, some 1,400 miles from Adelaide.

Perth was a small, quiet provincial town in those days. The *Sunday Times* was losing money, but its price was not cheap. It was the only serious city paper for sale at the time, and Murdoch wanted it. "We had to buy the first thing that came along," he said. Expand or die was already his watchword. He persuaded the News board to agree to let him buy the paper with a loan from the Commonwealth Bank, offering the assets of both the *Sunday Times* and the *News* as collateral.

The deal done, Murdoch began haring across the continent to Perth every Friday, bucketing around in a DC-3 or DC-4, tumbling off the flight, driving straight into the *Sunday Times* office to tear up the front page and many others besides. He personally licked and kicked the paper into the shape he wanted. He did so briskly and without sentimentality, firing all those whom he considered dead wood and importing sub editors and reporters from Adelaide. The paper at once became more sensational, and its sales increased.

According to one of his most critical biographers, Thomas Kiernan, it was in Perth that Murdoch journalism was born.

The exaggerated story filled with invented quotes; the rewriting of cryptic, laconic news-service copy into lavishly sensational-ized yarns; the eye-shattering, usually ungrammatical, irrelevant and gratuitously blood-curdling headline ("Leper Rapes Virgin, Gives Birth to Monster Baby" read a typical early front page) . . . all wrapped in cheap, smudgy tabloid form and pro-moted with the apocalyptic fervour and energy of Bible Belt evangelism.

At the same time, wrote Kiernan, the Perth paper was heavily promoted in the loudest and most vulgar and entertaining fashion possible, in order to stress, and to reach, the lowest common denominator. Nelson Mews, the Perth journalist, said this inter-pretation was wrong, recalling that the *Sunday Times* had been tawdry before Murdoch bought it, and remained tawdry after-wards – though perhaps more sparkily so.

With the success of the *Sunday Times*, Murdoch marched forth to other properties. Some of them were little papers in out-of-the-way towns – Darwin, in the Northern Territory, Alice Springs, in the desert heart of Australia, and Mount Isa, a mining centre in Queensland – but all were acquired in his particular fashion.

The purchase of the *Northern Territory News* in Darwin was typical of the way Murdoch did business. Darwin was the north-ernmost of Australian cities and the most polyglot, with Greeks, Chinese, Italians and other immigrants as well as traders from South-East Asia. It was still an outback town, a frontier place of the kind which Murdoch liked.

Murdoch zigzagged his way up the country by DC-3. He boun-ced into town and haggled for the *Northern Territory News* with the owner Sir Eric White, who recalled later that they had quite a night of it.

I gave Rupert my end of the deal, but he didn't say yes, or no or maybe. He talked about everything else under the sun. I had to fly out myself early next morning. I got to the airport figuring that Rupert was in bed having second thoughts. People had told me he was temperamental. It was just after dawn. But there was Rupert standing on the runway with a big grin on his face. He put his name on a piece of paper – that's the way we did things then. We left it for the lawyers to clean up the details later and he was off the runway before me.

In the 1950s he could afford to indulge his gambling instinct, for pleasure. At Geelong Grammar he had frequently nipped off to one of the Melbourne racetracks with more approval from Rupert Greene than from Keith Murdoch. Now he took his fancy for horseflesh further and bought a couple of racehorses. And on weekend outings with the staff of the *Sunday Times* of Perth he used to organize betting pools on the fishing prospects. On visits to the *Barrier Miner* at Broken Hill, he used to play two-up, the popular Australian betting game. Two coins are thrown into the air, and players have to call correctly how they will land. "Come in, spinner," they shout, as the coins are thrown. Murdoch always believed there was a system by which he could win. "You bet on a run," he recalled with relish later. "You go in with a couple of quid, and two, four, eight, you double it all the time. If you're betting on say, heads, you can make hundreds if you get a run. Then it comes down tails and you're all through. The real game is the gamble on knowing when to stop."

That indeed was the difficulty. In the Wild West atmosphere of the isolated mining town, excitement was high. There was "the Boy Publisher", small, tubby and sweating into his shirt sleeves, in the midst of vast miners throwing their pound notes into the ring. "You'd get a couple of hundred people shouting and they could build up a terrifically inviting atmosphere," he said later. The thrill of the throw was what it was all about, in every part of his life.

AMERICA

By now the shadow of America was beginning to loom over Murdoch, as it did over the world as never before; and not only because of its military and economic might but also because of television. Early on, Murdoch understood the potency of the combination of America and the box. "In the 1950s you had to be in TV," he said later. And to be in TV you had to be into America.

He had grown up with an awareness of America. His family house in Toorak had been commandeered by General MacArthur's staff during the war. Indeed, the war turned Australian consciousness away from Britain to America. It was America which defended Australia in the Pacific, and American soldiers were stationed in the major Australian cities. In the 1940s Rupert Murdoch had reacted against his father's increasingly pro-American views, but he had understood the notion that ties between America and Australia were gradually replacing those between Australia and Britain. At Oxford, he had grappled with the complexities of the Cold War and had begun to understand the reach of American power.

By the end of the 1950s he was visiting the States regularly, particularly after he decided that News had to break into television. He immediately loved America, and especially New York. He would have agreed with Bertie Wooster who said, in 1925, "The fact is New York often bucks fellows up and makes them show a flash of speed . . . It sort of develops them. Something in the air, don't you know." The America that Murdoch found, and began in his guts to understand, was the America which came over the next forty years to dominate the world.

The 1950s were the cradle of the television revolution, which was to force fantastic social change throughout the industrialized world. Regular commercial colour television started in America in 1950, with an hour-long programme featuring Ed Sullivan and Arthur Godfrey. That same year, the centenary of the first cross-Channel telegraph cable, France and Britain were linked by TV for the first time. RCA developed the Vidicon, which was more adaptable, sensitive and cheaper than traditional TV cameras. The first high-definition video recording on magnetic tape was made by Bing Crosby Enterprises in the US. Wide-screen movies were introduced by Cinerama. Twenty-one European countries agreed to share VHF waves, thus providing a real alternative to congested medium wavelengths. The first pocket-sized transistor radio was made in Japan by Sony.

In 1953, there were only about eight million television sets throughout the world, most of them in the United States. Texas Instruments introduced transistors that used silicon in place of germanium. (It would take until the 1960s before the silicon version was perfected and supplanted germanium as the heart of the chip.) The first transistor radio (the Regency) came on the US market. Discoverer I, the first US satellite publicly acknowledged to carry photo-reconnaissance equipment, transmitted photography to earth. The first TV dinner sold for ninety-five cents.

Independent television opened in Britain in 1955 and broke the BBC's monopoly, reaching twelve million people: Britain's first TV ad was for toothpaste. In 1956 the first desk-sized computer, the Burroughs E-101, was made in Philadelphia and introduced in Paris and London. Quartz crystal was improved so that six times as many short-wave radio channels were now available. The stable frequency allowed radio channels to be more closely spaced.

In Chicago, Alexander Poniatoff demonstrated his Ampex video tape recorder. In November 1956, the first video recording was aired by CBS. Automated banking hit the US. Australia broadcast the Olympic Games in Melbourne to a very small television audience.

Subset, high-speed telex cable capable of transmitting 1,000 words a minute was introduced by Bell. The first electronic calculator to have a memory was installed at the British Atomic Energy Authority laboratories.

One of the most important technological and political events of the decade was the launch by the USSR in 1957 of Sputnik, a 184-pound bundle of radio transmitters. This event so terrified the United States that it led to massive investment in further technological change.

In 1958 the USA successfully launched the satellite Explorer, which weighed thirty pounds and provided information about the earth's shape and atmosphere. Eisenhower's televised Christmas message to Americans was broadcast through outer space.

Australia was several years behind America in the development of television. But from his trips to America, Murdoch could see that television would become big business. Commercial television was immediately seen, in the words of Roy Thomson, the Canadian oil and publishing millionaire, as "a licence to print money". "As a newspaper man," said Murdoch, "you had to be in television to protect your position."

There was no television in Adelaide until 1957, though both Sydney and Melbourne already had three stations, two commercial and one run by the Australian Broadcasting Commission. The commercial companies were run by the two most powerful newspaper families. The Fairfaxes controlled Channel 7 and the Packers Channel 9 in Sydney. In Melbourne, the Herald and Weekly Times group ran Channel 7 and David Syme and Co, the publishers of the *Age*, were partners in Channel 9. These four stations had already created two mini-networks. Now the government planned to grant licences in both Adelaide and Brisbane. At first it seemed likely that each town would get only one licence.

Murdoch presented himself as the champion of monopoly, arguing against competition in Adelaide television. He told the Australian Broadcasting Control Board that the losses caused by competition would be enormous. But his appeal was rejected, and the government awarded two licences each in both Brisbane and Adelaide. In Adelaide, the group sponsored by the *Advertiser* was given Channel 7, and Murdoch's group, Southern Television Corporation, was granted Channel 9. Determined to get on air first, Murdoch rushed off to America.

The previous year he had propelled his young wife Pat around North America. "We drove down to New Orleans, and across and back into British Columbia, visiting TV stations everywhere," he recalled. In 1958 he returned with Ron Boland, the editor of the *Sunday Mail* in Adelaide.

They started on the West Coast, and spent time at the studios in Los Angeles, on the lookout for programmes they could afford for the new station. In Las Vegas they sampled everything that the desert city had to offer. Murdoch plunged on to the tables; Boland said later, "I always used to try and get the money off him to stop him." Wherever they went Murdoch had Boland collect things like magazine racks, for ideas to exploit back home. There was a lot to grab hold of. So much was changing in America.

Mass culture characterized the 1950s. Drive-in movies and fast food became a way of life. Small towns flourished and large cities were cramming skyscrapers on to tiny plots of land. Rock'n'roll provided the background music. *Playboy* premiered at fifty cents a copy and attracted 1.1 million readers.

But it was the technology of television that dominated the decade. Just as intellectuals had deplored mass-market popular newspapers earlier in the century, so now many commentators thought that TV was the beginning of the end – the demise of culture, reading, thinking. By 1959 the average American family was sitting in front of their set six hours a day, seven days a week. As Edward R. Murrow, the award-winning political and social commentator, remarked: "If television and radio are to be used for the entertainment of all the people all of the time, we have come perilously close to discovering the real opiate of the people." Murrow's social conscience and mission to inform made his programme, "See It Now", original and immensely popular. Murrow was a thorn in the side of CBS, the Columbia Broadcasting System, rattling politicians, businessmen and various professionals. He was also an exception.

As he travelled in America, some of this was clear to Murdoch. Not all of it, however, was clear even to the most reflective analyst, and no one has ever called Murdoch reflective. He is a man with relentless, unceasing drive and energy and a brilliant flair for spotting trends in popular culture. From the 1950s on, trends surfaced in the United States, and were then exported abroad, at least to the English-speaking world. Murdoch understood instinctively the allure of America to the rest of the world, the allure memorably summed up by the English critic, Malcolm Muggeridge, who wrote,

What they all want . . . is what the Americans have got – six lanes of large motor cars streaming powerfully into and out of gleaming cities; neon lights flashing, and juke boxes sounding and skyscrapers rising, story upon story into the sky. Driving at night into the town of Athens, Ohio (pop. 3,450), four bright coloured signs stood out in the darkness – "Gas", "Drugs", "Beauty", "Food". These could have shone forth as clearly in Athens, Greece as in Athens, Ohio. They belonged as aptly to Turkestan, or Sind or Kamchatka ... There are, properly speaking, no Communists, no capitalists, no Catholics, no Protestants, no black men, no Asians, no Europeans, no Right, no Left, and no Center ... There is only a vast and omnipresent longing for Gas, for Beauty, for Drugs and for Food.

Murdoch developed a number of contacts at the American television networks in Los Angeles and New York, the most important of whom was Leonard Goldenson of the American Broadcasting Corporation. Goldenson had come to television through Paramount Pictures. In 1951 he had bought the American Broadcasting Co for $24.5 million. For the next twenty-five years he struggled to bring ABC up to a par with the two other national networks, NBC and CBS.

Of Murdoch's first trip to New York, Goldenson said later, "Fortunately he happened to come to see ABC first. I was very impressed with him from the start." He invited the young Australian to lunch at Sardi's and was so taken by his drive that he asked to buy a share of News Limited. Murdoch agreed to let ABC have 6 per cent.

From the start Goldenson had felt that television could and would become a worldwide medium. So he set out to acquire foreign television stations as partners. This was before the development of satellite communications, so he envisaged several international networks linked by cable.

Murdoch already had similar ambitions and wrote later that Goldenson was "in many ways a role-model, though we came from very different backgrounds ... " He thought Goldenson was twenty years ahead of his time. "Leonard's success was always an inspiration and encouragement. He proved you *can* buck the odds."

Murdoch wanted to start a weekly television magazine in Australia and for that deemed it essential to visit the offices of the American model, *TV Guide*. He and Boland hired a car in New York and drove down to Philadelphia, where the magazine had been published by Walter Annenberg since 1953. He found he was not the only visitor trying to understand and exploit the phenomenon of *TV Guide*: "They had all these boring foreigners coming to see how to copy them." Few of them were as well equipped as Murdoch to duplicate Annenberg's success. But in those days his ambitions were limited. "It never occurred to me then that I would ever be starting anything in America," he said later. "The thing was to get out of Adelaide. Into Sydney, Melbourne."

Back in Adelaide, he dashed around imparting what he had learned, bouncing ideas, barking orders. He started an Australian version of *TV Guide* but his main energies went into getting Southern Television off the ground. The man he chose to set up the new station was Bill Davies, who had until then been running a commercial radio station, 5KA. Davies was a British émigré; he had been a police prosecutor for South Australia and then won a talent contest to be a radio announcer. He had a fine voice and a stentorian presence to match, and was affectionately known to some as "Bullshit Bill".

Murdoch gave Southern TV an office at the *News*. His instruction was simple: beat Channel 7 on to the air. One of Davies's recruits was Graham King, a man who was to remain with Murdoch for decades. "I kidded Bullshit Bill that I knew all about television," he recalled. "In fact I didn't even own a TV. I couldn't afford it." He was appointed promotions manager. Davies hired a chief engineer, and made a deal with Pye, one of Britain's leading electronics companies, to provide him with equipment and back-up. A few nights before they were due to go on air in July 1959, however, disaster struck. The building caught fire and the air-conditioners filled the whole place with smoke. The firemen ruined the studio floor. The place was unusable.

"So we had to go to the air from the transmitter itself," said Davies. "Our first transmission was from a tape-recorder sitting on the WC seat bundled up with chicken wire."

They patched up the studio in preparation for the full commercial launch in September 1959, but then discovered that it had terrible acoustics. The night before the launch they hired sewing machines and Davies bought army blankets which they stitched into long strips to hang up as sound bafflers. "We were the first on the air as Rupert had always insisted we must be," said Davies.

"I think he was right that it made all the difference. This was a small town."

The station made a splash. Although Murdoch, typically, ran it as cheaply as possible, at one time it boasted a ballet and an orchestra. Graham King wrote all the continuity, trailers and scripts, and put emphasis on stunts and personalities. The station broadcast live breakfast television, live children's programmes and a magazine called "Adelaide Tonight". Southern TV liked to think of itself as the little guy, battling the might of Channel 7 and its *Advertiser* backers, a self-image that Murdoch has always favoured. The station began to make a great deal of money – enough to enable Murdoch to escape Adelaide.

THE ALICE

But before that, he became briefly and painfully involved in Aboriginal affairs.

By the late 1950s all the state governments pursued an official policy of assimilation towards the Aborigines. This meant in effect the replacement, if not the destruction, of Aboriginal culture by that of the European. Often the policy was resisted by the Aborigines themselves, particularly in parts of Western Australia where the Pilbara tribes had struggled against the white men since the 1860s.

Interest in Aboriginal problems on the part of the white majority tended to be cyclical, or at least to be excited only by unusual crises. In 1957 there was a spate of stories in the Australian press to the effect that hundreds of Aborigines were dying in the outback.

Murdoch decided to turn reporter. He chartered a twin-engine Aero-45 and flew up into the desert with John Fisher, then general manager of News, and Geoff Handbury, the farmer husband of his sister, Helen.

They landed first at Alice Springs, a desert town situated virtually in the belly button of Australia. "The Alice", as it was known, was born in the 1870s, when explorers first began to peer across the Macdonnell Ranges, where it lies. Soon after it was founded, Alice became a repeater station on the telegraph line which linked Adelaide to the northern world. (Sir Charles Todd, who was in charge of building the telegraph, named it after his wife, Alice.) Alice was then joined to Adelaide, one thousand miles to the south, by a railroad built by a team of Afghan camel drivers who were brought there for the purpose.

From Alice, Murdoch's party set off to hop across the heart of dryness. The country around is empty and magnificent with the purple mountains behind, and the desert floor scattered with small eucalypts, ghost gums, and grey-green bush. Murdoch and his friends visited many of the nearby missions and weather stations to try to find Aborigines who were starving or suffering from such serious conditions as trachoma. They slept in a spotless mission hospital which, Geoff Handbury recalled, had no patients. They had various hair-raising adventures with their plane, flying up to Darwin and down to Perth, and then Murdoch wrote his conclusions. "ALICE SPRINGS, TODAY: No Aborigines in the Central Australian reserves are dying of thirst or starvation – or disease," he began. "The great nationwide concern over these people has not been necessary."

He poured scorn on the idea that there was any crisis at all in the care of Aborigines in Australia. But he concluded that "the ridiculous scare" must be turned to good use. The Aborigines would come into more and more contact with white men, especially as international companies mined for minerals. "Action will have to be taken to protect these prime but totally unprepared people, and gradually set them up as fully self-supporting citizens capable of taking their place in the country as a whole."

The most significant story in which the Adelaide *News* was involved under Rohan Rivett's editorship was the Stuart case. Stuart, an Aborigine, was charged with murder, and Rohan Rivett defended him in the pages of the newspaper and against the South Australian state authorities. It was a severe test of his relationship with Murdoch.

Rupert Max Stuart came from central Australia and was employed by a travelling sideshow. In 1958 he was convicted of raping and murdering a nine-year-old girl at Ceduna, 500 miles west of Adelaide. He was sentenced to death by hanging. The conviction was upheld by the Supreme Court of South Australia, but questions were then raised about the authenticity of his confession. Stuart's lawyers appealed to the High Court of Australia and then to the Privy Council in London. Rohan Rivett became convinced of Stuart's innocence and began a fierce campaign in the Adelaide *News* on his behalf.

Under pressure, the South Australian Premier, Sir Thomas Playford, postponed the hanging and appointed a Royal Commission of three judges. But its terms of reference were narrow, and the *News* went on the attack, demanding wider terms and suggesting that the judges were not the ideal commissioners, since two of them had already been involved in the case. Mr Justice Reid was the original trial judge and Sir Lewis Napier, the Chief Justice of South Australia, had presided over Stuart's unsuccessful appeal.

The *News* campaign and the whole affair became a great talking point in Adelaide. Murdoch himself was personally involved; he saw the case as a weapon with which to attack the Playford administration and the Establishment of Adelaide which he so detested. James Cameron wrote a piece in England calling Rivett "the Zola of South Australia" – and Rivett reprinted the piece in the *News*. "There's no doubt Stuart didn't get a totally fair trial," Murdoch said much later. "Although it's probable that he was guilty. I thought this at the time. In those days, although less so now, I was very much against the death penalty."

As the case proceeded, the *News* published tough stories criticizing, amongst others, Chief Justice Napier. When Jack Shand, the Sydney QC representing Stuart, withdrew from the case because Napier had interrupted him while he was cross-examining a witness, the *News* covered the event sensationally. The paper put out two billboards that day. The first read: "SHAND QUITS: YOU WON'T GIVE STUART A FAIR GO". The second one read: "COMMISSION BREAKS UP/ SHAND BLASTS NAPIER". The paper's headline was: "MR SHAND QC INDICTS SIR LEWIS NAPIER/ THESE COMMISSIONERS CANNOT DO THE JOB".

Murdoch himself had approved the headlines and the stories;

indeed, he even drafted the second poster himself. Premier Playford asserted that they were a grave libel against Napier, and the Crown laid charges against Rivett and News Ltd, alleging seditious libel and defamation. The case went to trial, with Rivett, Murdoch and a number of other *News* employees in the witness box. Although, eventually, the charges were dismissed or dropped, it was a fraught and painful time. In a subsequent editorial entitled "An Aftermath", the *News* climbed a long way down. It claimed that the paper had never considered that any members of the commission were unfit to judge the issue and that since the number of judges in South Australia was limited, there were bound to be times when they had to sit in appeal against themselves.

A few weeks after the repentant editorial, the British Labour politician Aneurin Bevan died. Rivett, a great admirer of the rambunctious Welsh socialist, gave over the front page and two inside pages to a passionate eulogy. A few years before, in his Leninist mode, Murdoch might have shared such sentiments; running the Adelaide *News* had made him understand the requirements of capitalism and he thought Rivett's socialist sentiments out of place. From Sydney, where he was beginning to establish himself, he sent Rivett a curt letter ordering him to leave the office that very day.

The Bevan editorial was not the reason for Rivett's dismissal. Nan Rivett, his widow, later said that there would have had to be a showdown at some stage. They were both strong characters and the break would have had to happen. Murdoch explained it differently.

We'd won the Stuart case so I wanted to cool it for a while. It had divided the community terribly. Rohan agreed with me absolutely. Then a couple of weeks later he had a front page [on the case] denouncing [the government] more angrily than before. It became quite clear that what would be a reasonable partnership if I was there, was not going to work in my absence. So I decided it was time we parted company. Some people wondered why I hadn't done it before. But I liked Rohan. He was strange and egocentric, but a good, well-intentioned man.

Nan Rivett said that although she thought a break was inevitable, "Rohan couldn't believe that Rupert had sacked him. He was very upset about the Stuart case; he had borne almost all of it. After going through prison camp all this was too much. He hated losing the paper. The progress of Rohan's idealism and enthusiasm under Keith to his disillusion under Rupert was very sad."

It seemed that Murdoch had outgrown both Rivett and Adelaide. He felt he could no longer depend on his old friend. He replaced him with Ron Boland, who had been editor of the *Sunday Mail*, and who was much more of a nuts-and-bolts journalist. Under Boland, the *News* became less of a crusading newspaper. There were more cats up trees in Adelaide and fewer uprisings in Ankara. Murdoch had had enough of advocacy journalism. He was expanding his empire and was more interested in cash than in confrontation, in profits than in political positions. He wanted editors who were safe rather than scintillating, whom he could rely upon, however far away he might be. From now on that would almost always be so.

Chapter 4

SYDNEY

Sydney in the 1960s was thriving, expanding, pushing itself to become one of the great cities in the English-speaking world, a sparkling metropolis built around a spectacular natural harbour.

It was here that the Rupert Murdoch whom the world came later to know, was truly formed. He began to put together the foundations of a publishing company which would have been noticed far earlier had it been based in New York – it included newspapers, books, printing, newsprint and television. He did it by competing harder and more fiercely than anyone else. It was at this time, too, that he honed his instinct for the mass market.

Sydney journalism has always been one of the fiercest of newspaper battlegrounds. In the nineteenth century the first issue of *Truth*, an extraordinary journal, was described by its opposition *Democrat* as a "puling little rag . . . that circulated widely round the Bondi sewer and was much execrated by the rats therein". Another scandal sheet, the *Innocents of Sydney*, described *Truth* as "the promulgators of piddling, babbling, frothy, doting nonsense . . . [who] have made one more abortive, plaintive, miscarriage sort of effort to catchpenny a few threepences".

Before Murdoch entered the Sydney newspaper market in the late 1950s it was dominated, as it had been for most of the century, by three groups – with the Fairfax and Packer families still running the two largest. Much smaller was the group owned by Ezra Norton, the owner of the *Daily Mirror* and *Sunday Mirror*. Norton's father had given him astringent advice regularly to pour "a bucket of shit" over people who showed signs of being uppity. His papers had faithfully done so. In 1958 Fairfax bought Norton's papers, the evening tabloid *Mirror*, and its Sunday sibling, largely to keep them out of the hands of the Melbourne Herald group, which had become even more expansionist since the death of Keith Murdoch.

Knowing that, despite their mutual antipathy, the Sydney moguls were determined to keep trespassers out, Murdoch approached the city covertly. He had a Sydney businessman, John Glass, make an exceedingly good offer for a company called Cumberland Newspapers, which distributed some 400,000 suburban papers a week. Murdoch's identity as the real purchaser was revealed only after the deal was signed.

But that was small beer. What Murdoch wanted was a full-scale Sydney paper. In 1960 he got it. Rupert "Rags" Henderson, the managing director of Fairfax, decided to sell him the Mirror papers. They were not doing well against their competition – the *Sun* – and Henderson wanted to invest more heavily in Sydney's Channel 7 television station. Murdoch said Henderson was also embarrassed by the downmarket *Mirror* – even though Fairfax ran it through another company, "Everyone knew that it was a front. He didn't want Packer to have it, or the Melbourne *Herald*. So, he said, 'We'll let Murdoch have it and then handle him some other way!' "

Henderson apparently felt paternal towards "The Boy Publisher" and did not see him as a threat – certainly not on the scale of the Melbourne *Herald*. Members of the Fairfax family, who had battled with Sir Keith, had greater insight. Sir Warwick Fairfax himself advised Henderson against letting Murdoch into Sydney. None the less, Henderson, whose power in the company was considerable, decided to do the deal.

The Fairfax group made a capital gain of some £500,000 from the sale of the *Mirror*, but Murdoch knew that he had a steal: "I was amazed they agreed." He paid only £600,000 down and another £1.3 million over six years. "They were pretty sure that I'd never make the pay-offs, that I'd collapse." He knew he would not. At a bargain price, he had acquired printing plants in Sydney, Brisbane and Melbourne. On top of that, he had a Sydney Sunday paper and a daily evening paper that he was determined to make the best-selling evening tabloid in Australia. It was reported that he danced a jig when the final documents had been signed and called his friends in triumph.

Sir Warwick was out of touch, on board a ship, when this happened. In later years, as Murdoch made money with the *Mirror*, expanded and competed more directly with the Fairfax papers, Sir Warwick would always blame Henderson for letting him into the town in the first place.

Before the sale of the *Mirror*, Packer and Fairfax were collaborating to resist Murdoch's Cumberland Newspapers in the suburbs. They had been using the downtime of the *Mirror* in its building on Kippax Street to publish additional papers for suburban sale. Murdoch was dancing his jigs in Kippax Street now and they had to find somewhere else to print and compete with him. They alighted on a small religious printer, the Anglican Press, which was in receivership. Frank Packer's son Clyde made an offer for it and was authorized by the receiver to enter the premises.

However, one of the original directors of the Anglican Press was Francis James, an eccentric adventurer who had flown with the RAF during the war and now used the back of his Rolls-Royce as an office. He had no wish to lose his press and so he asked Rupert Murdoch to help him fend off Packer.

By now Packer and a gang of men had occupied the press and were changing the locks. James went home to change out of his suit. Murdoch called up *Mirror* photographers and his sports correspondent rounded up a group of toughs. At one o'clock in the morning they surrounded the Anglican Press, attacked the Packer gang and drove them from the building. Francis James called a prayer of thanks. The next day the *Mirror* published a story under the headline, "KNIGHT'S SONS IN CITY BRAWL". The knight in question was Sir Frank, not the late Sir Keith, and the sons were Clyde and Kerry, not Rupert. The row continued in court and Murdoch emerged the winner. So began a bruising year of fierce competition with Fairfax and Packer in the Sydney suburban market. "They started papers against us in every suburb of Sydney," he said later. "It was a real bloody battle. But they found it much more expensive than they thought. And it scared us a bit." After a year he, Packer and Fairfax made a deal carving up the suburban papers which left Cumberland with the profitable printing contract for the lot. It was another victory for Murdoch.

The *Mirror* building was a former chocolate works on the corner of Holt and Kippax Streets, in Surry Hills, an area of old residences and decaying small factories in inner Sydney. Murdoch knocked down walls and made a large office which he hung with the Australian paintings he was beginning to acquire. He was a bundle of energy and was at the offices all the time, involved in layout, subbing and the choosing of stories, all the business of editing.

Most of the journalists adored Murdoch. They had been expecting a fire sale before he bought the papers. "He started the paper on a new and heady climb to popularity and profit," wrote Betty Riddell, a distinguished journalist who had covered the Normandy landings and was now one of the paper's columnists. For a short time Murdoch tried to take the *Sunday Mirror* slightly upmarket, but the paper did not gain circulation. With losses mounting, Murdoch began to suggest to his editor that some "cheesecake" might not be amiss. The editor disagreed and left, and Murdoch had the Sunday paper brought downmarket again to increase its circulation.

Using the Cumberland distribution system, Murdoch confronted the Packer family's *Telegraph* in the suburbs. Sir Frank Packer, an extreme right-wing old bully, was furious and vowed, according to one account, to spend however many tens of thousands of pounds it took until Murdoch was "sent back to Adelaide with his fookin' tail between his fookin' legs".

Murdoch made one big mistake which almost caused Sir Frank's wish to come true. He refused to join the Sydney newspaper publishers' association, saying that he would deal with the *Mirror* print unions alone. "They all had nice cosy keep-off-the-grass deals with the unions. And I, as the wide-eyed boy from Adelaide, came in and tore the lot up and said, 'I'll deal with the unions myself.' That of course was a picnic for the unions which I regretted very soon." The unions, among the toughest in the world, realized that he was vulnerable. He was heavily in debt, and they risked nothing from the other owners if they threatened the *Mirror* with a strike for wage increases. When they did so, Murdoch had to capitulate. It was an expensive lesson.

One of the perks of owning the *Mirror* was that he now had an office and a man in New York, a base for his frequent visits.

In 1960 he and his New York correspondent, Zell Rabin, a lifelong journalist from a working-class Sydney family, made a trip to Cuba. Murdoch was impressed with Fidel Castro; and he wrote a rather starry-eyed article arguing that the United States must reverse its opposition to Cuba – the future of Latin America was at stake.

Murdoch brought Rabin back to Sydney to edit first the *Sunday* and then the *Daily Mirror*. A slight man, with cropped hair and a tendency to wear preppy New York clothes, Rabin was a ferocious worker. His American wife Regina found his obsession with the paper tiresome, and left him, taking their son. Rabin took to breakfasting in the office, on the child's abandoned stock of baby-food. Murdoch's own wife, Pat, was similarly impatient with her husband's devotion to the paper; she used to bring their daughter Prudence into Kippax Street in the evening, as a signal that it was time to go home to the house he had acquired on Darling Point. He often did so reluctantly.

A camaraderie developed among the staff, who found Murdoch alternately (and unpredictably) genial and irritable. "You could never get close to him on editorial matters; he was only interested in circulation," said Betty Riddell. "But he was a lot of fun, a lot of the time."

"All the young reporters thought it was terrific to have a young proprietor," said Doug Flaherty, another veteran of the *Mirror* newsroom. "He brushed aside the old public service attitude of promotion by death, and moved up people he wanted. We all benefited from it."

Murdoch's personal prejudices were developing, however; he ordered the sub editors not to wear coloured shirts and especially not suede shoes. He thought only "homos" (as he called them) wore suede shoes. He also disapproved of adultery, dirty jokes and women in trousers.

The day started early, as the *Mirror* was an evening paper. Rabin often shaved in the office, which Murdoch thought rather disagreeable. After the first edition was printed, bundled and trucked over the city, there was time for the journalists to relax, call their bookmakers or brokers, and to fiddle expenses, which they called "swindle sheets". These infuriated Murdoch, who considered that the hacks were robbing him – as undoubtedly they were. One payday morning he grabbed a bundle of them, stormed into the newsroom, climbed on to a desk, and angrily tore them into confetti. This had a salutary effect – for a week or two. More often, when Murdoch was in a good mood, Friday evenings would end with the boss taking a part in heated two-up games in the newsroom. Always, he needed to win.

A great deal of the old larrikin spirit of newspaper brawls which had prevailed at the end of the last century in Sydney returned to the city in the 1960s. The Fairfax papers offered a £5,000 guessing contest; Packer raised the ante to £10,000, and each of them promoted these games on their television stations. Murdoch doubled the odds and offered a game of £20,000 and then Packer and Fairfax joined forces and offered a joint game worth £50,000. The prices were cars – then swimming pools, then blocks of land, then houses. The competition was probably the fiercest in the world.

Murdoch was determined to have the *Mirror*'s circulation overtake that of the *Sun*. The *Sunday Mirror* became a byword for titillation, sensationalism and vulgarity. Even Sydney's hardened readers were surprised. Shock, horror, probe. Huge headlines, deep cleavages and wide smiles. The billboards of the time give the flavour. "WHIPPING FOR HUSBAND – Wife's Rage". "TENNIS STAR SHOCKS PRIEST". "GIRL 13 RAPED 100 YARDS FROM HOME". "GANG RAPES GIRL 10". "WHY MY SON IS A KILLER – Mother's Story". "PROWLER STRIPS WOMAN NAKED". "BANNED SEX BOOKS, Free for Some". "LASH FOR 3 RAPISTS, Judge's Sentence". "NUDE TOP IN BUS. SYDNEY SHOCK. PICTURE". "SEX OPERATION OR GAOL – Judge's order". "PROWLER STRIKES AGAIN – Woman Attacked". And much more besides.

Murdoch did not invent or impose this sort of journalism; it had always come naturally to Sydney. One of the greatest exponents of it, Steve Dunleavy, had been an ace reporter on the *Mirror* before Murdoch acquired it. Journalist clichés were made for Dunleavy, the epitome of the bad boy on the newsdesk, the assiduously smiling picture snatcher, the imaginative inventor of the quotable quote. Sleight of hand, charm, straightforward lies and a large chequebook were all tools of the Dunleavy trade.

Dunleavy's career has run parallel to Murdoch's since the 1960s. Indeed, there are those who have described him as Murdoch's *alter ego*. Dunleavy was a good-looking, hard-drinking, womanizing, roustabout swashbuckler, with an astounding gift for turning dross into lively cliché, drear facts into purpled prose. To some he personified the underside of Murdoch's operation, if not of Murdoch's own personality. "Mad Dog and Mogul", Dunleavy and Murdoch have been called.

Like Murdoch, Dunleavy was born into journalism. His father was a photographer on the Sydney *Sun*, where Steve started to work as a copyboy when he was fourteen. To get away from his father's shadow, and any suggestion of nepotism, he moved to the *Daily Mirror* and was on the crime beat by the time he was sixteen.

Caught up in the hysterical rivalry between the *Sun* and the *Mirror*, the two Dunleavys fought as hard as anyone else. Once Steve slashed the tyres of a car from the *Sun*, and rushed back to Sydney with the story, leaving the man from the *Sun* sitting by the roadside. Steve claimed later that he did not know it was his father's car.

His father had to wait three years for his revenge. One day they were both on the trail of a knife maniac called the Kingsgrove Slasher – Sydney's biggest tabloid story in years. Searching for traces, Steve rushed into a little shed behind a house; his father bolted him in, shouting, "Remember?"

"The Sydney competition was so fierce that reporters would do anything to get a story – literally anything," said Dunleavy later. "I lost count of the number of times I posed as a cop, a public servant or a funeral director." A doctor's white coat was always hanging in the editor's room, available to any reporter assigned to call upon some person in hospital. Like the sharpest hack, he would carry rosary beads, a Bible and a Star of David, and other artefacts which might be helpful in seducing individual sources.

The editors of the *Sun* and the *Mirror* did everything to "spoil" the rival's story in the next edition. They revelled in denouncing each other's credibility. They mocked each other's claims to have more readers. They scorned each other's posters and headlines. (There was much to scorn, for both were often misleading.)

There was also cruelty. There was one series on sexual antics in a Sydney school, which led to such headlines as "WE HAVE SCHOOLGIRL'S ORGY DIARY". The *Mirror* then reported that one schoolboy had been suspended. Soon afterwards the boy was found hanging from a clothesline, but the *Mirror* did not report that. The girl who wrote the diary was found to be a virgin; her diary was all hallucination. It was the *Mirror* which had driven the boy to suicide. Years later, Richard Neville, the leading 1960s counter-culture journalist, asked Murdoch about the story. "Haven't you ever made a mistake?" asked Murdoch.

Some brakes were applied, sometimes. Murdoch had brought in his father's friend and employee, Douglas Brass, as editorial director of News Ltd. Brass, who had known Murdoch since he was a boy, was a former war correspondent and latterly chief of News's London bureau. Some said that Brass was the conscience of the outfit, but Murdoch was keener on competition than conscience. He both supported and frustrated Brass, a technique he has always employed with executives, making them happy one moment, despairing the next, bypassing them when disagreement was in the air.

"I saw and still see myself as a friend of Rupert's," said Douglas Brass. "He is warm-hearted and generous, hyperactive and adventurous, and he has a superb mind. But of course he can be utterly ruthless and, I'm afraid, will tread people down when they get in his way."

Brass felt that Murdoch was not interested in money as such. "He was like a small boy – just like the baby in the old Pears soap ad, who 'won't be happy till he gets it'. I'm not saying he didn't enjoy power. Who doesn't! But his father wielded it in a much more gentlemanly fashion."

The *Sunday Mirror* was far more lubricious than the *Daily* which, though ruthless and cheeky, did make efforts to cover political and social news. It sent reporters, for example, to Indonesia during the crises of the 1960s, gave extensive coverage to US and UK elections, and accompanied Menzies on his foreign missions. Brass recalled that the paper did try to run crisp and intelligent editorials, modelled on those of the *Daily Mirror* in London.

Murdoch was always searching for promotions to boost sales. One idea was serialize new books which were getting a lot of publicity anyway. Morris West's *The Devil's Advocate* was a complicated work, and Betty Riddell's task was to pare it right back without loss of plot or characters. "I reported to Murdoch that I had solved the problem by cutting out the religion and the profundity, while leaving in the sex. 'Good,' he said."

Murdoch brought Graham King over from Southern Television in Adelaide, where he had become known as the "Prince of Promotion". "I told the editors, I won't fuck with your front page, if you don't fuck with my commercials." He began to build up his media department, trying constantly to get the paper mentioned on television and radio. Despite the Chinese walls he insisted upon between promotion and editorial, he would supply editorial with stories, football promotions, giveaways. King came up with the idea of celebrating the *Mirror*'s silver anniversary. Everything was silver: silver double-decker buses in Sydney, silver Rolls-Royces for winners of silver fox furs. "Everyone thought the idea was boring except for Rupert. He got on one silver bus and threw silver balloons at the crowd. It was a great success."

While he was developing and promoting the *Mirror*, Murdoch's real ambition was to get into Sydney television. His station in Adelaide was already making good money; it showed profits of some 40 per cent on paid capital in its second and third years of operation. As elsewhere, Australian commercial television was "a licence to print money".

In 1962 there were all of nine applicants for the new Sydney licence. In order to give its bid a local flavour, Murdoch put the News holding in his chosen consortium into the names of Sydney subsidiaries and kept it below 30 per cent. Among his carefully chosen partners were churches, trade unions and an American movie company which would supply films. Hearings for the licences in both Sydney and Melbourne were held in Melbourne.

All the applicants knew what the Australian Broadcasting Control Board liked to hear: they all promised children's programmes, religion, education, local content – all the necessary ingredients of apple pie. Murdoch gave evidence for three days, saying that his newspaper experience meant that his station would be good at gathering news. He said he thought he should have a licence because the other two Sydney newspaper groups, Fairfax and Packer, already controlled stations. But he denied that he had bought the Sydney papers in order to qualify for a licence.

In the end he lost; the Broadcasting Control Board awarded the Sydney licence to United Telecasters Sydney Ltd, a group thought to have impeccable, conservative credentials and no connections with any newspaper. Applications from newspapers were similarly rejected in Melbourne where the new licence was granted to Ansett Transport Industries, which ran one of the country's two domestic airlines. It seemed likely that part of Murdoch's problem was Prime Minister Menzies, an old man for whom Murdoch did not conceal his contempt. Menzies was rumoured to have said he would not give the steam off his piss for Rupert Murdoch.

Murdoch did not give up. Instead, he tried to come into Sydney television on a curve – from the suburbs, as he had with news-papers. He went sixty miles south to the steel and coalmining town of Wollongong, and bought himself a share of an ailing station, Channel WIN 4. A whole swathe of southern Sydney could, in theory, pick up WIN 4 – but only if they adjusted their aerials. The station was on its knees because both Packer and Fairfax had forbidden their American distributors to sell to it any of the programming supplied to them, on pain of losing their business. Packer had been particularly ruthless.

Murdoch bought 320,000 Wollongong shares for £160,000. The solution, he understood by now, was programming. He called his friend Leonard Goldenson at ABC in New York and flew straight over. Packer realized what he was up to, and flew after him, but too late. At that time there was a gentleman's agreement among Australian television companies that no one paid more than $6,000 for an hour. Murdoch told ABC to tear the agreement up. Harry Plitt, who ran ABC's worldwide syndication, said that if he did that, he would never be able to sell another show in Australia. So Murdoch agreed to pay one million pounds for everything that ABC produced or distributed for the next five years. He obtained over 2,500 hours of ABC programming, including such successful shows as "Combat", "Ben Casey" and "The Fugitive". But he had to take the dregs as well – "all kinds of crap that I couldn't sell to anybody else", said Plitt. Plitt did not entirely trust Murdoch not to renege on the agreement, so he insisted that Murdoch pay $5 million up front. "He was pissed," said Plitt later, but he agreed.

Back in Sydney, Murdoch made his challenge clear, declaring that he had no intention of confining the station to Wollongong. While Graham King and others transformed an old tram shed in the Sydney harbourside suburb of Rushcutters Bay into a studio, the *Mirror* openly plugged Channel 4. Murdoch told his own magazine, *TV Times*, "There are two million Sydney viewers within WIN's range and we intend to go after them."

The challenge was immediately successful. Sir Frank Packer chose not to fight. Despite their personal antipathy, he offered Murdoch a quarter of the stock of his Television Corporation and two seats on the board. In return Murdoch would share his newly acquired American programmes. Murdoch leapt at the chance. With this one bound he had broken the Fairfax-Packer monopoly of Sydney television. The episode confirmed to him that programming, which later came to be known as "software", was paramount. Ever since, he has been putting together a software empire to compete with the biggest European and American companies around the world.

In his ambition to grow, Murdoch had now taken on a financial adviser who was to remain with him for decades. Mervyn Rich was as solid as he looked, and talked as little as a clam in a cloister. He knew all about feeding the maw of the entertainment industry, coming to Murdoch from Hoyts theatres, the biggest cinema chain in Australia.

In those days, Australians were the keenest cinema-goers in the world. Films were a special obsession in the outback, where television had not yet penetrated. Dusty little theatres were the main meeting place in small towns, and the weekly film, dropped off by bus, by truck or by plane, was eagerly awaited. Hoyts had to choose the right films to fit audiences in cinemas all around

Australia. This background appears to have given Merv Rich an unparalleled ability to run a worldwide news and entertainment company. He came into News as financial controller, quickly became Murdoch's business mentor and remained precisely that for more than twenty years.

One of the key management devices Rich introduced was the weekly "Blue Book". Most media companies in Australia had only a monthly reporting system; so problems took two months to fix. At News from now on, every part of the company had to put its figures into Kippax Street every week, so that Rich and Murdoch could immediately see where any problems – in sales, costs, profits, circulation, advertising, were developing. "The crucial thing was having someone who could read and understand what the figures were telling you," said Rich. "Rupert and I both could. Rupert liked them very much because they were something he could have on his desk and read when he had the time, and circle something that hit him." These weekly reports still come to Murdoch from all over the world today.

Rich's second major contribution was to enhance and institutionalize Murdoch's relations with his bankers, particularly the Commonwealth Bank of Australia, which was growing in significance alongside News. "We always had very good dealings with them, and always kept our word to them," said Rich. "We always kept them informed."

Murdoch's first flirtations with the world beyond Australia were, sensibly enough, in the Pacific. In 1963, he bought a 28 per cent share in a Hong Kong magazine publisher, Asia Magazines Ltd. He took only moments to consider and conclude the deal.

The next stop was New Zealand, where Roy Thomson, the Canadian press baron, was seeking to buy the *Dominion*, Wellington's major paper. The New Zealand government was nervous of any foreign owner, but in March 1964 Murdoch snatched it from the much larger and more prestigious Thomson group, quite a coup at that time.

1 LEFT *Rupert Murdoch's maternal grandfather, Rupert Greene, in 1936*

2 ABOVE *His paternal grandfather, the Reverend Patrick John Murdoch*

3 *Keith Murdoch's official farewell from Lord Northcliffe, in London. Keith Murdoch, holding his presentation golf clubs, is in the front row on Northcliffe's right; Billy Hughes, the Australian Prime Minister, is on Northcliffe's left*

4 RIGHT *Rupert Murdoch, aged 5, in a train window with Sir Keith*

5 BELOW *Sir Keith and Lady Murdoch, returning from a trip to Britain and the Middle East, 1942*

6 *Rupert Murdoch on his investigation into aboriginal affairs in February 1957, at Gordon McLeod's camp*

7 *Rupert Murdoch with Reg Polson on his yacht* Ilina, *in December 1960*

8 ABOVE *The day of Rupert Murdoch's marriage to Anna Torv in April 1967*

9 RIGHT *Rupert and Anna Murdoch arrive in London with their daughter, in December 1968, before his takeover of the* News of the World

10 ABOVE *Rupert Murdoch addressing the vital meeting of* News of the World *shareholders at the Connaught Rooms on the 2nd January 1969*

11 LEFT *The proprietor of* The Australian *defends the tone of his most successful paper in June 1970:* 'The News of the World *is in some ways an old-fashioned morality play.'*

12 *At the White House in 1962, left to right, Zell Rabin, who became editor of the Sydney* Daily Mirror, *President John F. Kennedy, and Rupert Murdoch*

13 *Graham King, News Corporation's promotional wizard from the 1960s*

14 *Max Newton, the first editor of* The Australian, *one-time pornographer and later economics pundit on the* New York Post

15 *The front cover of* Time *magazine, after Murdoch had taken over the* New York
Post, New York *and the* Village Voice

16 ABOVE *On Rupert Murdoch's purchase of Times Newspapers, 23 January 1981, with Harold Evans, on his right, and William Rees-Mogg*

17 LEFT *At* The Times *bicentenary celebration, on 11 July 1985 at Hampton Court, Rupert and Anna Murdoch greet Margaret and Denis Thatcher*

CANBERRA

On 14 July 1964 Rupert Murdoch celebrated his finest hour to date. Off a second-hand press in Canberra, the nation's capital, rolled the first newspaper he had actually created. *The Australian* was a broadsheet and its declared purpose was "to report the nation to Canberra and Canberra to the nation". It was also the continent's first major national daily and, as such, it was more than just a paper. It had a symbolic, emotional resonance. It was also a serious paper ("unpopular" rather than "popular" in Murdoch's parlance), and it remained so, losing money for Murdoch for many years to come. The courageous venture made Murdoch much loved, especially by Australian journalists, although many later came to dislike him.

It was often said then (and has been repeated many times since) that Murdoch's purpose in starting *The Australian* was to placate his mother, who had just been named a Dame of the British Empire in recognition of her charitable works. Dame Elisabeth was known to be embarrassed by her son's more sensational papers, especially the Sydney *Mirror*, and to compare his record and intentions unfavourably with those of his father. But when the suggestion was put to Murdoch that the idea for *The Australian* came from the desire to please his mother, he replied, "That's bullshit. If I got the idea from anywhere it would have been from my father." In any case his first plan had been to start a Canberra paper, not a national one, though he had always hoped to march upon the national stage.

Canberra was then a small town purpose-built for government, a pretty, cardboard capital, a place without much life or soul. Until 1927 the Australian Federal Parliament had been in Melbourne, and in 1964 some federal offices were still there. In the late 1950s sheep still grazed close to Parliament in Canberra, but by the early 1960s the city was growing fast – from 15,000 at the end of the Second World War to over 80,000. The only paper, the

Canberra Times, was a gentle, sleepy affair owned and run by Arthur Shakespeare and his family. Advertising in Canberra was a rich seam, and the paper was a little goldmine, earning some £80,000 profit per year before tax by the end of the 1950s.

To Murdoch the *Canberra Times* was not an attractive family affair, but "a tiny little very underdeveloped rag". He said that his father had always wanted to buy it, "and make it an important paper and maybe some sort of national". But he knew the Shakespeares would not sell it. In early 1964 he slipped quietly into town. He bought up a giveaway paper, the *Territorian*, which had been started by Ken Cowley, a former compositor on the *Canberra Times*, who stayed on to work for him. He also purchased a piece of land just down the street from the *Times*. When Parliament opened in February that year, Arthur Shakespeare and Murdoch met at a party. Shakespeare asked the young man what he wanted to do with his new land. "Run you out of business," said Murdoch without a pause.

Shakespeare was no fool; he had already made a secret agreement with Rupert Henderson of Fairfax, by which Fairfax could buy the *Canberra Times* should Shakespeare retire or die, or should any other company take steps to publish a paper in Canberra.

After Murdoch's threat, Shakespeare alerted Henderson. On 1 May 1964, the *Canberra Times* announced that it had been bought by Fairfax, and that the paper would be developed as a national daily. Fairfax at once began to fly high-powered teams of editors and journalists to Canberra. "They turned the paper from a shabby little tabloid, nearly all ads, into a very good-looking broadsheet in a month," said Murdoch. "It was a remarkable achievement. And a pretty rough welcome for us."

That was an understatement. It could have been a devastating blow to Murdoch's ambitions. His new paper would now never get the advertisements in Canberra needed to finance its publication. It looked as if Henderson, a brilliant operator, had taught Murdoch an expensive and humiliating lesson.

Murdoch would not be defeated. He decided that the only thing he could do was to go for the big time, and publish a national paper at once, instead of in two years or more. "We never thought of pulling the plug. We just said, 'Well, we'll have to go national right away.' "

As editor Murdoch had chosen Max Newton, a legend among Australian journalists, described in one profile as "a man who rolled dice with governments and redirected the careers of Prime Ministers". For twenty-five years he flashed in and out of Murdoch's galaxy, a troublesome, brilliant, neurotic, burning comet.

Newton was the son of a lead-burner in a sulphuric acid factory in Perth. He won a scholarship to Perth Modern School, where, showing an early interest in sex, he gave seminars to other boys about the merits of masturbation. He obtained exhibitions to the University of Western Australia in Perth and started to study economics – and to drink. The night before his final exams, he was picked up dead drunk and naked in a park. None the less, he managed to win a scholarship to Clare College, Cambridge. At Clare he sobered up. His neighbour was a young American student, Norman Podhoretz, later the editor of *Commentary*. Newton taught Podhoretz French and Podhoretz taught him "how to be honest in one's thinking", said Newton later. After two years without alcohol, he got blind drunk in the middle of his finals. Even so, he was awarded one of the two firsts given in economics that year, and was subsequently made an honorary Fellow of Clare.

While at Cambridge, he married Anne Robertson, a young woman whom he had met in Perth, and who had come to England after him. They returned to Australia and Newton held various unsatisfactory jobs before the *Sydney Morning Herald* hired him and sent him as political correspondent to Canberra. He began drinking heavily again but when Anne threatened to leave him, he gave up. For ten years he went on the wagon. Fairfax made him editor of the *Financial Review*, which Newton expanded from a twice-weekly paper to one appearing five days a week, doubling its circulation to over 20,000. But it still did not do well enough for Fairfax, and Newton, a manic depressive, became discontented. Early in 1964, he went to see Murdoch, who offered him the editorship of his new Canberra paper. Newton bounced into Kippax Street, where the paper was being devised, and then on to

Canberra, in great spirits. He even hired several Fairfax journalists and brought them with him.

When the *Canberra Times* and Fairfax announced their alliance against Murdoch, Newton was convinced the game was up. But, he wrote later in *The Australian*, "in those terrible hours and days, when we realized our predicament, Rupert showed some of the steel, the gambler's recklessness and the foresight that have since grown to such immense maturity on the world stage".

Together they toured the country to find advertisers, and to work out the immense logistical problems of producing a paper in Canberra and getting it around the continent by breakfast time. They went together to the Commonwealth Bank for further backing. The chairman, Warren McDonald, and the managing director, E.B. Richardson, told them, "You can have the money but you must not put the whole group into loss."

In less than four months they got the paper published and distributed across the continent – a remarkable achievement. The first few editions were, as with many newspapers, a mess. The paper carried a horoscope – because the stars have always been an obsession with Murdoch. Born on 11 March, he was Pisces, and Pisceans were urged in the first issue to "step into an area where you are most useful. Your poetic approach rings the bell of success." The problem was that the charts were from a London paper – and showed the northern sky. But the criticisms were quibbles. Murdoch had created not only a good paper but also an important paper to Australia.

The Australian was a fabulous adventure to all those who worked there in the early days. The editorial offices were unfinished when they started; the wind rushed leaves around the desks. They felt like roughneck frontiersmen in a very prim town. Max Newton recollected: "It was such a wild idea, a mistake, a dream of such compulsion, that I was, and still am, astounded that every journalist in Australia did not jump up as one and shout, 'Good Christ, let me be at it, let me be in it.' " Almost all of their tales embrace Murdoch, and with great affection. His energy seemed to *will* the paper into existence, and his courage sustained its losses. There was Murdoch in the composing room, recalled Owen Thomson, a reporter who was a close friend in the 1960s; Murdoch making and criticizing layouts; Murdoch hiring staff from all over the country; Murdoch rushing around the office in his sweater and chinos after he came straight from his boat; above all Murdoch at the airport.

To ensure daily distribution to all the state capitals, paper matrices, one of the oldest printing technologies in the world, had to be flown to printing plants in Melbourne and Sydney. The winter of 1964 was one of the coldest anyone in Canberra could recall, and the airport was constantly closed by fog rising off Lake Burley Griffin, the artificial lake in the new capital. Murdoch created a little airline – called Mickey Mouse airlines by the hacks – to fly the precious matrices out. He often used to drive them to the airport himself, sometimes in his dressing gown and pyjamas. The planes were supposed to be all gunned up with the pilots ready to roar down the runway as soon as the "matts" were flung aboard. There are stories of Murdoch in his night clothes trying to cajole the airport officials to let the planes go. "It's not fog," he would promise the control tower and the doubtful pilots – "it's just a light mist." Pilots, who were thus charmed by him into taking off against their judgement into a pea-souper, used to kiss the ground on landing.

"We got there ninety-nine times out of a hundred," said Murdoch, but some of those times it was by truck and the papers were hours late on the streets in other state capitals. It was two years before this Mack Sennett style of distribution ended, after coaxial cables were laid across the country, and the pages could be faxed down the wire.

The pressures of trying to run a national newspaper out of Canberra were immense. Australians are fiercely jealous of states' rights and in the 1960s there was no real, overwhelming sense of nationhood. It was hard to interest the denizens of Darwin in the mores of Melbourne. There were already well-entrenched regional papers which carried quite enough "foreign" news for most readers.

Circulation did not hold up as hoped. A total of 250,000 copies were printed at first and large numbers were given away free in the capital. But by November 1964 sales were down to only just over 50,000 copies a day and the southern summer "silly season", when there was much less news, was beginning.

Losses rose and rose – to $45,000 a week. Murdoch had to take the company into a trading loss, something he had promised the Commonwealth Bank would not happen. He began to question his choice of editor. Newton was brilliant, but he was also erratic, and most important, he was not producing the sales. In the last resort Murdoch was never good at accepting wayward intellectual independence. For his part, Newton grew increasingly disenchanted with having Murdoch constantly on the stone remaking pages and ordering new headlines.

"Rupert and I drifted apart," said Newton later. "Rupert became more worried about his business." They also had serious political differences. At that time Murdoch supported protectionism, and still had some liberal views. "He was violently opposed to the war in Vietnam, which I thought was a very important thing for Australia," said Newton later. "I remember recommending that we support the bombing of Haiphong harbour. Rupert was appalled . . . I don't blame him for being frightened, he had bloody good reason to be frightened."

Newton became more and more depressed, Murdoch increasingly worried. The survival of News Ltd depended on the sales of the *Daily Mirror* in Sydney. It was the source which sustained *The Australian* (as later, the *Sun* and *News of the World* in London were to sustain less popular and less profitable ventures). As *The Australian* continued to drain money, tensions on the paper grew unbearable. Murdoch tried to make more and more changes.

In March 1965 Newton resigned, or was asked to do so. He told the *Canberra Times*, "Perhaps I was wrong, but the experience of editing *The Australian* under complete direction in recent times has, in my view, made it impossible to achieve the essential principles, aims and standards of quality which fired the enthusiasm and dedication of a large team of men and women, including myself." Later he said that in firing him, Murdoch "did me a big favour. He sacked me because really I was an impossible bugger, wasn't a team player at all."

Murdoch appointed a new editor, Walter Kommer, a Dutchman to whom English was a second language. The paper continued to do so badly that, not for the last time, he seriously considered closing it. Many of his associates, including Bill Davies in Adelaide, wished that he would – it was such a drain on their own operations in other parts of the company. But in the end Murdoch's fear of defeat was too great and he kept the paper going.

In 1966, he appointed Adrian Deamer assistant managing editor, in charge of producing the paper. Deamer's father, Sidney, had been a distinguished and senior editor of the Melbourne *Herald* in the early 1930s, under Sir Keith. Adrian had inherited his serious aspirations for journalism, and he combined them with a mild manner and a waspish tongue.

Murdoch said later that *The Australian* was "an idealistic effort. You've got to look at the *Melbourne Age* and the *Sydney Morning Herald* and all those papers at the time we did it. They were being ground out by managers. Very poor papers. It was a way to open it up, have a national debate." He hoped that *The Australian* would give him a seat at the debating table, which it did.

He deserved that reward. Merely by coming into being, *The Australian* had an important impact on Australia. It attempted to conquer "the tyranny of distance" which dominated Australian life in so many ways. Murdoch had hoped that it would sink the *Canberra Times*, seize the capital's rich advertising market and undermine the *Financial Review*. Although it did not achieve this end, *The Australian* did ginger up the Canberra Press Gallery, producing strong and informed ideas about technological advances (an obsession of Murdoch's) which later won it a great deal of the lucrative computer advertising market, and it forced considerable improvements upon its rivals. Ranald Macdonald, Murdoch's cousin and the managing editor of the *Melbourne Age*, who had little affection for Murdoch, said later, "*The Australian* brought change at the *Age* by example. It covered at a national level issues in greater depth; gave much greater emphasis to foreign news and provided much better economic reporting than the *Age*." It tried to give Australia a sense of nationhood. Even the *Sydney Morning Herald*, one of its greatest rivals, subsequently acknowledged that "the launch of *The Australian* was the most significant event in post-war Australian journalism. It was a force in opening up

Australian society and preparing the ground for great changes in Australia after 1972." That force came from Murdoch.

CAVAN

As he established himself as a national power in Australia, Murdoch's life was changing. He was spending less and less time with Pat and their daughter Prudence. They had remained in Sydney when he was starting *The Australian* in Canberra. When he was not building his empire – which took most of his time – he played with others. Later, he said of his first marriage, "I was probably too young and married on the run. I was totally involved in the business – probably very inconsiderate. One grew apart, and outgrew, I think."

He would drink with the lads, but he rarely got drunk. The night of "the Big Chuck" lived as a prototype story of Australian journalism. Murdoch and two journalists, one a senior editor of *The Australian*, went out "on the grog". Murdoch stayed fairly sober; the others got pretty full. In the taxi to the hotel, Murdoch fell asleep in the back seat, and the editor vomited all over his employer.

The hotel commissionaire was appalled when they arrived and demanded to know who they were. He was told that the man covered in vomit was the owner of *The Australian*, while the other was the paper's editor. Next day, Murdoch called his editor, sounding very apologetic. He said, "I really must have had too much to drink last night. I chucked up all over myself."

He had in those days a splendid wooden ketch named *Ilina*, which he used to sail with friends and courtiers. He competed in the Sydney-Hobart race on several occasions. There was a certain element of abandon in his yachting: *Ilina* once went aground on a reef off the Queensland coast and was stuck for two days. One journalist remembers Murdoch declaring, with characteristic bravado, "I bet, if I was going to be shot at dawn, I could get out of it." He also went horse racing, he took hair-raising flights in small planes all over the country, he went fly fishing in the Snowy Mountains, and he spent a lot of time with the boys.

Then he fell in love with an exquisite-looking young cadet reporter on the *Daily Mirror*. She was similar to Pat only in that she too came from a far poorer background than Murdoch. She had had to fight.

Anna Torv was the child of an Estonian father and a Scottish mother. Jakub Torv left Estonia just before the Second World War, for Britain, where he served in the merchant marine. He married a Scottish girl, and together they ran a dry-cleaning shop in Glasgow. Anna was their eldest child, born in 1944. Three more children followed: Jan, Karin and Hans. In the early 1950s, Jakub decided there was no future for immigrants like himself in Britain, and when Anna was nine years old, they joined tens of thousands of other working-class Britons in taking assisted emigrants' passages to Australia. Anna thought this was a wonderful adventure. The highpoint of the voyage was going through the Suez Canal. One beautiful balmy evening she went up on deck. "I remember vividly feeling warm for the first time in my life."

But Australia proved not to be Arcadia. Life was hard for Anna's parents in Sydney too. They wanted to do something different from dry cleaning, and so they ran a picnic park just outside Sydney, in Easter Creek. It was a disaster, and they went bankrupt; they should have stuck to dry cleaning, Anna said later. Anna found life hard, too. At school the other kids thought she talked funny "and I rolled my eyes". They moved to a dreary 1950s high rise in Blacktown, a poor suburb in Sydney's outer west. Things grew worse still. Their mother, a feckless character, deserted them, and Anna became surrogate mother to her brothers and sister. "That's why I'm so bossy, because I had to do it from an early age," she has said. They had no money and Anna learned to slit open toothpaste tubes to avoid waste. They were Catholic and Anna was educated by the Sisters of Mercy; she worked in a department store to augment the family income.

She left school at sixteen. She wanted to be an actress or a journalist, but her first job was in a suburban crematorium. Knowing no journalists, she could see no way of getting a cadetship on a paper. But she was lucky, or determined: "I decided that I would take any job in newspapers. I was seventeen. I got a call eventually and I became a clerk in the finance department at the *Mirror* . . . The job paid $7. So I made it happen."

Once at the *Mirror*, it was not hard for her to get to know the journalists – for she was both beautiful and ambitious. Douglas Brass, the editorial director of News Ltd, took her under his wing. Anna, says Blanche d'Alpuget, another cadet journalist and later a novelist, was determined to do well. Blanche introduced her to rich "yachties" (eligible yachtsmen), and attempted to wean her from her strict Catholicism.

With help from Brass and others, Anna became editor of the cadet newspaper and decided to interview the boss, Rupert Murdoch. He said later, "I thought she was a very pretty girl. Her writing skills were not going through my mind." She said later that she found him very attractive from the start. "He was like a whirlwind coming into the room. It was very seductive."

The parting and the divorce from Pat were unhappy, especially for their daughter Prudence. (Murdoch won custody of Prudence, who then went to London with him and Anna. When she grew up, she made London her home. Pat married a man who owned a chain of hairdressing shops and went to live in Spain, but that marriage broke up and she moved back to Adelaide, where Murdoch helped support her.)

Murdoch and Anna married in April, 1967. They spent part of their honeymoon in New York, where Murdoch rushed around seeing Leonard Goldenson of ABC and other television warriors. Anna went bicycling in Central Park with Graham King, who happened to be there at the same time. Like Rupert, she loved New York. It was a city bursting with the turbulence of the 1960s and to any young foreigner involved in communications, it was clearly the cultural and scientific centre of the Western world.

Science fiction frequently became fact in the USA in the 1960s. In 1960 a scientist at Hughes Aircraft in California built the first laser beam – a pencil-thin, intense beam of light composed of a single wavelength that is coherent. A laser beam was sent from Kitt Peak National Observatory in Arizona and was easily spotted by the TV eye of Surveyor 7, an unmanned spacecraft on the moon. High-frequency laser light was modulated to transmit messages.

In 1960, the world's first weather satellite had been launched by the United States. So had Echo I, a balloon that reflected radio waves and linked earth stations miles apart. It proved conclusively that satellites could be used for worldwide communications, but this "passive" version was soon replaced with active versions transmitting signals, not merely reflecting them. Space flight was now a reality.

Nick Holonyak invented the light-emitting diode, destined to become the most popular digital display in pocket calculators and electronic watches. Electronic telephones were introduced. In the 1960s computers began to be widely used for adding up bank accounts, routing telephone calls, setting type, forecasting weather, directing city traffic, and guiding astronauts through space.

During the decade, 163 American magazines died, including the *Saturday Evening Post*, and 160 newspapers, including the venerable *World Journal Tribune*. The ghostly glow of television spread, but it was Marshall McLuhan who, almost alone, understood television and other electronic media as the beginning of the most powerful revolution to hit Western man.

The new media, he argued, were refashioning the world without boundaries. "Time has ceased, space has vanished. We now live in a global village, a simultaneous happening," he wrote in *Understanding Media*. This was a fantastic concept, but one which Murdoch was beginning to grasp.

In his own village, Murdoch had become a landowner. In the mid-1960s he had bought Cavan, an old one-storey stone house with several thousand acres not far from Canberra. About twenty miles out of the town of Yass on a paved, narrow road winding through the foothills, the estate sprawls along the banks of the Murrumbidgee river. In her first novel, *In Her Own Image*, Anna Murdoch gave this description of it:

> The green jewel of a garden . . . was an anomaly in the brown landscape. When the river was high they could pump water out continuously to keep it green but with the trickle the Murrumbidgee had become this season, watering was done by hand

when the sun went down. The river snaked lazily around the property creating a globular peninsula in which the houses and the stables, the yards and the shearing sheds were scattered with no apparent design. The trees in the bend of the river shimmered silver in the stillness and beyond the trees, the hills of the Murrumbidgee country lay gently and endlessly blue.

Cavan cost Murdoch almost A$200,000 and he subsequently spent a great deal of money on it, even building an airstrip there. For a time he considered becoming the local Member of Parliament. Anna redecorated the house, and Murdoch took great pleasure in developing the property, which carried about 6,000 sheep and 2,000 head of cattle.

Les Hewitt, his farm manager at one time, identified one of the things that he admired about Murdoch: "He'll fly down here out of a business conference in New York and stand and have a discussion with me and he's very much in touch with our wool market and our beef market. This is his home. He is Australian."

In the late 1960s and early 1970s there were constant house parties at Cavan. Murdoch was a generous host. The wine cellar was excellent and though by the late 1960s he rarely drank much, this did not deter his journalist guests. He loved to play the country squire. Betty Riddell recalled that once when she was staying there, Murdoch woke her up at 7 a.m. and walked her all over the paddocks. There was frost on the ground and he pointed out to her all the things he was going to do with his land – a pool there, horses yonder. That same weekend a News executive came down and Rupert insisted that they play tennis together. The man had no shoes, but did not dare to disobey the command. Murdoch always played tennis as if the future of the world hung on his winning. At the end of a typically aggressive match, the executive's feet were raw; Riddell thought that Murdoch did not even notice. Nevertheless, Riddell, in common with most of his journalists, admired Murdoch. "He was always around, both at the *Mirror* and at *The Australian*. He knew us all, loved us all, and he took our advice. When he made mistakes, he got rid of them fast. He could always be talked to and argued with. Now it's all gone. Why? Power, power, power, not money."

On those weekends Murdoch talked shop constantly – in the pool, on horseback, driving his four-wheel-drive car, which he revved up and down hills, terrifying his passengers. He paused only on the tennis court, or to discuss the estate with Les Hewitt.

As he grew richer, the paintings at Cavan grew more numerous and more expensive. Like his father, he was a patron of Australian artists; his collection included pictures by Tom Roberts and George Lambert, as well as work by contemporary artists such as Arthur Boyd and Fred Williams; the latter became a friend.

By 1967, the circulation of *The Australian* had risen to a high point of about 75,000 but only 3,800 of these sales were in Canberra. Closing the paper was still an option, but Murdoch decided instead to move most of the editorial staff to Sydney. They descended on the chocolate factory in Kippax Street. Adrian Deamer was still the editor, and was putting out an intellectually interesting paper. Walter Kommer had been moved to the commercial side of the company – and became involved more in the mineral exploration leases which Murdoch had just acquired. Murdoch invited a clever young Labor Party cadre, John Menadue, to be his executive assistant. Menadue had become bored with Canberra politics, and newspapers seemed to offer a wider range of public and policy issues. Attracted by Murdoch's energy, Menadue took the job.

He came to believe that the source of all that energy, the reason for the drive, was, at least at that time, a craving for recognition. In those days many politicians, and some papers, still referred to Murdoch disparagingly as "the Boy Publisher", merely as the son of Sir Keith, an adolescent of no substance. He appeared to Menadue to be a frustrated politician, fascinated by political processes and the power associated with them. Later on, in the mid-1970s, he discussed with Menadue the possibility of running as a candidate. Murdoch was attracted to the Country Party's nationalist republicanism and protectionism. Its leader John McEwen paid attention to Murdoch, while Menzies did not. "Rupert sought recognition," said Menadue, "but I never saw him seeking political favours or financial advantage. Just personal acceptance." Murdoch later said that his support for McEwen and protectionism was mistaken: "It was a different world then."

In January 1968, Max Newton, former editor of *The Australian*, became the subject of the paper's front-page lead. *The Australian* described him as a "foreign agent" – because he advised the Japanese government's export agency on Australian economic affairs. Newton, unlike Murdoch, was utterly opposed to protectionism, and in his economic newsletters he constantly attacked McEwen.

However, as George Munster, one of Murdoch's biographers, has pointed out, Newton's Japanese connection was a very small part of his work. "There was no suggestion that he had received information in his task from the Treasury." The story also damaged William McMahon, who with John Gorton was a candidate for the prime ministership after the drowning of Harold Holt. McMahon, a free trader and an associate of Newton, was defeated by John Gorton, and Gorton developed a close relationship with Murdoch. Gorton became a frequent visitor to Cavan – until, that is, Murdoch decided that he was no longer an effective Prime Minister.

Newton's office was raided by the police. It was an extraordinary scene. Newton made a great party out of the raid on his office, which lasted twelve hours. He was laughing, telling the policemen stories in his typically foul-mouthed fashion, making them cups of tea, and seeming to have a whale of a time, while he made sure that incriminating documents were spirited away. He then sued the government on the basis that the search was illegal – and won.

Jockeying between the Sydney publishers remained intense. Early in 1967 Sir Frank Packer let it be thought that he was anxious to sell his Australian Consolidated Press, the holding company for his magazines and papers. Both Fairfax and Murdoch made offers, even considering a joint offer. But then, while Murdoch was abroad, he heard that Packer had sold Consolidated Press to another of his companies, Television Corporation. His earlier feelers to both Murdoch and Fairfax had been put out merely to get accurate valuations of Consolidated Press. Although Murdoch was on the board of Television Corporation, Packer's move put the papers out of his reach. It also diminished the proportion of News Ltd's holdings in Television Corporation. Murdoch therefore decided to cut his losses and sell his stock in Television Corporation. Later in the year he bought the outstanding stock in Southern Television. None the less, he found himself, by mid-1968, with cash in hand and anxious, as ever, to expand.

Chapter 5

LONDON

Murdoch was at the races when the door to Fleet Street opened to him. Despite his conceit that he has always been a foe of the Establishment, the concierge was Stephen Gordon Catto, the second Baron Catto of Cairncatto.

Catto was a director of Morgan Grenfell, a leading and aggressive merchant banking firm, and of Australian United Corporation, an associated company. He had been introduced to Murdoch by Sir Norman Young, a colleague on the AUC board and at that time chairman of News Ltd. Murdoch told him he had long had a dream of buying the *Daily Mirror*, now controlled through IPC by Cecil King, Northcliffe's nephew. Some time later he saw Catto again in London, when Murdoch said that he had built up News Ltd to escape from Adelaide, and that he now wanted to escape from Australia. Catto told him that IPC would not sell. So Murdoch suggested that he might buy IPC itself. Catto thought that was slightly mad, he recalled later, and asked to see some money before he started buying anything. Shortly afterwards, Murdoch transferred around two million pounds to Morgan Grenfell.

"We started buying slowly," said Catto. "We thought we might pick up about 10 per cent. In those days you did not have to make any announcements of less than that." Catto was impressed that Murdoch seemed able to produce money as and when it was needed.

But in 1968 Catto called him about another property, the *News of the World*, one of Britain's longest-established popular newspapers, which might be available.

"The News of the Screws", as it is often called, was Britain's most salacious Sunday paper. It specialized in stories of randy

vicars, homosexual housemasters, threesomes in bed, stolen knick-
ers, misplaced virginities. Stories were told with a feigned air of
shock. The vicars rarely performed quite as vigorously as expected,
the deviant scoutmasters were larger in the headlines than in life.
The paper also had excellent sports pages, and sponsored various
sporting events. It was an institution of a rather British kind, and
successful, even though its circulation had fallen from 8.5 million
in 1950 to about 6 million in 1968. Although it published articles
by politicians of all parties, it combined its interest in sex with
devout support of the Conservative Party.

It was run on a shoestring, with only a handful of reporters
under a Falstaffian editor named Stafford Somerfield. He was
regarded as a genuine "Fleet Street character" who loved to pander
to all the most blimpish of British prejudices. The offices of the
paper were in Bouverie Street, just off Fleet Street. They were not
very modern; but through its subsidiary, Eric Bemrose, the News
of the World group had invested heavily in new colour presses in
Liverpool.

The company had been managed since the 1890s by one family,
the Carrs, who were the largest shareholders. Sir Emsley Carr had
been editor for fifty years and his son, Sir William, chairman for
sixteen years by 1968. Sir William was a powerful man who had
a long love affair with alcohol, which he indulged at midday at
the Savoy Grill. Although difficult and complex, he was intensely
proud of his position and had the capacity of inspiring loyalty
amongst those who knew him well.

With the paper came about thirty subsidiaries, ranging from
Greyhound Express and *International Hotel Review*, to *Men Only*,
the Walton Heath Golf Club, printing establishments and a paper-
making firm. In the late 1960s, the assets had trebled, but the
profits of the company had fallen, as had the share price. None
the less, the Carrs thought that they were impregnable, because
they owned 27 per cent of the voting shares themselves, while
another 25 per cent were in the hands of a cousin, Professor Derek
Jackson.

Jackson was the wild card, a bizarre and brilliant scientist with
a romantic history, who lived in tax exile in Paris and Lausanne
with his sixth wife. He had gradually become estranged from the

rest of the family, was disgruntled by the poor performance of his shares and wanted to sell.

Sir William offered him the market price of twenty-eight shillings a share, but Jackson rejected this with contempt: he wanted twice that. Carr could not afford it. Moreover, to have paid Jackson a higher price than the market value would, under British company law, have necessarily triggered a bid for the whole company. To Carr's horror, Jackson instructed his bankers, Rothschilds, to search for an outside buyer. They found Captain Robert Maxwell, MC, MP. No prospect could have been more terrible to the Carrs: Maxwell was a foreigner, a boor and a Labour Member of Parliament. And there were other reasons why he aroused mistrust.

Maxwell was born Jan Ludwig Hoch in Slovakia. After several other name changes he became Robert Maxwell and served, with distinction, in the British army against the Germans. He was decorated with the Military Cross.

Maxwell's first business coup came in occupied Germany after the war. He acquired a mass of German scientific documents owned by Julius Springer, brought them to Britain and began to sell them, very profitably, to librarians around the world. He then took over the bankrupt book wholesaling firm of Simpkin Marshall. He raised finance for Simpkins, on which he paid interest, and then advanced substantial sums from Simpkins, interest-free, to his other private enterprises. He was effectively using the company as a bank even though it was insolvent. When a director tried to raise the alarm, Maxwell silenced him with a "gagging writ"; throughout his life he used the law of libel to intimidate critics – unlike Murdoch, who nearly always allowed his critics to say their worst. After four years Simpkins collapsed leaving debts, mostly to publishers, of £475,000. Many publishers never forgave Maxwell.

Maxwell renamed his own company Pergamon Press, and built up a successful trade in specialized scientific texts and magazines. He also ventured into the twilight zone behind the Iron Curtain, whence he had emerged before it descended, signing up Russian scientists to produce articles very cheaply, and using East European printing companies, at very low contract prices. Having bought cheap, he sold dear. He would establish a near monopoly in a scientific discipline and then sell his works in small numbers at remarkably high prices; all that was required was that every library should need to buy one Pergamon edition.

In 1959 he decided to move into British politics. He helped establish lotteries which transformed the finances of local Labour parties, and was elected to Parliament as Labour MP for Buckingham in 1964. By 1968 he had a reputation for being loud and domineering; he liked to compare himself to Beaverbrook, and played upon his position as an outsider, seeking to disarm criticism by complaining that it was anti-Semitic, which often led people to give him the benefit of the doubt.

Maxwell and Murdoch had already crossed paths in 1967. Maxwell had persuaded Murdoch to buy 50 per cent of Pergamon in Australia. Merv Rich had the job of resolving the details of the agreement. This did not prove easy. Rich flew to London and Maxwell sent his Rolls-Royce to meet him at Heathrow. None the less, Rich found it impossible to get reliable figures out of Maxwell. "He was very hard to pin down," said Rich. So he left. "I arrived from the airport in a Rolls and went back on a bus."

On 16 October 1968 Maxwell offered three Pergamon stock units for four ordinary News of the World shares, together with redeemable stock in Pergamon. News of the World stock was divided into voting and non-voting shares. Maxwell offered more for the voting shares, thirty-seven shillings and sixpence, than for the non-voting – thirty-six shillings. The total value of the offer was some £26 million. He was in a strong position. Not only had the company been doing badly, but he had already obtained pledges from Derek Jackson, for his 25 per cent of the voting shares.

Sir William Carr was seriously ill when the bid came in. He sent a message from his sickbed to the boardroom, describing Maxwell's bid as "impudent". He had no faith in Maxwell, either as an individual or as a businessman. He thought Pergamon's share price was artificially high and that Maxwell intended to sell off News of the World assets in order to save Pergamon. To defend the company against the predator, the Carrs' bankers, Hambros, bought up shares on the open market and forced the price up to forty-five shillings. The board advised shareholders to do nothing for the time being. But clearly a very serious effort would have to be made to resist Maxwell's money.

It was at this stage that Catto telephoned Murdoch, and suggested that the *News of the World* might be an easier purchase than the *Mirror*. He also talked to the Carrs' banker, Harry Sporborg, at Hambros. Murdoch was immediately excited. The *News of the World* at once became his new obsession. With its 6 million circulation, its string of provincial papers and its printing plant, he thought it should be a very profitable acquisition. Graham King recalls him jumping up and down all over his office in Kippax Street, working out the figures, what they meant and what they could do for him. The *News of the World* appeared to be his ticket north and west.

On the afternoon of Friday, 18 October, Sporborg called Catto and suggested he bring his man over quickly. Murdoch proved hard to find. Eventually he was traced to the racetrack. He had gone to attend the Caulfield Cup, one of Australia's most important races. Catto told him to get on a flight at once. Murdoch called Anna in Sydney and asked her to meet him at Sydney airport with a bag of clothes and his *News of the World* files. From there he took a Lufthansa flight to London via Frankfurt, arriving secretly at Heathrow on Sunday, 20 October. Catto met him and drove him to his home in Huntingdon where they planned their strategy.

That Sunday the *News of the World* published an editorial by the editor, Stafford Somerfield, which instantly became notorious. All over the front page, it derided Maxwell's qualifications to be owner of the paper. He was a socialist, but above all he was a foreigner.

> Why do I think that it would not be a good thing for Mr Maxwell, formerly Jan Ludwig Hoch, to gain control of this newspaper which, I know, has your respect, loyalty and affection – a newspaper which I know is as British as roast beef and Yorkshire pudding? . . . This is a British newspaper, run by British people. Let's keep it that way.

Somerfield was widely excoriated for this assault.

Catto recalled, "We thought the sensible thing was to appear to be the white knight coming in to help the Carrs. The difficulty was to match any bid which Maxwell might be going to make. The easiest way of not paying too much for something was in fact to persuade them to buy shares in something which Rupert owned."

However, it was quite clear to both of them that Murdoch did not want to be merely a chivalrous white knight. At the end of the day, he wanted to control the *News of the World*. Catto suggested that he be cautious and not frighten Carr. First, he must get Carr to agree to his becoming managing director in order to see off Maxwell. Once that had been accomplished, he could issue a new block of shares in the name of News Ltd to override Carr. It was a brilliant, assured and relatively cheap way to break into Fleet Street.

On Monday night, Murdoch and Catto had dinner at the Mirabelle, one of London's smartest restaurants, with William Carr, the son of Sir William, his cousin Clive, and their wives. The Carr contingent wanted to inspect Murdoch's shining armour. He displayed all his charm. "I couldn't see any angle with him, or any chink in the armour," said William Carr later. They recommended to Sir William that a deal be explored.

There was no way in which Murdoch could have raised the cash to match Maxwell's original offer, let alone to surpass it. But Catto proposed that some of News Ltd's Australian assets be transferred to the News of the World. In exchange, the News of the World would issue new stock to News Ltd. Sir William Carr could now call upon some 30 per cent of the votes and with the new ones issued to Murdoch they would be, jointly, unassailable.

By now Maxwell had satisfied himself that none of the other British newspaper groups would bid against him. He knew nothing about Murdoch's arrival. But as the shares climbed steadily, it was clear that there must be a mystery buyer – and Maxwell was compelled to raise his bid to fifty shillings each for the voting stock. This set the overall value of the company at £34 million, even further out of Murdoch's reach.

On the Wednesday Murdoch went to breakfast at Carr's flat in

Cliveden Place. According to one version of the breakfast, Murdoch blurted out his demands rudely to Carr, and when Carr did not immediately agree to step down as chief executive, Murdoch said, "Let Maxwell get it, then," and stood up to leave.

At this Carr declared of Maxwell, "He's an evil man, you know."

"Well I'm not an evil man," replied Murdoch, "I'm here to help you if you want it. But I don't like to waste my time on dither."

At the threat of the loss of his knight, white or otherwise, Carr told Murdoch to sit down again, and agreed to many of his demands.

Murdoch asked that he should be joint managing director with Sir William's nephew, Clive. Sir William agreed. He had a seven-year contract as chairman and so felt secure. Moreover, he had long known and admired Murdoch's mother, and felt he could rely upon her son. (Not for the last time, affection for the irreproachable Dame Elisabeth swayed people in Murdoch's favour.)

They agreed that enough new shares would be created to give Murdoch 40 per cent of the voting stock. Then he and Carr would jointly control over half of the stock. Murdoch also agreed that he would not buy further shares in the company to raise his stake above 40 per cent, and that a member of the Carr family would remain chairman to support him in his role of joint managing director with Clive Carr.

By now news of Murdoch's presence in London had leaked. On the afternoon of Thursday 24 October, he gave a press conference to announce that he intended to acquire 40 per cent of the *News of the World* – he would buy 9 per cent on the market and get the rest in exchange for Australian assets. There were many questions. He was asked whether the minority shareholders would not suffer? Would the stock not soon fall well below its present value? Why would he not match Maxwell's offer? Because he did not have enough money, he replied. The man from the *Wall Street Journal* accused him of "watering the stock to swing this deal" and another questioner said that the City's Takeover Panel, which was supposed to regulate bids and protect the interests of shareholders, was being blatantly disregarded.

The panel was indeed in an absurd position. It could have ruled against the proposal – as Maxwell demanded. But the chairman, Sir Humphrey Mynors, cleared Murdoch to go ahead with his bid while advising him to transfer News Ltd's assets to the News of the World as soon as possible. The panel did insist that first Morgan Grenfell and then everyone else stop buying News of the World shares. Dealings were suspended for two months. Murdoch said later: "I could *smell* that the Establishment would not let Maxwell in."

The next few weeks were not easy for the Carrs. Sir William's health worsened dramatically, with the first signs of an aneurism. Lady Carr began to have doubts about Murdoch. She took him out to lunch at the Coq d'Or and was appalled when he asked her to provide him with a cigar, and then started smoking it before the meal. Lady Carr said he clearly needed a little polishing, to which Stafford Somerfield later commented, "Maybe that was true, for he proved as hard as a diamond."

A special shareholders' meeting at which the offers would be voted upon was fixed for 2 January 1969. Robert Maxwell then demanded that any stock purchased since the battle began should be excluded from voting. The Takeover Panel agreed, and the Murdoch-Carr axis suddenly found its holding reduced from 51 per cent of the eligible stock to 38 per cent. Maxwell had 32 per cent and about 30 per cent was undecided.

For some reason Maxwell did not move in fast enough. He did not make a formal offer until late November. By then the value of Pergamon's own stock had declined. More intense legal manoeuvring followed.

In December Sir William set out for shareholders the details of the deal with Murdoch – the News of the World would issue 5.1 million voting ordinary shares, which would amount to 35 per cent of the expanded voting stock. News Ltd would then hold over 40 per cent of the votes. In return it would inject into the company assets providing a guaranteed income of £1.1 million a year. Murdoch would become managing director. He had already insisted to Carr that his previous agreement to be merely joint managing director with Clive Carr was not enough. He would not proceed unless he was made sole managing director. Carr had protested, but by this time felt he had no choice. It was astonishing but, in their desperate bid to stop Maxwell, the Carrs were evidently prepared to sign over their company to another outsider who had only 3½ per cent of the shares.

The game grew rougher. Maxwell tried to dig up dirt in Australia about Murdoch, and Murdoch's papers there began to attack Maxwell. Then Maxwell attempted to buy News from under Murdoch, but Murdoch was protected by the shares held by ABC Television in New York. His friend, Leonard Goldenson, told Maxwell that ABC supported Murdoch, and then agreed to sell back to Murdoch the shares he had bought a decade earlier. Murdoch's Sydney *Mirror* denounced Maxwell's techniques of selling encyclopedias in Australia. Maxwell slapped in a writ for libel.

In December Murdoch returned to England and was photographed arriving at the airport with Anna and their baby daughter Elisabeth. "This boy doesn't miss a trick. Everyone will fall for the baby," wrote Somerfield.

On 2 January 1969 the crucial shareholders' meeting turned into an extraordinary gladiatorial encounter, the first of many, between Robert Maxwell and the hitherto unknown young Australian. Maxwell started with 32 per cent and Carr with 38 per cent of the shares. Lady Carr and her family had spent days and days trying to persuade as many of the smaller shareholders as possible to attend and vote the Carr-Murdoch ticket. They suggested to those who could not attend the meeting that they sign over their shares temporarily to *News of the World* staff who would be present and could vote them. Lady Carr gave her friends one share each so that they could attend and vote against an adjournment. Under the articles, an adjournment could be passed on a show of hands – so the turnout of shareholders might be critical.

The meeting took place at the Connaught Rooms, familiar, slightly *déclassé* territory for AGMs and chicken banquets. The family arrived in a fleet of cars, led by Sir William's company Rolls-Royce. Many of the women were in their fur coats. Sir William looked appalling; he had come back on a special flight from Portugal under his doctor's supervision. He was in great pain, and he should have been operated on in late December, but he had insisted on postponing this until after the meeting. He did not expect to survive long.

The room was packed with about 500 shareholders. They gave Sir William a long ovation when he appeared on the dais. His voice was reduced almost to a whisper. After him, Murdoch spoke briefly, modestly and nervously, stressing that News was a fine organization. He was delighted that Sir William would stay on as chairman.

It was almost like a pantomime, with the old king and his family, the crown prince from a far-off country, and the big foreign villain, threatening in an electric-blue suit. Maxwell was booed when he stood up. In his booming voice he stressed that his offer was now worth fifty-two shillings per share and that if it were refused – as by now he knew it would be – the shares would be worth only thirty-nine shillings and falling.

Carr replied, "What is money when you can get so much more out of life?" He compelled Maxwell to sit down. Maxwell accused the board of rigging the meeting. The audience needed no cue cards. Shareholders shouted "Go home" or "Go back to the Old Vic" – a reference to Maxwell's theatricality.

Carr and Murdoch won the day overwhelmingly with 299 votes for the issue of the new shares and only 20 against. From Paris, Derek Jackson said he thought the board was raving mad. "The law of the jungle has prevailed," declared Maxwell. Most financial journalists agreed that he had been shabbily treated. But when it later became clear that Maxwell's company Pergamon was worth much less than he had claimed, the Carrs could show that their suspicions of him were justified. However, it was also evident that they could have seen him off without the help of Murdoch. The day after the meeting, Sir William was taken into hospital for a series of major operations.

It was a bruising battle in which almost everyone had lost something. Maxwell had lost at least £200,000 and a lot of prestige, though he had gained some sympathy. The Carrs had lost some £2 million on paper and, more importantly, control of their company. Professor Jackson had lost his chance to sell his shares. The banks had lost, at the least dignity, if not shareholders' money. Only Murdoch had won – he now had a beachhead in one of the most important publishing centres of the world. For him it was a famous victory.

Anna Murdoch's second novel, *Family Business*, contains a thinly disguised account of the *News of the World* takeover. Her heroine, Yarrow McLean, a doughty American publisher (whose character seems to contain some parts Dorothy Schiff, the publisher of the *New York Post*, some parts Katharine Graham, the publisher of the *Washington Post* and many parts Rupert Murdoch), goes to London to buy the *Sunday Enquirer* from the Randolph family. Like the Carrs, the Randolphs are threatened by a takeover bid – from Piers Molinksi, who had come to England after the war as a displaced person and become a rich Labour MP. "There were unsubstantiated rumours about his political allegiances, and about the state of his business."

Battle is joined between McLean and Molinski and it follows much the same course as that between Murdoch and Maxwell. When the crucial shareholders' meeting takes place, five hundred people turn up and applaud the Randolph family as they enter, exactly as happened with the *News of the World*. "Yarrow wondered why, since the company was doing so badly."

She knows that Molinski's bid, which looks better than hers on paper, is falsely inflated. Her banker has told her Molinksi's business methods are suspect. "How could you evaluate a shipment of rubber condoms that had been sitting on Indian wharves in the sun for the past twelve months? 'Their offer is full of holes,' said Yarrow."

Yarrow "spoke modestly and kept it short" – like Murdoch. Molinksi is given three minutes to speak – as Maxwell was. "Molinski's voice and presence were more British than the British, but Yarrow could sense the hostility in the room." Molinksi – Maxwell – however, "thunders" on. The motion on the proposed merger is carried overwhelmingly – with just twenty people against – exactly the same number as in the case of the News of the World. The next day, Yarrow is discovered in the antiquated, empty pressroom by one of the Randolph sons who had never been there before.

Yarrow knows what she will do: start a daily, so as not to have the plant idle for five days a week. "But she didn't tell young Randolph that. It was none of his business. By the time she would be ready to move, none of the Randolphs would be around to be involved."

Like Yarrow McLean in the novel, Rupert Murdoch had no intention of being a mere partner. As soon as he had won the takeover battle, he unbuckled his knight's white armour and revealed a different person. As far as he was concerned it was just a question of getting down to work. But to the Carrs it was an appalling shock.

On the day after the takeover, he (like Yarrow McLean) swept into the *News of the World* offices in Bouverie Street at 8 a.m., "and found the SOGAT cleaning ladies having tea on the chairman's desk". He also insisted that he found the real state of the company to be far worse than the Carrs had revealed. "It could have made us broke," he said later. He therefore had to embark on a radical overhaul.

William Carr, Sir William's son, later commented, "This is rather cynical. Obviously if Murdoch made the wrong decisions, it could have broken him, but in practice the deal he obtained from the Carr family was one of the major leaps forward in his life."

Despite the democratic spectacle of the cleaners drinking tea at the chairman's desk, Murdoch decided that the class divisions on the paper were part of the problem. "The social attitude. You went into the *News of the World* and you went through a glass door and into an executive corridor. And if you weren't a Cambridge blue, you didn't get through. Or a member of the Carr family. Senior production officials were kept outside the door." (When, twenty years later, this author pointed out to him that there was just such a locked glass door opened only with a special pass-card key on the executive suite at his Wapping headquarters, he agreed: "That's true. Good point. We should take it down. It's theoretically there for security. I can never find my bloody card." It was taken down in 1992, after the offices of the *Sun* were moved away from the same corridor.)

After Murdoch's victory, Derek Jackson still wanted to get rid of his shares, even though the price had fallen. On 20 January,

Murdoch went to visit Sir William, recuperating from his operation. In a "My dear Bill" letter next day, he wrote:

> I did enjoy seeing you again yesterday and thought you looked *much* better . . . Bill, this is to tell you that I am now planning to buy *some* of the Jackson shares, probably about a million. I haven't worked out my cash situation yet, but I have to take them now or miss out . . . I don't want to worry you at the moment, but I thought I must tell you first. It does not change our understanding in any way.

Soon Murdoch controlled 49 per cent of the stock.

He embarked upon a total transformation of the paper's structure and staff, explaining that this was urgently needed because of the Carrs' old-fashioned, unsuccessful management style. He said that as the new chief executive he had to answer to the shareholders and make sure that the company was properly and profitably run.

In fact, the decline of the paper could not all be blamed on mismanagement by the Carrs. The spread of commercial television was a major cause. A better-educated population and the growth of the middle class was arguably another. The 1960s was the decade of new colour magazines and other supplements in the more prestigious Sundays; quality was the growth market of the time. The *News of the World*'s eclectic mix of prurience and preaching, tracts and Toryism, had begun to seem arcane.

Murdoch had Clive Carr sidelined and began to weed through the staff. Sarah Carr, Sir William's daughter, said, "It was a touch of the Carrbrush. Anyone associated with us had to go."

On 7 March, Murdoch wrote another letter to Sir William to complain that now he was out of hospital, Carr was having too much contact with senior executives: "The plain fact, which I am sure you are as aware of as I am, is that a company of this nature can have only one executive boss. As managing director (and in control of a virtual majority of the voting shares) that person has to be me." Although many of the executives were Carr's lifelong friends, in future he must contact them through Murdoch *alone*. He asked Carr to resign from the subsidiary companies in the group. He did not want there to be any confusion about the chain of command, he said. And he was sending William Carr, Sir William's son, to Australia for at least a year and perhaps eighteen months "for intensive training". This had the effect of removing him from his father's side. In Australia the younger Carr was given almost nothing to do.

Twenty-four hours later, Carr was dashed by helicopter from Sussex to London for emergency surgery. A plastic tube in his aorta had ruptured. It was removed, the aorta sealed, and the blood supply to his legs was redirected through tubes which came down from under his arms.

Next, despite his written promises, and his assurance to the shareholders that Sir William would stay as chairman, Murdoch drove down to Carr's Sussex home where he was convalescing, and told him that he wanted him to relinquish the job. Carr, too ill to fight, decided reluctantly to accept the ultimatum. He told Somerfield, "I had known our paper for many years as a happy place. It could not be happy if Murdoch and I did not agree. I decided to go." In June 1969, he resigned. At a meeting of the board, Murdoch was elected chairman. The resolution was moved by Clive Carr, who said that Murdoch had the full support of the Carr family. This was received by the board in silence.

The Carrs felt that they had been betrayed. Murdoch had originally agreed that he would not raise his stock above 40 per cent, and that a member of the Carr family would remain chairman. It was on this basis that the Carr family had voted its shares at the extraordinary meeting, said William Carr later, but the family felt that Murdoch abrogated the agreement within one month by purchase of the Jackson shares, leading ultimately to the exclusion of the Carr family from the business. "This deal was the heart of the matter," said William Carr later, "and the Carr family fought so hard for Murdoch in the expectation that he would honour it."

The editor of the *News of the World* was tougher than Sir William. Somerfield had been with the paper since the end of the war. Under Sir William he had been allowed to do things his way. Murdoch felt that this was part of the problem. He had no respect for Somerfield – he saw him as a pompous, complacent snob. For his part, Somerfield was determined to hang on to the editorial independence which he had always enjoyed – and to make sure that if he had to leave, he would be adequately recompensed. Murdoch felt that Somerfield was trying to engineer his own dismissal – so that Murdoch would be compelled to pay off his contract in full.

The notion that a proprietor must not lay his hands upon an editor and that an editor must be allowed to express the views and publish the stories he chooses was never one that Murdoch could tolerate. That has been one of the most constant sources of irritation, both to him and to many of the journalists who have worked for him.

"As proprietor I'm the one who in the end is responsible for the success, or failure, of my papers," he said in 1969.

Since a paper's success or failure depends on its editorial approach, why shouldn't I interfere when I see a way to strengthen its approach? What am I supposed to do, sit idly by and watch a paper go down the drain, simply because I'm not supposed to interfere? Rubbish! That's the reason the *News of the World* started to fade. There was no one there to trim the fat and wrench it out of its editorial complacency.

Murdoch ordered Somerfield to fire some of the paper's columnists, such as Douglas Bader, the Battle of Britain hero who wrote on aviation, and a number of reporters. He chose their successors. He started changing advertising posters that Somerfield had approved and told him not to send correspondents abroad without his agreement. When Somerfield complained about such interference, Murdoch said, "I didn't come all the way from Australia not to interfere. You can accept it or quit!"

In summer 1969, when Somerfield was away in Spain on holiday, Murdoch began to make large-scale changes to the layout of the paper. Somerfield rushed back to London and countermanded Murdoch's instructions.

They were, however, more or less united on the first big issue which involved Murdoch in a major controversy in Britain – and helped him to acquire from the satirical magazine *Private Eye* the name "Dirty Digger", which has remained with him since. It was a traditional *News of the World* story.

Christine Keeler was the beautiful call girl whose affairs with both the then Secretary of State for War, John Profumo, and a Soviet naval attaché, Eugene Ivanov, in 1962, had seriously embarrassed the government of Harold Macmillan. Profumo lied to the House of Commons in denying the affair, then, when he had to admit it, he resigned.

The *News of the World* had paid Keeler £23,000 for her memoirs at the time of the scandal. For this it had been censured by the Press Council. In the summer of 1969, Keeler hawked around a new version of the story. To boost sales, as he knew it would, Somerfield wanted to run it again. Murdoch was at first concerned. Profumo had spent the last six years working among the poor in the East End of London; he was widely respected for this arduous and sincere penance. None the less, Murdoch agreed and the *News of the World* paid £21,000 for the recycled story.

The outcry was enormous. The Press Council, encouraged by Denis Hamilton, the editor in chief of Times Newspapers, instituted an enquiry, which Murdoch and Somerfield refused to attend. The council condemned the *News of the World* once more. Hamilton said later, "I thought it important to show Murdoch that this wasn't the way to go in England, that it was a different place from Australia."

Cardinal Heenan, the country's leading Catholic prelate, withdrew from an agreement to write an article for the *News of the World* on the permissive society. Somerfield was uncontrite. He told the *Daily Mail* that he was surprised that the Cardinal did not wish to address fifteen million sinners through the pages of the *News of the World*.

Murdoch, who was beginning to see that he might have made a mistake, was appalled to read Somerfield's rebuke of the Cardinal and dashed off a letter of apology to Heenan. He told Somerfield that he had to clear any statements with him in future. More was at risk than just the *News of the World*.

But Murdoch was hardly more successful in his own defence. He was quoted as saying, "People can sneer as much as they like, but I'll take the 150,000 extra copies we're going to sell." This was certainly frank; the memoirs were bought precisely in order to sell newspapers. In one television interview he acknowledged that Profumo could be forgiven, but said that his actions should not be forgotten. His worst moment came when he was interviewed by David Frost for London Weekend Television.

At this stage of his career, Frost had developed the reputation as Britain's foremost television prosecutor. He interviewed his guests before a studio audience, which performed as a *de facto* jury.

Frost took the high ground and stayed on it. Murdoch tried to say that the articles would concentrate on the parliamentary side of the scandal, the role of the Labour Party, and so on. But Frost pointed out that the first week's extract had been mere sexual titillation. Murdoch claimed that there were important new facts in the series – but he could not name them. Worse was to come.

After the commercial break, Frost screened an interview he had filmed earlier with Cardinal Heenan. This was a different Frost. In the studio was a combative inquisitor facing down his victim, Rupert Murdoch. On the screen with the Cardinal, Frost appeared solicitous. The Cardinal expressed his shock at the *News of the World*'s cynicism and greed, and his concern for "this excellent man" Profumo.

Murdoch, trapped in the studio, was visibly angered by the homily. He said, "This easy glib talk that the *News of the World* is a dirty paper is downright libel and I resist it completely." People only said that, he maintained, because the paper was so successful.

As Frost moved in for the kill, Murdoch appeared shifty and equivocating. He said the row had been "whipped up by some members of the Establishment that don't want to be seen with Mr Profumo anywhere".

After the interview, Frost took the seething Murdoch to join Anna in the hospitality room. He offered them a drink, but Anna snapped at him, "We've had enough of your hospitality." Murdoch left the building vowing that he would buy London Weekend and dispose of Frost.

Murdoch complained that Frost had misled him into thinking that they would be having a "pally chat". Frost disputes this, saying that he had alerted Murdoch earlier that day to the Heenan interview. Even so, Ian Hamilton writing in the 9 October 1969 edition of the BBC's weekly, *The Listener*, felt a little sorry for Frost's victim: "There's a point at which the legitimately tough grilling of a public figure starts shading into blood sport."

The incident hurt and angered Murdoch. He felt that he was once more a victim of British hypocrisy, as he had been at Oxford. It coloured his whole attitude towards the British, and in particular towards that amorphous and uncertain entity, the British Establishment. Anna Murdoch felt that he had been outrageously abused by Frost. She was finding it hard to make friends in England, a fact which she attributed partly to the aloof nature of the British, and partly to the Keeler affair. Both of them began to nurture two seemingly conflicting ambitions: to get out and to get even.

From London they were able often to visit New York. They found it both more exhilarating and more friendly and were determined eventually to move there. But first there was another battle to be won in London.

FLEET STREET

At the end of the 1960s, there was probably no British industry so arcanely and badly run as newspaper publishing. The power of the print union barons over management had grown enormously since Murdoch had last worked in Fleet Street in the early 1950s.

There were about 140,000 people, including 26,000 journalists, employed in the publishing industry. Their turnover was about the same as that of the brewing or the aerospace industry but the methods of production were archaic.

There were then ten national newspapers, including eight Fleet Street dailies, eighty-nine morning and evening papers produced in the provinces, plus over 1,000 weeklies, 2,500 trade, technical and professional journals, and almost 2,000 magazines devoted to leisure or "women's" interests. Many of these were produced either at a loss or with far less profit than would have been possible if reasonable agreements had existed between management and unions. Instead there was a grotesque state of constant war.

The problem could be traced back to the 1950s, and in particular to the Beaverbrook press. After wartime newsprint rationing was lifted, the 1950s were a boom time for Fleet Street. Circulations and advertising revenues both soared. The money was pouring in, and proprietors could afford to ignore restrictive practices in the print unions. Indeed, the richer owners, like Beaverbrook, were pleased to let wages be pushed up – in order to drain resources from their competitors. As a result, the Newspaper Publishers' Association, which represented the national newspaper owners, was never able to unite. The proprietors would meet, agree some proposal which was meant to modify if not control union abuse of power, and then individually capitulate at once to the next union demand, whether or not it subverted any agreement.

On the *Express*, Beaverbook virtually invented the idea of "ghost workers". The paper's machines could not print enough pages under the agreed union procedures, so *Express* management agreed to invent (and pay to run) ghost machines, to explain away longer runs on the real presses. The existing workers would share the money paid to the ghosts on the fictitious machines. Thus union chapels (chapters) of, say, eighty men were paid the wages of 100. In return, they did a little more work than had been agreed. It was not uncommon for men to draw a second or even a third pay packet under fictitious names, such as Mickey Mouse, Abraham Lincoln, or Douglas Fairbanks.

The "Mickey Mouse" employees were just one of many so-called "Old Spanish customs" in which the Fleet Street printers were immersed. These were bizarre, often picturesque, and they meant that the London print workers were among the highest paid but least-taxed in the land. Management had in effect allowed the unions to take charge of employing labour on each paper. Printing staff often came in on a casual basis, particularly on the Sunday newspapers, where labour was needed only once a week. The union leaders on each paper began to accumulate enormous power. Each union's chapel fought against others, within the paper, as well as against management. Thus the men from the National Graphical Association (NGA) were in a constant state of warfare with those from NATSOPA, the National Society of Operative Printers and Assistants, later SOGAT, the Society of Graphic and Allied Trades. If one received a marginal benefit, the other at once demanded reciprocity on pain of shutting the paper. While profits were high in the 1950s, the proprietors usually caved in.

In 1955 the Newspaper Publishers' Association had abandoned its "one stop all stop" pact, in which all agreed to cease production if any was stopped by industrial action. Each owner was too anxious to increase his own circulation at the expense of his rivals. Then in 1964 price fixing for newspapers ended; from now on cover prices could float freely and proprietors could undercut each other at will. The jungle grew fiercer. In 1968, comprehensive wage agreements were reached with the unions to set basic rates for print work. They should have cut back on overtime and other extra payments but in effect they increased the power of the union chapels which ran their own labour exchanges to hire and fire workers. Management opted out.

In the *News of the World* building in Bouverie Street, Murdoch found a combination of expensive working practices and ancient machinery. "It was an unbelievable mess. We would have gone broke with all the bits and pieces of rubbish they had," he said later. He was desperate to get the presses and the men working all through the week. That meant buying or starting a daily paper. He failed to persuade Lord Rothermere, owner of Associated Newspapers, to sell him the *Daily Sketch*, a middle-market tabloid which was seriously sick. "So we thought we'd start one. And then the *Sun* thing opened up."

The *Sun* was the worthy, left-wing child of Hugh Cudlipp, the chairman of Mirror Newspapers. It had been created in 1964 out of the corpse of the *Daily Herald*. The *Herald* had been a serious-minded left-wing paper half owned by the Trades Union Congress with a bigger circulation than any other paper in Britain in the 1930s. After the war, it had lost ground and in 1961 it was bought by IPC, the owners of the *Mirror*. IPC guaranteed to keep the *Herald* alive for seven years and not to merge it with the *Daily Mirror*.

Hugh Cudlipp of the *Mirror* said later that no one sane would have wanted to publish the *Herald*. It was compelled to laud not only the Labour Party but also the trade unions, whatever the absurdities of their conduct. It had fewer women readers than any other national morning newspaper, and like the Labour Party it was losing the young.

In desperation IPC relaunched the *Herald* as the *Sun* in 1964. Their hope, based on massive market research, was that the new and better-educated working class wanted a more sophisticated paper than the traditional tabloids. They believed that there was a brand-new market of upwardly mobile young people longing for a new popular paper to reflect their values. IPC's marketing people called these readers "the growth generation". Apparently, they were young, bright and enquiring. But if they ever existed, they made it very clear over the next four years that they did not wish to buy Cudlipp's *Sun*.

By 1969 the *Sun*'s circulation had fallen from 1.5 million to 850,000. Together with the *Herald*, it had cost IPC over £12 million and the board were now free to sell it or close it. (They could not merge it with the *Mirror* – first because they had originally pledged not to, and second because the government would have referred them to the Monopolies Commission.)

The first nibble came in summer 1969 from Robert Maxwell. He said that if he bought the paper it would reflect the Labour Party attitudes. He planned to cut the budget and the personnel levels, and keep circulation low so as not to threaten the *Mirror*. IPC offered Maxwell the paper for almost nothing – £50,000 down and further instalments amounting to between £250,000 and £500,000, depending on how it prospered.

The unions, however, did not wish to lose several hundred jobs, and rejected Maxwell's terms. They made it clear to IPC that selling the paper to Maxwell could cause labour troubles on the other papers in the group. By midsummer 1969, Maxwell had other problems.

He planned to sell his company, Pergamon Press, to a New York conglomerate, Leasco, for £25 million. But then Leasco withdrew; its bankers, Rothschilds, explained that they no longer had confidence in the Pergamon figures. The Takeover Panel intervened to protect those shareholders who had not yet sold their

Pergamon stock. Leasco agreed to renew its bid, provided that the price was now based on a multiple of the average profits for 1968 and 1969, rather than on the 1968 disclosed profits, now in question. Then Leasco withdrew its bid altogether. Maxwell's position grew precarious during the summer. *News of the World* shareholders could already be grateful that their company had not been bought by him.

Murdoch now entered the second round of the long contest between the two men. "IPC had said they would give it to Maxwell for nothing if he could do a deal with the unions. And I said, 'If he can't, will you give me a chance?' They couldn't say 'No.' "

In August 1969, Murdoch flew to Rome to see Richard Briginshaw, General Secretary of NATSOPA, one of the most intransigent of the print unions which had divided Fleet Street between them. "That was typical of Briginshaw," said Murdoch later. "You know, 'Come and see me in Rome.' It was a way of getting a couple of his aides down there for a weekend to enjoy themselves, I think. But it worked." The problem he had to settle was which union would run the *Sun*'s presses – Briginshaw's men, or those from the NGA. In most Fleet Street papers, Briginshaw's men had the job. But at the *News of the World* the presses were controlled by the NGA. So the question was, which union would get the *Sun*? "In the end," said Murdoch, "it was split 50-50, which was an uncomfortable compromise, but all right."

Hugh Cudlipp said later, "It was the Maxwell deal we wanted." But once Maxwell had fallen, Cudlipp preferred to sell the paper to Murdoch than to close it down. Like the Fairfax management a decade before in Sydney, he did not see Murdoch's entry into daily tabloid journalism as any threat. Moreover, once Murdoch had declared himself interested, IPC was in a Catch-22 situation. The unions simply would not permit the company to close the paper and lose jobs which Murdoch was prepared to save. None the less, some members of the IPC board were against selling the paper to him at any price.

On the back of an envelope, Murdoch calculated the price he could pay to make the paper work as a decent investment. IPC had hardly given itself a strong bargaining position by agreeing a give-away price with Maxwell. Naturally, Murdoch wanted similar terms. IPC refused. Even so, in the end, Murdoch did have a bargain. He paid only £50,000 down and further instalments of £2,500 a week, up to a minimum of £250,000 and only rising above that to a maximum of £500,000, if the paper continued in profit. Eventually, when he had won a circulation of over 4 million and a far greater readership than that, Murdoch could say that he had gained his readers at only a few pence each. By contrast, in the United States, newspapers have sometimes changed hands for as much as $1,000 a reader. Murdoch felt he was off to the races.

Murdoch needed no market research to tell him what the *Sun* should be: a daily version of the *News of the World*. He considered the *Mirror* the prime example of the "gentrification of the press". Cudlipp had tried to take it upmarket and it now offered serious, investigative sections on contemporary political and social issues which Murdoch saw as pretentious. He thought readers wanted more fun in their tabloid, and that they hated being preached at. The *Mirror* was the soft underbelly of the tabloid market. Murdoch was a true disciple of his father's old guru, Northcliffe. "Explain, simplify, clarify!"

The first problem was overstaffing. The *Sun* had a staff of 3,161 in London and Manchester. Murdoch was determined to run it as leanly and cheaply as possible. The unions did agree to some cutbacks.

He wanted a tabloid. The printers told him that the *News of the World* broadsheet presses could not print it, at which Murdoch displayed his detailed knowledge of his trade. He informed the printers that their presses had originally been supplied with bars which would fold the pages to tabloid size. The head printer denied it. So Murdoch took off his jacket and climbed on to a press. In a box at the top of the machine he found the bar in question wrapped in sacking and covered in ink and grime. The printers were impressed.

Murdoch considered several Fleet Street candidates for editor of the new *Sun* and then, after a four-hour dinner with him at Rules in Covent Garden, he chose Albert "Larry" Lamb.

Lamb, the son of a Yorkshire colliery worker, considered himself a left-wing, boiler-room journalist. He had just accepted the job of northern editor of the *Daily Mail*. When he changed his mind and came to work for Murdoch, he decided that IPC's *Sun* hardly existed as a paper – his task was not to rescue a paper but to create one.

Murdoch brought over from Australia some of the more hard-bitten and experienced tabloid journalists who had made the Sydney *Daily Mirror* a financial if not an intellectual success. Among other key people were two IPC veterans, Bert Hardy and Alick McKay, an Australian Scot who had once worked for Sir Keith. Murdoch made him deputy chairman in London. McKay thought that Murdoch wanted him because of his age and his links to Sir Keith. "Rupert always liked father figures . . . He said I'd have to join him." McKay's association with Murdoch was to have tragic consequences.

In the last issue of the old broadsheet *Sun*, Murdoch published a signed editorial which promised, "The most important thing to remember is that the new *Sun* will still be a paper that CARES . . . The new *Sun* will have a conscience. It will never forget its radical traditions. It will be truly independent, but politically mightily aware . . . It will never, ever sit on fences. It will never ever be boring."

The reborn tabloid's first issue, published on 17 November 1969, led with the headline "HORSE DOPE SENSATION/ *Sun* exclusive". It seemed an odd choice, but not to Murdoch, an inveterate racing man. And, indeed, racing did sell papers in Britain.

Inside, on page three, was a fully-clothed young Swedish model, followed by an interview with the Prime Minister, Harold Wilson, a serialization of Jacqueline Susann's novel *The Love Machine* and a photograph of Anna Murdoch starting the presses rolling. She had to be made an honorary union member to be allowed to touch the machine at all, and even then the presses did not roll as commanded. Production problems meant that the first edition was two hours late – a common occurrence in Fleet Street in those days.

On the first night, Murdoch's public relations man, John Addey, organized a big party of advertisers and Fleet Street names. Disappointingly few turned up because Hugh Cudlipp was throwing a similar party at the *Mirror* a few streets away. One of the few outside journalists to accept Murdoch's invitation was Bill Grundy from the *Spectator*. He wrote of Murdoch, "The first impressions are that he is a very likeable man. He has a directness of approach that is like a breath of fresh air. He also seems a very open man."

When the first copies of the new *Sun* were carried over to the *Mirror* late that evening, Cudlipp glanced at the smudged pages and the typos and the spreads and threw it down on the table shouting confidently, "We've got nothing to worry about." He was wrong. Murdoch and Lamb mixed a brew of sex, fun and sensationalism that proved very attractive. Within twelve months the *Sun*'s circulation had doubled and was still climbing. Most of those readers came from the *Mirror* – and they gave Murdoch the profits which allowed him to establish another bridgehead westwards, across the Atlantic.

Right from the start, there was British antagonism to Murdoch and his *Sun*. The *New Statesman*, the voice of the established Left, referred to it as Murdoch's "shit sheet". When the *Sun* was criticized for having no principles, Murdoch stated what they were. It was opposed to capital punishment, apartheid, racism and the Vietnam War, and it was in favour of the permissive society. Some of these liberal positions were later to be renounced by Murdoch. But there was one attitude of his which remained constant. The *Sun* soon made plain his impatience with the British Establishment.

In January 1970 the paper called for the abolition of the honours system, by which thousands of people are annually awarded various medals or citations for their services to the country or to their profession. Murdoch had started attacking the honours system in the Sydney *Mirror* over a decade before. His theme song was and remained the boast: "We are not going to bow to the Establishment in any of its privileged enclaves."

Murdoch was always as lavish on promotion as he was tight on editorial expenditure. He spent almost as much on the *Sun*'s launch as he had on the downpayment for the paper – some £50,000. And he kept on spending thereafter.

A lot of the *Sun*'s success was due to marketing. Perhaps even more important than the journalists he imported from Sydney was the marketing maestro, Graham King. "Rupert called me over for a visit in summer 1969. We didn't go much for Britain in those days – we still thought of Australia as the Lucky Country. So he really had to seduce me." Murdoch knew that King had a fondness for antiquities. He picked him up in his Rolls-Royce in London and drove him up to the Cotswolds and then down to see Oxford. It was British tourism in style and at its most tempting. King agreed to move to London to market the re-created *Sun*.

"We worked out how to make it jump, like the Sydney *Mirror*," said King later. "It was a promotionally-oriented paper. We had no research about what the market was, but we clearly struck a chord." They sold the paper through bright television commercials, many of which seemed designed to irritate the Independent Broadcasting Authority, which had to approve them. "The ITA went ape over 'Pussy Week in the *Sun*'," said King. "It was all about cats." The promotions worked.

In January 1970, Murdoch sacked Stafford Somerfield, the editor of the *News of the World*. It was an expensive move. But it was worth it; Murdoch could now control the paper as he wanted. Somerfield was quite pleased too. He missed the good, easy, paternalistic old days of the Carr family in which he had ruled the paper.

Murdoch's politics were in a state of flux or redefinition at this time. He was still somewhere on the Left, but by now not very far off centre. On election day, 17 May, Murdoch published a front-page editorial which reaffirmed the *Sun*'s traditional loyalty: "WHY IT MUST BE LABOUR". Edward Heath, leading the Conservatives, won an easy victory. The *Sun* was generous and used a racing analogy. "Well done, Ted Heath. The British love to see an outsider come surging up to pass the favourite." Murdoch had always liked to be on the same side as the party in government. Since the days of Rohan Rivett in Adelaide, his papers had rarely taken stands on political principle.

By the middle of 1970, the *Sun* was gaining readers in their hundreds of thousands. The *Daily Sketch*, in despair, started to imitate the *Sun* by offering free televisions and other inducements to its readers. But it remained a lacklustre paper.

To begin with, the *Sun* gave more space to most subjects, apart from foreign news, than the *Mirror*. There were more pictures, twice as many pin-ups (mostly clothed) in the *Sun*, more about TV and radio, more features, more home news, much more sport, even more City news – and many more competitions. "Win a champagne wedding" was a typical *Sun*-style giveaway. The *Mirror* had almost twice as many advertisements as the *Sun*, which devoted the extra space available to sport and competitions.

Its extra feature space was filled with titillating articles like "The Affair" and "In Praise of Older Men". Sex was a great sales aid. There were numerous divorce reports, articles on the pill, and on sexual techniques. "HOW GOOD A LOVER ARE YOU? The questions and answers that can make your marriage happier". "HUSBANDS, HOW IMPORTANT DO YOU RATE PRE-LIMINARY LOVEMAKING?" "Tomorrow: WHY MAR-RIAGES GO WRONG IN BED: ASTONISHING NEW STUDY OF UNFAITHFUL HUSBANDS AND WIVES". The paper was constantly denounced and banned from libraries. Many people were even more enraged when it paid money to the children of the Great Train Robber, Ronald Biggs, who had fled to Brazil, for his self-serving story.

Page-three girls were introduced to the world, with bras in place, in early 1970. They were known then as Sunbirds. The first bare-breasted pin-up on page three was revealed to a breathless world on 17 November 1970. The caption announced: "From time to time some self-appointed critic stamps his tiny foot and declares that the *Sun* is obsessed with sex. It is not the *Sun* but the critics who are obsessed. The *Sun*, like most of its readers, likes pretty girls."

By the end of 1970, sales of the *Sun* had climbed to 1.7 million, only just behind the *Daily Mail*. Murdoch thought that the first important thing about its success was that it was a tabloid. "The broadsheet is just not part of modern life and the rush and the tubes and the buses. We were right to go for the *Mirror* of ten years ago. People wrote to say that they hadn't a paper they could understand until we came along." The *Mirror*, he said, had "turned their backs on the working class. We came along – brash, young and uninhibited."

The *Sun* was named Newspaper of the Year at the beginning of 1971. To meet its challenges, the *Mirror* was forced to abandon its more serious pages. Hugh Cudlipp was bitter. "Someone will always be found to scrape the bottom of the barrel," he said. Many others were shocked by the *Sun*'s sexual titillation. Richard Ingrams, editor of the satirical fortnightly paper, *Private Eye*, embarked on a long-running campaign against "The Dirty Digger" for his "vandalizing" of the British press.

Murdoch himself complained that there was far more sexual innuendo in the upmarket papers than in the *Sun*, citing as an example an article in the *Observer* about women horse riders and masturbation.

At the same time as the *Sun* was "soaring away", to use its own words, Murdoch was taking his first steps into British television. Commercial television franchises were then awarded every six years by the Independent Television Authority. In 1968 two companies were given the franchise for London: Thames TV was given the weekdays and London Weekend Television (LWT) the weekend from Friday to Sunday night. Thames TV had two main owners; London Weekend's ownership was more dispersed. Among the shareholders and leading lights were David Frost, and Arnold Weinstock, head of General Electric.

The company had intellectual aspirations but little commercial skill. By 1969 it was losing money heavily. Weinstock sold his 7.5 per cent of the voting shares to Murdoch, who thus became a non-executive director. True to form, Murdoch reckoned that viewers wanted relaxing weekend entertainment. He saw that the company was under-capitalized and offered to inject £500,000. The Independent Television Authority, alarmed by the thought of page 3 girls on LWT, allowed him on to the board on condition he would not involve himself in programming. He agreed but, once on the board, found it impossible not to intervene.

He started to propose new programme schedules and ways in which the staff could be streamlined and production costs lowered. When the chief executive, Tom Margerison, complained, Murdoch encouraged the board to remove him and said that he himself was now going to chair the executive committee of the company.

The Independent Television Authority bridled: it insisted that a new chief executive, not Murdoch, be appointed, and that programmes be submitted for its review. Despite their enmity, David Frost and Murdoch agreed to appoint John Freeman, former editor of the *New Statesman* who had recently been British Ambassador to Washington. Freeman was a great success, and London Weekend began to make money. But Murdoch was angry that the Independent Television Authority should have the power to exclude him. He saw it as another example of Establishment hatred of him. He was determined that one day he would break into British television.

None the less, in many ways Murdoch had good reason to be delighted with his first two years of battles in Britain. Commercially they had gone well for him. With the success of the *Sun*, his empire was growing fast. But he had been infuriated by the abuse which was heaped upon him during the Keeler episode; and David Frost's assault left him raw and angry. He was also horrified by the extent to which the print unions seemed to be out of any proprietor's control. "As soon as the *Sun* began to be a great success, the unions were all over us, squeezing us to death. Life became a misery."

There were endless phone calls in the middle of the night requiring him to intervene in a dispute that threatened the night's production. Like other newspaper owners, Murdoch usually gave in. Anna saw the unions as his persecutors, and came to hate London more and more.

An appalling event had also occurred. A few weeks after the launch of the *Sun*, Rupert, Anna and Elisabeth returned to Australia for Christmas, leaving their Rolls-Royce in England for the use of his executives. One day, Alick McKay's wife Muriel used it to go shopping in the West End. She then disappeared from their home in Wimbledon. McKay began to get messages claiming to be from "M3, the Mafia", demanding a ransom of a million pounds. The kidnappers had apparently assumed that the single woman in the Rolls was Anna Murdoch and that her husband was well able to meet such a ransom demand. When they discovered their mistake, the kidnappers murdered Mrs McKay and disposed of her body so effectively that it was never found. It was believed to have been fed to the pigs.

Eventually the murderers, Arthur and Nizam Hosein, two brothers from Trinidad, were arrested, tried, convicted and imprisoned. The event had a profound effect upon everyone involved. Murdoch did everything he could to help Alick McKay, who continued as his vice-chairman. But, although McKay remarried happily, he never really recovered from the ordeal. Outside the McKay family, the worst affected was Anna Murdoch. She already disliked England and the way in which she was ostracized by so many people in London. Now she had reason to be terrified as well.

SYDNEY

Murdoch's empire has always had an odd shape. The nucleus of News Ltd remained in the South Australian capital of Adelaide, but Sydney was now the real centre of the Antipodean operations. At the beginning of the 1970s, it was in London that the real money was being made – every evening of the week, in Bouverie Street, when the *Sun* and the *News of the World* were thrown into vans and trucked to the railway stations that took the papers to the ends of the land.

Murdoch was continually shuttling between the hemispheres, but inevitably he was spending more time in London now. Indeed, he often seemed an absentee landlord in Sydney. This is not to say that he left the place alone – he was constantly on the telephone from London, sometimes several times a day, giving orders, cajoling, flattering, seeking information and gossip.

The Australian was now quite a fine paper. Adrian Deamer had become editor and circulation had risen to over 143,000. It was a coherent national, slightly radical voice, much loved by journalists. Deamer was also popular with most of his staff. But he did not have good relations with the management, in particular with John Menadue.

Murdoch said later he thought that Deamer had "great talent, and was a great technical editor. And he brought a lot of young people through." But his tongue was altogether too fierce. And Murdoch was uncomfortable with his politics. Deamer and his editorial director Douglas Brass saw to it that *The Australian* was the first serious broadsheet to demand the withdrawal of Australian troops from Vietnam, and Brass wrote an impassioned column on "the shame" of My Lai. Murdoch was still against the war – but he was uneasy at *The Australian* being seen as a voice of radicalism. He began to worry that he could not depend on Deamer any more than he had been able to rely on Rivett. Deamer was too strong, too independent, a loose cannon, a journalist's editor, not a proprietor's editor. As his empire grew, Murdoch felt increasingly that he needed men on whom he could rely – men whose judgement would not be different from his own. And thus, over time, he came more and more to appoint rather colourless editors who would not disturb the outposts of empire.

It was almost impossible for him to keep in touch with both the paper and its readers. He came roaring in for short visits to make snap decisions, not all of them good. In the middle of 1970 Murdoch decided, without adequate research, that he wanted a Sunday edition of the paper. It lasted a year and a half. He launched a financial paper, *Finance Week*; it folded in six months.

He did not complain directly, but Murdoch clearly did not like the way Deamer was editing *The Australian*. In June 1971 *The Australian* took a strong stand against the South African Springbok rugby tour, asserting that it would divide the country. When the new Prime Minister, William McMahon, offered an air force plane to fly the team across the country, Deamer was outraged and published a front-page editorial headed, "CYNICAL MISUSE OF THE PRIME MINISTER'S POWER". Queensland declared a state of emergency.

When Murdoch came to Sydney in July he called in Deamer, thumbed through the stack of recent papers – always his way of terrifying editors – and complained bitterly about the Springbok editorial. It was, he said, the worst thing that had happened to

The Australian for years. Then, on 22 July, he told Deamer he was no longer producing the sort of paper he liked. Perhaps he would like to move to another part of the organization? Deamer replied that he would either edit *The Australian* or nothing. Murdoch called Owen Thomson in Melbourne and told him to come and take over the paper, at least for the time being.

To many of *The Australian*'s young journalists, Deamer had been the liberal conscience of the paper. Deamer himself asserted that Murdoch had a whole slew of complaints about the paper under his editorship.

It was anti-Australian, it preferred black people to white people, it wanted to flood the country with Asians. He complained it took up every "bleeding heart" cause that was fashionable among the long-haired Left. It was not interested in the development and progress of Australia. It criticized the political leaders he supported. It was dull, it was a knocking paper, and it stood for everything he opposed and against everything he stood for.

After Deamer, *The Australian* declined, and lurched unsteadily towards the right. Years later, in the 1980s, a newly-appointed editor, Frank Devine, asked Murdoch who he thought had been its best editor. "Oh Deamer, I suppose," Murdoch replied rather sourly. When Devine told Deamer of this belated imprimatur, his reply was concise. "Rotten bastard," he said, with a thin smile.

In May 1972 Sydney journalism was subjected to a new upheaval. The Packers decided to divest themselves of the *Daily* and *Sunday Telegraph*, which were losing money – unlike their television and magazine interests. Murdoch bought them for the asking price of A$15 million. The purchase brought him Sydney's second morning paper (after the *Herald*) to complement his afternoon *Mirror*.

The *Telegraph*s were moved into Kippax Street and the *Sunday Australian*, which had been losing a great deal of money, was absorbed into the *Sunday Telegraph*. The economies of scale immediately became effective and the operation at Kippax Street began to move out of the red. Profits were helped by a fantastic deal which Merv Rich cut on newsprint supplies. While the international price doubled over the next four years, Australian News-print Mills had to hold the price to News almost steady.

The Prime Minister, William McMahon, was alarmed when he heard the news of the sale to Murdoch. He was a close friend of Sir Frank Packer and the Packer press had always supported him. He wanted to know how Murdoch would treat him. Murdoch said that he would give him a "fair crack of the whip", but to many that sounded like McMahon's death knell. Murdoch thought McMahon ineffectual and was moving towards his opponent, the Labor Party leader, Gough Whitlam. Later Murdoch said that he never really liked Whitlam; but at the time he thought that Australia was overdue for change.

McMahon called an election for December 1972. For the first time the Murdoch press showed its clout, coming out wildly in favour of Whitlam. *The Australian* declared that Whitlam's policy proposals were "exciting" and "a radical alternative to the Australia which exists today". Whitlam promised to take Australian troops out of Vietnam, a major issue at the time.

On the night that Whitlam made his final rally speech, Murdoch flew to have dinner with him in Melbourne. Murdoch later had to testify to a hearing on television licences about the occasion. He said that among the things they discussed were who would be the next High Commissioner to London. Murdoch said that he mentioned jokingly that it would not be a bad job for himself. But Whitlam later claimed that Murdoch had made a serious bid for the job. Murdoch has always categorically denied this and indeed it is hard to see how it would have fitted into his plans to make himself a leading international publisher. But the story that he lobbied hard for the job has never died.

Whitlam won the 1972 election and Murdoch was quoted as claiming that he had "single-handedly put the present government into office". Subsequently he asserted that he himself had become "far too deeply involved" in the election. "Looking back we did some dreadful things to the other side . . . A lot more happened than even they have managed to find out." And on another occasion, he said his papers were perhaps unprofessional and certainly quite unfair to McMahon. "I should have had more reserve, but I got emotionally involved. I allowed, with my eyes open, some of the journalists to go beyond being sort of partisans into almost being principals. They became foot soldiers in Whitlam's campaign to some extent."

He also said that the *Daily Telegraph* in particular "went overboard". That had been a Liberal Party paper for a long time. "We all really threw ourselves into the fight, to get a change. It did break twenty years of conservative government. Not a bad thing to do."

TEXAS

In 1973, to Anna's delight, Murdoch made his first major move from Britain across the Atlantic. His first American purchases were three papers in San Antonio – the *San Antonio Express*, the *News*, and their combined Sunday paper.

He had been trying for years to establish a really firm beachhead in America. He did not believe he could have an English-language media empire without a strong presence in the States. Moreover, he and Anna were heartily sick of England. Although the *Sun* had continued to soar in Britain they had both become increasingly irked by the continued intransigence of the print unions and what they saw as the snobbish hypocrisy of the British Establishment. Their feelings of exclusion had increased since 1973, when Murdoch once again caused offence by publicizing upper-class British sexual shenanigans, as he had done with the Keeler memoirs. The *News of the World* had become involved in a good old-fashioned vice story, embracing a government minister, call girls, deviation, defence secrets, exactly what was needed to raise circulation. However, the price had turned out to be higher than Murdoch had anticipated.

Lord Lambton, a languorous but witty Conservative Member of Parliament, had become a junior defence minister in the Heath government. He had also acquired the habit of visiting a prostitute named Norma Levy in spare moments from the Ministry.

Norma Levy's husband brought pictures of Lord Lambton in

bed with his wife to the *News of the World*. The paper at first appeared to behave with restraint. In May 1973 it reported that the Home Secretary was investigating the vice connections of public figures. Lambton was told that there existed photographs of him in bed with Mrs Levy and another woman. He resigned.

Then, however, it emerged that photographs had been taken not only by Mrs Levy's husband, but also by a gentleman from the *News of the World*, who had hidden in the apartment. The encounter was tape-recorded as well as photographed. Eventually, after deciding not to buy or to run the story it had helped create, the *News of the World* handed the prints and the tape back to Colin Levy.

The paper was censured by the Press Council in an official report prepared by Lord Justice Diplock. He wrote:

The action of the *News of the World* resulted in two men with criminal records being supplied with convincing evidence, which they previously lacked, of the involvement not only in sexual irregularities but also in criminal offences in connection with drugs of a junior Minister who had access to SECRET and TOP SECRET information of value to the intelligence services of a foreign power. These potential instruments of blackmail they handed over to Levy and his associates to whom it was therefore open to make what profit they could out of them.

The *News of the World*'s conduct seemed to many to be a revolting combination of intrusion and hypocrisy and Murdoch was personally excoriated even more fiercely than he had been after the Keeler affair.

This fracas coincided with another traumatic event for Anna. Driving her car, she knocked down and killed an old woman. It was an accident and the coroner's court found it to be so, but it was none the less shocking and distressing. Anna saw it as part of the misery that seemed always to attend her time in England. She was therefore relieved by the prospect of Rupert expanding into, and perhaps moving to the New World.

Murdoch chose San Antonio only because it had properties available at a time when he had an ability – backed by the cash flow of the *Sun* and the *News of the World* – to buy. He had looked at a pair of free newspapers in California, at the *Washington Star*, at *Look* magazine and other properties. None had seemed right. San Antonio was in fact an appropriate place for him to start in America, a sunbelt town, with enough elements of the Australian outback for him find things familiar – it was raw, raunchy and growing fast. It was more advanced than Perth had been when he first descended on the *Sunday Times* back in the 1950s, but it had a similar frontier feel about it.

The San Antonio papers in which he was interested were the property of the Harte-Hanks corporation. The morning *Express* had sales of about 80,000, the evening *San Antonio News* sold about 63,000 and their joint Sunday sold some 135,000. The major competition, for the *News*, was the evening *Light*, a fairly lurid sheet which was owned by the Hearst corporation, and had a daily sale of about 135,000. So once again, Murdoch was doing what he liked and what was becoming a pattern: swooping on a town and buying the weaker paper in order to set it against the leader.

He paid $19,700,000 for the three papers, the *Express*, the evening *News*, and their combined Sunday paper. This represented a multiple of fifteen times earnings, which was high, particularly given the amount he would have to borrow. On the other hand, the purchase gave him a foothold in the US, and any profits could be set against the losses he expected to incur on starting another paper.

Murdoch did to the papers what he almost always tried to do. He livened them up or dragged them down, depending on the viewpoint of the observer. He made them more sensational, more trivial, more readable, more commercial. He also backed them with his customary massive burst of promotion – television commercials and contests for the readers. Among the favoured headlines of the new regime were "ARMIES OF INSECTS MARCHING ON SA", "UNCLE TORTURES PETS WITH HOT FORK", "HANDLESS BODY FOUND", "ARMY TO POISON 350 PUPPIES". The most famous of all, which passed quickly into journalistic legend, was "KILLER BEES MOVE

NORTH'', written to describe an imminent invasion of monstrous bees flying up from Latin America to assault the good citizens of the United States. It was complete nonsense.

Subsequently, Murdoch insisted to Alexander Cockburn of the *Village Voice* that all he had done to the *News* was to strengthen its paper's coverage of local affairs. People were certainly not getting good, hard local news from the Hearst papers, he said. "We studied the TV programmes. The leading channel by a mile was a station that put on two hours of local news every afternoon and was just following the cops around with mobile cameras . . . blood and guts. And so we turned the *News* pretty sharply, with lots of crime reporting and the courts. It's a pretty violent city, San Antonio." And it was used to newspaper circulation wars long before Murdoch hit town.

Murdoch was not immediately successful. Despite all the hoopla, he managed, over two years, to lift the *News* circulation, by some 12,000 only, to 76,000. American readers did not respond to his formula with quite the same enthusiasm as the British had done. Still, by 1983, he was well ahead of the Hearst *Light*, and the *News* and *Express* were set to earn over $5 million profit.

While taking over and remoulding the San Antonio papers, Murdoch had also been preparing to launch his own national paper in the USA, the *National Star*, a supermarket tabloid modelled deliberately on the *National Enquirer*.

The *Enquirer*, an American institution, was the creation of a former CIA psychological warfare officer, Generose (Gene) Pope. Throughout the 1950s and 1960s, the *Enquirer* had sold over 4 million copies a week on a lurid, not to say fantastical mix of crime, science fiction and the doings of Hollywood stars. For a time Murdoch had toyed with the idea of buying the *Enquirer* itself, but Pope refused to sell it at anything like a price that Murdoch considered reasonable. And so, with the help of well-tried Australian tabloid performers like Steve Dunleavy, he set about trying to improve upon it. Larry Lamb, the editor of the *Sun*, was also brought over and wrote later, "Since only the merest handful of American journalists were willing to talk to us, let alone join us, we staffed it with people from London and Sydney." That was indeed one reason. Another was that Murdoch simply felt more comfortable with old familiar faces around him. Among those he imported was Graham King, his promotions wizard, who had been with him in Adelaide, Sydney and London. "What we wanted to do was make a weekly *Sun*. But we hadn't figured out the logistical problems of distribution throughout the USA," said King later.

Murdoch threw himself into the paper with gusto. He was to be seen shifting desks, pasting pages on mock-ups, rewriting stories, side by side with Dunleavy. During the pre-launch publicity he spent some energy abusing and criticizing mainstream American journalism, claiming that it was boring and complacent and that his new paper would be a fresh new *Time* or *Newsweek*. He was playing his favourite tune – that he was not an elitist snob, unlike the pipe-sucking professors of journalism and their effete former students on most American papers. His new paper was going to give the people what they wanted. "We are not interested in the publishing judgements of Madison Avenue or professors of journalism," he declared.

The first issue of the *National Star* carried the story "THOUSANDS KNEEL TO MIRACLE BOY MICHAEL", but the paper's launch was less than miraculous. Despite a massive budget for television advertising, Murdoch was unable to get the space in supermarkets that he needed, and the *National Star* barely limped along. The paper was being promoted, but could hardly be sold. Murdoch himself was effectively the editor for the first few months; other editors came and went as if through revolving doors.

Murdoch had not realized that the *Enquirer*'s audience had changed over the last twenty years – it had become more middle-class and the *Enquirer* had moved (slightly) away from sagas of violent crime and sexual perversion and towards Hollywood gossip, diets and sexual self-help tips.

Graham King helped organize a relaunch, together with Marty Singerman, who had come to Murdoch from Triangle, Walter Annenberg's company, which published *TV Guide*. Singerman made it his business to ingratiate the paper with all the wholesalers, town by town, state by state. In 1976 the "National" was dropped from the title and the paper was given the subtitle "The American

Women's Weekly". Most of its readers were indeed working-class women, and Murdoch, like the *Enquirer*, fed them a diet of fantasy about space, their weight and looks, Hollywood and their sex lives. Eventually the paper began to prosper; indeed, it became one of the most profitable parts of his empire – a cash cow as invaluable as the *Sun* in London. By the early 1980s it had a circulation of 4 million, a million less than the *Enquirer*, and was making about $12 million a year.

SYDNEY

As he began to establish himself in the USA, Murdoch became increasingly disillusioned with the Whitlam government back home in Australia. In 1975 his opposition to the Labor Party helped fan a constitutional crisis and caused a serious upheaval in his own empire, from which it took years to recover. *The Australian* in particular was badly damaged.

Murdoch claims his disillusionment had political causes. Personal, or rather commercial, reasons have also been alleged. On the political side, Whitlam's government became considerably more radical than expected. Australian troops were withdrawn from Vietnam, as promised, but the government also began to attack American policy. One minister denounced President Nixon as "corrupt" and called for boycotts on American goods. Australian unions refused to unload American ships. The government began to break long-established agreements between the CIA and ASIO, its Australian counterpart. There are grounds for the belief that the United States was alarmed by the radical direction of the Whitlam government and that the Central Intelligence Agency had a hand in "dirty tricks" to destabilize it.

As the Whitlam government moved to the left, so Murdoch was moving in the opposite direction. His experiences with the printers in Britain, in particular, had sapped his patience with both trade unions and political ideology to do with "welfarism". In America, he was finding friends among the Republicans rather than the

Democrats. He had thought that Nixon was unfairly victimized by the "liberal press" during Watergate, and his earlier opposition to the war in Vietnam had now evaporated.

He said to this author that in 1972 he had hoped that Whitlam would "sweep away the cobwebs" of the Liberal years. "But he just went mad. 'Crash through' was his motto. He was an egomaniac and self-indulgent. He pushed every trendy thing through. And he was very much into having a good time as PM. A chaotic government." This was a widely held view.

On another occasion Murdoch explained that he was opposed to Whitlam because he was imposing on Australia "a European type of socialism which has caused ruin and misery in other countries". On another, however, he said he thought Whitlam had "chickened out" of making Australia a republic.

He also had commercial quarrels with the Whitlam administration over the development of mineral concessions in which he had an interest.

In April 1974, Whitlam called an election. The Murdoch papers were neutral. Certainly they were not unfair to Whitlam, who won the election with a reduced majority in the House of Representatives. He was still short of a majority in the Senate. Jim Cairns, the leader of Labor's left wing, became deputy Prime Minister.

At this time, Whitlam persuaded John Menadue to leave Murdoch and come back to work for him as head of the Prime Minister's department. Menadue had brought Ken Cowley, the printer who had joined *The Australian* in Canberra, into the top management, and Cowley then took over as general manager. He remained Murdoch's point man in Australia for years to come.

A few months later, Murdoch appointed Bruce Rothwell editor of *The Australian*. This was an unpopular move, partly because of Rothwell's abrasiveness, partly because his right-wing views were antipathetic to many of the journalists.

By now, the Opposition held enough seats in the Senate to block the supply of funds to the government. In October 1975, Malcolm Fraser, who had recently become Opposition leader, announced that the Senate would do so – in order to force Whitlam to call another election. This was an unprecedented attack, and fiercely controversial. *The Australian* supported Fraser and demanded that Whitlam call an election. The paper announced in one lead story, "Governor General will act soon, says Fraser". The next two weeks saw the paper firmly encouraging Fraser and portraying the Governor General, Sir John Kerr, who had the power to force an election, as neutral between the two sides. Many of the journalists on *The Australian* felt that the paper's editorial line was far too close to Fraser; on 2 November three of his journalists sent a protest to Murdoch, complaining about "the deliberate or careless slanting of headlines, the seemingly blatant imbalance in news presentation, political censorship . . . " They had the support of over seventy other journalists.

They said they believed the paper's policy was being implemented in a "blind, biased, tunnel-vision, ad hoc, logically confused and relentless way". Murdoch did not reply and on 12 November one of the journalists, Barry Porter, wrote to him again. Murdoch was angry and replied, "If you insist on providing ammunition for our competitors and enemies who are intent on destroying all our livelihoods, then go ahead."

On the national stage, Whitlam made no secret of his contempt for Kerr and his viceregal office, which he saw as a vestige of colonial rule. He refused to call an election and proposed to destroy for ever the Senate's power to block funds. Fraser remained publicly adamant that the Governor General might have to use his powers to dissolve the government and call an election. But he was nervous, and Murdoch later acknowledged that *The Australian*'s support might well have shored him up. He was "damn close to losing his nerve two or three times".

On 11 November Kerr summoned Whitlam to his study and dismissed him, installing Fraser as caretaker Prime Minister. This action was greeted with widespread fury. To vast numbers of people, the idea of the Queen's representative being able to dismiss a constitutionally elected government in the last half of the twentieth century seemed ridiculous.

When Kerr's secretary read out the proclamation dissolving Parliament, Whitlam cried out to the crowd, "Well may we say 'God Save the Queen', because *nothing* will save the Governor

General." He exhorted the people to "maintain your rage" and called Fraser "Kerr's cur".

In 1975 Australian newspapers still belonged to dynasties. There were the Fairfax family papers, the News group, where the Murdoch family exercised control, the Packer family group which, since the sale of the Sydney *Daily Telegraph* to Murdoch, was concentrated in television, radio and magazines, and the Melbourne Herald group, which had once been run by Keith Murdoch. Outside of these dynasties was the state-owned Australian Broadcasting Commission, which controlled more than half of the country's 132 television outlets and rather less than half of its 202 radio stations.

In 1975 the dynasties were united in their opposition to the Whitlam government and in their support for Fraser, when Kerr forced an election to be called.

During the election campaign *The Australian*'s coverage was not totally one-sided, but it clearly favoured Fraser. The paper published misleading unemployment figures, and many of Murdoch's journalists on both *The Australian* and the *Daily Telegraph* became convinced that their copy was being slanted by the sub editors. The Australian Journalists' Association (AJA) built up dossiers detailing the alleged fixing of the news. Thus one story changed between editions from "Gough's Promise – Cheap Rents" to "Gough's Panic – Cheap Rents".

Whitlam publicly claimed that the hostility of the Murdoch press was the result of the government's initial refusal to approve Murdoch's mining ambitions. "Now Mr Murdoch wasn't pleased. But we were right and it is just as well that the public, I believe, should know what may be behind his vindictive campaign against the Labor Party in this election, why he's turned against us."

Murdoch described these remarks as "highly irresponsible and entirely false". He insisted that the consortium in which News had a small share had gone ahead with its application at the suggestion of Whitlam's own advisers. "The fact that he didn't get it through Cabinet is another matter." In any case, the government had subsequently dropped its opposition.

The bitterness of these exchanges between the Prime Minister and the mogul were extraordinary. One of Whitlam's attacks on Murdoch was said to be so abusive that it was deleted from a current affairs programme.

The row between the two men inflamed the unions. Dock workers in Perth blacked News newsprint. On the weekend of 6–7 December, a week before the election, the *Sunday Telegraph* and *Sunday Mirror* each published fierce anti-Whitlam editorials. Members of the AJA at News's Sydney office circulated a petition calling for an emergency meeting "to protest repeated and continuing bias in the reporting and presentation of political stories during the election campaign".

On 8 December 1975 a group of News journalists in Sydney resolved that all AJA members employed by News should go on strike, in protest against the deliberate slanting of the news by Murdoch's papers.

Brian Hogben, the News group's editorial manager, countered by claiming that the real problem was the bias of journalists on *The Australian* in favour of Whitlam. It was true that many younger journalists on *The Australian* did find it impossible to adjust themselves to Murdoch's own switch from favouring Whitlam in 1972 to his virulent opposition in 1975. But the complaints of bias were also made by older, more conservative members of the sub editors' tables on both *The Australian* and the *Daily Telegraph*. The protesters were from all parties, not just Labor.

A court ordered the strikers to return to work and directed that Murdoch and the journalists should meet to discuss each other's complaints. When this meeting took place, a furious slanging match developed. Murdoch refused to accept that there was bias in the news columns; he accused the journalists of incompetence and inaccuracies.

Whitlam and Labor were roundly defeated in the election on 13 December. There were allegations of CIA interference. Kerr was rumoured to have links with the Agency through his membership of various South Pacific cultural and legal groups.

In February 1976 Murdoch himself wrote an extraordinary scoop in *The Australian*. He reported that just before the election, Whitlam had met in Sydney with two Iraqi officials from whom the Labor Party was soliciting funds. Many Labor Party sup-

porters saw Murdoch as such a Satanic figure that they instantly
dismissed the revelation as a lie. However, the meetings had taken
place and the *Sun News Pictorial*, a rival paper, carried it also.

The stories were immensely damaging to Whitlam. He refused
at first to answer the allegations. This helped persuade many
members and officials of his own party of his guilt: he had evidently compromised his party and a possible future Labor government by accepting funds from one of the more notoriously
obnoxious Arab governments.

At the end of 1977, Whitlam resigned from leadership of the
Labor Party and was succeeded by Bill Hayden. Whitlam sued
News but he and Murdoch reached an out-of-court settlement.

The fights with Whitlam hurt *The Australian*'s circulation. Murdoch thought that this was because Labor supporters saw it as
"the paper which had torn down their God". He was certainly
never forgiven in Australia for his sacrilege. From now on he was
seen by many on the left of Australian politics as a right-wing
monster, in the pocket of the Americans, if not of the CIA. As
for *The Australian*, it was the end of the age of innocence. Many
journalists and readers felt personally betrayed by the former
"Boy Publisher" who had given them "their" paper a decade
before. Scores of journalists cleared their desks and left.

In a real sense *The Australian* had lost its soul. For the next
seven years, one editor after another came and went, tried and
failed to find a formula that both attracted readers and pleased the
profit-oriented managers of News. In 1983, almost twenty years
after Murdoch launched it, the paper finally broke even, moved
into profit and began to become a little calmer. By the end of the
1980s, it began to show a sense of purpose once more.

Chapter 6

AMERICA

Dorothy Schiff, known to everyone as Dolly, was one of the major figures of American newspapers. In 1976, utterly charmed by Rupert Murdoch, she happily handed him one of the oldest newspapers in America.

When the American press had begun to operate, at the end of the eighteenth century, its problems had been cost, and access to technology. When the Governor of Pennsylvania wanted to set up Ben Franklin as a printer, he had to send Franklin to England to acquire the presses with which to polemicize against the King.

The literacy rate in New England in those days was probably higher than it has ever been in the world – as high as 95 per cent among males in some parts of Massachusetts and Connecticut.

Tom Paine sold 100,000 copies of *Common Sense* in three months at the beginning of 1776, among a population of only some three million. In the late twentieth century, a book would have had to sell two million copies in two months to match that extraordinary circulation.

Conversation and communication across the continent of the United States and across other continents began in 1844 after Samuel Finley Breese Morse invented the telegraph, sending the message "What hath God wrought?" from Washington to Baltimore. He united the United States, shrank the old world and set the stage for the new one. Thoreau's appalled comment in *Walden* on this unwelcome revolution is worth recalling:

We are in great haste to construct a magnetic telegraph from Maine to Texas; but Maine and Texas, maybe, have nothing important to communicate . . . We are eager to tunnel under the Atlantic and bring the old world some weeks nearer to the new;

but perchance the first news that will leak through the broad flapping American ear will be that Princess Adelaide has the whooping cough.

It was probably the telegraph which first made information into a commodity, something that could be bought and sold irrespective of its uses or meaning. Within four years of Morse opening the first telegraph line, the Associated Press was founded and news from everywhere, about anything and nothing, began to crisscross and entertain every state. People began to feel the first twinges of what became a serious disease in the twentieth century: a glut of information about crimes, wars, disasters and misdemeanours far afield that rendered them both horrified and powerless.

American mass media as such began in the first half of the nineteenth century in New York with the fierce competition between James Gordon Bennett's *Herald*, Horace Greeley's *Tribune*, Henry Raymond's *Times*, and Ben Day's *Sun*. By the end of the century, mass production and mass marketing of all sorts of goods became the norm, and with that came a vast increase in advertising.

In the early part of the twentieth century almost all American city newspapers fought continual fierce and often brutal wars with each other. The battles were vicious and ill-tempered, shrill and bloody, pandering to the excitability and anxieties of an immigrant and volatile society. William Randolph Hearst, Joseph Pulitzer and Colonel Robert McCormick were true barons who ran their papers as personal fiefdoms and propaganda sheets. They gave no quarter and they played by their own rules.

James Gordon Bennett and Horace Greeley in New York, McCormick in Chicago, and Hearst all over the nation had personal visions which they wished to impose on the world. They talked about the public interest but they wanted personal power. Their journalists were largely unknown, raffish, working-class, heavy drinkers, cynical, fun – or embittered. And so they remained until the Second World War – which was when Dolly Schiff acquired the *New York Post*.

Schiff was the grandchild of Jacob Schiff, one of the most successful of the German-Jewish bankers whose wealth and power grew in New York throughout the industrial revolution of the nineteenth century. As well as being rich, she was happily unconventional, within certain limits. She had a passionate relationship with Max Beaverbrook in the 1930s. Early in life she rejected her family's Republican affiliations and become an ardent supporter and friend of Franklin Delano Roosevelt; and in 1939 Roosevelt encouraged her to buy the *Post*.

Her then husband, George Backer, assured her that although it was losing money, the *Post* could be saved with an extra investment of only a couple of hundred thousand dollars. That proved to be nonsense, and she began writing monthly cheques for a hundred thousand for her husband, who had made himself the editor. She did not at first think of herself as a newspaper owner at all, "I was just a woman who had gotten sucked into another sort of monstrous country house." She grew disillusioned – but more with her husband than with the paper.

She became involved in the editorial side, and when she decided she would take over the paper, her husband went back to his mother in a fury. Next she married one of her editors, Ted Thackrey. Together, they remade the paper, turning it into a tabloid, but still with a liberal and indeed often left-wing slant. After the war, Thackrey became both passionately Zionist and increasingly left-wing. In the 1948 presidential election he supported Henry Wallace's newly formed Progressive Party. His marriage to Dorothy ended shortly afterwards; but her relationship with the paper endured. Her money was constantly needed to save it. In the 1950s the paper took a lonely and courageous stand against Senator Joe McCarthy, and her editor, James Wechsler, was hauled before McCarthy's notorious Permanent Sub-Committee on Investigations, to name names.

The war had forced changes on newspapers, and television was now forcing more. During the war, radio had come into its own. Families received fast news of what was happening to their men on the other side of the world. Facts became more widely valued than sensation. News was complicated, but readers wanted it to be right. American journalists had to retrain themselves. From being good ol' boys and drunken hacks, they had to become serious commentators, or at least serious reporters. Papers began to move upmarket. Then, after the war, commerce and advertising began to push papers even further away from their yellow origins. Advertisers no longer wanted merely numbers. They wanted numbers with money to spend. As the costs of producing newspapers rose, so the need for advertising became greater.

Tension grew between the public and the private interests of newspapers. Democracy needs a free and a vigilant press – that is its public purpose. Citizens need to understand the world in order to decide how they should be governed. But the private commercial imperative of the press became more and more the question of how to make itself attractive to advertisers. And the *New York Post* was hit as much as any other city newspaper by these pressures.

Between December 1962 and the middle of 1963 New York newspapers were changed for ever by a strike over, as usual, wages and hours. Print unions struck on the *Times*, the *News*, the *Journal-American*, the *World Telegram* and *Sun*; the proprietors of the *Post*, the *Herald Tribune* and the *Mirror*, suspended publication in sympathy. However, Dorothy Schiff then broke with the other publishers and made her own settlement with the unions, thus coming back on to the streets well before her rivals and peers, in March 1963. She tried but was unable to get union agreement to computerize part of the typesetting process.

By 1966 the sapping effects of industrial struggle, the haemorrhage of costs, and the loss of readers, especially in the suburbs, to television, forced the merger of the *Journal-American*, an evening paper, and the morning *Herald Tribune* into the *World Journal Tribune*. Schiff was terrified lest this powerful new evening paper destroy the *Post*. But the *Post* had a large Jewish readership who did not abandon it.

The "Widget", as the new three-headed paper was known, lasted only just over a year. On its collapse, the *Post* picked up a lot of readers, its circulation increasing from 400,000 to 700,000 at the end of the 1960s. But Schiff needed new plant on which to handle the extra runs. The *Journal-American* refused to rent her its idle machines, and she was forced to buy them, though they were largely defunct and very costly. Throughout the early 1970s the *Post*'s circulation fell away again, and the morning *News* and the *Times* got the bulk of the advertising.

One weekend in 1974 Schiff met Murdoch out in the Hamptons on Long Island. She was always susceptible to charming men. He told her what a rotten paper the *New York Times* was. The *Post* was just the sort of property for which he yearned and in 1975 he asked her if it was for sale. It was not, but Dolly Schiff's enthusiasm for the newspaper business was clearly fading. She had tried to get good new editors, but was increasingly out of touch with the rates now being paid. In the early 1970s, the story went, she even offered the job to Ben Bradlee, editor of the *Washington Post*. She offered him $20,000 a year. "But Dolly," he replied, "some of my own reporters make more than that."

In the middle of 1976 she was told by her lawyers that new tax laws would mean that her children could not afford to keep the paper. Moreover another strike by the print unions was looming. At seventy-three she decided she had had enough. Her lawyers made a number of calls to elicit interest. One was to the New York publisher S.I. Newhouse, but he was not interested in adding the *Post* to his Condé Nast empire, reckoning that the union problems of the paper made it a hopeless proposition. It had a circulation of almost 500,000 at this time, and was losing about $50 million a year. She asked Murdoch to lunch.

"I sensed she was very tired," Murdoch told Alexander Cockburn of the *Village Voice*. "She knew what was necessary to turn the paper and get it done right but she felt she just didn't have the energy left." Energy was a commodity of which Murdoch has always had a surplus. At the end of 1976, the year that the first Apple computer was built in a garage, and shortly after Jimmy Carter beat Gerald Ford in the presidential election, the *Post* announced that Dolly Schiff would sell to Rupert Murdoch.

Schiff said she was happy. "Rupert Murdoch is a man of strong commitment to the spirit of independent, progressive journalism. I am confident he will carry on vigorously in the tradition I value so deeply," she announced.

For his part, Murdoch declared, "The *New York Post* will continue to serve New York and New Yorkers and maintain its present policies and traditions." Murdoch said he was "very happy" that Schiff had agreed to stay with the *Post* as a consultant for the next five years.

Many staff members of the *Post* regarded Murdoch's purchase as a reprieve. "If nothing else, I feel pretty good that the paper will survive. God knows in what form, but the guy is not pumping in millions to fold it," said one.

Others were apprehensive. "People who have the decent journalistic beats like government and politics are shaky," said one reporter. "They don't know if they're going to be asked to write stories about two-headed babies, or what."

Murdoch was immensely excited. He described having the *Post* as like having both the *Sun* and the *Mirror* in Sydney – and New York was many times the size of Sydney. He said that there were masses of changes to be made, columns to be scrapped, reporting to be improved. It would be his command post in America.

While his men in New York inspected the *Post*'s books, Murdoch was diverted back to London. The *Observer*, one of the oldest and most prestigious Sunday newspapers, was for sale. Like the *Post* the *Observer* was owned by a liberal millionaire who was now facing greater financial problems than ever before. David Astor felt, as Dolly Schiff had, that his family trusts could no longer sustain the paper's losses. By September 1976 the paper faced closure. Astor and his legal adviser Lord Goodman contacted Murdoch. He was regarded in London above all as the persecutor of Profumo and Lord Lambton, but Astor had been impressed with his conduct on the board of London Weekend Television and by his effective management methods. Astor's opinion was that an "efficient Visigoth" was better than no buyer at all.

When news of the negotiations was leaked, the journalists and their editor, Donald Trelford, were less sanguine. Clive James, the paper's TV critic, announced that Rupert Murdoch was one of the main reasons he had left home in Australia and come to Britain. Another, anonymous journalist was quoted as declaring, "Giving the *Observer* to Rupert Murdoch is like giving your beautiful daughter to a gorilla." Questions were tabled in the House of Commons, the unions complained, the journalists planned to strike.

Murdoch was not pleased. After all, the *Observer* management had sought him out, he had not solicited them. From New York he sent a statement: "In view of the breach of confidence that has taken place, together with the deliberate and orchestrated attempt to build this into a controversy, News International is no longer interested." Eventually the *Observer* was sold to the American oil company Atlantic Richfield. The paper published glowing profiles of its new proprietor and congratulated itself on having escaped Murdoch's clutches.

The "gorilla" in New York was not amused. He thought that once again the British Establishment had rallied around to deny him one of its best-loved prizes. In the long term he had reason to be glad of it.

In the New World, by contrast, he was still advancing. While the *Observer* dithered and dropped him, the *Post* purchase was completed. The deal was masterminded by Stanley Shuman, a banker with Allen and Company, which Murdoch had chosen as his principal investment bankers in New York. The final price agreed was around $30 million; this was on the high side, but Murdoch wanted it. He said he would pay over the odds to satisfy himself.

He raised one-third of the money in Australia, by the sale of investments and by borrowing. One-third came from London – the earnings of the *Sun* and the *News of the World*. Merv Rich said later that at that time it was not easy for News to borrow in America – "We were not known there." The final third was an unsecured loan from the European-American Bank and Trust Company. Murdoch explained that it was important that News International in Britain and News Ltd in Australia each took only a half share: "In this way, a central bank in London or Australia can't order you to pay dividends, since you don't have control of the stock. It means you can plough back the profits."

On 20 November 1976, the day that the deal was finally agreed, Murdoch dined with Clay Felker, the publisher of *New York* magazine and *Village Voice*, and a friend of Murdoch's for several years. Murdoch discussed his problems with the *Observer* and Felker told Murdoch that he was having trouble with the board of *New York* magazine. It was not for the first time. Felker was a gifted editor, but he was the despair of his more commercially-minded colleagues. Felker considered this a private conversation between friends, but it soon became apparent that Murdoch had seen another prize.

With a small group of investors, Felker had started *New York* magazine in 1968; it was a lavish, glossy weekly whose writers included Tom Wolfe, Jimmy Breslin, Pete Hamill, Aaron Latham, Richard Reeves, and Gloria Steinem. The magazine was a great success and Felker became a celebrity.

He was a connoisseur and an eclectic collector of information. He was obsessed with politics, film, art, style. According to Gail Sheehy, the New York writer who was later his wife, he liked to call himself an "information sponge". He was also volatile and could be irascible.

Felker did not own *New York* magazine – he had never had enough money. He had partners: the sort of people whom Murdoch loathed and would never tolerate. They did not all appreciate his social and editorial success, or the lavish spending in which he indulged. Alan Patricof, a venture capitalist and one of the original investors in *New York* found Felker particularly irksome, Gail Sheehy wrote in *Rolling Stone*.

In 1974 *New York* acquired the *Village Voice*, the liberal weekly published in Greenwich Village and devoted to the lives and causes of those who lived there. It was more of a merger than an outright purchase; two of the *Voice*'s controlling stockholders, Carter Burden and Bartle Bull, received 34 per cent of the stock of the new company between them. There was an agreement that Burden had to give Felker first refusal on his 24 per cent. Felker therefore felt he retained control of the publications. But Burden, a Vanderbilt heir, became an ally of Patricof in the struggle against Felker.

In 1976 Felker started a new magazine, *New West*, published in Los Angeles. It did well at once, but it did so expensively; the cost overruns were unwelcome. At the same time Felker was negotiating for a large pay increase for himself. His partners were not amused. They did not feel part of the editorial enterprise. Patricof decided the only thing was to find a buyer for the magazine.

Sheehy believed that Murdoch had deliberately cultivated Felker since 1974 – since he had learned that Carter Burden had received mainly stock rather than cash in the merger of the *Voice* and *New York*, and would be looking to sell: "His patience was rewarded."

Three days after their dinner, Felker and Murdoch had lunch together and Murdoch warned him, "You and I could never work together." Felker agreed – each of them liked to run his own ship. Murdoch also told Felker that what really mattered was one-hundred-per-cent ownership. "Then you don't have to take any crap from anybody." The next day, Stan Shuman called Patricof, who realized that he had a potential buyer.

On 9 December, Murdoch astonished Felker by telling him he wanted to buy the company. He offered Felker $5 for shares that were currently quoted at $2. He offered to spin off *New West* and sell a third to Felker for $3 million. Felker refused and turned to Katharine Graham, owner and publisher of the *Washington Post*, for advice and assistance. She promised help if needed.

Meanwhile Stanley Shuman began what was called a "creeping tender"; he contacted the stockholders one by one and made oral agreements that each would sell to Murdoch under certain circumstances. After Christmas, Carter Burden called Felker to tell him he had been offered $7 a share and Felker, anxious to exercise his right of first refusal, agreed to pay Burden that himself. The *Washington Post* would finance the purchase and would buy all the other outstanding shares for the same price. The *Post*'s investment banker, Felix Rohatyn, confirmed this offer to Burden's lawyer. Rohatyn thought he had a deal.

On the last night of 1976, Murdoch and Shuman and Burden's lawyer, Peter Tufo, flew out to Sun Valley, Idaho, to do a deal with Burden, who had been "on the slopes" whenever there had been inconvenient telephone calls from the Felker or *Washington Post* camps in recent days. Tufo had told Shuman that there was a provision in the first-refusal clause which could become a loophole; Burden did not have to offer the stock to Felker if the company had made a loss for four consecutive quarters. On 1 January 1977, a new quarter began and that condition was fulfilled. In Sun Valley the malleable Burden agreed to sell to Murdoch for $8.25 a share.

In New York, Felker went for a temporary restraining order. He had another important weapon on his side: the writers. Like the *Observer* journalists in London, they had all recoiled in horror at the idea of being taken over by the obnoxious Murdoch. They met together and were unanimous. Felker told them that he intended to fight, and they all agreed to support him. They were convinced that "the spirit" of the magazine would have no chance of survival under Murdoch. They called a news conference to announce to other reporters that they were a "talent package" that could not be bought or sold at will. The takeover became a major event, just the sort of media bonanza with which to launch the new year.

Suddenly the life and times of Rupert Murdoch were big news. In the first week of January both *Time* and *Newsweek* rushed to compile cover stories on the invader – an unusual double accolade. *Time* featured him as King Kong, seizing newspaper properties as he climbed skyscrapers.

On the night of Monday 3 January, a board meeting took place in the offices of Ted Kheel, the union negotiator. The journalists waited in an anteroom. Patricof had voted off the board two directors known to be on Felker's side, and then summarily disposed of Kheel as company counsel. Then Patricof nominated two new board members – Murdoch and Shuman. Murdoch slipped calmly and quietly into one of the two empty chairs.

Eventually a delegation of writers from the magazines was allowed to put their views. The meeting exploded with charges of "fucking liar" and illegality being traded. The old hatred between the writers and the board was given full rein. Only Murdoch and Shuman remained calm and detached. Murdoch told Felker he was the most brilliant editor in America and asked him to carry on editing *New York*. One of the writers, Bryan Dobell, the managing editor, protested to the board: "You don't have the right to sell people." To which a board member, Thomas Kempner, replied, "You don't understand. In America, anyone can sell anything he wants, at any time. You're going to have to get that straight. That is just American capitalism."

Murdoch asked Felker to meet him. The writers implored Felker not to, but the Federal Court, hearing his case against Burden and

Tufo, ordered him to do so. Felker asked Murdoch to pull out, but Murdoch said he could not, for a reason which was both surprising and revealing. "I can't back down. After losing the *Observer*, I'd be a journalistic untouchable around the world. I can't lose."

Late that night Felker's lawyer met Murdoch and in the small hours of 7 January, Felker agreed to settle. He came out of it all with around three-quarters of a million dollars. Later that day, he met with many of his writers gathered glumly in a restaurant across from his office. He was brief and bitter: "Rupert Murdoch's ideas about friendship, about publishing, and about people are very different than mine," he said. Close to tears, he continued, "He should know that he is breaking up a family, and he does so at his peril."

That night the next issue of *New York* magazine was due to go to bed. There were almost no staff available to Murdoch. He put the magazine out himself, with the help of executives from the *Post* and some of the board of *New York*. He cancelled a cover by David Levine showing himself as a killer bee. About forty of the magazine's best writers and other members of the staff resigned. Murdoch installed his own editor, James Brady, and began to slash costs. The magazine continued to make money.

At the *Village Voice*, Murdoch tried to replace the editor, Marianne Partridge, despite a previous commitment that he would not do so. When some of the *Voice*'s most valuable columnists, in particular Jack Newfield and Alexander Cockburn, threatened to make a great deal of trouble, he allowed Partridge to stay.

Murdoch did not renew her contract when it expired two years after the purchase. But he understood that the paper's radical views were essential to its success and he did not seek to impose a conservative editor. Instead he chose David Schneiderman, a journalist from the *New York Times*, who remained editor until Murdoch eventually sold the paper in 1985. The *Voice* ran frequent attacks on Murdoch and the *New York Post*, particularly in Cockburn's "Press Clips" column. For the most part Murdoch ignored them. Schneiderman received the occasional irate telephone call, protesting against the more savage criticisms, but otherwise Murdoch left the *Village Voice* alone. Its massive classified advertising base grew and the paper thrived.

Clay Felker went on to edit *Esquire* and then *Tonight*, the *Daily News*'s evening attempt to challenge the *Post*, which failed. Subsequently he became publisher of *Manhattan Inc.* Much later he described himself as just one on the list of people damaged by Murdoch's advance. Felker thought Murdoch had two motives in all his actions: "To beat his father, Keith. And to run the world." But Murdoch did not destroy either *New York* or the *Village Voice* as Felker and the writers had predicted.

At the *New York Post*, Murdoch was a major presence from the start, and he immediately made that presence felt in the city. Within months Dolly Schiff's staid liberal backwater had become a roiling, clamorous torrent of news, mostly conservative opinion, and hucksterish entertainment.

It was very much Murdoch's own paper; no one who worked there could have any doubt about that. He surrounded himself with a number of the Murdoch "mafia", those men (few women) who had charged with him through Sydney and London, and set about revitalizing the paper in his own particular fashion. He was constantly on the stone, fiddling with stories, rewriting headlines. He was to be seen in the newsroom answering the phones and directing reporters. At once the paper became unsettled and changing, reflecting his own restlessness.

Stories became shorter, sharper and louder, the headlines garish. "BEHEAD THREAT!" told of an unfounded rumour during a Washington siege by Hanafi Muslims. A peaceful demonstration by less than a hundred people in Utah, protesting against the execution of Gary Gilmore, became "THREAT TO STORM GILMORE PRISON". Farrah Fawcett-Majors, the star of the TV series "Charlie's Angels", was chosen as a sexy mascot of the paper; story after story about her began to appear. Many of the paper's older readers were appalled and left it.

The *Post* newsroom erupted in protests that were both general and specific. There was bad blood between many of the old Schiff reporters and the new men, in particular the Australians. A group of reporters sent Murdoch a petition complaining about the cartoons of Paul Rigby, an old colleague of Murdoch, which they claimed were offensive to minorities and women.

Since he knew that there were some journalists who would always hate working for him, and since he wanted to bring in more of his Australian team, Murdoch extracted from the Newspaper Guild a once-only right to fire staff members he thought "incompatible with the new management". This became known as the "Auschwitz clause"; Murdoch used it to dismiss 122 out of 460 members of the guild.

By the 1970s newspaper economics throughout the land were changing fast. Production and distribution costs had soared. Thousands of papers had folded. Some 1,500 cities still had daily papers, but almost all of them were local monopolies, and many of them were part of monopolistic chains belonging to Gannett, Knight-Ridder, Hearst, and Times-Mirror. Newspapers were becoming increasingly bland, centrist and dreary, all marching to similar tunes written by executives of the chains. Even in New York, the *Times* and the *News* were ostensible competitors, but each in effect had monopoly control of its own market.

Murdoch believed that the American media had become increasingly stuffy and self-satisfied. Journalists from the *New York Times*, particularly foreign correspondents, often behaved more like ambassadors than journalists. Too often the power and the glory turned into pomp and circumstance. Most papers, needing to attract the big advertisers, like the New York department stores, were anxious to increase their share of upmarket readers at the expense of those lower down the scale. He insisted that the interests of blue-collar workers were being ignored. In 1977 he accused his fellow newspaper publishers of preaching "elitist journalism" and warned them against relying on the top end of the market. "A press that fails to interest the whole community is one that will ultimately become a house organ of the elite." This was a familiar Murdochian refrain.

Perhaps because the *Post* itself had no monopolistic security, Murdoch was determined not to accept what he saw as an insipid and prosaic formula. His blood-and-guts presentation had not yet proved very profitable in San Antonio, or with the *Star*, but he seemed determined to try it in New York. He came roaring into town and, as one writer, Chris Welles, put it, he was like "a throwback, a late nineteenth-century Hearstian figure who had seemingly materialized in the New York City of the late 1970s through some curious time warp". Most press barons of the time wanted merely to acquire comfortable monopoly papers with which to increase their cash flows and their dividend cheques. Murdoch had, by contrast, always delighted in taking over secondary, ailing properties and turning them around by making them shout and scream as necessary.

No one made a louder noise than Steve Dunleavy, whom Murdoch transferred from the *Star*. Dunleavy came to widespread attention in New York very soon after Murdoch acquired the *Post*. That year, 1977, had a long, hot and infamous summer, ideal for Murdoch to make his mark with the paper. There was a fiercely fought race for City Hall, with candidates elbowing each other all the way to the finish, and there were Puerto Rican nationalist bombings. During a heatwave in July the New York power supply failed for twenty-four hours – during which there was some looting and arson, and the *Post* was off the streets. It came back with a screaming "Blackout Special" with a vast headline proclaiming "24 HOURS OF TERROR" – an inside section described "A CITY RAVAGED".

Even more enticing was the story of Son of Sam, which might have been tailor-made for Murdoch's *New York Post*.

For a year a homicidal killer with .44 pistol had been on the loose in New York. The ghastly story began on 29 July 1976, when an eighteen-year-old girl called Donna Laurie was shot dead as she sat in a car in front of her home. Another girl was wounded at the same time. By March 1977 the maniac had murdered two more people and injured three others. At this stage the police started to call him "Son of Sam", a sobriquet which was taken up with equal enthusiasm by the media and by the killer himself. In April two more people were murdered and the killer actually left a note signed "Son of Sam" by their bodies. It was clear that he was enjoying himself.

The *Daily News* understood and exploited the potential of the story before the *Post*. Its star columnist, Jimmy Breslin, began to write open letters to Son of Sam and in his column of 5 June printed what purported to be a reply from the killer himself. This of course excited considerable attention. Murdoch was determined to catch up and Dunleavy was put on to the case.

On 26 June Son of Sam struck again and wounded a young man and a young woman. As the first anniversary of the death of his first victim approached, journalists on all papers speculated that the killer would mark the day. The anniversary issue of the *Post* carried a headline "GUNMAN SPARKS SON OF SAM CHASE" and told the story of police pursuing a man over the Cross Island Parkway. It was mere titillation. Only in the penultimate paragraph did the paper reveal "police say the mystery gunman was definitely not Son of Sam".

On 31 July, two days after the "anniversary", Son of Sam killed another woman and injured her escort. The *Post* ran the headline "NO ONE IS SAFE FROM SON OF SAM". Murdoch had insisted that there must be a new angle every day. On 4 August the *Post* declared, with no evidence, that New York's mafia dons had declared that Son of Sam must be caught and had put their resources behind the chase.

Like Breslin, Dunleavy made a personal appeal to the killer to give himself up – to Dunleavy. Asked by the *New York Times* whether this was such a good idea, Dunleavy replied, "There are no rules when it comes to appealing to a killer." He compared his "Open Letter to the Son of Sam" to an editorial that made an appeal to a head of state.

When the police arrested a man called David Berkowitz, the *Post* shouted triumphantly "CAUGHT!" in bright red letters – sales shot up by 400,000 to over a million for the afternoon.

The next day reporters and photographers from several papers, including the *Post*, were arrested for breaking into Berkowitz's apartment. All notions of guilt needing to be proven were cast aside – "INSIDE THE KILLER'S LAIR" read the headline over pictures of his rooms. Then the *Post* ran its most notorious headline in the case: "HOW I BECAME A MASS MURDERER by DAVID BERKOWITZ".

In Britain a newspaper editor would have been prosecuted for such a flagrant contempt of court. The headline was also misleading; it referred to letters which Berkowitz had written five years before, and which had nothing to do with the later killings. The same letters had been sold to the *News*, which also ran them, but under headlines to which no one took exception – and which no one remembers. Murdoch subsequently acknowledged that the headline "How I became a mass murderer" was wrong and inaccurate. "I didn't write it, but I certainly approved it. I think it was wrong. But that's hindsight."

Later the *Post* published an illegally obtained photograph of Berkowitz sleeping in his cell. Murdoch insisted that he played no part in securing this picture and did not know that it was improperly acquired.

By this time Murdoch had aroused the ire of his peers. The *New Yorker* attacked both the *News* and the *Post* for "transforming a killer into a celebrity". The *Times* published a front-page article questioning the *Post*'s propriety. The magazine *New Times* called Sam "Murdoch's favourite son". The writer Pete Hamill now likened the *Post* to a guest who throws up at a dinner party. "He is looked upon with alarm and pity, but no one really knows what to do to help."

Murdoch was not going to let him get away with that. Hamill at that time was escorting Jackie Kennedy Onassis, and, in revenge, Murdoch reprinted in the *Post* excerpts from an unflattering column Hamill had written about her some years before. Hamill, Murdoch said, was suffering from sour grapes, because he had wanted to be editor of the *Post*. "Pete's a nice guy, but I don't think he'd make an editor. I don't think he'd make an editor's bootlace."

He was generally dismissive of all critics and criticisms. They were merely "counter-attacks from the powerless left-wing fringe still in New York City".

Journalists on the *Post* began to complain, as they had on *The Australian* in Sydney, about the paper's political bias. Soon after the Son of Sam was caught, the *Post*, like other papers, wished to endorse a candidate for mayor. Murdoch took the election seriously and looked over all the candidates. He was impressed with Herman Badillo, the Hispanic candidate, and thought of endorsing him. He was less enamoured of Mario Cuomo, the liberal Secretary of State of New York. The *New York Times* came out for him. Three weeks later, the *Post* endorsed Ed Koch, in an unprecedented front-page editorial. Murdoch's choice was, as always, pragmatic. When he was asked why he chose Koch over Mario Cuomo, he was reported to have replied, "It's very simple. There are two and a half million Jews in New York and one million Italians." He told *More* magazine that he had been impressed with Koch and found him "very specific".

Murdoch's choice showed in the paper's coverage of the elections. A subsequent analysis confirmed the fears of journalists at the time – that the front-page stories up until the primary were far more favourable to Koch than to any other candidate. Indeed, there were quite simply no unfavourable stories about Koch.

Many journalists felt that the news columns were being prostituted by Murdoch's desire be on the winning side. They protested to him. "It was a very mildly worded thing, really," said Lindsy Van Gelder, one of the reporters who signed the protest.

We called up the ghost of Thomas Jefferson on the integrity of the press, but didn't ask for any heads to roll, and didn't mention any names. The basic sentiment was that Murdoch can say whatever he wants in his editorials – so long as they are labelled as such – but that the integrity of the news columns should be protected.

"This should have been accompanied by letters of resignation," Murdoch said when the protest was delivered. "Anyone who thinks I don't have integrity should resign." When the reporter suggested that if that were to happen the paper might have few reporters left, Murdoch riposted, "I can get better than you in a week. It's not your paper, it's my paper." Some of the more sensitive among them departed.

The Koch experience was instructive for American politicians. They came to understand that an endorsement by Murdoch was not just a peck on the cheek, as it would be from the *New York Times*, but a bear hug. As Mario Cuomo said, the *Times* might, after long deliberation, give you a column. "With Rupert, he turns the whole paper over to you." Koch understood this and Murdoch had a grateful friend in City Hall almost from the day he took over the *Post*.

Then came the incident which earned Murdoch the enduring anger of his peers: the 1978 newspaper strike.

The dispute which afflicted many newspapers in the 1970s and 1980s was over the introduction of new, computerized technology to replace the old linotype system which had been in operation for almost a century.

Dolly Schiff had not been prepared to form a united front with the other publishers in demanding concessions from the unions. Now the *Times* and the *News* were anxious to have Murdoch on their side. The *Post* stood to gain less from a successful deal with the unions than its rivals. None the less, Murdoch agreed to lead the publishers, and appear as their spokesman. He later said that he did this because it gave him "a chance to be seen a lot on TV in a different role, instead of always having to answer first about some crappy headline in the *Post*".

However, at the end of September 1978, Murdoch broke with his colleagues and agreed with the unions that if they would print the *Post* now, he would eventually settle on whatever terms they managed to get with the *Times* and the *News*. On 5 October, the *Post* was on the streets with a run of a million copies. "WEL-COME BACK!" it shouted to itself. While he left the painful and costly bargaining to the other proprietors, Murdoch spent hours on the telephone cajoling and charming major advertisers. For a time, he cornered some of those who had previously eluded him. On the spur of the moment he decided also to start a new Sunday paper to compete with the *News*.

Eventually the publishers did obtain concessions on featherbedding from the union pressmen (described by Murdoch as "an ornery bunch of bloody Irishmen"). And when the other two papers came back on to the streets in November, they went after his advertisers like piranha fish. The advertising department at the *News* organized a "Bury Murdoch" campaign. News salesmen were given hefty bonuses for every *Post* account they could lure back as an exclusive *News* account. They showed no quarter and within weeks the *Post* had shrunk and Murdoch was forced to concede defeat. He closed the Sunday edition.

The *Times* was as savage as the *News*. And *Newsday*, the suburban daily published in Long Island, New York, put up a fierce fight against Murdoch in Queens, where the *Post* was threatening to make inroads into *Newsday*'s readership. Otis Chandler, the owner of *Newsday*'s parent company, the Los Angeles *Times-Mirror*, announced, "We are waiting to see how long it's going to take him to fail in this country."

By the end of the 1970s, Murdoch was regarded as a fiend in New York publishing. It was as if Dracula had come to Gotham and was sucking newspapers dry. Josef Barletta, the general manager of the *Daily News*, acknowledged in 1979 that New York newspaper publishing was not a gentleman's club.

But you still don't have to become a dirty street fighter. I and my associates feel that there are some rules of good behaviour. In Murdoch's world there are no rules. His world is amoral . . . Now that he has shown how he works, we'll do it too. We're willing to play the game with him by his rules if that's what he wants.

Abe Rosenthal, the outspoken executive editor of the *Times*, announced that Murdoch was "a bad element, practising mean, ugly, violent journalism". Even an airline magazine wrote of him: "MURDOCH – the very name triggers chills and palpitations among many members of the American press, as if it were some dark, evil, contaminating presence slinking out of the night – the Grendel, the Blob." A writer from the *Daily News* complained in the *Washington Journalism Review* about the *Post*'s "S curves of Sex, Scandal, Sensation and Screw the facts". The *Columbia Journalism Review* claimed that the *Post* had turned white against black, the comfortable against the poor, the First World against the Third World. "The *New York Post* is no longer merely a journalistic problem. It is a social problem – a force for evil."

Murdoch's response was combative: "If these people are going to get up and score off me all the time," he said, "if they want to have a fight with me, they may as well know before they're through that they've been in a fight."

THE CLARKE RING

After his juvenile interest in Lenin, Murdoch did not honour many prophets. He was not known for reading books. His life was too packed with reaction, with the seizure of opportunities and the building and running of structures, to allow time for great reflection. But one man whose vision he constantly applauded was the science-fiction writer, Arthur C. Clarke. He was fond of quoting Clarke's prediction that "In the struggle for freedom of information, technology not politics will be the ultimate decider . . . "

Clarke was not only a distinguished writer of science fiction, he was also a gifted interpreter of the "facts" of science, so much so that there is an area of the galaxy named after him. Circling the equator, 22,300 miles above the earth, are satellites, parked on the Clarke Ring. It is a place of great importance to Murdoch.

Clarke was the man who first conceived the idea of satellite communications. In doing so, he redefined sovereignty. He had become obsessed with the new world of science fiction in the 1930s. In 1938, long before the discovery of nuclear fission, Clarke predicted that "the release of nuclear energy will make space travel not only possible but imperative". During the war, Clarke joined the Royal Air Force and worked on ground-controlled approach radar; his work there led him, while still a flight lieutenant, to publish a famous paper on satellites in the magazine *Wireless World*.

At that time, the only way to get a radio news report or to make a phone call across the Atlantic was by short-wave or undersea cable routes which were notoriously crackly and unreliable. Television was hardly born, but engineers already understood that because of the curvature of the earth, broadcasts would not reach more than a few score of miles from an antenna. Any notion of international TV exchanges seemed to be impossible.

Long before the technology existed to build satellites, Clarke worked out what in theory they could be. The crucial fact was that any satellite has to orbit the earth in order to stay aloft. The lower down it is, the faster it has to go round. A satellite just a couple of hundred miles up orbits once every 100 minutes or so, whereas the moon, a quarter of a million miles away, strolls around the earth once a month.

Clarke calculated that at 22,300 miles above the earth a satellite would take just twenty-four hours to orbit it. Since the earth itself spins on its axis once every twenty-four hours, a satellite above the equator at that height would seem to be motionless above the ground. Clarke later downplayed his vision. There was nothing new about the geosynchronous orbit, he said. "Any fool since Newton could have seen that . . . My contribution was to realize that the satellite was the answer to the global broadcast distribution problem and that that was the place to put it."

Despite such modesty, Clarke was a genius. At that time no one had demonstrated that it would be possible to build a rocket to lift anything beyond the earth's atmosphere. Yet Clarke suggested putting a team of radio engineers into a spacecraft 22,300 miles up. They would, he said, be able to pick up signals in New York and beam them down to London. With just three satellites spaced around the equator, the whole world could be covered.

There were developments which even Clarke did not foresee. In 1945 there was still no obvious alternative to vacuum tubes, which needed constant replacements. Clarke could not predict that solid-state electronics would soon appear and then advance to the point at which satellites could operate automatically, unmanned. Without the transistor, there would indeed have had to be teams of engineers zooming around indefinitely in geosynchronous orbit.

Satellites, or "birds", now dash along the Clarke Ring at 7,000 miles an hour, or 168,000 miles a day. They have a lifetime of up to ten years and in that time they cover something like 400 million miles. They only need tiny amounts of power. Once a satellite is positioned properly, its solar panels are spread and turned towards the sun. As the satellite travels, the panels move to catch the solar energy that both powers the housekeeping functions of the satellite and enables it to receive signals bounced up from the earth, amplify them, transfer them to a higher frequency to avoid interference, and bounce them back to earth. They travel along a beam with less than one degree of arc and each transponder needs only 50–240 watts power – about the same as a light bulb.

Communications satellites are in geosynchronous orbit, and make "footprints" on the earth below. These footprints, like those of some great, misunderstood monster, are the areas into which each satellite can beam information down. They are no respecters of national borders, any more than of garden fences.

In the 1940s Clarke predicted:

> Most developing countries will be concerned neither with building nor with launching satellites, but merely renting facilities in them . . . There will be more and more specialized satellites shared by countries in the same geographic region. Even countries which down on earth are not very friendly with each other. Radio waves have never respected frontiers and from an altitude of 36,000 kilometres, national boundaries are singularly inconspicuous. The world of the future will be an open world.

Or, perhaps, a world in which some societies recoiled from the monstrous footprints being stamped upon them.

In 1945, Clarke had thought that realization of his idea was at least half a century away. Even he had reckoned without the fantastic pace of technological change that the next few years would bring.

The first low-orbit satellite was Sputnik, launched by the Russians on 4 October 1957 to the horror of the United States. Telstar, the first international communications satellite, went into orbit in 1962. Reception dishes could track it across the sky for only an hour or so before it dipped below the horizon.

In the space adventure, Australia had an important part to play. Its clear sky and vast largely uninhabited deserts were unique, and crucial to the new science of rocketry and satellites. One of the world's largest test missile ranges and satellite tracking stations was established at Woomera. By the early 1960s Australia provided locations for satellite communications systems and deep space tracking stations that enabled the United States to orbit the earth and send missions to the moon.

In 1964 Intelsat, the International Communications Satellite Organization, was formed in Washington, to organize the world around the new technology. At that time it seemed inconceivable that anyone other than governments, and rich ones at that, would be able to launch and to maintain satellites. The Soviet government refused to join the consortium. Instead Moscow began to develop its own satellite network, Intersputnik, whose members were limited to the communist countries.

By the end of the 1970s Intelsat had almost 100 member countries and controlled fourteen satellites in various positions on the Clarke Ring. It channelled television, telephone calls and other data between 171 countries and territories around the world. The organization carried two-thirds of the world's international communications traffic and almost all international television transmissions. Intelsat offered over thirty different services, from telephone calls to sophisticated computer-to-computer exchanges and video conferences across the world. But Intelsat's satellites were never designed for direct reception in homes. They needed huge dishes, scores of feet across, located in remote areas.

During the 1970s, satellite technology developed dramatically. The "birds" became cheaper and more powerful. By the mid-1970s, five-metre dishes were able to pick up a good picture from the sky. By the late 1980s two feet was adequate.

The system was dominated by the West and the USA in particular. A large proportion of US military and diplomatic communications were carried by Intelsat, as was the hot line between Moscow and Washington. However, in the 1970s US influence over Intelsat diminished when the board of governors was expanded.

In Washington, the Nixon administration recognized the potential of the new generation of satellites, establishing an office of Telecommunications Policy in the White House, run by Clay T. (Tom) Whitehead, a graduate of MIT and a researcher at the Rand Corporation. One of his tasks was to fulfil the White House's longstanding responsibility for the allocation of government frequencies in the communications spectrum.

Whitehead was ambitious. He tried to sort out the tangles into which cable television was developing and drafted a new satellite policy within the United States. He wanted to introduce competition into the entire communications business. So the White House pressed the Federal Communications Commission (FCC) to allow an "open skies" policy for domestic communications satellites. As a result, in the next few years, dozens of privately-funded and -operated satellites were blasted up to the Clarke Ring to cater for a host of domestic services from television to mail order to banking. In Washington direct broadcasting to the home was seen as a fantastic opportunity to footprint Western broadcasts all over the Soviet empire.

The first country to use direct broadcasting by satellite was India. A one-year experiment in 1975–6, using an American satellite, was billed as an attempt to see how far the service could be used to provide isolated rural communities with information and instruction. The antennae were literally chicken wire and sticks. Technically the shortlived experiment was a success, and was seen as such by the CIA.

In 1976 Canada and Indonesia both began to experiment with direct satellite broadcasting. The Russians also started direct broadcasts to the inhabitants of Central Siberia and the far north when they launched the Ekran spacecraft up to a position of ninety-nine degrees east. Japan conducted similar trials.

In January 1977 the International Telecommunication Union, hosted a meeting in Geneva, the World Administrative Radio Conference, whose purpose was to carve up the Clarke Ring in order to allocate national satellite spots and to divide the spectrum into broadcast frequencies to different countries.

European governments were nervous. They knew perfectly well that the footprint of any satellite 22,300 miles up would cover more than one country. So French programmes would be beamed into Britain, and British jokes into Germany. The French in particular were frightened of their airwaves being swamped by American imports beamed at them by one of their neighbours. It was already becoming apparent – and not very welcome to governments – that the telecommunications revolution was, as Clarke predicted, redefining the nature of sovereignty.

Six hundred delegates from 111 countries attended the conference. They drew up an international plan for broadcasting satellite services in the 12 Ghz "downlink" band, chosen because it was the simplest bandwidth for available technology to receive. That simplicity was important if less developed countries were, in fact, to be served.

The conference had to discuss both physical space on the Clarke Ring and frequencies. If two nearby satellites use the same frequency, they will interfere with each other. So they have to be placed about two degrees apart and their frequencies have to be shared just as carefully as with terrestrial stations.

The task was to find an appropriate spot in geosynchrononous orbit for each of the countries that wanted satellite service. Most satellites are positioned just a few degrees west of the country they are designed to serve. This is because they are powered by sunlight, and the "eclipse season" means that during part of the year the satellite is hidden from the sun around midnight. By shifting the satellite a little west, they will be eclipsed in the early morning rather than late at night, and less interruption or inconvenience will be caused to earthlings. (In theory the satellites could provide twenty-four-hour service, but only with huge and heavy batteries.)

The satellite world of the Clarke Ring was divided into three regions. Region One contained Europe, Africa, the USSR and Mongolia. Region Two covered all the Americas and Greenland. Region Three embraced Asia, Australia and the Pacific. WARC 77, as the conference was inelegantly known, reached agreement only for Regions One and Three. The United States refused to cut any deals for Region Two. The conference developed into a fight between the *dirigistes*, led by France, and the open-skies advocates, led by the USA and Canada. The French insisted on a very rigid plan for Europe, whereby each country had only five channels. The Americans thought such restrictions absurd, if only because the technology was racing ahead.

In Region One, the Europeans had difficulties, because countries are so densely bunched. Everyone wanted approximately the same slot – nineteen degrees west, because it is high in the sky viewed from a European back garden. Those who argued least forcefully received inferior slots. Thus Britain was given thirty-one degrees west – this meant that the satellite would be lower against the horizon and strike the earth at a more oblique angle than was optimal. Mountains, skyscrapers, even trees and houses would interfere with reception much more than if the angle to the satellite had been more acute.

The conference gave each country just five frequencies, which usually meant three for operations and two for reserve. Slots were handed out regardless of the size of the countries or their probable needs. San Marino and the Vatican, Andorra and Luxembourg, were given rights along with everyone else.

The problem with WARC 77 was that it was an international treaty which tied governments to existing technology. In 1977, broadcast satellites were expected to need high power (220–300 watts) to transmit clear pictures to 60cm domestic dishes. WARC 77 awarded five-channel high-powered satellite slots to every country, regardless of its need or ability to exploit them. At that time satellites were almost all in the hands of governments.

Predictably, the technology moved on. Within a few years much lower-powered satellites with many more channels could be beamed down to smaller dishes. But governments were tied by WARC 77 to high-powered satellites with only five channels.

By the end of the decade it appeared that almost any satellite could be used to transmit direct into people's homes if only they had a small dish – and, of course, a television. The transnational opportunities that this offered to an international media empire like News Corporation appeared to be limitless. To Murdoch, satellites offered the same prospects that the railroads had provided for the barons of a previous era. This time the tracks led around the world.

AUSTRALIA

On the morning of Tuesday 20 November 1979, Rupert Murdoch strode into his father's old office at the Melbourne *Herald* on

Flinders Street – the office where, as a child, he had first been entranced by newspapers and by his father's power – and told the chairman that he intended to buy the paper.

It was an emotional moment for Murdoch – or perhaps it would be more accurate to say that it was the sort of moment which caused his adrenalin to flow. Here he was, trying, after more than a quarter of a century, to recapture the business his father had spent his life in building. The *Herald* had been part of the spirit of his family, but it had been an opponent ever since his father's death. Together with Fairfax, the *Herald* had set itself to curb his growth wherever possible. For decades the Herald group had thought itself invulnerable to takeover, because of its cross-ownerships with Advertiser Newspapers in Adelaide and the Queensland Press in Brisbane. But by now their shares in the *Herald* had fallen to less than 1 per cent of the company.

Murdoch believed that in recent years the Herald group, and the Melbourne *Herald* in particular, had been in appalling decline. The board had appointed not journalists, but managers and accountants who had no understanding of newspapers. As a result, the Melbourne *Herald* was the "dullest" of all papers "in its mindlessness", and he thought it his duty to shake it up. He was also convinced that he needed the group. Although others had different analyses, Murdoch regarded News as terribly fragile. "We were always in the position of being much weaker than people outside realized. We had an evening paper in Adelaide, an evening paper and a morning paper in Sydney and *The Australian*. No classified revenues anywhere. The prize of the Melbourne *Herald* was always the classified morning monopolies in Brisbane and Adelaide. Not the *Herald* itself."

Murdoch's move to recapture his childhood memories came at a time when he was trying to expand his group hugely. His acquisitions were being financed principally by profits from the *Sun* in London. Its racy formula of snappy news, pungent editorials and bare-breasted girls on page three continued to win readers. In 1978 the paper finally managed to overtake the *Mirror's* circulation of 4 million a day. Despite the ceaseless problems between management and unions, the *Sun* was now the financial engine of Murdoch's empire. In 1979 pre-tax profits rose by £7 million to £25 million.

Under pressure from Anna, Murdoch had turned his attention back to Australia. He was planning to settle there – or at least to make it more of a permanent base. Asked whether this was for business or personal reasons, he said:

> Purely personal. I think it is a lottery whatever happens to your children, but quite a compelling reason is not to have my children educated in the public-school system in England because I feel they could never get the old school tie off their necks. If they want to lead a life in newspapers, if they choose that, they will grow up with better values in Australia than anywhere else I can think of.

He intended to send them to boarding schools in Melbourne and to treat Cavan as home.

In 1978 he could not resist having News Ltd buy one of the largest sheep farms in the country, the Boonoke and Wanganella merino sheep station in the Riverina district of New South Wales. The 250,000-acre properties, together with 60,000 sheep, were being sold largely because protracted drought had brought them almost to ruin. The price was therefore very low. Once more the extraordinary Murdoch luck held; within days of the deal being completed the best rains in two years started falling in the Riverina.

He also developed his gambling investments. By the end of the 1970s gambling was beginning to acquire big-business respect-ability – largely because of the technological revolution. Com-puters and electronic gadgetry completely transformed some of the mysterious workings of gambling and especially the most ubiquitous of all games, the slot machine, finally making it possible to get a grip on the inherent cash control problems of the industry.

Long-odds gambling, known as soft gambling, and popular newspapers have always gone hand in hand. In the early years of the century Lord Northcliffe had caused riots in Threadneedle Street by offering cash payments for life to readers who correctly guessed the money value of the gold in the Bank of England. In the

1920s the British soccer pools were created, in part, by newspapers competing for readers.

Gambling, the addiction of Rupert Greene, had always been part of both Murdoch's leisure and working life. For decades he has been seen by headline writers as a gambler: "RUPERT MURDOCH – THE GAMBLER'S ROLLING HIGH"; "MUR-DOCH, THE GAMBLER WHO CAN'T BEAR TO LOSE"; "MURDOCH, THE GAMBLER WHO ALWAYS WINS".

In the 1970s his newspapers became involved in the simplest forms of gambling – soccer pools, Lotto and, for readers of the Sydney *Mirror*, the *Sun* and the *New York Post*, some form of bingo.

By the early 1980s, gambling was a huge and vital part of the international entertainment industry. Vernons, one of Britain's biggest betting firms, had made its mark in Australia. Its principal owner, Robert Sangster, made a deal with News Corp. "With his distribution system, his knowledge of marketing and his printing plants, Murdoch was the natural partner," said Sangster. By 1974 they were granted licences as sole operators of soccer pools in four states, the Northern Territory and Canberra.

In 1977 they expanded into the United States. New York State was anxious to develop a new low-stakes long-odds game. Sangster and Murdoch competed for the contract, choosing as their US partner Mathematica Inc, a Princeton think tank founded by the games theorist Oskar Morgenstern. It had produced many math-ematical designs for the US government, including blueprints for the space shuttle. Together they won the right to operate Lotto – a new version of the old game which was becoming a worldwide craze – throughout New York State.

Back in Australia, Murdoch and Sangster then went into part-nership with a far more seasoned gambler, Kerry Packer, to form Lotto Management Services. They planned to compete in every area of long-odds gambling across the continent. The stakes were high; in Victoria alone the right to run Lotto meant a revenue of some $30 million. The consortium first won a partnership with the government of New South Wales to run Lotto there. Next they obtained the rights to an instant numbers game in Queensland. In

1983 Australians alone spent $12 billion on gambling, the British $20 billion and the Americans $80 billion.

Murdoch was also expanding his television interests. At the end of the 1970s Australian television had been enjoying a period of fabulous profit making. Murdoch still had his stations in Adelaide and in the steel town of Wollongong, south of Sydney. Now he made a play for one of the three Sydney commercial stations, Channel 10, which he had failed to acquire in 1961. This was owned by United Telecasters Sydney Ltd, and had made more than A$4 million post-tax profit in 1977–8. It was part of one of the three big Australian commercial networks – in Melbourne and in Brisbane its chief partner was owned by Ansett Transport Industries, and in Adelaide its station competed with Murdoch's Channel 9.

Murdoch already owned just under 5 per cent of Channel 10 through WIN 4 in Wollongong. In mid-1979 he had his Australian finance director, Merv Rich, buy several packages of shares in Channel 10 – bringing his total shareholding up to 48.2 per cent. This made good commercial sense – but it brought with it legal complications.

Australian television was administered and controlled by the Australian Broadcasting Tribunal, which had superseded the less powerful Control Board in 1977. Under the Broadcasting Act one "person" was not allowed to hold more than 5 per cent stock in two television licences – unless he had already done so before 1965. Since Murdoch had already owned two stations (Adelaide and Wollongong) before he bought into the Sydney station, he knew he would have to sell one of them. He chose to dispose of Wollongong.

Murdoch's acquisition of Channel 10 was fiercely resisted. The New South Wales branches of the Australian Journalists' Association protested in the strongest possible terms – as did the Australian Labor Party. Both these organizations had been united in opposition to Murdoch since the 1975 election, when journalists had protested against alleged anti-Whitlam bias in his newspapers.

The hearings were presided over by Bruce Gyngell, who was famous for being the first man to appear on Australian television.

He was therefore thought by some to be too much of an industry man. Gyngell refused to allow the New South Wales branch of the Journalists' Association to appear formally, but the Labor Party was represented by Senator Gareth Evans.

A key issue was the question of where Murdoch lived. The Broadcasting Act prevented a company from holding a television licence if 15 per cent of that company was controlled by someone who was "not a resident of Australia". The Labor Party proposed to show that in 1979 Murdoch was not such a resident. Senator Evans, a lawyer, also sought to show that it would be against the public interest for News to control Channel 10 because the group's record showed that its news and information services would no longer remain independent and objective. Moreover, giving News the Sydney licence would create "a wholly unhealthy aggregation" of media ownership in Sydney.

Murdoch decided to take the stand himself and go on the offensive. He insisted that a connection between newspapers and television news was beneficial, not harmful. He described himself, as was his custom, as "the little guy" standing up to established interests, the big Sydney and Melbourne proprietors, Fairfax and the Melbourne *Herald*. "My life has been spent fighting them, starting with a very small newspaper, standing up to attempts to push me out of business at the age of twenty-three in Adelaide." He asserted that successive Australian governments had helped "the big guys" against him. Fairfax had run "a gutter campaign" against him. And he demanded to know: "Who in this room can say that I am not a good Australian or a patriotic one?" Nor was that all:

Who else chooses to be battered and bruised ten months of the year in being an Australian when it would be easier not to be one? Who else has risked everything to start a national newspaper which goes across the length and breadth of this country? Who employs more than 15,000 people, giving them opportunities to work throughout the world? I started *The Australian* fifteen years ago as a dream. Nearly thirteen million dollars has gone into making that dream a reality.

Asked if he intended to change the management of Channel 10 if he acquired it, he insisted categorically that he did not. Sir Kenneth Humphreys, he said, had done a magnificent job. Channel 10 would not be touched. "It will remain totally independent . . . We will not be interfering."

He told the tribunal that he would spend three months a year in Australia in the current year, that the previous year he had spent two months there, and three or four months in 1977. He had a "green card" enabling him to live in the United States, but he had no intention of becoming an American citizen.

He also said there was "no substance" to the rumour that he was planning to buy Channel O in Melbourne. "I do not see why I should give up a profitable station in Adelaide for a loser in Melbourne."

It was a robust performance. Gyngell decided that despite his sojourns in the northern hemisphere, Murdoch was adequately "resident" and could legitimately have Sydney's Channel 10 licence. He immediately began to dispose of the Wollongong station.

He had said he would make no management changes, but two weeks after he acquired Channel 10 he replaced its general manager with a director of News. Soon afterwards Sir Kenneth Humphreys resigned as chairman. Murdoch said much later, to this author, that he'd "had no alternative" but to fire the management because of the way it was ruining the company.

The other assurance he had given the tribunal was that he had no intention of trading his Adelaide station for one in Melbourne. None the less, he made a full-frontal assault on Melbourne and had bought Channel O within months.

America was welded together by the railroads, but no such close-knit grid could be built across the Australian desert. It was not until the arrival of the aeroplane that Australia really began to forge a sense of unity. Later, it was television which linked Perth to Darwin to Alice to Melbourne more closely than anything else.

Channel O in Melbourne was owned by Ansett Transport Industries, which ran one of Australia's two domestic airlines. The other, Trans Australia Airlines, was owned by the government.

Between them they monopolized Australian air routes. The idea of real competition was anathema to both of them and they made substantial profits. But in recent years the "Great Australian" who had chaired Ansett for years, Sir Reginald Ansett, had made mistakes. The company had lost large sums on real-estate transactions and its share price had fallen. By 1979 it was vulnerable to predators – as Murdoch was not the only one to understand.

Among those interested was Sir Peter Abeles, the chief executive of Thomas Nationwide Transport (TNT), who had been a major shareholder of Ansett in the mid-1970s. Robert Holmes à Court, a Perth businessman and head of the Bell Group, was also buying into the company. Sir Reginald Ansett took fright and made a defensive alliance with Ampol Petroleum Ltd; they each bought 20 per cent of the other's stock and pledged to keep their holdings at that level.

In September 1979 Murdoch entered the fray and bought just under 10 per cent of Ansett. He invited Abeles and Holmes à Court to Cavan to discuss how the impasse could be resolved. This meeting marked the burgeoning of a long friendship and close business association between Murdoch and Abeles. By the end of the day, Holmes à Court had agreed to buy the stock owned by Abeles, Murdoch and the two banks, for A$2.50 a share. He intended to make a similar offer to Ampol. He would then own over 60 per cent of the company. But he stipulated that Ansett had to buy the operating assets of the Bell Group – so that he would have the cash to pay for the shares. Once he was in control, he would offer Channel O in Melbourne to News, and the Brisbane channel to Ampol.

Murdoch was delighted and told Merv Rich to find a buyer for his Adelaide station; it would be much easier to get quick approval for the purchase of Channel O if he owned only one other station in the country at the time – Channel 10 in Sydney. By the middle of November, Rich had arranged the sale of Murdoch's first television station, for a price of A$19 million.

But the deal between Bell and Ampol was being delayed, and Murdoch now had some $50 million cash in hand from the sale of News Corporation's bauxite holdings. Murdoch next decided to engage battle on a new front, going after his father's old paper, the Melbourne *Herald*. On 19 November he declared a bid for 50 per cent of the stock at A$4 a share.

The next development happened with the speed of southern summer lightning. Before Murdoch's bid was announced on the evening of Monday 19 November, the Herald shares stood at $2.78. The following morning as he walked into his father's old office on Flinders Street to tell Keith Macpherson, the chairman of the Herald, of his plans, the share price rose to $3.75.

Murdoch said that he was shocked by what he learned of the group. "The *Herald* hasn't had an idea in thirty years. You talk about freedom of opinion – they haven't got an opinion."

Despite such contempt for the management, Murdoch told Macpherson that if he won control of the *Herald* he would want him to stay on as chairman. Macpherson was sceptical.

On Wednesday, 21 November *The Australian* carried a front-page story headlined, "Murdoch moves closer to the biggest conquest", and another, "After a long struggle, the chance to realize a dream", alongside a picture of Dame Elisabeth. Interviewed by *The Australian*, Murdoch declared, "Even before the idea of the Herald offer came, my wife and I decided we would make our base in Australia. The children will go to school here – although they haven't been told that yet. We will be back here, whatever comes of the Herald affair." He told the *Financial Review*, a Fairfax paper, "I think it completes the building of a tremendous Australian base for a worldwide company."

It was not to be, at least not yet. In panic, the Herald management turned to its old rival and partner, John Fairfax and Sons. Macpherson called Robert Falkingham, who had succeeded Rupert Henderson as Fairfax's chief executive. Falkingham had advised against selling Murdoch the Sydney's *Daily Mirror* back in 1960 and he had no wish to let Murdoch have the Herald group now. Quite apart from anything else, that would make him a partner with Fairfax in Australian Newsprint Mills, the company Keith Murdoch had helped found, as well as the Australian Associated Press. Fairfax was determined to deny Murdoch the 51 per cent he was after, and started to buy shares in the *Herald*. The Queensland Press did the same. In just two days Fairfax spent over A$52 million to acquire 15 per cent of the *Herald*. The *Herald* also managed to get the Trade Practices Commission, which was entitled to prevent the domination of the newspaper market by any single proprietor, to agree to investigate any successful bid. Murdoch had not anticipated quite such effective opposition and by Thursday he had decided to abandon his beachhead. "I got frightened. Too much money in it. If the market kept on going up, we would have had to offer that price to everybody."

He began selling shares, but he hid what he was doing. "I employed a different broker to sell. They were still buying, thinking they were buying against me." His normal brokers made noises as if they were still interested. Thus Fairfax and the *Herald* thought he was still in the market and kept on buying – the shares that Murdoch was secretly selling. "It was a period of extreme excitement in the marketplace and their operator was told just to put his head down and buy anything and everything," said Murdoch. "He bought four parcels from us totalling three and a half million in the space of a minute and a half."

Suddenly the Herald and Fairfax brokers realized the full horror of what they had done. In a matter of moments, Murdoch made a profit of over three million dollars. He then declared that his bid was at an end. The share price immediately fell to A$3.45, from a high of A$5.52. Even so, Fairfax management apparently felt that its enormous losses were worth carrying for having kept Murdoch out of Melbourne newspapers. Murdoch denounced the Fairfax-Herald partnership as "two incompetent managements throwing themselves into each other's arms at the expense of their shareholders".

His Australian enemies continued the fight to prevent him acquiring and holding on to Channel 10 in Melbourne. Protracted hearings were held by the Australian Broadcasting Tribunal.

The Australian Journalists' Association asserted that Murdoch "is a person whose history is such that any enterprise in which he has influence is not fit to have influence in the running of any further television station". The AJA portrayed him as an autocratic and unprincipled proprietor who had debased standards of journalism. They accused him in effect of demanding that his lackeys publish distorted accounts of the news when it suited him.

Giving his own evidence, Murdoch displayed both avuncular

charm and irritation. He said he thought politicians were "para-noid" about the media, but that maybe there were two sides to that question. He would not say what his politics were, beyond: "You'd be surprised."

The hearings turned into a reprise of the 1975 journalists' protest about Murdoch's anti-Whitlam bias and his alleged slanting of news against Labor. The final Appeals Tribunal proved uncon-vinced by the allegations. Mr Justice Morling, who presided, con-cluded, "I do not have any doubt that *The Australian* gave the Labor government a bad press in 1975. The evidence suggests that, in this respect, it was not unique. [The] evidence does not persuade me that there was culpable distortion of news in *The Australian* or in the other News Group publication."

Eventually, the tribunal decided that the purpose of the section was to prevent the control of Australian television stations "falling into the hands of persons who are un-Australian in outlook or sympathy or who may not be subject to the regulation and control of the Australian Broadcasting Tribunal".

The tribunal accepted Murdoch's argument that he had "to get overseas businesses on their feet" and that Cavan was his main home, "the home we always go back to". The tribunal also accepted that "that is the place he prefers to be. He said that, once his overseas businesses are running satisfactorily, it is his intention to return full-time to live in Australia. His daughter is at boarding school in Victoria and his sons will go there when they are old enough . . . I see no reason to doubt any of this evidence."

It was two years before the tribunal decided in favour of Mur-doch. Then he had his Australian network assured at last. He could concentrate on the problems in London.

LONDON

As the 1970s ended, the Western world began to shift towards the right – the direction Murdoch now favoured. In the 1979 election the *Sun* came out resoundingly in support of Margaret Thatcher and the Conservative Party. They won the election. For the next decade and more the paper remained astonishingly loyal to her, and that loyalty was rewarded. Throughout the 1980s Murdoch and Thatcher had a symbiotic relationship in which the one consistently and almost constantly encouraged and reinforced the other. The Thatcherite revolution and the Murdoch revolution strode hand in hand across the decade.

When Lamb and Murdoch had devised the formula for the *Sun* in 1969, they and the paper had been to the left of centre. In 1970 the paper backed Harold Wilson. In 1972 it supported the miners in a strike, and opposed Edward Heath's attempt to curb the trade unions. In the February 1974 election, it hedged and in the second election of that year, in October, the *Sun* reflected Murdoch's own view of himself: "The *Sun* is a radical newspaper. All our instincts are Left rather than Right. We would vote for any candidate who could properly describe himself as a social democrat. This much is sure. Neither Heath nor Wilson will do. They are tired and discredited. They do not inspire."

By the end of the 1970s, production of the *Sun* was constantly being stopped by union disputes. The unions complained that, despite the profits the paper was turning in, Murdoch refused to invest in improvements to the plant. There was some truth in this. The pressroom, the newsroom, the canteen, the latrines, and almost all the other facilities at Bouverie Street were among the filthiest and most primitive in Fleet Street. But, as more millions of copies were lost each year through strikes, Murdoch became more and more impatient. "The Fleet Street print unions, dominated by politically-motivated thugs, could probably claim to have unmade more socialists than all Labour's Prime Ministers put together," said Lamb.

Larry Lamb says that he saw the virtues of Mrs Thatcher before Murdoch himself. After she became party leader, Gordon Reece, the director of publicity at Conservative Central Office, persuaded Mrs Thatcher that tabloids like the *Sun*, the *Mirror* and the *Daily Mail* were far more important than the more serious papers in influencing voters. The *Mirror* would always be pro-Labour, but he had her cultivate the editors of both the *Sun* and the *Mail*.

Reece became a fairly frequent visitor to Bouverie Street, where he and Lamb used to drink champagne and discuss politics. The champagne was essential (the party's treasurer, Alastair McAlpine, once said of Reece, "If you have a car you have to run it on petrol. If you have a Gordon Reece, you have to run it on champagne.")

Neither Lamb nor Murdoch liked to call themselves Tories. But they both considered the Callaghan government a disaster. By 1978 Lamb thought "there was no alternative to Thatcher", but Murdoch was more nervous about alienating the paper's Labour readership and used to ring him up and ask, "Are you still pushing that bloody woman?"

In the winter of 1978–9 public-sector strikes led to rubbish overflowing through the streets and bodies being left unburied. Lamb borrowed from Shakespeare a headline which stuck to the government – "THE WINTER OF DISCONTENT". In early 1979, when Callaghan returned from a summit in Guadeloupe and seemed to be unaware of the extent of that discontent, Lamb had him say, "CRISIS? WHAT CRISIS?" in the paper's banner headline. The fact that he said no such thing did not in any way diminish its effect.

As the election approached, Reece and Lamb met fairly frequently. Mrs Thatcher also came to Bouverie Street. Lamb said she "accepted a glass of whisky, kicked off her shoes and engaged us all in spirited debate for several hours. We were all impressed, not least by the fact that she listened." Lamb also went to see her at her house in Flood Street, Chelsea, "to talk about the kind of campaign she planned, who she felt might emerge as the star performers, and which members of her team we should stick close to. She was most helpful." The chat, he said, was not all one-way. "I offered all the advice she asked for about popular communication."

On Election Day, 3 May 1979, the *Sun*'s massive editorial, covering the entire front page and continuing inside, was headlined "VOTE TORY THIS TIME. IT'S THE ONLY WAY TO STOP THE ROT." According to Lamb, Murdoch had had reservations and had asked Lamb to substitute "this time" for Lamb's first preference "today" – arguing that this would suggest that the *Sun* was not committed to the Tories for ever. The editorial asserted

Rupert Murdoch

that the *Sun* was a radical paper and was therefore urging a vote for the Conservatives.

The biggest swing to the Conservatives was among the lower-income group, known to market researchers as C2s, which included many *Sun* readers. A victorious Mrs Thatcher wrote Lamb what he called an "affectionate" letter and thanked him for his help.

A few months later, on the tenth anniversary of Murdoch's purchase of the *Sun*, the Prime Minister sent the paper a message. "Many congratulations on your first ten years. May you long continue to set out in plain, basic English the issues which confront Britain as we try to arrest and reverse our decline . . . It is in communicating the awkward truths that the *Sun* will, I am sure, play an invaluable part in the years ahead, in helping to restore our national fortune."

At the beginning of 1980 Mrs Thatcher revived a tradition which lasted through her reign – of handing out honours to journalists and newspaper proprietors who served her well. In the 1980 New Year honours, John Junor, the editor of the *Sunday Express*, was given a knighthood. Victor Matthews, the owner of the *Express*, was given a peerage. Larry Lamb was also knighted. This honour was described as being for services to journalism. Lamb told Murdoch of his award before it was announced, but did not ask his views. He knew that Murdoch despised the honours system. By now Murdoch had decided that Lamb was becoming pretentious.

Their relationship had already lasted over a decade. Like everyone else, Lamb was still trying to decide what made Rupert run. In the end he too came back to Keith Murdoch: "Some people live for ever in the shadow of distinguished fathers. Whatever else, Rupert was always determined that he would cast the longer shadow."

Lamb also tried to explain that despite the page-three girls, Murdoch was something of a Calvinist. He once complained to Lamb about what Lamb called "a delicate, beautifully written account of some fairly innocent schoolgirl-groping in the bicycle shed". At the same time, Lamb recalled, Murdoch was unable to understand the hostility that he aroused in Britain. He was a good

212

husband and father, a patron of the arts and the employer of thousands of people. Yet he was regarded as a monster. Why?

Lamb himself sometimes thought Murdoch a bit of a monster. Especially in the early days, he found Murdoch's criticisms painful. "Eventually we reached an unspoken truce. He ceased to be so unrelentingly critical, and I tried harder not to take offence when he was." Perhaps most disconcerting of all for an editor was the fact that Murdoch knew far more about every aspect of newspaper publishing than anyone he ever employed. And his determination could be ruthless. Sir Larry Lamb also claimed to be upset by Murdoch's constant denigration of the English and their class system. Murdoch used to love repeating the joke that the sun never set on the British Empire because God didn't trust the Brits after dark. On Lamb the joke wore thin, just as he was wearing thin on Murdoch.

WASHINGTON

The 1980s, the decade in which the technological, political and financial revolution enabled Rupert Murdoch to transform his company into one of the world's most important media empires, began for him with two significant adventures: the rescue of Maxwell Newton, the first editor of *The Australian*, and an interrogation before the United States Senate. They were hugely enjoyable successes; Newton once again became entranced, and the senators were charmed by him.

The rollercoaster of Max Newton's life had taken him down rather more often than up since he and Murdoch had parted company in Canberra in 1964. After being denounced as a Japanese spy and raided by the Commonwealth Police in 1969, he had tried to build up his own small newspaper empire. He started a mining newspaper and purchased a small country paper, the *Daily Commercial and Shipping News*, and then the *Sunday Observer* in Melbourne.

The *Sunday Observer* made Murdoch's tabloids look tame. "I

WAS THE POPE'S BOYFRIEND". "BILL'S NOT A HOMO"
– (this allegedly from the wife of the Prime Minister); "THANK
BLOODY CHRIST" – (when the Whitlam government fell),
"PREMIER'S POOFTER SCANDAL" – were some of the front-
page banner headlines that screamed at the citizens of Melbourne
in the early 1970s. The paper was also sustained by pages of
advertisements for sexual services.

Newton continued to live in style, with his pompadour hair,
his sharp shirts with their metal wing tips, a large house in the
Melbourne suburb of Toorak, and a Rolls-Royce. He had borrowed and bartered so much to support such a way of life that
the house was known to his friends as "Contra Castle".

His business prospered for a couple of years, but Newton was
unable to control it. He became addicted to Mandrax, and his
marriage to Anne, which had weathered so much, collapsed.
Newton had always lived on the brink of despair – these misfor-
tunes drove him close to insanity. Suddenly, after twelve years as
a teetotaller, he started drinking again.

He married once more, and the rival paper, *Melbourne Truth*,
published a photograph of bride and groom with the caption: "We
hope the bride has got some money because the bridegroom hasn't
got enough to pay the wedding bill." His addictions and his sexual
meanderings soon took their toll on the new marriage. The drink
problem was alleviated by Alcoholics Anonymous, but his financial problems grew worse. He over-invested in plant and then an
unexpected leap in newsprint prices plunged him into financial
chaos – with the tax department as well as the banks. By 1976 the
receivers had moved into the *Sunday Observer* and they began to
repossess his personal property. One day he called a friend in a
voice of doom, "The world has ended," he said. "They've taken
away the Rolls."

By now he was publishing straight sex papers. Through one of
them he met Olivia Mader, who had placed a small ad. saying that
a bored housewife was prepared to entertain gentlemen in the
afternoons. She said she fell in love with him at once. Their
afternoon trysts became regular; he moved in with her and she
became his third wife. She too was a member of AA. From running
sex papers, they diversified into sex shops and then into brothels.

They began to make a lot of money, all in cash. "Max bought condoms by the thousand and sold them to his girls at a substantial mark-up," said Olivia Newton later. "He used to ferry them to and from their tricks."

This Hogarthian life led Newton near to suicide, and he developed cancer and diabetes. In 1979, he backed slightly away from the abyss when he was asked to write a series of political and economic analyses for *Penthouse*. His flair had not deserted him; the articles were well received and he was given a slot on a Sydney television chat show. He became a pundit. When Murdoch made his move for the Melbourne *Herald* that same year, Newton's views were widely asked.

He was expected to denounce the man who had sacked him, and whom he had in the past described as capricious and superficial, but he did not. He praised Murdoch's vigour and said he would do the *Herald* a lot of good. Murdoch invited him to dinner, and they discovered that their friendship was renewable. They now shared a conviction that only right-wing politics and totally free markets could make the world safe, free and prosperous.

Murdoch decided to rescue Newton. He asked him to write for *The Australian* and then in 1980 invited him to America to advise him on economics and on the direction of the *New York Post*. He sent him and Olivia tickets but no cash. They borrowed A\$1,000 from her ex-husband and flew to New York, where Murdoch put them up at what Olivia called "the wonderful Plaza". Newton never went back to Australia, partly because the taxmen were still chasing his spoor around Melbourne.

In America his life began again. Murdoch made him chief business columnist for the *Post*, and he began to write like a fanatic. His passionate promotions of Reaganomics were a great success, and his punditry began to give the *Post* a presence (and sales) on Wall Street. His column was syndicated throughout the Murdoch empire. He also started writing private financial newsletters, as he had in the 1960s.

In 1982 he suffered agonizing operations for cancer of the prostate. This, said Olivia, made him work all the harder; words were a substitute for sex. "He wrote 7,000 words a day in the 1980s –

he would finish his first column before breakfast." At the end of the day she would pick him up at the *Post* building in a Transit van and he would sit at a table in the back, bashing out a "Maxwell Newton global currencies report", another article for the *Post*, or a chapter for his book on the Federal Reserve, on his computer as she drove him home along Route 1–95 to Connecticut.

The 1980s were Newton's most productive decade. He stayed sober and he knew he owed his salvation to Murdoch – who continued to treat him generously. Newton made the best of his new life and enriched himself from his prodigious output, but the black dog of despair was never far from his side.

After his 1979 retreat from the purchase of the Melbourne *Herald*, Murdoch turned his attention back to acquisition of ATI, the company which owned Ansett Airlines and Channel O in Melbourne. In a complicated but swift series of steps, he acquired enough shares to be appointed chief executive of ATI. He then made a deal with the other suitor for the company, Sir Peter Abeles of Thomas Nationwide Transport, whereby they each ended up with 50 per cent of ATI shares. Abeles, a resourceful businessman, had arrived in Australia as an immigrant from Hungary, and since built TNT into a very successful transport company. He and Murdoch became joint chiefs. Abeles was always fulsome in his praise of Murdoch. "I am a normal businessman, but he is a phenomenon. Rupert is well above all of us in capacity and speed. I have never seen anyone working so fast and so precisely. He can cover so much ground – no other human being in the world could do it."

At the end of 1979 both Australian domestic airlines, Ansett and TAA, were renewing their fleets. In the past, they had flown the same equipment and in December 1979 TAA ordered Airbus 300s, the main European competitor to American medium-range passenger jets. On past form Ansett would have done the same, and indeed Airbus gave an undertaking to supply the planes to Ansett at the same time as to TAA.

Murdoch, as usual, had his own ideas. If the terms were comparable he wanted to buy American.

Boeing recommended that he pitch his case personally in Washington to the president of the Export-Import bank. Murdoch asked if the meeting could be held on 19 February, when he had to be in Washington anyway, for a lunch with President Carter. This was a date which Murdoch had already twice rescheduled to suit his own plans. Carter wanted the support of the *New York Post* in the Democratic primary against Teddy Kennedy.

That morning, Murdoch arrived at the Ex-Im bank building on Vermont Avenue with a telex in his pocket confirming the Airbus offer for four planes. Airbus had offered loans in a basket of currencies at a blended rate of less than 8 per cent and he would need the same for the Boeings. He made it very clear that unless the Ex-Im loan were under 8 per cent, it would not fly.

After telling Ex-Im bank officials that the loan must be at a rate of under 8 per cent, he went to lunch with President Carter. He insisted later that the loan was not discussed between them. He told Carter that the *Post* would endorse him, against Teddy Kennedy, for the New York primary, but he refused to commit the paper to him for the actual election. Three days later, on 22 February, the *Post* did indeed declare for Carter.

In the end the bank offered Ansett a total loan of some $290 million, less than half what Murdoch was asking. He won his 8 per cent only on five aircraft, not twenty-five as he had sought.

But the speed of the deal, the low rate of interest and the coincidence of Murdoch's lunch with and support for Carter led to intense speculation. In Washington journalists and congressional staff alike attempted to find evidence of a corrupt deal – cheap money for political support. They were unable to discover any such thing. The incident came to seem more significant for the light it shed on Murdoch's access and influence, and his tough bargaining tactics with bankers, than for any improper political deals that were rumoured to have taken place.

Murdoch volunteered to testify to the Senate Committee on Commerce. He explained that it was Boeing's idea that he should meet with Ex-Im bank officials. The fact that he lunched with Carter the same day as meeting with Ex-Im bank officials was pure coincidence. Finally, he pointed out that the *Post*'s endorsement of Carter in the primary was no surprise. His opponent was Edward

Kennedy, and Kennedy was not one of the *Post*'s favourite politicians.

Senator Proxmire pointed out that the media's influence on the public was enormous. Senators had an ethics code designed to avoid even the appearance of a conflict of interest. Did Murdoch?

"Of course we do, sir. And I sympathize with you in what you're saying about the media, in particular watching television and what a job they did on me the last couple of days. There is no conflict of interest here unless it's in the eye of the beholder."

Asked why he had chosen Boeing, when Airbus was offering an identical deal, Murdoch replied that there were a number of arguments. "I have a large investment in this country. I have an admiration for the Boeing company, for their airplanes. And I believe the Australian public has a trust in Boeing airplanes."

In conclusion, Proxmire threw Murdoch a bouquet. "Well, I want to say that you are a remarkable man, Mr Murdoch. We have had a lot of witnesses before this committee, but I was especially impressed with what a quick study you are. You seem to know a whale of a lot about an industry you've just gotten into. You are very refreshing, intelligent and an effective witness, and responsive."

In the end the committee chided the Ex-Im bank, saying that the application had been handled sloppily, that not enough care of public money had been shown, and that too much of the bank's money went to the aircraft industry anyway. But Murdoch had already been given the loan. In the end the whole investigation seemed to be fuelled more by fervour than by facts. There was never any likelihood that the *Post* would support Ted Kennedy in the primary; "Teddy is the Toast of Teheran", the paper had declared early in the hostage crisis – a switch from its usual emphasis on his drinking and womanizing. Carter did not need to give Murdoch lunch to have his support, but neither lunch nor even the Ex-Im bank loan was enough to win the President Murdoch's support for the actual presidential election.

To Murdoch, Carter was an ineffectual liberal and he thought it high time that liberalism be decently buried. A sense of crisis gripped America in 1980. America's ally of thirty-seven years, the Shah of Iran, had been driven from his country. Much worse,

American diplomats had been seized as hostages and the Carter administration seemed unable to do anything about it. Since OPEC's second oil price "shock" of 1979, the price of crude oil had risen by over 50 per cent in six months. Cars were lined up at gas stations for hours. Inflation had soared over 10 per cent and was still rising.

Carter made what came to be called his "malaise" speech, in which he talked about a "crisis of confidence . . . that strikes at the very heart and soul and spirit of our nation's will". But he appeared to many Americans to be inadequate. The Soviets marched into Afghanistan and Carter's response was a humiliating declaration that Brezhnev had betrayed him personally.

It is hard to remember now that few people expected Ronald Reagan to be elected President, even up to the last minute of the campaign. But Reagan was the only person selling what has been called "pure strength". He told the Americans what they wanted to hear, and his election seemed to be, in the end, America's final rejection of the 1960s solution to the great problems of the 1970s – economic stagnation, social fragmentation, the need for a new world order.

Carter on the other hand represented the idea of a scaled-back America, a nation that would live modestly, renouncing its restless mobility, withdrawing from full engagement with politics around the globe, focusing only on issues of international importance. Carter's vision did not appeal to the American imagination. Reagan's did. It appealed also to Murdoch.

With the election of Ronald Reagan in November 1980, Murdoch had kindred spirits in both the White House and 10 Downing Street. The 1980s turned out to be the era of Reagan and Thatcher – and Gorbachev. It was a decade which shook the world. Murdoch liked to see himself as part of that process. He was.

Chapter 7

LONDON

In February 1981, Rupert Murdoch, in direct line of succession from his father's friend Northcliffe, became owner of *The Times* of London. When the deal was completed he called Anna who was in Australia – at home, as she thought. She still detested England and, although she liked New York:

> I still had a hankering to go back to Australia. Indeed we had sent our daughter Elisabeth to Geelong Grammar School for a term. I had fixed up the house [at Cavan], putting in a new kitchen, and I remember being there, trying to get the house together and Rupert called to say he had bought the London *Times*. And I burst into tears, because I knew I was on the wrong side of the world.

She asked him where they would spend most of their life from now on. "He thought about it and said, 'More than half in the northern hemisphere.' So I thought: Well! That narrows it a little bit."

The battle for *The Times* and the *Sunday Times* and their subsequent evolution have been crucial to perceptions of Murdoch both in Britain and around the world. This occurred in particular because of his well-publicized rows with one of Britain's most famous editors, Harold Evans.

The Times and the *Sunday Times* were, in different ways, two of Britain's most distinguished papers, but they were blighted by the atrocious state of relations between Fleet Street management and unions.

The *Sunday Times* was bought by Roy Thomson, the Canadian press baron, from Lord Kemsley, in 1959, when its sales were under a million. Thomson appointed a fine editor, Denis Hamilton, an urbane former brigadier, and allowed him to recruit a first-rate staff. In 1967 the paper's circulation touched 1.5 million, far ahead of each of its rivals, the *Observer* and the *Sunday Telegraph*.

Then a greater prize fell to Roy Thomson – *The Times*, the most influential paper in Britain, an institution sometimes called "the noticeboard of the Establishment". Its greatest hour had been in the mid-nineteenth century. When its legendary war correspondent, William Howard Russell, was dispatched to cover the American Civil War in 1861, President Lincoln said to him, "*The Times* is the most powerful thing in the world, except, perhaps, the Mississippi."

The twentieth century, and the development of mass audiences, drained away its power. Northcliffe had bought it in 1908. He lowered the price and raised the circulation but did not keep his promise not to interfere with the editor's judgements. The paper lost its high moral tone. After Northcliffe's death the paper was bought by the Astor family, in partnership with John Walter IV, a descendant of the founder, and the family ran it for the next half century.

"Top People Take *The Times*" was the slogan which the advertisers coined for the paper in the 1950s. But there were never enough such people to make the paper commercially viable. *The Times* crossword, the Letters to the Editor, the gravitas and the not infrequent wit of the leading articles, the self-conscious but honourable attempt to make *The Times* the journal of record, all these were what distinguished *The Times* – and made it unprofitable.

Under the Astors, concessions were reluctantly made to the vulgar spirits of the age. News and photographs replaced classified advertisements on the front page. But by the mid-1960s the Astor family decided that it had subsidized the ideal for long enough. The problem was whether anyone else could be found who would be willing to take it over.

The man who really wanted to do so was Roy Thomson. To some directors – and many readers – the Canadian was altogether too uncouth for *The Times*. There was much anxious debate as to whether he was a suitable custodian, and as to whether one man should be allowed to own both *The Times* and the *Sunday Times*. Long enquiries by the Monopolies Commission and other bodies were mounted.

But *The Times* directors understood that Thomson had the money to assume the burden of the great paper and together with the government they devised safeguards against his abusing it. The avuncular Thomson was happy to accept the conditions; he described the purchase of *The Times* in his memoirs as "the greatest thing I have ever done".

In many ways Roy Thomson was the journalist's perfect proprietor. He was creative, and yet he never interfered. He had fairly pronounced right-wing views of his own, but he reckoned that it would be absurd to try to impose them upon all the newspapers that he owned. He allowed his editors freedom.

After Thomson acquired *The Times*, Denis Hamilton became editor in chief of both *The Times* and the *Sunday Times*. William Rees-Mogg, an erudite writer on the *Sunday Times*, became editor of *The Times* and Harold Evans was made editor of the *Sunday Times*.

Evans, the son of a North Country engine driver, had been a journalist all his working life. He first edited the *Northern Echo*, where he distinguished himself by successful campaigning journalism. Denis Hamilton spotted him and in 1966 brought him to London as his chief assistant. One year later Hamilton handed over to him a superbly functioning, profitable newspaper with as gifted a team of journalists as was to be found in London. The *Sunday Times* was a paper, as Evans himself later said, "vivid with personality and excitement".

Under Hamilton, and then Evans, the *Sunday Times* developed a technique of journalism by a team of reporters. They were collectively known as Insight, and the fruits of their labours came to personify the paper. Evans made insight into a full-time investigative unit and throughout the late 1960s and 1970s the paper published massive enquiries into areas of public concern. These included the life and crimes of Kim Philby, the Soviets' most important agent inside the British Secret Intelligence Service, MI6; an enquiry into the DC-10 disaster in northern France, and an analysis of how the company Distillers came to market the drug

Thalidomide. This investigation was accompanied by a sustained and ultimately successful campaign for generous compensation for the victims of the drug.

Evans saw journalism as a social weapon and it was one which he deployed with enthusiasm, forever taunting government and trying to push back the laws of contempt, of libel and especially of governmental secrecy. Evans's *Sunday Times* had many critics who saw its style as abrasive, pinchbeck journalism with more glitter than substance. Evans and his supporters argued that his paper saw the citizen as victim, in need of defence, and that it was politically neutral, assuming a critical, quietly radical suspicion of all administrations.

It was, for all these and more reasons, a paper with a certain *esprit de corps*. Evans hired skilful journalists and allowed them their head. Among the most brilliant and combative was Bruce Page, editor of Insight and then features editor, a man who would study eighteenth-century German history or molecular physics in order to get a story right.

The paper's serious investigations – of the economic decline of Britain, of the country's union problems, of the banking system, for example – continued. But by the end of the 1970s, some of the spirit had faded. Evans could be as capricious as he was stimulating. He was not good at delegating and yet he was often too distracted to make a decision. He was a bundle of nervous energy, often on the run – or on his motorbike, or on his skis, or in a squash court. He liked to portray his *Sunday Times* as some kind of Camelot, but not everyone was allowed to sit at the round table. Tensions developed between feature writers on the sixth floor around Evans and those in the newsroom one floor below. One of those, Tony Geraghty, complained, "While the great and the good were pursuing their obsessions upstairs, us sherpas of the fifth floor had to see to it that we produced a newspaper each week." One senior editor, Don Berry, described Evans's sudden flashes of enthusiasm in the production process as "journalism by orgasm".

Evans's own life was changing. He was in the process of divorce and remarriage. He had co-authored a successful picture book on skiing, and later helped edit the memoirs of Henry Kissinger –

which some thought an odd extramural activity for an editor who prided himself on his independence from politicians.

While the *Sunday Times* prospered in the 1970s, its sibling *The Times* did not.

Since the Thomson takeover, William Rees-Mogg, an intellectual with an air of preoccupation, had remained editor. He began to modernize the paper, with bigger headlines and shorter sentences. The changes were not very drastic but they were none the less too much for some of the young traditionalists on the paper and in the early 1970s they complained. Since revenues were not rising with circulation – indeed the new readers were costing the paper money – many of the changes were abandoned.

While Roy Thomson's commitment to journalistic endeavour had always been beyond reproach, the company's management was lacklustre. In the early 1970s Thomson decided that there would be savings if *The Times* were moved from Printing House Square by Blackfriars Bridge where it always had been published, to a building next door to the *Sunday Times*, in the drab no-man's land of Gray's Inn Road. They sold Printing House Square much too cheaply, and carelessly included in the sale, for nothing, the sundial which the sculptor Henry Moore had made for *The Times*. Up in the Gray's Inn Road, *The Times* men lost some of their spirit and their conviction. Many of them felt contempt for the more raffish, more vulgar and much more successful *Sunday Times* next door. *Sunday Times* men felt for their part that the commercial failure of *The Times* was a drain upon their own success. Relations between management and print unions deteriorated. Production, especially of the *Sunday Times*, was constantly disrupted. By the second half of the decade the *Sunday Times* was no longer able to cover the losses of *The Times*.

When Roy Thomson died in 1976, everyone at Gray's Inn Road wondered what would happen next. People knew that whereas the Old Man was tickled pink by owning *The Times* even if it lost him money, and that he loved England, his son Ken had no such romantic notions. He lived in Canada, and found London much less congenial than his father had.

Throughout the 1970s British newspaper managements were nervously considering how to introduce the economical "new technology" – the computerized methods by which reporters and advertising copytakers could type copy straight into the system. The beauty – and the problem – of it was that this process would cut out the typesetters, who belonged to the National Graphical Association (NGA). The NGA refused to countenance any such revolution, unless the management agreed to "double key stroking" – this meant that anything already typed in by non-NGA members must be retyped by their men. After endless negotiation, and endless stoppages by the unions which lost millions of copies, Thomson managers lost patience. They told the unions that unless they would agree to uninterrupted production, and the introduction of new technology, they would close the papers down at the end of November 1978. Thomsons were convinced that a "short sharp shock" was all that would be needed. They were wrong.

In a whole year of closure the unions made no concessions of any value. In the end, it was management resolve that collapsed after a shut-down costing £40 million. When the papers did reopen in November 1979, with almost nothing gained, both management and journalists, who had been paid to remain idle during the shut-down, were utterly dispirited. Thomsons had even conceded double key stroking to the NGA.

The print unions continued their disruptive behaviour through 1980. Times Newspapers was losing money heavily – by autumn pre-tax losses were expected to be around £15 million for the year. Ken Thomson was in despair. He felt he had honoured his father's love for the papers but wondered how long he could support such losses. In August 1980, the *Times* journalists went on strike for a large pay increase. For Thomson, this was too much: if the journalists were not loyal, why should he bother?

He put the papers up for sale on 22 October 1980. Bids had to be submitted to the merchant bank Warburgs by 31 December. If no sale were agreed, then the papers would close between 8 and 14 March 1981. Thomsons were anxious to avoid such closure because it would have meant the company having to make redundancy payments of some £36 million.

Now there began a fine old story of brinkmanship and competition. Among the possible buyers were Lord Rothermere, descendant of Northcliffe and the owner of Associated Newspapers, which included the *Daily Mail*; Lord Matthews of the Express group; Robert Maxwell, the owner of Pergamon Press and perpetual suitor of any likely newspaper bride; and Atlantic Richfield, the American oil company, which had bought the *Observer* when Murdoch had hoped to buy it. Then there was Murdoch himself.

But was he really interested? As recently as 1979 he had said that he would "never" do so, and that "to buy *The Times* would be a highly irresponsible thing to do for your shareholders". When the sale was announced, Murdoch said publicly that he had no real interest; he had a lot on his hands already; he doubted whether there would be any buyers; Times Newspapers was "a snake pit".

He also knew that the rules had been changed since he had bought the *Sun* in 1969. He was already a British newspaper owner, which meant that if he sought to buy another paper, his bid would almost certainly have to be examined by the Monopolies Commission. That could be lengthy and disagreeable. There was, however, one loophole. If the paper concerned was clearly commercially unviable and was otherwise threatened with closure, then a bid by an existing proprietor could go ahead unchallenged. On this crucial question much came to hang.

Both Rees-Mogg and Evans decided independently that they must try to put together consortia to rescue their papers separately. Rees-Mogg was first off the mark and flamboyantly flew off to North America hunting for backers. None of significance could be found, but Rees-Mogg did meet Murdoch in New York and was pleasantly surprised by the man's gentle demeanour. Perhaps he was not the monster that "quality journalists" so feared. Murdoch was apparently full of praise for Harold Evans.

Evans was at first more circumspect than Rees-Mogg. He enlisted the help of his friend Bernard Donoughue, a member of the Economist Intelligence Unit who had been a senior adviser to both Harold Wilson and James Callaghan. Evans had long been impressed with his political acumen and, furthermore, "He knew his way round the City, so he was a natural ally," said Evans, "in the search for honest money."

Evans himself searched hard. In America those he approached felt newspapers should not be run by consortia, or were appalled at the idea of being confronted by the London print unions. He returned without commitments. In London, however, the *Guardian* expressed interest in forging links with a *Sunday Times* freed from the conservative *Times*.

In early December Murdoch came to London for a Reuters meeting. He met Gordon Brunton, managing director of Times Newspapers, at the flat of Lord Catto, Murdoch's London merchant banker. Brunton had encountered Murdoch often at meetings of the Newspaper Publishers' Association, that group of owners which had tried vainly for years to unite in defence of its interests against the print unions. He used to say that Murdoch was one of the few publishers who would keep his word. Brunton was a manager, not a journalist: he admired Murdoch's business acumen, and saw him as an honourable man. He wanted Murdoch to buy the papers. By contrast, he loathed Maxwell, and distrusted Rothermere, two of the other obvious candidates.

Murdoch made a bid for £1 million, just to get his foot in the door before the 31 December deadline laid down by Thomsons. Murdoch, like other bidders, knew that Brunton had a gun to his own head. If a deal was not done and Thomsons closed the papers in March, they would be liable for the massive redundancy payments.

Among the bids were those from both editors. Rees-Mogg had put together a consortium with a group of journalists called Journalists of The Times (JOTT) to buy *The Times* and its supplements. On the last day of the year Morgan Grenfell put in a bid "on behalf of Harold Evans, Editor of the *Sunday Times* and Chairman of the *Sunday Times* Executive Committee and his close associates on the Staff". But Evans's hopes were quickly dashed. First the *Guardian* pulled out of the partnership, and then the unions, whom James Callaghan, the former Labour Prime Minister, had tried to line up for Evans, decided they preferred Murdoch. He had saved jobs on the *Sun* and created more; he was tough but he was reliable.

Evans now realized that for the Thomson board, too, Murdoch was the favourite. "It was a bitter thought that they should favour an outsider, and one for whom they had expressed contempt in the past," he wrote later.

Then Evans had a call from Gerald Long, the managing director of Reuters. He told Evans in utmost secrecy that Murdoch had asked him to become managing director of *The Times* and that Murdoch wanted to talk to Evans. Evans gave Long his home number. That evening Murdoch called.

"It's all mine," he said at once. "Unless Harmsworth [Rothermere] comes up with a bigger offer. What do you hear?" He told Evans he was going to make a clean sweep of management and asked Evans to lunch the next day. Evans says he was unhappy to accept, but did so because he wanted to know what was going on. "Murdoch had become a prime source," he wrote in his memoir, *Good Times, Bad Times*.

"Would you like to edit *The Times*?" Murdoch asked Evans over lunch. In his book, Evans wrote that he ignored the question and that he was "quietly angry" at the way in which Murdoch was disregarding his consortium bid. He says he told Murdoch that the consortium wanted to continue to run the *Sunday Times* as a campaigning, investigative paper. "Sure, sure," said Murdoch.

Asked later (in an interview for this book) how Evans reacted at that lunch, Murdoch said, "I want to be fair to Harry. When I said it to him, he did not jump at it, he said he was thinking about his future. I thought he was just being coy. I think he wanted it as much as anything . . . "

On Saturday 17 January Murdoch invited Harry and his fiancée, Tina Brown, to his flat in Eaton Place. In his book, Evans quotes at some length from the relevant passage in Tina Brown's diary – in which he says Tina noted Murdoch's "alarming charm".

I had to admit I liked him hugely. He was in an American country gentleman's three-piece suit and heavy shoes, and was by turns urbane and shady. His face seems to have been made for the cartoonist's distortion – the gargoyle lips, deep furrows in the brow, the hint of five o'clock shadow that gives him such an underworld air when he's sunk in thought. But when he was standing by the fire with one foot on the fender laughing uproariously he seemed robust and refreshing. There's no doubt he lives newspapers. They are not merely seen by him as assets, as Ken Thomson sees them. At eight o'clock, when the first editions arrived, he fell upon them with childish excitement. I warmed to him when he read the *Observer*'s hostile account of his bid and instead of being cross burst into gales of laughter: "The bastards!" he shouted, throwing it to the floor.

The truth is that, although he'll be trouble, he'll also be enormous fun and H. has had so many years of Thomson greyness this vivid rascal could bring back some of the jokes. "I sacked the best editor of the *News of the World*," he said at one point. "Stafford Somerfield was too nasty even for me!"

What had happened in the space of two days seemed clear to those who knew Murdoch. Harry Evans had fallen in love, and so perhaps had Murdoch. There was nothing unusual about that. Murdoch would become immensely, sometimes disproportionately, enthusiastic for a new recruit or adviser. For them his attention could be overwhelming. His charm was so intense and yet so unaffected, so natural and yet so strong, that few people came away from their early meetings with him other than mesmerized. Harry Evans was susceptible.

When his associates in the consortium, Bernard Donoughue and Donald Cruickshank, urged Evans to lead a Stop Murdoch campaign, he refused. Later he wrote, "in the light of events they were right, and I was badly wrong to resist them". But at the time he argued that the thing to do was to tie Murdoch's hands as they had never been tied before. Evans's decision, in effect if not yet in public, to throw in his lot with Murdoch was important. It is likely that if Evans had publicly opposed Murdoch's bid, it would, at the very least, have had to be referred to the Monopolies Commission.

On 20 January, Denis Hamilton had Rees-Mogg and Evans to lunch to ask which of the possible buyers they preferred: they said that on margin they favoured Murdoch, but that he would have to give guarantees of editorial independence. So they had to decide just what guarantees they wanted from Murdoch and then to extract them from him.

This was harder than it sounded because the practices of editorial freedom of *The Times* and *Sunday Times*, were, like the British constitution, unwritten. When Roy Thomson had taken over *The Times*, four independent national directors had been appointed, but they had never had to be summoned to protect an editor from interference by the proprietor – for Thomson never interfered. Thomsons had never come near suggesting that the newspapers should promote the company's other commercial interests. Murdoch, by contrast, was known to have encouraged or at least allowed the promotion of Ansett in his Australian papers since he bought the airline.

And how far would he interfere in other matters of editorial policy? Would he, in pursuit of financial stability, drive the paper into that dreaded abyss "downmarket" where the *Sun*, the *New York Post* and other monsters lurked? Reporters began to scour the world for evidence of his malfeasance. The story of the Ex-Im bank loan was re-examined; as was the 1975 journalists' strike at *The Australian*. The *New York Times* noted with distaste that the *New York Post* had published a picture of John Lennon's body in the morgue. Roger Wood, one of Murdoch's assistants, denied that the picture was sensationalist, because it showed Mr Lennon "very much at peace and at rest".

On 21 January, less than a week after Murdoch had offered Evans the editorship of *The Times*, a committee created by Thomsons met to vet Murdoch's journalistic attitudes. It included three of the four national directors: Lord Dacre, better known as Hugh Trevor-Roper, the historian; Lord Roll, an economist and chairman of Warburgs Bank; and Lord Greene who, as leader of one of the rail unions, had been Sid Greene. (Lord Robens, the other national director, was abroad.) With them were Denis Hamilton, Evans and Rees-Mogg.

When Murdoch came in, Evans said he noticed for the first time the thick black hair on the backs of his hands. According to Evans, Murdoch walked quietly, and spoke softly, "like someone visiting a friend in hospital".

Hamilton set the discussion rolling by telling him what high standards they set at *The Times*. Murdoch then told them all about himself. According to Evans's account, he said he had learned the traditions of editorial freedom from his father and was used to producing different papers for different markets. He stuck with papers that were losing money – look at *The Australian*, he said. He would expect the national directors to be a court of appeal for the editor. He spoke self-confidently but not arrogantly; altogether, he gave a good account of himself.

He agreed to everything they asked him. There would be six national directors, not four. They would approve the appointment of editors. Hamilton was anxious that Times Newspapers should remain separate from News International and not come under the *News of the World* and the *Sun* in Bouverie Street. With some reluctance Murdoch agreed to that as well. He agreed that the editors should set the political policies of the papers and that in all other matters too the editors should have authority. After an hour and a half he had accepted almost all conditions. The committee was impressed.

After that ordeal was over, Murdoch went back upstairs to talk money. His was by no means the best offer Thomsons had received. Rothermere had offered £25 million for the *Sunday Times* alone, and £20 million if he had to take *The Times* as well. But Rothermere also insisted that he must retain the right to close *The Times* if he wished. Meanwhile, Murdoch's original offer of £1 million had increased to £12 million on the understanding that apart from the buildings in Gray's Inn Road, the company had almost £18 million worth of assets.

At one point Murdoch's people thought Thomsons' figures were wrong and Murdoch accused Thomsons' financial director of cheating. Brunton secured an apology at once. At another point, according to Richard Searby, News's chairman, "We told Brunton that Thomsons' declining to warrant or represent any figures to be correct plus or minus 20 per cent meant that we did not know what News might be buying and that the whole deal was off unless he agreed within fifteen minutes to produce figures he was prepared to stand by." Brunton coined a phrase with which he later described how tough negotiations had been. He was still using it almost a decade later. "The walls dripped with blood," he said.

In the end, soon after midnight, the deal was closed at £12 million. Murdoch was jubilant. And well he might be. The *Sunday Times* building in Gray's Inn Road alone was worth at least half of what he had paid for the whole company. Murdoch also retained the right to pull out if the deal were referred to the

Monopolies Commission. He thought that once more he had run rings around the English in his negotiations.

Murdoch appeared next day at a press conference. Flanked by Rees-Mogg and Evans, he was anointed by Denis Hamilton as "one of the greatest newspaper executives in the world today".

Purchase was contingent on Murdoch's making a deal with the unions. But they were eager for him; Joe Wade, leader of the National Graphical Association, praised the sale, saying that he knew Murdoch was ruthless but he was also fair. He did not push them far; in the end they agreed some 700 redundancies and to *The Times Literary*, *Educational* and other supplements being printed outside London. Murdoch gave in on the issue of key stroking, which would remain in the hands of the NGA.

A few weeks later Murdoch revealed to an Australian trade paper how well he thought he had done. The constraints imposed by the national directors were no problem: he could still appoint his own editor and a veto would be "highly unlikely if I go about it in a sensible manner". He confirmed that the price had been a steal. "We paid less than half the book value of its tangible assets, so we can always close it down and still be ahead."

The only remaining hurdle, but the highest one, was the possibility of a reference to the Monopolies Commission which had a special responsibility for newspaper takeovers. Under the 1973 Fair Trading Act all, or almost all, newspaper mergers must be referred to the commission.

Michael Foot, the leader of the Labour Party, wished to refer the sale to the commission, but the print union leaders asked him not to rock the boat. In a *Times* editorial Rees-Mogg dismissed the idea of a referral. In the *Sunday Times* of 25 January 1981 Harold Evans was more equivocal; in the first edition he wrote an editorial opposing referral and then, under pressure from his colleagues, proposed further parliamentary scrutiny of Murdoch's guarantees, in later editions.

If the Monopolies Commission had taken up the issue, its investigation would inevitably have delayed the purchase beyond the deadline set by Thomsons. Both Brunton and Murdoch had already been to the Department of Trade and Industry to argue that the sale should not be referred. Brunton had warned that if it were, the papers would both close. "I had £36 million redundancy payments to worry about. I told the government I would rather close the papers than go through a referral. Murdoch told them he would withdraw in those circumstances. I got him to do that." On behalf of Thomsons, Warburgs presented the ministry with figures which showed that together *The Times* and the *Sunday Times* were losing money.

The matter of referral was considered by an informal meeting of Cabinet ministers. There was apparently tension at the top. Unconfirmed gossip began to circulate in Fleet Street that his own departmental lawyers had advised John Biffen, the Secretary of State for Trade and Industry, that the sale might have to be referred to the commission, but that Mrs Thatcher had decided otherwise. Evans later alleged he heard of "Mrs Thatcher's determination to reward Murdoch for his political support, especially at the 1979 election". But Biffen himself said, in an interview for this book, that he had no reason to believe that this was so.

Biffen said that he would approve the sale providing the editorial safeguards which the vetting committee had proposed be written into the Articles of Association of Times Newspapers. They would have the force of law and Murdoch would risk going to gaol if he broke them. Evans praised this move and told the Press Association: "No editor or journalist could ask for wider guarantees of editorial independence on news than those Mr Murdoch has accepted and which are now entrenched by the Secretary of State." Biffen said that he was greatly influenced by Evans's remarks. But later he privately conceded that there were political arguments either way about a decision to refer.

Harry Evans said later that as the deal went forward he was still unhappy that the *Sunday Times* had been portrayed as a loss-making paper. In his memoirs he recalled being deeply upset as he sat in the House of Commons on 28 January listening to John Biffen describing the *Sunday Times* as not a going concern. "It was for me, sitting gagged and bound in the Press Gallery, perhaps the most bitter and frustrating moment of the whole affair."

But Evans, with Murdoch's assistance, had gagged and bound himself. As Magnus Linklater, one of his close colleagues on the *Sunday Times,* later pointed out, "Evans knew in advance that the whole object of the exercise was to steer Biffen in that direction. He knew the figures would be shaped to portray the papers as loss makers. If he felt so strongly about it, did he not have a duty as editor of that paper to reveal them?" At the time Evans appeared committed to Murdoch; some of his associates on the *Sunday Times*, still anxious at the idea of the wolfish Murdoch taking over their paper, were disappointed in his attitude. Most of the "cardinals", the senior journalists whose opinions Evans had been seeking and those who were his associates in the consortium, still hoped that the consortium could succeed. Harry Evans had now decided not to give them public support but says he secretly fed them his director's financial reports.

Some journalists remained unwavering in their hostility to Murdoch. From Washington, the *Times* correspondent Patrick Brogan sent a long telex to Rees-Mogg to warn that Murdoch's promises were meaningless. He asserted that the *Sun*'s reports in the 1979 election were utterly corrupt, because they were designed to present a Tory view of the world "rather than a description of the way the world in fact is. This is Mr Murdoch's doing." For Brogan the bottom line was that "Mr Murdoch runs very many, very bad newspapers". From London Rees-Mogg replied that he disagreed. Brogan told the *Baltimore Sun* that "no honest journalist could work for Murdoch" and resigned on principle.

When the *Sunday Times* journalists' chapel met at Gray's Inn Road, many of them argued, as did the *New Statesman*, that there was an obvious conspiracy between the government, Thomsons and Murdoch, to force the sale through. Thus Thomsons had set an artificial deadline, the government was accepting this as written in stone, and Murdoch was saying that if the Monopolies Commission were invoked, he would withdraw. And that, said Thomsons, would mean the end of *The Times* and *Sunday Times*.

The journalists voted to use legal action to force a referral to the Monopolies Commission. They hired solicitors, put together a dossier on Murdoch, and prepared a financial prospectus to show that the *Sunday Times* was definitely a going concern. The minister had said that the *Sunday Times* losses in 1980 had been £600,000. The journalists' figures showed a profit of £1,240,000.

Murdoch, according to Evans, was exceedingly nervous at the

prospect of the court action. The journalists, worried about their own costs, decided they should approach him again. One of their problems was to decide what they really did want. Did they really prefer Rothermere and the *Daily Mail* as owners? The one thing they could agree on was the need for more serious undertakings on additional independence, and those fast became the central issue.

On the evening of Friday 6 February, they met Murdoch, and found him impressive and straightforward, "a refreshing change from the ineffectual Thomson management people we were used to", said Linklater. He appeared to make some concessions. The national directors could have a special voting share to protect their status, and to give them some "teeth". He would allow two journalists on the board, but he refused to give journalists any say in the appointment of the editor. "I'm not having elections," he said.

The journalists' committee drew up what he had agreed in as tight a legal form as possible. They saw him twice more on Saturday and persuaded themselves that he had made further significant concessions. But Murdoch made it clear that if they still went to court the following Monday, then "all bets are off" – he would withdraw even the undertakings he had already given.

That put the fox among them. On the evening of that Saturday, 7 February, as the paper was being put to bed, another NUJ chapel meeting was called to discuss whether, in the light of the new undertakings that Murdoch had given, the court action should go ahead or be called off.

It was an emotional occasion. Some journalists were afraid that they would all be bankrupted and Murdoch would win anyway; others argued that they would be bankrupted and the paper then closed; others that if Murdoch did not get the paper, Associated Newspapers would – and might be even worse employers.

John Barry, a brisk writer, and one of the journalists who had negotiated with Murdoch, had dropped his opposition. He said of him privately to Harry Evans, "The man's charm is *lethal*. One minute he's swimming along with a smile, then *snap*! There's blood in the water. Your head's gone." None the less, Barry, along with Hugo Young, the political editor, now advised voting for Murdoch and dropping the court action.

Their change of heart swayed many people. One of the few executives to stand out against Murdoch was Magnus Linklater. Almost in tears, he argued passionately against caving in. They had gone this far, he said, because they did not trust Murdoch. That was the issue. In the end, however, the journalists voted to stop their action and to accept Murdoch as the least of the many evils confronting them. Fourteen people voted against. Later they called themselves the Gravediggers Club and had T-shirts made, printed with the slogan: "Don't Blame Us. We Voted Against".

It was all over. Murdoch would be the next owner.

Rees-Mogg had made it clear that he would not stay as editor of *The Times* under any new proprietor and on 17 February Murdoch formally offered the job to Evans. "I wanted to get the energy of the *Sunday Times* into *The Times*," he explained much later.

Harry Evans accepted. "Ambition and conceit were two of the elements," he admitted later. "I wanted to edit *The Times* of London. It was the most famous paper in the world. Nobody could resist it." He also thought that he could deal with Murdoch. Revealingly, he later said,

> Every editor, and many a politician who deals with Murdoch, thinks that they're the one who is going really to change him. They're like a woman who goes out with a womanizer. She thinks, "This time, this time he really means it. He really loves me. He'll really marry me." Well, Murdoch's like a womanizer in that sense. He has this fatal capacity to instil the confidence in you that you and he have a special, exclusive relationship. It's a wonderful con trick.

Enraptured, Evans went to lunch with Murdoch at the Savoy, made a tearful speech of farewell to the *Sunday Times* staff and prepared to cross the bridge to *The Times*. That afternoon, Murdoch had to persuade *The Times* board of the wisdom of his choice. He had already agreed to the appointment of two new independent national directors; he now proposed that these should be Denis Hamilton and Sir Edward Pickering, the man who had taught him the rudiments of popular journalism on the *Daily Express* in the early 1950s, and who was later editor of the *Daily Express*. After some protective snarling by the old-time dogs, Pickering was absorbed into this exalted company. They were then able to get down to the business of approving the new editors.

Dacre, who disliked Evans and felt he had lowered the tone of the *Sunday Times*, believed he was quite unsuitable as editor of *The Times*. Hamilton agreed. He later wrote that he had told Murdoch that "it would turn out disastrously", but he did not speak out forcefully at this meeting. Murdoch was granted the man he described as "the best journalist in Britain".

There was no problem about the man whom he wanted to edit the *Sunday Times*. To the surprise of many journalists, Murdoch had plumped for Frank Giles, the honourable sixty-two-year-old deputy editor of the newspaper.

Though startled into glory at a late age, Giles comported himself well. He had once worked in the Foreign Office for Ernest Bevin and had hoped to be an ambassador. He always retained something of the air of a diplomat, an impeccably dressed gentleman who would be thought quite at home in St James's Palace or the Quai d'Orsay. He was hardly an obvious Murdoch man, but he was a professional journalist and was flattered by Murdoch's invitation. He went to see his new employer and found Murdoch leaning back in his chair, twiddling his glasses round and round by their side pieces. Giles wistfully recalled later, "I told him I had known his father. He did not seem particularly interested."

THE VILLAGE

With Times Newspapers, Murdoch had also bought himself 5 per cent of a goldmine. "I did not know it at the time," he says. "Nor did Thomsons."

The goldmine was Reuters, the traditional news agency, suddenly transformed in value through its importance as a tool of the international financial services market.

In the first half of the 1980s, Reuters was floated as a public company, with the purpose of enriching its owners, newspaper proprietors of Great Britain, Australia and New Zealand, Murdoch prominent among them. "Reuters," says Murdoch, "is a key story in the information revolution. A real key." And it was a key to much more than newspapers. It was also integral to the arguments promoted by UNESCO in the 1970s and early 1980s about "cultural imperialism" and "information sovereignty".

Reuters was created in the 1850s by a German Jew who became a Christian and changed his name from Israel Beer Josaphat to Paul Julius Reuter. Telegraph cable had just been laid under the Channel and Reuter saw an opportunity to link the London and Paris Stock Exchanges. But he did not restrict himself to share prices. He used the cable to transmit other news as well and thus soon became a power in British journalism. He insisted on limiting news to verifiable facts. As a result, Reuter's organization soon developed a reputation for terse accuracy on which it prided itself ever after.

The news agency was not itself profitable – at any time in its history. Reuter made money by supplying commercial information to private subscribers and by a private telegram service. Reuters became a public and rich company.

During the First World War, there were shortlived fears that it could fall under German influence, and a group was formed to privatize it again. In the 1920s, rather than being refloated on the market, it was sold to the Press Association. A new crisis arose during the Second World War when the loss of its Axis subscribers put the operation in financial jeopardy. Despite parliamentary misgivings, the Fleet Street press barons, the Newspaper Publishers' Association, agreed to buy 50 per cent of the company for £170,000, and created the "Reuters Trust" to manage the agency.

After the war, Reuters continued to build on its reputation as a safe, sober and reliable purveyor of the news from around the world, but made very little money. In 1963, Gerald Long, a former correspondent, became chief executive as the company teetered on the edge of bankruptcy. There was talk of accepting a subsidy

from the British government. Long rejected that and decided to
follow the lead of the company's founder – "Follow the cable."

At the end of the 1950s, a new generation of international
cables had been laid, much more reliable than short-wave radio
transmissions, which were crackly and apt to break. Reuters had
already leased land lines over Europe, and in 1960 it leased its first
transatlantic cable circuit. It was able to transform its transatlantic
circuit, to carry telephone as well as teleprinter traffic. The circuit
could be split into twenty-two teleprinter channels in each direction. But now technical changes followed each other with dizzying
speed; within a year that number of circuits was doubled. By the
end of the decade Reuters was leasing two million miles of teleprinter line. Soon even that was a tiny number.

Until then ticker tape had been the standard means of transmitting stock exchange prices; it was reliable, but cumbersome and
slow. The nascent computer industry was beginning to change all
that. Long bought the rights from a US firm to supply stock
market quotations to subscribers through video terminals linked
to a central computer.

After the 1971 collapse of the Bretton Woods pegged exchange
rate system, money became a commodity to be traded like any
other, and the volume of trading grew enormously. Commercial
firms needed to hedge their positions. Speculation became a
growth industry. Long realized that banks and money traders
needed faster information on market movements, and Reuters
devised a computerized system called Monitor which would use
computers to make currency trading instantaneous worldwide,
creating a global market-place.

The system was launched in the aftermath of the 1973 Middle
East war, during the Arab oil embargo, when currencies were
unusually volatile and trading volume high. Within a few years
Reuters' financial services had over 15,000 subscribers in 122 countries and carried quotes on more than 100 currencies, over 135
commodities and over 40,000 stocks and bonds. In 1980 Reuters
refined the service to allow hundreds of its subscribers to negotiate
confidential currency deals on a one-to-one basis. Dealers all over
the world could conclude transactions on their screens in just four
seconds – at least eleven seconds faster than by telephone. Within

a decade, Reuters' revenue had grown from £13.8 million a year to £180 million. Reuters was spinning money for itself and the world's financial markets.

When Murdoch bought his share with Times Newspapers in 1981, there was already discussion among the other shareholders, the Fleet Street proprietors, of taking the company public so that they could all profit from their suddenly very valuable holdings. The most eager was Lord Matthews of Express Newspapers.

Glen Renfrew, who succeeded Gerald Long as chief executive of Reuters after Long went to work for Murdoch, recalled speaking to Murdoch about the profit potential in early 1981. Murdoch was fascinated by the whole business of information services, and by the use that Reuters was making of satellites; in New York he would visit Reuters' satellite farm outside the city. He was keen to see Reuters grow as fast as possible and for it to go public, so that he could offset the losses from Times Newspapers. But unlike some of the other barons, he did not seem to Renfrew to be merely intent on stripping the assets of Reuters for his own company. Renfrew found him a useful ally on the board in face of the greed of some of his peers.

Reuters' sudden new profits coincided with increasingly polemical attacks, from the Soviet Union and some Third World governments, upon the role of the international news agencies and the spread of information from the West. In the 1970s and early 1980s they mounted a campaign against "Western cultural imperialism" and in favour of "information sovereignty". In retrospect it could be seen as a desperate Soviet attempt to halt the spread of information carried by computerization and by satellites. But at the same time real concerns were expressed in Tunisia and many other developing countries.

It was true that Western organizations dominated the news flow. At least 80 per cent of international "news" was supplied by Reuters, Associated Press, United Press International and Agence France Presse. The daily output of these four agencies was vast. They were increasingly accused of selecting and distorting news about the Third World in order to pander to the prejudices of their predominantly Western markets. To Third World governments which controlled their own media, it seemed absurd to allow Western news organizations unlimited freedom. By the mid-1970s more and more such governments, encouraged by the Soviet Union, were insisting that news was a commodity which they should control. Their demands took form in a series of polemical UNESCO resolutions which were to prove disastrous for that organization, if only because they were contrary to the basic tenets of freedom of information enshrined by the United Nations after the Second World War.

The Russians also saw satellite broadcasting as a threat to their sovereignty – or rather to their ability to deny information to their citizens, and the citizens of the states they dominated. UNESCO agreed, over the opposition of the US, Britain, Canada and West Germany, that there should be no satellite broadcasts without the consent of receiving countries. All programmes should "respect . . . the right of all countries and peoples to preserve their cultures".

One study conducted for UNESCO in the 1970s showed that while Western Europe imported a third of its television programmes, Africa, the Middle East and Latin America imported about half. Asian countries, apart from Japan and China, imported more. The bulk of all imports came from the United States, which even then was exporting some 150,000 hours a year, most of it TV series and feature films.

The idea that television was a form of American "cultural imperialism" was widespread as early as the 1970s, and not only in the communist bloc and Third World. There was also concern in Australia. And in France, Jack Lang, the Minister of Culture, accused the USA of advocating "the freedom of the fox in the barnyard".

A UNESCO report, directed by Sean MacBride, suggested, ludicrously, that while journalists should be free, they must understand that their duty was to uphold friendly relations between states, enhance national dignity, promote peace, disarmament and other worthy causes. And so it continued. UNESCO seemed unable to understand that with information becoming more and more important a world commodity, governments would impoverish themselves all the more by cutting themselves out of the loop.

Rupert Murdoch's guru, Arthur C. Clarke, was sanguine about such attempts to stop the tide. In 1983 he suggested, in words which were prescient of events in China and Eastern Europe at the end of the 1980s, that the debate on the free flow of information would be settled by engineers, not by politicians. Governments would not for long be able to conceal the evidence of their crimes.

The very existence of new information channels, operating in real time and across all frontiers, will be a powerful influence for civilized behaviour. If you are arranging a massacre, it will be useless to shoot the cameraman who has so inconveniently appeared on the scene. His pictures will already be safe in the studio five thousand miles away and his final image may hang you.

That was somewhat optimistic, as the history of the rest of the decade showed. But Clarke did predict the way the communications revolution reported on and, in part, created images and events such as the young man facing the tanks in Tienanmen Square at the end of the decade.

AUSTRALIA

One of the happier events in Murdoch's fiftieth year was the birthday party which Anna organized at Cavan, soon after he acquired Times Newspapers. A small plane circled overhead, trailing a banner reading "HAPPY BIRTHDAY RUPIE". Parachutists plunged to the ground with a letter to Murdoch from the artist, Fred Williams, accepting a commission to paint his portrait. (Despite his admiration of and friendship for Williams, Murdoch did not like the finished picture. Like that of Winston Churchill by Graham Sutherland, it disappeared.) But from then on, 1981–2 was an unnerving year. Interest payments shot up from the equivalent of 36 per cent of operating income to 80 per cent. News

Corporation's pre-tax profits crashed from £26.1 million to £3.2 million. Earnings were poor and the income from Ansett became essential.

Times Newspapers was the big new drain, but the *New York Post* was still shedding money fast. Circulation had increased, but not enough for the paper to become profitable. Closer to Cavan, the strike-prone *Australian* continued to provide an object lesson in labour relations at their worst.

The Australian newspaper operations were under the charge of Ken Cowley, the printer who had joined him in Canberra – now managing director of News. Cowley was utterly loyal to Murdoch and rarely questioned his judgement. Working for him was "an adventure that eclipsed all my little dreams", he said much later.

The years since the 1975 strike had been turbulent, partly because of the hatred of Murdoch that had been engendered. Editors came and went quickly, and the paper's continued losses were irritating to News Corporation's managers who saw it, in Cowley's words, as "a bit of an indulgence by Rupert". The culture of News was resolutely profit-driven. The paper was also constantly hit by strikes, because as Cowley pointed out, "it was the most vulnerable paper, and the closest to Rupert's heart".

In the late 1970s Murdoch had come near to closing the paper. Cowley had persuaded him to keep it going. Many of the journalists who remained since the early, heady days of the paper had grown disillusioned with its lack of any direction except towards the right ever since. The difficulty was to find an editor who would prove to be effective. At one stage, Murdoch even gave the job to Sir Larry Lamb, the former editor of the *Sun*. This was not a success.

Still more frustrating was the long rearguard battle he had throughout 1981 to keep Channel 10 (as Channel O had been renamed) in Melbourne.

Everywhere there were problems. Every day Murdoch had to solve or at least alleviate them, in different parts of the globe. He was constantly on the phone, calling London, calling New York, calling Sydney, calling San Antonio, calling Adelaide, asking, demanding, shouting, ordering, soothing (sometimes), threatening with long silences (at other times). The empire was run, as one of his editors later put it, "by phone and by clone". On whatever continent he was, he phoned his influence, his personality, his force, down the line to his representatives and editors on the other continents. The time zones were the only control upon him, and as often as not he disregarded them, calling across the world at all times of day and night.

All the same, complications would arise. In London, the problems at *The Times* became insupportable to almost everyone involved.

LONDON

Harold Evans assumed his duties as editor of *The Times* just as Murdoch celebrated his fiftieth birthday. He was suffering from flu, but he visited the various departments and addressed the journalists in the reporters' area, making a powerful and, on many, a favourable impression.

He was very happy to be there, he said; it was a great honour to be editing *The Times*. It was a "splendid" paper and he intended to dedicate himself to its stability, independence and high quality. He hoped that the paper could end its reliance on subsidies. Murdoch's ownership gave it a great hope of getting on its feet.

In answer to questions, he promised that he would not make it look like the *Sunday Times*, which had a more theatrical layout. It would be wrong to inject similar drama into *The Times*; he wanted to reassert the paper's authority. His relationship with Murdoch was very good. The most impressive thing about him, said Evans, was his enthusiasm and his excitement with Times Newspapers. "In those first months Murdoch did everything and more to support me editorially," Evans later acknowledged in his book *Good Times, Bad Times*.

Evans also wrote, however, that he was unhappy about the way in which Murdoch fired many of the company's advertising executives soon after he took over. Evans described the sackings as insensitive, unjust and bad for the business. Murdoch, for whom

The Times was an editorial and commercial "graveyard", was unapologetic and explained: "The people trying to sell space in *The Times* really had their hearts broken in the Thomson years." Gerald Long, the chief executive of Reuters whom Murdoch persuaded to become managing director of Times Newspapers, thought Murdoch's decision was the right one, and that the firings were reasonably undertaken.

The worst problems, though, would arise on the editorial floor. Although Evans promoted some *Times* journalists – notably Charles Douglas-Home, who had hoped to be editor, and who now became his deputy – he also imported a number of close colleagues. Among them was Anthony Holden, a former *Sunday Times* journalist and biographer of Prince Charles, who became features editor. From outside journalism, as an adviser and leader writer, came an associate of former Prime Minister Callaghan, Bernard Donoughue, whom Gerald Long described as a "saloon bar Machiavelli". Their arrival, their close relationship with the editor and their generally higher salaries were widely resented by many of the old *Times* men and women, who felt they were being shifted aside by a new mafia. The new men made no secret of their intention to change everything by yesterday. As Evans began to impose his ideas and his vigorous if somewhat chaotic methods, the division between old and new blood increased.

There were undoubtedly major problems on the *Times* staff in 1981. Whole areas of interest were poorly or inadequately reported. Stories, according to Evans, would be lost in some Bermuda Triangle in the newsroom. Many journalists on the paper feared changes even before they began. Some of the opposition to Evans was from traditionalists who disliked the larger photographs and headlines that he introduced. But some of it was more considered. Murdoch felt that the editorials became erratic, even inconsistent. Gerald Long said: "Harry lacked the mental and physical stamina needed: the pressure of running a daily paper is enormous." When editions of *The Times* missed the trains, Evans became rather unpopular among News International's circulation managers.

By the autumn of 1981 many of the *Times* journalists were very unhappy, Charles Douglas-Home among them. At one stage,

Edward Mortimer, a leader writer of the old school, went to Lord Dacre, one of the independent directors, to complain. Dacre said: "Our job is to protect the editor from the proprietor if need be. What can we do if the editor himself is ruining the paper?"

More and more people volunteered to take the severance payments Murdoch was offering in order to cut staff – one month's pay for every year worked – and leave the paper. By the end of 1981, over fifty people had gone. That was fine with Murdoch: the trouble was that Evans hired as many new people – some of them on higher salaries than those they replaced. That had not been Murdoch's plan. Although circulation started to rise, Murdoch began to have doubts about Evans's vaunted brilliance. He felt that Evans was spending freely but not always consistently. For his part, Evans was frustrated by the fact that Murdoch had still not given him his formal editorial budget, an important issue as the guarantees allowed the editor independence within a set budget. Evans complained that Murdoch gave him no idea what the figures of the paper really showed. Gerald Long was critical of both men: "Harry's idea of a budget was having the accountants on the floor below, pushing up five-pound notes through the cracks. Rupert had his own ideas of financial control which, in my view, did not produce true control or reliable forecasting. Rupert is a gambler: he had a martingale and it worked, most of the time."

Evans became both more suspicious of his proprietor and yet more anxious to please him. Murdoch, Evans said, created an aura – one of scorn for the Social Democrats, and bleak hostility towards the Tory "wets" who did not like Mrs Thatcher's toughness. The Labour Party was of course beyond the pale. He would send Evans right-wing articles marked "Worth reading!" and would jab his finger at *Times* headlines which he thought should have been more supportive of Mrs Thatcher, saying, "You're always getting at her!" According to Evans he hated "balance" and "objectivity" and kept calling for more "conviction", which, Evans thought, meant more Tory cheerleading. "None of this," wrote Evans later, "represented a reasonable exchange of views between editor and proprietor, unexceptional in any newspaper. The tone was assertive and hostile to debate."

Murdoch, who had never accepted the Divine Right of Editors, remembered the problem differently. "Harry used to come to me and say" – (he mimicked a fast and mouse-like whisper) – " 'I'll do anything you like. Just tell me what you'd like.' And I'd say, 'Harry, nothing. Please get on with it. But please be consistent.' " Evans, he claimed, was forever switching the paper's policy on big issues. "The only thing I did say, and I put it into writing, was: 'You must have some underlying philosophical direction and follow it. Consistency is what we need.' " Evans claimed that by "consistency" Murdoch meant pro-Thatcherite views. Not so, said Murdoch, "I never discussed politics. I used to complain if it was anti-American, which it wasn't much."

Deprived of the glow of Murdoch's affection, Evans became more and more nervous. Murdoch later told an Australian journalist that Evans would come into his office and speak rapidly and disjointedly. "You've done all this and what can we do . . . you don't know . . . what we are . . . You must come here more often. It's wonderful to have you here." Murdoch then imitated Evans returning to his own office, laying his head in his hands and saying, "My God, the *pressure* I'm under. You don't know."

When Murdoch was not in town he often dealt with Evans through Gerald Long. Long was to become an instructive casualty of the News Corp style. A cultivated, military-looking man, he indulged a passion for French wine, food, language and literature, was highly opinionated and did not suffer fools easily.

At Reuters he had been an inspired, if maverick and gruff chief executive. With a small group of expert colleagues he had brought the agency to the front line of the information revolution. He considered Murdoch a friend and had joined him as managing director of Times Newspapers on a handshake and a brief word about salary and pension rights. Now, in the Gray's Inn Road, he became, in a sense, Murdoch's *doppelgänger*. Murdoch exerts such a strong force that those around him constantly try to please him, and to foresee his wishes. Long became aggressive, suspicious, and cantankerous. Richard Searby commented, "It's pretty difficult being one of Rupert's direct line managers, when he is involved on a daily basis. Gerry was used to being really chief executive, but he couldn't run Times Newspapers like Reuters."

Murdoch's presence was too powerful. Edward Pickering, whom Murdoch had chosen as national director, suggested, "Perhaps some of Rupert's boundless energy and aggression rubbed off on Gerry." Another thing which rubbed off was the kick-butt management style which seemed to characterize so many Murdoch operations yet which Murdoch, by virtue of his remote-control techniques, often appeared to be above.

The butt that all were free to kick belonged to Frank Giles at the *Sunday Times*. According to Evans, Murdoch allegedly declared on one occasion that Frank Giles and his wife were "communists". They were as unlikely a pair of revolutionaries as has ever graced a London dinner party, but they were certainly more pro-*détente* and less passionately anti-communist than Murdoch. To Murdoch, this looked like limp-wristedness.

Giles shared Long's enthusiasm for France, occasioning an initial friendly exchange on the origins of French words, but soon the relationship deteriorated. Long, according to Giles, began writing him memos of "boorish rudeness". Giles even opened a "Long insult file" which soon became quite fat.

When Murdoch was in London on a Saturday evening, he would often bound across the bridge from *The Times* to pick up the first edition of the Sunday paper. If there had been no industrial action by the printers, this usually appeared off the presses at around cocktail time.

The fastidious Giles began to dread these occasions. Murdoch tore through the paper, page by page, growling at anything he disliked, criticizing headlines, pictures, layouts, snarling, "What do you want to print rubbish like that for?"

Murdoch never gave explicit instructions to Giles about the political direction of the *Sunday Times*. But, like all his editors, Giles came soon to know Murdoch's views. When reading a piece critical of Reagan's policies in Central America, he would complain of the reporter, David Blundy – a fine war correspondent who was eventually killed in El Salvador – "That man's a commie." If there were others in Giles's office, then Murdoch could appear even more aggressive. Giles said that in front of such an audience, "Murdoch's bitter animus, stridently voiced, became especially hard to bear . . . "

One Saturday afternoon Frank Giles saw Murdoch when he was clearly happy – he told Giles that he and Anna had just had lunch with the Queen Mother. Giles knew too that Murdoch was capable of acts of private kindness. When his chauffeur was diagnosed as dying of cancer, Murdoch did everything possible for him and his family. When the other drivers thanked him, he seemed embarrassed by their knowledge of his generosity.

Throughout 1981 the fortunes of the Thatcher government, and of News, were ebbing. Britain was experiencing one of the worst recessions since the Second World War. Murdoch and Long were at pains to impress upon both Evans and Giles how much money the company was losing. Crisis hit in September when the *Sunday Times* branch of one of the two main print unions, the National Graphical Association, threatened "to withdraw co-operation" in support of another pay claim. Murdoch had not acted aggressively against the unions when he took over the papers. Now, however, he declared that if the NGA would not work normally, then everyone in the newspapers would be locked out. No one would be paid, not even the horrified journalists, who were used to being cosseted by Thomsons.

In the event one issue was lost and the NGA climbed down. But the gulf between many journalists and Murdoch grew.

He demanded that the unions agree to shed 600 jobs within "days". The papers were "bleeding to death", he said, and without such cuts he would have to close them. At the same time, to protect the trademarks in that event, Murdoch was quietly trying to remove the titles of *The Times* and *Sunday Times* from Times Newspapers Limited to News International, his company which owned the *News of the World* and the *Sun*.

On 5 February Murdoch met with senior *Times* executives to brief them on the financial crisis and to warn them that the papers might have to close if the unions were not more co-operative. Charles Douglas-Home asked if the titles would be available to a liquidator. Murdoch replied simply that they "might not be". This elliptical answer rippled around Gray's Inn Road and *Sunday Times* journalists went to Companies House to check the Times Newspaper mortgage register. They found that in the list of Times

Newspaper assets there was now no mention of "titles and copy-rights". They had been transferred to News International.

The effect of this transaction was to strip Times Newspapers of its principal assets, the titles. If the company were liquidated, the titles would remain part of the Murdoch stable, to be dusted off and republished at will. Sir Edward Pickering later agreed, "It was done to give Rupert protection if anything went really wrong. It's true that it was moving the assets." Searby later said:

> The losses we were sustaining at Times Newspapers were huge for News to bear at that time. We were much smaller then. The unions thought they had us over a barrel. So we thought, sup-pose we take the trademark and simply transfer it to News. Then if there was a terrible strike, we could simply close Times Newspapers and then at once start up a new subsidiary called New Times Newspapers. We wanted to preserve the papers, not destroy them. Our solicitors, Farrers, told us in writing that this would be OK.

Both Evans and Giles had been at the board meeting in December 1981 at which the removal of the titles had been approved. Neither of them had then objected. However, when their journalists pointed out the significance of the matter, Evans authorized *The Times* to investigate. In February 1982, the paper published a detailed story. Lord Dacre, who liked and respected Murdoch but questioned his methods, declared that the lack of previous consultation was a *prima facie* violation of the terms under which Murdoch had acquired the papers. William Rees-Mogg called for the transfer to be cancelled. Denis Hamilton was furious. The government said that it was studying the affair.

Murdoch asked Richard Searby to come over from Melbourne and sort out the mess. On 17 February, News International announced that the titles were being transferred back to Times Newspapers.

In his memoirs, Evans subsequently accused News International of "fraudulent" behaviour over the titles, a charge which the company categorically denied. The affair marked the death of the relationship between Murdoch and Evans. Rumours to this effect began to circulate in Fleet Street and Evans demanded that Murdoch publicly deny them. Murdoch did so, praising the improvements Evans had made to *The Times*.

There had been improvements, but the last year had wrought havoc among the staff. Their discontent coalesced around Charles Douglas-Home, Evans's deputy. In his memoirs Evans accused Douglas-Home of conniving with Murdoch against him; Douglas-Home denied this and Gerald Long maintained: "Charlie was loyal to the paper, not to Harry, but he never connived with Murdoch against Harry – he was an upright and honest man."

Communication from editor to proprietor now tended to take the form of barbed memos loaded with surface flattery. On 21 February, Evans wrote, "May I say how much I admire and support the battle which I feel sure we are going to win [with the unions] . . . "

Evans's note was written with an eye to Murdoch's prejudices. Commenting on a rise in circulation, "We collect the usual cheap sneers for being competitive and wanting readers." He went on to drop a name, and a possible opportunity for the proprietor. "By the way, Henry Kissinger offered to write pieces (for paying his fare or something like that). He is president of the US football league and knows a lot about the game. If you like the idea I'll take it further – or you can meet him when he comes here in April on his delayed trip."

Evans wanted to recruit "an intelligent polemicist". "I did talk to Alexander Chancellor (the editor of the *Spectator*) but came to the conclusion he represents part of the effete old tired England" – the class Murdoch most despised.

Evans concluded, "There's more but you have a lot on your plate. Thank you again for the opportunity and ideas. We are all 100 per cent behind you in this great battle and I'm glad we're having it now."

Murdoch replied coolly, complaining that several well-known journalists had recently decided to leave *The Times*. He went on:

My chief area of concern about the paper is one I have raised with you several times: the paper's stand on major issues. Of course it takes attitudes, but I fail to find any consistency in them, anything that indicates unmistakably the clear position of conscience that a great newspaper must be seen to hold. Just what that position is, it is your duty to define, and it cannot be mine. But it must be defined with clarity and authority and even repetition.

In a formal "Dear Chairman" reply, Evans was more combative, though he ended: "But of course, while being consistent in our editorial position, we have deliberately opened the paper to a diversity of views in the belief that truth will triumph and that our readers, especially, want a fully informed debate rather than a monolithic line of propaganda." The letter was signed "Yours loyally, Harold".

On 24 February, Evans sent a memo asking Murdoch for his views on how the paper should cover the impending budget, which all British papers always covered extensively. Murdoch replied cordially enough,

Dear Harry,

I don't see why we should be writing notes to each other when my door is always open to you . . . The sports pages look terrific . . . I don't know how to advise you about the budget . . . Surely you need to know the size and content of the budget statement before committing the exact amount of space.

The staff was in turmoil. Both Charles Douglas-Home and John Grant, the managing editor, decided to resign, but stayed at Murdoch's request.

On 1 March Harry Evans's father died. He was deeply affected. Murdoch wrote him a note of condolence saying that it was thirty years since his own father died and he remembered it as yesterday. "A good father-and-son relationship is one of the best experiences in life. You must take any time you need to attend to the necessary family arrangements."

Then, four days after the funeral, on 9 March, budget day, the busiest day of the year for any newspaper, Murdoch called Evans to his office and asked for his resignation. Evans said he refused and asked Murdoch why. Murdoch said, "The place is in chaos.

You can't see the wood from the trees . . . Your senior staff is up in arms."

Murdoch had already seen Douglas-Home that morning at his flat in St James's, for breakfast, and had asked him if he would take over the editorship. Douglas-Home had accepted. Later that day Evans went to his deputy and told him he had no integrity, no honour. According to Evans, Douglas-Home replied, "I would do anything to edit *The Times*, wouldn't you?" Douglas-Home also allegedly told Evans that he was "too close to Murdoch, too desirous of his approval, too ready to do his bidding".

By now, having secured almost three-quarters of the reduction in the workforce he had demanded, Murdoch announced that the papers were safe after all. But Gray's Inn Road was now riven by rumour. On 12 March *The Times* report on a successful outcome of the talks with the unions noted: "Mr Harold Evans, the editor of *The Times*, said he had no comment to make on reports circulating about his future as editor. He was on duty last night as usual." However, according to Searby, he had decided to leave and the only thing being discussed was the size of his golden handshake.

Next day, Evans agreed to resign, but then reconsidered and went back to the newspaper. Crucially, however, he made no attempt to rally the staff. If he had done so, and had challenged Murdoch directly for interfering with the paper's independence, he might have secured the support of the journalists, though many were as dissatisfied with him as others were with Murdoch.

Murdoch made a statement denying all reports of editorial disagreements between Evans and himself.

Evans was continually on the phone to the national directors for advice. One of them, Lord Robens, pointed out in a radio programme that he was "the most protected editor in the world". He could not be forced to resign if he thought he was under improper pressure. He had only to complain formally to the directors. In fact he made no formal complaint on which they could act.

Murdoch flew back to New York for a fifty-first birthday party, leaving Gerry Long and Richard Searby to negotiate Evans's terms. Searby said later, "There was no question of Evans's departure being conditional on agreement or compensation, because under his contract what he was entitled to was fixed: Murdoch had indicated a willingness to pay more and that was the subject of discussion." He added, "I told Rupert that it would be hard for Harry to get another job comparable to *The Times*, and it was basically our mistake for hiring him in the first place. We wanted to be generous and to make the pay-off as tax efficient as possible."

Evans was understandably emotional and uncertain what to do. His talks with Searby were painful. He described the Australian lawyer as having the debonair charm of a riverboat gambler. Long, however, found Searby meticulous, and totally honest.

On Saturday, 13 March, a group of *Times* journalists representing Journalists of *The Times* issued an extraordinary statement calling for Evans to resign and for Douglas-Home to take his place. "Our concern is that the gradual erosion of editorial standards from within might leave us with no paper worth saving. The way the paper is laid out and run has changed so frequently that stability has been destroyed." Only a few of the journalists had approved this statement, but it was clear that at least a part of the staff sided with the owner against the editor. Others, said Edward Mortimer, "were as dissatisfied with Murdoch as anybody. But Harry's fault was the greatest. He never asked for our support because he never made a decision to fight. Most of the damage Murdoch had done to *The Times*, up to that point, he had done through Harry." Evans was in a lonely place – rejected by both his proprietor and a large number of his staff.

Evans hung on through the weekend, wrestling with his nerves and his conscience. On Monday 15 March, he signed. News International paid £120,000 into the company's pension plan, gave him another £150,000 in cash, extended an interest-free mortgage for another year, and gave him his company car.

That evening Evans read to the press a short statement that had been agreed with Searby and Murdoch, saying he should not prolong the differences between himself and Murdoch and was therefore now resigning. He went home, where Tina had organized an impromptu party, filled with friends who toasted Evans and cursed Murdoch.

Tony Holden left the paper in solidarity with Evans, without a pay-off. Bernard Donoughue was fired with a redundancy payment. He subsequently went to work as a financial adviser to Robert Maxwell, resigning some months before Maxwell's death in 1991. In an interview for this book in 1990, he compared Maxwell favourably to Murdoch and declared that the damage Murdoch had wrought to the fabric of British society was greater than that done to Britain by Hitler's bombs. Gerald Long, whom Murdoch removed as managing director of Times Newspapers soon after Evans's dismissal, also retained unhappy memories and said that working for News was the worst time of his professional life. He thought Evans did not have the necessary talents to edit *The Times*, but he too found Murdoch's management methods unbearable.

THE FALKLANDS

A few weeks after Evans resigned, Argentina invaded the Falkland Islands, and Britain went to war.

Murdoch himself shared Mrs Thatcher's determination that the islands must be recovered. On 22 April, when he was made the first "Communications Man of the Year" by the American Jewish Congress in New York, he told the audience that the conflict between Argentina and Britain should be taken as a reminder of what might happen in the Middle East: the issue was democracy versus dictatorship and the case for supporting Britain was the same as that for supporting Israel.

All of Murdoch's British editors reacted characteristically. At the *Sunday Times* Frank Giles published a measured response in which he hoped that a peaceful solution could be negotiated and tried to exonerate the Foreign Office, which many others were blaming for having failed to predict the invasion.

At *The Times*, Charles Douglas-Home, Harry Evans's successor, called the attack "Naked Aggression", unparalleled since the days of Adolf Hitler, and then declared, "We are all Falklanders now." The paper questioned the ability of the Foreign Secretary, Lord Carrington, to carry on in the face of Foreign Office failure to predict the invasion. That same day Carrington resigned. The *Sun* declared that the Foreign Office had been a haven of appeasers since Munich.

The *Sun* fought a famous war which clearly reflected the personality of its editor, Kelvin MacKenzie, whom Murdoch had appointed in place of Sir Larry Lamb. Murdoch was looking to MacKenzie to liven things up, and he was not disappointed.

MacKenzie was born in 1946; he was a man of stout suburban origins who liked to affect a working-class yobbishness in person and in print. His parents were both journalists and they sent MacKenzie to Alleyns School, a good middle-class establishment. He left with only one O-level pass in English – an unusual, indeed distinguished, rite of passage – and decided to become a journalist. By the mid-1970s he was a sub editor on the *Sun*. From the subs' desk MacKenzie would scream abuse at the reporters who turned in copy he thought inadequate.

Murdoch liked his bloodymindedness and sent him for a spell to the *New York Post*. Back in London, he was lured off to the *Daily Express*, but when, in 1982, Murdoch disposed of Lamb, he invited MacKenzie back as editor. MacKenzie took to the editorship of the *Sun* as to the manner born. Using Cockney rhyming slang, he called the paper "the Currant Bun", and later "Curranticus Bunnicus".

The MacKenzie era was from the start very different from that of Sir Larry. For the *Sun* reporters, it was like being on a roller coaster with a crazed fiend at the controls. He immediately plunged the paper further downmarket or, as Murdoch would put it, made it more popular, in pursuit of the *Star*, which Express Newspapers published to undercut the *Sun*. MacKenzie soon became a legend for his abusive, scatological language and for the crude, witty, sometimes untruthful and sometimes brilliant paper he edited. Sex, violence, sport and Thatcherism were the essential ingredients of his brew. Walter Terry, the *Sun*'s distinguished political editor who survived beyond the Lamb regime, recalled being struck by the new editor's violently right-wing views and hatred for what he called "fucking foreigners".

MacKenzie had a fearsome temper and he would bawl out his reporters in the most ferocious "bollocking sessions". As far as

Walter Terry could see, MacKenzie had no time for politics and Terry's parliamentary work. "He was fond of saying he supposed we had to fill the paper with my kind of crap." Hyperactive, like Murdoch MacKenzie hardly slept and would ring news editors at 6 a.m.

His whole public persona was one of demonic brutishness and a disdain for Murdoch's pet hate, the Establishment. Next to that, he despised the socialist sympathies of the *Daily Mirror* and the liberalism of the *Guardian*, which he called "the World's Worst Newspaper"; other "upmarket" papers were merely "the Unpopulars".

Like Murdoch, MacKenzie was personally puritanical, and devoted to his family. He drank very little – because he had a very low alcohol threshold. He functioned best on a high charge of adrenalin – so he continually tried to create emergencies. He loved to force massive changes on to the front page so that he was always in the midst of rescuing the show, proving that the other "fucking cunts" were just "hopeless fucking wankers". His motto, and one by which he abided tenaciously, was "SHOCK AND AMAZE ON EVERY PAGE".

Murdoch seemed to treat MacKenzie like a wayward son, an erratic genius who had to be humoured. He once told Charles Wintour, the doyen of Fleet Street editors, that he had never really understood him. "MacKenzie is what he is. He's out there, screaming and shouting, and he's good. Somehow it works."

After the invasion of the Falklands, war fever gripped the *Sun* as nowhere else. *Sun* reporters gave themselves military ranks, a picture of Winston Churchill was hung up in the newsroom and, when the task force set sail for the South Atlantic, a new slogan was coined: "The paper that supports our boys". After a spate of leaks to other papers, MacKenzie stuck up a poster next to Churchill saying, "Careless talk costs jobs".

When the paper's reporter in Buenos Aires filed a story on hopes for peace, the *Sun* ran the story skilfully distorted under the headline "STICK IT UP YOUR JUNTA". On another occasion, the *Sun* announced: "The first missile to hit Galtieri's gauchos will come with love from the *Sun*. And just in case he doesn't get the message, the weapon will have painted on the side,

'Up yours, Galtieri' and will be signed by Tony Snow, our man aboard HMS *Invincible*." This slapstick type of coverage was satirized by *Private Eye* with a *Sun*-type competition, "KILL AN ARGIE AND WIN A METRO". But MacKenzie was immune to middle-class mockery. He plunged on, featuring the best "Argie bargie" jokes his readers could devise, sternly calling for a ban on Argentinean corned beef, and captioning one of his page-three girls with: "Britain's secret weapon in the Falklands dispute was revealed last night – it's undie-cover warfare."

The most infamous headline, "GOTCHA", to be splashed over the front page during the war, announced that the Argentinean cruiser *General Belgrano* had been attacked by a British submarine. It represented a visceral reaction in the newsroom to the news, which came through just before the first edition went to bed. As more stories came in during the night and the reporters realized that the *Belgrano* had been sunk with a crew of over 1,000 men, MacKenzie changed the front page totally: "DID 1,200 ARGIES DROWN?" read later editions. Next day the *Sun* tried to make further amends with the headline: "ALIVE! – Hundreds of Argies saved from Atlantic".

After HMS *Sheffield* was hit, passions became more inflamed. The BBC, which tried to give impartial accounts, became, as usual, a whipping boy for some right-wing Members of Parliament and their supporters in the press. The *Sun* published an editorial, "DARE CALL IT TREASON". Its first sentence, underlined, read, "There are traitors in our midst". The *Sun* also attacked the *Daily Mirror*, which had argued that "MIGHT ISN'T RIGHT" and had proposed a compromise settlement. "What is it but treason for this timorous, whining publication to plead day after day for appeasing the Argentinean dictators . . . " asked the *Sun*.

The *Mirror* responded with an editorial: "The Harlot of Fleet Street", which asserted that the *Sun* was said to be a "coarse and demented newspaper . . . It has long been a tawdry newspaper. But since the Falklands crisis began it has fallen from the gutter to the sewer . . . The *Sun* today is to journalism what Dr Joseph Goebbels was to truth. Even *Pravda* would blush to be bracketed with it . . . "

Writing in the *Sun*'s sister paper, *The Times*, Simon Jenkins agreed that the *Sun*'s editorial would have made Senator McCarthy blush. Soldiers in the Falklands seemed to agree; many were offended by the trivial, ghoulish jingoism of the *Sun*'s reports and headlines. All the same, MacKenzie was happy with his war record and the backing given by his proprietor.

MacKenzie continued the war with the *Mirror*. When its rival secured an exclusive interview with the widow of a war hero, the *Sun* simply fabricated its own WORLD EXCLUSIVE interview to spoil the *Mirror*'s story. The Press Council later came out with a stinging rebuke of this invention and called it "a deplorable, insensitive deception on the public", and the *Mirror* denounced the *Sun* as "a lying newspaper", declaring, "The *Sun* is to truth what the Borgias were to chastity."

The next Murdoch paper to stumble was the *Sunday Times*; indeed it took a spectacular fall, wittily described by Robert Harris in his book *Selling Hitler* – which subsequently became a TV mini-series, in which Barry Humphries played his compatriot, Rupert Murdoch.

In the spring of 1983, the so-called Diaries of Adolf Hitler were offered to the *Sunday Times* and *Times* by *Stern* magazine, one of Germany's largest mass-market weeklies. *Stern* would not permit full independent verification of the diaries. News Corporation then insisted that Lord Dacre, who was not only one of the independent directors of Times Newspapers but also the author of *The Last Days of Hitler* and former Regius Professor of Modern History at Oxford, be allowed to examine them.

At first Dacre was sceptical, but changed his mind when he saw the diaries in the bank vault in Zürich. He was assured by the men from *Stern* that the paper had been tested and the provenance established.

Murdoch, Richard Searby and others flew to Zürich to look at the diaries, and shook hands on a deal of $3.25 million for American, British and Commonwealth rights. But *Stern*, which had also been negotiating with *Newsweek*, informed Murdoch that the price had gone up another half million dollars. Murdoch was furious. He and *Newsweek* both began to walk away from any deal. When Murdoch was begged to return, as he knew he would be, the sums had become more realistic. He got what he regarded as a bargain-basement price: $400,000 for British and Commonwealth rights. Only $200,000 was to be paid at once (refundable if the diaries were proved to be not genuine) with the balance spread over two years.

On the evening of Thursday, 21 April, Murdoch called Frank Giles to tell him that he wanted the *Sunday Times* to carry news of the diaries' discovery the coming Sunday and extracts in the weeks thereafter. Giles asked about authenticity and Murdoch replied that Dacre was satisfied. Giles was elated at the prospect of the scoop. Other *Sunday Times* men, alarmed, warned Giles that the authentication process was incomplete. Murdoch himself had little sympathy with this line of enquiry.

By now he was very excited. When his old Oxford friend, Harry Pitt, dined with him and his mother in London, Murdoch said, "I'm not allowed to tell anyone, but I'll tell you. I've got the greatest journalistic scoop ever: Hitler's diaries!"

Dame Elisabeth was sceptical. "Rupert, you've been sold a pup," she said.

On the Saturday 23 April *The Times* published Dacre's testament to the diaries' authenticity:

When I entered the back room in the Swiss bank and turned the pages of those volumes and learnt the extraordinary story of their discovery, my doubts gradually dissolved. I am now satisfied that the documents are authentic, that the history of their wanderings since 1945 is true; and that the standard accounts of Hitler's writing habits, of his personality and even, perhaps, some public events may, in consequence, have to be revised.

But that very morning, as his article was read across the country, Dacre called Douglas-Home to tell him that he had begun to have doubts. Inexplicably Douglas-Home did not warn Frank Giles. And so the *Sunday Times* put together the first of the articles based on the diaries: "WORLD EXCLUSIVE: HOW THE DIARIES OF THE FUEHRER WERE FOUND IN AN EAST GERMAN HAYLOFT". The article claimed: "Hitler's diaries, which the *Sunday Times* is to serialize, have been submitted to the most rigorous tests to establish their authenticity. One of the world's leading experts on Hitler and the Nazi period, Hugh Trevor-Roper, Lord Dacre of Glanton, has staked his academic reputation on his conclusion."

That evening, after the first editions of the paper had been printed and were already on the trains, Giles called Dacre in Cambridge. Dacre told him that he was beginning to worry that he might be wrong. Giles was horrified: "I hope you are not going to make a 180-degree turn, are you?" he asked.

Dacre's reply led Giles to say, in front of a room crowded with *Sunday Times* journalists, "Oh, you are, are you?"

It was a moment of horror, if also one with a comic side. Some of the journalists felt that the presses should be stopped at once. Giles's deputy, Brian MacArthur, called Murdoch in New York for advice. The owner's reply was concise: "Fuck Dacre," he said. "Publish."

The following week, Dacre denounced the diaries as fakes. Soon after came the news that the diaries had been forged – by Konrad Kujau, a dealer in Nazi memorabilia.

Charles Douglas-Home apologized to Giles for not having relayed to him Dacre's doubts that fateful Saturday. An apology was due. If he had called Giles, the *Sunday Times* could have pulled the entire story, or at least have tempered its enthusiastic endorsement of the diaries. There was now no way, in the short term at least, of salvaging the paper's prestige. "What's happened to the *Sunday Times*?" asked the *New York Times*, and answered its own question: "Rupert Murdoch has, for one thing, with his talent for turning what he touches into dross."

But Murdoch was not particularly distressed. He lost no money at all: Stern had to refund the $200,000 he had paid in advance, the circulation of the *Sunday Times* rose 60,000 while the controversy raged, and 20,000 of those readers stayed with the paper. "After all, we are in the entertainment business," he said. It had merely been a Rupert Greene-type gamble which had not come off.

In England Hitler fever was rapidly overtaken by election fever. In May 1983, less than a year after her triumph in the Falklands War, Mrs Thatcher asked the country for a renewed mandate.

Given that there were three million unemployed at the time, this was anything but a foregone conclusion.

The *Sun* featured Mrs Thatcher as the Falklands heroine, contrasting the decisive nature of her leadership with the shambolic condition of the Labour Opposition. The Tories were said to be making a new Britain: it was "GOODBYE TO THE OLD SCHOOL TIE" under Maggie. The Conservative manifesto was spread over two pages with the headline "MAGGIE'S VISION OF GREAT DAYS FOR BRITAIN". In 1979 the paper had advised "Vote Tory", but now it was "VOTE FOR MAGGIE . . . Carry on Maggie! All the way to the GREAT Britain that a great people deserve." Similar if slightly more judiciously worded sentiments were expressed in *The Times*. The *Sunday Times* was less enthusiastic about Mrs Thatcher; Frank Giles said Murdoch never interfered, but, in the end, it too endorsed the Conservatives. Mrs Thatcher won.

Soon after the election, Murdoch called Giles and told him that he wanted him to make way for a younger man. Murdoch proposed that Giles should assume the title of Editor Emeritus, for the two years until his retirement. It was said that Giles had asked Murdoch exactly what his new title meant. "It's Latin, Frank," Murdoch was reported to have replied, "E means exit and meritus means you deserve it." The story was apocryphal.

In place of Giles, Murdoch appointed Andrew Neil, a relatively unknown thirty-four-year-old journalist from the *Economist*.

Neil, a man with a roughly-hewn face and a substantial but tender ego, was very much a man after Murdoch's heart. First of all, he was a Scotsman, and Murdoch liked to say that the Scots were the only decent Britons and, in America, the only decent WASPS. Like Murdoch, Neil saw himself as a leader of the new Conservative meritocracy, forever jousting with the effete English Establishment. He soon set about remaking the image and the behaviour of the *Sunday Times*, destroying, in effect, the last vestiges of the reign of Harry Evans which Frank Giles had elegantly retained. In doing so, Neil aroused dissatisfaction among the staff and among a section of the paper's readers.

Eighteen months later Evans brought out his book *Good Times*,

Bad Times of which the latter were almost all spent with Murdoch. The proprietor appeared, in Evans's account, the incarnation of evil.

The story was well paced and many reviewers praised the narrative, as well as Evans's courage in resisting and now denouncing the ogre. Even Murdoch's own papers were generous. But to some critics, the book seemed flawed by bitterness, self-pity, special pleading and the verbatim recollection of entire conversations, which others remembered differently. In his review, Magnus Linklater complained, "At vital moments, it shies away from the truth" – in particular the truth about the early courtship of Evans and Murdoch. In response, Evans wrote an angry letter to Linklater, accusing him of a pusillanimity similar to that of intellectuals in the Weimar Republic. Evans was equally upset by other criticisms made in the *Washington Post* by Patrick Brogan, who had resigned from *The Times* in protest at its sale to Murdoch. Evans wrote to Brogan to denounce his comments as "the product of a mean and fatuous mind . . . so frivolous . . . second-hand smears . . . "

Murdoch was much cooler about the whole matter. Unlike Robert Maxwell, who would have issued dozens of writs against Evans and his publisher, he largely ignored the book. In an interview in the *Sydney Morning Herald* just after it was published, he was asked if he had no desire to set the record straight. He answered, "We've issued a statement denying three of the most important lies in the book . . . Harry wanted to be loved by everybody. But he ended up being loved by nobody."

At *The Times*, Evans's successor Charles Douglas-Home was regarded with more affection. The literary editor, Philip Howard, once pointed out that Douglas-Home had taken over *The Times* "in a raging storm, with mutiny and panic below decks, and the ship in danger of foundering". As captain, he had quelled the mutiny, and quietly calmed the staff after the trauma caused by the bitter contest between Evans and Murdoch. He tried to give the paper a renewed sense of itself. Most of the journalists liked him, but not everyone approved the Thatcherite and more populist course on which he tried to steer the ship.

Under Douglas-Home *The Times* ran more crime stories and paid more attention to sport. It also introduced a top person's version of bingo, called Portfolio, which used stock-market share prices as a means of gambling. A similar game had been proposed by Harold Evans, but he had not had time to start it. When Douglas-Home did so, he and Murdoch were widely attacked for taking *The Times* irretrievably downmarket. But circulation rose.

According to some of the staff, Douglas-Home found it easier than Harry Evans to be robust with his proprietor. Instead of being appalled or terrified by a suggestion from Murdoch, he would either accept it or say simply, "Rupert, I'm sorry, but I just won't do that." This has always been the best way for editors to deal with Murdoch; he responds better to a show of decisiveness than to floundering. However, like many others, Douglas-Home often found Murdoch remote and used to say, "Rupert's not on receive." Murdoch's constant air of preoccupation could mean that even while talking, his mind had already moved to another problem, perhaps thousands of miles away.

The relationship was eased by the fact that, like Murdoch, Douglas-Home was a Conservative and admired Mrs Thatcher far more than Harold Evans had done.

Murdoch rarely gave Douglas-Home direct instructions. As always, his wishes and views merely emanated from him, rather like ectoplasm. His editors knew his opinions, and they knew his financial interests also. Many of them were constantly anxious to please him and there is no doubt that one way of doing so was to anticipate his views. Thus, from the mid-1980s on, *The Times* and the *Sunday Times* would not only be generally in favour of Mrs Thatcher (which they might have been anyway, whether or not they were owned by Murdoch), but they also carried constant sniping criticisms of such Murdoch *bêtes noires* as the BBC and the British television establishment in general.

Murdoch himself professed to be still unsentimental about *The Times*. Asked in the US about its bicentenary, he said, "I'm not letting myself be trapped into thinking I'm a trustee of some historic British institution that must be kept alive at any cost. It's no good having a great name on the top of a newspaper if it's sending us into the poorhouse."

Perhaps the crucial fact about Douglas-Home's editorship, and certainly the most tragic, was that, throughout it, he was suffering from an excruciating and incurable bone cancer. Many editorial meetings were conducted with the editor lying on his back on the floor.

He died in October 1985 and was buried near his home in Gloucestershire. News was generous to Douglas-Home's widow, Jessica, and paid for the education of their sons. Jessica Douglas-Home remained devoted to Murdoch – as a man, as a proprietor and as a friend. She later became involved in helping dissidents in Eastern Europe, and solicited Murdoch for assistance, which he gave.

Chapter 8

BOSTON

In the early 1980s Murdoch was determined above all to build up his presence in America. Just as he was fortunate in his relationship with Mrs Thatcher in Britain, so he was blessed in having Ronald Reagan and his free-market philosophy reigning in Washington. Murdoch's political views continued to move further to the right, as Anna's had done already. The process, he said, was "accelerated by five years in London watching the welfare state and watching what's happening in New York, which has a welfare state without being able to print money".

Murdoch cherished his relationship with the White House, though once, when he went to lunch with Reagan in the early 1980s, he was surprised by the President's age and fragility. Reagan actually fell asleep during the meal; the other guests went on eating and the waiters continued to take the plates away. Eventually Reagan awoke, bright and cheerful, as if on cue. Murdoch later described the experience as "awful".

Murdoch was also becoming friendly with Richard Nixon. He believed that Watergate-type investigations were not the purpose of journalism. "I differ from the vast majority of my peers in this country in that I believe the new cult of adversarial journalism has sometimes been taken to the point of subversion," he told a group of Boston businessmen. "It is a disgrace that we can and do read thousands upon thousands of words about our national defence and our foreign policy every day without so much as a nod of recognition to the enormous risks to our freedom that exist today – to the terrifying consequences of Russian and Cuban bases on this continent . . . " He also argued, "It is a sorry fact that the media as a whole . . . unquestioningly embrace a welfare state which divides and embitters our society without helping the truly poor and needy."

Murdoch's family holding company, Cruden, still owned 40 per cent of Australia's News Ltd, which in turn owned 49.3 per cent of his British company, News International. These two public companies were partners in News America publishing company. At this stage News America was not required to publish its results, because it was not traded on the New York Stock Exchange.

In America, Murdoch had taken on Donald Kummerfeld as president and chief operating officer of News America. Kummerfeld had previously been First Deputy Mayor and Budget Director of New York City. As a Democrat, Kummerfeld was a little uneasy with some of Murdoch's friendships, particularly that with Roy Cohn, who had been Senator McCarthy's aggressive lawyer during anti-communist investigations in the early 1950s, and had since acquired a sleazy reputation.

Through the 1970s, News had been globally run by Murdoch on a wing and a prayer. As it grew in the early 1980s, it was inevitable that a more structured organization was needed. Kummerfeld, with his budgetary experience, attempted to supply this.

When Kummerfeld started with News America in 1978 the company was worth some $300 million. By the time he left in 1985 its value was nearer $2 billion. Kummerfeld felt that more order was required, and insisted on stricter budgets and quarterly budget reviews. A financial committee consisting of Merv Rich, Kummerfield, Murdoch and Stan Shuman of Allen and Co, Murdoch's principal American banking advisers, was created. With Jeff Leist, an American accountant, Kummerfeld helped set up a computerized system for dealing with all the currencies in which the company traded. (Murdoch loved to gamble on the foreign exchange markets.) With Bruce Matthews, Murdoch's powerful manager in London, Kummerfeld also set about co-ordinating the purchase of newsprint for papers around the world. The News group became the world's largest newsprint consumer.

Kummerfeld also worked on Murdoch's image, enlisting the help of Howard Rubinstein, one of New York's most successful public relations wizards. Together, they tried to turn Murdoch into a social force in the US, as well as a supporter of the Zionist cause. He and Anna became involved in civic events in New York, where she felt easily at home. "I belong here," she said to Beth Kummerfeld.

As their New York world changed, so Murdoch had less time for some of the original colleagues he had brought from Australia. Or, at least, so it seemed to them. Paul Rigby, the cartoonist, had been a friend since the wild Sydney *Mirror* days. "He expected a lot of patriotism from his Oz mafia, but he wouldn't pay much for it," said Rigby later. "I had five kids at school but Rupert would never recognize that." This parsimony with old stagers contrasted with his tendency to offer large salaries to new recruits. Eventually, Rigby accepted a more lucrative offer from the *Daily News*. The *Post* reacted by employing his son, also a cartoonist, so that it could still proclaim that Rigby was in its pages.

On a public level, Murdoch used the paper as almost every baron of the media has done, to exert political influence. The *Post* gave him a unique and valuable platform in one of the most important cities of the world. He had used it to help elect the Mayor of New York and he had wholeheartedly supported Reagan for President in 1980.

Later Murdoch said that when the *Post* endorsed Reagan, "we expected a firestorm. In fact, the letters began running very strongly, first 50-50 for and against, then within a week they were running three to one in our favour. It was then I knew there was something on. It was not such a brave thing to do after all."

After Reagan's victory Murdoch was almost as supportive of Reaganism as he was of Thatcherism. Max Newton's enthusiastic encomia to the "Reagan Revolution" were influential. Murdoch helped both Reagan and Thatcher define the spirit of the 1980s. He was in a sense their amanuensis. Reagan responded. When he visited New York in spring 1982, he gave the *Post* an exclusive interview. It was only one of many favours from the administration.

Murdoch also continued the *Post*'s enthusiastic support for Ed Koch in New York, and in 1982 urged the mayor to run for governor. Once again reporters grumbled that their stories were chopped around to reflect the paper's endorsements, that balancing quotes were removed, that new and slanted leads were added. It was Steve Dunleavy of whom they complained most often. He was described in the *Columbia Journalism Review* as Murdoch's point man in the city room.

"The *Post* became what amounted to a political pamphlet for thirty days," observed Koch's opponent, Mario Cuomo. "That has to be important. The small political community that controls the early stages of every campaign is disproportionately influenced by something like the *Post* campaign; they read everything." None the less, Cuomo won.

In fact there was nothing new about the massive support that Murdoch extended to his preferred candidates. American publishers like Hearst, Greeley and Pulitzer had behaved even more brazenly.

Murdoch believed that tabloid journalism had to be alive to thrive. And he quoted H. L. Mencken's warning to tabloid papers. "Every tabloid, as soon as it gets into safe waters, begins to grow intellectual. The bold, gaudy devices that launched it are abandoned and it takes on decorum. I know of at least two that are actually liberal. This, I fear, is a false form of progress. The tabloid, so lifted by its bootstraps, becomes simply a little newspaper." And little papers, Murdoch added, disappear in big markets.

But he was wrong about the New York market. Despite his love for the wilder shores of journalism, the *Post* was not working properly. Whereas most British and Australian tabloids were only thirty-two pages, and had a relatively high cover price, Americans were used to fat papers at low prices. Advertising revenues were vital to American dailies, and offset the costs of low circulations. In almost all cities the local stores were crucial advertisers. But they were concerned not so much with numbers of readers as with their buying power. Although the *New York Times* had half the circulation of the *Daily News* in the mid-1970s, it carried almost twice as much advertising. Thus the *Times* was profitable while the *News* was always on the verge of going under. In San Antonio, Murdoch found that gains in circulation were actually losing him money – advertisers were not interested because they thought that most of the new readers were Mexican Americans too poor to buy the goods advertised.

In New York he never managed to win for the *Post* the better-heeled readers the advertisers wanted. There was a widely quoted story that a senior executive of Bloomingdales explained to Murdoch why the store did not advertise in the *Post*. "Rupert, your readers are our shoplifters."

This tale was only just apocryphal. A man from Bloomingdales did indeed tell the *Wall Street Journal*, "It's immaterial to us if the *Post*'s circulation is 600,000 or six million. Our customers are sophisticated and urbane and don't want to hear about the violence and sex the *Post* touts." By 1982, the *Post* still had only 6 per cent of the advertising in New York papers – the *Times* had 56 per cent and the *News* 38 per cent. Even the supermarket chains, which cared less for demographics, on the grounds that everyone has to eat, were doubtful about the *Post*.

Murdoch was forced to acknowledge that what he called "the cheeky working class" who bought the *Sun* in Britain did not exist in quite the same form in New York. In fact, he came to the conclusion that New York did not have a working class at all.

> This is a middle-class city. Everybody in this country wants to get ahead, get a piece of the action. That's the fundamental difference between the Old World and the New World. There's not the self-improvement ethic in England that there is in this country. If you drop below that level, you're talking about the ghettoes. And there's a question as to whether those people can even read, let alone afford a newspaper.

Murdoch still had his sights fixed upon the *New York Daily News*. He intended to launch a morning tabloid, the *Daily Sun*, against its soft underbelly – just as he had launched the *Sun* against the *Daily Mirror* in London. Despite his realization that New York was different from Britain, he still argued that the *News* had become too respectable, edited by people "who wish they were working for the *New York Times*".

Murdoch's analysis was not dismissed at the *News*. The editor, Mike O'Neill, acknowledged that after the disastrous 1962–3 strike, "we decided to move closer to the *Times*, occupying the centre". It was a mistake. The new generation of journalists hated over-simplification. "We'd love to get back irreverence without sacrificing credibility," said O'Neill.

Soon after Harold Evans's stormy departure in London, Murdoch offered to buy the *News*. The Tribune Company of Chicago, which owned the paper, was then negotiating its sale to the Texas financier Joseph Allbritton. The idea that Murdoch should buy it was not appealing. They expected that he would close it to ensure the profitability of the *Post*. The company said "No" to Murdoch, which enabled the *News* to display the headline, "TRIB TO RUPERT: DROP DEAD", an echo of its famous headline, "FORD TO NEW YORK: DROP DEAD". In the end the paper was sold to Allbritton – and it carried on losing money.

Undeterred, Murdoch continued to search for more North American papers. Later in 1982 he made a lunge at the *Courier Express* of Buffalo, New York. But the unions refused to agree to the scale of cuts in the workforce he thought essential to staunch its losses. The paper was closed. One reporter was quoted as saying, "We voted to die with dignity," an odd endorsement of suicide. Murdoch continued his quest in Boston, where the city's second paper, the *Boston Herald*, was the underdog to the established, mighty and somewhat preachy *Boston Globe*. This was a situation made for Murdoch.

The first *Boston Herald* had been founded in 1846 by printers in the city. In 1912 it had absorbed the *Boston Traveler* to become the *Boston Herald-Traveler*, and was until the end of the 1950s the pre-eminent broadsheet in the city, outselling and outclassing the *Globe*. But in the 1960s it had declined and in 1972 was bought by the Hearst Corporation who merged it with their tabloid *Record American*. This marriage of a blue-collar tabloid with a blue-blooded broadsheet produced an ever thinner and more dreary paper. Editors came and editors went. Advertisers just went. The paper had no idea of its readers or of itself.

In 1979 a gifted editor, Donald Forst, was transferred across country from Hearst's *Los Angeles Herald Examiner*. He improved it, but circulation continued to fall – below 200,000 on weekdays and to 329,000 on Sundays in 1981. The *Globe* now had almost half a million in daily sales and almost 800,000 on

Sundays. The *Herald-American* was losing at least $10 million a year.

Forst induced Hearst to make one last attempt to save the paper by investing another $3.5 million and turning it into a tabloid. The paper became much sprightlier and produced some notable headlines such as "HINCK'S SHRINK STINKS" – about John Hinckley's unsuccessful insanity plea during his trial for the attempted murder of President Reagan, and "CLAUS IS A LOUSE", referring to Claus von Bulow's celebrated trials for the attempted murder of his wife.

Circulation rose – but only by a few thousand. The Hearst Corporation began to cut costs and it seemed clear that they wanted to get rid of the paper. Forst contacted Murdoch, who had once offered him the editorship of *New York* magazine.

After a lunch in Boston, Murdoch invited him to his house at Chatham in upstate New York, and pumped him for information on the paper. Like so many others, Forst was disarmed by Murdoch. "He charmed me out of my underwear," he said later to Murdoch's biographer, Michael Leapman. But Murdoch took Forst for a walk in the woods with his children and told him that, notwithstanding Forst's valiant efforts for the paper, he would want a new editor if he bought the *Herald-American*.

Even so, Forst retained fond memories of Murdoch: "He was wonderful with his kids . . . And he seemed to have a nice relationship with his wife . . . How can I get angry with him? If a man pulls a rabbit out of his hat, he's entitled to do with it what he will. Make stew or skin it or turn it into another felt hat. That's the ball game."

Murdoch offered Hearst a million dollars for the *Herald-American*, plus another 7 million from future profits, if any. Since the paper's building alone was thought to be worth $8 million, he considered he was on to another winner. On 17 November, 1982 Hearst announced the negotiations, describing Murdoch as "the buyer of last resort". Murdoch insisted that he would go ahead only if the unions made significant manning concessions by midnight on 3 December. The *Globe* at once tried to wrest similar concessions from the unions and Murdoch accused them of trying to sabotage him. He threatened to sue the *Globe*.

As so often, the talks went right up to the wire, so that each side could demonstrate its resolve. Right till the end, it looked as if at least one union would hold out and scupper the deal. "MURDOCH AND THE UNIONS. GOING DOWN TO THE WIRE", ran the last headline of the Hearst ownership. Just ten minutes before the deadline on 3 December 1982, Murdoch got the concessions he wanted and acquired the paper.

He agreed to invest some $16 million, at the same time as cutting staff in all departments. He changed the paper's name to the *Boston Herald* – which was what most readers had called it anyway. He brought in new editors from New York, put bright yellow *Herald* vending machines all over town, spruced up the building, installed computers and changed the layout from four broad columns to seven narrow columns a page. And, of course, he took the paper into that netherland where he always goes – downmarket. More sports, a bit more sex (not too much in Catholic Boston), more competitions – in particular Wingo – more bizarre reports, more of everything that Murdoch thought Boston working-class readers should like. Headlines were reversed out of black boxes, stories were made shorter and were given fancy borders. Often the entire front page was given over to a headline designed to seize the reader by the scruff of the neck. It was all part of a deliberate effort to convince people of the truth of the headline on the day Murdoch clinched the deal: "WE'RE ALIVE".

The *Herald* gained over 100,000 readers in the first year Murdoch owned the paper. Tom Winship, the editor of the *Globe*, dismissed the *Herald* as "circus journalism". But the competition was good for the *Globe*, which began to cover more local stories and expanded its foreign reporting. David Greenway, the *Globe*'s associate editor, took a more considered view. "Murdoch saved a paper, he found a whole lot of new readers in Boston and he kept us on our toes." He thought Murdoch had benefited Boston.

Murdoch hoped to outsell the *Globe*. He thought that in some ways Boston would be an easier city for him to succeed in than New York. "Boston is a very passionate city. It's a very direct, no-nonsense city. You don't have the fakery and glitter here of Madison Avenue . . . I think it will be easier for us to find an identity here than it was in New York."

Most of the journalists on the *Herald* enjoyed working under Murdoch. Andrew Gully, the city editor, said later:

> The great thing about Murdoch is that we are left completely free to assign stories as we want to. There's no one ringing us from New York telling us, "I want this covered," or "I want that covered." We do what we think is best and that is a real luxury in any kind of business . . . The image is that Rupert is very heavy-handed, but it just hasn't been the case here.

When Murdoch bought the paper he said that it would not try to influence political life as strongly as the *Post* had endeavoured to do in New York, but "our politics will certainly be a lot less liberal than the *Globe*'s". That naturally extended to strident criticism of Massachusetts's senior, liberal Democratic senator, Edward Kennedy. He was to be a dangerous enemy for Murdoch.

THE CLARKE RING

While he was negotiating for the *Herald* Murdoch also climbed aboard the Clarke Ring. In November 1983 the space shuttle Columbia launched a private communications satellite owned by Satellite Business Systems (SBS), a combine which included Aetna Insurance Co, IBM and Comsat. Murdoch bought into Inter-American Satellite Television Inc, a company which leased five transponders from SBS for six years at a total cost of $75 million. There was to be a movie channel and a sports channel and subscribers would pay a monthly fee for the programmes which were to be beamed to backyard dishes. Murdoch called his company Skyband, and declared optimistically that it would soon be broadcasting to 100,000 subscribers.

At this time cable was also snaking across most of the United States, but Murdoch made a conscious decision not to invest in any franchises. He found the whole idea of cable television boring, and this disdain led him to ignore its huge commercial potential.

18 *A security guard patrols behind the barbed wire fence at 'Fortress' Wapping, just before the presses rolled on* 25 January 1986 *to produce the first copies of the* Sunday Times *and the* News of the World *to be printed at the new headquarters*

19 *More than 12,000 people demonstrated at the Wapping printworks on 24 January 1987, the first anniversary of the move there from central London in 1986*

20 *The proprietor holds the first copies of* The Times *and the* Sun *of 27 January 1986 to be printed in Wapping*

21 *Press barons, left to right, Viscount Rothermere, Rupert Murdoch and Robert Maxwell at the Reuters annual lunch, 30 April 1987*

22 *Some classic* Sun *headlines*

23 *Rupert Murdoch is congratulated by his mother, Dame Elisabeth, after his successful bid on 3 December 1986 for the* Melbourne Herald, *the paper which his father built*

24 BELOW *Rupert and Anna Murdoch with their children, James, Lachlan and Elisabeth*

25 *Charles Wilson, editor of* The Times, *Rupert Murdoch, and Mervyn Rich, former chief financial officer of News Corp, at the Aspen meeting, 1989*

27 *Richard Searby, QC, Geelong Grammar schoolfriend of Murdoch, and Chairman of News Corp, in 1989, Aspen*

26 *John Evans, futurologist and head of Murdoch Magazines in 1989, relaxing with the Murdochs at Aspen*

28 RIGHT *Alan Sugar
with Rupert Murdoch,
launching Sky Television to
the strains of* Carmina
Burana *in the auditorium of
the British Academy of Film
and Television Arts in
Piccadilly, 8 June 1988*

29 BELOW *Andrew Neil,
editor of the* Sunday Times
*and Chairman of Sky
Television, with Rupert
Murdoch in 1989*

30 OPPOSITE *Part of
BSB's campaign against
Murdoch's cross-media
ownership in 1990 when
BSB was launched in
competition with Sky
Television*

W NEIL
n Sky Television

RUPERT MURDOCH
Chief Executive News International

Who do you think will be the most influential person in Britain in the 90s?

If a politician, whatever his or her bias, turns out to be the most influential person of the 90s, at least some of the people will be happy about it.

Because, in Britain today, politicians are elected according to the rules of democracy.

They don't buy their way to power.

Unfortunately, given the current loophole in our law, the title is much more likely to go to someone who is doing just that right now.

The contender we have in mind is Rupert Murdoch.

Mr Murdoch's company owns 100% of The Sun, Today, The Times, News of the World and The Sunday Times.

Mr Murdoch's company also owns 98% of Sky TV.

Some say that by 1991 he'll control over 35% of our national newspaper circulation. And, by his own forecasts, he'll have six million people watching Sky. Or, to put it another way, more than currently watch Yorkshire, STV, Harlech, Tyne Tees, Anglia, TSW or TVS.

We're not alone in finding this worrying.

An editorial in The Economist succinctly identified the danger:

'The media have moved beyond being mere providers of entertainment and information. They have become a forum that rivals parliaments'.

Already, Mr Murdoch's company is abusing this power as a cross-media owner by running editorials for Sky TV in his newspapers that would make passable advertisements.

While, at the same time, running editorials attacking the BBC and ITV in his newspapers under headlines like 'BBC pipped as Sky goes Moonlighting' and 'Sky lifts cloud over our awful TV'.

How long will it be before he decides to flex his media muscles and start influencing the way in which we're governed?

In a recent survey, 80% of MPs questioned said they believed cross-media ownership to be undesirable.

We call on every one of them to oppose the Broadcasting Bill as it now stands, loophole dangling.

CHECKS & BALANCES
THE CAMPAIGN AGAINST CONCENTRATION OF MEDIA CONTROL

31 *Rupert and Anna Murdoch at their meeting with President Gorbachev in Moscow, May 1991*

32 *At the party to celebrate Kelvin MacKenzie's tenth anniversary as editor of the* Sun *in June 1991, left to right, Jacqueline and Kelvin MacKenzie, Anna and Rupert Murdoch*

By the end of the 1980s, the cable operators were mining gold from the monopolies they had established.

Satellite broadcasting seemed much more exciting to Murdoch. It did have promise. In the United States one of the huge steps on to the Clarke Ring had been taken by a Time Incorporated executive, Gerry Levin, who had risked putting Home Box Office "on the bird" – on to a satellite. A whole new era in communications and media began at that moment. Home Box Office was a regional pay TV service in the northeast US till the mid-1970s. Once aloft it was suddenly national, broadcasting its signal to regional cable systems all over the continent. And all because Levin understood the magic of satellite television. The idea apparently came to him with the broadcast of a few seconds of the Frazier–Ali fight from Manila – the so-called "Thrilla from Manila".

Levin was taking a considerable gamble. When he began, there were not many cable companies with satellite dishes. But once Home Box Office was up there, they began to proliferate. In 1977 there were some 500 cable system dishes in the country. By 1982 there were 5,000. Cable was driven across the land by Home Box Office and by Ted Turner's Super-Station. Like Levin, Turner was a pioneer. The fact that each of them used low-powered satellites to transmit to cable heads transformed the economics of cable. Super-Station eventually became CNN, the station that revolutionized the reporting of the world. One of Murdoch's most serious misjudgements was to ignore cable.

He believed that there was a large market for satellites because, while there were 83 million TV households in the United States, only 55 million of them were in areas being wired for cable. The others, mostly in rural areas, would never be wired. He expected Skyband to gross almost $325 million a year by 1986. The market was entirely new but, he said, "There was never any doubt it was going to happen. The real question is, are the advantages of being first in very great? We think they are."

Only after the deal was done and the first payments were made did Murdoch discover that his thinking was premature. The dishes required were still large and it was hard to persuade people to accept them in their yards. There were not enough programmes to attract viewers, and furthermore the satellite itself was already becoming obsolete. A new generation of more powerful satellites and smaller dishes was on its way. Jim Cruthers, an Australian television pioneer who was one of Murdoch's close advisers on the project, said, "The more we looked at it, the more we realized that it was extremely difficult to get programming of a sufficient quality that would make us competitive in the US, where there's so much TV."

In 1983 Murdoch backed out of Skyband, taking losses of $20 million. But he was still determined to take to the skies, in America and elsewhere; at the same time, he was making his first move on to the European section of the Clarke Ring. He bought into Sky Television, the system that was ultimately almost to destroy his empire.

Sky Television was born in Europe in 1981, as Satellite Television plc. It was fathered by an English television producer named Brian Haynes. On the frontiers of the Clarke Ring, Haynes, an infectiously enthusiastic man, was a true pioneer.

He had made programmes for Thames Television, and had become interested in satellite broadcasting at the end of the 1970s, at around the time that Ted Turner and Jim Bakker had started using satellites to broadcast their respective creeds of baseball and religion to middle America. Haynes's vision was of a pan-European satellite-delivered TV service, first through cable systems and then eventually direct to dishes at home.

Haynes persuaded the European Space Agency (ESA) to allow him to use its Orbital Test Satellite (OTS) – which had been intended for telecommunications only. With some difficulty he then induced Eutelsat, an inter-governmental organization which controlled European satellite use, to allow him to broadcast. "They had visions of the horrible Haynes beaming pornography and Coca-Cola down on to purist European families," recalled Haynes. The satellite had several more years of life to run, but the space agency's funds were running low and it needed to find new income to keep the satellite going. The satellite was offered to Haynes despite the fact that it had been intended only for telephone communication.

The merchant bank Guinness Mahon helped Haynes raise some £4 million of risk capital and he began broadcasting to Malta in 1981. In those days, satellite time cost only £300 an hour, and Haynes bought programmes from all over the world for only about £100 an hour on average.

The whole operation was run on a shoestring and Haynes made very little money, but he began to sign up more cable systems, moving in from the fringe countries like Norway, Finland and Switzerland to the richer pickings of Holland and Belgium.

On its own tiny scale, Satellite, as the channel was called, began to work. Haynes thought it should remain a minute system, but by 1983, as expected, Satellite had burned up its first £4 million. Haynes then discovered that a second round of £6 million risk investment capital was not so easy to find.

The banks put out feelers and, through Lord Goodman, Murdoch responded. He paid an initial £10 million for a controlling interest in Satellite Television plc and renamed the channel Sky to give him a global link to his American Skyband satellite venture which he hoped might one day fly again. He immediately set about enlarging his new acquisition with more people and further tranches of cash.

Under Haynes, the financial projections had forecast break-even by 1987–8 with annual costs of about £10 million and revenues of perhaps £12 million, with 13 million homes connected. But Murdoch thought that paltry. He replaced Haynes's staff with much higher-paid television executives. Costs rocketed to nearer £20 million. The problem was that Murdoch had bought a distribution system, not a television company. At that time there was only a small number of pan-European brands which wished to advertise on an international basis. Even high-powered Australian advertising executives could not suddenly conjure more such brands into life. They were fired and replaced almost overnight. Patiently constructed deals, contracts and credibility were blown away. Haynes thought it was all a pity. "Murdoch's problem is that he is a dealer now, not a creator. He has enormous power for good, but does not use it. It's all a game, just paying off interest charges, not creating anything."

To Murdoch such criticisms merely showed the limits of Haynes's vision. He was trying to build the world's greatest international media empire, and was convinced that satellite broadcasting could be an enormously important part of it.

In the early days, Sky was a tax loss. Meanwhile, the technology was whirring ahead. The French and the Germans were trying to enter the market, but American companies were now developing much smaller, cheaper, medium-powered satellites whose signals could be picked up by smaller dishes, and which could transmit more channels than the Direct Broadcast Satellites (DBS).

Tom Whitehead, who had run President Nixon's Office of Telecommunications Policy, now appeared. By 1983, Whitehead was running the satellite communications department at Hughes Aerospace. He went to Luxembourg to persuade the government that they should fill the slot they had been given on the Clarke Ring at the WARC 77 conference with a medium-powered satellite rather than a high-powered DBS. He chose Luxembourg partly because it had a tradition of international broadcasting and because it is, in effect, an offshore banking centre.

But there was still massive opposition from other European governments, including France and West Germany, to the concept of an international and private "bird" on the Clarke Ring. What Whitehead called "the most violent and the most ridiculous" opposition came from François Mitterrand, who angrily dismissed the Luxembourg plan as "the Coca-Cola satellite", because it had Whitehead and other American business interests behind it. He declared that the French government would do everything it could to obstruct the Luxembourg plans in order to protect the integrity of French borders and French television culture. At the same time, France and Germany signed an agreement to manufacture two direct broadcast satellites to service their two countries with national programmes.

Threats came from other governments, from Eutelsat and from the post offices. None the less, Whitehead and the Luxembourgeois set up a medium-powered satellite broadcast system, called Coronet. But negotiations broke down, and Whitehead moved back to America. A consortium led by Luxembourg banks stepped in and kept Coronet afloat, until it was renamed Astra. It was this enterprise that eventually gave Murdoch his big platform in the sky, later in the 1980s.

CHICAGO

In the winter of 1983–4 Charlie Wilson, a former marine from Glasgow who carried himself like a lightweight boxer, arrived in Chicago. He was expected, he said, "to sodomize" Murdoch's latest acquisition, the *Chicago Sun-Times*, on his master's behalf. That, he was sure, was how the men on the paper expected Murdoch's commissar to behave. He was met by a gale of loathing with a chill factor at least as painful as the winds which roar through the Windy City off the Plains and Lake Michigan.

Chicago is a robust and vibrant town, with a history of fearsome newspaper wars. Yet, in early 1984, the arrival of Murdoch and his men provoked an extraordinary amount of whimpering. This was strange if only because he was Chicago's kind of man, ruthlessly and single-mindedly building an empire of information rather than of steel or railroads.

Through the city the El (elevated train) thunders along, a steeplechase ride that brushes up against bedroom windows, as it passes stockyards, iron buildings and one ethnic neighbourhood after another. It speeds past rooftops you can virtually touch with your hand, behind three- and four-tiered back porches crisscrossed with lumber braces.

At the beginning of the twentieth century, Chicago had twenty-five or more newspapers competing for readers in ruthless ways. Some of their unscrupulous methods were illustrated in Ben Hecht's famous play *The Front Page*. The most violent struggle took place between William Randolph Hearst's *Chicago Examiner* and Colonel Robert McCormick's *Chicago Tribune*: each paper despatched thugs into streetcars to grab its rival's pages from passengers' hands, and they would throw the papers and sometimes even the readers into the gutter.

The *Sun* was founded by Marshall Field III, heir to the first

Marshall Field, who had established one of the first and the most successful of American department stores in Chicago in 1856. Its legendary motto was, "Give the lady what she wants". The store, Marshall Field, became and remained a byword for its service – and for its shoppers' dining room.

Marshall Field III created the *Sun* in December 1941 as a New Deal alternative to counter the isolationism and right-wing policies of Colonel McCormick's *Chicago Tribune*. Three days later came Pearl Harbor and isolationism died. In 1947, Field bought the *Chicago Daily Times*, an afternoon tabloid, and soon merged it with the *Sun*. From then on a state of fierce war existed between the *Sun-Times* and the *Tribune*. Their offices were at either end of the bridge over the Chicago River, the *Sun-Times* in a ugly modern slablike building at the south end and the *Tribune* in a glorious gothic tower on the northern bank. All through the 1950s and 1960s there was ferocious competition: Chicago journalism had quite a lot in common with Murdoch's Sydney. The order of every day was blood, guts and deception; reporters thought nothing of impersonating policemen by flashing phoney badges; they stole photographs of dead relatives; they did whatever they needed to do to get The Story.

In the 1970s some of these excesses were abandoned across America as the profession of journalism became, post-Woodward and Bernstein, a fashionable activity, and one which attracted thousands of college graduates. The game was cleaned up, the job became more genteel. Far too much so, in the opinion of Rupert Murdoch. But the memory lingered on.

In 1980 James Hoge, a graduate of Yale who had been editor of the *Sun-Times* since 1968, was appointed publisher. He moved the paper upmarket to compete more directly with the broadsheet *Tribune*. He favoured both aggressive reporting and stylish writing and he made the *Sun-Times* a vigorous, campaigning local paper. He even took on the Cardinal of Chicago – a historic act in a town where the Catholic Church wielded enormous power. He assembled a good, and by Murdoch's standards, a lavish staff. By 1983 the *Sun-Times* had a daily circulation of some 640,000, with 30,000 more on Sundays; the rival *Tribune* had sales of 751,000 on weekdays and well over a million on Sundays.

The *Sun-Times* was clearly the second paper in Chicago, but it inspired much loyalty in a city of immigrants where loyalty was important. It was not dying – but its profits were unspectacular. In 1982 it made $3.5 million on revenues of $161 million.

By now the paper was owned 50 per cent by Marshall Field V, grandson of the founder, and 50 per cent by his half-brother Frederick "Ted" Field, who was not interested in newspapers. Frederick was described by the *New York Times* as "a bearded amateur race car driver who lives in southern California and invests in real estate and movies". By 1983 he wanted a much greater return on his inherited capital than the *Sun-Times* was providing and decided to sell out. Marshall Field V resisted him for a time, but the trust devised by their father's lawyers provided that in the event of a purchaser being found for the paper, one brother would have to buy out the other at top dollar – or agree to the sale.

Marshall was not happy, but neither did he wish to fight his half-brother. Various buyers sniffed around but decided that the *Sun-Times* was not profitable enough; the conventional view was that it would always remain the number-two paper in a highly competitive market. The *Washington Post* was interested. So was Murdoch. This struck horror into the hearts of the journalists and Jim Hoge began to put together a consortium, based in Chicago, to buy the paper.

In the end, the *Washington Post* offered $50 million and Hoge's consortium offered $63 million for the paper. There was also the syndication service which was worth $20 million. Murdoch offered $90 million for the paper and the service together, which in effect made his bid some $7 million higher than the consortium's. This was not a huge difference but Field Enterprises president Lee Mitchell rejected Hoge's offer "without explanation or bargaining".

The Fields had agreed to consider Hoge's counter-bid if it was over $55 million. Now that promise looked like a sham. Company officials had even told Hoge that they would not actually sell to Murdoch – his reputation was too awful – but would allow him to bid the price up. Later they qualified this by saying that they would sell to Murdoch, but only if his price was disproportionately higher than that offered by anyone else – high enough to compensate for his bad name, in other words.

On 1 November 1983, Murdoch signed a letter of intent to buy the paper. He wrote to the Field brothers to assure them that he had no intention of changing it significantly and pledged to uphold the highest standards of journalism. He said that he was "approaching the task of continuing the work of the *Sun-Times* with great seriousness and no little humility". The final documents were to have been signed on 15 December, but this was delayed by a dispute over the valuation of the pension plan. Belatedly, another Chicago group tried to save the paper from Murdoch. Marshall Field first stalled, and then made himself unavailable – rather as Carter Burden had done during the sale of *New York* magazine. He finally admitted through his lawyers that he feared court action by Murdoch if he entertained the new offer.

Murdoch had a deal. For $90 million he had the paper, and syndicated news and feature services, producing annual revenues of some $200 million. The buildings alone were worth $30 million.

At a press conference after the purchase was concluded, he was asked what he had to say to counter his reputation as someone "who sends chills up the journalistic spines". He replied, "Nothing at all. I'm very happy to stand on my record." Asked again about the "sleazy" reputation of his papers, he retorted, "You ought to look at them before you spout those myths."

The journalists on the paper were furious, especially with the behaviour of Marshall Field. One reporter was quoted as saying that Field was far worse than Murdoch "because he was so duplicitous. There's a moral defect in leading people on and appearing a civic figure . . . Here he has a legacy, a community trust, and he violates it." The paper's eminent movie critic, Roger Ebert, said Field "betrayed hundreds of people".

Nick Shuman, a senior editorial writer with thirty-two years' service on the paper, wrote a letter of resignation to Field, saying, " . . . the legacy left you by Marshall Field III and Marshall IV was honorable, creative service to their community. You have pissed on that legacy."

Murdoch made several visits to the paper. The *New York Times* reported that when he appeared in the fourth-floor newsroom, he received scattered applause for his promise to keep the paper "substantially" the same. He hosted a small dinner for the paper's editorial stars at a Chicago restaurant and repeated assurances that the *Sun-Times* would not be compromised. But he also told Jim Hoge that he wished to be able to intervene editorially – he hadn't spent $90 million to let someone else have all the fun. Hoge replied that he had heard that this was how Murdoch operated. Each doubted he could work with the other, but they agreed to try.

Donald Kummerfeld visited Chicago and told Hoge that the way News functioned was that Murdoch made flying visits, altered budgets and put on a million dollars here if he felt generous and trimmed a bit there if he did not. "My job is to come in with my executives and clean it all up." Around the world, editors and journalists often found the attitudes and orders of Murdoch's managers much harsher than his own.

Murdoch's acquisition of the *Sun-Times* came shortly after the publication of Harry Evans's memoirs *Good Times, Bad Times*, in which he portrayed Murdoch as restless, brooding, moody, aggressive, manipulative, petulant and very right-wing. This assault on the new boss was widely read in the newsroom of the *Sun-Times*. "It was a deterrent to everyone to stay," said Hoge.

One of those who decided to leave was Mike Royko, the paper's star columnist, and a Chicago institution. His column, which often featured an ordinary cussed worker named Slats Grobnick, was widely read and much-loved. Royko was seen as a defender of the little person against authority.

After the deal was completed but before Murdoch moved in, Royko started to refer to Murdoch in his column as "The Alien", and painted a picture of a kind of journalistic terrorist. For years Royko had said he would never work for the *Tribune* – that he could not stand the right-wing legacy of Colonel McCormick. But no self-respecting dead fish would want to be wrapped in a Murdoch paper, he said, and he went across the bridge to the competition. Murdoch immediately sued him for breach of contract. The action was big news in Chicago; teams of cameramen stationed themselves outside the courthouse and sales of the *Tribune* increased notably.

Royko of course relished the drama. In his first column for the

Tribune, he said that the thing he liked best about his job was that he could do it sitting down.

> Until today, I've been doing my sitting at another place about a block from here. And I was content until this fellow came into town with a large sack of money and decided to buy that place.
>
> As sometimes can happen between boss and employee, we didn't see eye to eye on a few things, so I decided to do my sitting over here . . .
>
> But now this international tycoon's aide says they are going into court to prevent me from doing my daily sitting here.
>
> What a problem. I don't want to do my sitting there. But he doesn't want me to do it here. Can you imagine a guy coming all the way from Australia just to tell me where to sit?

After a couple of days of massive publicity, the case was thrown out. Royko thought that Murdoch had brought this action just to create a news story.

Some *Sun-Times* journalists were prepared to be more open-minded about Murdoch. Irv Kupcinet, the columnist, wrote that journalists should wait and see what Murdoch actually did. Movie critic Ebert opted to stay because

> I would rather have Murdoch as an owner than Marshall Field. Murdoch is a newspaper man, a height to which Field never truly ascended . . . he could not have told you how many columns his paper ran to the page . . . [Murdoch] is smart and cynical, like all the publishers legends are based on . . . He is like [Citizen] Kane in inheriting a small family fortune of which the only part that interested him was the newspaper.

In the first days of 1984 Murdoch was in London. He called Charlie Wilson, the editor of *The Times*, up to his office in Gray's Inn Road and told him he needed someone he could trust in Chicago, and he needed him there immediately. Wilson thought he would be away about two weeks. He was gone three months.

Wilson was the antithesis of Jim Hoge. Hoge was handsome

and Ivy League. Wilson was a rough-edged, aggressive Glaswegian, given to brackish oaths. Both were smart, but in very different ways. When he arrived in Chicago, one local paper quoted Patrick Brogan, late of *The Times*, as saying, "Murdoch is always looking for tough, aggressive, unpleasant people to bring into his papers to whip them into shape. Wilson is very tough, unpleasant, rude to his subordinates. He puts the fear of God in them." Wilson pointed out later that Brogan had never met him.

Wilson said he was astonished by the wall of hostility with which he was confronted in Chicago. "It was a classic Murdoch-monster-myth situation," he said. But it was beyond even the classic – it was hysteria. The hatred bubbled off the desks, it seethed from the video terminals, it bounced off the walls. Wilson said he felt like the running dog of a Cyclops. It was as if Murdoch were some foul fiend that stalked and ravaged the earth, chewing up newspapers for breakfast and expelling them covered with filth later in the day. The questions the *Sun-Times* men asked – when they could bear to speak to him at all: would there still be a sports page? Was the Washington bureau going to be closed? What about photographs?

The centre of the cauldron of hatred was the newsroom of the *Sun-Times*, and from there the hatred spread through Chicago and Illinois and beyond. Wilson's job was made more difficult by the "window" that the Fields had opened, which allowed journalists two weeks after the change of ownership in which to decide whether to take high severance pay and leave the paper. "It was very tempting – the choice after all was to be sodomized or to do the sodomizing," said Wilson. "I spent my time trying to convince the staff that Murdoch was not Satan, that we were not going to make the *Sun-Times* into the *National Enquirer* and that when the window closed life would still be bearable."

Many journalists refused to be convinced. For the obvious "moral" course seemed to be to leave, rather than to work for the Monster. In all, over sixty people leapt through the "window" and out of the *Sun-Times*.

Wilson lived in a penthouse nearby and spent about eighteen hours a day at the office.

It was one of the most exciting periods of my life, a terrific challenge. People hated me. I worked out that the only way I could change them was by convincing them about my journalism. I had a deputy and a managing editor who helped. When people took the window, I promoted people from inside the paper to get their loyalty.

Together with two News America executives, Robert Page who came from the *Boston Herald* to be publisher, and Roger Wood from the *New York Post*, Wilson immediately began to apply some of the Murdoch prescription. He shortened stories, used more graphics and photos and paid more attention to the front page. He increased crime coverage, especially of murder and rape. Every day he changed the front page as often as possible between editions in order to give the readers at least the illusion of freshness. He frequently called the circulation department to see how different headlines fared on the streets.

Wilson thought he finally won acceptability in the newsroom with the death of the Soviet President, Yuri Andropov, in February 1984. He heard the news at 6 a.m. and realized that the morning edition was already an hour gone. "I instantly thought that we must do a special, a slip edition." Knowing there was a lot of background on Andropov in the computer, Wilson woke up two editors from Murdoch's *San Antonio News* who were working on the *Sun-Times,* and told them to get in. He rang the night production manager, and found there were enough people still cleaning the presses to start them rolling again. By breakfast time he had a special edition out on the streets. The first three pages were devoted to Andropov. "I made sure it was on sale outside the *Tribune* building by the time its staff arrived for work."

"From being a sodomite, I was now a hero," said Wilson later. "Chicago loves to think of itself as fulfilling the *Front Page* tradition. It takes itself very seriously. It had not seen a special for twenty-five years. I was being toasted by lunchtime."

In the end, those who feared the worst may have been surprised. After an expensive, self-congratulatory and ultimately ineffective attempt to boost circulation through a million-dollar Wingo game, the *Sun-Times* changed far less than had been predicted. "Gradually the hatred faded because the paper never became the *Sun*-type rag which had been feared," said Wilson. "But the image of Rupert did remain. The other media were always on at us; everything we did was construed as badly as possible. Many sources would as a matter of course go to the *Tribune*."

The Medill School of Journalism in Chicago made a serious attempt to assess Murdoch's impact. It compared randomly selected final editions of the 1984 *Sun-Times* with others from 1980 and from 1976, and made a similar analysis of the *Tribune*. The students also interviewed almost a thousand readers and some dozens of *Sun-Times* employees.

The survey found that readers of the *Tribune* tended to be better-educated, more liberal and better-off than those of the *Sun-Times*. *Sun-Times* readers were more conservative on the issues of abortion and prayers in school. "These findings suggest that the paper's shift to a more conservative editorial stance under News America's management may be well received by a large proportion of its readers."

Sun-Times readers were asked what changes they had noticed. "Sensationalism" was mentioned in more than one-fourth of the answers, but those polled were unable to tell the difference between headlines of the *Tribune* and the *Sun-Times* and also thought that the headlines from the earlier years' samples were more sensationalist than those of the Murdoch era. The survey showed that 13 per cent more of the editorial space was being devoted to graphics and photos than in the earlier papers. Similarly, there had been an increase (2 per cent) in the space devoted to crime news plus a 15 per cent jump in the number of crime-related items, but the average size of stories had decreased. The number of crime items in the *Tribune* had also increased.

Coverage of government affairs declined, while the space devoted to "*Sun-Times* self-promotion" increased enormously. There were 20 per cent more stories about the Chicago area under Murdoch, and more coverage of celebrities, entertainment, accidents and disasters.

In both Boston and Chicago, the hysteria about Murdoch was misplaced. Under him, both the *Boston Herald* and the *Chicago*

Sun-Times were effective tabloid newspapers. The *Herald* continued to keep the *Boston Globe* on its toes; in Chicago the *Tribune* continued to be the more comprehensive paper, but it was no longer the only "acceptable" paper in town. After Charlie Wilson went home to London in the spring of 1984, Murdoch brought in Frank Devine, a cheerful, radical right-winger from *Reader's Digest* as editor. He did away with such headlines as "RABBI HIT IN 'SEX SLAVERY' SCANDAL" and "MEN BEAR CHILDREN?" and began to let his reporters loose on local scandals. The paper became much more of an aggressive local watchdog – the kind of paper that Chicago had always known. And then, in order to move into American television, Murdoch sold it.

Chapter 9

1984

Thanks to George Orwell, 1984 was a landmark almost as important as Adelaide, New York, London, or the other locations in
which Rupert Murdoch enacted the various scenes in the drama
of his life.

It was also the year in which Murdoch began to burst upon
public consciousness in the United States. The year opened, appro-
priately enough, with the business magazine, *Forbes*, declaring
that Murdoch was "building the greatest communications empire
the world has seen".

Up to and during the year 1984, the landmark "1984" was
subject to constant and perhaps somewhat neurotic, if understandable, examination. In the event, the year turned out to be far less
terrible than in Orwell's vision. Totalitarianism, which had been
most tenacious in the communist world, had not yet collapsed but
nor had it extended as far as Orwell had feared. In retrospect the
year 1984 marked the turning point in the totalitarian nightmare;
the Soviet Union began the process of reform which led to its
collapse.

But there are those who argue that the state of society in 1984
should not be measured against Orwell's fears but against those
of Aldous Huxley's *Brave New World*. Huxley's fear was of the
world destroyed by trivia. In *Brave New World Revisited*, Huxley
proposed that those who were alert to the dangers of tyranny
were often asleep to the dangers of distractions. He warned that
people would be controlled by pleasure, not by pain; their cultures
would be made essentially inconsequential. Neil Postman argued
cogently, in his book *Amusing Ourselves to Death*, that this was
happening by 1984.

As Murdoch well understood, entertainment was more and

more the staple of Western and particularly American culture. In the global village, television was taking the place of the village green – a tiny but enticing green in every house. Visual images were beginning to replace arguments. Information was being presented as entertainment, and there was no one more skilled at marrying and mixing the two businesses than Rupert Murdoch.

Entertainment had even taken over religion by 1984. The evangelists were on dozens of TV channels. Billy Graham (whom Murdoch came greatly to admire) praised television as "the most powerful tool of communication ever devised by man ... In a single telecast I preach to millions more than Christ did in his lifetime."

Politics, too, was becoming a form of entertainment. "Politics is just like show business," Ronald Reagan had announced as far back as 1966. By the mid-1980s a basic medium for American political discourse was the television commercial. In it, deception became an art form, and thus part of a show. "Sound bites" were a far more effective and evasive a method of distortion than anything promulgated by Orwell. In *Nineteen Eighty-Four* history went down the memory hole in the Ministry of Truth. Instead, by 1984, television was becoming an effective memory hole. Totalitarian politics in communist regimes might still demand that truth be forgotten, as Milan Kundera showed in his novel *The Book of Laughter and Forgetting*. But capitalism could impose the same condition, and with a smile.

By 1984 it was possible to argue that television controlled and trivialized the flow of public discourse in America. George Gerbner, Dean of the Annenberg School of Communication, suggested, "Television is the new state religion run by a private Ministry of Culture (the three networks), offering a universal curriculum for all people, financed by a form of hidden taxation without representation. You pay when you wash, not when you watch, and whether or not you care to watch ... " Or, as Neil Postman put it, "By ushering in the Age of Television, America has given the world the clearest available glimpse of the Huxleyan future."

The other world revolution which took place throughout the

decade of the 1980s was that of computers. It utterly transformed the nature of government and information; one cannot exaggerate the scale or the importance of this change. In the 1960s the computing industry still relied on IBM mainframes or other electro-mechanical monsters. It was thought that there might be a market for some fifty of these machines in all the world; they would sit at the centre of enterprises in their own huge sanctuaries, guarded and tended by a multitude of keepers, and they would dominate and control the world. The computer was then seen "as a leviathan instrument of Big Brother . . . " Predictions of a totalitarian 1984 gained credibility from the image of the men from IBM in suits of grey. Not only would computers gravitate to the hands of the state and other large bureaucracies but the computer would give the state new powers to manage the economy and manipulate individuals.

In the event the opposite had happened, and in a flash. Thanks to the development of the silicon chip, computers had become smaller and smaller, cheaper and cheaper, and more and more powerful. The firms that developed these personal machines were not the big corporations but smaller companies, such as Fairchild and Intel, which developed the first microprocessors and computer arcade games in the early 1970s. By 1976, dozens of companies had joined the competition, microcomputer conferences were being held, and the Apple I was born in its garage.

But it was in the 1980s that the explosion took place. When Ronald Reagan was inaugurated, the IBM PC had not even been announced. But from then on a vast new software industry grew exponentially to meet the possibilities that the new hardware had created. It was software that transformed the computer from a machine into an integral part of more and more homes and almost every business.

In 1977 nearly 100 per cent of the world's computer power had still been commanded by mainframes and other large computers in government or corporate hands. In the flash of ten years all this changed. By the mid-1980s less than 1 per cent of the world's computer power was in mainframes. The vast bulk of it was not in government, but in private hands. US companies controlled two-thirds of a vast new global computer market of some 90 million personal computers, more than half in the USA. "The resulting array of personal computers, engineering workstations, database servers, desktop publishers and silicon printers emerging in the real year of 1984 unleashed forces of liberation that would foil every tyrannous portent of 1984 and other industrial fictions," noted George Gilder, the writer and apostle of technological liberation. The pace of change was barely credible. Between 1961 and 1989 the speed of a computer operation increased 230,000-fold.

This fantastic revolution was accompanied by widespread deregulation of finance, telecommunications, trucking, energy and air transport in the United States. The supporters of such liberalization argued that it had massive and overwhelmingly beneficial effects on the US economy, helping to create 15 million new jobs during the 1980s.

By 1984, another consequence of the computer revolution was becoming apparent. The first Industrial Revolution vastly increased the value of raw materials. The coal and steel of the Ruhr basin had been crucial to the balance of power in Europe. No longer. Gilder suggested that whereas a steel mill was the symbol of the first Industrial Age, a similar symbol today is that of one man alone at a single computer workstation, with access to databases all over the world. Information was becoming one of the world's most valuable commodities.

At the same time, the combination of scientific and technological advances had by the mid-1980s produced a totally new kind of international financial market, quite unforeseen by either Orwell or Huxley. Computers and satellites meant that the world was now awash with new waves of money.

Banking, of course, had always been a branch of the information business. In the sixteenth century, Jacob Fugger built the principal financial institution in Europe on fast couriers bringing news from agents in Spanish America, Mediterranean Africa and the Orient. The Rothschilds established a fortune at the time of Napoleon on the ability of their agents to obtain and transmit information as swiftly as the times would allow. Paul Julius Reuter too had appreciated this. His money-by-cable remittance system, set up during the financial crisis and gold rush in Australia in early 1892, transferred funds much less expensively than did the commercial banks at that time. And, as we have seen, Reuters, with its fantastic instant flow of information across the screens of the world, was leading the revolutionary changes of the 1980s as well.

So were the banks, and among them, one of the most important in New York was Citibank, where the chief executive officer, Walter Wriston, was a close friend and supporter of Rupert Murdoch. After Murdoch had bought the *New York Post* in 1976, Wriston had asked him to lunch. He admired Murdoch's drive, vision and commercial acumen.

Through the 1980s, the decade of debt, Citibank was marching alongside News. The one was building a global banking empire, the other a global news and entertainment empire. Citibank became one of News's principal bankers. Wriston believed that the vast new financial trading market which grew in the 1980s "is not just more of the same: it is something new in the world. It has changed the world." The long-bow had changed the course of military history at the battle of Crécy. "Today, the financial long-bow is the linking of the satellite, the computer and the cathode ray tube." Wriston and Murdoch shared (with Reagan and Thatcher) an absolute, almost obsessive belief in the virtues of the free market, and in its eventual triumph, largely through its technological superiority, over communism.

This possibility was by now understood in the Soviet Union, and an event right at the end of 1984 symbolized the beginning of the end of the communist state. The new Soviet Prime Minister, Mikhail Gorbachev, met Mrs Thatcher. She was impressed with his rational, undogmatic attitudes and declared, in a phrase which came to have resonance, "I like Mr Gorbachev. We can do business together." Most crucially, she sought to help him do business with Ronald Reagan.

Within months of his cordial reception in Britain, Gorbachev had become Secretary General of the Soviet Communist Party. He came quickly to understand the USSR's desperate failure to take any part in or to benefit from the information revolution which was driving Western progress in the 1980s. Soviet leaders had always had a terror of communications technology and had sought to control it. Trotsky had apparently proposed a modern telephone system to Stalin, who had dismissed it saying, "I can

imagine no greater instrument of counter-revolution in our time."
In *Cancer Ward*, Alexander Solzhenitsyn described at great length
Stalin's attempt to record telephone conversations. The legacy of
Stalin's paranoia had had a disastrous effect on Soviet scientific
advancement.

The simple telephone was crucial to the computerization on
which the West was embarked in the 1980s. When Gorbachev
came to power the Soviet Union's telephone system was one of
the most primitive in the industrialized world; there were only
ten telephones to every hundred citizens, a far lower ratio than in
any other industrialized country. People had to wait for hours in
PTT offices for calls. Lines were almost always busy, down, or
so filled with static as to be inoperable. In the United States, by
contrast, there was almost a 100 per cent correlation between
telephones and people, connections were instantaneous and quality
excellent. In most industrialized countries at least 60 per cent of
people had direct access to telephones.

Gorbachev quickly began to lay plans to double the telephone
system by 1990, to start to computerize the society and to make
the next generation of Russians halfway computer-literate. He
understood that such policies would inevitably lead to the government losing its control over information. But he also understood
that the exchange of information is crucial to a modern society.
By 1984, as we have seen, the West was rushing helter-skelter
through a technology-driven period of extraordinary expansion.
It was undergoing the sort of creative destruction which Joseph
A. Schumpeter, the economic historian, identified as characteristic
of periods of major technological change. The Soviet Union was
experiencing nothing of this. In 1960 Khrushchev had promised
that Russians would have the highest standard of living in the
world by 1980. But in the 1980s the Soviet economy approached
total collapse.

As soon as he took office, Gorbachev began to attack those
officials and methods standing in the way of high-tech progress.

The most alarming thing, perhaps, is that we began to lag behind
in scientific and technical development. At a time when countries in the West had begun broad-scale restructuring of the

economy with emphasis on resource saving, the use of the latest technologies, and other achievements of science and technology, our scientific and technical progress was retarded. This was not because of the absence of scientific groundwork but chiefly for the reason that the national economy was not receptive to innovations.

There were then almost no computers in Soviet society outside of large institutions. The society was starved of the resource it most desperately needed: information. The Western world, by contrast, had almost a surfeit of it.

While Gorbachev was first grappling with the disaster of the Soviet Union, News Corporation was becoming one of the most important and most interesting of the stateless, international corporations of the Western world. Murdoch now owned a truly multinational media corporation. News Corporation's worldwide revenues for the fiscal year 1984 were expected to be $2.1 billion, only just behind the Times-Mirror's $2.5 billion and not very far behind Time Inc's $2.8 billion. And it was by far the most international of the world's media companies. It owned some eighty magazines and newspapers and was the Western world's largest newsprint consumer. The company was entirely a reflection of Murdoch himself and of his intuitive business genius. But there was a monkey on his back. Its name was Debt. So far, however, it seemed a friendly creature – indeed, one which was essential to Murdoch's method of operation.

He had a reputation among his business peers for honouring his commitments. Editors and journalists might distrust him but he inspired confidence among his brokers and his bankers. Everyone wanted to give him concessions and favours. He had the smell of success, and he could be trusted. His reputation was that once he shook hands on a deal, that deal would stick. Even if he had made a mistake in the figures, he never reneged.

Murdoch started to appear regularly on the covers of American financial and news magazines. In America, Public Television made a critical two-part series informed by the attacks of Harold Evans who was crusading against the man he called "the mighty Molloch". For the first time people understood that Murdoch owned as a personal fief one of the world's largest media empires, stretching across three continents. But if it was large now, it was less than half the size it would be by the end of the decade.

With his papers in San Antonio, with the *New York Post*, the *Boston Herald* and the *Chicago Sun-Times*, the *Star*, the *Village Voice*, and *New York* magazines, Murdoch was by 1984 a major American publisher. He approached Hearst to see if he might acquire the *Baltimore News American*, an afternoon paper which he considered making into a morning paper for distribution in Washington, which lies only an hour away by road or train. He also considered buying the *Los Angeles Herald Examiner*. Neither purchase went through. He claimed that he had no more newspaper peaks to climb; there were no more *Boston Heralds* that interested him: "I'm not going to run around buying little papers in little country towns all over America." Like many other people, he would have liked to buy the *Washington Post*, and change its liberal policies, but he could not afford it and, moreover, he said, "It ain't for sale."

American pundits were beginning to compare him with Pulitzer and with Hearst. The *Forbes* cover story was written by Thomas O'Hanlon, one of the first American journalists to spot the implications of Murdoch's imperial ambitions and business genius. "WHAT DOES THIS MAN WANT?" asked the headline. The answer was "Lots". O'Hanlon praised him, saying, "While most media corporations today are run by relatively colourless, numbers-oriented businessmen, Rupert Murdoch . . . almost alone among them combines a zest and a feel for the product with a shrewd sense of the bottom line."

He described Murdoch as "part accountant, part gambler, part brilliant marketer, part shrewd journalist . . . By the time Rupert Murdoch retires to his Australian farm in the twenty-first century, his current vulgar image will have faded, and he will be regarded as a sage who followed opportunity where it led and put together a global empire in what may be the twenty-first century's greatest industry, communications."

Fortune magazine was more critical: "Murdoch's tabloids luridly depict a world in which fiendish criminals prey on women and children, evil immigrants menace the natives, and most government affairs are too tedious to note." Murdoch was quoted as saying,

> I don't know any better than anyone else where the electronic age is taking us, or how it will affect a large newspaper company. But I do know that . . . you will have to be a major player in the production of entertainment programming.

Anna Murdoch remarked, "I don't think Rupert has finished yet. I don't think he has any plan that he follows, but I do believe that he still has things he wants to accomplish. I wish he would stop. I wish it would all slow down – we could have more time together. But I don't think that's going to happen."

Murdoch agreed in 1984 to authorize an official biography by Thomas Kiernan, author of books on Jane Fonda and Yasser Arafat. Kiernan wrote a detailed synopsis in which he said Murdoch was more controversial than any other media baron since Hearst. He had been called "a sinister force", "a piranha", "an evil element", "a foul odor"; he had affected millions of American sensibilities and made no secret of wanting to shape American culture. He had star quality. He was a throwback, the stuff of "Dallas" and "Dynasty". "He is the personification of all the fundamental contradictions of the American experience: selfishness vs altruism; ambition vs reticence; publicity vs privacy; daring vs caution."

Murdoch had agreed to give Kiernan total access in return for merely being able to comment on the accuracy of the manuscript. But the collaboration collapsed and Kiernan's unauthorized *Citizen Murdoch* portrayed Murdoch as an amoral thug, interested only in making money out of sleaze. His Murdoch, like that of Harry Evans, was a monster.

No man sees himself as a monster. Murdoch considered himself a newspaper publisher, and a crusader against established pieties, rather than as a mere businessman. However, he did not believe that a publisher had any duties that were sacred. There was nothing special about newspapers as a business. "The buck stops with the owner. Whether the presses break down, whether there are libels in the paper, or anything else."

Murdoch was interested above all in cash flow. He needed to have revenue flowing all the time to finance expansion and to feed his monkey. It was fair to say that News was driven by economics rather than by journalism, as well as by opportunities rather than a plan. Synergy between the various elements of News, if synergy there was, happened by chance, not by design.

In Australia, Fairfax, his main competitor, was very different. It had always been an innovative company, with a strong journalistic tradition, and had frequently created new journalistic products. It looked at the market to see where new products could be launched. Once Murdoch had been like that in Australia but he was no longer so.

His editorial or journalistic policy was oriented towards the market. His papers tended to be grey broadsheets or racy tabloids. Neither attracted excellent journalists. The ethos of News discouraged independent investigation or troublesome journalism. As a landlord who was absent everywhere most of the time, Murdoch was generally disinclined to upset the established order, especially if it was an order from which he benefited.

Measured in Australian dollars, News Corp's revenues had jumped by 41 per cent over the previous two years, and the share price had increased by five times between early 1983 and early 1984. The debt to equity ratio was much higher than in most large publishing companies. Richard Sarazen, News's financial controller, explained that this was because Murdoch was still absolutely refusing to dilute the 46 per cent of News owned by his family company, Cruden Investments (a stake worth some $340 million). To explain this, Sarazen summoned the ghost of Sir Keith: that Murdoch had seen his father make a fortune for others without much benefit to himself and he was determined not to make the same mistake. In fact the family's share of News was probably even greater than the 46 per cent owned by Cruden Investments. Another 14 per cent of News equity was held by nominee companies, including 2 per cent owned by News nominees.

Other companies were vulnerable to shareholder pressure to produce short-term results at the expense of long-term strategy. This was never a problem for Murdoch. He was able to borrow as much as he wished and to ignore short-term problems because of Cruden's control of the group. He did not risk either shareholder discontent or exposure to a predator. But he claimed that he was none the less still accountable. "If you screw up, the shareholders may not throw you out but the bankers will. Whatever happens you're subject to the disciplines of the marketplace. What it does mean is that you can take long-term risks, like *The Times*, and back your judgement, take a bad year or two, and nobody's going to run at you." His competitors had no such luxury.

At that time it was Murdoch's policy to try to keep long-term debt equal to or preferably below the level of shareholders' funds. Even so, at over $80 debt to every $100 of net worth, this was about twice as high as that of most publicly-owned publishing groups. Sarazen told the *Economist* that long-term debt had sometimes exceeded shareholders' funds by as much as 50 per cent. Murdoch said that a ratio of 1:1 was the ceiling.

His bankers were sanguine and said that instead of concentrating on News Corp's debt to equity ratios, they looked at its ability to pay interest charges and to make capital repayments if it ran into trouble. The beauty of newspapers, which generated most of News Corp's revenues, was that they were the supreme cash flow businesses.

The empire was still administered personally by Murdoch, using the weekly reporting system devised by Merv Rich over twenty years earlier. Every week he received the key figures for every business in the group and was thus able to tell at a glance where costs were rising too sharply, where revenue was falling, and would give instant instructions by telephone throughout the world to get the numbers back up to where he thought they should be.

Murdoch was spending less time in Australia. "If a company grows a lot, as we've done, there's got to be a limit to how much you can grow in Australia. For practical, political, social reasons, and everything else." In 1982 he had been there four times; in 1983 he spent only around eight weeks there altogether. However, he still said that he would retire and die in Australia. "Even if I semi-retire, I would start spending half my time in Australia." Asked when that might be, he replied, "When I'm 133 or something . . . " He could not bear to think about handing over to a chief executive. "It makes me quite miserable. But that's human and everyone has to face that some time in their lives."

The profits on his Australian newspapers and television stations were fair but not fabulous. He did not own any of the richest sources of classified advertising. These still belonged to Fairfax and the Melbourne Herald group. He would not be allowed to own more than the two television stations he already had and competition in newspapers was fierce and very expensive. Ansett Airlines was his most profitable Australian investment; he had bought it for $80 million and it was now worth some $500 million. His flagship, *The Australian*, was still in an unhappy state. It had inadequate journalistic resources – thirty-nine journalists had been fired in 1982 – and was not encouraged to upset the status quo. But it was beginning to make money, which meant that News Ltd's managers allowed the editor, Les Hollings, a little more leeway. A Labor government was riding the international political wave to the populist radical right, and Murdoch was becoming an ever closer "mate" of Bob Hawke, the Prime Minister.

All over the world News had become a political company in the 1980s, embracing the deregulatory policies and ethics of the Reagan-Thatcher era.

In the United States, News America had lost money till 1983, largely because of the *Post*; *New York* magazine, the *Village Voice*, the *Star* and the Texas papers were all profitable. But to Murdoch the losses on the *Post* were worth taking for the thrill of owning a paper in New York – a city of enormous power and patronage and one of his principal homes. He could not contemplate living in a city in which he did not publish a newspaper.

The *Post*'s sales had soared as high as 960,000 – an astonishing rise from the 485,000 when he bought the paper – but they were no longer rising. And its share of the advertising market had continued to fall, from 11.3 per cent in 1977 to 7.6 per cent in 1983. The *Daily News* share, by contrast, had grown from 25 per cent to 32.7 per cent, while the *Times* had fallen from 63.6 per cent to 59.7 per cent. The *News*'s advertising revenues in 1983 were over four times those of the *Post* – $225 million as against

$50 million. Murdoch acknowledged that the *Post* would never make money unless he managed to launch and sustain a Sunday edition.

His problem in Chicago and Boston, as well as New York, was that, whereas most American city papers were profitable monopolies, the three which he had bought were all locked in competition with bigger and better-positioned rivals. That was the way he liked to operate, but given the overall decline in newspaper readership, there was little reason to suppose that he would make much money from them.

None the less he seemed to have no liquidity problem. The previous year he had raised some $68 million by selling off oil interests. Ansett Airlines was providing significant revenue. And Reuters was, amid great controversy, about to go public. News Corp's share of that would be worth some $150 million. In November 1984 he spent $350 million on buying Ziff-Davis's travel publications.

The biggest money-spinner in the empire was still the *Sun* in London; it earned a staggering $50 million in 1983 – British working-class readers were providing 40 per cent of News Corp's worldwide operating profit. When the earnings from the *Star* and the Sydney *Telegraph* were added to that, almost 60 per cent of the company's operating earnings were accounted for.

However, in 1984 the *Sun*'s position was a little less secure. Its circulation had fallen by 51,500 in 1983 while that of its main rival, the *Daily Mirror*, had risen 90,000. This had happened partly because the *Sun* had cut its promotional advertising. Seventy per cent of the *Sun*'s revenue came from its cover price and Murdoch was loath to raise that for fear of losing readers. In 1984 the *News of the World* was also falling back and Times Newspapers continued to lose money, largely because of the labour problems which Murdoch had inherited from Thomsons, and which he had till now failed to confront.

Like Roy Thomson before him he had agreed not to interfere in the editorial policy of *The Times* and *Sunday Times*. He expected his other papers to stay within certain guidelines, but he did not demand that they obey daily instructions from him.

He hated the allegation that he had bought *The Times* to buy respectability. "All newspapers are run to make profits. Full stop. I don't run anything for respectability. The moment I do I hope someone will come and fire me and get me out of the place – because that's not what newspapers are meant to be about."

He was puzzling his way through the new technology maze and bazaar that confronted everyone in the 1980s. "Let someone else *own* the satellites. I wish someone else would own the printing presses." He believed that satellites had an immense role to play in the delivery of entertainment, in the future if not now.

He argued that the *Sun* was a testament to the success of the printed word in an age in which television was becoming more and more dominant. The *Sun* could and did handle all the big news, but it tried to do it in a way that was entertaining as well. He thought that popular papers did so well in England because television was so elitist that the English were deprived of choice on the screen and needed popular papers more than did the Americans. In New York he had to take on the *News*, because there was no room for a second *New York Times*. It was not hard to compete with the *News*, he said, because American journalists simply did not know how to compete. "They all go to journalism school and listen to failed editors dressed up as professors."

Perhaps the most revealing statement he made at this time was to Barbara Walters of ABC Television. When Walters asked him if his newspapers did not appeal to the baser instincts of their readers, he replied, "Well, there's nothing wrong with talking to the masses. You know, William Shakespeare wrote for the masses. I think if he was writing today, he'd probably be the chief scriptwriter on 'All in the Family' or 'Dallas'. They'd certainly be a little bit bawdier."

HOLLYWOOD

In the beginning was the photograph. Then came the phonograph, the radio, the moving picture, the talkies, television, VCRs, satellite broadcasts, and more movies and more television.

By the mid-1980s, entertainment was the second largest export business in the United States – after aerospace. Each technological advance increased the power which American entertainment products exerted over an increasingly large portion of the world's population. It was indeed J.R. Ewing, not Hamlet, who was the symbol of international culture.

Entertainment was one of the few really global industries. There were other international products – especially foodstuffs like Coca-Cola, Pepsi-Cola, McDonald's hamburgers – but music and images from the Beatles to Michael Jackson, to South Fork, from Luke Skywalker to Indiana Jones, were beamed over large parts of the world. And almost all those images came from America. As the *Economist* put it, America was to entertainment what Saudi Arabia was to oil. And the Hollywood studios were among the biggest gushers of all.

When he bought *The Times* and *Sunday Times* in 1981, Murdoch had told Anna that they would now be spending most of their lives in the northern hemisphere. By 1984 he had come to realize that his future lay in America. He thought like an American, saw his values as American. He also believed that entertainment and the electronic media were becoming more vital to his empire than news and publishing. Information alone was commercially unviable; it had to piggyback on entertainment. And the Rupert Greene in Murdoch was more interested in entertainment than in education.

Throughout the early 1980s Murdoch became increasingly anxious to acquire one of Hollywood's major film studios. Twentieth Century-Fox eluded him at the beginning of the decade. In 1983 and early in 1984, he made a lunge at Warner Communications, which owned the old Warner Bros studio and film library. His assault upon the company and the angry response of Steve Ross, Warner's chairman, did more than anything else to draw Murdoch to the attention of Wall Street.

In 1982 Warner Communications shares had been as high as $63 25 cents but by early 1983 the price had fallen to under $20. The main reason for this fall was the collapse in the sales of Atari, the video games division of the company. The company was vulnerable.

In August 1983 Stanley Shuman took Murdoch to see Steve

at his holiday home. Ross did not object to Murdoch's proposal that he buy a holding. He therefore began to do so, financing the purchases through short-term capital borrowings – which meant monies available through News overdraft facilities in the UK. He also used acceptance facilities from UK banks; these are like notes – facilities which UK banks make available to companies by taking an acceptance signed by the company, and selling it on the open market.

In September Murdoch announced that he had purchased a million Warner Bros shares; this amounted to less than 2 per cent of the company, considerably less than the 5 per cent threshold at which the Securities and Exchange Commission required a buyer to disclose his interest. As Warner's losses accumulated in the last quarter of the year, Murdoch went on buying. In December 1983 he revealed that he had spent another $98 million and now owned 6.7 per cent of the company – much more than Steve Ross or indeed than all of Warner's management together. He stressed in his filing to the Securities and Exchange Commission that he was not trying to control the company, nor did he even want a seat on the board. It was merely "an investment", he told the *New York Times*; he did not want to take over Warner.

None the less, Ross became alarmed. Meeting with Murdoch on 9 December he tried to warn him off, telling him that his purchases "might adversely affect Warner's relationship with certain of its creative personnel". In other words, some of the company's Hollywood stars and directors might not want to work with a man of Murdoch's reputation. Murdoch was not impressed; he did not think very much of Ross's own reputation.

Ross was also concerned lest Murdoch's growing share in the company jeopardize its cable television franchises in New York and Boston. The Federal Communications Commission did not allow cross-ownership of newspapers and television in metropolitan areas and Murdoch owned papers in both cities.

Ross immediately devised a complicated scheme to prevent Murdoch from increasing his stake. At the end of December Chris-Craft Industries announced that it was planning to buy over 25 per cent of Warner while Warner would acquire a 42.5 per cent stake in a Chris-Craft subsidiary, BHC. This was the fourth largest non-network television company in the country. The beauty of the transaction lay in the fact that aliens like Murdoch were not allowed to own more than 20 per cent of an American television station. So the arrangement not only diluted Murdoch's existing share in Warner, it also precluded him from pursuing any hostile intentions towards Warner at all.

Murdoch immediately filed a complaint with the Federal Communications Commission and then went to court in Wilmington, Delaware. He complained that the share swap between Warners and Chris-Craft was a breach of the commission's cross-ownership rules – because Warner already owned cable television services and BHC owned six television stations.

In court, News argued that the deal was against the interests of the shareholders, including News, and that Chris-Craft derived far more benefit from the swap than Warner. An incompetent and overpaid management was quite improperly protecting itself, the suit declared. News also charged Warners with engaging in "a pattern of racketeering".

Warner filed its counter-suit, describing Murdoch as a disreputable and untrustworthy Australian scandal-sheet printer. Drawing on Harold Evans's memoirs, Warner accused Murdoch of being "deceptive and manipulative" and asserted that he was well known for changing papers "into a sensationalist format, emphasizing violence, scandal and sex. Murdoch has already destroyed the journalistic reputations of the [New York] *Post* and the [Boston] *Herald*."

Before the Federal Communications Commission Warner argued: "What is really involved here is the effort of News Corporation and its controlling individual, Australian newspaper publisher Rupert Murdoch, to manoeuvre themselves into control of Warner." Warner quoted Harold Evans as saying: "Murdoch issued promises as prudently as the Weimar Republic issued marks."

Murdoch preferred Swiss francs. He flew to Geneva to discuss with his bankers the bond offering he intended to issue to finance the purchase of further Warner stock. There he told the press, "We feel very hard put upon by what has happened there. We're extremely critical of that management. We're going to go on and our present plan is that if we're successful in the courts or before the regulatory authorities we will certainly have a proxy fight to remove that management."

Richard Sarazen told the court in a sworn deposition that, until the Chris-Craft deal, Murdoch had intended only to be a passive investor, but after this public insult he decided to seek to exercise some influence if not control over the company.

Both the Delaware court and the Federal Communications Commission found for Warner; neither saw any need to stop the asset swap between Warner and Chris-Craft from going ahead. Murdoch vowed that he would continue to fight. Ross shrugged off the threat. Each of them continued to collect as much dirt as possible on the other. Ross hired a team of investigative lawyers in Washington. Murdoch's method was less orthodox. He deputed Steve Dunleavy to lead a team of reporters from the *New York Post* to investigate Steve Ross's background.

In public, Murdoch struck his usual combative attitude. In one speech he vowed that he would "oppose and expose gross misman-agement, racketeering and abuse of shareholders' funds". To the *New York Times* he said, "When someone's trying to run you down, you try to protect yourself. So that, the next time, someone else doesn't try to run you down."

However, in March a settlement was reached. To get rid of him, Warner paid Murdoch $31 a share for all of his stock. Thus he emerged with a profit of $40 million. Soon afterwards, the price of Warner stock collapsed, to the dismay and in some cases fury of the other stockholders.

Shortly afterwards, Murdoch went after another company, St Regis Corporation, a producer of paper and building supplies, whose share price had fallen sharply. Burdened by long-term debts of about $900 million, its prospects were being downgraded by analysts, and it was an obvious takeover target. Having bought just under 6 per cent of St Regis for some $65 million, he denied that he was interested in either "greenmail" or in acquiring the whole company. None the less the board of St Regis filed a lawsuit to prevent News acquiring any further stock or attempting a takeover. The company lost that legal battle in July 1984 and

Murdoch then told the board that he was willing to pay $52 a share or $757 million in cash for 50.1 per cent of the company. The money had been provided for him by a consortium led by the Midland Bank of London. To escape him, the board rushed into the arms of Champion International Corporation, another forest products company. The two companies merged in a $2 billion deal – entirely through fear of Murdoch – and Murdoch himself made a profit of about $37 million on the stock he already owned.

He later said that he had not liked the bad publicity that he received for his hostile Warner takeover. "I'm about building a company, I'm not about making money in the stock market. I thought I was getting quite the wrong reputation."

He told the *Economist* (which published another cover story on him) that he had wanted to diversify from newspapers into another branch of the entertainment industry. He claimed: "We didn't want to get control of Warner. We wanted to come along and have a look at it, take a ride and see, and maybe in our wildest dreams – if someone had made a run at it and given it to us ... But the major thing is the studio, and they've got a great film library ... "

But the failure with Warner was shortlived. Once again Murdoch's extraordinary luck held. A few months later an equally fabulous slice of the legend and reality of Hollywood became available. Twentieth Century-Fox was on the block again.

The company, founded by Hungarian-born William Fox, started as one nickelodeon on Broadway just after the turn of the century. Fox then went into making movies.

By the middle of the First World War, these were big business, and in 1917 Fox opened his first studio on Sunset and Western in Hollywood. Throughout the 1920s, Fox expanded his empire; in 1924 John Ford made *The Iron Horse* for him, establishing the genre of the big Western.

By the end of the 1920s there were a hundred million moviegoers a week in the USA. When sound arrived, Harry Warner said, "Do you realize what this means? From now on we can give every small town in America and every movie-house its own 110-piece orchestra."

Fox was well ahead of the pack in the development of newsreels. In May 1927 he showed, on the very same day as the event itself, sound footage of Charles Lindbergh taking off on his historic flight to Paris. This feat brought the house down. Fox was an early forerunner of Murdoch in that he understood well the potent combination of news, film and entertainment. By 1929 he had seventy newsreel units in the field, turning out four films a week, and he had opened an all-news theatre, the Embassy, in Times Square. Eventually, Movietone News served fifty-one countries.

Fox overreached himself when he tried to combine Fox with MGM to make the greatest movie company of the era and he was forced out of his own company. Without him, the Fox company began to lose money and was saved only when it merged with a smaller outfit, Twentieth Century Co, run by a young man named Darryl Zanuck.

After the war, Twentieth Century-Fox had to come to terms with its new competitor, television; the company made a deal with the R.J. Reynolds company for a five-days-a-week version of Fox Movietone News. That year there were 127,000 television sets in New York, 22,000 in Philadelphia and 15,000 in Los Angeles. By 1950 these numbers had trebled and when coaxial cable linked the coasts in 1951, live network TV became first a possibility and quickly a reality.

In 1952 Spyros P. Skouras, the president of Fox, sensing that TV would be a major competitor, tried to buy the ABC network, but his board would not agree.

Movie attendance continued to drop in the face of the competition from the box. The studios turned to the wide screen of Cinemascope and colour to save them. Twentieth Century-Fox made *The Robe* for $4 million in fifty-two days – and in its first four months the film grossed $20 million. Marilyn Monroe also did well for the studio with *Niagara, Gentlemen Prefer Blondes* and *There's No Business Like Show Business*, but it was almost destroyed in the early 1960s by the fiasco of *Cleopatra*, which cost the studio $35 million.

Zanuck recouped some of the losses with *The Longest Day* and in 1966 *The Sound of Music* outgrossed *Gone with the Wind* to become the biggest money-spinner of all time – till then. The company's great success story in the 1970s was *Star Wars*, which earned Fox at least $500 million worldwide, together with another $200 million from such spin-offs as clothes, toys, games and bubblegum. The sequel, *The Empire Strikes Back*, also did well. Flushed with this success, Fox launched on to a buying spree which included the Pebble Beach resort at Monterey for $72 million and the Aspen Ski Corporation for $48 million.

By 1980 the company's overall assets were worth far more than Fox's current stock market value, of around $35 a share. The board decided to try to effect what later became commonly known as a leveraged buy-out, but the deal came unstuck in January 1981. The publicity generated put Fox "in play" and made it vulnerable to a takeover bid.

This came from an oil man, Marvin Davis, and his silent partner, an oil and gas broker named Marc Rich. In April 1981 they bought the company for about $70 a share, or $703 million in all.

Davis had struck lucky as a wildcatting oil man in Wyoming in the 1960s, and his riches were vastly enhanced by OPEC oil price rises of 1973 and 1979. He was a mixture of shrewdness, even toughness, and joviality. He had always loved movies and enjoyed "fun" businesses. In 1981 he sold about 850 of his oil wells and had a pile of cash worth some $630 million.

His partner, Marc Rich, was less straightforward. He was under investigation by the Justice Department for tax evasion and for illegally selling oil to Iran, which was under embargo since its seizure of the American Embassy hostages in 1979. In 1982, he fled to Switzerland and the US government froze all his assets, including his half share of Fox.

Davis established himself as a flamboyant presence in Hollywood. Though he became disillusioned by the failures of Fox's films in the early 1980s, he and Rich did well out of their purchase. By 1984 Davis had taken out of the studio most of the money he had put in and millions in profits as well. The studio was still deeply in debt.

In 1984 a key figure arrived. Barry Diller was brought into Fox from Paramount where he had had an extraordinarily successful ten-year reign as chairman. Diller terrified many of the people who came into contact with him, and made others perform very well. When his relationship with the chairman of Paramount's parent company, Gulf and Western, deteriorated so much that Diller decided to leave, he called Marvin Davis and asked him to sell him half of Fox. Davis refused, but said he might sell him 25 per cent if he would agree to run it. They began to negotiate.

By October 1984, Diller had negotiated himself a splendid contract. His basic salary was to be $3 million, together with 25 per cent of any increase in the equity value of the studio during his tenure. Davis also loaned him $1.5 million interest-free, to pay off a similar loan from Paramount. His expense account was vast. The contract also stated that Davis would step aside and allow Diller the day-to-day running of the studio. Davis was not even allowed to talk to Fox employees "in such a manner as shall derogate, limit or interfere with Diller".

Once the deal was done, Diller and Davis found they could not tolerate each other, let alone collaborate. Davis was a raunchy, emotional, bluff man, who did not know much about films, beyond the fact that he liked them – especially *The Sound of Music*, to which he wanted to make a sequel. Diller was cool, crisp and fearsomely aggressive towards his staff. And he knew a lot about the movie business. In Hollywood the relationship became known as "the Hitler–Stalin Pact".

Moreover, by early 1985 Diller had begun to realize the size of the studio's financial problems. Its debt of $430 million required $70 million a year just to service it. There was not enough money to make good new products and Davis was unwilling to invest more. He suggested that Diller approach Mike Milken at Drexel Burnham Lambert to arrange additional monies.

Part of the enormous process of expansion and change in the communications industry in the 1980s was financed and made possible by the creation and sale of junk bonds in particular by Milken and others like him. Indeed, his supporters claimed that by the mid-1980s Milken had become an extraordinary force in American business life. Drexel Burnham Lambert was attracting some $2 billion to $3 billion in foreign funds every year into America – thus doing something to reverse the capital flight from previous decades. Milken's activities were crucial in the development of the new industries which were transforming communications – fibre-optic networks, the growth of Ted Turner's network, CNN, and Fox itself. Milken later pleaded guilty to six charges of felony and, at the time of writing, was serving a sentence in a federal penitentiary. Nevertheless Milken understood more than almost anyone else (save, perhaps Murdoch) the speed at which technology was transforming the world and in particular the world of communications. Changes which used to take ten years to effect were now taking place overnight. He had begun his career doing credit analysis of what were even then called junk bonds – high-yielding paper that had less of an equity cushion behind it than most people thought adequate. In ten years he had transformed junk bonds into a vast and mainstream financial instrument which he employed to open the capital markets to clever and aggressive entrepreneurs.

Despite Fox's problems, Milken agreed to try to raise $250 million by selling junk bonds. But that deal misfired because Diller demanded that Davis give him real equity in Fox. When Davis refused, Diller scotched the Drexel issue.

In early 1985 the Justice Department agreed to allow Davis to buy the 50 per cent of Fox which the US government had seized from the fugitive Marc Rich. Because of Fox's atrocious results, Davis was able to persuade Justice that the half share was worth only $116 million. Although he had also to shoulder Rich's half of the debt, it was the sort of bargain which Marvin Davis was famous for making.

Then, after further rows with Diller, Davis decided to resell Rich's half share. There was one man interested in buying: Rupert Murdoch. He agreed to pay Davis an effective price of $250 million. Davis clearly made a large profit and the general perception was that Murdoch had paid a premium price because he considered this a rare opportunity to acquire a major film library which could both provide the foundation of a fourth major American television network and also supply programmes for his television enterprises abroad. Murdoch described Fox as "one of the world's great film and television companies" and said that he was confident that it was about to grow significantly.

Murdoch had never been very interested in partnerships of any kind; it is a relationship that does not suit him. None the less, he felt that half of Fox was better than no part of any studio at all. He reckoned that for all Fox's obvious problems, Diller was a good bet and that he could help sort the studio out. Diller, however, was concerned about his own position. He did not know Murdoch well, but knew that his reputation was as fearsome as his own. He demanded the right to be able to terminate his contract at any time within the first year of Murdoch's ownership. Davis was alarmed that this might frighten Murdoch away. But Murdoch was blithe about it. He understood that, given Diller's dislike of Davis, he, himself, would soon be in an overpowering position at Fox. Diller told Murdoch that as he did not know him well, he wanted "exit rights" in case things did not work out. Murdoch gave them.

For Murdoch the purchase of Fox was a triumphant and essential step towards creating a worldwide media and entertainment empire. "A really integrated media company has to be in the production of entertainment," he said.

It also has to be in news reporting. For both, the question is one of how do you present it? In magazine form or television form? For all those things, you've got to have a foot in the creative processes. Making movies is part of that. I went to entertainment not to get into entertainment. It was part of a broad strategy to get into the media industry, the heart of the media industry. I know you can't really talk about one global economy, but there really is. There are certain things that are common. Hollywood is still the magnet for the most talent. Studios here still have the pre-eminent position. So if one owns a studio, it's a great opportunity.

Now what he needed were television stations. A few weeks after he had purchased his half share of Fox, they came his way, by an extraordinary stroke of serendipity.

In the spring of 1985, Murdoch went to China. His herald was the Australian Prime Minister himself; a few weeks before, Bob Hawke, who had reconciled the leadership though not the rank and file of the Labor Party with his friend Rupert, visited Peking and spoke warmly to the Chinese leadership of Murdoch and his projects. When he arrived, Murdoch was treated like some new capitalist demi-god by the Chinese communist authorities who, at that time, were moving China towards a market economy while attempting to sustain political orthodoxy. Like many anti-Soviets, Murdoch came away from China enthusing about the country and its progress. He also understood its unique commercial potential: 800 million new consumers. He wanted to extend his empire behind the Great Wall.

His first idea for an international hotel and media centre was eventually dropped, and Murdoch pursued a more primary interest – tapping the vast, untouched Chinese market for entertainment. The Chinese evening television news reached over 500 million people. There were hundreds of millions of homes in China. What they needed above all was a bit of fun. The problem was that they had no money to pay for it. To get his foot in the door, Murdoch made a deal for Fox movies to be shown all over China. A committee of official censors came to Hong Kong to vet and to choose those films which were deemed politically, culturally and socially "acceptable". The most popular in villages all over the country were subsequently said to be *The Sound of Music* and *Patton*.

On his return from China, the weekend after Easter 1985, Murdoch stopped off at his newly-acquired Fox lot, where he met a friend, John Werner Kluge, the owner of a chain of independent television stations called Metromedia, which had rented a studio at Fox for a financial presentation. They talked and, said Murdoch, he decided within minutes to buy Metromedia.

John Werner Kluge's was a great American Dream story. He had come to America from Germany as a fatherless child of eight, and had since made himself one of the richest men in the world. In 1941 an educational consultant named Clarence Lovejoy wrote a book entitled *So You're Going to College*, in which he appraised the prospects of one John Kluge. "Kluge," he wrote, "can't be President of the United States because of his birth, but he won't stop far short of it."

He started as a food broker and bought into radio. By 1959, when television was beginning to expand hugely, he had made enough money to buy the controlling share of Metropolitan

Broadcasting Corporation, a poorly-run company which owned TV stations in New York and Washington, and two radio stations. He changed the company's name to Metromedia and began to acquire independent television stations in big conurbations. Kluge swiftly built Metromedia into a corporate empire which grossed over $100 million in 1964.

He hoped to be able to start a fourth national TV network himself, but this dream died. The first half of the 1970s were comparatively lean but in 1976 advertisers began to deluge both the networks and the independent TV stations with money. Kluge's stations did well; in New York, Metromedia staged reruns of "M*A*S*H" against the evening news on the networks. By this time the three national networks, ABC, NBC and CBS, were beginning to lose their audience share, as cable TV encouraged people to switch channels more frequently. Kluge had Metromedia begin to buy up some of its own shares. In 1978 Metromedia offered ten-year non-convertible debentures for 1.5 million shares. By the early 1980s the shares had risen from under $40 to over $150. Metromedia was now the nation's largest independent broadcasting company.

In many ways Kluge operated like Murdoch. He kept a firm control over costs – his headquarters were in New Jersey rather than New York in order to avoid the city's taxes. Like Murdoch he also insisted on receiving weekly profit and loss reports from each division of the company. He liked to act alone – without a big board or an excess of executives to hamper him. Thus in 1983 he negotiated the purchase of WFLD in Chicago in just one day – though the station was not even for sale. He paid $140 million.

By the early 1980s he was much richer and had bought, among other things, the Harlem Globetrotters. In 1981 he married his third wife, Patricia Gay, who was part English, part Iraqi, wholly Catholic and a former model for his men's magazines. They had a splendid society wedding at St Patrick's Cathedral New York; the groom converted to Catholicism for the occasion and Anna Murdoch was one of the matrons of honour. (When they were later divorced in 1990 Patricia Kluge was said to have been given $80 million a year.)

At the end of 1984 Kluge embarked on his most astonishing

deal to date. He made a leveraged buy-out of Metromedia, and while pocketing $115 million in cash and securities, increased his share of the company from 26 per cent to 75.5 per cent.

The banks agreed a loan of $1.3 billion and the Prudential Insurance Company, which led the way by buying $125 million of the preferred stock, seemed delighted to help him. The deal enabled the banks to place large amounts of money at a rate which was pegged to the prime, which was more than most corporate borrowers were willing to pay. The only snag for Kluge was that this allowed the banks, led by Manufacturers Hanover, to keep Metromedia in line – not something he enjoyed. Under the banks' terms he had to pay back a first instalment of $200 million by June 1985. The idea that he should meet his interest payments from Metromedia's cash flow and pay back the principal in stages was not unusual, but it did not appeal to Kluge. It might mean that he had to sell some property, perhaps even one of the TV stations.

He began to replace his bank debt with $1.3 billion of new junk bonds created by Michael Milken and Drexel. Drexel issued four kinds of junk bonds with a total value of $1.35 billion against all the assets of Metromedia, including the radio stations and the cellular telephone systems in which Kluge had become interested. As in the real-estate and TV businesses Metromedia was worth more as a private company, in which Kluge could manage to maximize cash flow, than as a public company which had to maximize reported earnings. It was clever. Allan Sloan pointed out in *Forbes* that Kluge was in effect doing "a leveraged leveraged buy-out."

Kluge had to pay a higher rate on the new paper than he was paying the banks, but Metromedia's cash interest payments were lower because $300 million of the new money came from zero coupons. The original bank loan had cost Kluge $14.5 million in front-end fees – and he had kept it for only six months. But he probably reckoned it was worth it to rid himself of his shareholders. Now he was also rid of the banks, had deferred his principal repayments and had improved his tax position. He was, said *Forbes*, well on the way to his first billion.

He was betting that the value of the stations would compound faster than securities Drexel sold for him were accruing interest.

By the time he met Murdoch, and then Barry Diller on the Fox lot, Kluge wanted to get out of television and concentrate on new technological products such as cellular phones and a paging device. He thought that cable, pay television and video recorders would all conspire to devalue television networks. He also felt that the demand for television stations would never be as great again, because the Federal Communications Committee had just changed the rules to allow a single company to own a maximum of twelve stations, as opposed to seven, provided that together they did not cover more than 25 per cent of the national market. And so he told Murdoch and Diller that he might sell some of the Metromedia television stations, but not the one in New York.

The next day, at a meeting also attended by Michael Milken, Kluge said he wanted $1.05 billion for his stations in Los Angeles, Chicago, Dallas–Forth Worth, Houston and Washington DC. The Boston station was already pledged to Hearst and he again insisted on keeping New York. The price he asked for the other stations was about fifteen times cash flow, whereas standard ratio would have been ten to twelve times earnings. (This meant that Murdoch would have to pay $15 for every $1 a year that the stations provided. He would then pay 74 per cent to borrow the $15, which worked out at $2.10. Add another 20 per cent for transaction costs, also financed by borrowed money, and he was paying something like $2.50 for every $1 of station cash flow.)

Diller thought this price absurd, but Murdoch told him not to worry about it. Murdoch saw that to get a group of stations in major American cities was a unique opportunity. He realized this was a key moment in the development of News. His overwhelming ambition now was to be a force in global communications, and to achieve that he needed US television stations at the core of his empire. To seize them, he would pay whatever was the going rate. He argued, "You're paying a premium for them all coming together. It's the one time in life when wholesale is more expensive than retail." Never again would there be a chance to buy such a string of well-placed stations, offering the chance to start a fourth network. But he had to have New York as well. He told Kluge that no deal was possible without it, and Kluge conceded.

Marvin Davis presented difficulties. He was reluctant to expand his commitments, and he too thought Kluge's price was exorbitant. He told Murdoch he would only go in to Metromedia on a short-term basis and would want Murdoch to buy him out soon thereafter. However, he kept changing his mind about the price at which he would want that to happen.

Apart from the price and Davis, there were two other obvious and serious problems. The first was the rule preventing cross-ownership of television and newspapers in the same city. The second was the law that no alien could own an American television station. Murdoch was undisturbed by either problem. He would apply to the Federal Communications Commission (FCC) for a temporary waiver of the cross-ownership rule, and he would deal with the citizenship problem in the only possible way.

The agreement between Metromedia and Fox was announced on 6 May 1985. Murdoch and Davis (who remained on the masthead, but was little more than a name) agreed to buy Metromedia's seven television stations for just over $2 billion. They formed a separate company, Fox Television Inc (Fox TV, formerly News America Television Inc) to make the purchase. At the same time Murdoch also established Twentieth Century-Fox Holdings Inc (Twentieth) as the umbrella company for Fox TV. Both new companies were incorporated in Delaware. Twentieth would buy and keep WITG in Washington DC, WNYW in New York, WFID in Chicago, KTTV in Los Angeles, KRIV in Houston, and KDAF in Dallas. The Boston station, WCVB TV, would be immediately sold on to Hearst.

It was the second largest deal in the history of media so far – after the purchase of ABC by Capital Cities just one month earlier. With the resale of the Boston station for $450 million, the effective net price was about $1.855 billion, including all the fees and transaction costs.

Fortune magazine said that the sale could be "the worst deal yet" in a spate of high-cost US TV takeovers. But the financial writer, Allan Sloan, pointed out in *Forbes*: "When you have ambitions like Murdoch's, and when you have his grasp of media realities, you don't worry about quarterly earnings or even annual earnings. You fix on the big picture. Which is another way of saying that, yes, Murdoch overpaid in the short run but not necessarily in the long run."

Richard Sarazen gave another reason for Murdoch's branching into television and away from his first love, newspapers. "If you are an arch-conservative, fighting a world of left-wing journalists, particularly in this country, wouldn't you want to have another influence, another say?"

Murdoch himself acknowledged that he was betting News on the success of the deal. It was a gamble he could make because he, not institutions or shareholders, controlled News. "Apart from the normal motives of greed, it's the stability of the company. We've been able to take the years when we've got things wrong, and not look over our shoulders at Alan Bond or Robert Holmes à Court, thinking someone's going to take us over."

In its first filing with the FCC after buying the stations, Fox said that it believed the stations reached 22 per cent of American television homes and 23 per cent of the US advertising market. But FCC rules allowed that when accounting market shares, UHF stations could be discounted by 50 per cent. Therefore, for the purpose of calculating Fox's total market share (which had to be less than 25 per cent), the six Fox stations were said to cover only 18 per cent. Fox estimated that after the purchase of WXNE in Boston, this would rise to 19 per cent. Fox could therefore buy up to five more TV stations provided that their aggregate market share was 6 per cent or less.

Another problem with the purchase was how to deal with the junk bonds that Drexel had issued. These bonds were secured by the television stations, and some other assets as well. This meant that Murdoch had to satisfy the holders of Kluge's debt that the television stations alone, without Metromedia's other properties, would be adequate collateral for their bonds. They would need to give their permission for the sale. Only Drexel knew just who had the bonds, and that knowledge was an expensive commodity.

Drexel informed Murdoch that they could not get the agreement of all the original Metromedia bondholders, and that he could not simply assume Kluge's junk bonds. This put Murdoch at Drexel's mercy. Milken suggested instead that Fox TV issue $1.15 billion in convertible preferred stock. Then came the knife. Murdoch was offering the holders of Kluge's paper either a cash payment or an exchange of his preferred stock for their bonds. Assuming that Kluge bondholders wanted to roll their investment over into Murdoch paper, which many of them undoubtedly did, it made no difference to them whether they sold the Klugebonds to Murdoch and used the proceeds to buy Murdoch preferred stock, or whether they swapped the bonds for the Murdoch preferred. But it made a big difference to Drexel and to Murdoch. If Klugebond holders took the exchange, Murdoch and Drexel paid a fee of 1 per cent of the preferred stock thus swapped. If new preferred stock had to be underwritten, Murdoch would pay Drexel a fee of 3.5 per cent. In the event all the Kluge bondholders took the cash – including Drexel, whose trading desk seems to have owned several hundred million dollars of the Klugebonds. Thus Drexel got a 3.5 per cent fee for virtually the entire issue, rather than a mix of 1 per cent and 3.5 per cent fees. Drexel made many extra millions out of Murdoch – altogether Drexel's fees came to around $50 million. Milken was one of the few people who had outsmarted him on a financial transaction; and that angered Murdoch.

He was also angry that the preferred stock was three-year stock, and if not paid off in those three years it would convert into News Corp stock. Such an idea was anathema to Murdoch. He had always refused to dilute his stock, because he wished to retain his family's share, just under 50 per cent. The risk of losing this control if Fox did not develop as well as he hoped in the next thirty-six months was enormous. He was furious with Milken for having, as he saw it, misled him.

Richard Sarazen devised clever tax advantages in these series of transactions. In the USA the dividend payments on the Fox preferred shares were considered as debt, and were allowed as tax deductions, almost as if they were interest payments. In Australia, by contrast, preferred stock was treated as equity rather than debt and Australian banks lent money on the basis of that equity. So in Australia News Corp's assets had now increased by $1.6 billion. Australian accounting rules, unlike American, allowed companies to revalue their intangible assets like mastheads. This could automatically and almost miraculously transform a company's debt to equity ratio overnight.

To raise some cash to put towards the Metromedia purchase Murdoch began to sell assets that he considered tangential to the global empire he was building. He had never been comfortable with the radical political and sexual philosophies of the *Village Voice* – but he had known better than to interfere with its successful formula. Now he put it on the block. One of the people keenest to buy it was John Evans who, as the publisher of the *Voice*, had built up its classified ads and therefore its vast profits. He was now head of Murdoch Magazines. When he asked Murdoch if he would mind if he put together a consortium to buy the *Voice*, Murdoch gave a rather grudging consent. But Evans was unable to match the $55 million offered by Leonard Stern of Hartz Mountain Industries. Even though some of this payment was deferred, it represented a fabulous profit on the $7.5 million which he had paid for *New York* and the *Voice* in 1978. Murdoch was amused when the *Voice*'s staff asked the new owners to promise the same editorial independence as they had enjoyed under Murdoch.

Murdoch also agreed to a management buy-out of the *Chicago Sun-Times*, which was put together by the paper's publisher, Robert Page. Murdoch had bought the paper for $90 million in January 1984; just two years later, he sold it for $145 million, another substantial profit. At the same time he also disposed of a part of his Reuters stake.

Then Marvin Davis struck a blow at the whole scheme. In June 1985, he pulled out of the deal. "We have decided not to exercise our option," he said. "Instead we will concentrate on the development of our other investments, including Twentieth Century-Fox." This left Murdoch to find another $775 million to pay the full cost of $1.85 billion for Metromedia, which would increase News Corp's debt burden by six times from the $408 million in the 1984 annual report to over $2.3 billion.

On top of that, there was the problem of what to do with Davis. He said he looked forward to continued association and partnership with Murdoch at Fox. But that, of course, was hardly to be expected. Murdoch now liked him no more than Diller did.

"You can't rely on anything he says," he complained later. Davis came to realize that he was powerless against the combination of Murdoch and Diller and had best get out.

According to Murdoch, Davis suggested that they flip a coin to see which of them should buy the other out of Twentieth Century-Fox. Murdoch said he accepted the challenge but Davis then backed out. Throughout the summer of 1985 they argued, with increasing dislike for each other, over the price which Murdoch would pay Davis for his 50 per cent of Twentieth Century. Eventually they agreed on $325 million, but that included the $88 million he had already put in as a loan to the studio.

Davis kept 2.7 acres of the 56.7-acre lot in Hollywood, the Aspen Skiing Company and the Pebble Beach resort in Carmel, assets with an estimated value of some $100–$150 million. He subsequently sold Pebble Beach at a huge profit.

Quite apart from the financial cost, Murdoch had to pay a heavy price to establish a TV network. First he would have to renounce the *New York Post* – because the cross-ownership rule prevented one person owning a television station and a newspaper in the same town. Despite its lack of commercial success, Murdoch was almost besotted with the *Post*. It was his paper in his town, and that town was the hub of the world media. A major newspaper office, with the roar and the smell and the grime of the presses and its power on the community had exhilarated him all his life: they reminded him of his childhood and of Keith. Indeed, he derived the essence of his personality and his power from a newspaper's environment. As Alexander Cockburn put it in the *Wall Street Journal*, for Murdoch to sell the *New York Post* "would be like Dracula selling his coffin".

Second, there was the obligation to revoke his Australian citizenship and become an American. The US Communications Act was quite specific. No corporation could hold a broadcasting licence if any officer or director were an alien or if more than one-fifth of its capital stock were owned of record or voted by aliens, or if it were directly or indirectly controlled by any management with alien management, ownership or control.

To Murdoch even such high prices were worth paying. The

acquisition enormously increased the reach of News Corp. Murdoch's venture was seen as one of the most ambitious that any media magnate had ever attempted. No one else had managed to build a fourth US national TV network. And no one before had ever attempted to build a global communications empire as large and as complex as News was becoming. With the stations, he now controlled ninety-three publishing, broadcasting and other operations with assets of $4.7 billion and annual revenue of $2.6 billion. He would reach a quarter of the world's English-speaking population.

But first he had to make a similar journey to that which millions of immigrants had made before him, through today's equivalent of Ellis Island.

ELLIS ISLAND

For two centuries now, America has seemed the best and the bravest new world, the lodestar or the safe haven, the Eldorado, for millions of people around the globe. That is still so today, just as it was in the nineteenth century. No other country in history has exerted such a fierce gravitational pull.

At the end of the twentieth century, the world is on the move as never before. Before the Second World War there were just 2 million international travellers. Now 400 million people travel abroad every year. At the beginning of the 1980s there were 10 million refugees in the world. At the beginning of the 1990s there were over 17 million. There were many millions more migrants, both legal and illegal. For millions of Asians, Latin Americans and citizens of the Soviet empire, the United States was the dream destination, with Europe, Canada and Australia trailing behind. Migration has always been one of the great engines of human history, as the poor, the wretched and the tempest-tossed flee poverty and persecution in the hopeful pursuit of human happiness and wealth.

In one sense Murdoch was doing the same; he too believed in

the American Dream. But to his critics his motives seemed so material that he was merely a caricature of the millions who had landed in the New World with optimism and trepidation, and of many of those who were with him in the District Court in Lower Manhattan, on 4 September 1985.

The ordinary immigrants, dressed in their best clothes, waited in the corridors and then, as the time for the ceremony drew near, were shepherded into the courtroom, clutching their copies of the Oath of Allegiance.

Rupert Murdoch, Anna and their children Elisabeth, Lachlan and James, now aged seventeen, fourteen and twelve, arrived in two limousines and drove straight down into the underground entrance of the court. From the parking lot, they rose into the courthouse by elevator, avoided the press, and were ushered into the courtroom where everyone else was waiting. They were shown into the jury box. Judge Shirley Wohl Kram entered, took her seat and made a rather moving speech about the rights and responsibilities of new citizens.

The Australian papers recorded that at exactly 10.55 a.m. New York time, on 4 September 1985, Rupert Murdoch became an American by placing his hand over his heart and pledging allegiance to the flag of the United States of America and to the Republic, so renouncing the Commonwealth of Australia, where he had been born in 1931.

After the ceremony, the *New York Post* took pictures for that day's edition, as Murdoch and his family (who had not changed their citizenship) shook hands with Judge Kram and slipped out of the courthouse the way they had arrived. Murdoch climbed into one limousine, Anna and the children took another.

The reporters, mostly Australian, foiled so far, rushed after the cars. Say a word to Australia, Citizen Murdoch! How does it feel not to be an Aussie, Rupert? Bye-bye Bondi Beach! For a moment it looked as if the traffic would bear the Murdochs away upon its flow, but their cars were caught at a red light. An Australian television reporter dashed up to Murdoch's limousine. Murdoch's window was tightly closed. The Australian banged on the roof of the car to make the American inside open up. Murdoch smiled, but his car drew away.

Anna Murdoch was less prudent; she had her window down. Microphones were pushed into her face. How did she feel about her husband's change of citizenship? the jostling reporters shouted. "I'm very happy for him," she said.

Others were outraged. Jimmy Breslin, the tempestuous columnist for the *Daily News*, described Murdoch not as a man for all seasons, but as "a man for all occasions. He regarded New York as a town without sense, a place of damaged palates where nobody can taste, and he presented the great city with headlines about killer bees and newspapers filled with pictures of blacks in handcuffs. He gave you thuggery and called it a newspaper."

Breslin thought that Murdoch had incited racial hatred in the city. "We are a mixed population and he tried so blatantly to use race to sell his newspapers that he became known as 'Tar baby Murdoch'. I can't believe that we're so easy in this city that an act like Murdoch's can get by. You have more right to own a television station in this city than Murdoch does."

In similar vein, William Safire had already expressed his misgivings in the *New York Times*. Safire acknowledged that Murdoch "is just the sort of entrepreneurial type the country wants to attract – one who will generate jobs and pay taxes and challenge the powerful". (In fact Murdoch's critics considered that he usually befriended the powerful rather than challenging them.) "Isn't it true that his main reason for becoming a citizen is simple greed and lust for power?" Safire had no problem with that, but he felt that Murdoch was in fact the opposite of a nationalist. "He is the multinational man, a true 'citizen of the world'. He is at home in London, New York and Sydney and he pays homage to no political prince . . . Americans should remind him that allegiance means loyalty, sometimes passionate loyalty."

Mike Royko, the Chicago columnist, who thought Murdoch's papers unsuitable even for dead fish, demanded to know how Murdoch could be welcomed so easily when poor Mexicans and Haitians were turned back at the frontiers or on the high seas? He was not fleeing communism or any other kind of tyranny. "Nor does he have a skill that is in short supply. By profession, Murdoch is a greedy, money-grubbing, power-seeking status-climbing cad. Since when is that skill in short supply?"

To Royko, Murdoch's only motive was to get even richer and more powerful. He was "a bloated millionaire", a sacker of American workers and breaker of unions, "a proven ingrate", "a proven liar". Murdoch obviously had contempt for Americans.

> In his heart, if such an organ exists, Murdoch thinks we're boobs. That's why he publishes boob-mentality newspapers. He thinks that's all we can understand . . . So, if Murdoch is allowed to become a citizen while we're turning away people who are running from death squads or starvation, then we should make one small change in the plans to renovate the Statue of Liberty. Get rid of the torch. Just have the lady hold up her hand with the middle finger extended.

On the other side of the political spectrum, the views were rather different. Within the Reagan administration, Murdoch's move was widely welcomed, nowhere more so than on the Federal Communications Commission, which was undergoing its own Reaganite revolution at the hands of its chairman, Mark Fowler.

From Murdoch's point of view, there could have been no better chairman of the FCC than Fowler – they were ideological soulmates, united in their love of the free market and their abhorrence of regulations. Fowler admired Murdoch's own freebooting philosophy and welcomed his desire to create a new television network. Indeed he did everything he could to ease Murdoch's passage. Murdoch later called him "one of the great pioneers of the communications revolution", and "perhaps the most successful of any Reagan appointee".

Fowler was a forty-three-year-old communications lawyer who had worked in Ronald Reagan's 1980 campaign and was then given the chairmanship of the Federal Communications Commission. He was jovial fellow, a showman, who kept in his office a Mao cap, adorned with a red star, which he used to put on the head of any of his officials who came up with a suggestion he deemed "collectivist". He was an unabashed Reaganite and defined his mission as "pruning, chopping, slashing, eliminating, burning and deep-sixing" as many as he could of the regulations which the FCC had created and imposed upon communications throughout

America in the half-century of its existence. Fowler's enemies, many of them public-interest groups concerned with broadcasting, saw him as "the mad monk of deregulation". One former commissioner complained that Fowler saw regulation "as a kind of evil empire, and he's Luke Skywalker".

In the first four years of Fowler's chairmanship, the commission had allowed many more automatic renewals of broadcast licences, and had begun to deregulate radio and television. It had authorized direct broadcast satellites, and raised the number of AM, FM and TV stations a single owner might have from seven to twelve of each. This last change was important in the takeover of the ABC network by Capital Cities, and in Murdoch's purchase of Metromedia.

Fowler thought Murdoch an exciting challenger of the entrenched networks. He was coming in "to provide new choices". He commented, "That is something we certainly want to encourage as a generic matter." If Fowler had had his way, Murdoch could have had the Metromedia stations without the inconvenience of becoming an American citizen; after all, his nationality had not prevented him from buying his American newspapers, and Fowler wanted the freedom of print to be extended to the air.

Fowler had forced the commission to catch up with the technological revolution. But the change went deeper than merely adjusting to the revolution in computers and telecommunications. It was ideological. Under Fowler the commission sometimes appeared to be no more than a mere bystander in private industry disputes. Even some of the other commissioners thought this could go too far. James H. Quello, the dean of the five-member board, warned that "the FCC is not here to serve fast buck artists who buy broadcasters to bust them up".

It was upon Quello that Murdoch and Kluge had together made a formal call to inform the commission of the intended sale. Quello said afterwards that he liked Murdoch, whom he found quiet-spoken and persuasive. He did not think he was going to "bust up" Metromedia. "There was a good feeling at the commission about having an Australian turn American and becoming a big player in the communications industry," he said later.

Murdoch now saw himself above all as an American international citizen. His expansion promoted his world view and reinforced the power structures of which he was a part. He considered that he had a mission, or at least an opportunity to spread and to propagate the free-market-version American Dream wherever his empire stretched.

Nations are now increasingly defined by the extent to which knowledge is a tradable commodity in their economies. In America by the end of the 1980s, half of all jobs were related to information processing of one kind or another. In developing countries like the Soviet Union, and many in sub-Sahara Africa, primitive communications were inimical to development. Mark Fowler asserted: "Just as coffee beans will be grown in the most conducive environment, communications and computing traffic will move to those nations that can handle it fastest and cheapest."

This argument held that communications determined national identity. But at the same time communications were making national identity "less significant". Murdoch's belief, and Fowler's, was that the spread of communications around the world was in itself a good, but this conviction tended to ignore two corollaries of the communications revolution. Its threat to national identity is making that identity all the more jealously guarded, particularly in the Islamic world. And, conversely, the revolution is attracting more and more people towards its centre. In the years to come, mass movements of people, towards the United States and Western Europe, the communications hubs, will become overwhelming.

In Australia such perceptions were secondary. Reactions to Murdoch's change of citizenship were emotional. The nature of citizenship and national identity is always a live and troubling issue among the 16 million inhabitants of the huge, remote continent. Murdoch's main concern had been how his mother, Dame Elisabeth, would take the news. She had been uneasy at the prospect, and even admitted to Fairfax's *Sydney Morning Herald*, "It was quite a bit to swallow at first blush." When the Metromedia deal was finally arranged, Murdoch called her from a hotel in Arizona. John Evans was with him and said later, "Rupert was pretty anxious before he made that call. Finally he summed up the courage and did it. He came back greatly relieved and said, 'She said it's OK so long as I can keep the Australian papers.' "

Murdoch bore out some of William Safire's fears when he told the Australian press that News Corp remained an Australian company, giving employment to many Australians; however, "Communications technology is shrinking the world in a way no one envisaged just a few years ago." He said he was proud to be an Australian, and always would be, but he was building "what we hope will be a great and considerable media corporation" and American television stations were integral to that. He insisted his feelings for Australia were as strong as ever. "I am not severing any links with Australia. I continue to have the same emotions and feelings about Australia," he told the *Sydney Morning Herald*. "If I have to change the colour of my passport, then so be it. I don't put the same stress on it as some other people do."

Anna Murdoch, too, was privately dismayed by her husband's abandonment of his Australian citizenship. "I was shocked. I never thought he'd do it. I realized then how strong his ambitious drive was," she said later.

She too had her ambitions, and as her husband changed citizenship, she attracted attention to herself by publishing her first novel, *In Her Own Image*. It was a book about women, and the courage that they need in a world of men. The story tells of two Australian sisters, Liz and Josie, their relationship with their selfish mother and their attempt not to be crushed by the tensions between them, especially by the fact that they both love the same man – Liz's husband, Harry – who some critics saw as representing at least a part of Rupert Murdoch.

The book was written with passion. It seemed to show the pain of not being properly loved, the need for courage, and the belief that survival is more important than changing one's life to suit one's own nature. The fear of loss dominates the emotions of the two women, straining for places in a world invented and dominated by men. Anna's women have fierce emotions, her men merely ambitions and fears.

With the publication of *In Her Own Image*, Anna Murdoch came out. She was now a beautiful woman in her forties, elegantly dressed, with an air of coolness and a shyness that concealed determination. Her tongue could be sharp. It was clear that her life, often without her husband for long periods, had made her very independent. In interviews she gave to publicize the book, some journalists commented that for someone as well-known and seriously vilified as Murdoch, his family was kept surprisingly secret. She said that they had guarded their privacy jealously. "We have a very strong sense of ourselves. We don't need that sort of recognition that some appear to look for . . . I don't want to be a party-goer. I don't want to be a shopper. I don't want to be going to charity things all the time . . . You can take us or leave us," she said, "and we prefer it if you leave us." It was clear that they were able to protect themselves much more effectively than the victims of her husband's papers.

One interviewer pointed out to her that her demure manner sat oddly with the vulgarity of some of Murdoch's tabloids. She had to face a lot of questions about the *Sun*. "We *are* [good people]," she told the *Washington Post* rather defensively. The *Sun* was only "one of a vast empire of things, and one has to ask why this constantly comes up". Her answer was that it was used as a tool by people who were envious of Rupert or wished to destroy him. But she insisted that it had no effect upon them as a family.

> We know what he is like. People who work with him know what he is like. Of course, he has enemies. He doesn't suffer fools gladly. But he is a very good and moral human being, and we are bringing up our children that way. We know what we are about and time is on our side. There will be a great reversal. It's around.

She pointed out that whatever journalists thought of him, in the business world he had always had a fine reputation. He had never backed out of a deal. "Which is why people come to him with deals all the time, why banks lend him money."

She claimed that Rupert had a romantic side, but that he had no time for imagination. "I think that's a sadness. I've always said to him that was a side that was denied to him when he was a child."

In America, they now lived in an apartment overlooking Central

Park on 5th Avenue. She much preferred New York, she said, to London. It was a better place to be alone. She had been only twenty-six when her husband had bought the *News of the World* and they moved to London. He had taken her away from the Pacific, from the sunshine, from her family, and put her back into the drab country from which she had escaped as a child, where it poured with rain, where no one seemed to like him and where the unions made their life hell. "Night after night there would be phone calls from people who were blackmailing you. We were there six years. I couldn't wait to leave."

Anna had become practised at defending her husband. "He's very much misunderstood, he's much nicer than he seems," she had told *Time* in 1976. But she agreed he was a strange mix of modesty and ego. "I know in board meetings he can be very tough. I guess you could say that I'm a softy, but I can come over very tough and he's the other way around." He could be very impetuous and sometimes he regretted his actions.

Although good with the children, he was not always a very patient father, she said. "He's not a wrestly daddy. He'd rumple his tie." He could seem remote even at home. His son James sometimes asked her, " 'Is Daddy going deaf?' 'No,' I say, 'he's just not listening.' "

His children sometimes complained that Murdoch's aggressive competitiveness intruded even into his games with them. None the less, Murdoch was a committed family man, and enjoyed, when he found the time, taking his children on summer camping expeditions, as well as skiing with them in winter, at Aspen, where they had bought a house.

Anna said that his idea of relaxation was to read newspapers and talk about them or to watch the sort of trash television that Anna herself sneered at, the news and "corny musicals". His humour was, she said, "very basic. He likes slapstick." Her own tastes were both more highbrow and less constricted. She once said that she would have lived a much more bohemian life if she had not married him.

Their New York apartment was decorated with eighteenth-century English furniture – some of which had belonged to Sir Keith – and twentieth-century Australian paintings, especially those by Fred Williams. In the entrance was a painting of Dame Elisabeth by Judy Cassab, a Hungarian-born Australian artist.

They had domestic servants and, for a time, two rottweilers called Peaches and Melba. Anna had obtained these for security reasons, but Murdoch did not enjoy them sharing the apartment and eventually persuaded her to get rid of them.

In New York in the mid-1980s she had decided that the children were old enough for her to do something of her own, to be more of Anna and less of Mrs Murdoch. She also needed something to assuage the loneliness: Rupert spent so much time hop, skip and jumping around the world, and when he was at home he was usually on the telephone. "I suppose I could have just complained . . . and become a whining wife," she said. "But I didn't want to do that, so why not make it a positive thing and use the time?"

She tried the cello and the violin but felt she was not talented enough at either. So she decided to go to college and get a degree. She told Murdoch when they were together on a ski lift in Sun Valley. In one interview she said later that he gave her a "a really chauvinist argument" about why she should not do it. In another, she said more mildly, "He was a bit taken aback and said, 'What about the household and so on?' We have a very traditional household and marriage, and I think once he realized that everything was going to be fine, he actually took a great deal of pride in talking about what I was doing at the university."

Through the end of the 1970s and the early 1980s she studied mythology and then literature, first at Fordham and then at New York University. Along with other ladies of New York society she attended a literature course run by John Gross, a former editor of the *Times Literary Supplement*; he was impressed by her diligence. She started writing short stories, but Murdoch's criticisms were, she said, "devastating". "Here was someone who was not only my best friend and my husband and everything else, saying things about something I was really trying to do and not in a way that was helpful to me." She added, "What he said was so mortifying that I could never touch it again."

Despite his lack of support, she was determined to write a book before she was forty. She decided never to show him anything else until it was finished. She wrote the book over four years, scribbling and typing in spare moments, on planes and in their many homes. When her fortieth birthday came, the book was in type, though not yet in print. She finally gave it to Murdoch. He read it all the way through and, since his attention span was notoriously short, she was pleased by that.

She was well aware that the book, which some critics compared to *The Thorn Birds*, attracted more attention than most first novels, because of her name. She accepted and exploited that fact instead of decrying it. "I can't avoid being Rupert's wife, I'm proud of it," she told the *Melbourne Age*.

The novel explored how a woman can form herself "in her own image" and not that of her mother, her husband, or anyone else. But it was obvious to all who knew her that there was a lot of Anna's own history in the story of Liz and Josie. As a convent girl, Liz felt that she had been brought up to assume a secondary role to her husband – and she did not want that. She wanted a marriage *and* a career.

Anna called it a "book about forgiveness"; she had wanted to explore the negative aspects of motherhood. She was worried about how her own mother might take it – but it seems to have washed over her. Her sister, Karin, joked that it was a little over the top for Anna to have the mother incinerated at the dénouement.

In Britain the book was published by Collins, in which Murdoch had a substantial shareholding. (Later he bought it all.) Anna said that she was aware that this would lead to unkind remarks, and added that she had sold the book in the USA on its merits for many times what Collins had paid for it.

The book was well received, but some reviewers and interviewers were especially excited by its fairly raunchy sex scenes. Anna told Philip Oakes of the *Sunday Times* that these were difficult for her.

I'm a modest person, but I wanted to be honest in describing how women feel about things. And the difference between love and lust would have been completely lost if I'd stopped at the bedroom door and not gone inside. But there are special difficulties for a woman writer because there are some words used about parts of the body which are particularly male. A woman is limited in her use of verbs and nouns because they sound pejorative and sexist.

She said she thought it was a question "to which feminists could address themselves".

The *Melbourne Age* had fun with this dilemma. At the end of a sympathetic interview with her, they quoted from the book.

"Overcoming her modesty," Anna wrote, "they were slipping and sliding on each other up and down. His hands, her hands, his chest, her breasts, his face, her mouth, his buttocks, her lips. They were lost until he said, 'Now. Now.' And it was time.

"He bit her left breast with his teeth and they were bucking and rolling with each other, his arms no longer wandering over her but holding her firmly, one on each side of her hips, until he was pounding into her, and she could not shake him loose and she cried out, 'Harry. Harry. At last, at last.' "

She had shown it to Rupert.

"Who's Harry?" Rupert asked.

"It's you, darling," she said.

Chapter 10

WAPPING

None of Murdoch's endless battles was more ferocious than the one he waged at Wapping in London's Docklands through 1986. By the end of 1985, the debt incurred by the takeover of Fox and Metromedia meant that he needed more than ever to milk his British cash cows. He was exasperated by the intractability of the Fleet Street unions. The *Sun, News of the World* and *Sunday Times* were profitable, but if produced efficiently, they could be wildly so. What he needed was agreement on uninterrupted production and new technology. New technology for Murdoch, and other publishers, meant "single key stroking", by which journalists and advertising staff could set words in type without the help of printers.

The problem was not confined to Fleet Street. Murdoch had reconditioned a plant outside Glasgow where he had planned to print the *Sun*. This, he hoped, would save around £3 million a year, currently spent on airfreight, and also increase the *Sun*'s sales in Scotland. But the move had been resisted by Scottish journalists and print workers, on the grounds that the paper remained an English rather than a Scottish operation. They refused to accept papers faxed up the line from London, insisting that they must be written in Scotland. So the plant stayed empty, even though News actually offered to reset the entire paper in Scotland.

In 1982 his chief executive, Bert Hardy, persuaded Murdoch to build a new London plant outside of Fleet Street. Hardy had argued that the increased circulation of the *Sun* alone demanded this. Murdoch was not initially enthusiastic. It meant a large commitment of money and the clear risk of confrontation with the unions. He did not relish either, but eventually he agreed to build what he called merely "a printshed".

Hardy settled on a site in the old east London dockland area of Wapping. It was only a short walk from the Tower of London and a short taxi ride from the City, but to the men and women of Fleet Street it was so far east it might have been in Moscow. The site contained some of the finest Georgian warehouses in Britain. News obtained permission to knock most of these down, despite energetic protests from conservationists. The warehouses were replaced by one of the ugliest modern factories in London.

At first neither Murdoch nor Bert Hardy nor anyone else expected this new building to be anything but a printing plant. Pages would be typeset and made up in central London as before; the journalists would still not have access to the terminals. The unions had insisted that if they were ever to move into this new plant – or similar ones built by other managements – then all the old rules and practices of Fleet Street must move with them.

By the middle of the 1980s almost all London papers were suffering financially. The *Financial Times* faced nearly as much disruption from the machine minders of the National Graphical Association as Times Newspapers had faced from the Thomsons. But its management trembled on the brink of action against the unions. The example of Thomsons, after all, was too terrible to repeat. Telegraph Newspapers were in an especially parlous condition. Like Murdoch, the management was building a new plant out of Fleet Street, on the Isle of Dogs, which in terms of distance from "The Street" was Peking to Wapping's Moscow. By 1985, the company was practically bankrupt and its proprietor, Lord Hartwell, was forced to turn to a Canadian entrepreneur and newspaper owner, Conrad Black, for salvation. Exhausted by the struggle, Hartwell almost casually turned his family's business over to Black.

Murdoch liked to quote the *Times* columnist, Bernard Levin, as saying that Fleet Street newspapers were "produced in conditions which combined a protection racket with a lunatic asylum". He once complained that within his empire, he employed four men to a press in San Antonio, five men in Chicago, six in New York and Sydney, and in London – eighteen! "And all were paid salaries at least 100 per cent above the national average."

In the 1970s, provincial newspapers in Britain slowly began to adopt the new technology. The *Nottingham Evening Post* took the leap in 1976, with great success. Classified advertising increased, later stories could be carried and editions changed more frequently. Profits rose and so therefore did the wages. Managements in London took note, but remained far too frightened to follow.

A way out was shown to the proprietors of the established papers not by Murdoch, the self-proclaimed radical, but by a newcomer, Eddie Shah, who ran the Messenger group of free newspapers in Warrington in Cheshire.

Shah, a cousin of the Aga Khan, became impatient with the print unions' demands and tactics and determined to break them with the help of the trade union reforms passed by the Thatcher government in 1980 and 1982. The Warrington dispute became the focus of labour anger with "Thatcherism". More union members travelled to picket Shah's works, and the offices of his advertisers and of others involved with him. Some 4,000 dockers, miners and other activists joined the fray. The picketing became sometimes violent and always unpleasant; on 29 November there was a pitched battle with police. This time the National Graphical Association was fined over half a million pounds. Warrington was, as Simon Jenkins of *The Times* pointed out, probably the first time that an industrial dispute within the newspaper industry had cost the unions more than the owners.

Shah became a hero of the Thatcher age. He was particularly admired by Andrew Neil, the editor of the *Sunday Times*, who encouraged him to repeat his success by starting a national daily paper. Shah spent the next two years in preparation. Unwisely, he decided to buy expensive colour presses of his own rather than contract the work to outside printers. He also bought a state-of-the-art computer system to set type and compose pages on the screen. It was too sophisticated.

In the end Shah himself failed to make a success of the paper he had conceived. But *Today*'s gestation had an enormous impact on the industry. Shah made an agreement with Eric Hammond, the leader of the electricians' union (EETPU), to employ only his members in the printing and production process. Shah hoped that he would thus avoid the internecine fights which had so damaged the national press. Hammond agreed that the electricians would not impose a closed shop; and that there would be no demarcation, and no distinction between union and non-union staff. It was this deal, rather than the purring new technology in which he rather naïvely placed so much trust, that really constituted Shah's Fleet Street revolution. He also showed that the Thatcher union reforms really empowered managements.

The legal lesson was not lost on Bruce Matthews, Murdoch's new chief executive in London, who spent much of 1984 failing to reach agreements with the unions, SOGAT 82 and the NGA, over manning levels for printing the *Sun* and the *News of the World* in the new plants. Just before Christmas 1984 the talks broke down. One union negotiator proposed that the best thing Murdoch could do to his Wapping plant was burn it down.

Early in the New Year of 1985, Matthews and a small group of executives flew to New York to persuade Murdoch to go for a radical new operation at Wapping and Glasgow which would break the unions. It was a dangerous decision for Murdoch to make, because his whole empire depended upon the cash flow from Britain and the initial disruption was likely to be immense. But his friend Woodrow Wyatt arranged secret talks with Eric Hammond, and the electricians' leader agreed that his men could not only set up a new plant but would operate it as well.

The time seemed propitious. The government was not only providing the legislation but also setting its own example by resolute resistance to the miners' strike. And more reasons for trying to break the print unions presented themselves every day. The circulation of *The Times* under Charles Douglas-Home was edging up, and nudging the *Guardian* at just under 500,000. But to print more copies, the machine room staff in Gray's Inn Road demanded an extra seventy "jobs" – which would have added another £1 million a year to the losses of Times Newspapers. Murdoch's innate caution when dealing with the unions was finally overtaken by his exasperation. He agreed to start planning a move to Wapping.

In fact two plans were made. One was based on the premise that a deal would finally be struck with the unions to allow at least part of the printing of the *Sun* and the *News of the World* at Wapping. The rest of the plant might be used to produce a new paper called the *London Post*. The unions thought that the story of the *Post* was a smokescreen. They were not far wrong. Murdoch said later that he never wanted to publish a London evening paper – but he did like to put pressure on Robert Maxwell, who was planning a similar London paper, the *London Daily News* – which was launched and folded in 1987. If the unions refused to co-operate, Murdoch had decided he would move all his titles to Wapping. In that case, the *Post* would be a useful cover for the installation of computers and presses.

By the spring of 1985, as he was negotiating the purchases of Fox and then Metromedia, Murdoch became completely committed to the idea of the "Big Bang" – moving everyone and everything into Wapping and letting the devil take the hindmost. "It became *imperative* that we do it," he said later to Charles Wintour.

He was fed up, he said, with the fact that union leaders were so arrogant that sometimes they did not even bother to return calls. They had walked away from talks in 1984. He had no wish for all the grief and the "seventeen years of hell" in Fleet Street to be replayed in Wapping.

He still tried, ostensibly, to get some sort of deal. He called Bill O'Neill over from Australia to handle negotiations. O'Neill, a union man himself, had been the secretary of the Printing and Kindred Industries Union on the Sydney *Mirror*. He had been so good at upholding the rights of his members that Murdoch had hired him as News's industrial officer in Australia. Since then he had worked in both Bouverie Street in London, and the States. His negotiating style was to put his sneakers on the table and say, "What the fuck is this?" It was a far cry from Gordon Brunton of Thomsons.

By now Murdoch had stiffened the terms. He wanted a legally binding no-strike agreement with just one union. The closed shop would be killed. Management would have the right to hire and fire as it wished. Journalists and tele-ad sales girls would have direct input to computer terminals. In other words, the unions would have to drop everything upon which they had insisted over the last forty years. Management was demanding the right to change all the existing habits and actually to manage. And this time, that management (unlike Thomsons in 1978) had an escape route.

There were two tracks. While O'Neill talked with the established unions, Murdoch's Wapping team secretly set to work to equip the factory to produce not only a new London daily paper but all four of Murdoch's national titles.

The first thing that Murdoch decided on was the computer system. Despite his interest in technological progress, he was a man who could hardly change a lightbulb, let alone mend a fuse, or insert a cassette into a tape-recorder. Perhaps for that reason, he held the practical view that it was up to others to make the trials and suffer the errors associated with new equipment, as Eddie Shah had done. For himself, he wanted the most commonly used, off-the-shelf computer technology that had so far been developed for newspapers. This was Atex, a system created in 1972 by three men in a loft in New England. It had been bought in 1982 by Kodak for some $80 million, sold to over 500 customers around the world, and was especially well tried in newspapers across the United States.

In February 1985, immediately after agreeing with Matthews on the Big Bang, Murdoch had a meeting in his New York apartment with several senior Atex executives. Could they put together a huge computer system – at once and in secret, to be installed in London within months? It would have to be big enough to cope with four papers. Atex said that they could. Murdoch insisted that secrecy was paramount. Not even the company's London office could be informed of the project.

In March, News announced plans for the *London Post*, a new twenty-four-hour newspaper to be produced at Wapping. On 15 March a printing plate broke in the *Sun* machine room at Bouverie Street. There had been sixty such breaks in the last two years. This one ended in an eleven-day strike, during which the company took court action against the print unions under the 1984 Trade Union Act. An injunction was granted against the chapel.

The Atex team of about a dozen people was selected from regional offices around America. They began to arrive in London and lived anonymously in houses in Belgravia and Chelsea. Atex set up a separate company in London and News International activated a small company so that these two unknown firms could do business with each other without either name striking a chord, anywhere. News even asked that Atex purchase about $3 million worth of extra equipment, such as typesetters and graphic cameras, from other American companies and ship them over by the same secret system. Atex changed its usual shippers, so that this link would not be a risk, and used spray paint the colour of cardboard to delete the company's name on the outside of cartons. The Atex team worked in a disused shed – which they called the Bunker – in south-east London. There they began to put together the system.

Murdoch insisted on equal secrecy from his own people. Meetings of the key executives took place in different London hotels. There were usually no minutes; agendas were destroyed.

By early May, just as Murdoch agreed to buy Metromedia in the USA, the men and women in the Bunker in London had assembled the entire new system. It was taken to pieces again and put into boxes to be shipped to Wapping. Contractors were banned from the factory. Three large lorries came to the Bunker, picked up the crates, and carried them surreptitiously into Wapping. The rooms in which the computers were installed became the holiest of holies, off limits to all except the few who knew the extent of the revolution which Murdoch hoped to bring about. By the end of the first week of June the computers were all fired up and on line.

Murdoch was equipping Wapping with presses that were even less modern than the computers. They were Goss Mark One machines which he had bought more than a decade earlier, when Goss was offering them cheaply. They had been kept in their crates. Now they were literally dusted down and greased up and had new electrics and other parts fitted. Then they were installed in the vast printing hall that Murdoch had built – ostensibly for the *London Post*. When the button was first pressed on them they were both very old and shiny new.

Murdoch imported a number of his Australian employees to help. Among them was John Cowley, brother of Ken Cowley, who ran Murdoch's Australian operations. John Cowley had started as a printer's apprentice and subsequently oversaw the pressroom of *The Australian* in Canberra. Later he had taken over the night shift in Sydney and had remained on the production side of Murdoch's Australian papers ever since. Cowley was, by his own account, an arrogant and tough man, with whom people found it hard to work. When he arrived to become the operational manager of Wapping in July 1985, he joined a secret committee which included Charlie Wilson, the editor of *The Times*, Bill Gillespie and Bruce Matthews. Cowley thought that the enterprise was far less advanced than his English colleagues had told Murdoch. "Rupert kept putting more on to me. I set up the publishing room, the press room, the composing room and got involved in the technical department. I ordered walls taken down overnight. That caused tempers to flare." He liked to call himself the Mayor of Wapping.

As well as rebuilding the factory around the machines, Cowley got the "consumables" into the place. Originally the boilers in the building had been oil-fired, but in the course of 1985 the plant was converted to gas. "So we had these bloody great oil tanks under Pennington Street. We cleaned them out and filled them with ink." This gave the factory enough ink for three months' publishing.

Everything else – string, glue, wire, pencils – all came in under cover. Paper was the biggest item. Convoys would come in with one driver and manager. By the end of the year there were about 4,000 reels of paper available. But this was less than it looked; it would last all the papers for about a week.

Cowley had a dormitory built right under the remaining warehouses, in case the production staff, or anyone else, needed to stay on site for days (or more) at a time.

The most difficult problem was to decide who was to run the machines. Murdoch and Matthews decided, like Shah, to use the electricians' union, the EETPU. Eric Hammond, the electricians' leader, saw it as a way in which his men could break the stranglehold which the NGA and SOGAT had hitherto had over the London printing industry. A deal with News would be even more important than his agreement with Eddie Shah – and for that reason it would arouse even more fury among his comrades.

The electricians' union began to recruit men in Southampton on six-month contracts. They were bussed about a hundred miles every day to Wapping and were sworn to secrecy about what they saw and what they did. It was deemed especially important that they not understand the huge power of the Atex system. Astonishingly, they never did. Even though gossip began to run through the pubs on Fleet Street as to what Murdoch might be secretly planning behind the walls and wire of Wapping, no one really understood.

Cowley's rough ways became quite unpopular. He had particularly bitter rows with Bruce Matthews, scorning Matthews's view that the managers from Bouverie Street and Gray's Inn Road should come to take over. Cowley believed that "They had lost the art of management because of having had to work for the unions so long." Matthews by contrast felt that they had worked under appalling circumstances in Fleet Street and deserved an opportunity at Wapping. In the event, very few of the Fleet Street managers did survive the move to Wapping, and this contributed to a break between Matthews, who felt the company had been disloyal, and Murdoch.

With Atex and the presses and the electricians all installed, Murdoch had the means of production. There was still the question of distribution. Most national newspapers were distributed by train from London. But this would put him back into the hands of the unions. He decided to create a completely new distribution system – by truck. The trucks themselves were provided by "my friends and partners in Australia", Thomas Nationwide Transport. Murdoch paid £7 million towards the capital costs of 800 trucks and vans. TNT took on 2,000 new employees and began to practise the new delivery methods in the north east of Britain in the second half of 1985.

As usual, Murdoch was spending his time flying by Concorde back and forth across the Atlantic, often with his invaluable assistant Dorothy Wyndoe, who had been at the centre of his operations for fifteen years. On one of his running visits to London, in July, he met Brenda Dean, the leader of SOGAT 82, at the Waldorf Hotel and told her that his patience with the unions' "obstruction and delay" was running out. He said that the NGA was "impossible to deal with". Dean, who was the acceptable face of London print unions, would have been delighted to establish a single-union contract for SOGAT 82 inside Wapping, cutting out the NGA, which SOGAT loathed. But the NGA would never accept it.

A few weeks later, Murdoch completed the purchase of Metro-media in the States. In England the recruitment of electricians was stepped up. In September 1985, dummy issues of the *London Post* were printed in the Wapping factory. Copies were smuggled out to Fleet Street and the unions considered strike action but rejected it. This was a serious mistake by the unions. A strike at that moment would have caused Murdoch serious damage, given the new debt burdens of Fox and Metromedia.

Discussions continued. At a meeting with the unions at the end of that same month Murdoch insisted that any agreement on manning the *Post* at Wapping must be completed by the end of 1985. He said he planned to produce both the *Sun* and the *News of the World* there. The terms he offered for the *Post* were no closed shops, management's right to manage, dismissal for strikers and legally binding agreements. But even Brenda Dean could not deliver what Murdoch now demanded.

As the prospect drew nearer that Wapping would go live, News began to worry about the security of its staff. Key executives were advised to inform their local police who they were: "There are among us people who may be regarded as targets . . . Be sensitive to persons behaving in a suspicious or unaccountable fashion." They should avoid regular patterns of behaviour, at home they should fit locks to all doors and windows, remove trees or shrubs that could give cover, they should worry about car bombs and letter bombs, and they should shred all documents and letters and discuss nothing confidential on the telephone. John Cowley used to tell people that he had a pair of overalls hidden away. They were embroidered with the word "Gardener"; when the mob came over the wire, he would pretend to be cultivating the geraniums.

In the last quarter of 1985 the print unions began to shift closer towards a deal, but not with any sense of urgency. They believed they still had the upper hand and that, with his new American acquisitions, Murdoch could not afford a strike, which would stop the cash flow from Bouverie Street and the Gray's Inn Road. They had not yet grasped that Murdoch planned to move all four titles to Wapping.

Then a crucial element in the secret strategy leaked in the Communist Party daily, the *Morning Star*, just before Christmas. It had been outlined in a letter from Geoffrey Richards of Farrer & Co, News Corp's solicitors, to Bruce Matthews. Richards gave detailed advice on the most expedient method of getting rid of the London workforce: "The cheapest way of doing so would be to dismiss employees while participating in a strike or other industrial action". A striker would be in breach of contract, and "can thus be dismissed instantly." A striker would not be entitled to redundancy and would have no claim in the event of unfair dismissal, "provided *all* the strikers have been dismissed and *none* selectively re-engaged".

Richards noted that the managements operated complicated rota systems, "and many of the Sunday employees are different to the weekday employees". "The idea," he wrote, "is to catch as many employees in the net as possible, and it seems to me likely that that will be done best if the dismissals take place at the weekend rather than near the beginning of a week."

The picture was coming into sharper focus, but the print unions still could not entertain the idea of Murdoch being able to produce *all* his newspapers without them.

Murdoch went skiing in Aspen after Christmas 1985. Early in the new year, he flew to London. He had reserved four whole weeks for the Wapping campaign. News International announced that he was to take charge of the talks for the *London Post* for which publication was said to be anticipated on 17 March. The company was prepared to hold meetings with the journalists and the electricians. Negotiations with the other unions were at an end. The print unions still thought they were being bluffed. They knew that Murdoch's bargaining style was to go to the edge and then back away as he peered into the abyss.

On 19 January the *Sunday Times* published a special supplement produced at Wapping. Among a series of articles entitled "The Future of Fleet Street", Murdoch himself was interviewed and insisted that there was no dispute with the unions. "They have refused to work at Wapping and agreements are in place at our existing plants." He rejected claims that he was a union basher. "We don't have a print plant anywhere in the world which is not unionized . . . News Corporation employs more trade unionists than any other publishing company in the world." As for the claim that News had made money on the backs of union members, he said he had actually saved about 6,000 jobs on *The Times* and the *Sun*, where people earned rather larger salaries than was normal in the industry. The supplement deliberately repeated the fact that Wapping could produce "more than one" newspaper. The unions knew that the gauntlet had been thrown down.

If they had been wise, they would have done nothing. Then Murdoch would have had to pay the men in Fleet Street as well as the new men in Wapping. If they went on strike instead, Murdoch could at once sack them and so escape the obligation to make redundancy payments of about £40 million. The unions knew this. None the less, they voted to go on strike.

The Trades Union Congress intervened, but Murdoch was no longer interested in any compromise. "It's all too late," he said. Now the fences at Wapping were topped with coils of razor wire, bought from Germany. More guards were stationed around the site. The government was briefed; Mrs Thatcher was said to be delighted with Murdoch's plan. The Metropolitan Police sealed off side streets and practised tactics to defeat picketing and to keep the trucks running out of Wapping every night. It was the duty of the police to keep the highways open, but Murdoch was fortunate to have friends in high places. A Labour government would have been less helpful. Almost everything was now in place.

In the final weeks of 1985 and the first days of 1986, Murdoch was at Wapping as often as he could manage, cajoling, bullying, flattering the men who were struggling to get the plant ready to go live and produce four newspapers a night. "Bloody exciting, ain't it. Bloody exciting," he would say, when he was on a high. When he felt lower, because something was going wrong, he would shout, "Fix it," and would curse people, crying, "You're bloody incompetent. You've let me down." The key question now was whether the journalists would do the same.

FLEET STREET

Going to Wapping without printers was no problem – indeed, it was the whole point – but going there without anybody to fill the pages would be disastrous. The National Union of Journalists was instructing its members not to go until a deal with the print unions had been concluded, and the message had percolated down through the ranks. On 22 January the journalists' chapel committees in the *Sun* and the *News of the World* voted to obey their union's instruction. Then talks between management and the printers broke down and the print unions called a strike on the evening of Friday, 24 January 1986.

It was one of the few times in the industrial history of newspapers when the journalists possessed real power. And the novelty of it was reflected in their bewildered response. In fairness, many were genuinely divided between their suspicion of Murdoch and their distrust of the printers.

Murdoch flourished both carrot and stick: if the journalists agreed to go to Wapping, they would be paid £2,000 a year extra and be given private health insurance. If not, they would be considered to have gone on strike and would therefore be dismissed. The legality of this ultimatum was very much in question, and many of the journalists were infuriated by its tone. It seemed to them to betray, more than any previous action, the contempt Murdoch had always felt for journalists. He often seemed to treat them like taxis – if one is gone, another will soon come along.

Much unnecessary unhappiness might have been dissipated if Murdoch had addressed the journalists himself and made them feel he cared for them. But there were problems to this which Murdoch's old friend, and director of news, Sir Edward Pickering, put his finger on later: "The trouble was that Rupert was regarded as the Supreme Satan."

At Bouverie Street, Kelvin MacKenzie called a meeting of the *Sun* journalists. He was, as a tape of the meeting quoted by the author Linda Melvern shows, on top form. "This is a momentous day for the newspaper," he told them. Seven years ago, Murdoch had decided to build a new plant at Wapping. Ever since, the unions had bullied, blackmailed and threatened the management. For six whole years nothing had happened. There was resistance all the way. "In a minute-by-minute industry, when they've got you by the balls, you've got to listen. Well, they haven't got us by the balls any more."

MacKenzie insisted that the print unions did not matter now. The only people who mattered were the journalists. "I personally want every single one of you, including those who are ideologically at the opposite end of the pole from me, I want every single one of you in Wapping."

Almost shouting, he told them to make up their own minds and to think in terms of "enlightened self-interest".

The journalists were still worried. Their union had instructed them not to go to Wapping. Would they be thrown out of it if they obeyed Murdoch? MacKenzie was contemptuous of the union. "What the NUJ has done for you would safely fit up a gnat's arse."

The journalists debated among themselves and then called him back for more questions. Would their four-day working week continue or would hours become longer? MacKenzie promised them there would be no eighteen-hours-a-day, seven-days-a-week regime, even though he had proposed it to Murdoch (laughter). "I am quite happy to assure you that the agreement will be standing another year, right? So there we are, game, set and fucking match. I'll drop my trousers . . . OK? . . . If I bend over any further, I'll be in *Gay News*."

After he left the newsroom, the journalists were addressed by Harry Conroy, the general secretary of the National Union of Journalists. Conroy told them that they had no right to go to Wapping, because they were bound by the Trades Union Congress to take collective action with the printers. The notion was hard for some of them to swallow. After all, only eighteen months before, the NGA had walked through the NUJ's own picket lines. Most of those who spoke were critical or even abusive of Conroy. Then they voted. Their resentment of the printers, their fear for their own salaries and pensions, their dislike of the cramped and dirty conditions of Bouverie Street – these were all factors that combined to persuade them to leave. They voted 100 to 8 to go to Wapping, and began to fill black rubbish bags with their files and other belongings. So did the journalists from the *News of the World*.

Up in the Gray's Inn Road, *Times* journalists were summoned by the new editor, Charlie Wilson, who had recently taken over on the premature death of Charles Douglas-Home. His Glaswegian profanities were unusual in an editor of *The Times* but Murdoch had been impressed by his fierceness in facing down enemies at the *Chicago Sun-Times*. Since then, he had been Douglas-Home's deputy, had served as editor of the ghostly *London Post*, and had been intimately and secretly involved in the planning of Wapping. (Almost all journalists had been kept in the dark to prevent an anti-Wapping momentum from developing.)

Private Eye called him "Gorbals" Wilson and delighted in stories of his allegedly thuggish behaviour, describing him as screaming abuse or throwing telephones at his staff. But Murdoch was always partial to choleric Scots. Some people knew him as the "arse-kicking machine" – just the sort of quality which Murdoch had always wanted on *The Times* – and, indeed, in most other places. But he was also known as a newspaper man to his fingertips.

Standing on a table in his shirt sleeves, Wilson told *The Times* journalists that their colleagues on the *News of the World* had just reversed their previous decision and voted to go to Wapping. He apologized for not having spoken to them earlier – it had been impossible. "The storm has broken tonight," he said. "*The Times* will only survive and continue production if it can be from Tower Hamlets." Tonight's paper would be lost, but no more. Monday's paper would be written and published on Sunday at Wapping. "I am here to invite you to come along and help us do it." Those who did not would be fired.

As in Bouverie Street, some of the journalists were infuriated by the ultimatum, but as a group they were unable to reach an immediate decision on how to respond; they agreed only to meet the next day, to pick at the anguish further. It was that night that SOGAT called its members, who included secretaries and researchers as well as machine minders, out on strike.

Murdoch was now at Wapping full-time. Wearing old trousers, a cardigan and sneakers, the owner and the boss was totally in charge of the operation. Adrenalin pumping through his small, lithe frame, he was everyone and he was everywhere, cajoling, cursing, praising, rushing about like a kid with a complicated toy which he was assembling for the first time. He had lost Friday night's *Sun* and *Times*; on Saturday he was determined to get the Sunday papers out. The *Sunday Times* and the *News of the World* were being written by a handful of journalists who had already come through the wire or from stories prepared earlier and brought in by executives. That Saturday evening at about eight o'clock, he stood with his senior executives and pushed the button to set the presses into motion. Everyone clapped and cheered.

Shortly after 9 p.m., the first TNT lorries came down the ramp and roared through the East End. Others left Kinning Park in Glasgow just after 10 p.m. That night, 25 January 1986, News published 4 million papers in its new plants, without any help from the traditional craft unions. The papers were distributed around the country by the fleets of TNT vehicles which bypassed the rail network and its unions. The Wapping revolution had begun.

On Sunday, at a hotel in Bloomsbury, the *Times* chapel met again. The journalists spoke passionately and angrily. Tony Bevins, the young political correspondent, wanted to go to Wapping. "But not like this." Someone else shouted, "I want to go. But I want to go with my head up . . . not on my knees, eating Murdoch shit." Almost everyone was in despair, hating both the printers and Murdoch, despising themselves. Once again, they deferred a decision.

Some fifty *Times* journalists did go to Wapping that Sunday to prepare Monday's paper. At another meeting that Sunday evening, they were denounced by some of their colleagues, but one of them replied, "Apart from the barbed wire, there's not much wrong with Wapping," to which someone at the back shouted, "That's what they said about Belsen."

None the less, after more emotional argument that evening the journalists voted, by three to one, to move to Wapping. The NUJ's chapel committee resigned. Many journalists were in tears; no one was happy.

Next morning, Monday, 27 January, the front page of the *Sun* read "A NEW SUN IS RISING TODAY" and announced underneath it, "WE BEAT STRIKE THUGS". The story began "Good Morning Britain", and described how the papers were being produced "despite the biggest print strike since the war". The *Sun* said Murdoch was jubilant. The *Times* story described him as "relaxed and cheerful" and "delighted with the success" of the move.

Now it was the turn of the *Sunday Times*. Of all his newspapers, the *Sunday Times* was the most iconoclastic and independent of Murdoch, and the one most at odds with its own editor. Since his appointment as successor to Frank Giles over two years earlier, Andrew Neil had made no secret of his contempt for the liberal traditions established in Harry Evans's day. As a result of Neil's changes, the newspaper had acquired a right-wing tone that was uncongenial to many of its journalists. Hugo Young, the serious-minded political editor, resigned and denounced the paper's new hard-line cheerleading for Reaganism, Thatcherism and associated nostrums. He argued that under Murdoch and Neil, the paper no longer represented the citizen and gave little space to discussions of poverty, inequality, injustice or other moral issues. The paper "accepts an agenda laid down by someone else, namely the government, and originates little that disturbs current assumption". Many journalists agreed with Young, and a good number left the paper.

When Neil announced to his staff that Monday morning, "I am one of you", many of those who remained just didn't believe him. There was a widespread suspicion that Neil had been deeply involved in the Wapping schemes from the start. The meeting went on for most of the day. One speech was memorable.

This was made by Don Berry, a moderate man who was a gifted and popular managing editor and superb at production – the sort of journalist upon whom editors always depend utterly and usually reward inadequately. Berry hated the way in which, Saturday night after Saturday night, the print unions had destroyed the paper he and others had laboured over all week. He had not been absolutely opposed to Neil from the start; he considered him a serious journalist from a respected paper, the *Economist*. He had agreed that the *Sunday Times* needed to change from its 1960s' preoccupations. But he had been disturbed by the way in which Neil sometimes bullied writers and failed to get the best out of them. Now, forsaking his usual moderation, he excoriated Neil and the management for deceit in their campaign against the unions – "They have compromised the paper's moral stance," he said. As for the journalists, Berry said to Neil, "You have treated us with contempt." His speech was given an ovation.

When, at the end of the day, the vote was finally taken, it was remarkably close: sixty-eight journalists were in favour of going to Wapping and sixty were against. Most then went along with the majority decision to go in, but some felt they still could not stomach it.

Those most determinedly against called themselves the "refuse-niks". Murdoch was anxious to keep some of them, especially Don Berry, and the management offered them a special deal, on condition they kept it a secret. Berry was not interested. Among the veterans who left the paper with him were Lewis Chester, one of its finest feature writers, and Claire Tomalin, its distinguished literary editor. Tomalin would write to Neil: "You have become the mouthpiece for a ruthless and bullying management which regards all employees as cattle."

In the end, only sixty journalists from the four titles refused Murdoch's inducements and instructions to move to Wapping. The others went along, though some regretted the fact that they had not fought harder. They could have realized how important they were to the papers, if not to Murdoch. They could have felt more sympathy for other workers. They could have asked for time. Or for more money.

At first the pickets came slowly to Wapping. But it soon became clear that Murdoch had embarked on the most significant challenge to the British unions since the government faced down the miners' strike in 1983–4; and that he would enjoy Mrs Thatcher's full support in the struggle.

Those journalists who first made it through the lines were astonished by the spectacle of their new workplace – by the fierce fencing topped with razor wire, the gigantic gates, the floodlights, the ramp for the trucks, and the huge, hideous newspaper factory itself, towering over the middle of the compound, alongside the old rum warehouse which was to house the *Times* and *Sunday Times* editorial offices. There were security men patrolling the camp, and demanding ID cards. Surveillance cameras swivelled from every convenient vantage point. Into this high-tech encampment would thread the armoured buses, the safest and most humiliating method of crossing the picket lines.

There was more razor wire inside the fences. Its function was said to be to break up mass charges if the pickets should get in. "What would happen then?" someone asked. "Fall back to the rum warehouse with the editor on the steps, like Gordon at Khartoum?" They heard rumours that there was a helicopter pad on site. Someone said it would be like the last helicopter out of Saigon as Murdoch and his dearest scrambled out and left the hacks to the vengeance of the printers' mob.

On every desk inside the old warehouse where *The Times* and *Sunday Times* were now based, were the new Atex terminals, and bright American trainer/hostesses – "Hi, I'm Cindy" – who were there to lure the hacks into the late twentieth century. Despite the kind Cindys, many of them missed their old typewriters, and a scouting party was sent back to Gray's Inn Road to collect armfuls of the faithful mechanical beasts on which so many millions of words had been clattered out over the years.

On day one, they discovered, to their horror, that there was no library and therefore no cuttings from which to cull and rewrite stories. The television had no plug, there were no coffee machines to give comfort and, for the photographers, there was no working darkroom until one was fashioned out of the editor's shower.

The magazine office seemed like a classroom, bare save for a large poster depicting fifty years of Donald Duck – "So that's what they think of us." The newsroom, sports features and picture desk were all together in one huge concourse. A Matisse poster hung over the sports department and Hockney's sets for *The Rake's Progress* at Glyndebourne were behind the news editor. There were a few rubber plants and potted palms scattered around. The windows were high and small and someone said it felt like a

New York garment factory – no exit in case of fire. The only view – an inch of the Tower of London – was said to be from the editor's window.

The *Sun* and the *News of the World* were housed, together with the advertising and executive staffs, in the factory that towered over the warehouses. There was a decent-looking canteen, much nicer than the dismal cellar at Gray's Inn Road, and infinitely preferable to the rat-infested hell's kitchen at Bouverie Street. It was for printers, journalists and Murdoch alike – directors' dining rooms and executive suites were anathema to him – but some of the hacks were dismayed to learn of one of Murdoch's new rules: there was to be no alcohol inside Wapping.

If the humour inside the gates was black, outside there was none at all. Most industrial disputes start fiercely and tend to ebb away. Wapping, in contrast, seemed to grow progressively uglier.

The strikers, almost 5,000 strong, were desperate from the outset. In industrial terms, the battle was over almost before it had begun. Murdoch had quite simply outwitted them, and in holding on to what he had achieved, he had the full backing of the Prime Minister. Wapping was seen by Mrs Thatcher herself as an all-out offensive in the third Industrial Revolution. The first had begun a hundred and fifty years ago, with the rise of Victorian, industrial England. The second followed the Second World War, with the creation and development of the welfare state and the politics of "consensus", in which the unions grew into apparently invincible baronies. Now the third was intended to cut union power in the interest of liberating more competitive technologies.

By 1986 Mrs Thatcher saw her reform of the labour laws as among her most significant accomplishments. She had provided management with the weapons to fight the unions, which were required to hold secret ballots of members to elect their leaders and to vote on any industrial actions rather than permitting wildcat strikes. Picketing was limited to those workers on strike and could take place only at their own place of work. All forms of secondary picketing or boycott were declared unlawful.

None the less, few private sector employers had yet taken advantage of their right to fire striking workers; they preferred to have a labour force at the end of the dispute. Murdoch, by contrast, did not, at least not the same labour force with which he started. Murdoch simply took the law to its logical conclusion, as employers throughout the nation looked on in amazement and usually admiration.

While Murdoch could count upon all the resources of government and, in particular, of the Metropolitan Police, the printers could not count on their comrades in their own union, let alone others. They had for years made so much money, and had behaved so arrogantly towards fellow unionists as well as towards their employers, that around the country, SOGAT and NGA members refused to support their London colleagues by blocking the distribution of Murdoch's papers.

Murdoch's careful preparations – in terms of both the physical and the legal defence of Wapping – meant that the strikers had little room for manoeuvre. He had shrewdly diversified his operations under a series of newly registered, separate companies, to maximize the difficulty of secondary picketing. In February all SOGAT's £17 million worth of assets were ordered to be seized by the High Court, and held until the union's leader, Brenda Dean, apologized for the union's contempt of court. Then the NGA was fined £25,000 for defying an injunction. These setbacks had the effect of making the picketing even more angry and sometimes violent.

The striking printers wanted reinstatement, something that Murdoch had no intention of giving them. Money, or its equivalent, was a different matter. In early April, he offered to give the unions the *Times* and *Sunday Times* plant in the Gray's Inn Road to produce their own newspaper. Interviewed "live" from Wapping he explained: "We feel they have been misled and gave us a bad time . . . this gives them the opportunity for jobs and addresses the question of whether or not the Labour movement gets its own paper . . . We have no use for it . . . and we will risk the competition." In the end the proposal died.

By now the roads around Wapping were closed even to local residents and, at night, the traffic lights were synchronized on green to give the lorries a straight run out of the area. None the less, on the night of 3 May there was appalling, unprecedented violence outside the plant. Over 250 people were injured.

Next weekend the violence was repeated. Scotland Yard said that about 3,000 people had been picketing the plant. The evening began relatively quietly, but at one point, mounted police charged into a group of about 400 pickets trying to stop the TNT trucks. Demonstrators hurled rocks, bottles and smoke bombs at police. Police in riot gear moved into the area at about 1 a.m. to quell the trouble.

The violence was horrific, but it was quite clear that the new machinery of production and distribution could withstand any weight of picketing. Secret talks between Murdoch and SOGAT 82 leaders in Los Angeles failed. On 26 May, Murdoch flew in from New York and met with the Trades Union Congress leaders at an hotel near Heathrow. He told them that he would never tolerate at Wapping the different chapels and closed shops that had flourished in Bouverie Street and the Gray's Inn Road. "I have just been released from that nightmare. I don't intend going back." He made a "final offer" which proffered redundancy payments totalling £50 million.

That evening, he said in a television interview: "We are under no obligation to pay any money at all and we are putting this forward in an attempt to close down the picketing." It was an "extremely high price for bringing the dispute to an end".

On 6 June, the London branches of the unions rejected the offer. Murdoch described their decision as "a second suicide". The first had been when the unions had gone on strike in the first place. The printers were now left with nothing, he said, "no jobs, no recognition, and now no money".

So the bloody dispute dragged on. Murdoch became more detested by the political Left in Britain than any other employer had been for decades. He seemed to many to personify all that was most ruthless about the Thatcher revolution. He was already despised by the liberal intellectual establishment of Britain. Now he became the ultimate demon, with a forked tail and cloven feet for all to see. His newspapers were banned from college common rooms and by Labour local authorities all over the land, and leaders of the Labour Party refused to give interviews to journalists from Murdoch newspapers. His effigy was everywhere. One protest group called "Women Against Murdoch" marched on Wapping chanting, "Burn, burn, burn the bastard." Publicly, Murdoch was cool. "It's a very localized thing," he said. "And it's become very emotional. And it's natural, when things get emotional, they get personalized." Privately, such reactions confirmed his dislike of "soft-centred" and "appeasing" British attitudes.

More serious for him was the haemorrhage of journalists from Wapping, particularly from *The Times* and *Sunday Times*. Some left because they could not abide their editors and the politics they were imposing. Others had long been uncomfortable about working for Murdoch, and Wapping was the last straw. Many could not stand crossing the picket lines and the anti-labour violence that the dispute both embodied and involved. Even though most journalists abhorred the printers' past history, many sympathized with their present predicament. And it was not only the printers who were on strike; the journalists' own secretaries and researchers in SOGAT were out on the picket lines as well.

Many now sought new jobs on a new paper, the *Independent*, which three former journalists on the *Daily Telegraph*, Andreas Whittam-Smith, Stephen Glover and Mathew Symonds, were planning to launch in the autumn. The new paper promised to live up to its name. By July, a third of the 115 journalists it had hired came from Wapping; many more followed later.

Murdoch claimed to be delighted by the exodus – it "was probably twenty years overdue" – but the drain of journalists became too fast even for him. Huge salary increases were offered as an incentive to those who would stay in Wapping. Some journalists accepted, many did not. "Murdoch could have kept the loyalty of the journalists if he had been seen to want to make *The Times* a better paper," said Edward Mortimer, a leader writer on the paper, who was among those who left. Morale in the fortress was mixed.

Although a Murdoch victory would benefit all Fleet Street managements, other newspapers were slow to praise, let alone support him. The *Observer* even bowed to union pressure to deny work to casual staff who also worked on other days for Murdoch. It also censored a review by Bernard Levin, a long-time contributor to the paper, because he was a columnist for *The Times*. The *Daily Telegraph* refused to accept an advertisement from News.

Auberon Waugh, the *Spectator*'s resident iconoclast, praised

Murdoch, "a hairy-heeled, tit-and-bum merchant from Oz", for rescuing British newspapers from the tyranny of the unions, but was outraged that he had banned alcohol from Wapping. "Free drunks produce better newspapers than sober slaves, as the wretched Murdoch's performance in this country now proves." Referring to Murdoch's exhausting ceaseless travel around his empire, Waugh announced:

> When I was in Adelaide (where he owned his first newspaper and where he is still venerated as a patron saint), I was told that he survives this form of existence by having an enema before every flight, and by eating nothing on the day of flying. What sort of life is that for a man of fifty-six? Does he not realize how short is our existence on earth? For all his success, all his wealth and power, he is not a free man. It is the life of a slave.

It was also the life of a winner. In January 1987, Murdoch obtained the final settlement he wanted at a cost of £60 million and the pickets trudged away. When the money was divided, the strikers received between a third and a half of what their entitlement would have been if Murdoch had been obliged to make them redundant in the first place. For him it was a famous and fantastically inexpensive victory. And he could proudly claim that he alone had cut the noose the unions had tightened around the industry. He had liberated all of Fleet Street.

Drexel Burnham Lambert estimated that the value of Murdoch's four London papers rose from $300 million to $1 billion just by moving out of Fleet Street and into Wapping. By the beginning of 1987 Wapping and Glasgow were producing almost 33 million newspapers a week. Murdoch had reduced the number of print workers from over 2,000 to just 570; 132 people now packed the papers in the publishing room – a task for which in the old days 1,469 men had been employed. The factory was said to be generating £2 million a week. His UK profits were up 85 per cent to £34.5 million. Bankers throughout the world were full of admiration for his ruthlessness and his success. Their accolades were important to Murdoch. "The financial world, the industrial world and a lot of the rest of the world are impressed that we've been able to change the industrial environment in Fleet Street. And of that we're very proud."

He could fairly claim that Wapping brought a new "Silver Age" to British journalism, and he pointed out that not only could the *Independent* not have begun but for Wapping, but it also benefited in other ways. "The *Independent* was a total beneficiary because we became the public enemy of the Left and the Labour Party. Also the soft centre didn't like us. I don't mean the Liberal Party or the Social Democrat Party. There's a soft centre there in Britain. Always has been. There were the appeasers – the sort of Tories I don't like . . . they saw our actions at Wapping as a measure of enormous harshness. This gave the *Independent* a bit of a break."

The battle of Wapping was a strategic defeat for the labour movement in Britain, and a victory for Thatcherism. The profits that derived from it would flow like blood through the arteries of Murdoch's empire all around the world.

Chapter 11

MELBOURNE

On the morning of 3 December 1986, Rupert Murdoch marched once again into the office of his father's old paper, the Melbourne *Herald*, on Flinders Street, and announced to the chairman, John Dahlsen, that he was making another bid for the company.

At that moment, the shares were selling for A$8.50. Murdoch offered A$12 per share, or two News Corp shares or convertible notes for every three Herald shares. The total value of the bid was A$1.8 billion. He gave the board just five hours to accept his offer.

Before nightfall, the board of the Herald and Weekly Times recommended that shareholders accept the offer "in the absence of a more attractive offer from anywhere else". The *Herald*, an afternoon paper, printed a special final edition that day announcing the news with a banner headline.

That evening Murdoch gave a press conference with his mother, Dame Elisabeth, beside him. He said that he had been welcomed by the Herald board "somewhat like Father Christmas". When he said he had only decided to make the bid over Thanksgiving in America someone asked him if this was the biggest turkey he had ever swallowed. He laughed.

Murdoch admitted that the deal had great emotional significance for him. When asked the perennial question, "What makes you run?" he replied, "It's the challenge of the game. It gives me a great thrill and it would be very wrong to deny that it is emotional."

He and his mother were photographed alongside the bust of his father in the lobby of the *Herald* building. Once again, Dame Elisabeth said that Rupert was "a modern-day version of my husband . . . He's very much like his father."

"Rupert is not ruled by his heart, but there is a great deal of heart in everything he does, particularly in this instance," she said in a television interview. "It is naturally sentimental. I am very happy that Rupert has managed to take his place back in that organization. That is what his father might have wished for him."

She went on to propose a motive for her son's ceaseless, frenetic, acquisitive activity. "His father dying so young was a great challenge to Rupert. Subconsciously, he wanted to prove he was worth all his father's trust and worth all his praise. It was a challenge. And that is probably the secret of his success."

A writer in the *Melbourne Age* compared Murdoch with Citizen Kane. "It may be drawing too a long bow, but with his mother by his side, there seemed to be a feeling yesterday, that just as the tycoon in Orson Welles's film pined at his death for his childhood toboggan, so Rupert Murdoch had always believed the *Herald* was his by birthright."

Others pointed out that if the deal went through, Murdoch would have control of major daily newspapers in every Australian capital city, which meant more than 60 per cent of the total daily newspapers throughout the country. Why should Australians tolerate such power in one man's hands, just so that he could prove himself to his father's ghost? Among a wide section of the Australian population Murdoch's ambitions became more feared and disliked than ever.

This particular battle in his personal, unending war of the worlds had begun on the slopes of Aspen. The Australian government gave him advance warning that it was planning a radical change in its broadcasting and press policy. In the words of the government's treasurer at the time, Paul Keating, it was offering media owners the choice between being "princes of print or queens of the screen". In Australia Murdoch would take the role of the prince.

After dozens of his usual daily phone calls to New York and to Australia, he broke his holiday on Saturday 29 November. He flew to Los Angeles, where he was met by a secretary who had flown post-haste from New York with his new American passport. From Los Angeles Murdoch took a commercial flight to Melbourne, and began to plot his strategy in the Regent Hotel.

Since his change of citizenship he had been fighting to hold on to his Channel 10 television stations in Sydney and Melbourne. There was nothing new in such a struggle. Problems of citizenship and ownership had always been among the most intractable that Murdoch faced everywhere while trying to build his international empire. This was particularly true in regard to television stations. Governments take television much more seriously than they take newspapers, and the price of having a TV station is usually paid by accountability and agreement to serve the public interest. And so Australian broadcasting law, media and even politics had been in turmoil ever since Murdoch's decision to take out American citizenship.

When he had first sought to buy Channel 10 in 1979, one clause of the Broadcasting Act had prevented any company from holding a television licence if 15 per cent of that company was controlled by someone who was "not a resident of Australia". The Labor Party had endeavoured to show that Murdoch in 1979 was certainly not such a resident. Murdoch had put up his usual self-defence of being the little man taking on huge established interests.

Eventually, the tribunal decided that he was adequately *resident* and could legitimately have the Channel 10 licence. Then the law was changed. It was no longer necessary to be "resident" in Australia – instead an owner of a television station had to be a *citizen* of the country. This had been seen at the time as advantageous to Murdoch and thus an example of his influence over the government of the day. It was widely called the "Murdoch amendment". But when he became an American, such a change obviously worked against him. By the middle of 1986, it seemed clear that he would have to sell off his two Channel 10 television stations in Australia.

Nevertheless, Murdoch sought to retain them. He saw them as an important if not crucial part of the global news and entertainment web he was weaving around the world from its centre on the Fox lot in Hollywood.

In Australia that was seen as part of the problem. "Our cross-ownership rules were vital because they stopped Murdoch having both papers and TV all over the world," said Deirdre O'Connor, the chairman of the Broadcasting Tribunal. "It broke the circle. I think Murdoch was very anxious to keep Channel 10 at that time. He had just bought Fox and said it would be of great mutual benefit to Australia and the USA. That's what we feared – we didn't want to be swamped by US material." Once again, fears of omnivorous American culture had been raised.

In Canberra the problem generated heated internal debate within the Labor Party. Prime Minister Hawke was reported to be strongly in favour of changes that would assist the Packer and Murdoch organizations. Hawke's declared motive was "national reconciliation" – almost as if Murdoch were a sovereign state.

Like the United States, Australia had become more and more deeply in debt in the 1980s; assets were shuffled and redealt. One industrialist called it a "casino mentality". The Australian macho concept of "mateship" between Labor leaders and tycoons was an insidious part of this process. Murdoch and Packer were among the mates. Hawke called Packer "a close personal friend and . . . a very great Australian".

Fairfax and the Melbourne *Herald*, by contrast, were seen as representing the old Establishment and being irredeemably pro-Liberal and anti-Labor. This was in part because Fairfax had a reputation for troublesome investigative reporting, rarely a forte of Murdoch newspapers. As Paul Chadwick pointed out in his book, *Media Mates*, the Fairfax papers had subjected almost everyone who was anyone – Bob Hawke, Paul Keating, Peter Abeles, Murdoch's Ansett partner, among others – to scrutiny. After one article, Keating was reported to have said, "Don't they realize it's a jungle out there, and I'm a tiger?" Hawke spoke of Fairfax as "the natural enemy" of Labor and of the Melbourne *Herald* as a "violent, virulent anti-Labor journal". Murdoch's campaign against Gough Whitlam was forgotten by Whitlam's successors.

When he became an American citizen, Murdoch's Australian lawyers had announced plans to transfer control of the Channel 10 network to the public shareholders of News Corporation and to a new trust. The purpose was to quarantine Murdoch's personal interest in the two stations and keep it below the maximum 15 per cent allowed to an alien. Under the proposal a new company called Network 10 Holdings would own the two stations.

The tribunal's hearing into the new structure was delayed from November 1985 until April 1986. This was just as well for Murdoch, who in late 1985 was heavily involved in preparing the move to Wapping.

When the tribunal did meet, News Corp proposed that it would have less than 1 per cent of the voting rights of Network 10 Holdings. The tribunal's enquiry focused on the degree of control News Corporation might be able to exert on the board of Network 10. The Journalists' Association which, as usual, opposed Murdoch, asserted that whatever the appearances, "the American still remained in effective control".

Conspiracy theorists expected that Murdoch's close relations with the Labor government would enable him to sail through the hearings. But then, while the tribunal was still pondering the problems, the government suddenly announced its "queens of the screen" and "princes of the print" changes to the broadcasting system, modelled on the American cross-ownership rules.

From now on, owners could buy as many television stations as they wished – but could not also own a newspaper with more than half its circulation in the same catchment area. In other words a television station owner in, say, Melbourne, could not also own a major Melbourne paper. These new rules would not be retrospective, but they would be brought into play whenever a TV station or newspaper changed hands.

This scheme would not hurt Murdoch or Packer, but it would penalize the Melbourne Herald and Weekly Times group and the Fairfax group. The Herald had daily newspapers in many markets, including Brisbane, Adelaide and Perth, and these would prevent it from developing a national television network. If it wished to acquire a Melbourne station to match Sydney's Channel 7, it would have to sell its Melbourne flagship, the *Age*.

Kerry Packer had no newspapers, only magazines. So the new rules were of no concern to him. For Murdoch the situation was different. Assuming that his attempt to keep his Channel 10 stations failed, and he had to sell them, he was now likely to get a much better price. If there was no longer a two-station rule, the value of leading stations in both Melbourne and Sydney would increase enormously to anyone seeking to establish a national network. One analyst reckoned that the changes increased the value of Packer's and Murdoch's stations from $800 million to $1.8 billion.

On 24 November, after long discussion and some heated debate, the Labor Cabinet finally approved the Keating proposal. At a subsequent meeting of the Labor Party caucus, Keating attacked the *Herald* and said that it would be good if it were split up because it was not "one of us". Left-wing members of the caucus complained that a deal had been done with Packer and Murdoch; this was angrily denied by Hawke. One member pointed out that in the past industrial barons had exercised power in Australia. "True power in the future will be exercised by those who control the means of information," he pointed out.

Keating had had dinner with Murdoch in New York several weeks beforehand and told him of his plans. Murdoch said later that it sounded so fantastic that he thought it would never get through Cabinet. Keating also alerted Packer but gave no such advance warning to either the Herald or the Fairfax groups. When the Cabinet agreed the Keating plan and it was announced, Murdoch knew that this would be the best possible time to sell his television stations and to become an even more powerful Prince of Print. He made his dash from the slopes of Aspen back to Australia to try and buy the *Herald*.

The group had been vulnerable to a takeover for some time. It was an old-established company, with valuable assets and a cautious management. The flagship of the group, the Melbourne *Herald*, had once been the biggest-selling newspaper in the city, but its circulation was in decline.

In July 1985, John D'Arcy, an extrovert Irish accountant, had given up the management of the successful Queensland Press to take over as chief executive of the Herald group. He began to grapple with the company's problems. He improved the management and bought papers in Sydney, New South Wales and the Melbourne suburbs.

D'Arcy realized any threat was most likely to come from Murdoch. News was not now financially strong in Australia – Murdoch's papers simply did not have the classified-advertising market that Fairfax and the Herald group enjoyed in different cities. A large part of his cash flow came from the earnings of Ansett Airlines.

D'Arcy tried to defend the group with a series of cross-shareholdings with other companies, the Brisbane-based Queensland Press and Adelaide-based Advertiser Newspapers, two of the largest shareholders. But rumours of takeover abounded. Many brokers who examined the Herald group's assets calculated that its break-up value was $9.28 a share – well above the current share price of $7.60. D'Arcy himself acknowledged: "Everybody knows the Herald and Weekly Times could be grabbed if the price is right."

In early November 1986, Murdoch had a drink with D'Arcy, who recalls him saying, "The world is awash with money and it's inevitable the Herald will be a takeover target. I don't want to be in a three-way fight." He proposed that they should merge News and the Herald group. D'Arcy was not keen. "I thought it would create too big a company for Australia. The Trade Practices Commission and the government wouldn't allow it. Rupert's citizenship was another problem." He came away from the meeting more concerned than ever that Murdoch would pounce.

At 7 a.m. on 6 December, Ken Cowley called D'Arcy asking if Murdoch could meet with him and the Herald's chairman, John Dahlsen, at Flinders Street at 9 a.m. "I knew what it was, obviously," said D'Arcy.

When he came in, Murdoch was friendly, but he insisted on an answer by 5 p.m. The board discussed it all day. Some felt they could have rejected the offer. But they had to consider their duty towards their shareholders. "It was a bloody bonanza. He was paying forty times earnings!" said D'Arcy later. Keith McDonald, the managing director of the Queensland Press, said later that he had another reason: "I thought the share register was very unstable. Better to be taken over by someone who understood and loved papers – better to be swallowed and digested than chewed up and spat out. I suppose also there was a bit of sentiment on my part. When I first came to Queensland Press in 1946, Sir Keith was the proprietor."

That evening the board recommended acceptance of Murdoch's

offer of $12 per share, in the absence of a better offer. This was deliberately phrased in order to bring Holmes à Court into play.

After the *Herald*'s announcement, Murdoch gave his press conference. On the way to it, Ken Cowley warned him to make no promises about the *Herald* itself. It might be that the demographics of Melbourne and the problems of all afternoon papers were such that it just could not be saved.

Murdoch told the press that his price was fair and generous. He said he would sell off the Herald's interest in the HSV-7 TV station in Melbourne and its interest in the Adelaide TV station, ADS-7 if the bid succeeded. This would be necessary under the proposed cross-ownership laws, but it also suited Murdoch financially.

Asked about his plans for the Melbourne *Herald* itself, Murdoch ignored Ken Cowley's advice and said: "One has to design what will be a proper publishing strategy for the *Herald* . . . the *Herald* will continue in its present traditions, and I hope greatly improved. I believe that the *Herald* is at the point where it is worth going upmarket again." He said the *Herald* had always been the "quality act" in town and he wanted to restore that reputation. Next day, *The Australian* headlined the story of his bid "MURDOCH'S OFFER TOO GOOD TO REFUSE".

If the takeover succeeded, it would give Murdoch immense and unprecedented power over Australia's newspaper business. His Australian empire was already wide. In Sydney, News Corporation owned the *Australian*, the *Daily Telegraph*, the *Sunday Telegraph* and the afternoon *Daily Mirror*. In Perth, News owned the *Sunday Times* and in Brisbane, the *Daily Sun*. In Adelaide, he still owned the *News*, his first paper, and the *Sunday Mail*. With the Herald group as well, he would control major daily newspapers in every Australian capital city and would have a monopoly in Perth, Brisbane and Adelaide. Seventy-five per cent of daily circulation would be in Murdoch's hands.

His bid was therefore widely greeted with both fury and concern. His biggest rival, Fairfax, felt especially threatened. An editorial in the *Sydney Morning Herald* warned that Murdoch would transform the group from a "benign, loosely managed media giant to an extension of Mr Murdoch's ego and a very closely managed instrument of his ambition". The *Financial Review* complained: "The Government is encouraging a near national monopoly – and an absolute monopoly in some places – by an American citizen who has a history of using his newspapers to manipulate politics as it suits him." Murdoch denounced this as "a filthy libel".

Such criticisms of Murdoch were dismissed by many members of the Labor government. The Prime Minister, Bob Hawke, said that Murdoch had been kind enough to come and tell him of the bid, and attacked the Fairfax press for its complaints. It became clear that the government had no intention of standing in the way of the bid. Hawke said that the old Herald management was "viciously anti-Labor, so if Mr Murdoch were to fire a few salvoes at us, it couldn't be worse than what we have been enduring". The only body which could step in to prevent the bid was the Trade Practices Commission, which did not do so.

Murdoch did not get his way at once. On the stock market, shares in the Herald group began to rise after he made his bid. There was strong suspicion that Robert Holmes à Court, who already owned 4 per cent, was behind the buying. Ron Brierley's Industrial Equity group was also known to be interested in raising its 12 per cent stake. Brierley had been buying shares for months. Others speculated that Fairfax might once more come to the "rescue" of the Herald group just as it had when Murdoch lunged for it in 1979.

On Christmas Eve, 1986, Holmes à Court made a A$1.95 billion offer, or A$13 a share, for the Herald group. Some thought that his bid was a negotiating ploy to get Murdoch to deal out some favourable assets in the Herald group. But Murdoch insisted, "In no circumstances will we deal separately with Mr Robert Holmes à Court." When Holmes à Court increased his bid to $13.50 a share, the board recommended the offer to shareholders.

On 4 January 1987, Fairfax entered the contest. It did not launch a bid for the Herald group; but for Queensland Press Limited, which had a vital 24 per cent stake in the Herald. This was a relatively cheap – but somewhat uncertain – method of putting pressure on Murdoch. Fairfax bid $20 cash for Queensland Press shares, which had closed the previous trading day at $17.20. It was a condition of the offer that Queensland Press should accept Holmes à Court's offer of $13.50 for the Herald group. This condition suggested that Fairfax and Holmes à Court were working together to fight off Murdoch and carve up the Herald group.

Murdoch responded by increasing his offer to A$15 a share. The deal also included an offer to top the Fairfax bid for Queensland Press by offering $23 a share, through his family company, Cruden, not News. Fairfax leapfrogged him with an offer of $24 a share for Queensland.

On 15 January, Holmes à Court and Murdoch made a deal, despite Murdoch's earlier insistence he would do no such thing. Holmes à Court agreed to drop his bid for the Herald in return for being allowed to buy the Herald's TV station (HSV-7 in Melbourne) for $260 million and West Australian Newspapers Limited, publishers of two newspapers – the *West Australian* and the afternoon *Daily News* – for $200 million. Holmes à Court would also make $100 million in trading profits from the sale of his shares to Murdoch.

Fairfax then made another offer for the Herald, topping Murdoch's bid, and proposing to carve up the group. However, the Herald management decided that this offer had come too late and that Murdoch was now unstoppable.

Murdoch finally had the house his father built.

All this while he had also been fighting to keep his television stations, despite everything that seemed to disqualify him from ownership. News announced yet another change to the proposed ownership structure. Murdoch would resign from the board of News Limited, the Australian company, in a further attempt to quarantine himself from the stations. It was still not enough. On 20 January 1987, the federal court ruled that Murdoch would still be in a position to control the TV stations.

Once the Herald deal was finalized, Murdoch moved quickly to sell off the group's television assets to avoid another threatened hearing of the tribunal to look into the implications of the takeover and his American citizenship. In February 1987 he announced he would be selling the TV and radio stations for $820 million to Northern Star Holdings, a small media company based in northern

New South Wales. Northern Star was backed by a Sydney investment company called Westfield Capital Corporation.

Murdoch made one last visit to ATV 10 in Sydney in February 1987. He pointed out that he had not been allowed to come to the studio for eighteen months – since becoming an American. He said News was "very sad" to be selling Channel 10 and he hoped none the less there would be some opportunity to network programmes to 10 from the US. There were "no formal links at this stage", he said, between News Corp and the new owners, Northern Star. However, a few weeks later, Murdoch announced that News would be taking a 15 per cent interest in the new company formed by Northern Star to operate the stations. (This was the maximum a foreigner could own in an Australian TV station.) Murdoch's Australian managing director, Ken Cowley, was to join the Northern Star board.

There were other links between Northern Star and News Corp, which came about because the Trade Practices Commission imposed some conditions on the News takeover of the Herald group. Murdoch was to sell his old newspapers in Adelaide and Brisbane to an acceptable purchaser who would assure their continued viability. The commission's aim was to ensure continued competition for Murdoch's new (Herald) papers, the Adelaide *Advertiser* and the *Brisbane Courier-Mail* in these two cities. So the Adelaide *News* (Murdoch's first paper) and the *Brisbane Daily Sun* and the *Sunday Sun* were all sold to Northern Star. Under the arrangement, the papers would be produced on News Corporation presses in both cities. Northern Star TV stations were also given the first right of refusal to Fox Film productions.

When he took control of the Herald group, Murdoch removed the chairman, John Dahlsen, from the board, and retained the chief executive, John D'Arcy, making him chairman as well. He appointed his sister, Mrs Janet Calvert-Jones, a director – the first woman ever on the board. "Newspapers have been in my blood from the day I was born," she said. "We are all very proud of Rupert and what he's done. And I share my mother and my brother's excitement, or emotion, about the *Herald*, about something that Dad built up."

Reviving the *Herald* would be a major task. Its circulation had once been over 500,000 but it had since fallen to some 238,000. Murdoch was ambitious: "We're going to turn it around, get it back into the homes of Melbourne. It will have authority, polish and professionalism." The *Herald*, he said, would be "the best-written paper in Melbourne . . . a young middle-class paper".

Murdoch raided Fairfax, and made Eric Beecher, the editor of the *Sydney Morning Herald*, editor in chief of the Herald group, and editor of the *Herald*. Beecher saw himself as a serious journalist, not a popular one in the prevailing News Corp tradition. He had done his early training on the *Age* in Melbourne, where he was held to have great promise. However, after being passed over for a promotion, he had left and joined the *Sydney Morning Herald*. Now, the rumour mill had it that Murdoch wanted to groom Beecher for greater things and that within two years he would be in London, editing either *The Times* or the *Sunday Times*.

It was clear at once that Murdoch had given Beecher considerable financial freedom to turn the *Herald* around. Beecher said that he was not intimidated by stories of interference from Murdoch, whom he found "extremely charming and intelligent". He had a mandate to report directly to Murdoch or to Ken Cowley, if Murdoch was not in the country. Once ensconced in Melbourne, Beecher poached some of the top Fairfax journalists, and stories about the high salaries being offered swept newsrooms round the country.

In July 1987, Murdoch officially "relaunched" the paper. There was to be a multi-million-dollar advertising campaign. Edition times were to be brought forward to 10 a.m. It was a brave effort. In the months to come Beecher certainly succeeded in taking the paper upmarket to rival the *Age*. Melbourne society was approving; Dame Elisabeth was delighted. But the relationship between owner and editor soured and Murdoch's hope of restoring his father's flagship to the glory that he remembered as a boy proved forlorn.

THE VILLAGE

In those days, though, Murdoch was bursting with self-confidence. Bankers from all over the world were falling over themselves to fawn upon him and to praise his famous victory at Wapping. They were almost begging to recycle their money through his miraculous machine. In the heady financial atmosphere of the mid-1980s, over which the clouds of the October '87 crash seemed to pass quickly, Murdoch appeared, to others and to himself, to be invincible.

By early 1987 News Corp was one of the world's largest communications groups, with some 250 subsidiaries. Apart from newspapers, books and television, the company had interests in aircraft, oil, bauxite wool, and games management or gambling. Turnover and profits of the group had both risen enormously fast after Wapping – they were up 56 per cent and 83 per cent respectively in the second half of 1986. But debt was beginning to burgeon as well – by 30 September 1986 it was close to $3 billion, a total approaching the company's annual revenues. (By contrast the Columbia Broadcasting System, which many people considered overburdened by debt, had debts amounting to less than a quarter of its revenue.) News's debt was serviced by the cash flow of the company's newspapers, particularly those from Wapping. In the fiscal year 1986 the interest payments doubled, to more than $160 million, but cash flow was up to $364 million.

In 1989 loan maturities and redemption of preferred shares would total $425 million, in 1990 $560 million, and in 1991 $1.2 billion. None the less Richard Sarazen, News Corp's financial officer, was sanguine. He said early in 1987 that the principal could be renegotiated when the time came, and if interest rates started rising, "We are prepared to swap into fixed-interest debt at a moment's notice. We have lines of credit and standby agreements to do that when we think it is appropriate."

Murdoch and Sarazen also constantly played the foreign

exchange markets, in effect gambling on the prices of the various currencies in which the company traded. They usually did this to good effect; in 1986 the company recorded currency exchange profits of $64 million.

Nothing could keep Murdoch still. Even as he completed the purchase of the Herald and Weekly Times in Melbourne in early 1987, he was planning a Sunday edition of the *New York Post*, despite the fact that the FCC had required him to sell the paper to comply with US cross-ownership rules. In fact, he was still doing everything he could to find his way around these rules, or to obtain another temporary waiver. He detested the idea of losing the *Post*.

At the end of 1986 Murdoch outbid Pearson, the publishers of the *Financial Times*, and paid $260 million for the *South China Morning Post*, Hong Kong's most profitable daily newspaper and one of the best in Asia. Michael Sandberg, the chairman of the Hong Kong and Shanghai Bank, said that Murdoch had told him that he saw the *Post* as "*The Times* of South East Asia".

More than that, perhaps. Murdoch had long had his eye upon China, since his first visit there in 1985; he understood that English was the second language in China and that a vast market for books and films beckoned there. Hong Kong's own economy was booming, and so were its commercial links with the coastal cities of China, especially Canton province, which was increasingly becoming an extension of Hong Kong industry. The classified advertisements of the *Post* seemed to Murdoch to be an almost bottomless mine of gold. Moreover, quite apart from China and Hong Kong, the entire Pacific was economically the fastest-growing region in the world and the *Post* gave him a media presence on a fourth continent. The fifth, Africa, was being left almost entirely out of the information revolution, because it seemed incapable of generating the wealth necessary to make it attractive to international corporations.

In America, Murdoch had managed to lower the cost of financing his infant network, Fox. News Corp had already redeemed most of the $1 billion-plus preferred stock issue, and the rest of it was expected to be bought in soon. Interest on the borrowed funds had been reduced from about 13 per cent to 7 per cent. The seven television stations were under-performing against earlier projections, but Richard MacDonald, an analyst with First Boston who followed News Corp stock, reckoned that their cash flow was already well up on their financing costs. Part of this success was due to skilled accounting.

Fox Broadcasting, carried by the seven stations, had already cost at least $50 million, but was still too young to have made a real impact. In Hollywood, Barry Diller was talking of "counter-programming". He said, "Anyone looking for an edge will try to offer what isn't being offered." He was looking for shows that appealed to the young. So far Fox sitcoms like "Small Wonder" and "9 to 5" had had some success, though neither was as popular as the reruns of "M*A*S*H", which was still the king of situation comedies and responsible for between $20 and $30 million of News Corp's cash flow.

Soon after the acquisition of the *South China Morning Post* and the Melbourne *Herald*, Sarazen declared that Murdoch would now consolidate rather than expand further. But Sarazen knew that Murdoch had spent his life saying that he had now bought enough. He never meant it. He simply could not escape, ever, the seduction of a deal. He had no game plan, no carefully devised strategy. It was just Murdoch against the world, trying to score whenever he could. He never stopped pulling in pieces and people as they were needed, in his everlasting attempt to create some extraordinary machine that straddled the globe and fed the world what he knew it wanted. As soon as Sarazen said he had stopped, he dashed after the New York publishers, Harper and Row.

This was, according to Stanley Shuman, his banker, another last-minute decision. The public reaction to it showed how American views of him had improved since he had become a citizen. He was now seen much more as the man trying to build a fourth national TV network than as the publisher of downmarket newspapers.

Murdoch considered book publishing an essential part of his growing global network of publishing, film and broadcasting properties. He had long wanted to have an American publishing house to be a partner to Angus and Robertson in Australia, and William Collins, the British house, of which he had owned over

40 per cent since 1981. The story of his interest in Collins is crucial to the purchase of Harper and Row.

Collins was one of Britain's oldest family publishers. The Collins family had controlled it for six generations. Collins authors included Alistair Maclean and the Holy Ghost, for Collins published the Bible in Britain and in British overseas markets. One of the principal executives of the company was Ian Chapman, a Scotsman who had trained before the war to become a musician and then gone into publishing. By the mid-1970s he had risen through the company to become managing director, to Sir Billy Collins's chairman.

Sir Billy died in 1976. His son Jan was appointed chairman, but was not a great success. From 1977 to mid-1979 Collins slid into loss for the first time since the company was first floated in 1949. In August 1979, Jan Collins was stripped of his executive power and made non-executive chairman. It was a blow to the Collins family pride which was later to provide Rupert Murdoch with his entry into the company.

Ian Chapman, the deputy chairman, and David Nickson, the vice chairman, set about putting Collins back on its feet. Much cost-cutting ensued. The freehold of the beloved head office in St James's Place in London was sold and 800 jobs went in Glasgow, where Collins had been founded. It was painful, but by the end of 1979 the company was breaking even. In 1980 it was scheduled to make £2 million in pre-tax profits, and the company was worth about £10.5 million.

In early 1981 rumours of an impending takeover spread. Robert Maxwell had been buying shares and now announced that his stake had passed the 5 per cent mark at which it had to be revealed. Immediately, Chapman received a call from Murdoch, who had just bought *The Times* and *Sunday Times*. According to Chapman, Murdoch said, "I see you've got a new shareholder. Are you looking for a white knight?"

Chapman says he replied, "Absolutely not, Rupert. The company can't be taken over. It's protected by two family trusts. So there's nothing to worry about. But thanks very much." Chapman reported his telephone conversation with Murdoch to the next board meeting.

In April 1981, one of the professional trustees on Billy Collins's trust died and Chapman lost the overall support of the trust. The family contacted Lord Goodman, Murdoch's London solicitor, and asked him to see if Murdoch was still interested. Murdoch replied that he was and the family decided to sell him their stock. Goodman and Murdoch both seemed to have assumed that the board and Chapman were aware of this move. In fact they were not.

The Collins board was not pleased. Jan Collins was persuaded to resign and Ian Chapman was appointed chairman and chief executive officer, with instructions to resist the takeover bid.

The shares Murdoch was buying from the Collins family constituted 31 per cent of the company's stock – the law thus obliged him to make a bid for the entire company. Meantime Maxwell had also increased his shareholding to about 9 per cent and in the early summer he rang Chapman to ask for a meeting. Chapman said that Maxwell insisted on a conspiratorial, clandestine encounter at which he told him, "I'm either part of your problem or part of your solution."

Maxwell wanted a seat on the board. Chapman said he could not grant him that; he asked Maxwell if there was any risk of his selling his shares to Murdoch.

Chapman recalled, "With his great big hairy hands, Maxwell thumped the table. The china was shaking, and he said, 'I'll never sell to that Australian bastard.'" But within seventy-two hours he did.

Murdoch's bid for the company was worth £25 million. Chapman mobilized his authors – Alistair Maclean, Jack Higgins, Hammond Innes, Ken Follett – against it. They all urged the shareholders to reject Murdoch and in July 1981 the shareholders did so. However, Murdoch was left with 41.7 per cent of Collins's voting stock and two seats on the Collins board; Chapman persuaded him to take one for himself; he gave the other to Sir Edward Pickering.

He took his defeat gracefully and, said Chapman, promised he would behave as non-executives should behave, representing all the shareholders, monitoring the performance of the executives, playing a part in the board's decisions, but beyond that, not interfering. In Lord Goodman's presence Murdoch assured Chapman he would not make a hostile bid for the company.

And that, according to Chapman, was how Murdoch behaved for many years. Under Chapman's direction, and with Murdoch's support, Collins thrived during the early 1980s. Profits rose from £4 million in 1981 to £15 million in 1986. Throughout all that time, said Chapman, "Murdoch was as good as his word. He didn't interfere, nor increase his holdings, as he was entitled to do, at 2 per cent a year."

In 1983 Chapman acquired Granada Publishing for Collins and renamed it Grafton Books. By the mid-1980s he was anxious to acquire an American publishing arm for Collins. In 1985 he came close to buying New American Library, but it was considered overpriced. Then in early 1987, Harper and Row came into play.

Founded in 1817, Harper and Row had published Herman Melville and Mark Twain. By the mid-1980s, it was one of the last independent publishers in New York but, despite its fine backlist, the board had been attempting to devise a defensive structure against takeover. The scheme had not been greeted with enthusiasm by the company's largest shareholder, Theodore Cross, a lawyer and editor, who held 5.3 per cent of the stock. On 9 March, he made a surprise bid of $190 million for the company – $34 a share against the market price of $24. That was at once followed by an offer of $220 million from Harcourt Brace Jovanovich.

Murdoch immediately saw this as the perfect opportunity to buy the American trade publishers he thought the News empire needed. He called Chapman, who had already been talking to Brookes Thomas, the chairman of Harper and Row, and invited him to dinner at Overtons, the fish restaurant in St James's. "Let's go for it," he said.

Chapman shared Murdoch's enthusiasm. He had personal connections with many in Harper's management and agreed that he should call Brookes Thomas and suggest Collins as a white knight. Thomas told Chapman that they would be delighted to have Collins ride in. After negotiations between Harper, Collins and News, a deal was struck, but then Chapman and Murdoch agreed that News would buy Harper outright and that Collins would have an option to buy 50 per cent of it after three or four months. Chapman, delighted with this deal, persuaded the Harper board that Murdoch was not to be feared – he had been a perfect partner at Collins.

Murdoch's bid of $300 million (A$428 million) valued the company at $65 a share – fifty-five times earnings, a generous multiple by any standards. Brookes Thomas said, "If somebody offers you more money than you think you could ever make through earnings, you have to take it." Murdoch also seemed less of a risk than Harcourt Brace Jovanovich – which was expected merely to take over the lists and dismantle the company. After a meeting at Murdoch's apartment on Fifth Avenue, Harper and Row's management accepted Murdoch's offer. A few months later Murdoch, as agreed, sold 50 per cent of the company to William Collins for $156 million. By linking Collins and Harpers, he was creating one of the largest and most powerful publishing companies in the English language.

The deal brought fever to the American publishing industry. "Anything that isn't pinned to the wall is being bought," said Roger Straus, president of Farrar, Straus & Giroux, one of the few companies to remain in private hands.

By the 1980s, book publishing was becoming more and more dominated by large conglomerates. William Morrow was bought by Hearst, Scribners by Macmillan, Simon and Schuster by Gulf and Western (now PCI). Bertelsmann bought Doubleday for $475 million and merged it with Bantam and Dell. The International Thomson Organization (the former owners of Times Newspapers in London) had been making acquisitions in the States, including South-Western Publishing, for which it had paid $270 million. Harcourt Brace paid $500 million for CBS Educational and Professional Publishing. Time Inc paid $520 million for the academic publisher, Scott, Foresman.

To many, the sale of Harper and Row to Murdoch seemed another blow to "quality" publishing. Fears were expressed that with fewer and fewer publishers, there would be an increasing demand for blockbusters of clear commercial, but not much literary, merit. Even Brookes Thomas, who had favoured the sale of Harper to Murdoch, agreed that being owned was not the same as being independent. "If somebody has your string – even if they never pull it – maybe it has some effect on you."

LONDON

Murdoch's next acquisition brought him once again into conflict with his old rivals. On Saturday 28 July 1987, Murdoch, in Los Angeles, received a telephone call from Robert Maxwell in England. It was a costly mistake by Maxwell.

For almost twenty years Maxwell had been consumed by his rivalry with Murdoch who, for his part, regarded Maxwell with bemused contempt. Privately he would say he was a mad crook. Maxwell's ambition was to build an international media empire bigger than Murdoch's. He had not succeeded, but his own empire had certainly expanded since he had lost their first battle over the *News of the World* in 1968.

In 1969 Maxwell had lost his company Pergamon after Saul P. Steinberg of Leasco pulled out of an agreement to buy it, insisting that Maxwell had misled him as to its real worth. The shareholders then ousted Maxwell from the board and a Board of Trade enquiry concluded, famously, that Maxwell "is not in our opinion a person who can be relied upon to exercise proper stewardship of a publicly quoted company".

None the less, in 1974, after reaching an out-of-court settlement with Steinberg, he persuaded the board of Pergamon that only he could save it – and was invited back. He claimed, falsely, that he had been exonerated of the Board of Trade charges against him. He issued writs against anyone who suggested otherwise.

In 1980 he had another success – he convinced the British Printing Corporation and its unions that, since it was nearly bankrupt, the company could be saved only if jobs were cut from 13,000 to 7,000. With its name changed to Maxwell Communications Corporation, it became profitable. But he was still after a newspaper. So far, he had been thwarted in his bids for the *News of the World*, the *Sun*, the *Observer*, and *The Times*. Three out of four of these had gone to Murdoch.

Finally, in 1984 he was able to buy Mirror Group Newspapers from Reed International. At last he had a daily tabloid and two Sunday papers. And not only that – he also had the tabloids which were pitted most directly against his rival's *Sun* and *News of the World*.

At once, he dominated the *Mirror* far more completely, and far more crassly, than Murdoch had ever aspired to do with his own newspapers. He himself was a constant subject of stories, whether he was conducting fawning interviews with East European dictators, or flying on a "*Mirror* Mercy Mission" to Ethiopia. Although he continued the paper's support for the Labour Party, it became, for a time, a vehicle for the blatant promotion of Maxwell.

In the spring of 1987 Maxwell and Murdoch both became interested in buying *Today*, the paper with which Eddie Shah had launched the revolution that was followed through at Wapping. *Today* had been an unhappy venture for Shah. He had planned a seven-day colour tabloid produced in London, using the very latest technology. This was a mistake, since as Murdoch argued, the newest machinery always went wrong. More fundamental, no one seemed to know who the readers were, or what the paper should say to them. With a sales target of one million and a break-even point of 600,000 (after cost-cutting) the paper was selling barely 300,000 copies.

In August 1986, Tiny Rowland, the chief executive of Lonrho, the Pan-African conglomerate which owned the *Observer*, had rescued Eddie Shah by buying a 90 per cent stake. A new editor and managing director were installed and sales improved, and in early 1987 the Lonrho board set a deadline of 30 June for a buyer to be found.

Murdoch met Tiny Rowland shortly after Easter. They were not on good terms. The *Sunday Times* and *Times* had published critical stories about Lonrho. None the less they agreed a deal whereby a million copies of the *News of the World* would be printed on *Today*'s presses. The deal relieved the pressure on

Wapping, and also allowed the *News of the World* to experiment with colour.

Murdoch had for some time wanted a middle-market paper to complete News International's presence in every sector of the British market. On Saturday 13 June, two days after the general election in which Margaret Thatcher won a third victory with the enthusiastic support of Murdoch's British papers, Murdoch went to see Tiny Rowland at his London home. Within the next few days, they agreed that Murdoch would buy *Today* for £40 million. The payment would be spread over a period of years and would be contingent on the paper reaching certain circulation targets.

Then Rowland changed his mind. An article on Lonrho in the *Sunday Times* apparently infuriated him. Details of the impending sale were leaked and sparked the interest of both Robert Maxwell and Lord Rothermere, the owner of Associated Newspapers. The latter would have liked to have bought *Today*, and closed it down to relieve the pressure on his own *Daily Mail*.

Maxwell wanted to increase the pressure on Rothermere, who had helped destroy Maxwell's own twenty-four-hour paper, the *London Daily News*, a few months earlier. He offered Lonrho £10 million in cash and promised to assume £30 million of debts. But Maxwell wanted 100 per cent of the shares, not just the 90 per cent which Lonrho owned. Company rules in Britain allowed a bidder with 90 per cent of a company's shares to compel the other 10 per cent to accept his bid, but Eddie Shah was reluctant to relinquish his 10 per cent holding. He had always preferred Murdoch to Maxwell. The writer Jeffrey Archer also controlled a minute but vital 0.01 per cent given to him as part payment for the serialization of his novel *A Matter of Honour*.

On Saturday 28 June, the *Financial Times* revealed the negotiations. It seemed that Maxwell had won, but in fact Shah was still being pursued around golf courses by Maxwell's men attempting to get his final signature. Only after Jeffrey Archer had accepted an offer of £100,000, and Maxwell had made three weekend phone calls to Shah, did the founder of *Today* tentatively agree to sever his connection with the paper for £250,000 plus a promised option in Mirror shares when the group was floated on the Stock Exchange.

It was then that Maxwell made the crucial mistake of phoning Murdoch in Los Angeles. "It's all over," said Maxwell. "Congratulations," said Murdoch. But as Maxwell talked, Murdoch suddenly became aware that the deal was not yet finally signed.

He now realized that he could either let Maxwell buy a paper that was losing nearly £30 million a year, or he could try to acquire it himself and make it into a success, just as he had done eighteen years earlier with the *Sun*. The challenge, added to the piquancy of pipping Maxwell at the post, was irresistible. Murdoch was not obsessed with his rival, but he was irritated that they were so often conflated and confused in the public mind – the two indistinguishable evil barons dominating the British media. And it was in Murdoch's nature to compete.

He decided to swoop. While his men in London traced Tiny Rowland to his yacht in the Adriatic, Murdoch flew to Aspen. From there, on Sunday, he spoke to his own people in London and to Lonhro executives. He made a new offer – of £38 million in cash, almost four times as much cash as Maxwell was offering. Discovering that the Maxwell signing was scheduled for 10.30 on Monday morning, he flew overnight to London.

At 7.15 on the morning of Monday 30 June, News International's senior executives and lawyers arrived at Lonrho's offices. Murdoch was to have been with them but his flight was delayed. By 10 a.m. they had thrashed out a deal to put before Rowland upon his return later that day.

Maxwell, enraged, pulled out, once more frustrated by Murdoch and leaving Rowland no option but to close the deal with "that Australian bastard".

The final price proved difficult to agree. On Wednesday 2 July, Murdoch said that he had had enough, that the deal was off and that he was leaving London. By the time he reached the airport this tactic had succeeded. His negotiators had finally settled with Lonrho – for £38 million cash.

The deal gave Murdoch his fifth British national newspaper. The 1973 Fair Trading Act required that it be referred to the Monopolies Commission. But Murdoch and Rowland gave an ultimatum to the Secretary of State for Trade and Industry, Lord Young. Unless he approved the sale within twenty-four hours,

Murdoch would withdraw. These were the same tactics as Murdoch and Thomsons had used over the sale of Times Newspapers in 1981, and they were seen by many as a brazen attempt to blackmail the government. Nevertheless, they worked. After consulting his officials, Young, who had been Secretary of State for less than three weeks, acceded. Accepting that the paper's existence would otherwise be threatened, he allowed its sale to Murdoch.

The Labour Party was infuriated and even the Press Council made a rare intervention, denouncing the deal. The critics argued that Lonrho's earlier decision to cease production required merely that a buyer be found by 30 June, not that the deal be concluded by then. Jonathan Aitken, a Conservative MP, asked, "Should we now give Mr Murdoch a free pass and have done with it?"

The Labour Party also claimed that during the recent election campaign Young had telephoned Murdoch to complain that the *Sun* was not giving enough support to the Tories. This phone call, said Malcolm Bruce, MP for Gordon, had had the desired response: "another scurrilous outburst – *Sun*-style support for the Conservative Party. The pay-off came when . . . Rupert Murdoch . . . asked for support for this takeover." Young totally denied this; he last saw Murdoch before the campaign and did not speak to him again. During the campaign, he spoke constantly to many editors, including Kelvin MacKenzie.

The night that Murdoch took control of *Today*, he appointed David Montgomery, till then editor of the *News of the World*, as the new editor. In the first edition, the outgoing editor, Dennis Hackett, had been running a story emphasizing the Labour opposition to the takeover. Montgomery immediately changed it to an attack on the critics of the sale. Next day's *Sun* labelled the criticisms "absolute balderdash".

Although Hackett left, many of the old executives stayed. The paper aimed itself more squarely at the young men and women who were doing well in Thatcher's Britain. City coverage was improved. There were more gossipy stories about TV personalities. Politically, the paper abandoned the Social Democratic-Liberal Alliance – easy enough now that that group was imploding – and adopted Murdoch's loyalty to Margaret Thatcher. Early in

1988, Granada TV awarded the paper the title "Newspaper of the Year", for its preference for news coverage rather than topless models, sex scandals and lurid details of violent crime.

In July 1988, *Today* announced that its sales had topped the half-million mark. This rise was phenomenal, but it was still losing £150,000 a week, and its circulation was only a quarter that of its main rivals, the *Mail* and *Express*. Murdoch himself remained dissatisfied with the paper.

The battles for Harper and Row and *Today* had scarcely been won when Murdoch opened yet another front. He staged a dawn raid on the shares of Pearson plc, the financial and publishing conglomerate whose most prestigious property was the *Financial Times*, arguably the world's best financial paper.

Like other newspaper managements Pearson had been galvanized by Murdoch's move to Wapping. In summer 1986 Frank Barlow, the chief executive of the *Financial Times*, pointed out that Murdoch had now established a completely new and much lower competitive base: "He now enjoys a huge cost advantage over the *FT*. Murdoch now has the ability – the financial ability – to reduce his advertisement rates, to reduce his cover price, to increase his promotional spend, or a combination of all three. The *FT* is extremely vulnerable . . . "

The *FT* embarked on a radical transformation to become a fully front-end newspaper, with copy set directly by editorial and advertising staff. These changes were inspired and demanded by Wapping. But Barlow said, "I do not intend to do a Wapping. I intend to do the very opposite of a Wapping. I intend to do an anti-Wapping" – change by agreement. The unions, their power destroyed by Murdoch, conceded.

Through 1987 the shares rose consistently amid persistent rumours that Murdoch was quietly buying. This was true, and by Monday 21 September his stake had reached 4.9 per cent, the maximum that could be held without public announcement. The very next day, News International staged a dawn raid and acquired 17.5 million shares at a cost of £161 million, which brought Murdoch's holding up to 13.5 per cent. A News spokesman said that they wanted to co-operate with Pearson, but ruled out any take-over bid. At Pearson headquarters on Millbank, Frank Barlow, whom Murdoch had once invited to be chief executive of News International, was adamant that they should not co-operate. He thought Murdoch an honest man, but a compulsive interferer. Indeed, Murdoch himself had told him so.

The news of Murdoch's raid aroused horror in some quarters. The Labour Party, which still had a policy of refusing to speak to Wapping journalists, was aghast. Bryan Gould, the party's spokesman on trade and industry, told the government that any bid by Murdoch must be referred to the Monopolies and Mergers Commission. Maxwell, who had recently failed in an attempt to acquire the American publisher, Harcourt Brace Jovanovich, then threatened to enter the fray. But if Maxwell made an actual bid, Murdoch would be released from his undertaking not to do so. It seemed clear that Murdoch hoped his stake would put Pearson "into play" so that he might do just that.

The underlying reality was that Wapping had transformed the finances of all British newspaper groups. They now looked under-valued by contrast with their counterparts in America, where newspapers and television stations sold on much larger multiples of their earnings. Murdoch saw the *Financial Times* as a fabulous and under-exploited franchise. He believed the company's resources should be much more dedicated to building up the *FT* as a really serious competitor to the *Wall Street Journal* and to Dow Jones.

Richard Sarazen publicly stated this view. "It is in a fantastic position to go global ... with the *FT*'s expertise and database, and our worldwide distribution, we could develop a great global business ... Murdoch's intentions are up-front. There is no ulterior motive." Max Newton said later that Murdoch did not want the *FT* as such, he merely wanted the right to publish it in the States.

On 1 October, Murdoch went to lunch with Lord Blakenham. The two men were not a likely pair. Their class backgrounds were similar, but whereas Blakenham enjoyed his, Murdoch had always attempted to paint himself as the enemy of the very Establishment from which he had sprung. Blakenham was proud to be leading an established family grouping of high-quality businesses quietly and soberly towards the end of the century, whereas Murdoch had built a career on mocking such established concerns and conventions. Blakenham stood for continuity, Murdoch rejoiced in change.

Blakenham told Murdoch that "new large shareholdings are unwelcome" and that Pearson did not want to be identified too closely with any one shareholder. Murdoch said that he saw himself as a long-term investor and hoped to be supportive of management as a whole. He put forward no concrete proposals for mutual co-operation. One of his anonymous and aggressive aides was quoted in the press as saying, "They should have called in the RSPCA – Murdoch ate him for lunch."

The affair reached the States. Anthony Lewis declared in the *New York Times* that the *Financial Times* was a superb independent newspaper, whereas Murdoch's name was "synonymous with slippery journalism". He quoted Peter Jenkins, the distinguished columnist who had recently resigned from the *Sunday Times*, as saying that although he had no complaint against Murdoch himself, he saw "how good newspapers, and once independent spirits, withered in his presence – or at 3,000 miles removed". Commenting on Murdoch's support for Mrs Thatcher, Lewis concluded that "those who believe in a free press" should support Pearson. In reply, Andrew Neil, the editor of the *Sunday Times*, pointed out that Peter Jenkins had been allowed to publish his anti-Thatcher views without any interference for almost two years.

Throughout the winter of 1987–8, speculation about Murdoch's intentions continued. Then an apparition was seen touring Wapping. It was Maxwell. This extraordinary sight – Montague in Capulet's house – convinced some people that Murdoch was preparing to sell Maxwell *The Times* so that he would be free to bid for the *FT*. News International denied that *The Times* was for sale. But Murdoch was known to be unhappy with the way in which so many of its writers had deserted it for the *Independent*.

At the beginning of 1988, Pearson announced that it was purchasing *Les Echos*, the leading French financial daily. But the French government raised objections because of the stake Murdoch would then have in *Les Echos*. Pearson also joined with Conrad Black, the new owner of the *Telegraph*, to take a 25 per cent stake in a new Canadian tabloid, the *Financial Post*. The effect of these and other purchases was to dilute Murdoch's holding in Pearson, but he then increased his share by buying Carlo de Benedetti's 4.9 per cent stake for over £85 million. The British government insisted that any takeover bid by Murdoch would be subject to scrutiny. Murdoch himself told the *FT* from Aspen that he had "no intention or ability to make a takeover offer in any way, shape or form ... we will never go above 25 per cent. I don't see it ever being possible to take over the *Financial Times*." However he also issued a warning to Pearson: "If they keep insisting I'm hostile, that could turn me into a hostile person."

The bulk of News shares in Pearson, 37.35 million shares, were held by News International, and the rest by News Publishers, a Bermuda-registered entity 100 per cent owned by companies within the News Corp group. In February 1988, Murdoch reduced the cost of holding his 20.5 per cent stake – and raised liquidity – by issuing £147 million worth of preference shares convertible into Pearson shares. The ten-year News Corp issue, convertible into a maximum 40 per cent of News Corp's stake in Pearson, was launched in dollars and Swiss francs. It was in the name of News Publishing Finance, a wholly-owned subsidiary. Its effect was to reduce the pain of holding the Pearson shares and to make any war of attrition against Pearson much less expensive.

In April 1988, Murdoch and Lord Blakenham had a second meeting. Murdoch was now saying he foresaw a partnership similar to that which he had with Hachette's *Elle* magazine, which News published in America. "It's a 50-50 partnership. We're very happy to go into partnership with people and help them market their products." He said that the *FT* should be selling 200,000 copies a day in America – 17,000 was pathetic, as was its 4,500 sale in Asia.

He was anxious at that time to become a major force in the booming new field of information services and was seeking to buy the 55 per cent of Australian Associated Press that he did not already own. With AAP's 13.5 per cent of Reuters added to News Corp's stock, he would be Reuters' largest single shareholder. Then he would be halfway towards being able to beam the contents of the *Financial Times* around the world on Reuters' screens. Unlike Pearson's management, he thought the *Financial Times* could and should be transformed into the principal daily price list of the global village. He was confident he would get his way. "You can't ignore your largest shareholder," he told *Forbes* magazine early in 1988. "It's not possible." But it was possible. Pearson formed further defensive alliances against him, and after being ignored for two years, Murdoch decided to sell his shares and move on. It was a setback.

NEW YORK

In 1980, Murdoch had charmed the US Senate. In 1988 he suffered at its hands another of his rare defeats. He was compelled to sell the *New York Post*. The sale caused him greater grief than almost any other business transaction in his life. He blamed it on Senator Edward Kennedy – and never forgave him. Max Newton said later that in fact Teddy Kennedy did him a favour in forcing him to dispose of the *Post*. But that was certainly not how Murdoch saw it at the time.

"We had never before lived in a town where we did not have a paper," said Anna afterwards. Murdoch was attached to the paper because it was the first major property he had bought in America, and because it afforded him an invaluable entrée into American political life. As such it was a continuing source of power, a base from which to mount all other operations. Moreover, a newspaper office is a very invigorating environment, and Murdoch was never happier than when he was immersed in the hubbub of a newsroom. Sitting in an ordinary, anodyne office would never compare to presiding over the roar of the presses.

Under the American law governing the "cross-ownership" of television stations and newspapers in the same city, Murdoch was bound sooner or later to sell the *Post* after he bought New York's Channel Five TV from John Kluge. But he had intended it to be later rather than sooner. Ever since the purchase was completed in 1985, he had searched, with some success, for loopholes in the regulations, and for some device by which he could continue to own both the paper and the station. It was Kennedy who put a final stop to that.

By the mid-1980s, the *Post* displayed the layers of Murdoch's life in New York. Some of the old Australian "mafia" had left, but others were still on good terms with the boss. Steve Dunleavy was the most prominent. His louche career continued to flourish. He had had a radio show in New York which he called Radio Dingo. He would sometimes pass the night drinking in bars in the fish market area of New York (the sort of place where one is apt to hear Frank Sinatra played on the jukebox) and would then straighten his tie and go right into an editorial conference at the paper. In 1986 he left the *Post* and moved to Fox, where he became famous as a "tabloid TV" reporter. Murdoch, in whom the Rupert Greene element still celebrated Dunleavy, spoke glowingly of him at his farewell party at the *Post*.

The formula which Murdoch had applied so well at the Sydney *Mirror* and had adapted with such success on the *Sun* in London did not work in New York, and furthermore Murdoch had serious labour problems on the paper. The paper handlers' union at the *New York Post* was heavily composed of Irish families who could trace their recent ancestry to County Kerry. If a union member retired or died – or was murdered – within days the union produced a young replacement fresh from Ireland, complete with green card. "It's all quite charming – except that they're being paid $1000 a week to do a job that could easily be mechanized," said Murdoch.

Later Murdoch said that he should have put more resources into the *Post*. "Should have kept a steadier course with it. It was such a difficult, impossible position being the third paper out of three." He said that the problem was not one of getting advertisers but of getting more of the right kind of readers. "If we had more readers than the *Daily News*, we would have taken all their business away. No problem about that at all." Circulation had risen, but never enough. He had never been able to get enough middle-class readers in Queens. "This is not a melting pot, this place, it's not a landing ground. I mean, it's very ethnic. It's very settled in its attitudes."

Among those attitudes were the city's politics. It remained –

just – a Democratic town, while Murdoch ran a Repub.
Ever since 1980, the *Post* had been supportive of Ronald .
In its 1984 endorsement the *Post* said that he had "unleashea
boundless energy, innovation and enthusiasm of America". The
corollary of that support for Reagan was denigration of his
opponents. Geraldine Ferraro, another victim of the *Post*,
explained the *Post*'s assault upon her by referring to "connections"
between Murdoch and Reagan. The *Wall Street Journal* quoted a
Washington official as saying that Murdoch was very useful. "He's
a great supporter of this administration and of the Western
alliance. He has a great deal to contribute." For his part, Murdoch
also benefited, in particular at the Federal Communications Commission. There was no reason to doubt the sincerity of his support
for Reagan's nostrums. And there was no reason why he should
not also seek to profit from it and to encourage the administration's deregulating spirit.

In 1986 he brought Frank Devine over from the *Chicago Sun-
Times* to edit the *New York Post*. Devine, a large and jovial man,
thought the basic problem was that "Rupert was trying to run a
lumpen proletarian newspaper in a country where there is no
lumpen proletariat. He hid this from even himself, because he is
such a good salesman." He also hid from himself the fact that the
chances of keeping both the *Post* and Channel Five were slim. He
hired the political consulting firm of Roger Stone, the north-
eastern director of the Reagan–Bush campaign, a man close to the
heart of the Republican Right, to help him bypass the cross-
ownership rule.

The rule, introduced by the Federal Communications Commission in 1975, was controversial. There is no doubt that the
rule, designed to prevent unscrupulous owners having too great a
stranglehold upon local opinion, had led to the closure of some
newspapers which had previously been subsidized by the greater
profits of local television. The Freedom of Expression Foundation,
a conservative Washington lobby group which Murdoch helped
fund, claimed that the rule had forced the closure of well over 100
papers. It argued that newcomers like Murdoch were penalized,
because they could not use broadcast to subsidize print.

When Murdoch had first proposed buying Metromedia in 1985,

he was challenged by public-interest groups concerned about his reputation for managing to bend rules to suit himself. Before the FCC approved the transfer of the stations, he was compelled to give repeated assurances that he would not seek a permanent change or waiver to the cross-ownership rule.

In July 1986 he sold the *Chicago Sun-Times* to a consortium led by Robert Page, the paper's publisher. In New York, where he had Channel Five, and in Boston, where he had more recently acquired station WFXT, his tactics were different. He sought and obtained temporary waivers from the FCC – they gave him two years in which to sell the *Post* and eighteen months for the *Herald*. Later Mark Fowler, chairman of the FCC, remarked that these waivers where amongst the best things he had done at the FCC. (Later still, he said this remark had been made jokingly.)

Murdoch considered Boston borderline. He would try to keep both the *Herald* and the TV station, but would not kill himself in the attempt. New York, however, was his town, and he wanted to do everything he could to keep the *Post*. "Instead of getting on with it and selling it then, we delayed and said maybe they would change the law," he acknowledged.

The *Wall Street Journal* reported that he intended to have the waivers extended further or even made permanent. The *Post* stopped all the giveaways and other circulation-boosting gimmicks for which Murdoch had always been famous. Promotion budgets were cut and the eight editions were reduced to two. Circulation began to fall, from 700,000 to under half a million, and by 1987, the paper was losing $100,000 a day. Buyers did not line up and the closer Murdoch moved towards the end of the waiver, the more it seemed as if the *Post* might be unsaleable. The Federal Communications Commission would then be faced with the choice of either seeing the paper close or letting Murdoch keep it.

In August 1987, the commission repealed the Fairness Doctrine, which demanded that television, unlike newspapers, attempt to be even-handed. Many Democrats in Congress, led by Senator Ernest Hollings, the chairman of the Commerce Committee, which over-saw the commission, were greatly opposed to this move. In November 1987 the Freedom of Expression Foundation filed a petition with the FCC to eliminate the cross-ownership ban. The president of the Foundation, Craig Seaton, said that the petition was not intended to help Murdoch as such, but it did have News Corp's full support. The FCC at once asked for comments. Fowler's successor, Dennis Patrick, appeared to share his deregulating philosophy.

However, under pressure from Edward Kennedy, Senator Hollings decided that the FCC should now be prevented from lifting the rule and thus giving Murdoch a permanent waiver. On 15 December 1987 Hollings inserted a rider into the Appropriations Bill which prohibited the FCC from repealing the cross-ownership rule and from extending any waivers to it. News America was the only waiver outstanding at the time. The bill passed the floor late at night on 22 December, the new wording at first unnoticed by almost everyone.

Murdoch was in Los Angeles when he learned the news. William H. Meyers, a *New York Times* reporter who was with him, wrote:

A fiery-red Lotus roars out of the driveway of the Bel-Air Hotel in Los Angeles. Knees tucked under the dashboard, Rupert Murdoch guns the low-slung two-seater through the twisting turns on Stone Canyon Road – simultaneously shifting, steering and tracking down his subordinates on the car telephone. At precisely eight o'clock on this balmy January morning, the Lotus rolls through the gates of Twentieth Century-Fox, Murdoch's television and motion picture studio.

Murdoch storms into his office, his double-breasted blazer flapping, and confronts the stack of letters and faxes on his mahogany desk . . . Normally Murdoch would devour these documents, but he impatiently shoves them aside. He wants to concentrate all his considerable energies and anger on the target of the day: Senator Edward M. Kennedy, Democrat of Massachusetts . . . Over the next days, Murdoch will mount the kind of brass-knuckle attack that has made the Melbourne-born publisher the most intimidating media mogul since William Randolph Hearst.

Murdoch told Meyers, "The process was an outrage." It was

"liberal totalitarianism", an attempt by Kennedy to kill off his critics.

It was the Patrick Murdoch, not the Rupert Greene, in Murdoch who hated Teddy Kennedy. He was appalled by his drinking and womanizing. But there was also an important political agenda. Kennedy was one of the mainstays of liberalism in the Senate; he was an effective senator and a leader in the fight against the Reagan revolution.

For years the *Boston Herald*, the *Post* and the supermarket tabloid *Star* had published editorials and columns revealing Kennedy's sexual misadventures, or re-examining the worst of them, the death of Mary Jo Kopechne at Chappaquiddick. Steve Dunleavy had written a muckraking book about the family. Kennedy was now becoming a target of Fox's "tabloid television" investigations as well. Howie Carr, a columnist on the *Herald*, delighted in calling Kennedy "Fatso" and, when space allowed, "that fat rich kid".

The language in the Appropriations Bill, which finally closed the door on Murdoch's *Post*, was seen by Murdoch as Kennedy's revenge. It led to a classic brawl. "Fat Boy versus the Dirty Digger," chortled *Time*. "Was it something I said, fat boy?" asked Howie Carr. Murdoch lined up his friends and supporters.

He called Charles Z. Wick, the head of the US Information Agency, a member of Reagan's kitchen cabinet and a friend of Murdoch. Wick offered his help and Marlin Fitzwater, President Reagan's spokesman, said that Reagan would have deleted the amendment, had he had the power to do so.

Murdoch also spoke to Mayor Edward Koch, who declared publicly that it revealed a "character flaw" in Kennedy, and, with more than a hint at Chappaquiddick, he said, "In the dead of night, and then by the way not to immediately own up to it. We've seen that before."

Kennedy acknowledged that he had encouraged Hollings to insert the waiver language in the Appropriations Bill. He explained, "The signals were abundantly clear that history was about to repeat itself" – just as the FCC had repealed the Fairness Doctrine, so it was now about to repeal the cross-ownership rule, and he and Hollings "were not about to be burned again". He claimed that "right-wing ideology is dictating policy and deregulation is running amok". The important question, he said, was whether Murdoch was "entitled to be the only publisher in America who can buy a television station and obtain an exemption to keep his newspaper under the anti-trust laws". He said that Murdoch had not seriously tried to sell the *Post*.

Murdoch replied that he was "shocked that the rules were changed in the middle of the game". He insisted that he had been looking for a buyer for the *Post*. Mark Fowler, who was now practising law in Washington, said that Murdoch was "a local businessman being intimidated and bullied by a politician". The First Amendment, he added, "was precisely designed to protect against that". Kennedy met with the *Post*'s unions and said he would agree to a further waiver only if a buyer for the *Post* had already been identified and more time was needed to complete the sale. Hollings insisted that he would continue to fight the legislation being prepared by New York's Senators Moynihan and D'Amato to repeal his Appropriations Bill amendment.

On 19 January 1988 the FCC decided to abide by the legislation and deny Murdoch's request for an extension of the waiver. On the 25th, the Senate defeated the Moynihan/D'Amato bill by a vote of 60-30 after a heated debate in which Senator Lowell Weicker, the liberal Republican from Connecticut who was often attacked by the *Post*, called Murdoch "the number-one dirtbag" in communications.

Senator Hollings wrote an editorial-page article for the *New York Times* in which he complained about the "unholy alliance" between Murdoch and the FCC. This, he said, had begun with Murdoch's purchase of Metromedia, and it had allowed him to delay the sale of the *Post* thus far. "The FCC and Mr Murdoch need to be reminded of three important principles of our democracy. The airwaves belong to the public. Concentration of media ownership threatens free speech. No man is above the law."

Murdoch responded with a full-frontal attack upon Hollings and the way in which the amendment had been surreptitiously slipped through Congress. He asserted that at first only Kennedy had really known what effect his amendment would have and that many of the senators who voted on the Appropriations Bill were quite unaware of the wording that had been covertly inserted and of its effect. This was undoubtedly true. Murdoch asked the Appeals Court to rule on his submission that the Kennedy-Hollings amendment was unconstitutional, because it singled him out.

Even though he knew now that he would have to sell the *Post*, Murdoch still delayed. Frank Devine, the editor, recalls that he became more and more depressed as the awful day approached. "He tried everything possible to hang on to it. His spirits would rise when some scheme seemed possible." One escape route he considered was to turn the *Post* into a national paper. He had often regretted that he had not started a paper such as *USA Today*.

By now no one on the News Corp board wanted him to keep the *Post*. Nor, really, did Anna. But Murdoch still found it almost impossible to let go. He was dismissive of most of those who sought to buy the paper, like a father rejecting his daughter's suitors. He considered that one bidder was untrustworthy, another was out for a pay-off, a third was merely seeking publicity. Eventually he entered into negotiations with Peter Kalikow, a New York real-estate developer and landlord. Given the losses of the *Post* – $17 million in 1987, according to Murdoch – Kalikow wanted to force the best possible deal from Murdoch. He demanded swingeing concessions from the unions.

As with the *Boston Herald*, it was uncertain till the very last minute whether the unions would make adequate concessions and the sale be completed. A deal was finally concluded on 5 March 1988. "WRITE ON", declared the splash on the front page. Murdoch could hardly bring himself to sign the final papers.

Just three weeks later, the Washington DC Court of Appeal ruled in Murdoch's favour on the waiver issue – two judges appointed by Reagan were on his side, the third, a Johnson appointee, dissented. Part of the majority decision read, "The Hollings amendment strikes at Murdoch with the precision of a laser beam." It was by now too late for the *Post*, but Murdoch said he would still press for exemption for the *Boston Herald* and his Station WFXT. In June he filed an application with the Federal Communications Commission to have the station placed in trust and beyond his editorial control. This was eventually approved.

Murdoch thought that the loss of the *Post* would be seen as a failure, and worse, a defeat at the hands of his enemies. It was "a nightmare", he said. In the Murdoch war of the worlds it was one of the most significant battles he had lost. He said that it sent him into a deep depression. The only way out of it that he knew was to go on what he himself called "an expansionary lunge". This one was to be almost fatal to his empire.

ASPEN

If there was a high point in the spread and the confidence of the News Corp empire, it was marked by the two conferences which Murdoch hosted for his employees and colleagues in the Rocky Mountain town of Aspen. At the first, in 1988, Murdoch was given the blessing of Richard Nixon. By the time of the second, in 1989, he was hailed as an architect of one of the most important developments of the late twentieth century: the global village.

The Aspen meetings were high councils of war, strategy sessions at which the officers of the News Corp army were summoned from their posts around the world, fitted out with uniforms, debriefed and rebriefed, inspired and invigorated and sent back to their commands filled (it was hoped) with renewed loyalty to their commander in chief and the sense of purpose of the worldwide organization.

The 1988 session began in Los Angeles. The general staff were welcomed by the Murdochs at their new hilltop house in Beverly Hills, the former home of Jules "Doc" Stein, the founder and head of MCA, Music Corporation of America. Murdoch impressed many of those whom he knew only slightly by his instant recognition of them and their names. The next day everyone was handed colour-coded boarding cards for one of several Learjets which were to fly, in formation, across the Rockies to the ski resort of Aspen, where Murdoch owned a house.

Aspen '88 had two parts. First, the assembled employees were addressed by outside speakers who represented different aspects of Murdoch's view of the world. There was Norman Podhoretz, the editor of *Commentary*, who had been at Oxford with Max Newton; Paul Volcker, the former head of the Federal Reserve; some officials from the Pentagon and an intelligence analyst from the White House. From Britain came David Owen, the leader of the Social Democrat Party. Murdoch admired his robust attitudes and may have thought him the best available alternative to Margaret Thatcher. Owen made a rather formal speech about European integration.

The star performer was Richard Nixon. The former President flew in on Murdoch's plane, stood stiffly at the lectern and impressed listeners by his cogent speech on the way in which the world was changing, particularly under the impact of perestroika. Murdoch glowed as he received the Nixon imprimatur.

There were obvious similarities between Nixon and Murdoch as they stood together, Nixon in his plaid jacket and tie, Murdoch in a short-sleeved blue T-shirt, bearing the corporate News logo. Murdoch was more relaxed than Nixon, but they shared a certain brooding quality. Both men were guarded and shy, both restless. Each had a global vision, some parts clear, some parts flawed, and was ruthless in pursuit of that vision. Each saw himself as an outsider, attempting to force an established world into new patterns. Nixon believed that "the Establishment" – by which he meant liberals in the Washington press and their allies – had destroyed him; Murdoch agreed with that – and his own fight against his enemies in what he called "the Establishment" was continuing relentlessly, wherever he found it.

In 1988 their shared beliefs seemed to be triumphant in the battlefields of both ideas and economics. As Nixon pointed out, Mikhail Gorbachev's reforms in the Soviet Union were among the most extraordinary and important acts of any government in recent decades. Already in 1988 it was clear that the world was on the cusp of revolutionary change, in which the spread of information was playing a vital role.

Murdoch could now see himself as an essential piece of the structure of Western power as close to the Republican leadership in the States as he was to Thatcher in Britain. His influence, and the power of the resources he deployed, had recently been recognized in America by his appointment to the board of the Hoover Institute, an increasingly conservative think tank based in Stanford. The Hoover board included such stars of the Reagan firmament as George Shultz, Jeane Kirkpatrick, and Caspar Weinberger.

This marked an important transition for Murdoch. A decade earlier in America he was seen as an alien, gutter-press lord and his *New York Post* had been denounced as "a force for evil". Now, as the American leader of a new army, a transnational media force, he was welcomed into drawing rooms and the councils of state of the American Right.

After Nixon and the other visitors' speeches, editors presented their papers to each other so that everyone could understand a little better the deployment of the different corps commanders in the international army.

Such a session was certainly needed, because the size of the army had been increased enormously in the last three years. In terms of assets, by the end of 1988 the company was six times the size it had been in 1985, and its assets were now valued at some $13 billion. Sales in the year 1988–9 were expected to be about $4.8 billion, not far behind Bertelsmann, the largest media conglomerate in the world. From now on the American properties would account for the majority of News Corp's total revenue, almost $3 billion.

Murdoch still ran this vastly expanded empire by studying the figures for each company and each property every week, though Merv Rich was no longer responsible for the weekly book. The old clam from Sydney had been replaced by Richard Sarazen, who was at Aspen to explain just how the system worked.

Among the editors at Aspen, Kelvin MacKenzie of the *Sun* was conspicuous by his absence. The news editor, Tom Petrie, came instead. The *Sun*'s presentation was as lavish as it was misleading – a John Wayne-type video which used clips from old Hollywood films to present the paper as an altogether happy-go-lucky and delightful place and product. There was even a sequence about how the *Sun* fought with its rival, the *Star*, over the rights to the life of a donkey in Spain; and another, which included clips from *Citizen Kane* and Busby Berkeley films.

Among the heroes of the 1988 conference was Andrew Neil, the editor of the London *Sunday Times*. His paper's circulation was increasing and the profits it was generating from Wapping were enormous. Its critics saw it as raucously right-wing, a broadsheet version of the *Sun*; Neil would retort that the paper was not always "Thatcherite", employed columnists who were left of centre and allowed them total freedom of expression. That was undoubtedly so. But, although Neil liked to distance himself from the *Sun* tabloid methods, many of the attitudes of the two papers were similar – for example, Neil and MacKenzie shared a disdain for liberals, for much of what the royal family stood for and did, for the BBC, and for the other myriad ways in which "the great and the good" still attempted to play their part in British governance. Both papers were also very sceptical of the notion that AIDS was a disease which threatened heterosexuals.

Among the other editors was Philip Crawley, editor of the *South China Morning Post*. Crawley had come to Murdoch from the *Daily Telegraph* and continued to run a serious paper, perhaps the best English-language paper in South East Asia. It was also increasingly profitable – as more and more people sought to leave Hong Kong before its return to China, the classified-ads section was growing exponentially.

Also present was Eric Beecher, still at the Melbourne *Herald*, but starting to reconsider his position. His attempt to take the paper upmarket had resulted in a further loss of circulation. News Corp's Australian managers were beginning to question his decisions, as was Murdoch.

Far more bullish was Max Newton, resplendent as ever in his metal wing-tipped collars. Newton had now retired to south Florida with his wife Olivia, but continued to write thousands of words a day for his various newsletters and publications. He was still an inspiration to Murdoch; both were convinced that a brave and wonderful new world was being fashioned by communications technology. As Newton put it: "Our fragile global village is knit more closely together today than ever in human history. The information explosion has produced a world where money flows virtually without barriers in and around all markets." Newton believed that this, and the diffusion of economic and financial power around the world, made the risk of international financial calamity far smaller than ever before.

Among the senior executives at Aspen was Carolyn Wall, one of the few women to be promoted very high in the News Corp army. (Even Murdoch's closest admirers have acknowledged difficulty in dealing with women as senior executives, let alone partners.) She had been the publisher of *New York* magazine since 1984. Although she had no experience of television, Murdoch had given her the job of running his New York television station, WNYW, a business with a staff of 450 and annual sales of $150 million. "Working for Murdoch is like being thrown into the water without knowing how to swim," she said, with obvious delight, to the *New York Times*. "He hires people who would not be thought qualified in other corporate environments."

Also at Aspen was John Evans, head of the magazine division and probably the only one of Murdoch's entourage who could boast of having been a hippie. He was a sturdy Welshman, with longish hair, and a worn appearance. There had been a lot of wearing; he was a little too old to be called a "Child of the Sixties", but perhaps he was a youth of the decade. In his hippie years, John Evans had wrestled with demons which nearly destroyed him – drugs, drink, racing cars and unhappy love affairs – and he was now a member of Alcoholics Anonymous.

Like many who worked for Murdoch, Evans said that it was hard to explain his task. "In true Murdoch style, no one ever tells you what your job is. You make it up as you go along. You may be given a title but you have to define the job yourself." Evans told a New York underground paper that News was "a very large family business" which worked on trust. "None of us have contracts, none have written financial security. All of us are given amazing amounts of trust and we pass that along. It's an amazingly elevating feeling to know you're trusted."

Evans was known as the futurologist in News. In terms of technology, Murdoch was almost a blind man, and Evans was his seeing-eye dog. He rhapsodized about the great marriage to come – the coupling of the TV and the PC. The PCTV of the near future would be programmed, he believed, with its owner's personality profile and would behave accordingly throughout the day. So that when you came home at night, the TV would say, "Hi, there's been seven minutes of news that you will be interested in. I expected to record the game between the Redskins and the Bears, but it was rained off. The good news is that *Citizen Kane* was playing on Channel 42; so I've got that for you."

Evans had a number of favourite lines. "Civilization is equal to bandwidth" was one of them. He talked about fibre-optics cables' vast capacity for transporting information, which he reckoned would transform the world more than almost anything to date, so that "the readers of tomorrow will be the editors of tomorrow", and they would be able to fashion newspapers after their own needs and desires.

Evans was trying to create electronic databases for News, and believed electronic publishing could double the value of the magazine division. He felt that News was still looking towards the past, and that electronic communications rather than print should be its future.

Aspen demonstrated that News Corp was an eclectic collection of companies, a reflection more of Murdoch's will and opportunities than of any business plan. All arteries led through Murdoch. Only he knew what everyone and every company was up to. What some at Aspen thought was needed was a middle way between an organization chart drawn by Jackson Pollock and one laboriously devised by IBM.

At the closing dinner, one Australian editor who had been hired, fired and rehired by Murdoch made a rather emotional speech in praise of his employer, who responded by saying that "we all share certain values", at which Barry Diller, the head of Fox and perhaps the only registered Democrat in the room, muttered to his neighbour, "Like what?"

Soon after the delegates had returned to their posts, Murdoch announced a new deal which staggered almost everyone. It was the deal too far, the one that created so much debt that it subsequently crippled his entire empire. He intended to buy *TV Guide* and other properties of the Triangle group from his friend Walter Annenberg.

Murdoch and Annenberg had known each other since the late 1960s, when Murdoch first arrived in Britain and Annenberg was American Ambassador to the Court of St James. They liked each other; indeed, it seems hardly fanciful to suggest that each saw something rather special in the other. Annenberg had lost his son. Murdoch had lost his father. Annenberg was in his eighties and, like Sir Keith, had made an extraordinary success in the publishing industry. Murdoch was doing just what Annenberg would have liked his own son to do.

Like Murdoch, Annenberg was born into media riches. Moses Annenberg made a fortune with the daily *Racing Form*, the betters' bible, which he had purchased in 1922 for $400,000. The previous owner, Frank Brunnel, had insisted on cash and Walter, then aged fourteen, later recalled: "I carried this huge package, one foot square all wrapped in old newspapers, to Brunnel's office."

Mo Annenberg also ran other racing papers, and a wire service which reported racing results. In 1940 he was jailed for tax evasion but *Racing Form* continued to flourish. Walter recalled that in the family it was known as the "Old Cow" because it gave such rich milk.

After Walter Annenberg took over the company, he spent much of his career trying to live down his father's reputation. He started *Seventeen*, a magazine for young women, which became known as "The Acne and the Ecstasy", and in 1953 he was one of the first publishers to understand the coming power of television: seeing independent television guides spring up in New York, Philadelphia and Chicago, he had the idea of making them national.

The first issue of *TV Guide*, on 3 April 1953, was symbolic of the nascent television culture. It displayed on its cover Lucille Ball's newborn child, under the headline, "Lucy's $50,000,000 Baby". At that time the magazine was distributed in ten cities in the east and midwest for fifteen cents and carried listings of all local stations and sold some two million copies at once.

As the network schedules became more fluid over the years, *TV Guide* became more important – to the networks themselves as well as to viewers. In the 1950s, the networks needed coverage

Rupert Murdoch

and advertising in the magazine – so much so that they based key decisions on programme scheduling on *TV Guide*'s deadlines. By the mid-1960s, *TV Guide* had become every viewer's favourite scorecard. It lived on the television set in almost every home.

In 1974, *TV Guide* became the first magazine to sell over a billion copies a year. By 1988 one of every five magazines sold in the United States was an issue of *TV Guide*. The magazine, costing seventy-five cents, had 106 regional editions and a new cable edition. Weekly circulation was around 17 million. In the first six months of 1988 it had advertising revenue of $162.8 million. Even so, 70 per cent of its total revenue came from circulation sales.

At the same time, *Seventeen*'s circulation had grown to 1.8 million and was thought to generate profits of some $10 million on annual revenues of about $150 million. The group also owned *Good Food* – a new creation which lost money – and the aforementioned *Racing Form*. Its circulation was not audited but it was thought to sell about 140,000 copies a day, at the huge price of $2.50 a copy. The *Form* was said to make $40 million profits on just $80 million in revenue. There were, as Murdoch was to discover to his cost, alternatives to *TV Guide*, but for race-goers there was no alternative to *Racing Form*.

By the end of the 1980s, Annenberg was an important and revered figure in the conservative Republican Establishment of the United States. He was a friend of Richard Nixon, and a generous supporter of his political campaigns. He had been a popular and successful ambassador to London – in part because of his generous contributions to such causes as the restoration of St Paul's cathedral. In 1976 the Queen awarded him an honorary knighthood, and in 1983 she stopped for lunch at his large estate in Palm Springs, California. When the Shah and his family were forced to flee Iran, Annenberg offered them hospitality at Sunny-lands, and in the 1980s he was as close to Ronald Reagan as he had been to Nixon.

When Annenberg decided to sell Triangle, he thought immediately of Murdoch. He said later that since his son Harry had died, "I had no one to carry on, and it was a family business. Rupert occurred naturally to me. He had Fox and Metromedia, and I sensed he was after the whole ball game."

Almost twenty years earlier, Murdoch had asked, through an intermediary, if Annenberg would sell *TV Guide*. For $1 billion, came the reply. In those days such sums were far beyond Murdoch, but their friendship developed. Annenberg said to this author, "I thought him very attractive and an immense gambler. A determined, dedicated fellow and a fearless competitor." He thought the outstanding thing about Murdoch was the courage he had displayed at Wapping.

The midwife of the deal in 1988 was John Veronis, the chairman of the New York brokers Veronis, Suhler and Associates. Annenberg wanted a fantastic sum, $3 billion in cash, for Triangle. Murdoch agreed. The profits were gushing in from Wapping. Mrs Thatcher had been re-elected and there seemed no threat to his British businesses. Interest rates were low. But even that sense of security would not usually lessen his attentiveness. Normally he subjected all potential purchases to close scrutiny. In this case, the biggest media purchase in history, he appeared to do nothing of the sort. It was all over very quickly.

"Maybe I was a bad buyer, too keen," acknowledged Murdoch later. "I should have beaten him down a few hundred million. He's a hard dealer. Wants his pound of flesh. Said he could sell to someone else, that the Japanese wanted to pay more."

Astonishingly, it seems that Annenberg had more doubts than Murdoch. He asked Warren E. Buffet, the legendary investor from Omaha, if he should sell for $3 billion. Mr Buffet replied, "Run to the bank, Walter, run to the bank."

Veronis said, "It was an understandable, natural conversation between two professionals, two giants in the field who have enormous respect for each other." Murdoch's public-relations man, Howard J. Rubinstein, added, "There is a circle of friendship here that really helped in this deal, because they had mutual respect and trust for one another."

The deal aroused front-page astonishment throughout the United States. The *Washington Post* commented, "No drawn-out negotiations. No takeover threats. No white knight defences or greenmail to complicate matters." Just two hugely successful entrepreneurs shaking hands. One question debated was whether Murdoch was an ideologue bent on taking over the world or merely a gambling man with an eye to the main chance. The *Washington Post* delivered itself of the view that, despite appearances, he was "not a wizard". The *Los Angeles Times* asked if he was "a global Citizen Kane". Another piece began, "In science fiction books, a handful of global corporations whose pursuits transcend any nation's interests or borders emerge to control modern society's most prized and powerful resource. The resource is information. This week, Rupert Murdoch took what many consider another step, whether intentional or not, into that science fiction fantasy."

Murdoch himself said that the deal made him the largest publisher of consumer magazines in the States. There were then about 3,000 magazines on the nation's newsstands, but only around 120 of them sold more than 100,000 copies an issue. Curtis Circulation, with *Penthouse* and *Ladies' Home Journal*, was the leader, with Warner Publishers Service, which distributed the Condé Nast publications, coming second. Both of these sold many magazines with circulations below 100,000. By contrast Murdoch, together with Triangle, sold relatively few titles, but they were large volume. What Murdoch bought with *TV Guide* was not only the magazines but also Triangle's distribution company, which handled *Reader's Digest*, *Newsweek*, and *Woman's World*. This huge clout would mean space at the supermarket counter and the newsstand shelves. The association with *TV Guide* would "piggyback" weaker Murdoch titles like *Elle* closer to the front of the rack.

Norman Lear, the television producer and publisher of the industry magazine, *Channels*, was outraged. "This is one of those events that makes me think that the last great war will not be fought between two countries but between two giant conglomerates that have already gobbled up all those countries."

Such concerns were understandable. The deal extended Murdoch's reach within the United States enormously. David Wagenhauser, an attorney at the Telecommunications Research Action Center, warned, "One of the best ways to influence public opinion without holding a political office is to control the media and from past experience it does seem that Mr Murdoch wants to influence public opinion." Similarly, Andrew Jay Schwartzman, executive director of the Media Access Project, a public-interest telecommunications law firm, said that joint ownership of Fox and *TV Guide* gave Murdoch too much power.

> Too few different voices is a threat to the democratic process.
> If there are several Murdochs out there, fine, but if there is only
> one Murdoch, look out. Murdoch has a bias for incumbency
> and an old-boy network. The broadcast medium has enormous
> power shaping public taste . . . Murdoch has not kept all his
> promises. He is someone for whom citizenship is matter of
> business convenience.

While Murdoch's potential "threat to democracy", was being debated, many of his colleagues saw the purchase more pragmatically as a commercial disaster.

If, as was thought, Triangle had revenues of $700 million and an operating profit of some $200 million, he had paid some fourteen to fifteen times cash flow – a high multiple. Time Warner's board had looked at Triangle and decided that it was not worth more than $1.5 billion – half what Murdoch was paying. But Murdoch argued that *TV Guide* was unique. It went into 17 million homes every week, and took in $12 million in gross revenue. After the supermarkets and others had taken their cuts, this probably left about $6 million revenue. Then there was another $6 million a week in advertising. The magazine would also provide an enormous database for the electronic publishing company he was planning; it had computerized summaries of 20,000 movies and 150,000 programmes. In the future, he might be able to use the listings as the basis for an international television magazine. He already owned his own version of *TV Guide*, *TV Week*, in Australia.

Despite this, many of those who knew anything about the finances of Triangle and of News were aghast. One colleague who said he tried to talk him out of the deal was John Evans, head of Murdoch magazines. He and others at News thought Murdoch was captivated by Annenberg, "the Ambassador".

Evans argued that *TV Guide*'s day was gone. Its circulation had already fallen from 20 million to 17 million and there was nothing to stop it dropping further. Readers were dying off. New immigrants did not buy it. "You had to grow up with *TV Guide* to use it. Even Rupert couldn't use it." There were now so many channels that the magazine needed to be A4 size, but then the advertising rate per square centimetre would fall, and it would lose its miracle slots at the supermarket checkout. Evans told Murdoch that the price was at least $250 million too high, but Murdoch would not hear of offering a lower price. He had made his agreement with "the Ambassador". In those days, Murdoch appeared sanguine, almost cavalier about his level of indebtedness. He said of *TV Guide*'s purchase, "Dick Sarazen fixed it with short-term debt. I don't know where the money is coming from." News Corp spokesmen said that he would raise about half the purchase price by selling existing assets and the other half by increasing his debt. The purchase would probably increase the company's overall debt from $5.5 billion to $7.6 billion, requiring annual interest payments of some $760 million. In addition to that, the company had $960 million of convertible notes on which annual interest payments totalled $48 million.

Murdoch raised some $320 million by the sale of a building in Los Angeles, and in London, the treasurer of News International, Colin Reader, organized another $2 billion. "I went to our good friendly bankers and arranged for ten of them to provide $200 million each. It was done on the basis that half the money would be repaid by the following June. The other half we did with a general bank syndication." Despite a last-minute hitch with the financing, the deal was completed on 7 November 1988. (The $1 billion repaid by June 1989 came primarily from the sale of travel magazines to Reed.)

After the purchase had been completed, and when Murdoch had begun to realize that Triangle would not in fact make enough to service its own debt, Evans suggested that he should resell the company promptly – perhaps along with a couple of magazines like *Star*. Murdoch would not consider it.

Publicly he remained enthusiastic. "These publications are the most valuable and prized publishing properties in the world," he said. Perhaps he believed it, but for Murdoch there was a sense of pleasure in paying Ambassador Annenberg, the friend of Presidents and a pillar of the information society and the conservative elite, what he asked.

Chapter 12

SUN COUNTRY

Stepping out of the elevator on the sixth floor of the factory at Wapping, the visitor would be warned by a sign which read, "You are now entering Sun Country".

This was a fantastic place. At its heart (if it had one) lay the legendary goldmine which Murdoch had discovered in 1969. Ever since then he had hired gangs of more or less wild men and women to excavate its precious seams. They had dug, lower and lower, but still the ore came out. For over two decades Sun Country had been Murdoch's Eldorado, a place of fable and riches, where fantasy passed for real life, jokes for news, falsehoods for facts and nothing was as it seemed. Only one thing was certain: as Mae West said with a wink at her cleavage, "There's gold in them thar hills."

Many of Murdoch's critics would claim that, although he was born with silver type in his mouth, and was bred with the ambition to be at least as great a newspaper man as his father, he had rarely been able to produce outstanding newspapers, or even outstanding journalists. They would argue that there was a mediocrity about most of the papers in every corner of his empire.

One very important exception to this notion was the *Sun*, the second paper he purchased in Britain. The *Sun* became a paper touched by genius, both commercial and editorial – it was the genius of the late, mad Lord Northcliffe, the inspiration to Rupert's father, Keith.

At the end of the 1980s and in the early 1990s the *Sun* was the largest-selling English-language daily in the world. It carried a good deal of news, though some of it was so succinct as to be almost invisible, its editorials were crisp, its headlines often superbly inventive. It was witty, it was ideological, and it was often cruel. On the spectrum of news to entertainment, it registered far over to the side of the latter.

On any day, and at almost any hour, its remarkable editor, Kelvin MacKenzie, could almost be guaranteed to be in Sun Country, and on the rampage around his terrain. MacKenzie was like an inspired schoolboy terrorist, forever lobbing stink bombs and banana skins in the way of those he disdained. He achieved his results with ranting and raving, twirling his arms like windmills, and occasionally lapsing into brief interludes of self-deprecating charm. The *Sun*'s turnover of journalists was high, but nothing like as high as might be expected. Most stayed on, awed, perhaps browbeaten but utterly fascinated by the King of Sun Country. People would shake their heads wisely and say, "Bloody Kelvin – he's mad, but a genius."

Through the 1980s, which saw the *Sun* continue to outstrip the *Daily Mirror* as Britain's best-selling tabloid, MacKenzie established himself as Murdoch's favourite editor. Murdoch considered the *Sun* along with *The Australian* as his original creation, and felt that it was in good hands.

MacKenzie was always reverential about "The Boss". For him, Murdoch was a man who "achieves more in half an hour than any other human being achieves in a whole day", and who was "as smart as a wagonload of monkeys".

"Shock and amaze on every page" was the MacKenzie clarion, though his critics would translate this as "Nothing succeeds like excess". The Press Council, which monitored the behaviour of the British press until the end of the 1980s, frequently censured the *Sun*'s approach to the news. At various times this was said to be sexist, racist, xenophobic, exploitative and just plain fabricated. Many people sued the *Sun*, among them Queen Elizabeth II. But the most spectacularly successful action was brought by the pop star, Elton John, who earned libel damages of one million pounds – a British record.

Though happily married, MacKenzie seemed to have no other life than the office, and he expected others to show the same dedication. He took an obsessive interest in the lives of his staff as well as in their work. At the first sign of one office romance, he took the man on one side and advised, "Don't dip your pen in the company ink."

His management style did not come out of any known textbook. A woman reporter begging for the consolation of "E for Effort" for a failed piece was told that it only merited "F for Fuck Off". Journalists going through a rocky patch would be made to feel still less secure by their editor saying, "You're still 'ere then, eh? Haven't you gone yet?"

Opinion divided over whether MacKenzie was an "ogre" or a "manic genius". Essentially, he was both. As a newspaper man, his natural bullying instinct gave him a sure grasp of those groups in society which could be abused with relative impunity. These groups constituted what was known as his "scum" agenda. *Stick It Up Your Punter*, a lively history of the *Sun* written by Peter Chippindale and Chris Horrie, listed the "scum" as: "prisoners, criminals, drug-takers, football hooligans, most blacks, homosexuals, militant trades unionists, muggers, students, peace campaigners, demonstrators, hippies, dossers, tramps, beggars, Social Security scroungers, squatters, terrorists and especially the IRA, vandals, graffiti artists, prostitutes, gypsies, winos, various foreign groups *en masse* and all deviants, particularly sex offenders".

MacKenzie's authority for his actions, aside from Murdoch, was a near mystical understanding of "the readers". He would invoke them much as Richard Nixon would invoke the "Silent Majority" in the United States. MacKenzie, and MacKenzie alone, was the great arbiter of their tastes, desires, fears and frustrations. When a trendy young executive suggested that *Sun* readers might be interested in a piece about the argument for legalizing marijuana, MacKenzie exploded at the very thought. "You must be fucking joking," he screamed, jabbing the executive in the chest.

You don't understand the reader, do you, eh? He's the bloke you see in the pub – a right old fascist, wants to send the wogs back, buy his poxy council house, he's afraid of the unions, afraid of the Russians, hates the queers and weirdos and drug dealers. He doesn't want to hear about that stuff. When you can imagine that bloke saying, " 'ere, I tried that marijuana last night – not bad!" – then we'll write about it. And not before.

The problem for those who wanted to strangle MacKenzie was that he could often make them laugh just as their hands were approaching his throat. Though his demand for loyalty was intense, solemnity was not prized. MacKenzie would satirize everything.

When a reporter eagerly rushed in with a story that was also said to be true, MacKenzie pranced around the office raising the alarm: "True story alert, folks! True story alert! We have a true story here." He affected the language of a south London barrow boy and deployed it with some skill – "If that's a story, my prick's a bloater."

As editor, he exhibited an acute humbug detector. Never trammelled with ideas about the need to "educate" readers, he gave them what his gut told him they wanted – sex, scandals, TV soap dramas and the royals.

There was nothing especially original about this formula but the zest with which it was pursued and the punchy brilliance of the packaging had not been previously equalled. "Don't worry about the fucking writing," MacKenzie snarled to a new reporter he was hiring, "we've got subs to do that bit."

Most of Murdoch's reproaches of MacKenzie were of a fond, parental nature. Kelvin appealed to the Rupert Greene side of his nature, much as Steve Dunleavy did in New York. And MacKenzie instinctively knew that Murdoch liked him to be naughty. The only thing he could seriously do wrong would be to cease to be entertaining. This in itself was a stern discipline.

When he was away, Murdoch administered by telephone. These calls had a ritual quality. "Hello, Kelvin," Murdoch would say, "how's it going? What's your splash?" MacKenzie would fill him in on the front-page headline news. There would then be a pause, the length of which indicated Murdoch's degree of displeasure. One of the longest pauses came after MacKenzie announced that he proposed to lead the paper with "FREDDIE STARR ATE MY HAMSTER", which was to become one of the *Sun*'s most famous headlines.

The Murdoch calls would inform life on the paper. If Murdoch let slip any praise for the *Sun*, it would be sunshine all around in the office and a brief moratorium on bollockings. If Murdoch had voiced his most severe criticism – "You're losing your touch, Kelvin" – no one was safe. But MacKenzie's touch, even in the fabrication department, was, for the most part, deft.

In the early months of MacKenzie's editorship, Queen Elizabeth had invited the editors of all the papers to come to the Palace to discuss the boundaries between royal privacy and press attention. MacKenzie did not show up, pleading a prior appointment with Rupert Murdoch. In any event, MacKenzie saw no grounds for royal privacy and soon the Press Council was rebuking the *Sun* for a centre-spread headline "THE ASTONISHING SECRETS OF THE FUN-LOVING ROYALS". MacKenzie again could not make it to the council hearing, but he did say, through a legal go-between, that "affection and loyalty for our royals was sustained by the unceasing publicity about their lives".

Armed with such a self-serving constitutional theory, and backed by a proprietor who was totally unsentimental about the pretensions of monarchy, MacKenzie operated on a free rein. Anything from running the tittle-tattle of disaffected servants to climbing tropical trees in pursuit of the pregnant-princess-in-a-bikini picture, could be characterized as no more than an expression of loyalty to the Crown. It was ostensibly very matey, though not much appreciated by the royals or by thoughtful royalists, who saw it as the thin edge of a republican wedge. As far as Murdoch was concerned, that was just fine. His papers constantly reflected his own republican sentiments – few opportunities to mock, criticize or shame the royal family were missed. Such an attitude compelled the Queen to overcome her inhibition against going to law against her subjects. She used the law to block a *Sun* series of royal "disclosures" and sued when the *Sun* published a private photograph, depicting four generations of the royal family. Obsessed by the need to draw ahead of Maxwell's *Daily Mirror* and not be outflanked by the raucous rise of the *Daily Star*, a paper even more harsh and lubricious than the *Sun* itself and far less witty, MacKenzie had little time for the Queensberry Rules of journalism.

The free-swinging approach was also well manifested in the *Sun*'s chauvinistic attitude to foreign affairs. MacKenzie loathed the French. When he was in a good mood he merely mocked them. "Hop Off You Frogs" badges were awarded to readers contributing funny stories about their cross-channel neighbours. The Germans were funny too, but fearsome with it. The *Sun*'s editorial on the prospect of German reunification concluded with the thought: "One Germany. For Britain and the rest of the world it would certainly not be all reich on the night." Nor was the *Sun* inclined to forgive Germany's old comrade-in-arms. When the Emperor Hirohito died, the *Sun* announced, "Hell's waiting for a truly evil emperor." When Spanish air controllers went on strike, the *Sun* advised them to "take up bullfighting, bird-strangling or donkey-torturing".

*Sun*speak was often hilarious. But anyone whose daily fare was confined to *Sun* editorial columns might think not merely that the British were the best, but that they were the only nation with any brains at all. When Mrs Thatcher found herself in a beleaguered minority of one among forty-eight Commonwealth Prime Ministers on the issue of sanctions against South Africa, the *Sun*'s headline advice was, "WAVE GOODBYE TO THIS RAGBAG CREW, MAGGIE".

Damien McCrystal, the young writer recruited to start the *Sun* City page, bravely told MacKenzie that he was thinking of running stories to help the Third World and the cause of disinvestment in South Africa. "Get this through your fucking head," said MacKenzie with slow menace. "Nobody gives a fuck about the Third World." Such xenophobia blended naturally with prejudice against ethnic minorities in Britain, and the paper was accused of consistent racism, though only a minority of complaints were upheld by the Press Council.

Like his proprietor, MacKenzie had little sympathy for homosexuals, whom he described as "poofters" when he was not calling them "shirtlifters" or "bum bandits". Reporters who had the temerity to protest that Aids, the so-called "gay plague", was in no way confined to homosexuals merely invited his ridicule.

"Come out then, have we, eh?" MacKenzie would taunt, and shout across the editorial floor, "Watch out folks! There's a botty burglar about." As late as 1990, when the risk of Aids to heterosexuals was widely established, the Press Council had cause to rebuke the *Sun* for "gross distortion" with its headline – "STRAIGHT SEX CANNOT GIVE YOU AIDS – OFFICIAL".

Writers in what MacKenzie described as the "Unpopulars" would sometimes debate whether the *Sun* was serious (in which case it was assumed to be deeply misguided) or merely comic (which rendered it relatively harmless). In fact, the *Sun*'s skill was that it could be both comic and serious at the same time. This was exhibited particularly in what were known as the "Loony Left" stories which ran through 1986 as a thought-provoking prelude to the general election.

Their theme was the idiocy of Labour authorities. Not all the stories were true, but many of them were hilarious and all of them helped to hold up the Labour Party to ridicule and contempt.

The magazine *Marxism Today* shrewdly deduced that MacKenzie's talent for turning the news into a joke was immensely persuasive in an era grown tired of seriousness. And the jokes, of course, were all going one way. The spin put by the *Sun* on its social and human interest stories may have been a greater contribution to the right-wing cause than its more standard political writing. Not that it was deficient in this more formal area. MacKenzie helped keep Mrs Thatcher aloft through two general elections in the 1980s. "Thank God for Maggie", cried an editorial of 1988 vintage. "It doesn't matter a tuppenny damn who is the Opposition. She acts for us all. And that's why she'll be in charge until the year 2000. We wish it could be 3000."

The *Sun*'s political skill lay in its ability to attack Labour politicians with a vigour well outside the competence of the Tory machine and even the plain-speaking Mrs Thatcher. "Red" Ken Livingstone, the leader of the Greater London Council, was variously described in the *Sun* as "the most hated man in Britain", "the most odious man in Britain" and a "little twit". Tony Benn, another left-wing luminary, was subjected to *Sun*-style psychoanalysis and diagnosed as "greedy for power" with a tendency to confuse himself with God. In his farewell speech to the Labour conference the party leader, Michael Foot, once one of Beaverbrook's top journalists, reflected: "The debasement of journalism is worse in Fleet Street today than at any time I can recall. I do not say it is all due to the arrival of Mr Murdoch in Britain, although I think he bears his fair share of the blame."

Neil Kinnock, who succeeded Foot as Labour leader after the 1983 election, knew he would be in for a rough ride. He was soon featuring in *Sun* headlines as "THE NOWHERE MAN" and "A BORN LOSER" leading "A PARTY OF PLONKERS".

Just before the June 1987 election, Kinnock's first contest with Mrs Thatcher, the *Sun* produced a front page with the banner headline: "LABOUR WINS!" The illustration was a picture of Neil Kinnock, victoriously waving and grinning outside Number 10 Downing Street. Readers who detected the creative hand of the *Sun*'s process department in this picture were not wrong. "It's OK folks," announced the caption, "it's just a nightmare." The text went on: "But with all his lies and weasel words, he could . . . just could . . . fool us into voting for Labour . . . " The antidote was to turn inside to the "Nightmare Issue", where five pages were devoted to warnings about "life under the Socialist jackboot".

Among trades union leaders the *Sun*'s main bogey figure was the miners' leader, Arthur Scargill. During the long miners' strike of 1983–4, MacKenzie sketched out a front page with the bold words "Mein Führer" to accompany a picture of Scargill in rhetorical flow, with his arm upraised. All hell broke loose in the production department. The printers refused to touch the picture. Eventually, the *Sun* came out with a blank front page. When a subsequent leader alleged that many miners were now no longer the salt of the earth but "the scum of the earth . . . " the printers went on strike and four days' production of the *Sun* were lost.

MacKenzie found Wapping liberating. There were no printers around to censor him. And the new technology had the charm of making it much easier for senior executives to rewrite copy. His new office and those around bristled with motivating slogans along the lines of "Do it to them before they do it to us"; "Make it first, make it fast. Make it accurate." Alongside this an office sage inked in "Then go and make it up."

For some years, under MacKenzie's guidance, the *Sun* had been cutting the lead established by the *News of the World* as Britain's main kiss-and-tell paper, detailing the sex romps of celebrated persons. This was high-sales material, but also high-risk. In 1987, the year after both newspapers moved to Wapping, they faced a combined total of fifty writs.

In the area of what was known as "bonk journalism" – defined in the *Guardian* as "a cross between private investigation and porn" – the *News of the World* was still the more professional operation, but the *Sun* was coming boldly into the picture. Credit for the great leap forward was ascribed to Wendy Henry, MacKenzie's tough-minded features editor. Tired of reprocessing showbiz handouts, she told MacKenzie, "What I want to know is who's fucking who?"

The paper was soon telling its readers just that, particularly in their TV soap coverage, Henry's personal bailiwick. The *Sun* identified "EastEnders", a BBC saga of Cockney life, as the show for maximum celebration and penetration, and was well rewarded. After a year spent dovetailing the real and on-screen sex lives of its characters, the *Sun* nosed a million copies ahead of the *Daily Mirror*. By 1986 competence in this field had been extended into other regions of showbiz and national life, and as the older hands were shed by the Wapping move, there was a new zealotry in the reporting of such matters.

Murdoch appeared to be happy about the way in which things were going. In August 1987, he promoted Wendy Henry, still in her thirties, to be editor of the *News of the World*. She was rapidly into her stride, and the paper soon produced one of the more salacious stories of the epoch about Frank Bough, a popular, rather modest BBC TV presenter. He was banished from the nation's screens, until he was later given a job by Murdoch's Sky Television.

It was the *News of the World* which broke the story about Sir Ralph Halpern, the million-pound-a-year boss of the clothing chain, Burton, who was said to be the model of Thatcherite enterprise. "We had sex non-stop," said Fiona Wright, explaining her acquaintance with Sir Ralph; she also claimed that he had told her he had goosed Mrs Thatcher at a Downing Street party. "He thought she had an attractive bottom."

Maxwell's *Daily Mirror* rushed to the defence of Mrs Thatcher:

"Politically Mr Murdoch has been the loyal parrot on Mrs Thatcher's shoulder. Yesterday she must have thought he was more like a carrion crow."

Throughout the late 1980s the abuses of the *Sun* and the *News of the World* grew. In 1986 the Press Council upheld four complaints against the *Sun* and three against the *News of the World*; in 1987 the figures were fifteen and eight respectively.

Wendy Henry's taste for the macabre was almost as pronounced as her interest in the sex lives of the stars. Friends like Woodrow Wyatt suggested to Murdoch that the "News of the Screws" was going too far over the top. Murdoch told Henry to raise the tone a little. Henry refused – pointing to a circulation increase of 400,000 in her fifteen-month reign – and in December 1988 Murdoch let her go. Within three months she was editing Robert Maxwell's Sunday paper, the *People*, with the same gruesome panache – until he too fired her.

MacKenzie made history of a slightly different kind. In December 1988, News International was obliged to foot the record libel bill to Elton John, for having alleged that he consorted with rent boys. Murdoch was not amused, and there could be no doubt that his favourite editor was to blame.

"SORRY ELTON" ran the *Sun*'s breezy front-page headline above grovelling apologies. Including legal expenses, the episode cost News about £1.5 million.

Shortly after the settlement, Kelvin MacKenzie summoned the staff into his office for what they assumed would be a Christmas cheer-up. Instead, it was a diatribe on the recently discovered merits of accuracy. MacKenzie threatened that the next reporter who got a writ would be out. "It's got to stop," he said. "If I go, I'm going to take you bastards with me."

There was by now a powerful groundswell of opinion against what the tabloids did, not just the way they went about it. More than 300 MPs had expressed support for legislation designed to curb tabloid excesses and enshrine a Right to Privacy.

Murdoch's view was ambiguous. He told an American interviewer who asked him about the *Sun*'s sensationalism, "You have in Britain a society that is becoming extremely decadent. You don't have the underlying puritanical history that this country's got, an influence that is still there." Others could argue that tabloid excess contributed to any such British "decadence".

The *Sun*'s answer to these criticisms was powerfully, if oddly, expressed in its leader of 6 February 1989, the year of its twentieth birthday as a Murdoch publication. Rupert Murdoch played a part in its composition.

The Establishment does not like the *Sun*. Never has.

We are so popular they fear our success, since they do not understand the ordinary working man and woman.

There is a growing band of people in positions of influence and privilege who want OUR newspaper to suit THEIR private convenience. They wish to conceal from the readers' eyes anything that they find annoying or embarrassing to themselves.

LIVING LIES AND HYPOCRISY ON HIGH CAN HAVE NO PLACE IN OUR SOCIETY . . .

OUR READERS WANT US TO BE QUESTIONING, COURAGEOUS AND FREE.

THE "PRIVACY" LOBBY WOULD PREFER TAME, TIMID NEWSPAPERS THAT ARE AS MUCH THE HOUSE MAGAZINE OF THE ESTABLISHMENT AS *PRAVDA* IS THE PARROT VOICE OF THE KREMLIN.

FOR THE *SUN*'S PART WE SHALL FIGHT TO STAY EXACTLY AS WE ARE. IT IS NOT JUST OUR STRUGGLE.

IT IS THE STRUGGLE OF ALL THOSE CONCERNED FOR FREEDOM IN BRITAIN.

In fact, the *Sun*'s record of exposing corruption in high places was not impressive. Abuses of power and high-level financial chicanery were much more fully covered by the "Unpopulars".

The *Sun*'s investigations were more often concentrated on people in positions of weakness and vulnerability than those of influence and privilege. Indeed the most serious criticism to be made of the *Sun* and other tabloids was the wanton cruelty with which they treated ordinary people and stars alike. David Scarboro, a nineteen-year-old actor in the cast of "EastEnders", jumped to his death off Beachy Head three months after his "weirdo" ways were exposed in the *News of the World*. Russell Harty, the popular BBC talk-show host and *Sunday Times* columnist, was a homosexual who was hounded by the *News of the World*. When its story about him was published, Harty expected to be fired by the BBC. He was kept on, though he died within eighteen months of hepatitis.

Many tabloids, not only Murdoch's, behaved abominably when Harty was dying in hospital. One took a flat opposite his room and nurses would point out the telephoto lens to his visitors. A reporter posed as a junior doctor, infiltrated his ward and demanded to see his notes; others tried to bribe porters to snatch a photograph. The woman who had written the original story in the *News of the World* appeared on television to recount the tale of her triumph.

At Harty's memorial service Alan Bennett, the playwright, said: "The gutter press had finished him, because they had panicked him into working so hard that by the time he was stricken with hepatitis, he was an exhausted man." The *Sun* replied that such claims were absurd and nauseating, and then went further:

> Stress did not kill Russell Harty.
> The truth is that he died from a sexually transmitted disease. The Press didn't give it to him. He caught it from his own choice.
> By paying young rent boys to satisfy him, he broke the law. Some, like ageing bachelor Mr Bennett, can see no harm in that. He has no family.
> But what if it had been YOUR son Harty had bedded?

The *Sun*'s assertion that "living lies and hypocrisy on high can have no place in our society" itself had a hypocritical ring. Like the *News of the World*, the *Sun* was remorseless in its sexual titillation while preserving its pursed-lipped, phoney puritanism. Page-three girls were only a part of the titillation. "Are you ripe for a secret affair?" asked a "caring *Sun*" feature as it issued an invitation to readers to call its "Illicit Love Line" service.

Attacks on the *Sun*'s sleaze coverage increased, but MacKenzie came to grief in a quite different way. In April 1989, ninety-five people – most of them Liverpool football fans – were crushed to death in Sheffield's Hillsborough stadium, where the FA Cup semi-final between Liverpool and Nottingham Forest was to be played. Much of the horror was seen on television.

It soon emerged that the fault lay primarily with the crowd control failures of South Yorkshire police. On the MacKenzie *Sun*, the police force was almost as far above reproach as Mrs Thatcher. Football hooligans, on the other hand, were the dregs. They had featured in *Sun*speak down the years as "yobs", "scum" and "animals". The *Sun*'s story, run under the front-paper banner headline: "The Truth", began:

> Drunken Liverpool fans viciously attacked rescue workers as they tried to revive victims of the Hillsborough disaster, it was revealed last night. Police officers, firemen and ambulance crew were punched, kicked and urinated upon by a hooligan element in the crowd. Some thugs rifled the pockets of injured fans as they were stretched out unconscious on the pitch . . .

No evidence was presented for the specific allegations and none was ever produced.

In Liverpool, once a high-circulation area, sales of the *Sun* dropped like a stone. The Press Council's inevitable censure soon followed, but this time it was received with apparent humility. Rupert Murdoch's official comment on Hillsborough was: "At a time of great emotion and great tragedy, our coverage was uncaring and deeply offensive to the relatives of the victims. More thought on our part would have saved more anguish, which we deeply regret." Even more remarkably, MacKenzie consented to go on the record. In a radio interview he dutifully bit the bullet – "It was my decision and my decision alone to do that front page in that way and I made a rather serious error."

On the backbenches of the House of Commons the eagerness to curb the tabloids reached new levels of fervour. The two key exhibits in the legislators' rogues gallery were the *Sun* and the *News of the World*. When the Hillsborough tragedy occurred, two private member's bills, with strong cross-party support, were fighting for time in the Commons. One was intended to provide a statutory Right of Reply to press inaccuracies, the other to enact a Right of Privacy.

The press, "Populars" and "Unpopulars" alike, was becoming thoroughly alarmed, and with good reason. The great concern of the "Unpopulars" was that the process of sanitizing the tabloids could undermine hard-won press freedoms. As it happened, the government was also disturbed, though perhaps for other reasons. Murdoch's papers had been among the strongest supporters of the government, and it was Murdoch papers that were most under threat.

Eventually, the Home Office pre-empted a private member's bill by announcing its own review of the press. It gave notice to editors and proprietors that they were now all "on probation". David Mellor, the Home Office minister who took on the oversight of the review, announced: "The tabloids are now drinking at the Last Chance Saloon." In Sun Country, they began to tidy up their act – a little. But it remained a bizarre, alien territory, a Wild West in Wapping, a place where wit and dross, prurience, news and cruelty were all traded, where only the strangest people could thrive. Patrick Murdoch would have hated it. But Rupert Murdoch defended it against almost all criticism.

SPRINGFIELD, USA

At the very end of the 1980s, the respectable suburb, where Mr and Mrs Jim Anderson and their clean-cut children, Betty, Bud and Kathy had lived their perfect American life in the 1950s TV sitcom "Father Knows Best", was invaded. The wretched Homer Simpson and his unhappy, alienated family moved in and took over the American imagination. Fox Television had launched its animated sitcom, "The Simpsons".

With his perpetual five o'clock shadow and slovenly ways, Homer Simpson was an unmotivated worker at Springfield's nuclear plant, just down from the town's toxic-waste dump and prison. He and his good-natured, eccentrically coiffed wife Marge had three children: melancholic, existential Lisa; Maggie, a baby glued to her pacifier; and above all the incomparable Bart. Bart was the Dennis the Menace of modern TV, a renegade who would not tolerate acceptable behaviour and rules. He was bloody-minded and determined. He was street-smart. He was aggressive. He took no hostages and suffered fools very ungladly. He also had a kind and charming side to his character and he could use that charm to manipulate people. In many ways he was a miniature Rupert Murdoch. Only in one respect were the two characters unlike: Bart was an Underachiever – And Proud Of It.

Within months of the Simpsons' premiere on prime-time Sunday-night TV, young people – and many older ones – across America were trading Bartisms, donning Bart T-shirts. The family pushed Fox Television to the top of the Nielsen TV ratings, just three years after the fledgling station had begun to make its bid for a share of a dwindling national television audience. Bart and his parents spoke a language that viewers apparently wanted to hear, at a time when the American Dream seemed at least on pause, if not on rewind.

"The Simpsons" was the brainchild of a counter-culture artist, Matt Groening. In his America, values were not clear-cut, feelings were often thwarted or worse, ignored, and family relationships collided. In short, life was a struggle. Instead of the "normal" American family, reconciling all life's difficulties and getting what they want, the Simpsons battled and often lost. "The Simpsons" was the show that fanned Fox's flame and gained it the respect of the television industry.

On one hand, the show seemed to display the cynicism that Americans had begun to feel about their country by the end of the 1980s. On the other, it represented Fox's daring in putting together a slate of provocative programmes designed to target the lucrative market of people under forty years old. Either way, programmes like "The Simpsons" made Fox the darling of media buyers. By the autumn of 1990, 49 per cent of Fox's audience was aged twelve to thirty-four, compared to 37 per cent for ABC, 31 per cent for NBC, and 25 per cent for CBS. These figures helped Fox rack up $550 million in advertising sales for the 1990 season, up 75 per cent from 1989. Bart Simpson had done the impossible. He had created a fourth national network.

Bart had help. The credit for Fox's success lay principally with the strange partnership of Barry Diller and Rupert Murdoch. Diller was a special kind of Hollywood creature. Aggressive and touchy, he could be both charming and psychologically overbearing. Powerful motorcycles, heavy skiing, and Democratic Party politics were his style. Politically, he was the sort of person Murdoch might have detested. But he came with Fox and Murdoch realized that he knew his job. "Barry is one of those rare people who have a combination of great creative talent and a very sharp business head," he said. It was rare, he thought, to find in Hollywood someone so energetic and so honest as Diller. At Fox, Diller was Murdoch's Murdoch.

Diller was short, slight and meticulously dressed. He seemed aloof and had been described as having "the sly manner of a leprechaun", but he could cut people to pieces with his tongue. "Killer Diller" ran a tough ship and not many of his colleagues could take life before his mast for very long. He demanded full commitment. "Don't just nod your head. Go bananas if you like something. Don't take no for an answer. Do you love it? How much do you love it?" (One correct answer was "Enough to lie down on barbed wire.") But Diller worked people effectively, as well as hard, and many came to admire him. What he did, he did with flair. He did Hollywood.

Like Murdoch, Diller had always had money; his father was a Beverly Hills real-estate developer. Diller had started in the mailroom at the William Morris agency. Later he said this had been his school – he had read all the files on every star the agency had represented. It was a unique grounding in the entertainment business. He left Morris in 1966 to join ABC where, *inter alia*, he invented the television mini-series and made-for-TV movies. In 1975 he became chairman and chief executive of Paramount. By 1983 he earned $2.12 million a year. When Murdoch bought Fox, he gave Diller stock in News Corp of some $60 million.

Like Murdoch he was a gambler. He played poker with Warren Beatty, Johnny Carson and other friends; losses might reach over

d dollars an evening, but that was nothing to any of the
gathered in Diller's Coldwater Canyon home. At Caes-
e in Las Vegas, he once refused to sit at one table. "This
table is pathetic. This table stinks. This table has no heat." He
went to another table more to his liking and piled a whole stack
of chips on it. "There! Heat!"

Diller had long wanted to start a fourth network, and in 1984,
Murdoch's purchase of Fox and then Metromedia had given him
his chance. The three networks, ABC, NBC, CBS, had never had
it so bad and Diller saw that the stranglehold they had exerted
over American television and its audiences since the 1950s was
finally weakening. In 1977, on an average TV viewing night, 93 per
cent of America's 90 million television viewing audience used to
watch an NBC, ABC or CBS programme. By the end of the
1980s, it was less than 70 per cent and still falling. Competition
– from independent stations, cable, satellite – was taking away
audiences.

This was the context in which Diller and Murdoch launched
Fox as a fledgling fourth network on 1 March 1987. Many people
thought they were walking the plank. With a string of weak
independent stations, it was hard to imagine how they could reach
the markets that were necessary to lure rich advertisers. But, by the
early 1990s, Fox had helped transform the landscape of American
television. There were those who thought it a worse place. It was
certainly different.

Fox did more than spot where the networks were failing. Its
success at the end of the 1980s reflected the enormous changes
that had been taking place in American life. One needed to loop
back to the 1970s to see this. That was when American conviction
that they would always enjoy economic success – better housing,
more cars, more education – began to falter.

In retrospect, the OPEC embargo of 1973 could be taken as
the pivotal moment at which mass upward economic mobility in
American society ended. Average weekly earnings peaked in 1973.
Productivity abruptly stopped growing. The midwest went into
further decline; inflation soared. Until then, there had been an
American assumption that children would do better than their
parents. As Nicholas Lemann wrote in *American Heritage*,

"Upward mobility wasn't just a characteristic of the national ture; it was the defining characteristic. As it slowly began to ..... in that everybody wasn't going to move forward together anymore, the country became more fragmented, more internally rivalrous and less sure of its mythology." Above all, perhaps, the middle class lost confidence, and the nuclear family came under pressure.

In 1980 Ronald Reagan's certainties seemed reassuring. And yet the gap between the wealthiest and the poorest Americans continued to grow. So-called yuppies seized the imagination of American media and advertisers and made big money, but the backbone of America was bending. After taking into account inflation, the average hourly pay for US workers fell from $8.55 an hour to $7.45. Something strange, painful and unprecedented began to happen to the country that had sparked the world's imagination with its energy, vitality and bravado. By 1989, 70 per cent of American families had no disposable income.

The decade ended with retrenchment. Debt restructuring replaced leveraged buy-outs. People might still be mobile, but no longer only upwardly. The Simpsons reflected these truths but they were not the only reality which Fox purveyed. There were many others.

Fox went for the young. This was exactly the same strategy as Murdoch's friend Leonard Goldenson had adopted for ABC in the early 1950s. In 1955 he had given young families "Cheyenne" (one of the first western series), then "King's Row" and other series. "We selected in every case young, virile men and young attractive women in order to try and attract the younger families of America," he said later. By the 1990s tastes had become more jaded. But it was still just such families that were chased. By targeting kids and those who had quite recently been kids, Fox did better than anyone thought possible.

Diller's first move, however, was a mistake. He hired Joan Rivers away from NBC and "The Johnny Carson Show", to host her own "Late Show Starring Joan Rivers". At NBC she had been an occasional and welcome alternative to the steady-paced cool of Carson, the late-night talk-show king. At Fox her show was all brash, noisy Joan, and it bombed.

"Buy her contract out," Murdoch was reported to have snapped, barely looking up, as the show's numbers were read off to him by a station employee. "If we're going down, let's cut our losses and try something else." Rivers's settlement figure was reportedly $5 million.

Murdoch and Diller had hoped that Rivers would bring instant credibility, but their losses in 1987 totalled $96 million. A traditional series, "Mr President", starring George C. Scott, also failed. In the first two years, 1987–8, over $125 million was invested in broadcasting, with few signs of a return. "We were grafting an alien thing and it just didn't take," said Diller. They were forced to retrench, abandoning their plan to launch prime-time Saturday shows. They had learned a lesson. If Fox couldn't make it according to the networks' formula, it would take a rashly different turn.

"I tend to have things get worse before they get better," said Diller later. From now on, Murdoch and Diller tried consciously to make Fox's shows different – racier, and more provocative. Fox would be an "alternative" network. They went for lower costs and higher ratings, replacing failing programmes with inexpensive, news-oriented shows, some of which were developed by the stations that Fox owned.

The 1988 Hollywood screen writers' strike was a godsend to Fox. It cut the networks' stream of new shows; they had to air reruns. Fox was different. One of its first successes with younger viewers was "The Tracey Ullman Show", a sophisticated, offbeat comedy skit show, which attracted a loyal group of viewers who kept it on the air from April 1987 to May 1990. There was nothing that Ullman would not try. Her live show was smart, clever and hip, even politically savvy, walking the line between irreverence and condescension. Fox pulled in advertisers by offering cut rates. But still the viewers did not come fast enough. By summer 1989, Diller feared the fledgling network had only months to live.

The film company began to make money. "We cratered the old company," said Diller. "It was *so* bad. We got rid of every senior executive except one and then really juiced it up, and got it back into profits." In 1988 the film *Big* grossed more than $100 million; *Working Girl*, *Die Hard* and *Young Guns* helped studio earnings

grow 35 per cent in the second half of 1988, over the prev
year, to $35.8 million. It was quite a comeback from the nearly
$300 million loss that the Fox studio had incurred between 1982
and 1985.

Fox's style was to shout. "We had to do shows that demanded
your attention, that yanked you by the throat to get you to change
the channel." And they did. Diller and Murdoch continually tried
to push the boundaries of what was acceptable TV.

"Married . . . with Children" was an early sign of the new times.
No one was quite ready for the domestic reality the show ushered
in. It was the tale of Al and Peg Bundy and their kids Kelly, Bud
and a dog called Buck. The Bundys sniped at each other, bickered,
belched. According to her husband, Peg was the worst wife/cook/
mother ever to call herself a housewife, and she, it was clear,
considered Al a woefully inadequate provider/lover/father.

"Married . . ." was first carried by 109 stations in the spring of
1987. It was a modern version of "All in the Family", which had
inspired similar horror when it had first appeared on CBS. (In
an early episode of "Married . . ." Al, the henpecked husband,
suggested that the initials PMS stood for "pummelling men's scro-
tums". "Married . . . " led one mother from Michigan, Terry
Rakolta, to launch a letter-writing crusade against Fox. She
accused the companies that advertised on the programme of "helping feed our kids a steady diet of gratuitous sex and violence".

Fox sensed that some of the skits had gone a bit too far, and
decided to tone down the show. Still, Coca-Cola insisted that
they decide only on a programme-by-programme basis whether to
advertise. Other advertisers asked for tighter screening procedures.
The *New York Times* ran an editorial saying that Rakolta had
every right to launch her one-woman campaign, and Fox had the
right to run the show. But it urged that the show's time slot be
switched back an hour so that children were less likely to see it.
"Married . . . " gained two to three points in the ratings after the
Times made its case. It was the first syndicated success story since
"The Cosby Show". It did not matter what time it aired. Early
or late, it was a hit. Whatever early resistance advertisers had soon
dissipated as its ratings soared.

As Fox grew, it garnered the reputation of being a risk-taking

network. Like Murdoch magazines, it developed a name for allowing people their head, and was known to be receptive to new
ideas. The industry was ready for a new act to shake the town.
Between them, Murdoch and Diller pulled it off. Murdoch liked
to call Fox's ideas "subversive", though of just what was not quite
clear. Staff turnover was ruthless and the number of jobs was tiny.
Whereas the established networks each employed thousands, the
crew of Fox numbered only about 200. Within three years, Fox
turned a profit. It was doing what no American network had
done since 1953, when the American Broadcasting Company was
founded. "We're the little skiff slicing through the water, as the
big ocean liners are throwing off furniture and bodies to stay
afloat," boasted Diller.

Reality was the watchword by the end of the 1980s, and reality
rescued Fox from its early losses. "Truth", of a kind, replaced
fiction. No one understood it better than Barry Diller. To Diller
the realities at the end of the 1980s were appalling. He thought
the Republican years had depressed all that was good in America:
"This country is no longer about anything but memories and
myths." Politics was the fundamental difference between him and
Murdoch. "He is able to make more fun of it than I am," said
Diller. "I can't make fun of conservatives – I just get crazy,
tied up."

In the summer of 1986, Murdoch summoned Maury Povich,
the talk-show host of Fox's Washington station, to New York.
Povich had been told horror stories about Murdoch by Harold
Evans and others. The real Murdoch came as a surprise. "He
wore a serious and dangerous brow, and spoke softly, politely,
minimally, like a Mandarin demigod."

Murdoch told him that Fox was starting a new show, first in
New York and then perhaps nationally. Povich would be host.
Its name would be "A Current Affair", and it would begin to
air in a month or so. Povich, used to slow-moving television
bureaucracies, was astounded by "the sheer audacity of it all.
Nobody mentioned focus groups, or consultants or marketing
research. These guys were so casual, as if nothing could be easier.

They were fearless: Murdoch's daredevil squadron, heading into the unknown without parachutes."

At first "A Current Affair" ran late in the evening on New York's Channel Five. It was to CBS's "60 Minutes" as the *Post* was to the *New York Times*, or the *Sun* to the *Financial Times*. "We did stories about freeing dogs from pounds in Connecticut and putting them in witness protection programmes in Massachusetts, wet T-shirt contests and so on," wrote Povich. When he complained that they should be doing some serious stories as well, he was told he could make it clear on air that he thought particular stories frivolous.

Povich thought that what made "A Current Affair" different was that it never tried to be fair – and its bias could be absolutely obvious, as in the sentimental coverage it gave to Mary Beth Whitehead, a working-class woman who had borne a surrogate child which she then wished to keep. (She lost to the couple who had hired her.) Next, the programme staged a grisly re-creation of the Central Park murder of Jennifer Levin and then broadcast a tape, which it had bought, of her alleged murderer, Robert Chambers, pretending to strangle a doll. Good taste was never a problem to what Povich called "Rupert's outlaw gang of scoundrels". But they all needed Murdoch's approval: "There was always the threat of that raised eyebrow, which loomed like an open IBM silo over our future," said Povich.

In September 1987, after a favourable review in the *New York Times*, Murdoch immediately decided to move the show up to prime time, 7.30 p.m. Stories became more national. Boston, then Houston, picked up the show. It took off and became more aggressive. "It had been a nice, populist, sweet little tabloid," said Diller, "not mean-spirited but fun. Then it went right over the line. Rupert kept pulling it back." It was successful. By the end of 1989 it was making $25 million a year and its appeal to a nationwide audience propelled the network onward.

The next offering was even more "realistic". Like "A Current Affair", "America's Most Wanted", was born from the sensibility that informed tabloid newspapers.

While Fox was not the first station to use the genre, it developed the concept beyond anything that TV had so far done. "Real" criminals became prime-time stars.

The programme was hosted by John Walsh, a successful builder who had turned crusader after his six-year-old son had been kidnapped and murdered. He was not only an attractive TV host, but also an outraged American parent, who was out to see justice done – a cross between Charles Bronson and the Peter Finch character in *Network*. The premise of the programme was painfully simple: you, the viewer, wanted to see the scum caught. The show offered re-enactments of gruesome crimes, and encouraged TV viewers to confront their neighbours, or the stranger in the bar, and turn the criminals in. Questions of invasion of privacy abounded, and some people wondered how long it would be before the TV audience would see a criminal executed. But, instead of feeling threatened by the show, American law enforcers welcomed it with open arms. FBI director William S. Sessions made an appearance, announcing the FBI's three most wanted people. The calls poured in.

As a result, more than 100 criminals were captured and prosecuted. Fugitives as far away as American Samoa were apprehended. Crimes committed as far back as 1971 were solved. In 1989 "America's Most Wanted" became the second most watched programme on Fox, right behind "Married . . . with Children". It thrived on America's obsession with violent crime and with voyeuristic crime-solving. As the programme became more successful, its grislier aspects were diluted – a little. Advertisers started to call the show "pro-social" – that was Diller's term. "America's Most Wanted", he said, was the show which turned the corner for Fox Broadcasting. In 1989 Fox nearly tripled its 1988 advertising revenue, and pulled in about $325 million in up-front sales to advertisers. By 1990 sales were up to $550 million.

Diller and Murdoch realized that they had hit a goldmine, a string of raunchy, "realistic" programmes that the image-conscious networks, with their phalanx of censors and taste-makers, had never dared attempt. As well as finding new younger viewers, and the advertisers who pursued them, Fox was constantly pushing back the frontiers of what was acceptable to a living-room audience. In a sense Murdoch was doing for Americans with Fox what he had done for the British with the *Sun*.

"Cops", which hit the airwaves in 1989, was a programme unlike any other in prime time. Carrying police genre TV as far as anyone could imagine, the programme starred real cops, going after real criminals committing real crimes – hookers, hit-and-run drivers, thieves, peeping toms, wife-beaters and child-abusers. Each week a minicam crew dogged several members from a local sheriff's department. "No actors, no scripts, no bull," Fox boasted. Week by week the locale shifted to a different American town. The police loved it – they were its stars. Law enforcement departments across the country offered their own teams of crime-busters. Civil libertarians, were outraged. They pointed out that the rights of the "alleged perpetrators" were being seriously violated by the programme, which vividly identified them as criminals. Even though it carried the Constitutional disclaimer "innocent until proven guilty", the implication was otherwise.

The show reached a peak of sorts when it travelled to the Soviet Union in May 1989 for an hour-long special that aired in the United States and the USSR later in the year. The Soviets placed virtually no limitations on the American crew wandering through Moscow and Leningrad seeking the darker side of glasnost. Drunks being arrested and suffering cruel punishment, fragile families suffering in the strained Soviet society, a women confessing to killing her husband with the outburst, "I'm tired of life", a little boy turning in his father for possession of drugs.

"Cops" was reviewed by *New York Newsday* as "The Best New Crime Series of the Year" and it soon spawned similar shows on other networks. Ultimately it led to such confrontational live audience shows as that hosted by the abusive Morton Downey Jr. – who was then taken off the air. In the next tabloid TV stables were Phil Donahue's exploration of the sexual fantasies of housewives and Geraldo Rivera's screen adventures with Satanism and prostitution.

In all this cavalcade there was no greater star than the tireless Steve Dunleavy, whom Murdoch moved from the *Post* to Fox. As "The Simpsons" replaced "Dallas", Dunleavy was the man who silverplated the realism in "reality TV", and who crossed all the Ts in Tabloid Television. He was still the Mad Dog to Murdoch's Mogul, but he had turned fifty and was now almost an elder statesman in the Murdoch organization. At the Boss's request, he had transformed himself from a hot-metal, cold-typewriter legend in Murdoch's most important newsrooms into a charming caricature of a serious network newsman. He wore well-cut suits and he had polished his prose till the purple really sparkled. He carried a spare tooth to stick in the gap between his front teeth when filming.

Like the veteran reporter he was, Dunleavy talked to people, listened, called them back. He was unstoppable, and was known as "Street Dog". Policemen loved him; he was a hero in all the precincts which he visited and where he praised the man on the beat. But it was not only good ol' boys in the police who loved him. Good ol' boy journalists felt a little tenderness too. Jimmy Breslin, no slouch when it came to criticizing the way in which Murdoch shoved journalistic standards downhill, acknowledged, "At least Dunleavy's no goddamn TV clone. I can't watch one more Asian woman who talks like she's from Nebraska. He's got that 'fuck you' attitude and I love it." In the newsroom at Channel Five, most of the staff were kids who would die for Dunleavy's smile. He was the hero as well as the legend.

It was Steve they sent after Jessica Hahn when she revealed her affair with the Reverend Jim Bakker, the television evangelist. Despite serenading her from the street at 4 a.m., he failed to get an interview. But when ABC announced that she would be appearing in an exclusive that evening on "Nightline", Dunleavy rushed to her apartment on Long Island and screamed through the locked door, "How can you do this to me, Jessica?" When ABC's limousine pulled up, Dunleavy told the driver she was sick and had to go to hospital. The car drove away. Dunleavy called an ambulance and spirited her off. Dunleavy got the interview.

His hair was a little more grey and rather more coiffed, but the Steve Dunleavy who appeared on the screen for Fox was the same Dunleavy who had followed Murdoch around the globe scripting their shared tabloid vision. Like Murdoch, he still loved to stick in the craw of high-minded journalists and professors of journalism. When he was invited to attend a high-flown seminar in Princeton on the ethics of journalism, he showed up late and with a blonde on each arm. "It was a set-up and I loved it," he told Marc Rich, who profiled him in *GQ*. "The seminar reeked of wall-to-wall journalistic evangelists, who absolutely send me nuts. That's kind of arrogance . . . The only bosses are the public. That's who runs my life, next to Rupert Murdoch. Those over-indulged students left there firmly convinced they had stared into the eye of a journalistic Satan."

Tom Shales, the TV critic of the *Washington Post*, wrote: "Dunleavy makes Geraldo look like Eric Sevareid . . . This guy is a sleaze, and unfortunately that's no longer a problem on TV." Similarly, the *New York Times* said "A Current Affair" was "Nothing short of vile. What kind of people do we want to be?"

That was a question that the Mad Dog and the Mogul provoked in all the societies through which they ran. The answers were not easy to find. Bart Simpson's famous cry, "Eat my shorts", was one.

AUSTRALIA

Rupert and Anna Murdoch saw in the New Year of 1989 at their home in Cavan, New South Wales. They were in Australia for his mother's eightieth birthday party and to sort out some of the problems in News Corp, in particular with the Melbourne *Herald*, which had been a commercial disappointment since he had acquired it in 1987.

At 4 a.m. on 3 January, he was awakened by a call from Europe, where it was still the afternoon of 2 January. It was from Presses de la Cité, the French publishers who had been brought in by Ian Chapman of Collins to help him resist a full takeover by Murdoch. Murdoch already owned a large part of Collins and he had been angered by Chapman's reaction. He told the French that he would never give in.

Murdoch and Chapman had co-operated well since Murdoch's purchase of 42 per cent of the voting shares of Collins in 1981 and over their joint acquisition of Harper and Row in 1987. But by 1988, international conglomerates were taking over more and more of the publishing industry. Most significantly, Robert Maxwell bought the American publishers, Macmillan, for $2.5 billion. After his purchase of *TV Guide*, Murdoch told Ian Chapman that the financial pressures on him were now such that he would have to make a bid for the whole of Collins. Chapman resisted and told Murdoch that the Collins board considered this a hostile bid, which Murdoch had assured him he would never make. Lord Goodman, Murdoch's lawyer, said later that he understood Chapman's feelings – Murdoch's bid was clearly a breach of his 1981 commitment. On the other hand, said Goodman in an interview for this book, that commitment had been made seven years before and business circumstances had changed. Goodman added, 'Having known Murdoch for over thirty years, I cannot remember any other occasion on which he broke his word.' In November 1988, News International launched a cash bid for the 58 per cent of William Collins that it did not already own. In the City, the bid was thought low, valuing Collins at £293 million.

Collins was a profitable company, one of the last big independents in publishing. As well as its UK publishing operations and the 50 per cent stake in the American publisher, Harper and Row, which Murdoch had sold to them, Collins owned a large print plant in Glasgow, seven Claude Gill retail outlets and the Hatchards chain of bookshops. It also had publishing subsidiaries in Australia, Canada, New Zealand and South Africa.

In its offer document News International claimed that stronger direction was needed. The document asserted that staff morale was low, and that the performance of the company's core businesses was poor. Ian Chapman, the chief executive of Collins, told the *FT* that he was astonished by such claims. "The attack on the Collins management has been manufactured for this bid," he said. Chapman once again began to mobilize Collins's authors against Murdoch and to look for a new "white knight".

For a few weeks things went quiet. The night before the bid was due to expire on 23 December, News International announced it was extending its offer until 5 January. Then the Collins board announced that it was holding talks "which may lead to offers being made, at a level appreciably above the level of the News

International offers, for the whole of Collins". Murdoch moved immediately to scotch this initiative. News stated "categorically that it will not accept any competing offer in respect of its 41.7 per cent voting stake in Collins".

On 29 December the unknown bidder – which was in fact the French publishing group Presses de la Cité – announced that it would be prepared to make a £403 million bid for Collins, on condition there was a "significant number of ordinary share-holders undertaking irrevocably to accept the offer". They were looking for a reasonable indication that they were going to succeed before they committed themselves to a contest.

Murdoch wasted no time in repulsing the move. News now offered 880p cash for Collins ordinary shares and 735p for the A shares and called on the Collins board to recommend its offer. A News International announcement said it was clear from Collins's behaviour that the firm was prepared to relinquish its independence anyway. From Australia, Murdoch said: "The board of Collins and the possible offerer should now realize that we have no intention of discussing the sale of our stake in Collins, nor of our interest in Harper and Row." There seemed little question that Murdoch held the stronger hand. All Ian Chapman could do was reiterate that "News International's offers are not in the best interests of Collins's shareholders, authors, employees and customers."

Then came the 4 a.m. phone call from Presses de la Cité. Murdoch insisted he would never back down; honour was at stake. He would top any bid they made. Presses de la Cité believed him to be implacable and, on the strength of one conversation, withdrew. Days later Collins began talks with News International. The board had left itself with few options. To encourage Presses de la Cité's interest it had put a low value on the company and the French withdrawal effectively forced it to accept the News International bid. That was substantially higher than News's original offer, but business opinion held that, even now, News had got itself a bargain, in publishing terms. The purchase price reflected a price/earnings multiple of 17.8, compared, for instance, to the multiple of 29.8 in Pearson's 1988 purchase of US educational publisher Addison-Wesley.

Many of Collins's authors expressed their horror. Over 200 of them contributed "letters of support" to the company's management. "I feel a great sense of obligation to Collins," Michael Frayn told the *Guardian* on 6 January, but he would not offer a new book to Collins if Murdoch controlled it. "I think Murdoch has put a fairly foul imprint on a lot of things." "I do not like his style or the way he does business," said the thriller writer, Ken Follett. "He will vulgarize Collins, restrict its range and take it right-wing and bring it downmarket. We will end up with Miss Marple thrillers with page-three girls on the cover." Sir John Harvey-Jones, the former chairman of ICI and a Collins author, was more reasoned in his reaction, but still betrayed the singular mistrust that Murdoch could inspire:

I have three worries about Murdoch and Collins – firstly, that I wouldn't describe what has happened to most of his properties in the media as being the maintenance of standards. Secondly, I think you need to take risks in publishing, and if you go totally commercial the world is a poorer place. Thirdly, it would put an enormous amount of power in his hands.

Murdoch stated that he was "very much more interested in the 95 per cent of the authors who did not come out against the bid", adding succinctly that if writers did leave "we will find that other authors will come to us because we will sell more books". In the event only a handful left.

After Murdoch gave Collins guarantees regarding the company's future editorial and management autonomy, the board finally recommended the News bid. "I am sad that we have not managed to keep our independence," Ian Chapman was quoted in the *New York Times*. "We have, however, received assurances we sought regarding Collins's autonomy and editorial freedom. Above all, the Collins business is to be developed."

It was clear that Chapman, who was angry at Murdoch's démarche, could not stay on. Murdoch himself took over as Collins's chairman. George Craig, who had moved from Collins to be joint chief executive of Harper and Row with Ian Chapman, was now made group chief executive. He began to integrate the two companies, which Chapman felt was a breach of some of the guarantees Murdoch had given.

For all the emotive language it produced, the Collins takeover was ultimately about the business logic of the 1980s. It was part of a worldwide corporate strategy in which newspapers, printing works, film libraries, databases, books, satellite TV and magazines were converging on one another, in the expectation of global economies of scale for the parent company.

On 4 January, Murdoch flew to Melbourne. He spent the afternoon at the Herald and Weekly Times office. That evening there was a birthday party for his sister, Janet Calvert-Jones. Her husband was a British-born yachtsman and stockbroker whose Melbourne company handled business for News and for the Murdoch family company, Cruden. Their son was born deaf, and Janet herself, as well as being chairwoman of the Herald board, spent a great deal of time promoting the needs of the deaf.

There was much to discuss. Australia had still not digested his takeover of the Herald group and there was still concern about the way in which he had disposed of newspapers to satisfy the Trade Practices Commission. Both the *Brisbane Sun* and the Adelaide *News* (Murdoch's first paper) had been bought by their News Corps editors. Murdoch had helped arrange the financing of the deals and the papers remained in News buildings and were printed on News presses. He insisted this was the only way to ensure they remained alive. That may well have been true but it seemed to many people that they would obviously remain under Murdoch's influence.

An even greater upheaval was taking place at Fairfax. The twenty-six-year-old Warwick Fairfax had launched a takeover bid against the rest of his family for their company, John Fairfax Limited. Murdoch was full of praise. "I congratulate Warwick Fairfax on a courageous move. I wish I had had the guts to do this when I was twenty-six and perhaps I would not have to be standing here now," he told a seminar in Sydney. This was absurd, if not mischievous. Warwick Fairfax's bid was to prove catastrophic for his family's company, as Murdoch must have suspected it would be.

Early in 1988 Warwick Fairfax shut down the two loss-making

papers of his new empire – the *Times on Sunday* and the tabloid Sydney *Sun*. The closure of the *Sun* was a major victory for Murdoch. It had been locked into a fierce circulation war with his *Daily Mirror* for the Sydney afternoon tabloid market. Now Fairfax had handed that market and its potential profits to Murdoch. He was delighted; Fairfax had originally sold the *Mirror* to him in 1960 thinking that it would destroy him, but Murdoch had in fact outlived them.

He also tried to buy Fairfax's shares in both Australian Newsprint Mills and the Australian Associated Press. If these deals had gone through, he would have controlled almost 80 per cent of the country's largest supplier of newsprint, and more than 70 per cent of AAP. On this occasion the Trade Practices Commission intervened to stop him.

In January 1988 it emerged that News was planning to build a $120 million printing works and warehouse in Melbourne's docklands area. At the same time, News announced it was buying thirty-nine printing presses from Germany in a deal worth $800 million, reported to be the world's biggest press order. The presses, customized for Murdoch's plants at Wapping and in Australia, were renamed the "Newsman" by the German company in honour of the size of the order. They were designed to handle high-speed, high-quality colour production. Murdoch had been persuaded against his better judgement, and largely by the example of Robert Maxwell, that he had to have colour. This investment was one of the massive outlays which almost ruined him in 1990.

Equally unsatisfactory was the progress – or lack of it – of his father's old paper, the Melbourne *Herald* itself. Murdoch's unhappiness had become apparent to his senior executives.

His choice of Eric Beecher as editor, together with the return to *The Australian* of Paul Kelly, one of Australia's best political columnists, who had left the paper after the 1975 strike, suggested that Murdoch was now prepared to invest in more "upmarket" journalism. Both Kelly and Beecher had demanded and received guarantees of independence; Kelly was told that he could write precisely what he wanted, and that promise had been honoured. Beecher by contrast found through 1988 that the fast track he had ridden through the softer world of Fairfax had done little to prepare him for the realities of the Murdoch empire.

There was no doubt that he faced a difficult task. The *Herald*'s circulation had been free-falling from its high of 550,000 copies a day twenty years before. It was now selling only 220,000 a day, and several previous attempts to increase circulation had failed. It was losing A$15 million a year.

Beecher had emphasized good writing, improved the political and financial sections and the paper's overall layout. He put less emphasis on sport – a mistake in a city which was still as obsessed as it had been at the turn of the century with Australian Rules football.

Circulation continued to fall and the paper lost advertising market share to the *Age*. Rumours abounded that the losses were so high that Murdoch might consider closing it. In late 1988, the high-priced columnist Peter Smark jumped ship and went back to the *Sydney Morning Herald*, whence Beecher had lured him.

By the second half of 1988, News executives were dropping broad off-the-record hints that they were tiring of Beecher. They compared the *Herald* with the *Sun*, the morning Melbourne tabloid which had gained circulation since Murdoch took control. In News, circulation was still king, whatever Beecher might once have hoped.

In November 1988 Murdoch summoned John D'Arcy, the Herald's managing director, to London. D'Arcy had now worked almost two years for News. Murdoch had had the idea of making him and Cowley contend for supremacy on the continent. Warned that that would be destructive, he had desisted, but D'Arcy's relationship with Cowley was not happy.

D'Arcy had always felt Beecher was the wrong man for the *Herald* – "He had no feel for the city. Too prissy. He was a good writer of cricket books" – so he saw that Murdoch had a problem with the paper. When he was called to London, D'Arcy thought he might be promoted. Instead, Murdoch called him to his flat in St James's, offered him a whisky and sacked him. It took twenty minutes. D'Arcy was devastated, and his wife never forgave Murdoch. D'Arcy said later:

I was astonished by the culture of News. It was run like a corner store. No one makes a decision except Rupert. He doesn't care about conventions or customs. He prefers executives who never question him. When you answer back, Rupert says "I don't want to hear that." He wants to own the world. Everything he sees for sale, he wants to buy. Look at *TV Guide*. Madness.

In D'Arcy's place, Murdoch appointed a News journalist, Malcolm Colless, at the same time as he made his sister, Janet, chairwoman of the company. The two appointments meant that after two years of owning the Melbourne *Herald*, News Limited management was finally moving in to control it.

Colless had been chief executive of a network of suburban newspapers owned by News in New South Wales, Victoria and Queensland. He had also reported on industrial relations and on Canberra politics for *The Australian*. He was a News Corp man to his fingertips; a man who would be prepared to do exactly what Murdoch wanted.

Beecher could not stand him: "He wanted no foreign policy leaders. He just wanted sport on the front page every day," he said later. Before long Beecher and Colless clashed. News executives began to back Colless over Beecher.

When Murdoch came into the *Herald*'s office on 5 January 1989, there was already unspoken tension between them. Murdoch did what all his editors fear. He dashed in and stood at the desk with the sheaf of recent editions. "He began to flick through it," said Beecher later. "Actually he began to tear it apart."

Beecher did not react immediately and later said that Murdoch then complained, "You're too aloof! My friends in Melbourne are ashamed to read the paper." The next day Murdoch apologized, but a few weeks afterwards Beecher resigned. At first he insisted that he had no dispute with Murdoch himself, but later he said that News Corp's culture was antithetical to good journalism. "They over-promote people who would never have such chances elsewhere. They lock them in financially and give them bags of prestige. In Fairfax such people would not be able to interfere in editorial decisions."

Beecher said that he, too, had had a love affair with Murdoch.

When it soured, life became impossible. "Rupert is a great manipulator. He lets you grab his coat-tails and jump on the magic carpet. But the flight path may change in order to accommodate Rupert's needs for greater profits." (In similar vein, Anna once told a *New York Times* reporter, "If Rupert was a pilot, I would not board the plane – he cuts too many corners.")

"The basic problem," said Beecher, "is that Rupert has contempt for those who work for him, and total contempt for those whom he can bend. I used to get up and say, 'He's changed.' But he had not."

Murdoch's subsequent explanation of the débâcle was quite different. Beecher, he said, "ran all these Living supplements and whole pages on where to get the best croissants in South Yarra. As a result, he *shooed* away the readers. Evening papers are in terminal decline everywhere. Beecher simply sped the process."

On 6 January, Murdoch spent much of the day in talks with Sir Peter Abeles, his partner in Ansett Airlines. Through the 1980s Ansett had been a vital source of cash for News, and Murdoch constantly consulted Abeles.

That evening, they all went to Cruden Farm, his parents' house outside Melbourne, for his mother's eightieth birthday party. Tributes were certainly due, for Dame Elisabeth, sprightly and opinionated as ever, remained a prominent figure in many areas of Australian life – art, charities and not least, gardening. As a family, the Murdochs had been substantial public benefactors since Sir Keith had taken a leading part in strengthening the National Gallery of Victoria, where a wing carried the Murdoch name. There was still a Keith and Elisabeth art prize, and Rupert Murdoch himself had assisted many Australian artists by buying their work, sponsoring exhibitions, financing shows overseas.

News had helped finance an oral history programme at the museum of the National War Memorial in Canberra, and the company was underwriting the retrieval and cataloguing of early Australian films. News marked the twenty-fifth anniversary of *The Australian* by funding Rupert Murdoch scholarships at the Graduate School of Management at Melbourne University. Murdoch and his mother and sisters had joined in financing the Institute of Birth Defects at the Melbourne Royal Children's Hospital.

And in Oxford Murdoch had refurbished the library of his old college, Worcester. (This had prompted his old tutor, Asa Briggs, who was now Provost of Worcester, to remark that this was the first time he had ever seen Murdoch in the library. Murdoch had replied that in fact he had always gone there as a student to read *Sporting Life*.) In Melbourne and elsewhere, friends attested to other examples of Murdoch family generosity to institutions and to individuals.

The party was a great occasion. Indeed, it could almost have been a set piece in Anna Murdoch's second novel, *Family Business*, the saga of a newspaper dynasty headed by Ms Yarrow McLean, which had recently been published. All Dame Elisabeth's children, their spouses, and most of her many grandchildren were there. In fact, there was almost a full complement of the beneficiaries of the Cruden Trust, the principal owners of News. But it was not only a family party: the cream of Melbourne's Establishment – political, commercial, academic, social – was there. The governor of Victoria, the chairmen of the banks, directors of industry, vice chancellors of universities, and Murdoch's old Geelong Grammar headmaster, Sir James Darling. "Well, you get your way, Rupert," said Darling, as they shook hands.

Among them were some old-timers who had been offended by Murdoch's business "ruthlessness" and downright appalled by his taking of American citizenship, but who had maintained their affection and respect for his mother and family. The newspaper people were there, too. Richard Searby, the chairman of News, and his wife Caroline were there. The D'Arcys, though still fragile, came because of their friendship with Dame Elisabeth. So did Douglas Brass, who had been with Sir Keith before Rupert, and his wife Joan, a friend of Dame Elisabeth since schooldays. It was quite a party: like *Aida* with a cast of thousands, recalled one editor present. It was an open-air affair and the evening was chilly; everyone ate out of special pre-packed dinner boxes with a picture of the house on the lid. In his speech Murdoch paid teasing tribute to his mother's strong character and recalled his childhood.

The next day, Murdoch jetted off. This is how he himself listed his major engagements in the next few weeks:

SATURDAY JAN 7. Melbourne-Sydney-Los Angeles. Arrive Los Angeles 10.30 same day. Lunch with Barry Diller. Fox-TV affiliates dinner on Fox lot.

SUNDAY JAN 8. Black tie affair – TV Academy Hall of Fame.

MONDAY JAN 9–TUES JAN 10. Fox, Sky/Disney, Motion Picture Corp meetings.

WEDNESDAY JAN 12. LA – Washington DC on our plane, a Gulfstream 111. Black tie dinner at White House. President and Mrs Reagan. Late return to New York.

THURSDAY JAN 13. Meetings e.g. on Mirabella launch: . . . drink with Bibi Netanyahu, leading Israeli politician.

SATURDAY JAN 14. Concorde New York-London.

SUNDAY JAN 15. Meetings on Collins Publishers, Sky-TV, Times.

MONDAY JAN 16. Meetings on Collins, Sky. Concorde to New York, arrive 5.50 p.m.

TUESDAY JAN 17. Breakfast with George Ball at Prudential-Bache. Meetings at News Corporation.

WEDNESDAY JAN 18. NY-Washington-NY. I gave testimony in the Newhouse IRS case. Dinner: at the William Paleys for Sid Bass and Mercedes Kellogg.

THURSDAY JAN 19. Meetings, then major customers' conference on "free-standing inserts" – a subtlety of the media business.

FRIDAY JAN 20 (Inauguration Day). Meetings, bull sessions on Mirabella, TV Guide, Collins, Fox.

JAN 22 (SUNDAY). Concorde to London, dinner at Connaught.

JAN 23 (MONDAY). Meetings at Collins all day.

JAN 24 (TUESDAY). At Collins in Glasgow all day.

JAN 25 (WED)–JAN 27 (FRIDAY). Various meetings e.g. with Conrad Black in Wapping. Concorde to New York.

JAN 28 (SAT) New York-Washington DC Black tie dinner at Alfalfa Club, guest of Harry Byrd Jr.

JAN 29 (SUN) DC–Los Angeles.

JAN 30 (MON)–(WED) FEB 1 Los Angeles. Turf Racing Assoc dinner dance on Fox lot (a goodwill function for Daily Racing Form*).*

FEB 1 (WED). LA to NY.

FEB 4 (SAT). Concorde to London.

FEB 5 (SUNDAY). Launch of Sky-TV.

Chapter 13

THE CLARKE RING

It was the "Star Wars" over Britain which did more than any of his other ventures to put Murdoch's empire at risk. Emboldened by the adventure at Fox, he felt the need once more to take on his enemies in "the British Establishment".

In February 1989, he launched a new four-channel satellite service, Sky. It was the start of a war which cost both sides almost as much as the Channel Tunnel.

Like other countries, Britain had five Direct Broadcast Satellite (DBS) channels allocated to it in 1977 by the World Administrative Radio Conference (WARC). In 1982, two of these channels were allocated to the BBC alone, but the Corporation failed to get the project under way.

Early in 1986, the IBA reported to the government that there was renewed interest in the DBS franchise, which had now been extended to fifteen years. In April they invited applications to provide a commercial service on three of the DBS channels allocated to Britain.

Seven applications were received by August that year. One of the consortia included Murdoch and the Sky channel service on which he was already broadcasting to European cable systems. The other groups, among them Tiny Rowland's Lonrho, and Robert Holmes à Court's Bell group, all seemed to have one thing in common – they wanted to keep Rupert Murdoch out of British television. There was much talk about the danger of his putting the *Sun* on satellite and doing a Wapping of the air. The risks to both morals and established television practices seemed overwhelming.

In the end, the franchise was won by British Satellite Broadcasting (BSB), a consortium made up by Granada, Pearson, Anglia television, Virgin Records and Amstrad. BSB's impressive presentation emphasized programme-making. Each of BSB's four channels would cater to specific tastes. "Now" was a twenty-four-hour current affairs channel; "Galaxy" would provide light entertainment; "Screen" would show feature films; and there would be a Disney channel. The last two would, from the outset, be funded by subscription.

The overall watchword was quality: including many arts programmes and repeats of classic BBC and American series. The service made no qualms about being entrenched firmly in middle-class values. To Murdoch, it was uncompromisingly "Establishment-oriented", in that it fitted easily into the mainstream of British television. The *Sun* called it "toffs' telly".

The technology was expected to be high quality also. Under the terms of its franchise, BSB was compelled to use a new, and much more expensive transmission system, D-MAC, which was expected to produce a better picture than the old PAL system. D-MAC certainly seemed an advance on previous satellite technology, but it was untried.

Along with the Channel Tunnel, BSB became one of the biggest risk capital ventures the British markets had ever seen. The original estimates were that it would need over £500 million. The launch was first proposed for late 1990, although this date was quickly and optimistically brought forward to September 1989. BSB projected that it would by then be broadcasting to 400,000 homes, a figure that would rise to around 10 million by the end of the fifteen-year franchise. It hoped to break even by its third or fourth year and to be in profit in around six years. Initially it would rely on subscription income for most of its funding.

At first, the BSB consortium seemed not only financially strong but also a practical outfit – Amstrad could develop the dishes and receiving equipment and Granada could rent out equipment at a rate competitive with VCR rentals. Virgin, Anglia and Granada would assist with the programming of the channel.

By April 1987 the founding shareholders had pledged £80 million, with a further £120 million in letters of intent. The projected costs had now risen to around £650 million and the main shareholders cast around for other interested parties. Alan Bond's

Bond Corporation pledged between £30–50 million. The French company Chargeurs and Reed International (which had been part of the failed Sky bid) and Next also bought substantial shareholdings.

But in May 1987 a serious blow was struck at the integrity of the consortium. Alan Sugar, the creator and controller of Amstrad, failed to get the exclusive right to supply BSB's equipment. He became increasingly concerned that the technical problems of D-MAC had not been properly thought out, and he pulled out of the project altogether, leaving BSB to look elsewhere for the development and manufacture of its dishes.

Then, a year later, Rupert Murdoch arrived. Having had the front door closed against him, he decided to kick down the back door, and come into, or rather over, Britain on Astra, a private pan-European satellite operated from Luxembourg.

In spring 1987 Astra had been given a confirmed position at 19.2 degrees east on the Clarke Ring. Its plan to broadcast sixteen channels in different languages throughout Europe was an obvious challenge to established broadcasters and governments alike. Officials at Eutelsat, whose task was to allocate broadcasting and telecommunications frequencies in space, dismissed Astra with disdain, for wanting only to operate that part of the market which would make money. They complained that Astra's plans would interfere with unused frequencies, and that Astra would now be competing with Eutelsat itself.

Astra's technology was different. All the national satellites were using DBS "broadcast" frequencies with satellites of three to four 150–200-watt transponders. Since then satellites had become much more sophisticated; smaller dishes could now pick up lower-powered signals. The Astra satellite carried sixteen fifty-watt medium-power transponders.

During the 1980s the map of the European sky had changed radically. At the start of the decade the talk had been only of national, high-powered direct broadcast satellite systems. Now the future of the industry seemed to be assured by something quite different: low-powered commercial telecommunications satellites.

Apart from the European rocket Ariane, which was used to launch Astra, almost everything in the industry was American.

The Astra satellite itself was an RCA 4000. The BSB satellite was built by Hughes and was to be delivered into orbit by McDonnell Douglas. Much of the programming and advertising was American. Coca-Cola, Pepsi-Cola and McDonalds were all early and important advertisers on European satellite television.

By 1987, Murdoch had spent over £40 million on his European Sky Channel, in four years. He had increased its transmission from two to ten and then to eighteen hours day, and had extended it by cable into about 12 million homes in twenty countries including Hungary, the first country in the Eastern bloc to take Western television.

In Britain cable started slowly and did not really spread until the end of the 1980s, when the government relaxed the rules on investment by American companies which were flush with money from the monopolies they operated in the United States.

After Murdoch had decided to challenge BSB in Britain, he withdrew Sky from Continental Europe completely, and decided to move it on to Astra to be beamed to Britain. "Astra was not the only possibility. There were other things we could have done. Most importantly we could have done nothing," said his adviser, Jim Cruthers. But that would not have been Murdoch's style at all.

On 8 June 1988, the auditorium of the British Academy of Film and Television Arts in Piccadilly was dominated by a large stack of TV screens which filled the stage. A white satellite dish was attached to a paper red-brick wall. Emblems of Sky TV and Astra, "Europe's sixteen-channel television satellite" were displayed on a deep blue background. There were model satellites and a model yellow rocket.

When the audience was seated, the ecstatic roar of the chorus from Carl Orff's "Carmina Burana" filled the auditorium, a rocket took off across the screens and smoke obscured the stage. On the screens a satellite decoupled from the rocket. Clips from promised programmes ended with a jingle of girls singing "Sky Television".

Murdoch, soberly dressed as ever, walked over to the rostrum and spoke with his usual nervousness: "Thank you, ladies and gentlemen, for being here this morning, to hear these announcements, which we hope will cause a great deal of interest." He said that News International had spent £40 million developing Sky, "in the belief that the public of Europe and of Britain particularly had been deprived of choice of viewing". Now with new satellite technology he saw a great opportunity of getting to a mass audience in Britain as well as in Europe a lot faster. "So I'm happy to announce today that Sky will be leasing four transponders on the magnificent new Astra satellite which is due to be launched on 4 November of this year." He made a promise: "We are seeing the dawn of an age of freedom for viewing and freedom for advertising." He announced that Alan Sugar, who had abandoned BSB and was now on the platform with him, would manufacture the dishes for Sky.

His refrain was familiar. British television should be bust right open. "Broadcasting in this country has for too long been the preserve of the old Establishment that has been elitist in its thinking and in its approach to programming," he declared. So-called "quality" television merely reflected the prejudices of the narrow elite which controlled British broadcasting. He was now going to war not only with the terrestrial stations of the BBC and Independent Television, but also the new satellite service of British Satellite Broadcasting. For the first time, and after many frustrations, he was about to become a broadcaster in Britain. Hitherto, this had always been denied him because of the government's restrictions on newspaper and television cross-ownership. Those restrictions still applied, but Murdoch was sidestepping them by broadcasting from a satellite outside British jurisdiction.

His announcement was an unequivocal threat to BSB. Richard Branson, the founder of Virgin Records, and one of BSB's investors, immediately understood the scale of it. BSB costings had been based upon the premise that it would have no satellite competitors. Now it was clear that Murdoch was trying to beat them off the Clarke Ring with cheaper, existing technology. BSB might be able to promise better reception from their new-fangled D-MAC system, but customers would buy only one system – probably the first to fly.

Branson knew how resolute a competitor Murdoch was and he realized that Sky would be enormously boosted by support from all the News International papers. That plugging began at once.

In the months to come, Murdoch's papers, in particular the *Sun*, the *News of the World* and *Today* all became shameless cheerleaders for Sky.

Branson tried secretly to interest Murdoch in a merger. But Murdoch was too confident for that. And so Branson arranged to sell Virgin's shares in BSB to an existing BSB shareholder, the Australian, Alan Bond. Branson offered him his £30 million stake for just £31 million, in order to cover all Virgin's costs. Bond was delighted. The night the deal was done, Branson went out and drank champagne; he was enormously relieved.

The first managing director of Sky was Jim Styles, an Australian who had worked for Murdoch's Channel 9 in Adelaide in 1958. His Australian experience was invaluable in setting up the kind of lean, cheap operation that Murdoch liked. In Australia, with tiny audiences, every corner had to be cut and programmes were made many times faster and more cheaply than in Europe. That was how Murdoch wanted Sky to be. At BSB, a far more relaxed, expansive and expensive philosophy prevailed.

In October 1988, Sky signed the lease for a set of buildings on a business development park in Osterley, near Heathrow. It was little more than a building site, filled with mud. In the next four months, 77,500 square feet of offices were prepared to house 600-plus staff, state-of-the-art production facilities, studios, editing suites, transmission equipment, graphics studios and an entire self-contained, twenty-four-hour news service. Sony had originally said it would take eighteen months to plan and equip such a studio. Told that the deadline was six months, Sony thought again – and did it.

Much more difficult than arranging the hardware was obtaining the software. Both BSB and Sky reckoned that the success of their system depended on the lure of their movie channel. So, in the autumn of 1988, both of them sent teams of buyers to Hollywood to collar the gems of Dreamland.

In a town where excess is the daily fare, this bidding war seemed to the studios like an unbelievable Christmas. The British rivals were offering prices that were out of this world. The BSB team would sign up one studio, Sky the next, and then they would fight over the third. Each later blamed the other for pushing the prices into the heavens. BSB people said that Murdoch promised far too much money up front and insisted that, given his newspaper strength in Britain, it was certain he would eventually win the war.

In the end Sky signed up Fox, of course, Orion, Touchstone and Warner Brothers. BSB came away with Paramount, Universal, MGM/United Artists and Columbia. Sky was said to have spent £60 million and BSB £85 million .

The studios were concerned about how the films would be encrypted. Murdoch had originally intended to show films on an "all-advertising-funded" free film channel. The studios were unenthusiastic. Film sales are now such that the studios expect to milk a film at various stages: first of all at the cinema release; then at video release; then pay-TV release, followed by free-TV release; then library release. They were not eager to allow Murdoch to come in ahead of terrestrial TV with a free service to the British, especially if he was spilling it all over the continent of Europe at the same time, as the Astra footprint would do. They insisted that the films had to be broadcast in scrambled form, so that only subscribers with decoders could unscramble them. This meant another level of technology, and expense. Murdoch found and acquired a system from Israel.

The expenditure in Hollywood horrified Murdoch. He also began to worry that the development in Osterley was going too slowly. He summoned Andrew Neil, the editor of the *Sunday Times*, and an enthusiast for the television revolution, to be executive chairman of Sky. For several months Neil held down the two jobs. He said that Sky was chaotic when he arrived and had no sense of urgency. He brought in Jonathan Miller, the *Sunday Times* media correspondent, to be chief of corporate affairs. Miller set up a sign counting down the number of days to lift-off. Neil shouted a lot, moved and dismissed people – and succeeded. By February, the studios were all set up, the equipment was in place, the technicians were trained, and so were the presenters. Four channels were ready to start sending their signals 22,300 miles up to the Clarke Ring above the equator.

This was a technical triumph, and Sky's young staff liked to refer to the proverbial spirit of the Blitz. John O'Loan, the architect of Sky News, recalled:

> I can't remember a lot about our first bulletin to air. We went to air at 1800. We rehearsed all the half hours from ten o'clock in the morning, so the last one we rehearsed was the first one to air. We started bang on 5.30 with the new rehearsal and went to air just before six, so we had about three minutes to turn everything around again and get it set . . . I was numb for about forty minutes. I knew what was happening but it was just like watching a dream.

The only problem was that despite the undoubted success of getting four channels up to the Clarke Ring, there was almost no one watching when the signals came down again as broadcasts. There were virtually no satellite dishes to be had in the shops. This was partly because the unexpected demands by the studios for encryption meant that the Amstrad receivers had to be altered at the last minute. The fact that so much was being broadcast for so few gave rise to much merriment if not scorn among Murdoch's critics. They also mocked the poor quality of the American and Australian game shows and sitcoms on the channels that no one could watch. Still, by getting on the air in February 1989, only eight months after the launch, Murdoch had easily and amply beaten BSB up to the Clarke Ring and down again, and that had been his first objective.

The mockery continued, even though Sky News was a far more substantial undertaking than most of those who loathed Murdoch had predicted or could now believe. It had cost over £40 million to create, its budget for 1989 was £30 million and it attempted to provide news on a twenty-four-hour basis, as CNN was doing in America and, increasingly, around the world. It broadcast fourteen and a half hours of live news each weekday, and, like Fox, it was lean. It had a staff of 260 – ITN, by way of comparison, broadcast six hours each day with a staff of 930 and a budget of £64 million. The money, effort and time put into Sky News reflected its importance in deflecting the criticism that the more populist output of Sky's other channels attracted.

All the time, stories about Sky were vigorously promoted in Murdoch's popular papers. BSB submitted a large dossier of complaints on such cross-media advertising to the Home Office, the Department of Trade and Industry and the Office of Fair Trading, and then conducted and released a poll of Members of Parliament. Eighty per cent of those questioned thought it was undesirable for one proprietor to control newspapers, TV and radio. BSB argued that Sky should be subject to the same provisions of the Broadcasting Bill as applied to the ITV stations; these limited newspaper holdings in British TV stations to 20 per cent. Under pressure the Department of Trade and Industry announced an enquiry, and the News International papers reined back. The *Sunday Times* ran a long interview with Anthony Simmonds Gooding, the chief executive of BSB, and the space given to Sky programmes on the television listings page was reduced. The *Sun* and *Today* continued to boost Sky's rental offer and free trials, but they began to refer to all the Astra channels, not just to Sky alone.

By the summer of 1989 Sky's dishes were in the shops, but hot weather and continually rising interest rates discouraged consumers. There would have been similar problems for BSB, had it been on the air and had its dishes, known as "squarials", been for sale. But none of BSB's equipment was ready, not the dishes, nor the chips, nor the decoders. Their satellite was still on the ground. The D-MAC technology might eventually prove superior to the old-fashioned PAL systems that Sky was peddling, but that was little comfort when it was not available. BSB tried to shrug it off. What did a few months matter in a fifteen-year project? The answer was – "Everything."

Despite lagging at least a year behind Sky, BSB embarked on a £20 million advertising campaign designed to show that it would be much classier than Sky and that consumers should wait for a BSB squarial rather than buy a Sky dish now. "It's smart to be square," proclaimed one poster. Whether the campaign was smart or not was unclear. It certainly helped to sow confusion.

By the second half of 1989, it was clear that BSB was going to need much more cash to get on the air, and a new round of financing got under way. "We have come to regard £400 million as a minimum," commented Ian Clubb, the finance director. "I would like to get more than that as a facility in order to dispel doubts about BSB's viability. We think that overkill on the funding side is good sense. It is a form of insurance." But no insurance could cover the disaster that the two companies were now preparing for each other.

With far too few dishes moving out of the shops, Murdoch decided to "relaunch" Sky. Thousands of dishes were given away to readers whose homes were strategically selected for the copycat effect they might provoke. Then Sky launched its own rental package at the loss-leader price of £4.49 a week. Armies of unemployed doubleglazing salesmen were hired, dressed up in white coats and sent in smart vans on to housing estates all over the country. The combination of saturation promotion through Murdoch's popular papers and aggressive young men on the doorstep was irresistible for many, and rentals began to increase.

The sale of advertising time to companies was a disappointment. No real sales research had been done prior to the launch – Murdoch never believed in it. Throughout 1989 and 1990 Sky was compelled to downgrade the number of viewers it could deliver to advertisers. The Sky advertising department went through dozens of executives, all of whom were dismissed when they failed to achieve what Murdoch and Andrew Neil wanted. No one would say how much advertising Sky had garnered in its first year. Estimates varied from £10 million down to mere thousands. Sky tried to introduce a scheme that had worked well at Fox – that of charter advertisers. A commitment of £4 million spent over two years guaranteed advertisers slots at a fixed rate. In the first year only Beecham and Unilever signed up. Sky was a mess. But so were its competitors, terrestrial as well as satellite, as Murdoch himself was only too keen to point out.

On the last weekend of August 1989, Murdoch and Anna drove from London to Scotland in his Jaguar. His aides later said admiringly that his gearbox had gone and that he had had to do the trip without being able to reverse.

Murdoch's destination was the Edinburgh Television Festival. He had agreed to deliver the MacTaggart Lecture, named after the

Scottish drama director, a distinguished disciple of the public broadcasting ethic which Murdoch abhorred. The theme of this year's festival was "New Television", and Murdoch's speech was the big event.

It was an appropriate moment. That same weekend, Voyager 2, the American spacecraft launched with magnificent self-confidence and skill on its trajectory through the stars, was having its final planetary encounter in its grand tour of the outer solar system. It was passing Neptune, 4.4 billion kilometres from earth, and the pictures and information being sent back were stunning. Scientists at mission headquarters in Pasadena declared that in twenty-four hours they had learned more about Neptune than in the 143 years since the planet was discovered. In a state of some euphoria they talked about "rewriting all the textbooks of the solar system".

Neptune was the last known outpost in the solar system. From now on Voyager's journey was into infinity. Besides it, any other technological achievement was mundane. But that same weekend another "bird" took to the skies. BSB's satellite, Marco Polo 1, a twenty-four-foot "bird", built by Hughes Aircraft, was finally carried aloft to the Clarke Ring.

A few days before Murdoch arrived in Edinburgh, News Corp announced its results for the year ending 30 June 1989, which showed that Sky was losing the company £2 million a week, and had so far cost £75 million since the launch. These daunting figures were not included in that year's accounts; the losses were to be spread over several years. None the less, News International's pre-tax profits had dropped from £88 million to £20.1 million. Interest payments had more than doubled during the year from £61.7 million to £138.6 million.

The stock market still had faith in Murdoch. News shares rose when the results were published. But there was also bad news for Murdoch that day. He failed to break into the Spanish television market, which was reckoned to be one of the fastest-growing and most lucrative in Europe. He had had a 25 per cent stake (the maximum allowed a foreign partner) in Univision, a consortium which included Grupo Zeta, a Barcelona-based newspaper group, and other Spanish concerns. Their bid was unsuccessful. Instead two licences were awarded to groups headed by the Italian Silvio

Berlusconi and by France's Canal Plus. The third went to Antena Tres, an FM radio network in which Barcelona's *La Vanguardia* newspaper was the major shareholder. (However, in 1992, he and Grupo Zeta did manage to buy the Antena 3 station. He was expected to take it into more robust competition with Berlusconi's Tele 5, which had done well promoting game shows and soaps.)

At the same time, Murdoch was concerned that his growing share of the British media was about to come under scrutiny. The Office of Fair Trading had been conducting a preliminary investigation into media ownership of papers and television to see if the issue of media monopoly should be referred to the Monopolies and Mergers Commission. (His enemies said over half of all papers sold in the UK were owned by him. Murdoch himself produced figures to show that he owned about a third.)

Outside the ornate Victorian MacEwan Hall in Edinburgh, the evening air bristled with the first chills of autumn. Young people were darting around handing out flyers for a performance of David Hare's play *Pravda*, which satirized a Murdoch figure's cynical control of British newspapers and his manipulation of politicians. (When the play was first performed at London's National Theatre, Anna Murdoch went with a friend, and decided not to take her husband to see it.)

Waiting for Murdoch inside was row upon row of members of the British television Establishment. He came to the rostrum looking mild and nervous – as he does on such occasions. After praising Adam Smith who, 200 years before, had written *The Wealth of Nations* just a few miles away, Murdoch quietly delivered a forty-minute attack on British television, and the elitism of his listeners: "Much of what is claimed to be quality television here is no more than the parading of the prejudices and interests of like-minded people who currently control it."

Murdoch argued that Britain's public service television had had seriously debilitating effects on British society. Its programmes "are often obsessed with class, dominated by anti-commercial attitudes and with a tendency to hark back to the past". Most television drama, he declared, was "run by the costume department". (This raised an anxious laugh.) "The socially mobile are portrayed as uncaring; businessmen as crooks; moneymaking is to be despised." British television was an "integral part of the British disease, hostile to the sort of culture needed to cure that disease".

Murdoch agreed there was still a place for "public service television" in Britain, but it should be the subservient not the dominant factor. This would liberate broadcasters: "Public service broadcasters here have paid a price for their state-sponsored privileges. That price has been their freedom . . . I cannot imagine a British Watergate or a British Irangate being pursued by the BBC or ITV with the vigour of the US networks."

This was an odd argument. In fact it was American print media which had broken new ground in almost all major US scandals from Watergate on. Murdoch's papers had never been conspicuous in taking on governments, nor had they given much support to such investigative reporting on television as he was suggesting. For example, they had turned their fury upon Thames Television for its investigation of the SAS killings of IRA terrorists in Gibraltar, "Death on the Rock". News International papers had accepted the government's explanation, which the television station had questioned. (One *Sunday Times* reporter, Rosie Waterhouse, protested over the way in which she felt her enquiries were distorted by the paper, and subsequently resigned.)

Perhaps his most extraordinary remark was in comparing the British cultural Establishment to an authoritarian dictatorship. If the market, rather than public service, dominated television, freedom, he argued, would be safer. "The multiplicity of channels means that the government thought police, in whatever form, whether the great and good in Britain, of the jackboot-in-the-night elsewhere, will find it hard to control more and more channels."

He had expected tough questions. There were almost none. The failure of the assembly to defend its position seems more remarkable than Murdoch's intemperance. He must have walked out convinced that the British broadcasting Establishment was even weaker than he had suggested.

There was of course a defence against Murdoch's assault, though no one in Edinburgh had the wit to make it. The BBC and independent television could not rely on the popularity of their programmes for their integrity. They had to be defended as institutions. They had been established on the basis that the market was an inadequate guardian of the viewer's best interests. The BBC in particular had values and traditions that were part of national identity. It has for decades been a national resource, the heartland of politics, culture, literature, news and entertainment.

Murdoch spoke at a time when British broadcasting was under pressure, forced by the convictions of Margaret Thatcher, abetted by Murdoch and his papers, towards the open market. Those who valued the traditions established on both the BBC and independent television, feared that the commercial ethos embraced by Thatcher and Murdoch would drive out much that had been important – the single drama, the investigative documentary, freewheeling public affairs programmes, arts series, and other programmes based on British experience. All these would be replaced by entertainment purchased cheaply off the shelf in international markets. In the Murdoch-Thatcher plan for the future, it would become ever harder to maintain that there existed a separate and necessary public stake in television. Anthony Smith, the broadcasting expert and president of Magdalen College, Oxford, pointed out that from now on the viewer would be "not the Reithian citizen patiently waiting to be informed and entertained, but the Hayekian consumer, whose attention must be grabbed and held minute by minute".

Such fears were already being realized, but to Murdoch, with his contempt for Britain's "decadent society", this was not a problem. His own political and commercial imperatives, often stridently expressed by his newspapers, were utterly opposed to the "elitist" Reithian concept.

Murdoch's Edinburgh attack was fundamental. He was declaring the values of British broadcasters futile, snobbish, paternalistic. Yet no one really challenged him. This was perhaps because his audience was loath to see itself as an Establishment of any kind and was frightened to agree with the BBC's founder, Lord Reith, that there could be a value in institutions which could be described as Murdoch described them. The dilemma in which Murdoch placed his audience was perhaps displayed most charmingly by William Rees-Mogg, the editor of *The Times* whom Murdoch had replaced with Harry Evans. Rees-Mogg said he was not in the minority who had disagreed with the lecture. Yet he was worried about whether national cultures would be preserved in the new enveloping world of communications. "International market forces tend to break down national culture, and indeed Rupert Murdoch can be seen as a powerful agent of that change. Some aspects of these national cultures may be obsolete, some may even be bad, but people have a loyalty to them."

The problem he found most difficult was that of the relationship of market and quality. "The market does, as Mr Murdoch argues, give people what they want, and that is good. But it is a mistake to suppose that what most people want is necessarily what is high-quality. If that were so, Jeffrey Archer would be a better novelist than Jane Austen." Rees-Mogg acknowledged that the market was better than monopoly, "But I do not want the result to be a McDonalds culture, in which television provides the international fast food of the mind."

The scene in Edinburgh demonstrated nothing so much as the power of one man's will. That was impressive. The reaction to that will by the very people it threatened was less so.

Down the road, in a theatre on the fringe of the festival, *Pravda* ironically echoed the Murdoch effect later that night. In the play, the press baron Lambert le Roux (South African not Australian) attacks the English ruling class:

They are the Establishment. They think they have a right. They think they are England. They hate me because I'm an outsider. No Old Boy and Old Chap. I've broken their toys and now there are tantrums. But none of them are manly, none of them have the courage to fight . . . People disgrace themselves around me. Sell their property, emigrate, betray their friends, even before I ask them. Give in. "Oh, he's not as bad as I expected . . ." In England you can never fight because you do not know what you believe.

In the MacEwan Hall that had certainly seemed to be so. Murdoch knew full well what he believed in. He believed that "the McDonalds culture" was an elitist British phrase for the world's freest political and economic system, and that the more of it that could be beamed down from the Clarke Ring the better. "The freeing of broadcasting in this country," he said in Edinburgh, "is very much part of [the] democratic revolution, and an essential step forward into the Information Age."

ASPEN

By the summer of 1989, when News Corp officers marched again from all over the world to Aspen for another briefing from their commander in chief, it was clearer than ever that information was one of the crucial products of the time. The world of media was in turmoil – and the new media were reflecting turmoil around the world as communism began to break apart. It was a year which began with the announcement of a merger between Time Inc and Warner Communications, was savagely punctuated by the live coverage of the massacre of Tienanmen Square, and ended with Sony's takeover of Columbia pictures and the televised revolution in Romania.

It was a frustrating time for Murdoch. "I'm tapped out," he kept saying. Revolutionary changes were taking place, from which he felt excluded, his hands tied by debt.

News claimed that its ratio of debt to equity was 0.98, uncomfortably close to the ceiling of 1:1.1 which the banks had imposed. At the same time, it stated that its interest coverage (ratio of income to interest expense) was down to 1.6. (In 1985 it had been 2.9.) Standard and Poors had warned at the end of 1988 that this left "little margin for error in the company's ability to meet its debt-servicing obligations". In fact, News's figures were optimistic, and depended on Australian accounting rules. Under American rules, the debt to equity ratio would have seemed far worse.

In early March 1989 Murdoch announced the formation of a new company, Media Partners International (MPI). It was immediately dubbed Son of News and was hailed as a typical stroke of Murdoch genius.

The plan was for Media Partners to raise between $1 and $2 billion in a worldwide private placement, with minimum investments of $25 million. News Corp would then transfer its book publishers into the new company. These included Harper and Row, William Collins (it was now clear why he had wanted to buy the whole company), Bay Books and Angus and Robertson in Australia. The sale price would be set by outside appraisal, but was expected to be at least $1 billion. With the infusion of $200 million of News Corp money, this would reduce News Corp's debt by $800 million. Murdoch would retain control of the new company through a ten-year management contract and News Corp's initial 20 per cent stake might go higher. Murdoch would be selling his own assets to himself, using other people's money. Few people would dare even to try such a scheme.

"Son of News" was not an inapposite nickname. Murdoch himself said that his intention was to "start a second News Corporation" and that "the main purpose is not to be stopped from expanding". If the plan worked "it means we aren't tapped out . . . we can go on with everything".

Richard Searby told *The Times* that there were vast opportunities in European media markets and that Media Partners would allow Murdoch to seize them. Stanley Shuman said that the plan "allows Rupert to continue being as aggressive as ever without losing time – the media business is restructuring worldwide and he doesn't want to be sitting on the sidelines while that is happening". This was at the heart of it. Murdoch was approaching his sixtieth birthday. The world was in a state of extraordinary flux and he believed that opportunities had to be grabbed at once. He was not prepared to allow his debt to hobble him.

At first, Media Partners was seen as a brilliant new trick by the great master. The *Financial Times* commented: "The whole venture is a typical piece of Murdoch adroitness: if your own company is too loaded with debt to move, start again with someone else's money."

However, potential investors saw more problems. Murdoch put a great deal of time into Media Partners, travelling in Japan, Australia and Europe, explaining the proposal, answering questions. He found that he was constantly having to reassure institutions that he was not a raider but interested rather in building company values. He and Sarazen found most difficulty in Japan, where banks and institutions seemed to consider the *Sun*'s strictures about the evils of Emperor Hirohito a disincentive to investment.

Other investors also seemed unwilling to make a blind bet on the company. MPI was seen as highly leveraged – and by 1989 debt was beginning to be considered a worry, not a blessing. Moreover, there was a paradox: if News Corp's debt was reduced, then it would seem more attractive than MPI. After all, that was where Murdoch and most of the action would be. By the summer of 1989, he was forced to acknowledge that the idea would not work.

The short rise and fall of Media Partners coincided exactly with the announcement of the controversial and expensive merger between Time Inc and Warner Communications. The deal, announced in March 1989, was a proposal to create the dominant media company of the twenty-first century. The new company would be the biggest entertainment group in the world – $15 billion worth of films, TV programmes, pre-recorded videos, recorded music, magazine and book publishing and cable and pay-to-view television networks.

Murdoch was irritated at not being able to play an active role. He really would like to own Time, he told John Evans, the president of Murdoch Magazines. He wanted the gravitas that ownership of such an American institution as Time Inc would confer: "I want to be at the table and a player when they move the pieces around in America."

Talks had been under way between Time and Warner since 1987. Time Inc was particularly vulnerable. The fabulous creation of Henry Luce and Briton Hadden in 1923, it had become bureaucratic and timid. One of its own internal reports warned in 1988 that it was perceived as "uncreative, overly cautious, investor-driven and risk-averse". The break-up value of its assets was thought to be considerably greater than the value that Wall Street placed on the company through its share price.

The fashionable doctrine of "synergy" was given as one reason for the merger. This was a medical term used to describe a group of muscles working together to produce movement. At the end of the 1980s it was proposed that linking books, video, film, television and other media would create some sort of chain reaction which would reach critical mass and be enormously productive (profitable) for all of them. The vertical integration proposed by the Time–Warner merger was said to represent a whole new level of industry concentration, combining a rich pool of creative talent with just about every possible outlet for distribution and marketing it. Time was the second biggest cable operator in the States, and Warner already produced programming for its new partner. The synergy argument was that the combined Time-Warner would make fabulous profits around the world – for example, from the current deregulation of European TV and also from the vast growing markets in Asia.

In fact synergy turned out to be elusive. And this deal was, in any case, motivated less by the hope of synergistic lift-off than by concerns over corporate survival. It reflected the paranoia caused by the foreign invasion of the US media and entertainment industry. Richard Munro of Time acknowledged, "We see Robert Maxwell and Rupert Murdoch and Bertelsmann and Sony coming into our market and raising hell. We see [the merger] as an opportunity for an American company to get competitive."

In 1980 ten of the twelve biggest media companies in the world had been American-owned. By 1989, after several years of a weak dollar, which had encouraged foreign takeovers, three of the top five were non-American. Nick Nicholas, Time's president, said, "There will emerge on a worldwide basis six, seven, eight vertically integrated media and entertainment conglomerates. At least one will be Japanese, probably two. We think two will be European. There will be a couple of American-led enterprises and we think Time is going to be one of them."

This view was echoed by Steve Ross of Warner. He thought there was only one solution. "Unless American companies join together, there aren't going to be any American media companies. They are all going to be owned by foreign enterprises."

By the end of the decade, there were indeed around half a dozen major media and entertainment companies dominating different parts of the global village and competing with each other as well.

The most prominent were News, Walt Disney, Berlusconi, Bert-elsmann and Sony.

Each of them reflected its own specific history. Murdoch's jigsaw illustrated more the sense of his own frantic odyssey than anything else. Walt Disney had always been an international company with a clearly defined product; it saw the advent of the single market in Europe and other changes as offering huge new opportunities, particularly for its theme parks.

Until the Time-Warner deal, Bertelsmann was the world's largest media company. In addition to its US interests, it had magazines and newspapers in Europe and a West German TV channel, RTL Plus, the first privately-owned TV channel in the country. Bertelsmann's turnover was more than $6 billion. Its invasion of the USA was followed by that of Hachette, which paid $1.2 billion for Grolier, the encyclopaedia publisher, and Diamandis, the magazine giant. Hachette then displaced Time Inc to become the world's largest magazine publisher.

But although the invasion of the Europeans (and the former Australian) seemed threatening, it was the arrival of the Japanese that caused most angst and heart-searching in the United States.

In 1987, the Japanese media hardware manufacturer, Sony, had bought CBS Records for $2 billion; this had left Warner as the last big American record producer ever although, as Steve Ross put it, "this was an industry that America created". Through the first part of 1989 Sony was known to be seeking a film studio – RCA and Columbia were seen as likely targets. Nevertheless, when Sony did buy Columbia, the news was greeted with near hysteria in the United States. Hollywood was at the heart of the American Dream, and the notion that it could be owned by the Japanese seemed to many Americans to be insufferable. As fear of communism receded, with its failure and collapse around the world, it was being replaced by fear or envy of the extraordinary successes of Japan.

Then there was Maxwell. He was still trying to create an international communications company to rival News; in 1988 he had reacted to Murdoch's purchase of Harper and Row with another lunge into the United States. Frustrated in his attempt to buy Harcourt Brace Jovanovich, he finally managed to buy the American publishers, Macmillan, after a bruising fight with some of America's deepest-pocketed investors. Maxwell paid $2.5 billion which, even by the overheated standards of the time, was thought to be hugely expensive. He also paid $750 million for the *Official Airlines Guide*. It was these new debts which his ramshackle and dishonest business was unable in the long run to sustain.

But while most buy-out activity was taking place in the American market at the end of the 1980s, one of the most lavish prizes for the new conglomerates would be in Europe, where the new generation of satellites and deregulation would accompany the creation of a single market in 1992. The prospect of this new goldmine was one important reason why so many foreign companies wanted to buy up American studios – they needed the programming.

The move to television was crucial. Bertelsmann was already well placed in Germany. The flamboyant Silvio Berlusconi owned three commercial television channels in Italy, half a cable network in Germany, and a share of La Cinq, a new commercial channel in France. He was also expanding into Spain. Maxwell was increasing his reach through European cable. Murdoch was pinning his hopes on Sky. The Time-Warner merger showed that American media companies felt the pressure. More and more, media companies were beginning to see that television, not newspapers, would probably be their main source of income in the future.

Ben Badgdikian, a writer on media studies and former dean of the journalism school at Berkeley, warned:

> The lords of the global village have their own political agenda. Together, they exert a homogenizing power over ideas, culture and commerce that affects populations larger than any in history. Neither Caesar, nor Hitler, Franklin Roosevelt nor any Pope, has commanded as much power to shape the information on which so many people depend to make decisions about everything from whom to vote for to what to eat.

The enormous power of the new barons to disseminate the news of the village was being more and more dramatically demonstrated by the speed of political changes.

In the spring of 1989, communist dictatorships were being swept away in both Poland and Hungary and Mikhail Gorbachev's bold reforms were allowing unprecedented freedoms in the Soviet Union. The most dramatic and poignant of these upheavals was taking place in China, where students staged massive peaceful demonstrations in Tienanmen Square round a copy of the Statue of Liberty – their own Goddess of Democracy.

The ensuing massacre, on the night of 3–4 June, happened in what television officials call "real time" – and was the first such event to have been broadcast live. Cable News Network, CNN, gave a constant commentary. At once the slaughter of Tienanmen Square became a part and product of what is called the information revolution – the linking, but perhaps not the binding, of the world by satellite and by other brave new technologies such as the PC and the fax. After the massacre, people evaded Peking's censorship by faxing information into and out of the West.

Murdoch, along with Ronald Reagan, believed that this Information Revolution would be absolutely liberating. Certainly in this case, the impact of the technology was on the side of the oppressed. Murdoch thought, "Watching the events in China on CNN was the most amazing experience; it was an extraordinary moment in history, to know that what was happening in China was happening in part because we were all watching it." He hoped that in the next ten years Fox and Sky would become a major force like CNN.

The same week as Tienanmen, Paramount Communications tried to disrupt the merger between Time and Warner by launching a $10.7 billion takeover bid for Time Inc. Murdoch was not prepared to be left out and, despite the failure of Media Partners, he announced that he too was now looking at ways to intervene. Eventually, neither he nor Paramount succeeded and the Time-Warner merger took place, though at much greater cost to the two companies than they had originally envisaged.

Shortly afterwards, the News Corp colonels assembled in Aspen to discuss global and parochial issues. The weekend was extremely well prepared, with expensively printed booklets and brochures describing people, times and events, and even the weather patterns for the same weekend in the past two years. Participants were given clothes bearing the News Corp logo, and were informed before arrival that "Aspen is a city that requires casual dress. For men, a jacket at dinner is appropriate, but not a tie. For women, slacks will be appropriate at all times during the conference weekend."

The conference was divided into three principal groups. They discussed the synergy to be derived from a multi-media international empire, the impact of new technology, and the image of News together with journalistic ethics. As they talked it became clear that the company worked very differently in each continent where it was based.

Although Murdoch was preoccupied with debt, he was still talking growth rather than consolidation. He emphasized to the gathering of his officers that if they all got another 5 per cent on the bottom line, he could borrow another $2 billion and continue the expansion of his empire.

There was also considerable talk about Sky Television. Dish sales were still slow and the service still losing some £2 million a week. John Evans argued the virtues of cable television over that delivered by satellite, largely on the grounds that cable is much more interactive. Evans believed that the culture of television couch potatoes was a thing of the past and that once fibre-optic links were brought into homes, television would no longer be a mere shadow in the cave. On the other hand, he had to acknowledge that satellites were global in a way that cable never could be.

Grace Mirabella was there as testimony to the speed with which Murdoch moved. In 1988 she had been summarily fired by Condé Nast after years of success as editor of *Vogue*. Murdoch had immediately asked her if she would like to start a new fashion magazine with her own name, Mirabella, as the title. She had agreed, and so, with the minimum of fuss, it had been accomplished. In an organization like Time Inc, for example, starting a new magazine would take years of memos, planning and agony. Murdoch authorized it in moments, and it happened in months.

The editor of *Premiere*, Susan Lyne, had a similar story. She had been on the *Village Voice* when John Evans invited her to create a movie magazine. When she had shown him an early dummy, he had said that she did not need to consult him or Murdoch – they had hired her and trusted her. If her concept did not fly, that would be too bad.

Lyne's husband, George Crile, a liberal journalist who worked for CBS, was astonished by the creative freedom which News employees could enjoy – at least in Murdoch magazines. He saw the weekend as a gathering of local chieftains from around the world, summoned to hear the instructions of their controller. It reminded him of the James Bond novel *Goldfinger*. Crile thought the company was superbly flexible and responsive. One of the debates at Aspen was how to preserve that sense of spontaneity as News grew even larger.

But the issues which dominated the weekend were the image of News Corps and the ethics of journalism. The debates centred around the quality broadsheets versus the tabloids in Britain, and in America, Fox Film against the *Star* and Channel Five's investigative programme, "A Current Affair", and "The Reporters", where the inimitable Steve Dunleavy reigned.

The Hollywood people, led by Barry Diller, were particularly enraged by the tabloid mentality of much of News, and complained that movie stars were not prepared to work for one part of the News empire, while being abused by another. Later there was a report on page six of the *New York Post*, the diary which been a byword for intrusive enquiries when Murdoch had owned the paper, that the two sides almost came to blows at Aspen on this issue. That was an exaggeration.

A typical problem had apparently arisen with Arnold Schwarzenegger. At a time when Diller was trying to persuade the giant star to sign a large contract, the *News of the World* published a story alleging that Schwarzenegger's father had had Nazi connections. Another of those who felt themselves damaged by the tabloids was the actor William Hurt, who had been involved in a disagreeable child support suit. Still another was the comedian Danny DeVito, who had objected to the way in which he had been portrayed on the cover of *Premiere*.

Tabloid journalists in the empire resisted any call for a company-wide standard of ethics, while many of the broadsheet editors demanded that something of the sort was essential. Andrew Neil, the editor of the *Sunday Times*, said he felt that his paper was tarred by association with the *Sun* and the *News of the World*. He complained in particular about the *Sun*'s celebrated libel of Elton John.

After venting his spleen, Barry Diller roared into the mountains on a motorbike. He fell, breaking his ankle, and when he hobbled back, Murdoch said, "I hope none of you did this."

On the last day, there was a plenary session. The proceedings of the working groups were summed up by Irwin Stelzer, a wealthy American economic consultant who wrote a column for the *Sunday Times* and was an increasingly important adviser to Murdoch, as well as an Aspen neighbour. Stelzer said later that he had assembled all the criticisms of the company which had been made over the weekend in order to challenge Murdoch.

It was clear that the speed and ease with which decisions could be reached was one of News's greatest assets and competitive advantages over its rivals. Moreover, the company had access to major sources of capital, which Murdoch was willing to deploy in ventures that other companies might consider risky.

Stelzer put his finger on an important part of the News Corp culture. "Almost everyone in it views himself as a buccaneer; an outrider; an accident waiting to happen to his competitors; and as being involved with a highly unstructured, highly entrepreneurial organization."

On the downside, those same buccaneers were reluctant to criticize. People were afraid to question Murdoch's judgement, for example on such matters as the vast investment in colour presses in Britain and Australia.

The ethics of the company were tied to its image, which was different in each of the continents. It was worst in Britain, where it was seen as too powerful and monolithic, controlled by Murdoch, voicing a strident pro-Thatcher, anti-BBC line. In the States since the sale of the *New York Post*, News Corp and Murdoch had had no serious image problems – except for an emergent concern with "tabloid TV". Without the *Post*, News had no visible political power in the States, unlike in Britain or Australia. (In fact Fox

Broadcasting programmes often did display a political agenda, as in their vendetta against Edward Kennedy.)

The problem was that the papers which caused most of the problems also provided most of the money. Stelzer pointed out: "If there were no *Sun* and no *News of the World*, there would almost certainly be no *Times*, which when acquired was losing almost £50 million annually. And there would certainly be no Aspen meeting."

He suggested there were ways of alleviating the difficulty without "neutering" the tabloids, an idea which would have been anathema to Murdoch. A 5 per cent improvement in their accuracy could lead to a 95 per cent improvement in their image. There should be more UK citizens in top positions in News Corp, and more constructive answering of criticisms. This proposal was directed especially against Kelvin MacKenzie, who was famous for his bunker mentality.

There was disagreement as to how "the Murdoch problem" should be addressed. Stelzer recounted that officers at Aspen felt that if their leader would appear more often in public, "the Murdoch image problem" would disappear: he was so transparently decent and modest that he would win friends everywhere. However, the more cynical among them felt that "the liberals" in the press and television around the world were so irredeemably hostile that this would be a waste of Murdoch's time.

In his reply, Murdoch took the side of the tabloids, where both his heart and his pocketbook resided. "This is a media corporation. We are into news," he said. "There are two kinds of newspaper. There are broadsheets and there are tabloids. Or, as some people say, there are the unpopular and the popular newspapers."

That had always been his view. He still insisted that "downmarket" was the snob's word for "popular" and that elitist intellectuals spent altogether too much time denigrating the appeal of popular papers. But Aspen '89 demonstrated that News was no longer an overwhelmingly newspaper company. The British papers, the *Sunday Times*, the *Sun* and the *News of the World*, still sustained the rest of the empire, but Murdoch's focus was on electronic means of communication – especially film and television. Once more, Rupert Murdoch was reinventing himself, and as a result of Aspen '89 he started to try to present to the world a more responsive and responsible face.

ADELAIDE

Late in the evening of 9 October 1989, after an early dinner with his editors and associates in Melbourne, Rupert Murdoch flew back to where it all began, to Adelaide. Next day was the Annual General Meeting of News Corporation, which was still registered in the capital of South Australia.

Murdoch flew by private plane, half-owned by News. He had to: there was a national pilots' strike against Ansett and Australian Airlines, the country's two carriers. Murdoch's papers – 60 per cent of all those in Australia – had been fierce in their denunciation of the strike. Only *The Australian* had been a little more muted – its editor, Frank Devine, took a libertarian view which proposed that the pilots should be allowed to get whatever the free market would allow, and the government should not intervene.

As Murdoch arrived, the editor of the *Adelaide Review*, a tiny free sheet which was the Murdoch press's only competition in the city, and which attempted a spiky confrontation with News Corp's might, asked a visitor, "Do you smell a certain effulgence in the air?

"Rupert is here," he said. "Lucifer has come trailing smoke and sulphur."

The AGM was to take place in the tall, almost brand-new, pink tower of the Hyatt Regency, close by the fine railroad station. It stood exactly opposite the little white building of the *Adelaide News*, in which Rupert Murdoch had assumed his inheritance on the death of his father, and whence he had begun to build his empire, some thirty-five years previously. Now the *News* building, dwarfed by modern commercial blocks along North Terrace, was locked up and defunct. Murdoch had had to sell the *News* when he had bought the Melbourne *Herald*, which owned the other Adelaide paper, the broadsheet *Advertiser*. The *News* was now owned by Northern Star, though it was still published on the *Advertiser*'s presses.

By 11.25 there were around 100 people in the conference room, many of them brokers or from the press. There were probably only about sixty shareholders. Some were elderly retainers of the Murdoch empire who had worked for many years for Rupert and for his father before him, and had done well out of their shares. An original shareholder who had bought 100 of the original News shares at A$2 each in 1922, and had taken up every share issue since then, would have had 92,880 News Corp shares worth almost A$1 million by the end of 1988 in return for a total outlay of merely A$3,000 – which would itself have been covered many times by dividends.

News men in old tweeds, or in navy blazers with brass buttons, old retainers and shareholders, were proud of the company and of Murdoch. One elderly journalist said that his shares, first purchased in an employee option scheme in the 1950s, were now worth some two and half million Australian dollars (roughly two million US dollars). That should take care of the grandchildren, he said with sheer delight.

Anna Murdoch, wearing a simple, smart black dress with gilt buttons, came into the room and sat at the front. Close by were the two principal financial geniuses of News, the solid figure of Mervyn Rich, who had conjured with Murdoch's finances since 1960, and the dark, tough-looking man with curly hair, Richard Sarazen, who did so today. Both men understood well the importance of the Adelaide connection for News.

News Corp's figures were virtually impossible for a layman to understand. They skated and slipped between US and British and Australian accounting rules, with the same items described and evaluated differently in each place. There were about 400 different business units within the News Corp empire. Some were shell companies, but all had some purpose. Sarazen was now the man who shuffled them like cards, who pulled silk scarves out of sows' ears, and who put rabbits into hats and drew out peacocks.

An Italian American from Brooklyn, he had sometimes been described as the "invisible" man behind Rupert Murdoch. He was one of the handful of men who subsumed their own ego to that of the boss, and on whom Murdoch had relied completely throughout the recent years of hectic, helter-skelter growth. Sarazen was the man who provided the technical back-up to a dream, the know-how for a scheme. Thus in the summer of 1988, Murdoch called Sarazen one morning at his Upper East Side apartment, and, according to Sarazen, said, "I'm going to spend $3 billion for *TV Guide*. Where do you think you can get it?"

Sarazen replied, "Give me an hour." In fact he needed a day. By the end of it he had lined up verbal promises of $2 billion in Europe and $1 billion in the US. These were formalized into written agreements within the week.

Sarazen had joined News America as chief financial officer in 1974. "Murdoch," Sarazen would say simply, "is a genius." He thought, "The beautiful thing about working for Murdoch is that when mistakes are made, he never kicks the dog and says you recommended it." He had the same radical conservative philosophy as Murdoch. "If we criticize the rest of the world for inefficient bureaucratic government that may destroy the Western world, you can put the same criticism on bureaucratic US businessmen who are worried about jobs, position and doing poison pill deals. They don't give a stuff about US shareholders. They're selfish and inefficient."

Throughout the 1980s Sarazen had retained his wizard's touch. Some of his methods were made possible by the fact that, despite the growth of a global economy, there were still no internationally accepted rules of accounting. Few countries offered such lax or tolerant rules as did Australia – and the differences between Australian and American practices enabled News Corp to steal marches on its competitors.

Unlike the United States, Australia and Britain allowed a firm to revalue its intangible assets periodically. As a result News Corp could add its intangibles, like newspaper titles, to its balance sheet as assets, instead of gradually writing them off as almost all other countries, including the United States, required.

Australia also did not require a company to amortize the goodwill of any company it acquired. American firms had to do so, which meant that their earnings were hit when they made a purchase.

Australia allowed a company to add preference shares to stockholders' equity. American rules did not – in the United States such shares were classified as debt.

Australian rules allowed companies to capitalize interest payments on loans for investments. Under American rules such interest would be deducted from current earnings. This of course produced quite the opposite effect on earnings. By American rules, the Australian procedure overstated profits, assets and therefore equity.

In America, net operating losses were listed as extraordinary items. In Australia, they were viewed as a reduction of income tax expenses, and so the company viewed them as earnings. This tended to inflate reported profits, because the interest was not being charged to the operators.

In Australia non-current equity shares were stock held for long-term investment. News Corp did not recognize any paper losses in such stock. Thus, for example, it ignored fluctuations in the price of its shares in Pearson and Reuters. Under US rules, such falls would be treated as a reduction in shareholders' equity.

In 1989 one American commentator, Allan Sloan, proposed: "Sarazen's secret is that he treats financial reporting as a game to be won, rather than an obligation to be met. Instead of reacting to what regulators want, as most CFOs are wont to do, Sarazen forces them to react to him." This was exactly how Murdoch had always behaved.

In Australia, as the law allowed, Sarazen treated preferred stock as equity for the sake of the balance sheet. In the States, he was entitled to call it debt, and was therefore able to deduct the dividends from income tax. In the fabulous 1980s it became common practice for Australian companies to write up the value of their media properties in order to improve the balance sheet as if by magic. That legitimate wheeze began with Sarazen and News.

News Corp was a South Australian corporation. It had American Depositary Receipts (ADRs), traded on the New York Stock Exchange, which meant that US investors could buy News Corp just like any other stock. American shareholders were sent the glossy annual report of the Australian company. With it came a leaflet which was supposed to translate the Australian figures into officially accepted American terms. Naturally this package met American reporting standards but much significant information for American stockholders was contained in rather more obscure documents, such as financial reports filed by Fox Television or Twentieth Century-Fox with the Securities Exchange Commission.

For example, in several years in the 1980s, News generated substantial profits from currency speculation, little short of gambling. This was acknowledged in one line in the annual report and in the footnotes of the News America's 10K form filed with the SEC. It was not mentioned in the ADR leaflet at all. In other years, News Corp had lost money on the foreign exchange markets because of the decline in the Australian dollar. These trades were shown as extraordinary losses, which made it hard to understand why the 1986 profits were treated as income. Sarazen's answer was that currency spot trading was a profit centre.

Sarazen liked to use only banks who understood News Corp well. "If a bank wants to lend us $50 million tomorrow, we won't take it unless we're satisfied it knows we're a very complicated company with a lot of cross-ownerships and complicated flows of money." The bank also had to accept Sarazen's clever global accounting practices, and the fact that News Corp would not secure loans with its own holdings and would brook very few restrictive covenants. In the end it often seemed as if News Corp were doing the bank a favour by agreeing to borrow money. At the end of 1989, News Corp still had an unused credit line of $1.8 billion to draw upon if it wished.

Sarazen explained that the banks remained loyal because, "Regardless of where we borrow, ultimately the parent company guarantees virtually all the debt of all subsidiaries." In 1989 there were about 110 banks associated with and supportive of News Corp. They could expect good treatment from Murdoch, but he demanded quick responses from them. Thus in September 1989, when he suddenly (and briefly) attempted to bid for MGM/USA Communications, his bankers had to dash to their starting blocks. In the event, his interest lapsed.

Just as News used to inflate its assets and earnings so it used its international structure to minimize its tax liabilities. This was done by establishing what were technically legitimate paper companies in tax haven countries and washing profits through them, and by arranging affairs in Australia, the US and the UK to suit best the tax situation in each one of them.

Of the three, Australia had the highest corporate tax rate and had tended to do so over the years. The rate for the 1987–8 financial year was 49 per cent, well above the rates in the US, UK and Hong Kong at the time. It was reduced to 39 per cent as from 1 July 1988.

Australia's accounting standards meant that Murdoch was not forced to reveal a great deal about his financing. Sarazen could book a lot of the loans for News operations outside Australia to his Australian operations. This reduced the profits from his Australian operations – and even actually produced losses – so that his tax bill was reduced in what was the highest significant tax-paying country of operation.

News's annual reports showed a breakdown of operating profits in each of the three major areas before allocation of interest. Interest was shown as one figure for all the international operations. However, the losses reported by News Limited in the financial year to June 1988 (a year in which the Australian operations did very well) suggested that something like the allocation of overseas loans to offset his Australian profits had occurred.

This was where tax shelter companies like News Corp Cayman Islands, created in spring 1989, came in. The Cayman Islands subsidiaries could make loans to other News Corp subsidiaries in high-tax countries, such as Australia. News Corp Cayman made large profits but paid very little tax – because tax was not what the Caymans were for.

In 1989, News Corp Cayman issued $600 million guaranteed preference shares in three denominations, convertible into shares in Reuters or Pearsons. The reason, according to News Corp's deputy finance director, Dave DeVoe, was that it was tax-efficient. There were no corporate taxes in the Cayman Islands and the preferred shares could be treated as equity under Australian accounting procedures. Moreover, the rates were better than in the US. And finally, Sarazen had worked in a repeat of his scheme with the 1986 Fox preferred shares; if these funds were lent to an American subsidiary they would be regarded as debt, but by lending them to News International, the British company, News Corp could include the issue as shareholders' equity and reap a tax deduction.

By 1989, News Corp's technique of revaluing its "intangible assets" under the Australian Generally Accepted Accounting Principles was causing more concern to some American analysts. A report from Prudential Bache Securities showed that in 1988 News Corp revalued its intangibles upwards by $1.3 billion. This, the report claimed, resulted in shareholders' equity being overstated by 22.8 per cent as of June 1988. Moreover, under Australian rules, News Corp's profit increased in 1988; under American rules, it decreased.

The way in which the company exploited all possible tax breaks was well demonstrated in the case of the *South China Morning Post*. Murdoch had bought it for US$230 million (HK$1.79 billion) in March 1987. Through a Hong Kong vehicle named Asher Holdings, the *Post* immediately became a subsidiary of News Publishers Bermuda, which was in turn wholly owned by News Corp of Adelaide. In June 1987, News Publishers sold "the entire publishing business" – that is, the titles of the *Post* and *Sunday Post* – to a new Hong Kong-registered company called SCMP Publishers. SCMP Publishers bought the fixed assets of the old South China Morning Post Ltd for almost HK$46 million. Second it bought the titles of the daily and Sunday papers for HK$1.82 billion. According to the *Far Eastern Economic Review*, SCMP Publishers borrowed the cash from a shell company called South China Morning Post Finance which was a direct subsidiary of Murdoch's Bermudan vehicle, News Publishers. South China Morning Post Finance then borrowed the HK$2 billion from the banks and SCMP Publishers guaranteed these loans.

The beauty of this scheme was first that the "transfer" went straight to the bottom line of SCMP Publishers in Hong Kong. Registering a loss for tax purposes of HK$1.82 billion enabled Murdoch to make substantial claims against his Hong Kong taxes. Then SCMP Publishers had to pay interest to SCMP Finance. The interest payments were also claimed against tax. As a result of all this, the *Post* paid no tax in the three years after Murdoch took control of it, except for relatively small amounts still owed by the previous management.

Murdoch's tax situation was highlighted in Australia in a report by the House of Representatives Standing Committee on Finance and Public Administration tabled in May 1989. The report, entitled "Tax Payers or Tax Players?", found that News Corporation was the second biggest Australian avoider of tax as defined by the percentage of profits which were washed through tax havens. To be fair to News Corp, the percentage also included profits earned from its operations in Hong Kong, which was classed as a tax haven in the study.

The report found that all of News Corporation's profits of A$387.9 million for 1987–8 were earned through tax havens. The 1988 annual report showed that four subsidiaries of News Corporation in the Netherlands Antilles recorded profits of $149 million while another three in Bermuda recorded another $165 million.

These tax haven profits were in stark contrast to the losses made by three of Murdoch's most important operating companies in high-tax countries. News Limited, incorporated in South Australia, made a loss of over A$202 million; News International, London, made a loss of A$322 million in the UK; and Fox Inc, incorporated in the USA, made a loss of A$213 million.

Looking again at the 1988 figures, it seemed that the gross income from News Corporation's operations and the equity accounted profits from its associated companies (i.e. those in which News had less than 51 per cent, the major one being Ansett) were A$575.6 million in the year to June 1988. Tax paid on this by News Corp and its subsidiaries was A$52.9 million. Income tax paid by associated companies was A$49.9 million. Thus the total tax paid was $103 million. This represented a rate of 17.8 per cent, compared to the Australian corporate tax rate at the time of 49 per cent and a UK rate of 35 per cent.

News Corp declined the committee's request to comment on such findings and merely suggested to the committee: "There [are] a number of complex issues which would need to be examined to ensure that there is a balance between immediate changes in tax regimes and longer-term benefits accruing to the Australian economy from companies with significant global operations."

Just before half past eleven, Murdoch arrived at the Adelaide Hyatt for the AGM. He came into the conference room carrying a tan leather briefcase and looking slightly harassed, diffident, stooping. Wearing his customary dark blue suit, he walked up from the back, greeting old employees, shaking hands, remembering every name. He sat down to take notes while the chairman of News, Richard Searby, QC, opened the meeting.

Searby might well have been Chief Justice of Australia had he not agreed to his old friend Rupert's request that he become chairman of the group. Now he warned shareholders of the high level of interest rates, which had had a severe impact on advertising revenues in both the US and the UK, and told them of the losses incurred by Sky Television. So far it had cost about A$150 million and was now losing some A$4 million a week.

When Murdoch got up to speak, he wiped his handkerchief over his mouth and cleared his throat. In contrast to Searby's lithe figure, he looked crumpled and his voice was thinner and softer than Searby's. He spoke hesitantly.

Murdoch's family company, Cruden Investments Pty Ltd, still owned just under 50 per cent of the News Corp ordinary shares. Cruden's directors were Murdoch himself, his mother Dame Elisabeth, his three sisters, Kayarem Pty Ltd (Murdoch's own personal investment company) and Jack Kennedy, a retired accountant who had been associated with the family since 1947. Cruden's A shareholders had one vote for every share. The B shares had one vote for every ten shares. Of 700 million or so A shares, Murdoch controlled 287 million through Kayarem. On Sir Keith's death two trusts were established which held another 362 million A shares; the beneficiaries of these trusts were Dame Elisabeth, Rupert and his three sisters, and the sisters' children. (Rupert's own children were taken care of elsewhere in the complicated skein of family companies.) Dame Elisabeth and her daughters also held both A shares and B shares in their own names.

Rupert Murdoch told the Annual General Meeting that the

media were becoming more and more central to the functioning of the world – and that meant more valuable. However, under pressure to be realistic, his short-term message was not cheerful. The magazines were doing well, but Twentieth Century-Fox was "quite frankly . . . having a bad year". Not enough films, poor management. But next year would be better. Fox Television, on the other hand, was already going well, thanks to an increase in advertising revenues.

Sky Television, he said, "was our largest risk undertaking, perhaps ever". He blamed the high costs in good part on BSB for forcing up the price of "the product" – by which he meant the films which Sky had bought to transmit to viewers in England. "But that's life." The sale of dishes had been slow so far, but was now picking up. As for the new Sunday papers in Melbourne, they too were doing less well than had been expected. Generally, economic conditions around the world were "softer" and the company's revenues "are not what we expected".

He ended by thanking Richard Searby for his wise counsel, "and for keeping me out of trouble from time to time". As he sat down, he looked and sounded exhausted.

Searby asked the meeting if there were any questions. There was a short silence. No one stood. No one raised a hand. There were no questions.

The accounts were accepted unanimously, and the directors, who included Barry Diller, the head of Fox, and Charles Wick, the former head of the US Information Agency, a man who had helped Murdoch to forge close relations with the White House, were re-elected unanimously.

Within thirty-five minutes the meeting was over, completed without a murmur. In closing, Searby thanked the shareholders for coming, and invited them to have some refreshments.

Murdoch dived into another room for his favourite business tool – the telephone – while the shareholders accepted champagne, orange juice or beer at the bottom of the stairs to the lobby. George Main, an old Morse code and telex operator from the Adelaide *News*, recalled how he had bought News shares in 1955. He now had about 20,000 – worth some A$300,000, thanks to

Rupert Murdoch. Rex Clark, a photo engraver of the same vintage, nodded enthusiastically. Each man adored him.

Anna Murdoch was talking to Mrs Searby and Mrs Rich about the widows of powerful men. Many people believed that if Murdoch died, Anna would take over the empire – as regent for their three children, Elisabeth, Lachlan and James. Of the three, Elisabeth seemed the most eager to take over the family business.

After lunch Murdoch went off to see the State Premier, who had asked, as almost all politicians did, whether Murdoch could spare him a moment. Piers Akerman, the editor of the *Advertiser*, had warned Murdoch that the Premier would have several complaints about the paper, and when Murdoch returned to the office, he said that Akerman had predicted them correctly. He saw the key advertising staff on the paper and impressed them with his knowledge of what was going well and what not. A quick visit to the newsroom, where he delighted people by remembering their names – and then he was gone.

It was left to Richard Searby to round off the day, as guest of honour at a legal dinner at the Hilton. He made a rather cryptic speech in which he discussed the problems of citizenship and international businesses such as News. He ended by referring to Athens in the fifth century BC: "Alcibiades, a real mover and shaker, was ostracized and Socrates was sentenced to death." This classical reference was unclear. Could it be that these were Rupert Murdoch's role-models? Searby did not say.

Meanwhile, Lucifer, or Alcibiades or Socrates – or Rupert – had soared away again, to Sydney, to London, to New York, to Los Angeles, his visit to the financial heart of the empire completed in twenty-four hours.

Chapter 14

THE EVIL EMPIRE

In the evening of 21 January 1990, a Gulfstream executive jet circled in the dark over Bucharest. The passengers could see no lights, no sign of an airport, let alone of a town. Less than a month had elapsed since the execution of the Ceauşescus, still less since the end of the bloody resistance by Ceauşescu's secret police.

As the plane taxied to a halt, the passengers and crew stared into the darkness. At first there was nothing. "It was like landing on the moon," said one of them later. And then they saw dozens of headlights stabbing towards them through the dark. It felt a bit like a round-up and, remembering the brutal fighting in the streets of Bucharest only a few weeks earlier, some of those on board wondered whether they should not take off again at once.

When the door was opened and the steps lowered, the plane was surrounded by men in thick coats and fur hats. Above the headlights, TV arc lights were switched on. As the passengers descended they were smothered in unexpected embraces. Nothing like that had happened in Warsaw, in Prague, or in Budapest, from which they had just flown. But this was Latin Romania. And the man stepping out of the plane was Rupert Murdoch, entering into yet another battlefield in his lifelong war to become communications czar of the world.

The collapse of communism in Eastern Europe in the closing months of 1989 was one of the most startling upheavals in recent history. Murdoch believed the communications revolution had destroyed communism. "Eastern Europe," he had declared in a speech in Washington in 1988, "will be opened up by television, which in turn will certainly change the lives of tens of millions of

482

peoples. Global communications will prove to be the biggest cata-
lyst for peaceful coexistence. Perhaps that is already happening."

He thought that as an immigrant to America he could more
easily recognize a great truth: "Modernization is Americanization.
It is the American way of organizing society that is prevailing in
the world." What Murdoch perhaps failed to recognize was the
fear and alarm that this undoubted truth could provoke in many
societies. The only fear he had was of an "atavistic, authoritarian
response. This is the real danger in the present revolution. We
might be panicked by future shock into one of the inappropriate
and regressive schemes of regulation that are always lurking
about."

His tour of the battlefields had begun in Warsaw. The party
was not large. First there was Anna, who on this trip through the
debris behind the Iron Curtain was said to be collecting material
for a new novel. She had recently become a member of the board
of News Corp.

After the Murdochs, the most senior member of the News
organization on the flight was John Evans, whom Murdoch had
now made vice president for corporate development. Evans was
the man who decided which dark caves of the future Murdoch
should try to explore. He liked to see the new world just over the
horizon as a communications heaven, one in which all old orders
would change for ever.

Also aboard was Rafael Pastore. Hungarian by descent, Pastore
was now assigned to Murdoch's new "hit team", a group designed
to look at opportunities in Eastern Europe. (Until now, Murdoch
had resisted owning papers which he could not himself read and
that meant papers which were published in any language other
than English.) Another member of this "hit team" was Pio Cabin-
illas, a lawyer with News Corp in New York.

There was also John O'Loan, editor of Sky News, one of the
four channels on Sky, and Peter Smith, an engineer from Adelaide
who had known Murdoch ever since the 1950s and who had
worked for him for about six years, setting up new systems at Sky
and elsewhere. Finally, and perhaps most surprisingly, there was
Kelvin MacKenzie, the editor of the *Sun*, whose sense of comedy
had his fellow travellers rolling in the narrow aisle of the plane.

He did constant impersonations of Andy Capp, the working-class cartoon hero, and would frequently knock ash off the end of an imaginary cigarette cupped in his hand as he delivered a homily on the way of the world.

This expeditionary force flew out of London to Warsaw on 18 January, carrying dozens of boxes, each containing one of the newest and most useful pieces of communications technology – a fax machine. Other boxes were filled with coffee. All these were presents for those they were to meet. At Warsaw airport they were greeted by a young Polish journalist, Radek Sikorski, who later became deputy defence minister. Sikorski took them to the Marriott, a new and especially luxurious hotel, catering for the international business traveller and upmarket tourists who were doing so much to homogenize the world.

After a lunch with young journalists, many of whom had been dissidents, Murdoch and his group were taken to the printing works of the paper *Zycie Warszawy*. The presses and all the machinery had a tired, prematurely dead look about them. It was clear that, along with much of the plant of Eastern Europe, they needed to be replaced.

Until now, most of Poland's papers had been associated with the Communist Party, and were subsidized by the state. The Solidarity government's new economic policy had now opened the country to the world market, and the price of newsprint was hiked up 500 per cent. Hundreds of papers and magazines were threatened with closure. The party paper, formerly *Tribune of the People*, was now renamed *Tribune*. It had increased its sports coverage, abandoned its dogmatic line and was even carrying advertisements – from private house builders – on the front page.

That evening, the Murdoch party dined off roast pig in a private restaurant with officials from Polish television which, like the newspapers, was in some turmoil. The Poles wondered if Murdoch would like the station that used to broadcast in Russian. Murdoch was cautious.

After dinner, John Evans looked out of the window of his fifteenth-floor room in the Warsaw Marriott, through the grey-brown haze of coal dust and other carbons which had made

Eastern Europe into one of the most vilely polluted regions of the world. It seemed to him like a terrifying scene from the science fiction film *Blade Runner*. "There we were in our fur coats seeking out business opportunities in the middle of this nightmare. It was either sci-fi or Wagner."

Next day, they flew on to Prague, one of the most beautiful cities in Europe and, since the Soviet invasion of 1968, one of the saddest. After the communists had finally been overthrown at the end of 1989, Vaclav Havel, the country's new democratic President, said that they had used the people as mere rivets in a thrashing, smoking machine with no obvious purpose.

In January 1990 there seemed to be more satellite dishes on the sides of houses and apartments in Prague than were to be seen in the West. People spoke of how important CNN and then Sky News had become as alternative sources of information to those controlled by the government. Videos were also important. Before the revolution, an underground group called Video Journal had distributed samizdat video tapes documenting the work of the opposition. Now, as in Poland, the communists had lost their control of the newspaper industry and the plunge into the free market had begun.

Murdoch and Anna had lunch with the American Ambassador, Shirley Temple Black, who had been a vigorous supporter of Vaclav Havel and other dissidents. Before leaving, Murdoch gave an interview to a journalist from *Lidove Noviny*, which was fast becoming one of the most popular papers in Prague. It had been one of the best papers in Czechoslovakia between the wars, but after the communist takeover in 1948 it was banned. It had started again in January 1988 as a samizdat, underground monthly but now that the communists were gone, it was openly published.

Quoting Ronald Reagan, Murdoch told the paper that the events in Eastern Europe "are the last chapter in the history of the evil empire. It is one of the most hopeful moments in history."

Reminded that he used to be a liberal and even sported a bust of Lenin at Oxford, Murdoch replied, "I was young and even had other hare-brained ideas." He agreed with the maxim that a man who is not a socialist at twenty has no heart, while one who is still a socialist at forty has no head, adding:

But I have always been of the opinion that it is extremely important that everyone should have the same chance, the same opportunity ... A really first-rate society must not close the door to anyone.

When I was young I was of the opinion that everything that we want to achieve must be absolutely perfect. Nowadays I know that nothing in this world is perfect, that we only have to aim for the best possible. Real democracy must have both economic and political substance; one cannot exist without the other.

Murdoch was one of several Western publishers seeking investment opportunities in Eastern Europe. Wherever he went, the man whom some saw as his alter ego had gone before. Eastern Europe had long been a stamping ground of Robert Maxwell. His company Pergamon had had a monopoly on many Soviet scientific texts, and Maxwell had contracted a great deal of printing work out to Eastern Europe, where the rates were considerably cheaper than in the West.

But commerce was never enough for Maxwell. He also had to try to be a part of the ruling class wherever he was, and had made it his business to fawn upon the dictators of Eastern Europe. One way of doing this was to publish articles about his own encounters with them in the *Mirror*. He also published biographies and books of their speeches in the West.

He had praised General Jaruzelski and condemned Solidarity in Poland. He had serenaded the Czechoslovak President Gustav Husak, who had crushed the Prague Spring of 1968 and imprisoned Vaclav Havel, as "this impressive man" who "had brought stability and economic progress to his country".

The title of the book he had published on the Bulgarian despot was *Todor Zhivkov: Statesman and Builder of Modern Bulgaria*. In its foreword he wrote that the book was intended to show the Bulgarian people's "heroic struggle ... to build a prosperous and happy nation under the leadership of the Bulgarian Communist Party and its General Secretary Todor Zhivkov".

"What has, in your opinion, made you so popular with the Romanian people?" he had asked Nicolae Ceauşescu in an interview included in *Ceauşescu: Builder of Modern Romania and International Statesman*, published in Pergamon's "World Leaders" series (general editor Robert Maxwell).

By 1990, with the Soviet empire in collapse, other men might have been abashed by such a record of servility to dictators now dead or deposed. But Maxwell had no shame. He was now trawling the new democratic Eastern Europe for investment opportunities as energetically as he had when his former friends had been in power, and somewhat to Murdoch's chagrin, he was being welcomed back. From Prague, Murdoch's plane made the short flight to Hungary. At the airport in Budapest, they were met by the Hungarian representative of News Corp – Peter Toke, the editor of the weekly newspaper *Reform*, and the daily *Mai Nap*. On an earlier visit in 1989, Murdoch had already agreed to buy these two newspapers and had thus become the first Westerner to acquire a significant investment in the new free press of Eastern Europe. Indeed, the signing of the final documents was the original reason for this whole trip.

Reform had the sort of popular pizzazz that Murdoch liked, a splashing colour tabloid featuring an endless parade of nudes along with stories on political corruption and reform. Soft-porn stars, the Princess of Wales, the legacy of the Hungarian Revolution, and Soviet responsibility for the Katyn massacre were all topics in one issue. Toke described himself as "the Magyar Murdoch", and had persuaded the American one to invest in his paper.

Now, when they went into the newspaper's office, said Anna Murdoch, "there was something very familiar" there. "It was an old dress boutique turned into an office. They'd hung a wonderful Hungarian flag, and they're very lively, very interested in things, being journalists. That was really very exciting. You felt: this is really going to work."

Murdoch flicked through some of the recent back numbers. According to Peter Smith, he actually criticized some of the naked women, whose poses were more explicit than those on page three of the *Sun*. Murdoch said he liked to distinguish between pretty girls and sex.

With the contracts for *Reform* and *Mai Nap* duly signed, they flew off again, on the evening of Sunday 21 January, further towards the east.

Anna Murdoch later said that the landing in Bucharest was "surreal". Describing the darkness and the snow, she said, "It was just like a Le Carré novel. These cars just came across the ice towards the plane, with TV lights etc, most of the Romanian men with heavy fur hats on and beards. It was marvellous."

The next morning they were taken to Ceauşescu's home, a suburban villa where the bathrobes were still in cupboards, the toothpaste tubes still in the bathroom, and papers were still in his office.

They went also to an orphanage. This was largely Anna's idea and she found it moving. "Little children were running up to any woman saying, 'Mama, mama,' putting their hands around your legs. Very sad. I asked them about the selling of babies to the West. The doctor in charge said: we are not selling children; all the money given went to pay lawyers' fees."

Anna found the whole city extraordinary. "It was amazing to see young soldiers the age of my son with AK47s, clicking the bolts and listening to rock music," she said. "Only one little incident need take place and they'd blow up. It was very nerve-wracking. And very sad."

They went to the television station, where bullet holes and broken glass were everywhere. This was where the revolution had been fermented. The station was seized by the revolutionaries and from tiny Studio Four, extraordinary exhortations and events were broadcast continuously to the nation after the dictator's fall. Often a helmeted soldier stood with his rifle behind the announcer. Over and over, the people of Bucharest were asked to come and protect the television station from Ceauşescu's armed supporters. All in all, it was the classic type of television-led revolution that Murdoch might have dreamed.

But in its wake came the threat of another kind of mayhem. After Murdoch picked his way around the smashed building, he offered them access to Sky News and sport. A senior broadcasting official told him that that was not enough – what they really wanted was a powerful transmitter to beam their programming to ethnic Romanians in Soviet Moldavia. "We must get them back. The last ounce of blood into our country."

As the world is homogenized by just such organizations as News, nationalism may well become one of the overwhelming, killing forces of the twenty-first century.

On the evening of 22 January Murdoch and his party boarded the Gulfstream again to fly back to the West. They were suffering from culture-shock. It seemed clear to them all, particularly to Murdoch, that working in the new Eastern Europe would be commercially difficult.

Murdoch believed that, in the war against communism, Western businessmen deserved much more praise than intellectuals and journalists who had too often given the communists the benefit of the doubt. "There is now no social model anywhere on earth," he said, "to compete with that developed in the English-speaking world . . . [It] is composed of popular elections, limited government, a rule of law, private property, and free markets." For three generations it had been derided as mere "bourgeois democracy" by journalists, politicians and "chatterers", who also insisted that socialism worked and its people had better values.

"At least, that was what I learned and believed at Oxford and at Geelong Grammar. But it was all lies. Many people were clear-sighted enough to know, but only a few people were courageous enough to say so and suffer the exclusion and derision of the chattering classes."

They landed in Milan, where they were to meet Sylvio Berlusconi, another lord of the global information village. His lavish eighteenth-century villa outside the city was, said John O'Loan later, "a lot more tasteful than Ceauşescu's house".

Berlusconi was a man whom Murdoch admired and must to an extent have envied. He owned the fourth largest private television network in the world after CBS, NBC and ABC; one of the largest of Italian stores, Standa, which had 400 outlets; 305 cinemas; the rights to a huge library of Hollywood classics; and a football team, AC Milan. His company, Fininvest, had an annual turnover of $11 billion.

When Murdoch came to lunch, Berlusconi was involved in a

bitterly fought battle to take over Mondadori, Italy's greatest publishing house and the owner of the country's most important independent paper, *La Repubblica*. He was close to victory, and the deal would make him the most significant power-broker in Italy.

Murdoch was often said to have an intimate political relationship with Margaret Thatcher, but it was nothing compared to that existing between Berlusconi and Bettino Craxi, the former socialist Prime Minister of Italy. Like Thatcher, Craxi championed "independent" press and television. That meant market-led television, which in turn tended to mean the whittling away of the safeguards built up over decades around state systems like the BBC or the Italian RAI. When Craxi became Prime Minister in 1983, new decree laws enabled his friend Silvio to create an almost complete monopoly of television in Italy. Until then, Italy had had only three state-run television networks. The new law allowed new private stations to be set up, so long as they did not create an actual network. They key question was what defined a network; it was determined that it existed only when stations were connected by line. Nothing was said about motorcycles. So Berlusconi biked pre-recorded video cassette recordings around 800 local relay stations – a network in all but name.

Much of the programming was similar, sometimes identical to that which Murdoch used on Sky Television: American game shows and minor soaps, plus "Dallas", "Dynasty" and various Latin American telenovellas. His most famous show was called "Calpo Grosso", a game in which Italian housewives took off their clothes.

Berlusconi was ahead of Murdoch in the East European market. He had reached agreement with the Soviet Union in 1988 to have the exclusive right to package West European advertising material for Soviet television. Fininvest had an office in Prague and Berlusconi was negotiating with both Poland and Hungary to set up a new television station in each.

The meeting had been arranged in order for Murdoch and Berlusconi to be able to get to know each other better. There were no joint ventures as yet. But they had a lot in common.

After lunch, members of the Murdoch entourage flew in different directions to Spain, Luxembourg and elsewhere. Murdoch and Anna flew to Britain. As they approached Heathrow, Anna said, "I never thought I'd be so glad to see London again."

The next day, 24 January, the *Sun* ran a passionate editorial, saying that Britain should become much more deeply involved in Eastern Europe, otherwise the Germans would take it all. That same day Murdoch went around to Downing Street to see Mrs Thatcher. He told her the same.

LONDON

The new decade began with serious constraints upon News's vast and astonishing expansion. Australian Ratings downgraded News Corp's debt, for the second time, and Morgan Stanley International downgraded profit forecasts for News and put a sell recommendation on the stock, where only a few months before, the bank had been touting Murdoch as a man to back.

News earnings per share had fallen by 78 per cent in the quarter ending 30 September. The share price was diving – in New York it fell from $27 to $17 in just six months. News Corp's 1990 profits were expected to be even lower than in 1989. Ansett Airlines had been badly damaged by the Australian pilots' strike. Newspaper sales in Australia and the UK were sagging. Debt servicing costs were astronomical. And Sky was a gushing drain. News Corp's gearing – the ratio of debt to equity – was now a high 185 per cent and this resulted in net interest cover of around 1.6. Banks begin to get nervous when net interest cover falls below two. Financial analysts argued whether the debt was even higher than those figures the company acknowledged; it should have included the A$1.5 billion attached to Murdoch's book publishing vehicle, HarperCollins, which he had hived off after the failure of Media Partners International.

At the beginning of 1990, News Corp declared its assets to be worth A$19 billion. But of these, almost half were made up of intangibles such as publishing rights, newspaper mastheads and television franchises. Their actual market values were much harder to assess accurately than pieces of property – witness the helter-skelter changes in the price of Australian television stations in the past few years.

Moreover, the Australian government was threatening to tighten up its accountancy rules, in particular on the valuation of intangible assets. This could certainly cramp Murdoch's regular practice of revaluing his assets to enable him to borrow more. The last revaluation in 1987 had added A$600 million to the value of News Corps assets. At the start of 1990, a new revaluation was expected to add at least another A$2 billion to the declared value of the company.

It looked as if Murdoch's magic was beginning, for the first time, to wear very slightly thin on the fund managers and analysts whom he had dazzled for so long.

In Australia, the Hawke government was showing signs of strain as the economy went into recession. The airline pilots' strike had seriously harmed the underlying economy and tourism, as well as leaving Ansett and Australian Airlines with serious losses.

In Sydney, Frank Devine became the latest editor of *The Australian* to be removed. Among his errors, he had supported the pilots' strike and had also shown antipathy towards the management of News in Australia. But Devine did not rail against Murdoch; he stayed on the paper as a columnist.

In America, Fox Broadcasting continued to gather audiences and planned to extend its nine hours of programming to fifteen hours a week, the level set by the Federal Communications Commission as the threshold of a "network". Although Fox was expanding, and wished to be seen as the fourth network, Murdoch and Barry Diller were anxious to avoid it being defined as such, for then it would fall under one of the few remaining pieces of communications regulation, the so-called "fin-syn" rules. These limited the freedom of a network to produce its own shows and benefit from their subsequent syndication. Such rules were fatal to the synergies Murdoch was striving to create. As so often, he was seeking waivers.

The greatest problems were in London. In part they were problems of perception. In early 1990, Murdoch started to implement some of the proposals made at Aspen to give News a more human face. Rumours began to circulate that he was now a born-again Christian. These were not quite true, said his aides, but of course, they added, Rupert had always been religious, and he had become friendly with Billy Graham. He began to accept interviews in Britain, but when he said on a BBC TV chat show that the *Sun* knew how to speak to the common man, some of the studio audience groaned.

Murdoch's attempt to show the human face of Wapping was necessary. The press, both "populars" and "unpopulars", were alarmed by the growing criticisms of tabloid intrusions and abuses of power. The "unpopulars" feared that the process of sanitizing the "populars" could devastate press freedom in Britain. Murdoch did not wish the *Sun* and the *News of the World* to be the cause of new privacy legislation.

Kelvin MacKenzie had come briefly out of his closet in Wapping and entertained a group of media correspondents from the "unpopulars" to lunch. He performed in vintage style, telling them that he wasn't going to take "that feminist crap about page three being sexist". They should know that most Fleet Street editors couldn't edit a bus ticket. The *Sun* could edit the *Guardian*, but it certainly could not be done the other way around. Of *Guardian* editors, he said, "If they have a popular thought they have to go into a darkened room and lie down till it passes."

MacKenzie assured them that the *Sun* aroused hatred because "we represent a power outside the Establishment". Any idea that it was racist or sexist was "hogwash". The correspondents from the "unpopulars" were mesmerized.

Murdoch's line was more cerebral: that anyone anxious to put curbs on the press must have something to hide. Much of the feeling against his papers, he said on American television, was "orchestrated by people who can't cut the mustard". Like his redoubtable editor, he took the populist position – "It's the Establishment that criticizes, not the public." He still loved the *Sun* and wanted it to represent and appeal to the young working classes. The newspaper should be "a mixture of morality and hedonism; it sounds contradictory but we want them to have a good time and yet have very strong values".

Both Murdoch and MacKenzie gave evidence to the Calcutt Committee, set up by the government to review press conduct. Each argued that any new statutory machinery was unnecessary now the tabloids had reformed themselves. MacKenzie strengthened his case by presenting the committee with thirty recent issues of the *Sun*. These days, he said, there was nothing in it that he could not show his maiden aunt. (Their evidence smoked out Robert Maxwell; having disdained Calcutt, he insisted on testifying when he heard that his rival Murdoch had already done so.)

MacKenzie also signed the new Editors' Code, in which twenty Fleet Street editors solemnly pledged themselves to show respect for privacy, made a commitment to pursue stories "by straightforward means" and expressed a readiness to grant a right of reply, where reasonable.

This decorous behaviour produced a reprieve. The Press Council was replaced by a more representative and powerful body, the Press Complaints Commission, and the government shelved draconian remedies. The period of probation was extended and the Home Secretary, David Waddington, spoke of the industry being given "positively the last chance".

None of this did much for the *Sun*'s circulation, which had fallen from 4.3 million a day to 3.87 million. The *Mirror* combined its own sales with those of its Scottish sister paper, the *Daily Record*, and claimed to be ahead.

The *Mirror* had already installed colour. Murdoch had never believed that colour sold papers. But now he had reluctantly agreed to play catch-up-to-Maxwell for the first time in his life; Wapping was being re-equipped with new colour MAN presses from Germany. Some of his executives felt this £500 million investment was a mistake and that News should instead contract printing out, as the *Independent* did. To John Evans, with his vision of an electronic digital world, investing £500 million to run crushed trees through a vast plant of iron bears was to spit in the face of the future.

To supervise all of the Wapping operations, Murdoch appointed a new chairman of News International, Andrew Knight. This caused astonishment, since Knight seemed to many the antithesis of everything for which Murdoch stood. Whereas Murdoch had made a career out of contempt for "the British Establishment", Knight had spent his life as part of it.

A good-looking and impeccably dressed man, Knight was not without distinction. Most of his journalistic career had been spent on the *Economist*, where he was editor for eleven years and tripled the circulation. He would Concorde back and forth to the United States and he saw himself as the European interpreter of leading American politicians; he considered Henry Kissinger a close friend. He and his wife, Sabiha, gave important dinner parties at their Hampstead home.

Knight had left the *Economist* in 1986 to work for Conrad Black, the Canadian entrepreneur whom Knight helped to buy the *Telegraph* newspapers from Lord Hartwell when they were in apparently terminal decline. Seizing the opportunities created by Murdoch at Wapping, Black and Knight acquired new offices way beyond Wapping on the Isle of Dogs, introduced new technology, cut back on all staff and brought the papers into profit. By 1989 the parcel of shares which Knight had received when he undertook the job was worth £14.5 million.

Knight's languid style was not much appreciated around the new offices of the *Telegraph*, and the staff of the *Sunday Telegraph* was infuriated by the way in which he imposed on it a merger with its daily sibling – a process which served neither paper well. Throughout 1989 there were constant rumours that Knight was about to join Murdoch, but Black said Knight denied them. When he did move, Black was enraged, and faxed Knight an open letter describing his behaviour as "premature to the point of unseemliness". He continued: "Your prolonged (if sporadic) courtship with our principal competitor while continuing as the ostensible chief executive of the *Daily Telegraph*, leading to a consummation just eighty days after retirement (awkwardly) as a director of ours, and with your pockets loaded with a net £14 million of free *Telegraph* stock, raises substantial ethical questions." A profile in the *Sunday Telegraph* described Knight as "the constant smiler with the knife".

Knight dismissed the criticisms. "I can't think of a single thing which they are going to do [at the *Telegraph*] which would be remotely valuable for Wapping to know about," he said. Some of the *Telegraph* abuse rubbed off on executives at Wapping – many felt that Murdoch had simply fallen for Knight, as was his wont, and was blind to his shortcomings. Stories of the huge salary and stock options which Murdoch had reportedly given him alienated many who had worked for years at News for much less generous rewards. Knight's appointment showed that Murdoch realized the empire had now grown too large for his single-handed control. It also reflected the feeling expressed at Aspen that News needed a more "British" face in London. Knight was to be a high-class public-relations officer for News. One of Murdoch's London editors called him "Rupert's prophet on earth".

One of Knight's principal tasks was to ensure that Sky was exempted from the Broadcasting Bill, which was now passing through Parliament. He was to assure the House of Lords and others that Murdoch was not a ravening beast but a delightful human being who wanted nothing more than to be able to work in a market economy. He also had the difficult task of both controlling the behaviour of the tabloids and trying to halt their fall in circulation.

In an interview with the *Financial Times*, Knight praised Murdoch as "the greatest newspaper publisher in the world". News, he said, was "superbly run", but Murdoch had "so many balls in the air that he wants – and I think it's a very healthy thing – someone to catch some of them for him". Knight also argued that the quest for quality was essential; with more and more papers in competition, only the best would survive. Newspapers, he said, were like oil wells – they had depleting reserves but could generate a lot of cash if well run.

At the beginning of 1990, the gaiety of the nation was briefly but immeasurably enhanced by the spectacle of Andrew Neil, the aggressive but sensitive editor of the *Sunday Times*, suing Peregrine Worsthorne, the editor of the *Sunday Telegraph*, over an editorial written by Worsthorne about Mr Neil and his former girl-friend, Pamella Bordes. She had subsequently been revealed as a call girl. Neil's lawsuit was said to have infuriated both Murdoch and Anna.

The trial was gripping for the glimpse it gave into the day-to-day life of the man who described his pastimes in *Who's Who* as "dining out in London, New York and Aspen". Pamella, he said, had struck him as extremely well-dressed, "not in a page- three bimbo way" but in what his fashion editor would describe as "designer couture".

"You don't seem to have a very high opinion of the popular press, Mr Neil," said Mr Worsthorne's counsel. "I'm the editor of the *Sunday Times*," declared Neil. His performance revealed his sensitivities and his own interpretation of the Murdochian conceit of the outsider at war with the English ruling class. He denounced "the Garrick Club mafia who think they should be running everything", and after the jury awarded him damages of one thousand pounds, which Worsthorne declared would not be enough for a weekend with Ms Bordes, Neil declared the verdict "a victory for the new Britain against the old Britain". To many, this was a discouraging thought.

In the *Sun* newsroom, Kelvin MacKenzie, a rival rather more than a colleague, enjoyed it all immensely. He published front-page photographs of Pamella holding hands with both Neil and Donald Trelford, the editor of the *Observer*, under the headline, "DIRTY DON TRIED TO PULL MY PAM SAYS RANDY ANDY". The *News of the World* published a sanctimonious article by its reporter Stuart White, who had entrapped Pamella: "MOMENT THE EDITOR'S LOVE WALKED IN NAKED".

Despite such diversions, Neil was still very much in charge of the *Sunday Times* and liked to tell interviewers how he had fashioned it after his own image – there was very little of Harry Evans left there now. It was highly profitable, but Murdoch had sent his old promotions wizard Graham King to take some of the hard edges off the paper. "I felt we needed to re-establish ourselves in arts and writing," said King. "The first thing was the old anniversary trick – the silver jubilee of the magazine." There were various gimmicks, aimed at what King called "Young Aspiration-als". To curry favour among "the chattering classes" who loathed Murdoch (and read the *Independent*) King had had the *Sunday Times* promote concerts; it also began an annual literary festival in Hay-on-Wye, a Welsh border town famous for its bookshops.

By 1990, the paper's image and depth had improved considerably, and Neil sometimes felt he did not receive enough credit for this.

Murdoch thought *The Times* needed to change its image, too. On 12 March, he told Charles Wilson that he wanted a new editor. Wilson was shocked; he felt that for years he had done just what Murdoch wanted and was now being discarded – in his farewell to the journalists, he said he felt he was being sent to the gulag. Murdoch put him in charge of new projects in Eastern Europe – but then Wilson went to work for Robert Maxwell, as editor of *Sporting Life*.

In his place, Murdoch appointed Simon Jenkins, the thoughtful and somewhat iconoclastic star columnist of the *Sunday Times*. An author as well as a journalist, he had previously been editor of the *Evening Standard*, was highly regarded by his peers, and had received many awards. Although married to Texan film actress Gayle Hunnicutt, he was perhaps the most English editor Murdoch had ever appointed; his passionate concern for the country's appearance and history had led him to serve on such public bodies as the British Railways Board and English Heritage.

Jenkins told Murdoch, and the directors of *The Times*, that the success of the *Independent* proved that there were 300,000 bishops in Britain. To compete, he thought *The Times* must be quieter, should no longer try to appeal to fundamentalist right-wing prurience, and needed fewer vast headlines, less blatantly Thatcherite views. The directors were delighted. Murdoch did not demur. Jenkins agreed to take the job for two years. He did not want Murdoch to feel uncertain with him as he had with Harry Evans, and so he gave him an assurance: he would constantly criticize the Conservative government, but he would never propose that readers of *The Times* vote other than Conservative.

Jenkins was appalled by the physical conditions at *The Times*. The building was a listed warehouse, but the entrance was like that of a public lavatory. He found in the cellar the old war memorials and some ancient tombstone front pages. No one had wanted to display them before – they were not thought to be in the Murdoch image. Jenkins ordered a new entrance hall to accommodate them. He fired some columnists, ordered stories to be longer and headlines smaller, and began to improve the quality of the writing. Jenkins felt that for the first time Murdoch, now nearing sixty, was seeking a degree of respectability in Britain.

In early 1990, Murdoch also decided that he would now take personal charge of Sky, which was still losing £2 million a week. "It's my big gamble and I'd better see it through," he said. He gave Sky a five-year commitment.

BSB was finally about to get to air. At last the "Star Wars", predicted for months by the popular papers, were about to begin. BSB had been beset by both technical and financial troubles. For a time at the end of 1989 it had seemed that Murdoch's attempt to undermine confidence in BSB might have succeeded. But in January 1990, the four main shareholders pledged a new £900 million funding package to add to the £423 million already committed. The amount of money was extraordinary and, as the *Financial Times* pointed out, it was being committed with very little security.

Sky, said BSB's chief executive, Anthony Simmonds Gooding, was now looking down the barrel of "a well-funded gun". But Murdoch had had more lives than most cats and he was by now seen, as the *Guardian* put it, so much as "the master of mass communications" that his swoop back to London to take personal control of Sky was daunting for BSB.

One of his most obvious weapons was that the Sky team was lean, young and dedicated. By contrast, BSB was burdened with a big, highly-paid management. They behaved like established fat cats, spending huge amounts of money on office furniture, cars, lunches and the other accoutrements of good life. Two granite desks in the hall cost over £70,000. They insisted that they were also going to spend much more on programmes than Sky – some £200 million in the first year – and they claimed that they had a far superior movie channel. To most people, there would probably be very little to choose between the two lists of movies; each offered both talent and trash.

Sky also had Eurosport and Sky One, its least taxing channel, and Sky News, which was earning grudging approval from those who disapproved of Murdoch. BSB had already dropped plans for an all-news channel on grounds of cost. Moreover, Sky's satellite,

Astra, now carried sixteen channels and another sixteen would be available when its sister satellite went up. BSB, by contrast, had and would always have only five channels on its Marco Polo satellite.

BSB said that it hoped to have 3 million homes wired within two years. Early in 1990 it began a promotional campaign, costing £300 million, which was half as much again as any other British brand would spend on advertising in the next year. Two-thirds of this was to go on cleverly disguised subsidy – ensuring that the equipment was "attractive, competitive and well promoted". The other £100 million would go on direct advertising.

Sky's promotional budget was still a secret, but, as the *Guardian* pointed out, "Sky's big advantage has always been cross-promotion by Murdoch's five newspapers: the often outrageous editorial plugs and the special offers have all helped build the audience." This use of editorial columns was protested at by some journalists on *The Times* and *Sunday Times*.

In April 1990, fifteen months after Sky, BSB finally started its direct broadcasts. The launch was a fiasco. BSB could not even supply the high street stores with demonstration squarials. BSB needed to sell around 700,000 receivers in the run-up to Christmas. Sky already had about 750,000 dishes installed.

BSB executives and shareholders could be forgiven for feeling chagrined. When the company had been awarded the national franchise for direct satellite broadcast to Britain in 1986, no satellite competition was expected. As it staggered on to the air, BSB campaigned hard to pressure the government to bring Sky under the regulations of the pending Broadcasting Bill.

Under the existing Broadcasting Act (1981), no national newspaper proprietor or non-EC shareholder could control more than 20 per cent of a British television company. The Broadcasting Bill of 1990 was to include new terrestrial franchises and also satellite broadcasts, but legislation did not include broadcasts from medium-power satellites such as Astra.

BSB pushed hard to have this loophole closed. But the government, anxious not to damage Murdoch, asserted that since Sky came from a Luxembourg satellite, using frequencies not allocated by the British government, and a technology which could provide essentially unlimited channels, it was not subject to the spectrum scarcity argument which had required the previous restrictions. This was obviously not so, if only because Sky's headquarters and studios were in Britain. As BSB pointed out, public policy was constantly challenged by new technology; legislation had to be changed to preserve the long-established principles limiting cross-media interests. BSB argued: "Mr Murdoch has a position of unique power in British life that no other Western country would permit a foreigner to hold."

As part of its campaign, BSB began to circulate British "opinion formers" with glossy personal attacks upon Murdoch. "Who do you think will be the most influential person in Britain in the 1990s?" was one question posed under portraits of leading British politicians – and Murdoch. At least politicians were elected, BSB declared. "They don't buy their way to power."

Complaining that Sky had escaped regulation by a piece of "technological wizardry", BSB's advertising also condemned the blatant promotion of Sky in News International's papers. One thirty-one page document was called "Raising Kane"; it carried a picture of Orson Welles as Citizen Kane on its cover. BSB sought to convince people that the real Murdoch was as terrifying as the fictional Kane .

BSB argued – and in this it was correct – that Sky was now no longer a pan-European channel but an attempt to smash British broadcasting. It was driven by Murdoch's personal obsession that the British system was unforgivably "elitist" and that the British people were all desperate for American or Australian programming.

During the parliamentary debate on the Broadcasting Bill, Jonathan Miller was the most diligent lobbyist for News International, working out of a special Sky public relations office in Westminster. Andrew Knight was also involved. They argued that in the past, with a finite number of television channels available, it had been necessary to limit cross-media ownership to 20 per cent, but now, with a potential of unlimited channels, there was no such need. "The broadcasting spectrum is no longer an acutely scarce resource too dangerous to put into the hands of over-mighty men," said Knight. His glides through the corridors of Parliament undoubtedly helped Murdoch. An amendment to put Sky under the same regulations as all other UK broadcasters, which would have forced Murdoch to choose between Sky and his newspapers, was defeated.

In an attempt to improve his British image, Murdoch announced that News was giving £3 million to fund the Murdoch Chair in Language and Communications at Oxford. This news, coming on the same day as the *Sun* was once again censured by the Press Council – this time for calling homosexuals "poofters" – aroused some mirth among his critics. Murdoch was not well enough to go to Oxford's ceremonial lunch and Anna spoke in his stead. Kelvin MacKenzie also attended, sitting between two professors. A few days later, Murdoch was fit enough to attend a lunch at Chequers given by Mrs Thatcher for President De Klerk. (A year before he had been the only publisher invited to her tenth-anniversary lunch at Chequers.)

Meanwhile, during the summer of 1990, the world's economy was beginning to slide downhill. In the United States, banks started calling in loans instead of renewing them. Then the American advertising market began to slump into the worst recession in decades.

In Britain, the Sky–BSB battle to sell dishes increased in ferocity. BSB was thought to be losing £8 million a week, Sky still £2 million. The banks warned BSB that unless it had signed up a significant number of customers by Christmas, then the next tranche of operating capital, due in the New Year, would be withdrawn.

At this point John Veronis, who had brokered the deal between Murdoch and Annenberg over *TV Guide*, entered the fray. He had been shocked to discover from London taxi drivers and others how confused ordinary people were about the two systems. He arranged a meeting between Peter Davis of Reed International and Murdoch. They discussed a merger, but Murdoch showed no eagerness to make terms with his enemy.

In July 1990, Max Newton, the first editor of *The Australian*, one-time brothel keeper and pornographer, more recently Murdoch's economics pundit on the *New York Post*, and prolific writer, died of a stroke in Florida. He was sixty-one.

In his tribute, Murdoch said that Max was "one of the most colourful, prolific and brilliant journalists Australia has produced. Max was a man of extremes. He had both more friends and more enemies than any other living person . . ."

Frank Devine, former editor of *The Australian*, wrote that Max's best epitaph was Evelyn Waugh's description of Basil Seal. "[He] had been leader writer on the *Daily Beast*, he had served in the personal entourage of Lord Monomark, he sold champagne on commission, composed dialogue for the cinema, and had given the first of what was intended to be a series of talks for the BBC. Sinking lower in the social scale, he had been press agent for a female contortionist . . ."

Any account written by Max about his own life would have been dominated by sex, drink – and his relationship with Murdoch. These three demons together had virtually destroyed him in the past. But, thanks to Murdoch, his last decade in America was his most productive and stable ever, and right up to his death he was obsessed with trying to prove his value to him. Max Newton was obviously an extreme case, but many others in News Corp all over the world were bound to Murdoch by similar ties of gratitude, admiration, fear and a kind of longing that was never quite satisfied.

When Olivia, his third wife, saw Max for the last time, lying in his casket in his sharp suit, she took many photographs, "and, as I kissed him goodbye, I slipped his platinum American Express card into his pocket, just in case".

But it was Rupert Murdoch, not Max Newton, who really needed credit at this time.

THE VILLAGE

Later, to explain how he felt when News was nearly destroyed at the end of 1990, Murdoch quoted a verse from Rudyard Kipling.

Kipling, he said, was the poet laureate of the British empire, and "Nowadays I have a lot more sympathy for embattled empires!"

> The toad beneath the harrow knows
> Exactly where each tooth-point goes;
> The butterfly upon the road
> Preaches contentment to that toad.

Murdoch said that the restructuring of News, which he accomplished with the help of Ann Lane and Citibank at the end of 1990 and in early 1991, made him feel just like that toad, expecting at every moment to be crushed.

Through the previous decade he had devoted himself to acquisitions, and left debt management to his chief financial officer of more than a decade, Richard Sarazen. "We thought we had the year covered, though we knew we were tight." But in June 1990 the problems became acute.

The company tried to refinance a short-term bank loan of $750 million which it had raised in December 1989 and which was due for repayment on 30 June. News had expected to pay back the loan, as it usually did, out of asset sales. But it was becoming increasingly difficult to sell assets at a reasonable price. And so, at the end of June, News Corp tried to secure a three-year loan to refinance it, but found that impossible to arrange. The company paid back $250 million and asked its bankers to roll over the other $500 million for another three months. With various degrees of reluctance, they agreed.

Richard Sarazen was replaced by Dave DeVoe, only the third chief financial officer since the 1960s. The new man inherited an unenviable task. In the summer of 1990, News Corp began to enter its slide towards what seemed to many like oblivion. In its annual report to the year ending 30 June 1990, News showed massive losses and equally massive short-term debts. The drain of Sky seemed unending. The accounts also showed that News Corp had just revalued its own assets by A$3 billion. The largest salary was shown to be A$12.74 million. Many people assumed this was Murdoch's; in fact, it was Barry Diller's. Murdoch's salary was under A$3 million.

In London, the company had trouble paying its bills for the retooling of Wapping. All over the world, shareholders and institutions began to sell News Corp shares. The banks, which had previously begged Murdoch to borrow, started to panic. For years they had lent recklessly; now they were desperately trying to lower their exposure. Standard Chartered Bank suddenly called in money from News – "Bang," said Murdoch. "We were given ten minutes. I went to see the chairman, etc, but they were apologetic and said they didn't have the freedom to lend the money. They had their own problems."

Many Australian corporations were in trouble. In September Bond Corporation announced Australia's biggest ever corporate loss of £1 billion and Alan Bond at last resigned. At the same time John Elliott's Elders IXL revealed a £575 million deficit. That month News shares fell by 25 per cent and it seemed that the market's love affair with Murdoch was over. The cruellest cut was that some analysts remarked that the shares in Maxwell Communications were holding up better than those of News – not knowing that Maxwell was illegally supporting them.

Subsequently Murdoch tried to explain to a group of bank presidents just what it had felt like to be a toad. "From my humble reptilian perspective", he had had to watch, aghast, as the shafts of the harrow had come plunging down, one after another, through the autumn and winter of 1990–1.

Like Toad of Toad Hall, he had been carried away by his own enthusiasms. He admitted that he had been so busy with acquisitions that he had not paid enough attention to what was going on around him or around the world. Between 1985 and 1991 News had grown from total assets of $3 billion to $26 billion.

However, he had recently made some good sales too. News travel magazines had gone for 140 per cent more than he had paid for them just three-and-a-half years earlier. News's 50 per cent of American *Elle* had fetched $160 million, only two years after a start-up costing $5 million, and the supermarket tabloid, the *Star*, into which he said he had only ever invested $9 million, had netted over $400 million.

In mid-1990 Murdoch believed that these and other sales were enough to stabilize News's capital structure. He thought that real interest rates were historically high and that short-term financing was therefore preferable. He believed that he could continue to expand print capacity with lease finance. He did not believe that there was going to be one of the severest advertising recessions in recent history, a banking crisis in America, liquidity squeezes in the UK and Australia, and a war in the Gulf – all on top of the appallingly costly competition with BSB.

Explaining how the toad was nearly finished off, Murdoch said also that News Corp had always lived on "the risk frontier" – after all, that was how the company had grown from a small afternoon paper in Australia's fourth city to a worldwide empire in less than forty years. News Corp had "hopped" a great deal in that period and for most of the way the banks had hopped happily along beside it. The experience of 1990–1 taught Murdoch "that the fates of all of us – toads, butterflies and banks – are inextricably interlocked. We need the banks. And banks, if they are to make their way in a changing financial environment, need strong relationships with toads who know which way to hop."

In early October, Murdoch went to Australia for the AGM of News, in Adelaide. While he was there, he merged his morning and afternoon papers in both Melbourne and Sydney. In Melbourne this meant the death of the *Herald*, which he had watched his father build. When, predictably, he was asked if this hurt, he insisted, equally predictably, that it did not.

His influence in the continent was demonstrated (at least to his critics) by an invitation sent out by Ken Cowley, a director of News and the head of its Australian operations. Cowley wrote to the Prime Minister, Bob Hawke, members of the Cabinet and leaders of the Opposition:

Dear—,
    Rupert and I will be travelling to Canberra on business and would like to take the opportunity to meet with senior Federal politicians over drinks.
    Would you be available to join us between 6.30 and 8.00 p.m.

To the Australian Broadcasting Corporation and to Murdoch's

principal newspaper rival, the *Sydney Morning Herald*, this summons demonstrated Murdoch's power over Australian politics and politicians. The ABC stationed a camera crew outside the house where the party was given – they recorded that the Prime Minister and four ministers showed up. So did six senior members of the Opposition.

Earlier in the year, Murdoch had been the subject of a popular play in Sydney. Now ABC Television was broadcasting a television mini-series, "The Paper Man", which was clearly based upon his life. Soon afterwards, he and his massive newspaper ownership were denounced at a conference of some 1,200 people in the Sydney Opera House. The novelist Thomas Keneally was enthusiastically applauded when he said, "We don't want an unofficial minister of information." Keneally thought Murdoch couldn't help his acquisitive nature: he was like a killer who pleads "Stop me before I kill again." He needed help in the form of government regulation.

Among the other speakers was Eric Beecher, the former editor of the Melbourne *Herald*, who maintained it was an outrage that Murdoch now owned papers which had 70 per cent of circulation in the country. He said he had resigned because of pressure from within the company (though not from Murdoch himself) not to publish anything which might damage Murdoch's interests, including his holding in Ansett Airlines. "I found my sense of journalistic morality being questioned and tested very regularly," he claimed.

Asked to comment, Piers Akerman, a witty but aggressive journalist who was now editor of the merged Melbourne *Sun-Herald*, told the *Sydney Morning Herald* that Murdoch was "without doubt, the most pre-eminent newspaper man in the world". Murdoch for his part said later that he thought Akerman "wild but full of ideas".

It was now, as both Murdoch and his banks began to understand for the first time the extent of his financial crisis, that Ann Lane of Citibank came riding into his life.

As she began her investigation, she found News Corp's financial planning unsophisticated. The company had been doing standard top-down projections to give to the banks that backed them. They financed themselves with very short-term bank debt (one to three years), the kind of capital that was expected to roll when rolls were needed. Murdoch, she found, was focused on day-to-day operations, but had kept his eye off the financing.

Lane and her team devoted themselves to coming up with a plan to present to the banks. She kept telling the company, "You've got to tie yourself to this plan. And it can't be tops down, it's got to be tops up." This meant that the company must state what it thought its businesses were going to earn. Lane knew that the banks would demand to know that.

Looking at the task in front of her, Lane felt as if she had to build the Pyramids from scratch, without drawings. It was so daunting and complex that the only hope was an utterly simple plan which everyone would have to adopt. Hence Lane's twin slogans: "We are where we are" and, "Nobody gets out", and the fact that there was *no* Plan B.

As the banks began to hover, the fabulous losses of Sky were still the greatest strain upon the empire.

But the losses of BSB were even more dire. By the end of September, it had sold at most 120,000 squarials, against its target of 400,000 by Christmas. Some of BSB's backers were becoming nervous. At the *Financial Times*, Frank Barlow, the chief executive, had always been sceptical about BSB and he now believed that merger was essential.

John Veronis intervened again. Each side denied inviting him in. (He eventually collected a fee of $1 million from both, considerably less than he asked.) He talked to Peter Davis at Reed, who said BSB was still interested in discussing a deal, and he called Murdoch in Australia. Murdoch said he could not get back for a fortnight, so Davis's deputy, Ian Irvine, flew south and met in secret with Murdoch, at Cavan, on 15 and 16 October. A basic deal was worked out. It was to be a 50–50 merger designed to unify the company, stem losses and maximize profits.

At BSB the chief executive Anthony Simmonds Gooding was told almost nothing. At Sky's headquarters in west London, many people feared that the company was about to be shut down.

After Murdoch and Irvine had come to tentative agreement, further secret talks were held at a hotel at Luckham Park, near Bath. They were led for News by Andrew Knight, until Murdoch joined them.

The discussions were not easy – many BSB people saw Sky as an example of Murdoch philistinism; Sky considered BSB to be filled by effete British fat cats. BSB thought Murdoch had destroyed them, and that without Sky they would have succeeded.

The Sky men pointed out that the Marco Polo satellite had only four channels, whereas Astra's were almost unlimited. Disney was coming on to Astra, as was CNN. Had it had not been Murdoch, it would have been someone else. Sky thought that BSB deserved to die.

Eventually, however, an agreement was reached. Murdoch and the four chairmen of the BSB consortium had dinner in London but negotiations subsequently broke down. Murdoch was still reluctant to compromise. Although it was he who had created this competition, he had a visceral dislike of BSB, and wanted to win this battle outright. But for the pressure from his banks, he would have fought on. The blackout on the talks was still total. On 29 October Murdoch went secretly to Downing Street to meet the Prime Minister. He said later that they talked about international affairs and he only mentioned the impending merger in an off-hand comment at the end of their talk. He knew that it would throw British broadcasting into turmoil, and the merger needed the government's acquiescence, because BSB had no right to share its franchise with Sky.

On 2 November, final details of the deal were negotiated at the offices of Freshfields, the London law firm. (The firm was codenamed 'Greenacres' for security, Sky was 'Sox' and BSB 'Box'.) Murdoch brought his nineteen-year-old son Lachlan to the signing. "His son is learning the ropes and he witnessed a deal that probably has saved the empire," ran a *New York Times* article.

News International said it called the Home Office a few hours before the merger was announced, but Peter Lloyd, the minister responsible for broadcasting, was out of town and knew nothing of this until the following morning. Just one hour before the official announcement, the Independent Broadcasting Authority was informed of it. Andrew Knight said this had been at BSB's insistence.

Simmonds Gooding was summarily dismissed. Ian Irvine was named as chairman of the new venture. Sam Chisholm, Sky's tough Australian chief executive, became chief executive officer. Ian Clubb, BSB's finance director and Gary Davey of Sky were named as joint deputy chief executives. An executive committee was made up of Murdoch, Ian Irvine, Frank Barlow of Pearsons, and Andrew Knight. News International now controlled 50 per cent of the new company, Granada 11 per cent, Chargeurs 10.5 per cent, Pearson 11 per cent, Reed 10.5 per cent, Bond 3.5 per cent and others 5.5 per cent.

At first the merged channels would be broadcast on both systems, but eventually Astra, Sky's satellite, would prevail. The deal was designed to compensate for the market position Sky had reached; BSB was required to furnish at once an extra £70 million pounds, and News International a further £30 million. In substance it was a Murdoch victory.

Both relief and outrage greeted the news of the deal. The relief was felt by Murdoch's bankers and all others seeking to preserve News International. The outrage was more publicly expressed by his enemies. The merger was announced only days after the new Broadcasting Act received Royal Assent. The government had refused to include them within the terms of the act, on the grounds that Astra operated from Luxembourg. Yet again, Murdoch seemed to have cocked a snook at government regulations. Sky would still be a pirate ship.

Officials at the Independent Broadcasting Authority which, under the new Act, became the Independent Television Commission, were furious that it had not been consulted. The deal put BSB shareholders in breach of their contract with the IBA because the franchise was not BSB's to dispose of in this way.

In effect Murdoch – admittedly under financial duress – had at last seized control of a British television station, BSB, and was now daring the authorities to deny it him. Lord Thompson, the former IBA chairman, described the merger as a characteristically "brutal Wapping in outer space".

As always when matters Murdochian were discussed, the debate in the House of Commons was heated. Among the most important questions was why the Prime Minister had told no one that Murdoch had revealed the merger to her on 29 October. The Home Secretary, David Waddington, averred: "It certainly was no business of the Prime Minister to go phoning around the place to all and sundry, and me included, saying that she had been told by Mr Murdoch what everybody already knew."

This was unconvincing. For the Labour Party, Roy Hattersley said that it was an insult to Parliament to say that Mr Murdoch "just mentioned it to the Prime Minister and it wasn't regarded as being in any way important". Her tacit approval was hard to justify – the Home Secretary himself subsequently acknowledged that the deal was technically not legal; because under the Broadcasting Act, Murdoch could not own 48 per cent of the DBS franchise – which he now did.

The *Independent* commented, "The fact is that Mr Murdoch employs his media power in the direct service of a political party, which now turns a blind eye to what it has itself depicted in Parliament as a breach of the law in which Mr Murdoch is involved. So much for Mrs Thatcher's lectures on media bias."

To Labour's complaints that the merger made a mockery of the new Broadcasting Act, Murdoch replied, "Well they would, wouldn't they? The fact is, they hate the idea of a competitive society and it is only companies like ours that have the guts and strength to risk everything in building a competitor to the existing monopoly. That's what we're still about."

Murdoch had seen the battle as yet another personal struggle between himself as David, and the Goliath of the British Establishment. He said later, "I regard Sky Television's defeat of BSB, deploying maybe a third of the resources in the process, as my outstanding achievement as a journalist."

He was disappointed that his banking problems had forced him to negotiate a compromise peace "rather than pressing on to claim the whole prize, which was within only a few months of our grasp. It's too bad. But I will survive the disappointment."

He called the achievement "busting the British broadcasting

cartel" – and, most astonishingly, he said that it meant more to him than the defeat of the unions at Wapping.

The merger between Sky and BSB coincided with a fierce debate in Britain over the nature of sovereignty within the Common Market, and the consequent fall of Mrs Thatcher.

The *Sun* behaved characteristically. True both to its loyalty to Thatcher and to Kelvin MacKenzie's loathing of the French, the paper published a long series of anti-French jokes and campaigned against one of Mrs Thatcher's *bêtes noires*, the French European Commissioner, Jacques Delors. "UP YOURS, DELORS" shouted one of its most memorable front-page headlines.

By a curious coincidence, Murdoch's *Sun* was twenty-one years old in the week of Mrs Thatcher's leadership crisis. "YER CUR-RANT BUN IS 21" announced a box on the front page. Inside were tributes from some of those showbusiness and other personalities who had not suffered its abuse. Mrs Thatcher wrote, "Your twenty-first anniversary offers tremendous encouragement to a Prime Minister eleven and a half years into office. The *Sun* has become a great British institution. If it can come up fresh and bubbling for twenty-one years, then so can I, and I shall do so."

She did not.

As the pressure against her mounted, Murdoch's papers were not monolithic. *The Times* supported Mrs Thatcher temperately, but the *Sunday Times* published "A Reluctant Goodbye" editorial, saying it was time for her to go. Kelvin MacKenzie was appalled and the *Sun* published a riposte praising "Margaret Thatcher's unrivalled record of achievement in peace and war", and swiping at "the opportunists of the *Sunday Times* . . . At the first sight of the favourite finding the going tough, they switch horses . . ."

After Mrs Thatcher's resignation, the *Sun* ran a sixteen-page tribute and then backed John Major in the race to succeed her. Its reasons reflected Murdoch's view of Britain: "He is the only candidate who has totally made his own way. No public school, no university . . . He himself is the product of the years when Mrs Thatcher provided the opportunity for those of humble background to succeed without the benefit of privilege and connection."

The Village

In the same week as Mrs Thatcher's fall, and while Murdoch awaited with trepidation the impact of his worldwide roadshows upon the banks, another symbol of the 1980s fell further than before: Michael Milken was sentenced to a decade in prison.

His impact on the decade had been huge, particularly in the world of communications and information. Without Milken's assistance, MCI Communications, now the second largest long-distance telephone company in the States, and Turner Broadcasting, would never have grown so fast. But many other companies were damaged by the methods he pioneered and pursued, and overall, he left corporate America with a far greater debt burden. By the beginning of the 1990s, interest payments were devouring more than a quarter of the cash flow of the average US company, an all-time record which was sure to mount higher still as the recession continued to depress revenues. There were fearsome predictions that the high debt burden would lead to a chain of bankruptcies which themselves would deepen and prolong the recession.

Murdoch's refinancing problems coincided with a slowdown in the growth of Fox. It retained its air of cocky originality, but as it became established it found progress more elusive. Murdoch himself decided to move "The Simpsons" to challenge the most popular programme in the land, "The Cosby Show", head-on every Thursday night. But Bart Simpson had so far failed to catch Bill Cosby. The network had planned to expand from three to five nights a week in the summer of 1990. But its failure to attract adequate advertising prevented that.

Throughout November and December 1990, Murdoch was on the move, conducting his roadshows. Day after day he begged, cajoled and flattered bankers. He was virtually bankrupt – and would have been but for the Sky-BSB deal. Every week the company was battered by the rolls that came thundering along. All the time Lane was having to judge how to push the banks into line, when and if to "launch" upon them.

The pressure on Lane's team was fantastic. The images they used constantly were symptomatic: rolls, launching, cliffhanging, the death spiral and many more. They had only one another to take it out on. They all screamed, but Lane screamed loudest.

513

The only person Lane did not scream at was Murdoch. She was his guide away from the precipice. Or, to use Murdoch's own toad idiom, she hopped along beside him, pushing him away from the toothpoints of the harrow, as they came crashing down, again, and again, and again.

Secretly she feared that she could hardly see further than he could, but she knew that he needed to have confidence in her. She gritted her teeth and lied. It was going to work, she insisted.

She was not quick to laugh, but she understood the value of humour, bantering wit and smart, sarcastic comments which relieved the tension. While she screamed at DeVoe, she mocked Murdoch. She also urged him to make her a movie star, stressing that "the world needs more than Julia Roberts, maybe a middle-aged yup".

Against this extraordinary background, Murdoch continued his public life. He produced a synopsis for his autobiography, the US and Canadian rights to which were bought by Random House for $1 million. Then Random House announced it had a new publisher – Murdoch's old enemy, Harold Evans. Evans told the *New York Times* that he had written to Murdoch, saying, "The wheel of fortune makes me your publisher as you used to be mine. I think it will be a happier experience for you than it was for me. But please don't pull any punches." Murdoch was not amused.

By the beginning of December, financial news from around the world was worse than ever. In Australia Alan Bond had been arrested and charged with financial offences, and his Bond Corp had reported a A$2.2 billion loss. The Bell group, bought by Bond from the late Robert Holmes à Court, brought in a loss of almost A$1 billion. Consumer confidence had collapsed and shops on the main streets of Australian cities were having closing-down sales.

On 7 December, Murdoch had the most terrifying night of his life – when he thought that the Pittsburgh bank was not going to roll and the whole house of News would come crashing down like cards.

Later he said that he thought many of the lesser banks were so difficult because it gratified their egos. "Chief credit officers of small banks who were $2–$3 million participants had no qualms about telling us to liquidate the whole $20 billion of assets. In fact one or two seemed to enjoy it."

In the tense run-up to Christmas, Murdoch called his London editors. Not to tell them what to do, but for gossip. He had been anxious to know about Mrs Thatcher; now he was more interested in Gorbachev. On 9 December, he attended a cocktail party given by Simon Jenkins and his wife. He had seen Mrs Thatcher that day. She looked like a tired old housewife, he said; all the energy had gone out of her.

British newspapers then alleged that Mrs Thatcher had proposed an honorary knighthood for Murdoch in her resignation honours list, but that the committee which scrutinizes such proposals had turned him down. The story was a humiliating one and it stung him. Uncharacteristically, Murdoch made a public statement denying it and said that he would have rejected any honour had it been offered. He asked the *Daily Mail* to apologize.

Murdoch's December rolls over coincided with the end of the Fairfax family empire. On 10 December 1990, after 150 years of publishing often excellent newspapers in Australia, and providing the fiercest competition to their rivals, the company was placed in receivership, largely because of the recklessness of Warwick Fairfax, a young man who lived mainly in America. Fairfax was subsequently bought by Conrad Black, the Canadian media owner fast becoming a latter-day Beaverbrook.

The next problem for Murdoch was a television documentary, broadcast on Channel 4 in Britain, which criticized News Corp's accounting procedures. Even before it came out, leaks of the allegations it would make caused the share price to fall further. Murdoch had agreed to answer written questions from the reporter, Christopher Hird. (Maxwell by contrast would have taken him straight to court.) The film was entitled "Murdoch – The Empire", and it was presented in the style of *Citizen Kane*. Christopher Hird declaimed that it was: "The tale of an empire built on political influence and on avoiding media controls – an empire that has been kept alive by questionable accounting policies and tax dodging on a world scale . . . groaning under massive debts and teetering on the brink . . ."

The programme described News Corp's practice of revaluing

its intangible assets, and the network of tax havens that Murdoch used to enable News to pay average tax of less than 3 per cent on its declared profits. It insinuated that he had dealt in the company's shares at a time when he had possessed "price-sensitive information". But these transactions were already matters of public record and in Australia, unlike in Britain, there was no ban on directors dealing in options in their own company.

Although it was debatable whether the programme lived up to its claims, coming when it did, it helped send the shares skidding down by another 20 per cent on the Australian exchange. Murdoch was now being compared with other failed Australian financiers. No longer did he seem to be a communications visionary – he looked like another tycoon who had been too greedy and was fighting for his life.

Murdoch took no action against the programme, but he was upset that it appeared just as his negotiations with the banks reached their climax. He asserted that for weeks before its makers "were boasting to London dinner parties of what they planned . . . It was the sort of the thing that tabloid newspapers are supposed to do but don't dare. Only a government-protected television cartel can get away with it."

The toad continued to hop under the fearsome harrow through Christmas and New Year, as war in the Gulf approached. John Reed, the Chairman of Citibank, called upon the assistance of Bill Rhodes, Citibank's famous troubleshooter, sometimes called the Red Adair of the banking industry. He was the man who had renegotiated Citi's loans to bankrupt South American countries. He was the obvious man – after all, News's debt was as large as Ecuador's. He had dinner with Murdoch and Anna at Côte Basque in New York and was impressed with Murdoch's straightforwardness, and his ability to listen. Rhodes began calling bank presidents all over the world. He warned that News was so large, that its collapse could have a very serious impact on the international economy – particularly with the state of panic induced by war in the Gulf. They must help, he said.

The pressure was building. None of the deadlines for completion of the deal that Murdoch and others had incautiously promised would be met. About 90 per cent of the money was pledged. But the last 10 per cent was proving the hardest of all. The *Wall Street Journal* and other papers published predictions that the share price might fall to zero. One Indian banker, whose signature was desperately needed, could not be found – he had gone hunting tigers. Lane was infuriated by her British colleagues, who were taking a whole week off at Christmas! There was no holiday for the Citibank team.

She felt that Murdoch, by contrast, did need a holiday. He worked ceaselessly, getting up at 5 a.m. every morning. Balance sheets aside, she respected the company he had built and the people who worked for him. And she viewed him as a visionary who had used the industry well. She was also struck by his love for his family, and she admired Anna Murdoch, for being both independent and a remarkably supportive woman.

For Christmas, Murdoch and his family went to their home at Aspen. The skiing town in the Rockies had been transformed (and ruined) by 1980s money as it became one of the most fashionable resorts in America. Andrew Knight, the executive chairman of News International in Britain, accompanied them. He believed that throughout this financial crisis "Rupert showed fantastic qualities of generalship. How he and Anna remained themselves and were not warped, I do not know."

In Aspen, Murdoch had a daily regime. He made early-morning calls to Australia, London and New York and then turned all his energy to the ski slopes. Having exerted himself to the full, he then went back to the telephone.

On the slopes, Andrew Knight tried, rather too hard, to keep up with him. He smashed at speed into a rock wall and nearly died from internal haemorrhaging. Murdoch and Anna spent much of their Christmas visiting him in his hospital room. Their solicitude touched Knight. "I cannot imagine life without Rupert," he said early in 1991.

There was good news over Christmas. Fox's movie *Home Alone*, which had cost $18 million to make, was a runaway hit. Barry Diller, the head of the studio, was ecstatic; he reckoned it could bring in $225 million in America and at least $65 million overseas. (By 1992, *Home Alone* had in fact earned Fox $285 million.)

By early in the New Year 1991, many of the banks had caved in and agreed to roll over. Some had agreed conditionally on everyone else being brought in too. Meanwhile News Corp's maturing debts were rolling up until the deal was completed. As more became due, even more debt was short-term, which increased the risk that a lender would call the company into default. International bonds issued by News Corp were by now yielding up to 47 per cent because of investor anxieties. That was the sort of return usually expected only on the debt of such no-hope cases as Peru.

Now, the objective was to close by 31 January. It was a crucial date, because there was a termination date of 31 January on the document, at which time all $2 billion of debt, which had rolled, would be due. Lane knew that they could not keep rolling that $2 billion for ever. There was a point where the deal was either going to happen or it was not, even though four months was a record for closing such a mammoth agreement.

On 14 January, just before the allied coalition began its air attack on Baghdad, a new crisis of confidence hit News Corp. The company publicly acknowledged that it might be insolvent by June if it did not secure its $8 billion refinancing package. It could not generate the internal cash to meet its obligations at the end of June. It also became known that some of the banks were still holding out against Ann Lane and her terms. This sent shares falling once more on the Australian Stock Exchange. On 15 January, the price fell by 15 per cent, 50 cents, in the day. The shares of TNT, the transport company owned by Murdoch's friend Sir Peter Abeles, also dived. Together News and TNT owned Ansett Airlines, which operated domestic air services in Australia and New Zealand.

On 16 January 1991, sixteen members of the editorial staff of *The Australian*, the paper which Murdoch had created in 1964 and which remained the flagship of his fleet, were dismissed. At the same time about twenty others were fired from the tabloid *Telegraph-Mirror* in Sydney. They were required to leave not because they had worked badly or were troublemakers, but because of economies Murdoch was making. Many were people with long service. *The Australian*'s letters editor, Philip Pearman, who had been on the paper for twenty-two years, was told to pack his desk and go. So was the senior sub editor, Alastair Diffy, who had been there ten years.

The firings were done in the casual, almost brutal way that some people had come to expect of News Corp. That morning Diffy walked in, sat at his desk, booted up his computer terminal and was called by the editor, who was shaking. He was handed a letter which began "My dear Alastair" and was signed by someone on another floor whom he scarcely knew. He packed up and left. The Australian Journalists' Association, one of Murdoch's fiercest institutional critics in Australia, called a twenty-four-hour strike of his papers.

The first American attack on Iraq on the morning of 17 January was broadcast from Iraq, with great drama, by CNN. CNN's link to the world was a portable, independently-powered four-line telephone system which microwaved a feed from the roof of the Al Rashid Hotel to a satellite truck across the border in Jordan. From there the signal was bounced up to the satellite and down to CNN headquarters in Atlanta. All the other satellite feeds, from Washington, the United Nations, Moscow, Saudi Arabia, and elsewhere were being gathered there, bounced back up to the satellites and played instantly around the world.

This first night of the Gulf War was perhaps the most dramatic vindication ever of Ted Turner's decision back in 1980 to create a twenty-four-hour news service for the global village. He had lost $77 million on it in its first five years. By the time of the Gulf War it was valued at $1.5 billion and was seen in 65 million homes in ninety-three countries around the world.

The war established CNN as the most influential network in the world. More than any other station, it had helped to create the reality of the "global village", in which the manor house was the United States. By this time there were about 120 satellites available for commercial use worldwide – almost half as many again as a decade before. Intelsat alone had fourteen satellites, seven over the Atlantic, four over the Indian Ocean and three over the Pacific. Throughout the world, diplomats, politicians and statesmen would watch CNN to know what was happening everywhere else. Bush, Saddam and Gorbachev were all known to watch it. In Britain, Murdoch's own twenty-four-hour television news service, Sky News, though not in the same league as CNN, showed itself to be fast, efficient and reliable. At the same time, however, all the television companies allowed themselves to be manipulated and censored by governments. The war appeared as a stunning, bloodless video game.

In the midst of war the Japanese nearly pushed News over the cliff. The Citibank team found the Japanese banks hard to deal with; they could not make a decision except at head office. They had about 20 per cent of the lending altogether, most of it placed outside Japan. Lane and Murdoch had not thought a roadshow necessary in Japan. By January they regretted this decision. The Japanese could not understand why they were not being bought out. If it were a Japanese restructuring, they maintained, the smaller lenders would have been rescued. Why not now and in this case?

The week before the deal was supposed to close, fifteen Japanese banks made a move to pull out. Bill Rhodes and Ann Lane knew they needed someone on the ground in Japan. Neither of them could go. In the last week of January Lane sent Bill Sorensen from her team. He was not overjoyed. Fear of flying during the war added to the intense pressure, but Lane told him that he didn't have to "launch" on anyone. If the deal fell apart, it would be her fault.

On the first day in Tokyo, Sorensen made no progress. He became fairly frantic. One of his friends in the office in New York tried to cheer him up. "You're lucky you're not here. She's going crazy. She's going to kill us all." That, said Lane later, was an understatement. "I was completely APE that week." She was storming around the Park Lane office in her designer suit and sneakers, shouting people into line. They were working towards Thursday. On Monday forty banks were still out. If they didn't get to closure, they would face $2 billion of debt, which would cause a worldwide cross to fall. So they decided to roll for another two weeks.

Finally the signatures began to come in by the dozen. The last waves were breaking, smaller now.

Watching the Gulf war on several of the nine monitors in his Manhattan office, Murdoch told Peter Barth, the editor of the American showbusiness paper, *Variety*, that he had won his own battle. "This has been a chastening experience," he said with a pained smile. "There have been, shall we say, some unpleasant moments."

Murdoch was astonished at the volatility of the markets. Some 40 per cent of the capitalization of the company had disappeared in one trading week. He was sure that speculators had been feeding negative stories to the papers to drive down the share price. It was a feeding frenzy for short sellers.

Murdoch had begun to indicate, even in public, that he might change his ways, and admitted to having "taken my eye off the financial side". He said he would appoint a chief operating officer, and even suggested that he might issue more full-voting shares, which would dilute his family's control of the company. He promised to travel less and let other people do more of the work. The idea that he would do either – relinquish personal or family control – seemed radical to those who knew him and the company best.

In the end, the banks had rallied to News because they believed in Murdoch. In the last thirty years, some journalists and editors had disliked him, but he had built up relationships of trust in the business world. He was known to be a man of his word. He had never missed an interest payment. "Our credit record was unblemished," he said truthfully. To Murdoch, "relationships are at the heart of banking practice. Some of our principal relationships go back to my earliest days in business." He also thought that media and banks were both on rolling logs: business practices were changing so fast – because of communications technology and computerization. At such a time, trust was essential.

In the early hours of Friday 1 February, the final signatures of the 146 banks were appended to all the new agreements. This was one of the largest refinancings ever – it covered $7.6 billion of short- and medium-term debts, which were to be rescheduled over three years. By February 1992, the company would have to repay $800 million to the banks, $600 million to redeem the bridge, and $400 million in three six-monthly instalments after that. When the agreement expired in February 1994, $5.6 billion would fall due.

The cost of doing the deal was high – Citibank sent in a bill for $50 million.

They were where they were. Nobody had got out.

Murdoch knew that all this was only a stopgap. The harrow had passed – but it could return. To escape completely, he said, meant "managing ruthlessly and managing for cash. Regardless of how unpleasant this can be, there is no choice but to grit your teeth and get on with it." He had to sell assets even if the price was disappointing, squeeze extra margins wherever possible, sell still more assets, consider the possibility of diluting his family share by issuing new equity, cut back or eliminate developments today in the knowledge that there would be other opportunities tomorrow, do whatever else was needed to attract long-term debt, and fight his way out.

At the end of the January 1991, to reassure the banks, Murdoch appointed a new chief operating officer for News Corp. This was Gus Fischer, a Swiss businessman who was already managing director of News International, the British company.

Morale at Wapping was appalling. The circulation of the *Sun* was down – and Murdoch was berating Kelvin MacKenzie. Other editors were also unhappy. The *Evening Standard* ran a story that *The Times* was to be sold. It was not true, but no one called the editor of *The Times* to reassure him. All the papers were in effect on autopilot. Andrew Knight, the chairman, looked like a ghost after recovering from his near-fatal skiing accident. The day-to-day management of Wapping was more and more in the hands of John Dux, who had been moved from Murdoch's Hong Kong paper, the *South China Morning Post*, and whose beard had turned from black to grey in the preceding months. He told the editors that as a result of the deal with the bankers there would have to be severe cuts in all editorial budgets – perhaps as high as 16 per cent.

Production at Wapping was still in confusion. The new and vastly expensive colour presses were not effective. Pictures supposed to be in colour turned up every day in black and white. Some people blamed it on the British software which had been tacked on to the German presses to appease the anti-German sentiment of some of those who worked at Wapping. A German team was there trying, and so far failing, to put the problems right.

There was a knife-edge competition between *The Times* and the *Independent*, and between the *Sun* and the *Mirror*. But production problems were costing both Murdoch papers thousands of lost copies every night. The factory which had seemed so progressive when it opened in 1986 was now dragging the company down.

There was another problem. The empire had depended so much on Murdoch's personal touch that many officers felt not only bereft but also betrayed when he did not have time for them. He was like a lighthouse; people needed his beam to warm them from time to time. They began to talk ill of him. Thus, one of his lieutenants complained, "We are all driven by our character defects. Rupert is too greedy and too mean. He is only interested in control and power, not in building or improving things. He doesn't take enough care of our people. He is on the edge. His magic was vast ambition and energy. *TV Guide* marked the beginning of the end. Now reality has arrived." People noted that almost all those who had helped him expand his empire had been discarded or had fallen away. Bruce Matthews, whose work at Wapping had been crucial, was gone. And now even his oldest friend, Richard Searby, was falling out of favour. Searby was known to have told Murdoch that Andrew Knight's appointment and extravagant emoluments were a terrible mistake, if only for the effect on loyal, long-serving employees. Murdoch could not accept criticisms like that. Nor could he share power.

Before News's financial crisis, Anna had planned to take the whole family – the beneficiaries of the Cruden Trust – down the Nile to celebrate Rupert's sixtieth birthday. This was rendered impossible both by the war and the refinancing crisis. Instead, after it was completed, Anna insisted that Rupert go to the Canyon health ranch in Arizona for a complete rest.

Even there, this was impossible. Frank Barlow, the chief executive of Pearson, had to fly out to discuss a new crisis at BSkyB. Murdoch's fellow shareholders, Pearsons, Reed, Granada and Chargeurs, the former owners of BSB, now demanded he make a further investment of £100 million in a £200 million refinancing package. They knew that, following his agreement with the banks, he had no cash.

After furious rows, a deal was reached. Murdoch met most of his obligations by bartering film rights from Fox. Reed pulled out of any further funding and its stake dropped from 11 per cent to 4 per cent; its shares were taken up by Pearson and Chargeurs. By now, over £1.6 billion had been spent on the British satellite revolution.

The next and much more painful part of the News restructuring was looming. Murdoch had to sell some of the assets that he had been so pleased to acquire. The bridge that Citibank had put together was only just a bridge to that next step. "He knew he had to start selling at once. Now, not in two and a half years' time," Lane said. "He knew he was selling into a market that was a disaster, but he knew he had to do it."

Among the first assets to go on the block was Murdoch Magazines, his American group which included *New York*, *Premiere*, *New Woman*, *Seventeen*, *European Travel* and *Life*, *Mirabella*, and *Soap Opera Weekly*. Talks began with K3, a subsidiary of Kolberg, Kravis Roberts, the buy-out firm whose $32 billion take-over of RJR Nabisco had probably been the most astonishing corporate excess in the 1980s. K3 demanded that Murdoch include *Racing Form* in the deal, since it was a good daily provider of cash. He agreed and the deal was closed at $650 million, a good price.

He also sold the other 50 per cent of the *Star*, which had been his first American paper. Thus by the middle of the summer of 1991, News was in a position to repay the bridge and had a little breathing room to focus on corporate finance problems. Murdoch knew that even if he met the $2 billion payments under the override, he still had $6.4 billion coming due in February 1994. This meant more refinancing. There was no way that sort of debt could come due in one day.

While Murdoch was selling, Maxwell was still buying, trying to appear to rise as fast as Murdoch was descending. In particular, he was after the *New York Daily News*, which had suffered long strikes and which the Tribune Company of Chicago had finally decided to sell. Maxwell was still obsessed with Murdoch and found it sweet to own a New York paper when Murdoch was not allowed to do so. He flaunted himself as the saviour of the *News* and was hailed and embraced by the mayor and other functionaries of the city.

Tribune paid Maxwell $60 million to take the *News* off its hands – but the paper's obligations may have been as high as $100 million. And, although Maxwell's own debt problems were more completely shrouded than Murdoch's, it was clear that they were horrendous. Maxwell Communications and the private companies through which he juggled his finances owed at least $4.5 billion. Ever since his purchase of Macmillan Inc for $2.6 billion in 1988, he had been scrambling to raise cash. *Business Week* reported in March 1991 that at least a third of Maxwell's stake in Maxwell Communications had been pledged as collateral for loans. There was another element, sometimes called "the Max factor": whereas Murdoch's business associates trusted him implicitly, most of Maxwell's associates suspected that there was something unreliable about him, even if they tried to ignore it. He smelt bad. But because of fear, sycophancy, and the libel laws, not many people dared say so.

At the beginning of April, Murdoch closed the *Sunday Herald* in Melbourne. He had launched it as an upmarket broadsheet to compete with the *Sunday Age*, in August 1989, but its circulation had fallen to under 100,000, well below that of its rival. News said that it had been losing A$15 million a year. Seventy jobs were lost and the journalists in the Herald group went on strike.

Murdoch's sister Janet, the chairwoman of the Herald and Weekly Times, sent a photocopied handwritten note around the building to "all you wonderful people working through the strike". Thanking them for their loyalty, she said, "My brother, Rupert, telephoned this morning, asking me to thank you all on his behalf, and to say 'KEEP UP THE GOOD WORK – WE MUST WIN IN THE END'. You are all very much in my thoughts." The company was intransigent and, muttering abuse, the journalists were back at work after almost three days out.

In early May 1991, Murdoch flew out of London to launch his

latest newspaper – in what used to be East Berlin. The wall was now in fragments, and eastern Europe was the new jousting ground for the great information robber barons of our time. Murdoch had already bought a newspaper in Hungary, as had Robert Maxwell. Robert Hersant, owner of *Le Figaro* in France, the Italian Silvio Berlusconi, the German groups Bertelsmann and Springer, were all represented there too.

East Germans had had little recent experience of Western sex and scandal sheets. Now they had an abundance. Murdoch's offering was a tabloid called *Super!*, which played on the same emotions as the *Sun* in Britain, and was pitted against another new Berlin tabloid – *Berliner Kurier*, launched by Maxwell.

Like the *Sun*, *Super!* encouraged chauvinism. It stressed the accomplishments of East Germany and attacked West Germans, who were known as "Wessies". *Super!* had screaming headlines on the sins of the Wessies, rather as the *Sun* did on the alleged misdeeds of the "Frogs". "WESSIE BUYS VILLAGE: 256 CITIZENS IN PANIC"; "WESTERN OFFICIAL SEIZES FARMERS' LAND IN MECKLENBURG". Stories about the influx of pornographic videos blamed West German decadence for destroying East German marriages.

From Berlin, Murdoch, Anna, Andrew Knight and other members of his staff flew on to Moscow. This was Murdoch's first trip to the capital of the "Evil Empire". Recently, his own successes had been invoked in the Soviet press. "Why not learn from Murdoch?" one long Soviet analysis had been headlined.

Information is a great force today. Society's actions and people's actions are in many respects determined by the amount of information they receive . . . Instead of going to Murdoch for money, we must ponder how to learn the ability to manage the information business from people like Murdoch, Maxwell, Hersant and Springer. It is not at all compulsory to copy their gutter-press style.

Murdoch had been invited to visit Mikhail Gorbachev, whose fear of fundamental reform he had been privately decrying. Murdoch was all for Yeltsin; so, passionately, was the *Sun*. Now

Murdoch found Gorbachev, "full of energy, and making speeches at you all the time. He was still a communist. He would not grasp what it is all about." He seemed a tragic figure, commanding nothing real.

It became clear that one of the principal reasons Murdoch had been invited to Moscow was to make an offer for Raisa Gorbachev's memoirs. Murdoch and Anna found her a stunning performer. "She was coquettish, sweet, sexy, then brutal," said Murdoch. "Her attitude was one of anger against the world which has turned against her." She told them that she would not change a word of what she had written. She wanted $400,000. Murdoch agreed. This was what Harper had paid for Gorbachev's own book, *Perestroika*, which had sold well.

After Moscow, Murdoch and Anna stopped again in Berlin and then, following a brief stay in London, attended the Monaco Grand Prix. Anna went on to Sydney, where their eldest child, Elisabeth, was starting out as a journalist, in preparation for assuming a large part in News's management in the future. Anna Murdoch's third novel, *Coming to Terms*, part of which was based upon her father, was just being published. After doing publicity interviews, she flew across the Pacific to their home in Beverly Hills. Anna had pressed her husband to leave New York, in which she found it increasingly hard to live. Now that he no longer owned the *New York Post*, and since the centre of his American business, Fox, was in Hollywood, he could not refuse.

Then it was back to London, for a celebration of Kelvin MacKenzie's tenth anniversary as editor of the *Sun*. It was not an altogether happy milestone, for the circulation of the paper was down by over 300,000 from the previous year. There were those who wondered whether the *Sun* could survive the end of the 1980s and of Mrs Thatcher.

The party was a surprise for MacKenzie, who had been told he was to have dinner with some politicians. It was attended by other editors from Murdoch's empire, past and present, page-three girls and Steve Dunleavy, among others. Praising MacKenzie, Murdoch declared, "We've had a lot of fun producing popular newspapers." Warming to a favourite theme, he said, "We believe absolutely in our readers, the ordinary people of Britain, and it is a great pleasure to puncture the pompous or, at times, to brush aside the 'chattering classes' . . . "

In July 1990, "Dallas" was broadcast to Soviet television viewers for the first time, and the Soviet Union became the 121st member of Intelsat, the International Satellite Telecommunications Organization. This event was described by the president of the official American organization Comsat as "the last nail in the Cold War's coffin".

The coup against Gorbachev one month later showed that there were still those in the USSR who wished to open the coffin again. The failure of the coup demonstrated once more the power of communications. The US government had first realized that something was amiss when its spy satellites revealed that all telephone traffic from Mikhail Gorbachev's Black Sea villa had ceased – the lines had been cut by the plotters. But the attempt to isolate him failed: his guards, who remained loyal, found a radio in the basement and were able to listen to the BBC's and Radio Liberty's accounts of the resistance mounted in Moscow by Boris Yeltsin, hitherto Gorbachev's chief political rival, and now his saviour.

Soviet satellites carried the first pictures of military activity in the streets of Moscow. The image of Yeltsin defiant atop a tank was beamed instantly around the world. Visnews used a Soviet Horizont satellite to carry video from Moscow through London to its European affiliates; CNN utilized Sputnik Express. At the same time, American users of Internet, a worldwide computer network that links universities, sent summaries of the CNN evening headlines to Moscow.

The plotters shut down all the newly independent newspapers and broadcasting stations, but throughout the coup, accurate and uncensored reports from a news agency supporting Boris Yeltsin were distributed around the Soviet Union on private computer networks. Foreign newspapers were able to phone these networks in Moscow and, by modem, pick up messages and reports from the Russian Parliament building where resistance to the coup was centred.

As in the Gulf War, the theatre of news was global. When John Major called George Bush soon after the coup began, the American

President told the British Prime Minister that he had just seen him on CNN. Yeltsin was in frequent contact with Major and with other Western political leaders. They helped him rally resistance. Information was everywhere, the most powerful weapon of all. The coup collapsed. Viewers around the world watched the astonishing sight of Muscovites tearing down the statue of the spymaster, Feliks Dzerzhinsky, in front of the KGB's Lubyanka headquarters, amid cries of "Rossiya", "Rossiya". "We were literally watching the fall of the Bastille," said Murdoch. The global village had closed down its principal prison.

Chapter 15

ON THE ROAD

One morning in December 1991, Rupert Murdoch left his new *pied-à-terre* at the Museum Tower in New York before dawn. The last year had carved the ruts of his face into crevasses, and his hair was a chalky grey. "I'm off to humiliate myself again," he said with a grimace.

He was being sent by his bankers to dispose of part of his birthright – some of the Cruden Trust's share of News Corp – thus diluting his family's control over the company.

He looked tired, older than his sixty years. He climbed into the car with the morning's papers, and was driven in the dark through the streets of Manhattan, into the Holland Tunnel and out to Teeterborough airport in New Jersey, where his private plane, a Gulfstream III, was waiting to fly him to Hartford, Connecticut.

There his bankers had arranged a breakfast meeting and then another encounter with a firm of investment brokers to whom he could explain the restructuring of News.

En route Murdoch grumbled about recent falls in the company's share price. The price would determine how many shares he would have to sell, how much control he would lose. It had been falling for days, from $23 to under $20. Murdoch blamed this on short sellers who had been taken unawares by the stock's rise over recent months, and were now trying to force the price down. He was furious with a report by one New York "shorter", Kynikos Associates, which alleged that the shares "could be worthless".

Few others thought that News was "worthless". By most standards, its transformation over the past year had been extraordinary. At the end of 1990 it had been crushed by a debt of $8.1 billion and constant threats of imminent bankruptcy. By November 1991, the shares had leapt up on the New York Stock

Exchange by almost 300 per cent above their nadir just eleven months before.

News Corp's annual results had been published in the same week as the Moscow coup. The figures showed that in the year to 30 June, revenues had increased 25 per cent while profits, before abnormal items but after tax, rose 14 per cent. This was a considerable accomplishment in a time of recession. But its net loss for the year was A$393 million (£184.5 million) after abnormal losses of A$714 million. These included a write down of A$229 million on magazines which were sold for A$830 million, plus A$193 million spent on rescheduling the debts. As News Corp had to sell off more assets to meet its repayment schedules, there could be more abnormal items ahead.

Then there was tax. News Corp's tax payments on ordinary items rose considerably on the previous year – but it was still paying only 4.5 per cent tax on its profits – a far cry from the 30 per cent paid by most Australian companies. The Australian Tax Office was even now investigating its use of offshore tax shelters.

There was also the treatment of losses at BSkyB. Before Sky merged with BSB it had been treated as a subsidiary. After the merger, the 49 per cent stake in BSkyB was treated as a loan and therefore not equity-accounted. But when the group was refinanced in May, all loan interest was deferred; News Corp started to treat it as an associate company and reverted to equity accounting. On the other hand, the prospects for BSkyB were beginning to look good. Its losses had been cut from the £11 million a week of the year before to about £2 million a week. Costs had been pared to the bone, in the usual Murdoch fashion. The annual budget for Sky News had been reduced from £35 million to £20 million. Dish sales had already reached 2.2 million and BSkyB could claim a reach that made it a serious contender for advertising. It was now reported to be worth all of £2 billion.

The figures showed that News was well on the way to reducing its debt by $800 million by February 1992, as the bankers had demanded.

Analysts were praising Murdoch for having cut capital expenditures and reduced his workforce by 18 per cent. Murdoch himself, in a moment of unusual euphoria, had recently told the *Sunday*

Telegraph in October 1991, "We are the pin-up boys of the banks. Emotive words like bridge loans have gone."

None the less, the harrow could still threaten to the toad. Even if News met the $2 billion payments under the override, there were still repayments of $6.4 billion coming due in February 1994. Murdoch wanted to meet the override debt repayment obligations early. In exchange the banks would be asked to loosen the covenants imposed on News and extend debt maturities from 1994 to 1997.

He and Ann Lane chose to combine three methods – the sale of more assets, an equity offering and public debt offering. The hardest pill for Murdoch to swallow was the equity offering. He had always kept around 45 per cent of News Corp's shares in the hands of his family's Cruden Trust.

The premise was that if they could get $3.5 billion of debt extended for three years, the company had a realistic chance of refinancing and paying down the debt. Lane maintained, "And that's how we're going to get paid back, guys – by helping the company fix itself." Essentially they created an option on the company.

They paid a fee for a commitment to extend from 1994 to 1997, but the commitment was enforceable only if the company met certain conditions – by keeping to their business plan, successfully refinancing the other pieces of the debt. If they did not do so, all the repayment would come due in February 1994 and they would be back to square one. But by the early autumn of 1991, Lane thought Murdoch was well on the way to achieving what was needed. "He recognized that he was managing for cash and could not take a breather. He got on with it."

At the end of October, Murdoch's bankers, Citibank, Morgan Stanley and Allen and Company took the new deal to market. They asked the top forty-six banks to extend 60 per cent of their outstanding credit for an additional three years, from 1994 to 1997, and to loosen the override covenants that had been imposed in the agreement made by Ann Lane.

Murdoch announced the floatation of his Australian printing and magazine interests to raise A$682 million. News Corp would retain 45 per cent. News Corp also announced that it was planning to raise about $450 million by issuing 16.1 million American depositary receipts (each representing two shares) for US investors and 5 million shares elsewhere. It had already raised some US$180 million through the private placement of convertible preference shares. These were bought by friends – Hong Kong businessman, Robert Miller; William Thomson of the venture capital firm Boston Ventures; and TCI, the world's largest cable TV company. TCI's president, John Malone, said that News was an attractive investment for them. TCI bought programming from Fox and was now extending its cabling in Britain, where there would be close links with Sky.

These moves, together with the conversion of notes due in 1992, would dilute Cruden's control of News Corp to some 40 per cent. Even though the family, and he within it, would still retain overall control, that was a small death for Murdoch.

By Thanksgiving 1991, the schedule was getting tighter. The equity offering was supposed to take place in December. His bankers told Murdoch that he would have to go on another road-show: even the thought of interminable early-morning flights to bad breakfasts and poorly attended meetings with thirty-year-old analysts all over the United States and Europe nearly killed him. He insisted on covering Australia by a teleconference.

That December morning, Murdoch arrived at the airport before some of the young bankers who were to shepherd him around the country. He drank tea out of a styrofoam cup, and waited for them. On the short flight to Hartford, Murdoch talked about the death of Robert Maxwell and the revelations of his massive frauds.

He was convinced that Maxwell had committed suicide. "He must have been terrified of going to prison – as he would have done."

As Murdoch seemed to be pulling News out of his own financial abyss, Maxwell had been slithering into a far deeper one. No one knew how deep. The accounts of his many companies and holding corporations, registered in secrecy in Liechtenstein, Gibraltar and elsewhere, were infinitely more complicated and more covert than those of Murdoch.

Murdoch had loathed the way in which he had often been twinned (or worse, confused) with Maxwell in the public imagination. Indeed, right after Maxwell's death, the *Independent* magazine's diarist suggested it would have been preferable had Murdoch not Maxwell died, because although Murdoch was the nicer man, he was "much wickeder" – because of the damage his tabloids had inflicted on British society.

Having observed Maxwell at close quarters for twenty years, Murdoch was not surprised by what had now been discovered. "I'm only surprised by the fact that it's possible to steal so much money." He had long believed that Maxwell was both dishonest and totally unreliable. They had recently competed for Mrs Thatcher's memoirs. HarperCollins had offered £3 million for world rights. According to Murdoch, the negotiations had been made more complicated by the intervention of her son, Mark Thatcher. "He told us that Maxwell had offered ten million. It was never clear whether it was pounds or dollars, but I said fine, go ahead. In the end Maxwell produced neither and they came back to us."

Murdoch also thought that Maxwell was concerned about his KGB files. "He was an agent of influence for the Russians. They had been blackmailing him for years," he said.

One of the few political views Murdoch and Maxwell had shared was support for Israel. Maxwell had been buried with extraordinary eulogies on the Mount of Olives, while President Chaim Herzog described him as "a man of almost mythological stature".

After his death, the astonishing extent of Maxwell's thefts had begun to emerge and it became clear that he had robbed the Mirror pension fund of at least £500 million in an illegal attempt to support his private companies and the share price of Maxwell Communications. The British companies were placed in receivership, as was the *Daily News* in New York. The empire that Maxwell had spent his life building, and with which he had tried to rival Murdoch, collapsed almost overnight.

The *Sun* could afford to be exultant. One of its classic front pages asked,

MIRROR, MIRROR ON THE WALL,
WHO IS THE BIGGEST CROOK OF ALL?

Murdoch's plane landed in Hartford just after 8 a.m., at the private airport belonging to United Technologies, the defence contractor on whose board Murdoch had served since 1984. Immediately behind it, another Gulfstream III touched down, bringing Barry Diller, the president of Fox, from Washington.

Only about a dozen young men and a couple of women came to the Hartford breakfast. Murdoch's aides showed a video extolling News; in it Murdoch looked even more aged, his hair seemed white not grey, and he spoke haltingly. After the video he addressed the analysts himself, explaining the unique attraction of the company for investors. Its media assets, he said, were the greatest in the world: there was Fox, with its movie studio and television stations; there were News's coupons, the Free Standing Inserts, acquired for $80 million and now making about $100 million a year; and *TV Guide* which was being retuned to the proliferation of cable. Murdoch continued:

> The objective of this company is to make investment grade. We are not going through this again. As far as I am concerned, this company is my life . . . my time and my worth are in it. I'm taking a very big step here reducing [my holding] from 44 per cent to just under 40 per cent and could have avoided that by selling more assets. But we believe it is right to keep these assets together – they do make sense and do have very great potential.

Then Murdoch repeated an idea that formed the subtext of his life and the core of his philosophy: "As the world is modernizing, so it is Americanizing." And as America remade the world in its own image, so the world was demanding more and more American entertainment. Fox would meet that demand. Within the United States, the network share of the audience was falling. "We are still going to be the only game in town for people who want to reach the masses."

As he left for the next appointment, he asked quietly, "Did that go all right? I think that went all right, didn't it? There were a couple of reasonable questions." He seemed exhausted, but willing.

Down the road, at the office of George Weiss Associates, a small investment fund manager, there was a shock. After shaking hands, Mr Weiss said that he would not be able to listen to Murdoch and Diller.

Murdoch thought something terrible must have happened. Had Tokyo collapsed? he asked. He meant, Was his share price even lower than an hour ago? No, Mr Weiss replied, "Just the usual press of business."

He had Murdoch and Diller, two of the most powerful men in one of the world's largest industries, in his office and he did not want to hear them.

To some young analysts, Murdoch, Diller and Dave DeVoe told their story again. Asked about the dilution of his stock, he replied, "My entire net worth is here. That's OK! We don't want to sell more [assets] so we decided to dilute."

Diller sang the song of Fox. In film, he said, Fox had five competitors, the other Hollywood studios. In television, none. Fox Broadcasting reached 93 per cent of the USA. The other networks each had 5,000 employees. Fox had only 238. The others would lose $200 million this year, Fox would make at least $50 million. The Simpsons were now doing well against Cosby and would make a fortune when they went into syndication. And so would BSkyB, Murdoch added. Costs were falling and dish sales rising fast. "We have *all* the product of Hollywood for the next ten years."

On the other hand, Fox's new Bette Midler film, *For the Boys*, had just bombed. Fox had hoped the film would repeat last year's success of *Home Alone*, which had boosted the studio's earnings by 182 per cent in the year ending 30 June. But the Midler film, which had cost $40 million, had been panned. "We have written it off already," said Murdoch.

Then it was back to the United Technologies airfield for the short flight to New York.

Diller's plane was more lavishly appointed than Murdoch's. Coffee did not come in styrofoam cups, but was served by a steward in large pottery cups and saucers on tables beside lush tan leather seats.

Diller was furious that he had to be on the road. "On Sunday night I went to Minneapolis. Almost burned down my hotel room overnight, slept four or five hours, went to Chicago, went to a black-tie dinner in New York Monday night, went to the wrong building, did all day yesterday, flew to Washington to make a speech, and then got up at 6 a.m. today to come to Hartford."

Diller was certain that he and Murdoch could have sold far more shares from teleconferencing. Indeed, one teleconference alone to Australia had sold almost half the equity. "It's absurd to make me and Rupert traipse around like this." In his view, the whole process was merely intended to make yuppie bankers and analysts feel important.

Diller's relationship with Murdoch was complex and competitive. Diller bowed to no one in Hollywood; Murdoch tolerated no peers in News.

Playboy had once asked Diller what it was like to "to get your ass kissed all day long?" Diller had replied, "It's been true for so many years it really doesn't affect me."

When *Playboy* asked, "Do you ever have to kiss Rupert Murdoch's ass?" Diller replied, "The term kissing ass is not sophisticated enough because you're dealing in the sophisticated leagues. The only issue really is, do you use your charm to persuade people to do things? I suspect that anybody in any kind of structure does that." As well as charm, Diller sowed terror.

On his plane, Diller praised Murdoch's organizational genius. Politics, he said, was the major subject on which and Murdoch disagreed, and to Diller that was no laughing matter. His voice rose as he spoke with fury about the same laissez-faire conservatism that Murdoch revered. He thought twenty years of Republicanism had killed all ideas. "America is no longer about anything except memories and myths."

But Diller was also scathing about Japan's Hollywood adventure. Neither Sony nor Matsushita was making progress with Columbia and MCA, he said, because they had no understanding of the culture.

He expounded, in typically hyperbolic manner, on the mistake he thought that Sony's chairman, Akio Morita, had made in choosing the controversial team of Peter Guber and Jon Peters to run Columbia. Diller was convinced that American fears of losing its "Dream" to Japan were absurd. The Japanese would be defeated by Hollywood. "They're 6,000 miles away and it's not like having a little Sony Walkman plant in Des Moines, where language is irrelevant."

Such views were quietly dismissed by Akio Morita himself. A few weeks later the chairman of Sony said in an interview for this book that Columbia was doing quite well enough for Sony, that the investment was well worthwhile and Sony would never pull out of it.

Driving from the airfield back to New York, Murdoch constantly punched the car phone, calling his bankers, his lawyer and other advisers. He heard that his share price had fallen further. He would now have to sell another 1 per cent of the company to raise the cash he needed. He toyed with the idea of closing the deal that night, twenty-four hours early, before the price fell further.

Stuck in traffic, he and Diller jumped out at the Plaza Hotel to walk to their next roadshow. Scenes for Fox's *Home Alone Two* were being filmed at the Plaza. The original film had cost only $18 million to make; the sequel would be over $40 million. The child star would get $5 million, as against $200,000 for the first film.

All that day, through the night, and the next day, Murdoch continued to fret about the falling share price. The bankers would decide only at the very last minute at what price to offer the stock.

By Thursday morning, the day the deal had to be closed, the Australian market had moved up overnight and New York opened strong. The shares rose to about $20⅞, but to murdoch's fury, his bankers told him they wanted to make the offering at $19.25. This seemed a huge difference. The banks said they wanted the stock to be bought by institutions who would hold it; they did not want it flipped out quickly and into the hands of short sellers. This made some sense, but Murdoch was enraged; he thought they had been protecting themselves, rather than promoting News.

In the event, he was forced to sell 42 million new shares instead of 37.2 million as he had hoped. The price was $19.30 for the American Depositary Receipts (A$12.50) and with this he raised $404.3 million, instead of the planned $450 million. The extra offering would dilute his control of the company to 39.5 per cent. At the same time News would issue US$400 million worth of senior notes due in 2001, carrying an interest of 12 per cent.

Altogether Murdoch had now raised $1.5 billion since late October – through the equity issue, the preference shares, and the sale of 55 per cent of the Australian commercial printing operations.

The proceeds would be used to reduce the bank debt. As of 30 June, the company's net interest-bearing debt had stood at A$10.5 billion. By now News had repaid early about $2 billion of the debt due in 1994 and stretched out repayment of other maturities. The company's debt had now been reduced to about A$9 billion.

At the same time the banks loosened some of the restrictions that had been imposed in the package negotiated by Ann Lane. They allowed News Corp to increase the annual dividend payout and agreed to lift the ceiling on the funds News could commit to certain investments.

Within eleven months, Rupert Murdoch had begun to burst the bonds that the banks had imposed on him. It was an extraordinary achievement. But it would not be correct to say that he was free. There was now speculation that he would have to raise as much as $1 billion more in equity over the next year, which would dilute his controlling interest to well below 30 per cent. This was something which he would obviously resist with all the force at his disposal.

After the deal was completed, Murdoch flew back to his home in Beverly Hills, where Anna, following the example of Dame Elisabeth, was designing an English garden. Fully grown trees were dropped into holes by helicopter to give it a look of maturity. There were still not many other English things that Murdoch found tolerable.

His assistant, Dot Wyndoe, had also moved to Los Angeles, and taken up a new office on the Fox lot. She had now worked for Murdoch for thirty years, and still travelled constantly around the world as he did. She knew all the details of the imperial history and the surge of personalities within it. In a company which made the most effective use of personnel, she might long ago have been promoted. But as an assistant she was crucial to Murdoch.

Barry Diller was not. At one stage in News Corp's 1990–1 financial crisis, it had seemed possible that Murdoch would have to sell Fox. Diller would happily have bought it. But when he asked Murdoch to sell him at least a share of the company, Murdoch refused. Through 1991, Diller became increasingly frustrated and irritated by Murdoch sitting in on meetings at Fox. Murdoch himself began to chafe. Diller told Murdoch he wanted to be "a principal", an owner not an employee. Murdoch made it clear that in this company there was only one principal. By the second half of 1991, the two men had decided that they should part.

In February 1992, Diller issued a strikingly flowery and personal statement to announce his departure from Fox. He praised Murdoch fulsomely and insisted that he was leaving only because, at fifty, he now wanted to control his own company and his own destiny. In response, Murdoch praised him also. He was delighted that Diller was gone. Now he would have Fox all to himself.

Diller talked about the power of the communications revolution and its potentially harmful impact upon society.

Murdoch was restlessly reinventing himself once again. At almost the same time as he and Diller parted company, he disposed of Richard Searby. After fifty years of friendship and ten years in which Searby had diligently served the company as its chairman, Murdoch asked him to resign. He did not do this face to face; it became known in the company that he had sent Searby a curt note through Ken Cowley. Searby was philosophical; he thought Murdoch had finally tired of his relative independence and differences of style and values. Others thought that Murdoch merely felt he no longer needed Searby.

One of Murdoch's first acts, on taking full charge of Fox, was to promote Stephen Chao, to be head of the Fox News Service, and then of Fox Television Stations. There were those who thought Murdoch had once again sacrificed judgement to infatuation. Chao was a clever Harvard classics graduate of thirty-six, who had been a reporter on the *National Enquirer* and was credited with developing "America's Most Wanted" and "Studs". He delighted in being the enfant terrible of Fox: he would pretend to doze off in meetings, and he once walked out when Diller criticized him for not wearing a tie. In his office he had as decoration a phony soiled diaper and pile of fake excrement. On his appointment to head the news division, *Daily Variety* commented that perhaps he would invigorate TV journalism but, "Then again, those who see it as a sign that the nation is going to hell in a handbasket could be right, too." Murdoch would hear no criticism of him. Now that he had to be on the West Coast, he was determined to concentrate on the electronic side of his empire and to integrate Fox more tightly into News. He regretted that it had been Ted Turner, not himself, who had created CNN and he was determined to catch up by moulding Fox and Sky into a worldwide satellite service of news and entertainment.

At once he made it clear that he would try to slash the costs of film-making by attacking what he saw as the near fraudulent practices of Tinseltown, where agents and stars could command outrageous prices. He intended to increase the number of movies made for TV and he bought into Request Television, one of the new pay-per-view channels which were already threatening to replace the video cassette and the video store.

In reality global entertainment means the export of American entertainment. Films from Hollywood are shown on 86 per cent of Europe's cinema screens – the export of French films is as nothing by comparison. This has led to a continuing battle between the EC and the Motion Picture Association of America over cultural "preservation" in Europe. Jack Lang, France's minister of culture, has denounced the flood of American programming as "cultural imperialism".

By 1992 deregulation of television in Europe was having a huge impact. It was expected to expand EC television airtime from 125,000 hours to 300,000 hours a year. There was no way that those hours could be filled except by pulling in more and more low-budget and usually low-grade made-for-television movies and sitcoms – almost all of them from the USA. Murdoch understood that Fox was at the heart of a fantastic growth industry.

In the 1992 British election campaign, all of Murdoch's papers supported the Conservative Party. Commercial as well as political interests were involved. The Labour Party had promised to intro-duce cross-ownership rules to force him to surrender either his half share of BSkyB or his papers. Arguably no other company in Britain stood to lose so much from a Labour victory as did News.

The *Sun* campaigned fiercely. As usual, it exploited fears, warn-ing, for example, of a "flood of immigrants – including many bogus refugees and scroungers" if Labour won. It also displayed some sense of jollity in its distortions. It consulted a psychic who declared that Stalin and Mao Tse-Tung were for Labour, Elvis Presley was rooting for John Major, while Genghis Khan thought only Mrs Thatcher was worth anything. In a ten-page section headed "Nightmare on Kinnock Street" the *Sun* made dire and fanciful predictions of the horrors of life under Labour.

On the day of the election, 9 April, the front page was filled with the face of the Labour leader, Neil Kinnock, inside a lightbulb. The full front-page headline read: "IF KINNOCK WINS TODAY WILL THE LAST PERSON TO LEAVE BRITAIN PLEASE TURN OUT THE LIGHTS".

> ... We don't want to influence you in your final judgement on who will be Prime Minister! But if it's a bald bloke with wispy red hair and two K's in his surname, we'll see you at the airport.
> Goodnight, and thank you for everything.

On page three the paper published a colour photograph of a fat old woman in a swimsuit, warning: "HERE'S HOW PAGE 3 WILL LOOK UNDER KINNOCK!"

That night, when the Conservatives coasted to a surprise victory over Labour, Murdoch was quoted by *Variety* as saying, on the Fox lot in Hollywood, "We won!" It was a vital victory for him and for News.

A few weeks later, News Corp published figures for the first nine months of the financial year, showing a huge rise in profits. The sales of BSkyB dishes had already soared – by now they were on some 2.2 million homes in Britain – and its prospects were greatly enhanced when, in May 1992, it beat Britain's independent TV companies for the rights to broadcast Premier League football matches. This extraordinary coup infuriated the terrestrial commercial television companies. A satellite dish would now be as vital to millions of people in future as a television set had been in the past. It was now thought that almost 12 million homes would have dishes by 1997 and BSkyB might have an annual subscription income of over £1,700 million.

In his new headquarters at Fox, Murdoch had reason to be delighted with the way in which everything was moving. Orson Welles once said that a movie studio was the biggest train set a boy could ever have. The tracks of Murdoch's train set ran up into the sky and around the world. Now he had it all. Hollywood, and the global reach it has always enjoyed, was his future.

Chapter 16

THE VILLAGE

The making of this book has involved a long journey around Rupert Murdoch's past, present and future. When the research began, he had not bought *TV Guide*, he had not announced his plans for Sky, the Astra satellite had not even been launched – and no one had heard of Bart Simpson. While it was being written, his empire came close to collapse as a result of his expansion and a deepening recession. It was saved above all by his bankers' confidence in Murdoch himself. Now, his fortunes appear to have been restored, although he still has to meet massive debt repayments by February 1994. He is running one of the world's major film studios, his programmes are appearing on televisions in homes across two continents, and he has reinstated himself as one of the most powerful lords of the global village. In spring 1992 he sent his son Lachlan to visit China, where the teaching of the English language and economic reforms are creating a vast new market for his products. In June 1992 he summoned his lieutenants once more to Aspen in order "to tear down the walls of this company". He was determined to remake News to exploit more fully the opportunities of the 1990s.

As usual, the conference was well organized, with hot air ballooning, white water rafting and other pastimes. Murdoch and Anna were excellent hosts. But many employees thought that News had changed enormously since that last Aspen meeting in 1989. Fox and its concerns dominated Murdoch's attention. Some of the British participants felt that they were there merely to service the American broadcasting machine.

The US Secretary of Defense, Dick Cheney, Charles Powell, the former foreign affairs adviser to Mrs Thatcher, and William Rees-Mogg, the former editor of *The Times*, addressed the meeting on global issues. But the conference was punctuated by an incident which some saw as an extraordinary reflection of the contradictions at the heart of Murdoch's empire.

One of the stars of the conference was Stephen Chao, Murdoch's new protégé at Fox. That week, "Studs", Chao's creation in which young men and women make sexually suggestive conversation in front of a studio audience and a leering host, achieved its highest ratings ever. The show would gross $20 million in 1992 and was expected to make $60 million in 1993. Basking in Murdoch's obvious approval, Chao behaved at Aspen with an insouciance bordering on arrogance. As President of Fox Television Stations and Fox News, he took part in a panel discussion of "The threat to democratic capitalism posed by modern culture". The other panellists were Lynne Cheney, the chairwoman of the National Endowment for the Humanities and wife of the Defense Secretary, John O'Sullivan, editor of the *National Review*, Irving Kristol, conservative intellectual, and Michael Medved, film critic. Most of them were critical of the way in which social and moral values were being corrupted by film and television and warned that censorship might be on its way.

To illustrate his theme of the effects of sensationalism on news, Chao had secretly arranged that, while he spoke, a young male model would come onto the platform and take off all his clothes. The audience was astonished, and embarrassed. As the man undressed, Chao asked them not to look at the stripper but to listen to him. Few were able to do so.

After Chao had finished, and questions were taken, Patsy Chapman, the editor of the *News of the World*, tried to make a joke of it all by standing up and asking, "Can you give me the telephone number of the man on the stage?"

Nothing about the incident amused Murdoch. He sacked Chao that same day, and told the conference, "It's a terrible thing to see a brilliant career self-destruct. And it's a bitter loss. But the point is that there are limits."

The question of limits was at the heart of the matter. What were the limits of News Corp? Many people would argue that topless girls on page 3 of the *Sun* overstepped the proper limit. Others would say that the tabloid shows of Fox were often gratuitously sleazy and violent. Fox traded on being the network most likely to transcend good taste and constantly transmitted material which was outrageous and, to some people, vulgar. Murdoch liked its success. But he would not tolerate an outrageous and perhaps vulgar act in front of his wife and distinguished guests. Inevitably the charge of hypocrisy was raised. A columnist in the *New York Times* asked whether Chao would have been fired if he had shown a clip from "Studs" in which contestants asked of each other "Which is the guy who has bounce in his butt?" or "Which one is the more likely to find the G-spot?"

The question was hard to answer. As so often, and with so many issues, Murdoch was ambivalent. The fact that the panel discussion was held at all was evidence of his serious endeavour. He knew that the concerns expressed by Kristol and others were real. But the company – and his own ambitions – had always been financed by pushing the edge of the envelope of decency. His tendency to dismiss such criticisms as "elitist" evades the issue.

It is not possible to pass judgement on a career before it is ended. Any assessment made at this stage of Murdoch's life and empire is bound to be partial – all the more so because he never pauses. Moreover, he is in a business which is constantly in flux and which has forced revolutionary changes upon the world. Information and its dissemination underpins the fabric of our age. Murdoch is one of the most powerful brokers.

Since embarking, over thirty years ago, on his personal, ever-westward odyssey from South Australia to Southern California, Murdoch has encircled the world. In mid-1992 he directly employed 31,000 people, and published 60 million papers (including *TV Guide*) around the world every week. Sky TV was in 3 million British and Irish homes, while Fox Broadcasting was available to 86 million American homes. News was the largest publishers of Bibles in the English language, through HarperCollins and Zondervan Publishing. It also printed China's telephone directories, and Fox films were broadcast to scores of millions of Chinese every week. The annual revenue of the company increased from $5 million in 1960 to $8,546 million in 1991. By any standards, it was an extraordinary, unparalleled achievement. Yet, he was still restless. He was still after more.

He had won nearly every battle he had joined. His defeated enemies were numerous and, even more important, articulate. This in part explains why, in some quarters, he has such a fearsome reputation. If Murdoch had been running a chemical company and Harold Evans had been a dismissed foreman, his complaints would never have gained such wide currency. Much of the criticism of him by journalists and media experts has been repetitive, and uninteresting – or made by political opponents. Many of the direst predictions about his impact on papers – such as *New York*, the *Village Voice, Boston Herald, Chicago Sun-Times, The Times* – have proved wrong.

One could argue endlessly about the precise cocktail of emotions, fears, ambitions, fun, desires and visions that made him. He is a complicated, often ruthless, often charming, usually effective but sometimes uncomfortable mix of Patrick Murdoch and Rupert Greene. He has more than one personality. He can be prim and yet he is a "larrikin", an Australian troublemaker. He sees himself as a radical, he likes to provoke. But he has not always been careful of the consequences.

He is an entrepreneur of genius, and a dedicated publisher. Throughout his career, he has rescued or started papers and television stations. He sustained *The Australian*, the *New York Post* and *The Times* through many years of heavy losses; until his 1990 crisis the only paper he had ever closed was the *Sunday Australian*. However, he has not always improved the papers he has saved.

Murdoch succeeded because he dared. No British publisher had the courage to remove the hands of the print unions from his throat, as Murdoch did at Wapping. In so doing he liberated all British newspapers. Yet their praise for him was grudging.

He could think faster than most of his competitors and therefore often outsmarted them. His intuitive judgement was usually good – though better of situations and businesses than of people. He could see the potential of a business from a mere glance at a balance sheet, while he often misread the heart and the mind of an editors and executives.

As a manager, he was a constant interferer. He felt he could make many decisions better than the people he had appointed. He never liked to be second-guessed. Some of those who fell out with him believed that he regarded everyone who worked for him with contempt; others felt he used people and cast them away. Men like Rohan Rivett, Adrian Deamer, Harold Evans, Eric Beecher, Bruce Matthews and Gerald Long were all at first captivated and then disillusioned by him. Some argued that News was run merely as a machine to make money, and to sustain Murdoch's own astonishing ego and acquisitiveness, with inadequate regard for the fundamental responsibilities of a free press in a free society. Many Australian journalists complained that the culture of News was brutal and contrasted it unfavourably with that of Fairfax before its fall.

But even his antagonists had to acknowledge that Murdoch allowed them the freedom to speak. Unlike some of his enemies, he does not bear grudges. In 1991 he shelved his autobiography, saying he had no wish to re-fight old battles. And it is important to point out that a book like this could not have been written about Maxwell or, indeed, about many other tycoons. It is immensely to Murdoch's credit that he does not attempt to cow critics. (One of the few exceptions was in 1982 when his lawyers demanded excisions from Piers Brendon's book *The Life and Death of the Press Barons*.)

Within News, there were employees at every level who testified to his generosity, the extraordinary enthusiasm he inspired and his courage. Other Murdoch editors, such as Max Newton, Charles Douglas-Home, and Simon Jenkins, have had happy experiences working for him. Jenkins has said he can think of no publisher in Britain who would have allowed him such editorial freedom.

But News became a treadmill. As far back as the 1975 strike on *The Australian*, unhappy journalists asked him to spend more time on improving the paper and less time on foreign acquisitions. In 1991, Murdoch agreed that this was a problem.

I would always have liked to spend less time with the business and more with the product. And we did if you go back. When we started *The Australian*, it was intended to knock the *Can-*

berra Times out and build a base to go out from years later. Instead it was all done overnight. And we were in something that we did not really have the resources to support and make good enough. And equally, I think, the same was true of the *New York Post*. Our resources were spread too thin. But we never starved *The Times* of any resources, ever. You could argue that we tried to push it too fast in some ways.

The power that he has accumulated and deployed on the part of his allies is awesome to their enemies. Many in Britain see Murdoch's relationship with the Conservative Party as almost a symbiotic process in which each helps the other. Similar charges were made about his relationships with Bob Hawke's government and the Reagan administration. Murdoch would not be concerned – in Britain especially, he has rejoiced in the fact that he had helped Mrs Thatcher and John Major bury the socialist era.

He inherited from Rupert Greene the need to live on the edge and, like any successful gambler, he was blessed with luck. To some, his acquisitiveness seemed a kind of madness. Like Don Giovanni, he could never have enough. If anyone asked him why he had bought something new, he would mutter that News needed it, that it was there, and that he could do it better than anyone else.

Beyond the empire, he has no other interests apart from his family, to whom he is devoted. He finds it virtually impossible to relax. He does not read books, nor listen to music, nor enjoy museums. His wife keeps him on a strict regime – for his health he eats only white meat and drinks only white wine, sparingly. He does not sleep well. In his early sixties he is still a man possessed – and lonely. Only a few of those who have helped build his empire are still close to him. As the years have passed and he has driven the business – his business – harder and further, his ability to enjoy friendship, and the value he places on it, has clearly suffered.

His mother thought that "the ultimate aim of Rupert is to achieve. I suppose you have to say that power comes into it. But it's not that he's power-hungry, and he's not money-hungry. But there is that implacable drive in him . . . it's like a general with an army." Dame Elisabeth thought that her son loved the challenge more than anything else.

He himself has said, "I guess I enjoy most of all what little influence there is in publishing papers. I'm not about making money. Not in the sense of mega-money. It goes back to my father, to my background, having been brought up to believe that there was an opportunity to have influence and to do something with that influence."

Asked what drove him, he replied, "I think what drives me are ideas and what you can do with ideas. You can demonize me by using the word power. But that's the fun of it, isn't it? Having a little smidgen of power."

What did he want people to think he had done with his power?

To leave the world a better place, as I saw it. There'll be others who'll say it was a worse place . . . I think they'd be wrong. But the worst thing they can say about me now is that I have too much power. Have we backed some wrong causes? We've probably done so, made some mistakes. Have we had bad values? Certainly some of our papers have had horrible lapses of taste and done things which shouldn't be easily forgiven, but . . . Have we thrown ourselves behind things which today we could consider bad? No. Mistaken maybe.

Of his changing priorities, he said: "I was more of an Australian nationalist when I was younger. Today I would describe myself as being totally internationalist, free market, believing that most people will benefit most and the world will be a better place from having free markets. In ideas as well as goods." What this actually meant was that he thought the export of American values and products always a blessing. He loathed the strictures of feminism and the gay rights lobby, particularly in America, and felt that "political correctness" inhibited proper discussion of the problems of the black ghettoes. Far from believing that the *New York Post* had inflamed racial tension, he felt he had not allowed it to be forthright enough about racial problems. "You are not meant to talk about it in racial terms, but you can't avoid it. We have to face up to it."

He did not start with a hard and fast game plan as such; he was a brilliant opportunist, able to find vacuums and fill them. He identified and exploited social trends and technological possibilities before most people. He dealt in simplicities, by instinct, and his instincts were usually commercially correct.

But simplicities can also be dangerous. Murdoch has often been dismissive of values and institutions without having thought out the consequences of destroying them. His mother, his wife and others close to him have said that he has little imagination. Perhaps this explains why he finds it hard to understand the fear that his power arouses, or the fact that many believe his products transgress accepted limits.

In Britain the argument about him has often centred on the *Sun*. Millions of people buy the *Sun* (and the *News of the World*) each week and enjoy them. There is much that is concise, witty and pertinent in the *Sun*. There is also much that is tawdry, specious, sententious and hypocritical. The worst characteristic of all the tabloids, not just Murdoch's, is their cruelty, in intruding upon the lives of people unable to defend themselves.

When he first bought the *News of the World* and his mother, Dame Elisabeth, expressed unease, Murdoch explained that the poor Brits had to have such entertainment – their lives were so wretched. But the constant, salacious invasions of privacy that his papers have practised, and which have helped to finance the News empire, are not easy to reconcile with the walls of privacy that he and Anna erected around themselves and their family.

Those who fear and dislike Murdoch in Britain say that with the *Sun* he brought about a sea change and debased the values of the class which reads the paper on which his fortune was made. His supporters say that on the contrary he merely understood, at the end of the 1960s, the way in which the working class and its relationship to society was changing, and rammed home the hypocrisy on which the old British system rested. Either way, pointed out Anthony Smith, author of many books on communications, Murdoch has won the argument. The *Sun* and its values are an overpowering fact of British life. (Auberon Waugh proposed that "Kelvin MacKenzie is more powerful in shaping our lives than John Major . . .") In Britain today Reithian concepts are often decried as noblesse oblige, a foolish relic of a bygone age, anathema to the market-led classless society which the Conservative Party, with Murdoch's full support, says it wishes to create.

In Britain he has been particularly identified with attacks upon the royal family. His papers are not alone in constantly intruding upon their lives – indeed, it has become an ugly national blood sport – but in the *Sun* and the *Sunday Times*, there is often a hard edge to the attack. Any other citizens would have stopped such media assaults by use of the laws of libel, but the royal family has denied itself such protection. In June 1992 a new nadir was reached when the *Sunday Times* outbid the *Daily Mail* to serialize a book purporting to reveal the misery in the marriage of Prince Charles and Lady Diana. The intrusive revelations were also serialized and promoted in the *Sun* (though not in *The Times*) and on BSkyB by Andrew Neil. The editor of the *Sunday Times* had apparently abandoned his previous distaste for tabloid methods. It was not an attractive spectacle, even though the Princess of Wales appeared to have sanctioned the publication of this book. The *Daily Telegraph* asserted that Murdoch and his papers "have never made any secret of their republican leanings, nor of their indifference to whether the British throne continues to possess an occupant". Neil and Murdoch were described as "moral dwarves" in the *Sunday Telegraph*.

In an interview in 1991 Murdoch had described similar criticisms as "a bum rap", though he conceded that *Sunday Times* attacks on the royal family sometimes went too far because, he said, Andrew Neil was "a chippy Glaswegian who thinks the whole system is rotten". Asked if he would like to see the end of the monarchy, he replied,

> I'm ambivalent about that. I think you'd have to say No, because I don't think the country has the self-confidence to live without it ... But is the system holding the country back in this new competitive open global village that we talk about? Is it inhibiting the country's growth? I think it's debatable at least. And I think there is nothing wrong in debating it. But if you show yourself even to be thinking about it, that makes you

a figure of hate there, because some people get very excited about it.

People also became "excited" because they understood, often instinctively, that with the decline of industrial and agricultural society, rapid, unpredictable and often uncomfortable changes were being forced upon them. We are living through a revolution in working habits and relations and it will not always be pleasant. Many people rightly identified Murdoch as a powerful agent and advocate of such changes and they did not thank him for it. Others thought such changes long overdue and Murdoch's role useful.

As this book ended, there was reason to think that he was becoming more concerned with quality. "The good thing about running newspapers," said Murdoch, "is that you can always improve them." The *Sunday Times* still had a triumphalist and hectoring tone which many people found disagreeable, but he had ordered Kelvin MacKenzie at the *Sun* to be less aggressive. He had appointed one of Australia's most distinguished political journalists, Paul Kelly, as editor of *The Australian*. Kelly had demanded and received guarantees of independence and had begun to improve the paper. Simon Jenkins had done the same with *The Times* in London before telling Murdoch, in the summer of 1992, that he wished to stand down, as he had always intended; after a flirtation with a tabloid editor, Murdoch appointed Peter Stothard, the Washington correspondent, in Jenkins' place.

In 1992 he was beginning to free himself from the financial covenants imposed by the banks. The danger was that he would embark upon yet another series of enormous risks, in order to stretch the reach of News even further. A wiser policy might be to improve what he already had.

News Corp was filled with prime properties around the world, a fact of which the banks were well aware when they rescued him in 1990–1. But Murdoch was by far its greatest asset. It was *his* future, *his* drive, *his* understanding of markets in which the banks were investing. He believed that all successful companies are built by individuals, not by boards or committees. The corollary is that he has never entertained independent-minded colleagues around him. Rohan Rivett was the first to be unceremoniously set aside, and in 1992 Richard Searby was the latest. This impatience with other people's views and suspicion of their motives is perhaps his greatest weakness. It is unclear how the company will survive him. In 1989, he spoke of Andrew Knight as his successor – "if I should turn out to be mortal". But by 1992 there were few in the hierarchy of News Corp who expected Knight to succeed. Both Murdoch and Anna, who was now on the board, hoped that some or all of their three children would become involved in the empire. (His eldest daughter Prudence did not wish to do so.) Elisabeth was already working as a journalist, James was at Harvard and interested in archaeology, Lachlan was at Princeton. Whatever their qualities, it seemed unlikely that even Murdoch's genes could give his children the extraordinary competitive drive that inspired him. The problem of succession was becoming serious – as it must for any tycoon. The company might soon find itself in a similar position to John Fairfax and Sons over a century before; the second generation of Fairfaxes appointed a series of strong managers to run the business while the family retained control – until Warwick Fairfax lost it in 1990.

Whatever happens to Murdoch, he has an importance far beyond himself. The information age offers fabulous opportunities, but there is no guarantee that they will be seized. What matters are the choices of those barons who control the fantastic new holdings in the global village. Companies like News, Sony, Bertelsmann, Time-Warner, are now in a position to help set the agenda for the millennium. No one has elected them to such responsibility. Technology, the market and, in Murdoch's case, invincible energy and ambition have given it to them.

The age on which we are now embarked is impossible to map. The agricultural age was driven by the plough and draught animals, the industrial age by engines and their fuel. The information age is formated by computers, software, television, and the satellites and lines that link them. Marshall McLuhan expected that the Xerox machine would make Everyman his own publisher; he would have been astonished by the way in which personal computers, linked to networks, could expand this concept. In the next decade, the present generation of computers will be replaced by multi-media machines, processing voice, video and data inputs. Children take for granted an electronic environment in which their parents can only stumble around. What will happen is almost as hard to predict as it would have been in 1700 to anticipate the car or the plane.

In the past a nation's transport infrastructure controlled its wealth. Thus a maritime nation like Britain, with excellent deep-water ports, became the principal trading nation of the world, and its richest. Now a powerful new highway system for information is being created.

The optical-fibre networks that are currently being laid across the United States and, more slowly, elsewhere, are capable of carrying hundreds of thousands of times more traffic than the traditional copper wire. Four huge industries – computers, consumer electronics, telecommunications and entertainment – are now blurring and merging together. Digital electronics are marching ever onwards, converting everything – information, sound, video, text, and images – into a single stream of digits that are then encoded for endless transmission around the world.

For the makers of consumer electronic hardware the march means huge and changing markets. To stave off attacks by newly competitive industries, rather than by old rivals, defensive alliances are being constructed. Thus Sony, Apple and Motorola have teamed up to create pocket-sized cellular phones that double as electronic notepads. Time-Warner, the world's largest media company, and Toshiba, the world's largest computer company, are collaborating to develop the first interactive television system.

In typical Murdoch fashion, News is trying to go it alone and to embrace all at once digital software and hardware, networks and content.

What is not clear is whether these developments will meet today's real needs. Between 1945 and 1991 the world was dominated by the struggle between the West and communism. The victory of the West was well won but the struggle was enormously costly, not least to many of the Third World countries in which proxy wars were fought. The international challenges that the world now faces – such as pollution, global warming, refugees, terrorism, nationalism, Aids, poverty, crime and racial conflict – make the slaying of the communist dragon seem almost simple in retrospect.

During the 1980s the gap in wealth between the richest and poorest nations widened. It is still doing so. The information age has helped to break down tyrannies; but it seems less likely that the trade in information will disperse wealth around the world.

Information and its processing have less value in poor countries because there are few tangible goods to which they can lead. Yet Western consumerist culture is the only global culture – that is the most significant fact of any New World Order. The Evil Empire has been defeated and the Video Empire is spreading. Parts of it are alluring, but other parts are, by any standards, cheap, boring, violent – and overwhelming. Stalin is reputed to have said, "If I could control the American film industry, I could control the world." That industry is infinitely more powerful today.

In India and other parts of Asia, the poorest shacks have televisions and videos and, increasingly, satellite dishes. The Gulf War and the Moscow coup led to a huge expansion in demand for dishes right across the subcontinent: CNN became a worldwide household name during the war. In the autumn of 1991 a Hong Kong based satellite broadcaster, Asiasat, began transmitting MTV rock videos, all-day sports, the new BBC World Service Television, and much more besides. Asiasat's footprint spreads from Turkey through Indonesia and as far north as Korea. Its potential audience is reckoned to be at least 3 billion. All over Asia in villages where people had watched only the government channel on the communal television set, there is now a plethora of choice – of Western entertainment. Indian film-makers fear that their culture and business might be destroyed completely by satellites. But there is more news also, and that is liberating. In one of the most fractured parts of the world, the Middle East, satellites have begun broadcasting news in Arabic to peoples whose information has hitherto been rigidly controlled by vicious regimes, and that will undermine those regimes.

In Europe, it seems likely that there will soon be as many as forty-eight different satellite channels and cabling is racing ahead. Japan is doubling the number of channels through use of satellites.

It is not surprising that the Japanese have bought Columbia and MCA – for their libraries alone. The foreign appetite for American films seems insatiable. By the end of this decade, the film and television industries will probably produce annual revenues of $200 billion – at least half of which will come from abroad.

In 1990 the joint worth of the American film, television and global information businesses (including computers and telecoms) was said to be some $1.3 trillion. By 2000 it might reach $3 trillion – or roughly $1 out of every $6 of global GNP. Murdoch is determined to be one of the larger giants of this colossal enterprise. He is well on the way: in 1992 BSkyB held a virtual monopoly on Hollywood movies for pay television in the UK.

Murdoch believes that the Americanizing of the world is not only profitable for his business, but a great good in itself. But even he asked, in an interview for this book, "Are we going to homogenize the whole world with satellite and cable, with no room for local culture? I think there is a danger. One benefit may be that it is more peaceful. And more prosperous. But there will be fewer differences." In one speech, he told a story (possibly apocryphal) of how the North African tribesmen, the Tuareg, had delayed their annual camel caravan across the Sahara, in order to watch an episode of "Dallas". The individuality of Babel is threatened.

Americanization is bound to be, at the very least, an uncomfortable and unsettling experience. As people of the South have more and more understanding of the unequal division of resources in the world today, more and more millions of them will try to move to the Northern part of the village. Global communications will exacerbate one of the great crises of the 1990s – mass migration, to which Western governments have yet found no answer.

Moreover, America is exporting its culture at a time when American society is in crisis – from poverty, inner-city deprivation, falling education standards, drugs and Aids. By 1992, America, the repository of so much of the world's collective and individual hope, was in crisis at home and abroad. In the words of Murdoch's fellow Australian and resident of America, Robert Hughes, its culture "had replaced gladiatorial games, as a means of pacifying the mob, with high-tech wars on television that cause immense slaughter and yet leave the Mesopotamian satraps in full power over their wretched subjects".

The new video culture has to share the responsibility. Some of Fox's programmes, like "Studs" (now also shown on BSkyB), are outrageous (though funny), and all the American networks are becoming more violent. In 1992, Americans can tune into an HBO TV series called "Real Sex" and watch a striptease class. On NBC News's "I Witness Video" they can see a policeman's murder recorded in his car's camcorder. They can watch a pregnant woman plunge from a blazing building to her death. Throughout 1991–2, the video film of Rodney King being beaten by Los Angeles policemen was shown over and over again as, later, was the film of blacks beating up a white trucker during the Los Angeles riots. Drawing on these and other examples, the broadcaster Bill Moyers quoted W.B. Yeats in a 1992 lecture, saying, "We had fed the heart on fantasies, and it had grown brutal from the fare."

Walter Lippman, the great American journalist, once said that journalism is a picture of reality that people can act upon. Now society is acting upon reality refracted in a thousand different ways. Where is reality when films such as Oliver Stone's *JFK* purport to tell "the truth"? Much of what is being transported down fibre-optic cables is pap. Deregulation lowered the quality of all television channels in France. It threatens the end of serious drama and current-affairs programmes in Britain. They are disappearing also in America. In the free market, only the number of viewers matters. Yet, as newspapers decline in importance as most people's primary source of news, television needs, more than ever, to become the vigilant watchdog of a free society. That is not happening.

Murdoch has argued that "Anybody who, within the law of the land, provides a service which the public wants at a price it can afford, is providing a public service." By contrast, John Reith said at the founding of BBC radio, "He who prides himself on giving what he thinks the people want is creating a fictitious demand for lower standards which he will then satisfy."

Reith was undoubtedly right. But Murdoch can argue that his view is more democratic, and television is a democratic medium.

Moreover, "yellow journalism" has long been a vital part of a free press. It is also worth remembering that the printing press itself, the novel, the radio, the mass-market paperback were all in their time expected to cause the death of culture. The papers which Lord Northcliffe published for the newly literate British public at the turn of the century were denounced by British intellectuals much as Murdoch is denounced today. Yet intellectual life and culture survived.

None the less, there is a legitimate concern. It is the democratic right of millions of Americans to enjoy American culture. But by what democratic decision is that being imposed upon older cultures in Asia, the Middle East and elsewhere? Are people really being offered more choices than before? The phenomenon is so new that such questions cannot all yet be answered. But they need to be asked.

One thing is clear. Press barons like Lord Northcliffe, William Randolph Hearst and Lord Beaverbrook used to affect the views and policies of nations. Murdoch and a handful of others are now reaching and touching the lives of billions of people all over the world. They are building the foundations of the twenty-first century, the information age. Their power is awesome, and the responsibility is immense. It is a responsibility which Rupert Murdoch, grandson of the Reverend Patrick, great-grandson of the Reverend James, scion of the men and women from the dour beaches and the strict kirks of Aberdeenshire can understand. He has only to grasp it.

Source Notes

When $s are referred to in Australian sections of the narrative these are Australian $s, unless otherwise specified.

Prologue

ON THE ROAD

page

1–18.   The principal sources are the author's interviews with Rupert Murdoch, David DeVoe, Ann Lane, William Rhodes, and published accounts. Of these, the most important include: *Institutional Investor*, May 1991; *Australian Business*, 5 June 1991; Stephen Fidler, *Financial Times*, 4 April 1991.

2–3.   Murdoch on the problems with Pittsburgh: author's interview.

2–3.   DeVoe on the problems with Pittsburgh: author's interview.

6–7.   Growth of world financial market: Stewart Brand, *The Media Lab* (Viking, New York, 1988), pp. 230–5.

6–8.   The information society: the standard text on this is Wilson P. Dizard Jr, *The Coming Information Age* (Longman, London, 1989). See also Anthony Smith, *The Age of Behemoths: The Globalisation of Mass Media Firms* (Twentieth Century Fund, New York, 1991).

9.   Murdoch on short-term debt shock: *Financial Times*, 4 April 1991; author's interview.

10.   Banker in *Financial Times*: 4 April 1991.

10.   Story of September roll: author's interviews and published accounts.

10–18.   Ann Lane's story: author's interview and interview with Carole Kismaric.

13.   Annual general meeting, 23 October 1990: *Business Review Weekly*, Sydney, 2 November 1990.

13–14.   Sky-BSB talks and merger: author's interviews with Rupert Murdoch, Andrew Knight and Frank Barlow. Also *Sunday Times* magazine, 23 June 1991.

Chapter 1

CRUDEN

page

19.   Ian Mudie's poem: quoted in Mike Walker, *Australia: A History* (Macdonald Optima, London, 1987), p. 8.

20–2.   History of the Free Church and James Murdoch: I am grateful to George Rosie for research in Scotland on many of the facts in this passage; also to Paul Chadwick for research on Patrick Murdoch's ministry in Australia.

MELBOURNE

22.   Sir William Preece's remark: Walter B. Wriston, *Risk and Other Four-Letter Words* (Harper and Row, New York, 1986), p. 225.

23.   John MacDouall Stuart: Walker, *Australia: A History*, p. 66.

23.   Jeannie Gunn: *We of the Never-Never* (Blackwoods, London, 1908).

24–5.   John Fairfax story: Gavin Souter, *Company of Heralds* (Melbourne University Press, 1981), pp. 9–27.

25.   Melbourne life: Humphrey McQueen, *Social Sketches of Australia, 1888–1975* (Penguin Books, Ringwood, Victoria, 1978), pp. 14–15.

26.   Patrick Murdoch's ministry: *Australian Dictionary of National Biography*, Vol. 10.

26.   Church life in Melbourne: J. Stanley Martin, *A Tale of Two Churches: From West Melbourne to Box Hill* (Box Hill, St Andrew's Presbyterian Church, Melbourne, 1967).

26.   Patrick Murdoch on Camberwell flock: Trinity Presbyterian Church, Camberwell, 1885–1935, jubilee souvenir book (Osboldstone and Co., Melbourne, 1935), p. 17.

26.   "Full of Christian fun": *Australian Dictionary of National Biography*, Vol. 10.

26.   "Prince of preachers", etc.: Presbyterian Church of Victoria, obituary of the Revd P. J. Murdoch in Proceedings of the Assembly, November 1940 (continuing Presbyterian Church archive, Melbourne).

26.   *Laughter and Tears of God and Other War Sermons*: Arbuckle, Waddell and Fawckner, Melbourne, 1915.

27.   Patrick Murdoch's court case, the *Argus*, Melbourne, 16 March 1909; *Australian Dictionary of National Biography*, Vol. 10.

27–8.   Keith Murdoch's childhood: Desmond Zwar, *In Search of Keith Murdoch* (Macmillan, Melbourne, 1980), pp. 1–7.

27–30.   Keith Murdoch's life: *Australian Dictionary of National Biography*, Vol. 10.

28–9.   Henry Lawson: McQueen, *Social Sketches of Australia 1888–1975*, p. 8.

29–30.   Keith Murdoch in London: Zwar, *In Search of Keith Murdoch*, pp. 10–16.

30.   Keith Murdoch on Ellis Island: Ibid., p. 16.

GALLIPOLI

31–6.   Principal sources include Zwar, *In Search of Keith Murdoch*; John Moorehead, *Gallipoli* (Hamish Hamilton, London, 1956); John Robertson, *Anzac and Empire: The Tragedy and Glory of Gallipoli* (Hamlyn, Melbourne, 1990); C. E. W. Bean, *The Story of Anzac* (Angus and Robertson, Sydney, 1941).

31.   "The Journalist who Stopped a War": John Avieson, as "The Correspondent who Stopped a War", *Australian Journalism Review*, January-December 1986.

31.   Sidney Nolan on Gallipoli: *Nolan's Gallipoli* (Australian War Memorial, Canberra, 1978), pamphlet.

31–2.   Murray Sayle: *Spectator*, London, 10 October 1981.

32–3.   Patrick Murdoch's sermons: in *Laughter and Tears of God and Other War Sermons*.

33–6.   Keith Murdoch in the Middle East and London: Zwar, *In Search of Keith Murdoch*, pp. 20–61; Avieson, "The Correspondent Who Stopped a War", passim; Moorehead, *Gallipoli*, pp. 311–12.

36.   Dame Elisabeth on Keith Murdoch's bitterness: interview with Michael Charlton, BBC Radio 3, 2 February 1989.

36.   Rupert Murdoch interview with Gerard Henderson: *Australian Answers* (Random House, Milsons Point, NSW, 1990), pp. 249–64.

FLEET STREET

37–9. Northcliffe's career: Piers Brendon, *The Life and Death of the Press Barons* (Secker and Warburg, London, 1982), pp. 108–26; Charles Wintour, *The Rise and Fall of Fleet Street* (Hutchinson, London, 1989), pp. 1–29.

38. Views of T.S. Eliot, Aldous Huxley and others: John Carey, "Literature and the Masses", The T.S. Eliot Memorial Lectures, 1991, published as *The Intellectuals and The Masses* (Faber and Faber, London, 1992), passim.

39. Keith Murdoch on Northcliffe: Zwar, *In Search of Keith Murdoch*, p. 61.

39. C.E.W. Bean on Murdoch: *The Story of Anzac*, Vol. 6, pp. 6–8.

40–3. Northcliffe–Keith Murdoch correspondence: British Museum, Add. MSS. 4890, XXVII. Some of these memoranda are quoted in Brendon, *The Life and Death of the Press Barons*; Piers Brendon also supplied the author with others.

40–2. Keith Murdoch's influence on the Herald: Michael Cannon, "Shaping the Herald", the *Nation*, 29 June 1963; *Keith Murdoch, Journalist: A Biography* (Herald and Weekly Times, Melbourne, 1952), pamphlet.

42. Colin Ross story: George Munster, *Rupert Murdoch: A Paper Prince* (Penguin Books, Ringwood, Victoria 1987), p. 21.

42–3. C.E. Sayers: unpublished biography of Keith Murdoch, La Trobe library, Melbourne.

43. Northcliffe's visit and advice: Zwar, *In Search of Keith Murdoch*, p. 70.

43–4. Expansion of Herald group: *Keith Murdoch, Journalist: A Biography*, passim.

MELBOURNE

44–5. Keith's home: "A Bachelor's House in Melbourne", *Australian Home Beautiful*, 2 April 1928.

45. Courtship and marriage: Zwar, *In Search of Keith Murdoch*, pp. 76–80; author's interview with Dame Elisabeth Murdoch.

45. Nellie Melba at wedding: Dame Elisabeth Murdoch, interview in the *Melbourne Age*, 22 December 1986; author's interview.

45–6. Elisabeth Greene's family: author's interview with Dame Elisabeth Murdoch, Ranald and Patricia Macdonald and Mrs Ila Massy Burnside.

46. Rupert Greene's career: author's interview with Dame Elisabeth Murdoch, Helen Handbury, Rupert Murdoch; J. Pacini, *A Century Galloped By: The First Hundred Years of the Victoria Racing Club* (Melbourne).

46. No gentleman talked about money or age: the *Melbourne Age*, 22 December 1986.

47. Murdoch and Lyons: C.E. Sayers, unpublished biography of Keith Murdoch; *Australian Dictionary of National Biography*, Vol. 10.

49. Keith Murdoch's enemies: A.A. Calwell, *Be Just and Fear Not* (Lloyd O'Neil, Melbourne, 1972), pp. 88–95.

49. Keith Murdoch on *Sydney Morning Herald* people: Souter, *Company of Heralds*, p. 156.

Chapter 2

CRUDEN, VICTORIA

page

51. Rupert Murdoch and his parents: the most negative view is expressed in Thomas Kiernan, *Citizen Murdoch* (Dodd, Mead and Co., New York, 1986), pp. 14–20.

51–2. Rupert Murdoch on his parents: author's interview.

52. Dame Elisabeth on herself and Keith: interview with Michael Charlton, BBC Radio 3, 2 February 1989.

52. Rupert Murdoch on life as a publisher: author's interview; memoral speech at Helsingen Sanomat Centenary Seminar, 24 October 1989.

52. Rupert Murdoch on being "a chump": interview with Mary Goldring, Channel 4, London, 15 October 1989.

52. Dame Elisabeth on spoiling children: author's interview.

52–3. Anna Murdoch on Nanny Russell: author's interview.

53. Dame Elisabeth on Miss Kimpton: author's interview.

53. Rupert Murdoch's tree house: Michael Leapman, *Barefaced Cheek: The Apotheosis of Rupert Murdoch* (Hodder and Stoughton, London, 1983), p. 19; author's interview with Dame Elisabeth and Rupert Murdoch.

54. Helen and Rupert: author's interview with Helen Handbury.

54. Rupert Murdoch on Patrick Murdoch: author's interview.

54. Rupert Murdoch on his father's fear of his being like Rupert Greene: *Financial Times*, 1 February 1988; author's interview.
     Joan Lindsay on Cruden cavalcade: Zwar, *In Search of Keith Murdoch*, p. 95.

55. Rupert Murdoch on Wagga Wagga sheep station: author's interview.

56. Dame Elisabeth on Rupert Murdoch's liking links with reality: interview with David McNicoll, the *Bulletin*, Sydney, 24 January 1984; on his dislike of dissension and his gentleness, Zwar, *In Search of Keith Murdoch*, p. 96.

56. Dame Elisabeth on sending Rupert Murdoch to boarding school: author's interview.

GEELONG

56. Rupert Murdoch on hating Geelong: author's interview.

57. James Darling's aims at Geelong: author's interview.

58–9. Darryl Wardle on Rupert Murdoch: interview with John Wilcock, confirmed by author's interview.

61. Dame Elisabeth Murdoch's *noblesse oblige*: the *Melbourne Age*, 22 December 1986.

61. Rupert Murdoch on rebellion: author's interview.

61. Rupert Murdoch on James Darling: author's interview.

61–2. James Darling on Rupert Murdoch: author's interview.

OXFORD

62. Sir Keith's health: Munster, *Rupert Murdoch: A Paper Prince*, pp. 7–9; Zwar, *In Search of Keith Murdoch*, p. 122.

63. Rupert Murdoch and Rohan Rivett: author's interviews with Nan and Rhyll Rivett. Murdoch–Rivett correspondence courtesy of Nan Rivett.

64. Rupert Murdoch, Pat Gibson and *Birmingham Gazette*: Kiernan, *Citizen Murdoch*, pp. 25–7; author's interviews with Rupert Murdoch and Pat Gibson.

64–5. Aneurin Bevan: quoted by Thomas J. O'Hanlon in unpublished biography of Rupert Murdoch.

65. Keith Murdoch's letter to Rupert Murdoch in Birmingham: quoted by Dimity Torbett, speech to Australian Journalists' Association conference, "News Unlimited", Sydney, February 1989.

65–9. Rupert Murdoch at Oxford: author's interviews with Rupert Murdoch, Richard Searby, George Masterman, Harry Pitt, Asa Briggs, Nan Rivett.

69. Dame Elisabeth on possibility of withdrawing Rupert Murdoch from Oxford: author's interview.

70–1. Rupert Murdoch on farewell from Sir Keith and Crete: author's interview.

71. Rupert Murdoch on Australian Ambassador in Paris: author's interview.

71. Rupert Murdoch on rent reduction: author's interview.

71–2. *Cherwell* on Rupert Murdoch: 28 May, 11 June 1952.

72.   Gerald Kaufman on Rupert Murdoch: the *Listener*, London, 9 February 1984.
72.   Rupert Murdoch on Gerald Kaufman: author's interview.
73.   Keith Murdoch's plans: Munster, *Rupert Murdoch: A Paper Prince*, pp. 7–9; Zwar, *In Search of Keith Murdoch*, pp. 118–21.
73.   Hugh Cudlipp on Sir Keith Murdoch: Hugh Cudlipp, *Walking on the Water* (Bodley Head, London, 1976), pp. 202–3.
75.   Rupert Murdoch on Keith Murdoch's death: author's interview.
75–6. John Hetherington on Keith Murdoch: "The Man in the Paper Mask", in *Australians: Nine Profiles* (F.W. Cheshire, Melbourne, 1960).
76.   A.C. Watson on Keith Murdoch: *Keith Murdoch, Journalist: A Biography*.
76.   Rupert Murdoch on funeral: author's interview.
77.   Keith Murdoch's will: Munster, *Rupert Murdoch: A Paper Prince*, p. 8.
77–8. Rupert Murdoch's wish to keep *Brisbane Courier-Mail*: author's interview; Murdoch's letters to the Rivetts.
80.   Murdoch on the *Express*: author's interview with Ted Pickering.
80–1. Rupert Murdoch's telegram on Kinsey report: Nan Rivett's files.

Chapter 3

ADELAIDE

page

83.   Dame Elisabeth on Adelaide wilderness: the *Melbourne Age*, 22 December 1986; author's interview.
83.   Rupert Murdoch on *Brisbane Courier-Mail*: author's interview.
83.   Lloyd Dumas and Adelaide *News*: Munster, *Rupert Murdoch: A Paper Prince*, pp. 41–55; Leapman, *Barefaced Cheek*, p. 22; author's interview with Rupert Murdoch.
85.   Ron Boland on Rupert Murdoch: author's interview.
85–6. Rhyll Rivett on Rupert Murdoch: author's interview.
86.   Rupert Murdoch's criticisms of *Sunday Mail*: Nan Rivett's files.
86.   "Rupertorial interruptions": Nan Rivett's files.
86–7. Frank Shaw on Adelaide *News*: author's interview.
87.   Rupert Murdoch on Playford government: author's interview.
87.   Rupert Murdoch on Robert Menzies: author's interview.
88.   Rupert Murdoch and Commonwealth Bank: Munster, *Rupert Murdoch: A Paper Prince*, p. 41; author's interview with Merv Rich; telephone interview with Vern Christie.
89.   Rupert Murdoch on Perth *Sunday Times*: author's interview.
89–90. Thomas Kiernan on *Sunday Times*: *Citizen Murdoch*, pp. 50–2.
90.   Nelson Mews on *Sunday Times*: author's interview.
90.   *Northern Territory News* purchase: O'Hanlon, unpublished biography of Rupert Murdoch.
90–1. Eric White on Rupert Murdoch: Ibid.
91.   Rupert Murdoch on two-up: Simon Regan, quoted in *Time*, 17 January 1977.

AMERICA

93–4. Rupert Murdoch and Australian television stations: Munster, *Rupert Murdoch: A Paper Prince*, pp. 44–7.
94.   Rupert Murdoch on trip with Pat Murdoch: author's interview with Rupert Murdoch.
94.   Ron Boland on trip with Rupert Murdoch: author's interview.

Source Notes

95–6. Malcolm Muggeridge on allure of America: *Things Past* (Collins, London, 1978), p. 125, quoted in Dizard, *The Coming Information Age*, p. 18.

96. Leonard Goldenson on Rupert Murdoch, and Murdoch on Goldenson: Leonard H. Goldenson with Marvin J. Wolf, *Beating the Odds* (Charles Scribner's Sons, New York, 1991), pp. 214–34.

96–7. Rupert Murdoch on *TV Guide*: author's interview.

97–8. Creation of Southern Television: Munster, *Rupert Murdoch: A Paper Prince*, pp. 44–7; author's interviews with Bill Davies and Graham King.

THE ALICE

98–9. Rupert Murdoch's Aboriginal investigation: author's interviews with Ron Boland and Geoff Handbury.

99. Rupert Murdoch's report: Adelaide *News*, 1 February 1957.

99–101. Stuart case: Munster, *Rupert Murdoch: A Paper Prince*, pp. 47–54; author's interviews with Rupert Murdoch and Nan Rivett.

101–2. Rivett sacking: Munster, *Rupert Murdoch: A Paper Prince*, pp. 62, 64; Leapman, *Barefaced Cheek*, p. 26; author's interviews with Rupert Murdoch and Nan Rivett.

Chapter 4

SYDNEY

page

103. Nineteenth-century Sydney journalism: Cyril Pearl, *Wild Men of Sydney* (W.H. Allen, London, 1958), passim.

104. Rupert Murdoch's purchase of Cumberland Newspapers and Sydney *Mirror*: Souter, *Company of Heralds*, pp. 344–6; Munster, *Rupert Murdoch: A Paper Prince*, pp. 57–60; Leapman, *Barefaced Cheek*, pp. 26–8; author's interview with Rupert Murdoch.

105. Francis James and Anglican Press story: Munster, *Rupert Murdoch: A Paper Prince*, pp. 59–60.

106–8. Murdoch at Sydney *Mirror*: Ibid., pp. 60–71; Leapman, *Barefaced Cheek*, pp. 28–30; the *Bulletin*, 23 October 1990; author's interviews with Rupert Murdoch, Betty Riddell, Graham King, Doug Flaherty, Douglas Brass.

106. Frank Packer on Murdoch's tail: Kiernan, *Citizen Murdoch*, p. 70.

107. Doug Flaherty: author's interview.

108–9. Steve Dunleavy story: Marc Fisher, *GQ*, April 1990.

110. Schoolboy suicide: author's interview with Richard Neville; Richard Neville, *INK*, 1 May 1971.

110. Douglas Brass and Rupert Murdoch: author's interview with Douglas Brass.

111. Betty Riddell and Morris West: the *Bulletin*, 23 October 1990; author's interview with Betty Riddell.

111. Graham King on promotion: author's interview.

111–13. Murdoch and Sydney television: Munster, *Rupert Murdoch: A Paper Prince*, pp. 65–71.

112–13. Murdoch, Goldenson and Plitt: Goldenson, *Beating the Odds*, pp. 214–34; author's interview with Graham King.

113–14. Murdoch and Merv Rich: author's interview with Merv Rich.

CANBERRA

115. Rupert Murdoch on idea for starting *The Australian*: author's interview.

116. Rupert Murdoch on *Canberra Times*: author's interview.
116–17. Fairfax takeover of *Canberra Times* and early history of *The Australian*: Souter, *Company of Heralds*, pp. 353–9.
117–18. Max Newton biography: Clyde Packer, *No Return Ticket* (Angus and Robertson, Sydney, 1984), pp. 100–29; Munster, *Rupert Murdoch: A Paper Prince*, pp. 74–6.
118. Newton on Murdoch: *The Australian*, 15 July 1989.
118–22. *The Australian*'s teething troubles: Munster, *Rupert Murdoch: A Paper Prince*, pp. 77–81; Leapman, *Barefaced Cheek*, pp. 31–7.
120. Newton to *Canberra Times*: quoted in Munster, *Rupert Murdoch: A Paper Prince*, p. 81.
121. Newton on being "an impossible bugger": *Times on Sunday*, Melbourne, 31 January 1988.
121. Murdoch on *The Australian* as "idealistic effort": author's interview.

CAVAN

123–4. Anna Torv's background: author's interviews with Anna Murdoch and Karin Torv. Also, profiles of and interviews with Anna Murdoch, for example: Sally Bedell-Smith, *Time* magazine, January 1976; *Sunday Times*, London, 16 June 1985; *Sunday Express*, London, 7 July 1985; *Washington Post*, 23 October 1985; *Independent* magazine, London, 9 March 1991; *Good Housekeeping*, June 1988; *The Times*, London, 3 August 1988; *Telegraph* Sunday magazine, London, 7 August 1988; *Boston Globe*, 15 February 1989; *Sunday Telegraph*, Sydney, 9 June 1991; *Sydney Morning Herald*, 5 December 1986.
125–6. Anna Murdoch on Cavan: *In Her Own Image* (Collins, London, 1985), p. 11.
126. Les Hewitt on Rupert Murdoch: interview with John Wilcock.
126–7. Betty Riddell on Rupert Murdoch: *Bulletin*, 23 October 1990; author's interview.
127–8. John Menadue on Rupert Murdoch: author's interview.
128. Max Newton story in *The Australian*: Munster, *Rupert Murdoch: A Paper Prince*, pp. 85–7.
128–9. Frank Packer and Television Corporation: Ibid., pp. 83–7.

Chapter 5

LONDON

page

The story of Murdoch's purchase of the *News of the World* is told at length in all the biographies of Murdoch and of Robert Maxwell. The author has also interviewed Rupert Murdoch, Lord Catto, Lady Carr, William Carr (son of Sir William and Lady Carr), Sarah Carr, and Merv Rich.
130. Lord Catto on Rupert Murdoch, the *Mirror* and the *News of the World*: author's interview.
130–3. Carr family and *News of the World*: Tom Bower, *Maxwell The Outsider* (Mandarin, London, 1991), pp. 170–82; Munster, *Rupert Murdoch: A Paper Prince*, pp. 117–31; Leapman, *Barefaced Cheek*, pp. 41–9.
133. Merv Rich's encounter with Maxwell: author's interview with Merv Rich.
133–4. Carr family reactions to Maxwell and Murdoch: author's interviews with William Carr and Lady Carr.
134. Stafford Somerfield's editorial: Stafford Somerfield, *Banner Headlines* (Scan Books, Shoreham-by-Sea, 1979), pp. 157–60.
135. Catto's recollections: author's interview.
135. William Carr on dinner with Murdoch: author's interview.

Source Notes

135–6. Breakfast meeting: Kiernan, *Citizen Murdoch*, pp. 96–7; author's interview with William Carr.

137. Lady Carr's doubts: Somerfield, *Banner Headlines*, p. 169; author's interview with Lady Carr.

137–9. Shareholders' extraordinary meeting: Munster, *Rupert Murdoch: A Paper Prince*, pp. 123–4; Bower, *Maxwell The Outsider*, pp. 180–2.

140–1. Anna Murdoch's version: *Family Business* (Collins, London, 1988), pp. 547–65.

141. Rupert Murdoch on SOGAT cleaning ladies: Wintour, *The Rise and Fall of Fleet Street*, p. 225.

141. William Carr on deal with Murdoch: author's interview.

141. Rupert Murdoch on class system at *News of the World*: author's interview.

142. Sarah Carr's remarks: author's interview.

143–4. Murdoch's ownership of *News of the World*: Somerfield, *Banner Headlines*, pp. 183–94; Munster, *Rupert Murdoch: A Paper Prince*, pp. 124–7; Leapman, *Barefaced Cheek*, pp. 48–55; author's interviews with Rupert Murdoch, William Carr and Lady Carr.

146–7. David Frost encounter: Leapman, *Barefaced Cheek*, pp. 50–2; author's interviews and correspondence with David Frost.

FLEET STREET

148. Old Spanish customs in Fleet Street: Simon Jenkins, *The Market For Glory* (Faber and Faber, London, 1986), pp. 73–99.

149. Rupert Murdoch on mess at Bouverie Street: author's interview.

150. Maxwell and the *Sun*: Leapman, *Barefaced Cheek*, p. 56; author's interviews with Hugh Cudlipp and Frank Rogers.

151. Murdoch and Briginshaw: author's interview with Rupert Murdoch.

151. Hugh Cudlipp on Maxwell-Murdoch quandary: author's interview.

152. Murdoch leaping onto presses to find bars: "Inside Story", Public Broadcasting System, 27 April 1984; interview with Brian McConnell, former news editor of the *Sun*.

152. Larry Lamb's hiring: Larry Lamb, *Sunrise* (Papermac, London, 1989), pp. 6–8.

153–4. Early days of the *Sun*: Ibid., pp. 9–41; Munster, *Rupert Murdoch: A Paper Prince*, pp. 133–8; Leapman, *Barefaced Cheek*, pp. 58–9; author's interviews with Rupert Murdoch and Graham King.

155. Sacking of Stafford Somerfield: Somerfield, *Banner Headlines*, pp. 187–94.

157–8. Murdoch and London Weekend Television: Munster, *Rupert Murdoch: A Paper Prince*, pp. 140–2; author's interview with Tom Margerison.

158–9. Muriel McKay's murder: Munster, *Rupert Murdoch: A Paper Prince*, p. 138; Lamb, *Sunrise*, pp. 31–41; author's interview with Beverly McKay.

SYDNEY

160–1. Murdoch on Deamer: author's interview with Rupert Murdoch; Munster, *Rupert Murdoch: A Paper Prince*, pp. 87–92.

161. Adrian Deamer on complaints: author's interview.

161. Frank Devine on Murdoch on Deamer: author's interview.

161. Murdoch and Sydney *Telegraph*s: Munster, *Rupert Murdoch: A Paper Prince*, pp. 95–8.

162. Whitlam and 1972 election: Ibid., pp. 95–103; Kiernan, *Citizen Murdoch*, p. 141; Henderson, *Australian Answers*, pp. 254–6; author's interview with Rupert Murdoch.

162. Murdoch on "far too deeply involved": author's interview.

162–3. Murdoch on "I should have had more reserve": Henderson, *Australian Answers*, p. 256.

TEXAS

163–8. San Antonio: Munster, *Rupert Murdoch: A Paper Prince*, pp. 151–3; *Newsweek*, 14 July 1975; David Shaw, *Los Angeles Times*, 25 and 26 May 1983.

164. Report by Lord Justice Diplock: Munster, *Rupert Murdoch: A Paper Prince*, pp. 144–5.

169. Murdoch on Nixon's victimization: Kiernan, *Citizen Murdoch*, pp. 42–3.

169. Murdoch on Whitlam's "European-type socialism": author's interview.

169. 1975 election story: Munster, *Rupert Murdoch: A Paper Prince*, pp. 107–14.

169–73. The definitive account of the newspapers and the election is C.J. Lloyd, "The Media and the Elections", in Howard R. Penniman, *Australia at the Polls: The National Elections of 1975* (American Enterprise Institute for Public Policy Research, Washington DC, 1977), pp. 171–209.

Chapter 6

AMERICA

page

174–9. Dorothy Schiff's life story is told by Jeffrey Porter, *Men, Money and Magic: The Story of Dorothy Schiff* (Coward, McCann and Geoghegan, New York, 1976).

174–5. Tom Paine and literacy: Neil Postman, *Amusing Ourselves to Death* (Penguin, New York, 1986).

175. Glut of information: Ibid., p. 68.

175. Press baron wars: Brendon, *The Life and Death of the Press Barons*, passim; Richard C. Wald, *A Ride on the Truth Machine* (Gannett Center Journal, Columbia University Press, Spring 1987), pp. 7–20.

177–8. Schiff and *New York Post* history: Porter, *Men, Money and Magic*, passim.

178–9. *New York Post* takeover: *Time*, 17 January 1977.

178. Schiff–Murdoch meeting: Leapman, *Barefaced Cheek*, p. 81; Munster, *Rupert Murdoch: A Paper Prince*, p. 158.

178. Murdoch to Alexander Cockburn: *Village Voice*, 29 November 1976.

178–9. Murdoch on the *New York Post*: *Village Voice*, 29 November 1976; Munster, *Rupert Murdoch: A Paper Prince*, p. 158.

179. *Post* staff members on Murdoch takeover: *Washington Post*, 21 November 1986; *Wall Street Journal*, 22 November 1986.

179–80. The *Observer* fracas: *Sunday Times*, 24 October 1976; *The Times*, 15 November 1976; *Sunday Times*, 28 November 1976; *Cosmopolitan*, July 1986.

180–5. Murdoch and Felker: Gail Sheehy wrote in *Rolling Stone*, 18 July 1977, a very full account from Clay Felker's point of view. See also *Time* Magazine, 17 January 1977, and *Wall Street Journal*, 7 January 1977.

182. Peter Tufo's view: author's interview.

184. Felker on family being broken up by Murdoch: Sheehy, *Rolling Stone*, 18 July 1977.

184. Denouement: *New York Times*, 7 January 1977; *Washington Post*, 9 January 1977.

185. Felker on Murdoch's motives: author's interview.

185–7. Murdoch's impact on *New York Post*: *Time*, 24 January 1977; *MORE*, November 1977; *Columbia Journalism Review*, July–August 1982.

186. Murdoch on elitist journalism: *Washington Post*, 13 May 1977; *Cosmopolitan*, July 1986.

187. Murdoch's reported reasons for choosing Koch: *Esquire*, 22 May 1979.

187–8. Son of Sam story: Munster, *Rupert Murdoch: A Paper Prince*, pp. 169–170;

Leapman, *Barefaced Cheek*, pp. 105–7; *GQ*, April 1990; *New York Times*, 22 August 1977.

189. Murdoch's apology: *MORE*, November 1977.
189. Murdoch and Hamill: *MORE*, November 1977; *Washington Post*, 30 November 1977.
190. Murdoch on support for Ed Koch: *Esquire*, 22 May 1979; Munster, *Rupert Murdoch: A Paper Prince*, pp. 171–4.
190. Lindsy Van Gelder complaint and Murdoch's response: *MORE*, November 1977.
191. New York newspaper strike: Munster, *Rupert Murdoch: A Paper Prince*, pp. 175–83; Leapman, *Barefaced Cheek*, pp. 111–21.
192. Josef Barletta on Murdoch: Leapman, *Barefaced Cheek*, p. 120; Patrick Brogan, *New Republic*, 24 June 1985.
192. Abe Rosenthal on Murdoch: quoted by Leapman, Ibid., and Brogan, Ibid.
192. *Washington Journalism Review*: March 1984.
192. *Columbia Journalism Review*: January–February 1980, quoted by Rupert Murdoch in The 1990 Chet Huntley Memorial lecture.
192–3. Murdoch's response: *MORE*, November 1977; *Esquire*, 22 May 1979.

THE CLARKE RING

193. Murdoch on Clarke: speech to International Institute of Communications, 15 September 1988.
193. *Wireless World* article: see Ernie Eban, the *Listener*, London, 11 March 1982.
194. Clarke's history: *Sunday Times*, London, 22 October 1989.
194–7. Satellite history: Ernie Eban, the *Listener*, 11 March 1982; author's interviews with Les Brown, editor of *Channels*, Brian Haynes, Jonathan Miller, Jeff Hollister; John Burgess, *Washington Post*, 27 August 1989; *Washington Post*, 17 March 1985, 14 June 1988.
195. Clarke on the future in the 1940s: quoted by Rupert Murdoch, *Intermedia*, autumn 1988.
196. Clay T. Whitehead's actions: *Washington Post*, 7 November 1971; interview with Marc Champion, on behalf of the author.
198–9. WARC 77: author's interviews with Jonathan Miller, Brian Haynes; Marc Champion's interview with Tom Whitehead.
199. Satellite developments: Rosemary Righter, *Whose News Anyway?* (Burnett Books, London, 1978), pp. 217–28.

AUSTRALIA

200. Murdoch on deficiencies of Herald management and News Ltd's need for *Herald* revenue: the *Melbourne Age*, interview by Terry McCrann, 23 November 1979; author's interview.
200–1. *Sun* as engine of empire: *Esquire*, 22 May 1979.
201. Murdoch on children's schooling: McCrann, the *Melbourne Age*, 23 November 1979.
201–2. Gambling background and Robert Sangster on Rupert Murdoch: quoted in O'Hanlon, unpublished biography of Murdoch; O'Hanlon, *Fortune*, 6 November, 1978, 7 May 1979; James Cooke, *Forbes*, 6 March 1989.
203–5. Murdoch and television applications: papers from the Australian Broadcasting Tribunal, 1979–80; Munster, *Rupert Murdoch: A Paper Prince*, pp. 184–99; author's interviews with Rupert Murdoch, Deirdre O'Connor, Jim Cruthers.
205–6. Ansett story: Munster, *Rupert Murdoch: A Paper Prince*, pp. 189–94; author's interview with Rupert Murdoch.
207. Murdoch on no ideas at *Herald*: McCrann, the *Melbourne Age*, 23 November 1979.
208. *Herald* share price story: Munster, *Rupert Murdoch: A Paper Prince*, pp. 152–94.

208.   Australian Journalists' Association on Rupert Murdoch: Ibid., pp. 200–1.

209.   Murdoch on his politics: Ibid., p. 200.

209.   Justice Morling on *The Australian*: Ibid., pp. 200–3; Australian Administrative Appeals Tribunal (General Administrative Division), 17 December 1981.

LONDON

210–11.   The *Sun* and the 1979 Election: Larry Lamb, *Sunrise*, pp. 154–68; author's interview with Rupert Murdoch and correspondence with Gordon Reece.

212–13.   Lamb on Murdoch: Lamb, *Sunrise*, pp. 219–35.

WASHINGTON

213–16..   Max Newton's life: Packer, *No Return Ticket*, pp. 121–9; *Times on Sunday*, 31 January 1988; Sunday *Observer*, Melbourne, 18 August 1990; author's interview with Olivia Newton.

216–18.   Ansett-Boeing purchase: Ansett Loan and Export-Import Aircraft Financing Policies, hearings before the Committee on Banking, Housing and Urban Affairs, United Sates Senate, 12, 13 May 1980, passim.

Chapter 7

LONDON

page

220.   Anna on home: author's interview.

220.   Evans and Murdoch rows: see in particular, Harold Evans, *Good Times, Bad Times* (Coronet Books, London, 1984), pp. 280–493.

221.   President Lincoln on *Times*: quoted by Leapman, *Barefaced Cheek*, p. 152.

222.   Harry Evans's background: see Evans, *Good Times, Bad Times*; profile, *Observer*, 22 February 1981.

223.   Tony Geraghty on *Sunday Times* sherpas: letter to the author, 3 February 1991.

223.   Don Berry on "journalism by orgasm": Linda Melvern, *The End of the Street* (Methuen, London, 1986), p. 103.

224–6.   *Times* history: Leapman, *Barefaced Cheek*, p. 150.

226.   Murdoch's 1979 denial of interest in *The Times*: interview with Terry McCrann, the *Melbourne Age*, 23 November 1979.

226.   Evans on Donoughue: Evans, *Good Times, Bad Times*, p. 120.

227.   Brunton's views of Murdoch and others: author's interview.

227.   *Guardian* withdrawal from Evans's plan: Evans, *Good Times, Bad Times*, p. 150.

227.   Evans on Murdoch as favourite: Ibid., p. 153.

227–8.   Gerald Long call to Evans: Ibid., p. 161.

228.   Murdoch's call to Evans: Ibid.

228.   Evans on Murdoch as prime source: Ibid., p. 162.

228.   Evans–Murdoch lunch: Ibid., pp. 162–3.

228–9.   Tina Brown on Murdoch's charm: Ibid., pp. 164–5.

229.   Evans urged to lead Stop Murdoch campaign: Ibid., p. 167.

229.   Hamilton, Evans, Rees-Mogg lunch: Ibid., p. 168.

230.   Roger Wood on John Lennon's corpse: *New York Times*, 12 February 1981.

230–1.   Committee to vet Murdoch, and final *Times* sale negotiations: Evans, *Good Times, Bad Times*, pp. 172–80; author's interviews with Gordon Brunton and William Rees-Mogg; correspondence with Lord Dacre.

232.   Murdoch on how well he had done: *Editor and Publisher*, 11 April 1981.

233.   Brunton on referral: author's interview.

Source Notes

233. Referral considered at Cabinet level: Evans, *Good Times, Bad Times*, p. 186; author's correspondence with John Biffen.

233. Evans on Mrs Thatcher's determination to reward Murdoch: Evans, *Good Times, Bad Times*, p. 186.

233. Biffen's concession: in an off-the-record lobby briefing to journalists afer the publication of *Good Times, Bad Times*.

233. Evans's frustration in Press Gallery: Evans, *Good Times, Bad Times*, p. 186.

234. Linklater's criticism of Evans: *Journalist*, November–December 1983.

234. Patrick Brogan's telex: Leapman, *Barefaced Cheek*, p. 198–200.

234. *New Statesman* argument: 30 January and 6 February 1981.

235. Murdoch's nervousness over court action: Evans, *Good Times, Bad Times*, p. 197.

235. *Sunday Times* journalists' action: Ibid., pp. 196–9; author's interviews with Magnus Linklater, Geoffrey Robertston, Tony Geraghty, Hugo Young, Don Berry.

235. John Barry on Murdoch: Evans, *Good Times, Bad Times*, p. 199.

236. Murdoch on reasons for appointing Evans: author's interview with Rupert Murdoch.

236. Evans on his own ambition: "Inside Story", Public Broadcasting System, 27 April, 1984.

237. Frank Giles on accepting appointment: Frank Giles, *Sundry Times* (John Murray, London, 1986), p. 199.

THE VILLAGE

238. Murdoch on Reuters: author's interview.

238–40. The Reuters story is told in John Lawrenson and Lionel Barber, *The Price of Truth* (Mainstream Publishing, Edinburgh, 1985); also author's interviews with Gerald Long and Glen Renfrew.

240. Glen Renfrew on Murdoch's fascination: author's interview.

241. Receiving countries' consent: Righter, *Whose News Anyway?*, pp. 220–1.

AUSTRALIA

243. Profits crash: Munster, *Rupert Murdoch: A Paper Prince*, p. 246.

243. Cowley on Murdoch and *The Australian*: author's interview.

244. "By phone and by clone": author's interview with Eric Beecher.

LONDON

244. Evans's meeting with *Times* journalists: Evans, *Good Times, Bad Times*, p. 266.

245. Gerald Long on Bernard Donoughue: author's interview.

245. Evans's vigorous if chaotic methods: author's interviews and correspondence with Richard Williams, Edward Mortimer, Richard Davy, Gerald Long, Richard Searby, Jessica Douglas-Home, Adrian Hamilton.

245. Evans on *Times'* Bermuda Triangle and other problems: Evans, *Good Times, Bad Times*, pp. 309–49.

245. Gerald Long on Evans's lack of stamina and ideas of budgets: letter to the author.

246. Edward Mortimer and Dacre: author's interview with Mortimer and correspondence with Dacre.

246. Gerald Long on Evans's budgetary ideas: letter to the author.

246–7. Evans on Murdoch and politics: Evans, *Good Times, Bad Times*, p. 296.

247. Murdoch on Evans: author's interview.

247. Murdoch to Australian journalist: Terry McCrann, *Sydney Morning Herald*, 19 November 1983.

247. Gerald Long on working for News: author's interview.

247–8.   Richard Searby on Gerald Long: author's interview.
248.   Edward Pickering on Gerald Long: author's interview.
248.   Murdoch on Giles's Communism: Evans, *Good Times, Bad Times*, p. 358.
248.   Giles opens "Long insult file": Giles, *Sundry Times*, p. 208.
248.   Giles on Murdoch's "bitter animus": Ibid., pp. 202–3.
249.   Giles on Murdoch's kindness to chauffeur: author's interview.
249–51.   Affair of the Titles: Evans, *Good Times, Bad Times*, pp. 432–49; author's interviews with Richard Searby, Edward Pickering and Gerald Long, and correspondence with Harold Evans.
251.   Evans on Douglas-Home accepting the editorship: Evans, *Good Times, Bad Times*, p. 456.
252.   Murdoch on death of Evans's father: Ibid., p. 451.
253.   Searby on Evans's departure: author's interview.
254.   Evans on his resignation dilemma: *Good Times, Bad Times*, pp. 450–87.
254.   Unions demand for Evans to resign: Leapman, *Barefaced Cheek*, pp. 234–5.
254.   Edward Mortimer on Evans: author's interview.
255.   Gerald Long on Evans and Murdoch: author's interview.

THE FALKLANDS

A full account of the British press and the Falklands war is in Robert Harris, *GOTCHA! The Media, The Government and The Falklands Crisis* (Faber and Faber, London, 1983).
255.   Murdoch as Communications Man of the Year, and on parallel between Falklands and Israel: *New York Post*, 22 April 1982.
256–8.   Kelvin MacKenzie's life and times: A full and hilarious account is Peter Chippindale and Chris Horrie, *Stick it Up Your Punter* (Heinemann, London, 1990).
259–61.   Hitler Diaries story: Robert Harris, *Selling Hitler* (Faber and Faber, London, 1986) and Giles, *Sundry Times*, pp. 231–56; author's interview with Harry Pitt, Frank Giles, Philip Knightley, Brian MacArthur, Richard Searby and Gerald Long.
262.   Frank Giles's departure: Giles, *Sundry Times*, pp. 247–51.
263.   Magnus Linklater on *Good Times, Bad Times*: *Journalist*, November–December 1983.
263.   Harold Evans's letter to Magnus Linklater: 6 January 1984.
263.   Harold Evans's letter to Patrick Brogan: 29 November 1984.
263.   Rupert Murdoch on Evans: *Sydney Morning Herald*, 19 November 1983.
263.   Philip Howard on Charles Douglas-Home: in introduction to Philip Howard, *We Thundered Out: A Bicentenary History of The Times* (Times Books, London, 1985).
264.   Charles Douglas-Home's relations with Murdoch: author's interviews with Edward Mortimer, Richard Davy, Alan Franks, Jessica Douglas-Home.

Chapter 8

BOSTON

page
266.   Murdoch on welfare state: *Fortune*, 15 January 1979.
266.   Murdoch at lunch with Reagan: author's interview with News America executive.
266–7.   Murdoch criticisms of investigatory journalism: David Shaw, *Los Angeles Times*, 25 and 26 May 1983.
267–8.   Donald Kummerfeld's role: author's interview.

268.   Paul Rigby's departure from *New York Post*: author's interview.

268.   Murdoch on *Post*'s support for Reagan: *Editor and Publisher*, 11 April 1981.

268.   Murdoch and Koch: Michael Davie, the *Spectator*, 27 February 1982; Patrick Brogan, *New Republic*, 24 June 1985.

269.   *Columbia Journalism Review* on Steve Dunleavy: July–August 1982.

269.   Mario Cuomo on *Post*: *Columbia Journalism Review*, July–August 1982.

270.   Bloomingdales man to *Wall Street Journal*: quoted by Patrick Brogan, *New Republic*, 24 June 1985.

271.   Murdoch's interest in *Courier Express* and *Daily News*: Leapman, *Barefaced Cheek*, pp. 245–50.

271.   "Trib to Rupert: Drop Dead": 1 May 1982.

271.   Murdoch and the *Herald*: Lea Kivivali, "The Murdoch Influence on the *Boston Herald*", thesis submitted to the Royal Melbourne Institute of Technology, November 1988.

271–2. Donald Forst and Murdoch: *Boston* Magazine, May 1983; Leapman, *Barefaced Cheek*, pp. 250–3.

273.   David Greenway on *Boston Herald*: author's interview.

273.   Murdoch on Boston's passion: *Boston* Magazine, May 1983.

THE CLARKE RING

274.   Murdoch's move onto Clarke Ring: *Washington Post*, 6 May 1983; *Newsweek*, 6 June 1983; *Business Week*, 11 July 1983; author's interview with Jim Cruthers.

274.   Murdoch signing with SBS: *Washington Post*, 6 May 1983.

274–5. SBS background: *Broadcasting*, 13 March 1983; *USA Today*, 15 November 1983; *New York Times*, 15 November 1983; author's interview with Les Brown.

275.   Murdoch on missing cable: interview with Raymond Snoddy, *New Media Markets*, 17 February 1988; *Sydney Morning Herald*, 13 November 1989.

276.   Jim Cruthers on problems with Skyband: author's interview; Murdoch in *Fortune*, 20 February 1984.

276.   Sky television beginnings: author's interview with Jim Haynes.

277–8. Development of satellite broadcasting: *Financial Times* survey on broadcasting, 16 September 1985, and *Financial Times* survey on satellites, 29 May 1990.

278.   Tom Whitehead in Luxembourg: Whitehead interview with Marc Champion on behalf of the author.

CHICAGO

279.   Charles Wilson's account of the *Sun-Times*: author's interview.

279–82. Field family and growth and sale of *Sun-Times*: Chicago *Tribune*, 22 January 1984; Garry Wills, *Vanity Fair*, May 1984.

280–2. Jim Hoge's role: author's correspondence with Jim Hoge; Wills, *Vanity Fair*, May 1984.

282.   Sale of *Sun-Times* to Murdoch: *New York Times*, 2 November 1983; *Newsweek*, 14 November 1983; *Wall Street Journal*, 21 December 1983.

283–4. Royko's departure: interview with Carole Kismaric; *Washington Post*, 11 January 1984; *New York Times*, 14 January 1984; *Chicago Lawyer*, February 1984; *Washington Journalism Review*, March 1984.

284.   Roger Ebert on Murdoch and Field: *Vanity Fair*, May 1984.

285.   Wilson on Brogan: author's interview.

285–6. Wilson on changes: author's interview.

287.   Medill School study: "The *Sun-Times*: Before and After Murdoch", spring 1984.

288.   Frank Devine: author's interview.

Chapter 9
page

289.   *Forbes* on Murdoch: 30 January 1984.

289.   Neil Postman on Orwell and Huxley: *Amusing Ourselves to Death*, pp. 110–12.

290.   George Gerbner: Ibid., pp. 139–40.

290.   Huxleyan future: Ibid., p. 156.

290–1.   Computer history: Gene Smarte and Andrew Reinhardt in *Byte*, September 1990, pp. 369–400.

291.   Computer as "leviathan instrument of Big Brother", and growth of small computer companies: George Gilder, *Microcosm* (Simon and Schuster, New York, 1989), passim.

292–3.   Banking history: Anthony Sampson, *The Money Lenders* (Hodder and Stoughton, London, 1981), pp. 27–64.

293.   Walter Wriston on Rupert Murdoch: author's interview.

293.   Walter Wriston on communications revolution: *Foreign Affairs*, Winter 1988/9.

293–4.   Soviet leaders and telephones: Wilson P. Dizard and S. Blake Swensrud, *Gorbachev's Information Revolution: Controlling Glasnost in a New Electronic Era* (The Center for Strategic and International Studies, Westview Press, Boulder, Colorado, 1987).

294–5.   Gorbachev speech: Ibid., pp. 11–12; *Pravda*, 26 June 1987.

295.   News Corp's position in 1984: *Australian Business*, 30 November 1983; *Forbes*, 30 January 1984; *The Economist*, 25 February, 2 March 1984; *Fortune*, 20 February, 1984.

297.   Murdoch on direction of electronic age: *Fortune*, 20 February 1984.

297.   Kiernan-Murdoch agreement: signed 21 March 1984.

297.   Murdoch on buck stopping here: Terry McCrann, *Melbourne Age*, 21 November 1983.

298.   News Corp revenues: *Fortune*, 20 February 1984.

299.   Murdoch on "screwing up": *Economist*, 25 February 1984.

299.   Sarazen to Economist: Ibid.

300.   Changes at *The Australian*: author's interviews with Ken Cowley, Richard Searby and News Ltd journalists.

300–1.   *New York Post* figures, etc.: *Economist*, 25 February 1984.

301.   Murdoch buys Ziff-Davis publications: *Washington Post*, 22 November 1984.

301.   Murdoch acknowledging that Times Newspapers was different: interview with Terry McCrann, *Melbourne Age*, 21 November 1983.

302.   "Let someone else own the satellites": *Forbes*, 30 January 1984.

302.   Murdoch on failed editors: *Forbes*, 30 June 1984; *US News and World Report*, 27 May 1985.

302.   Murdoch to Barbara Walters: "20/20", ABC TV, 28 June 1984.

HOLLYWOOD

303.   *Economist* on American entertainment industry: *Economist* survey, 23 December 1989.

303–4.   Warner Communications story: *Financial Times*, London, 29 December 1983; *Wall Street Journal*, 4 January 1984; *Financial Times*, 7 January 1984; *New York Times*, 8 January 1984; *Business Week*, 16 January 1984; *Wall Street Journal*, 18 January 1984; author's interview with Rupert Murdoch.

304.   Shuman–Ross–Murdoch meeting: Richard Sarazen deposition, Court of Chancery, Wilmington, Delaware, 9 January 1984.

304.   Murdoch on "investment": *Wall Street Journal*, 18 January 1984.

304.   Warners' decline: *Fortune*, 13 January 1983; *New York* magazine, 24 January 1983.

Source Notes

304–5.   Warners and Chris-Craft: Jerome Tuccille, *Rupert Murdoch* (Donald Fine Inc, New York, 1989), p. 114.

304–5.   Murdoch–Ross meeting: *Boston Globe*, 18 December 1983.

304–5.   Murdoch launches campaign for Warner: *New York Times*, 4 January 1984; *Washington Post*, 6 January 1984.

305.   Murdoch files suit to block Warner–Chris-Craft deal: *Washington Post*, 7 January 1984.

305.   Warner attack on Murdoch: *Washington Post*, 11 January 1984.

305.   Murdoch in court: *Washington Post*, 12 January 1984.

305.   Murdoch in Switzerland: Leapman, *Arrogant Aussie* (Lyle Stuart Inc, New Jersey, 1985), p. 266.

306.   Murdoch on "pattern of racketeering" at Warner: *New York Times*, 25 January 1984; *Daily Telegraph*, London, 26 January 1984; Tuccille, *Rupert Murdoch*, p. 118.

306.   Steve Dunleavy and Ross: *New York Times*, 28 January 1984.

306.   Murdoch on not being run down: *New York Times*, 6 February 1984.

306.   Murdoch's $40 million profit: *Newsweek*, 26 March 1984; *Broadcasting*, 26 March 1984.

307.   Murdoch to *Economist*: 25 February 1984.

307–9.   Twentieth Century-Fox history: John Gregory Dunne, *The Studio* (Farrar, Straus & Giroux, New York, 1969), passim; Stephen M. Silverman, *The Fox That Got Away* (Lyle Stuart Inc, New Jersey, 1988), passim.

309.   Davis and Marc Rich: Alex Ben Block, *Outfoxed* (St Martin's Press, New York, 1990), pp. 15–16, 72–3.

309.   Marc Rich charged with tax evasion: Ibid., p. 82.

309–10.   Marvin Davis and Fox: Ibid., pp. 14–29, 59–83.

310–11.   Barry Diller–Marvin Davis relationship: Ibid., pp. 59–83.

310–11.   Milken and Drexel Burnham Lambert impact on industry: *Wall Street Journal*, 18 September 1989; *Financial Times*, 20 September 1989; *Sunday Telegraph*, 6 May 1990; *Business Week*, 31 December 1990.

310–11.   Milken's fall: Allan Sloan, *Newsday*, 22 April 1990.

311.   Murdoch agrees to buy 50 per cent of Fox: *Washington Post*, 21 March 1985; *New York Times*, 21 March 1985; Ben Block, *Outfoxed*, p. 82.

312.   Diller's "exit rights": Ben Block, *Outfoxed*, p. 82.

312.   Murdoch buys half of Fox: *Variety*, 25 September 1985.

312.   Murdoch on entertainment and news reporting: Ben Block, *Outfoxed*, p. 86.

312–13.   Murdoch in China: statement by Howard Rubinstein, May 1985; *Business Review Weekly*, 5 December 1986.

313.   Murdoch taking only five minutes to decide to buy Metromedia: interview with Trevor Kennedy in Trevor Kennedy, *Top Guns* (Sun Books, Melbourne, 1988), pp. 280–300.

313–14.   Kluge story: New York *Herald Tribune*, 6 September 1964; *Fortune*, 5 April 1982.

314–16.   Kluge's development of Metromedia: Allan Sloan, *Forbes*, 23 April 1984, 17 December 1984, 3 June 1985, and *Wall Street Journal*, 8 May 1985.

316–18.   Murdoch's financing of Metromedia: *Business Week*, 20 May 1985; Allan Sloan, *Forbes*, 3 June 1985; *Business Review Weekly*, Sydney, 23 August 1985; *Wall Street Journal*, 23 January 1986.

318.   Sarazen on Murdoch: *Business Review Weekly*, Sydney, 23 August 1985.

319.   Murdoch's anger with Drexel: Ben Block, *Outfoxed*, pp. 106–7.

320–1.   Davis withdrawal from Fox and Murdoch's reaction: Ibid., pp. 108–9.

321.   Alexander Cockburn on selling the Post: *Wall Street Journal*, 23 May 1985.

ELLIS ISLAND

323.   Citizenship ceremony: *New York Times*, 5 September 1985; *Financial Review*,

575

Sydney, 6 September 1985; additional background supplied by Glenda Korporaal.

324.	Breslin on Murdoch's citizenship: New York *Daily News*, 6 September 1985.
324.	William Safire on Murdoch's citizenship: quoted in *Media Week*, 24 May 1985.
324–5.	Mike Royko on Murdoch's citizenship: New York *Daily News*, 15 May 1985.
325–6.	Mark Fowler's background and views: *Broadcasting*, 18 February 1985; *Christian Science Monitor*, 20 May 1985; *Business Week*, 5 August 1985.
326.	Quello on "fast buck artists": *Business Week*, 5 August, 1985.
326.	Quello on Murdoch: interview with Glenda Korporaal, 1985; *Business Week*, 20 May 1985.
327.	Murdoch on Mark Fowler: "Implications of The Communications Revolution", United States Information Agency, International Council Conference III, May 1990, p. 16 of transcript.
327.	Dame Elisabeth to *Sydney Morning Herald*: 4 December 1986; *Daily Telegraph*, Sydney, 6 December 1986.
327–8.	John Evans on Murdoch informing his mother about citizenship: author's interview with Evans.
328.	Murdoch to *Sydney Morning Herald*: 6 May 1985.
328.	Anna Murdoch on Murdoch's ambition: William H. Meyers, *New York Times*, *Business World* Magazine, 12 June 1988; author's interview.
329.	Anna's sharp tongue: Murdoch told *Cosmopolitan*, "She can cut me off at the knees better than anybody else", July 1986.
329.	Anna Murdoch on not wanting to be a partygoer: *Washington Post*, 23 October 1985.
329.	"We are [good people]": *Washington Post*, 23 October 1985.
329.	Anna Murdoch on Murdoch having no time for imagination: *Melbourne Age*, 9 August 1985; author's interview.
330.	Anna Murdoch on nightly blackmailing calls in Britain: *The Times*, 3 August 1988.
330.	Anna Murdoch to *Time*: 6 January 1976, interview by Sally Bedell-Smith, cover story on Murdoch published 17 January 1977.
330.	Anna Murdoch on Murdoch's "deafness": *Sunday Express*, 7 July 1985.
330.	Anna Murdoch on traditional household and marriage: *Washington Post*, 23 October 1985.
330.	Anna Murdoch on Murdoch's sense of humour: interview with Sally Bedell-Smith, *Time*, 6 January 1976.
330.	Anna Murdoch on a more Bohemian life: *Melbourne Age*, 9 August 1985.
331.	Murdoch's "devastating" criticisms: *Washington Post*, 23 October 1985.
332.	Karin Torv on her sister's book: author's interview.
332.	Anna Murdoch on Collins and American publishers: *Sunday Express*, 7 July 1985.
332–3.	Anna Murdoch to *Sunday Times*: 16 June 1985.
333.	*Melbourne Age*'s fun: 9 August 1985.

Chapter 10

WAPPING

page

The best account of the Wapping story is Linda Melvern, *The End of the Street* (Methuen, London, 1986). Also essential reading is Simon Jenkins, *The Market for Glory* (Faber and Faber, London, 1986); David Goodhart and Patrick Wintour, *Eddie Shah and the Newspaper Revolution* (Coronet, London, 1986); Brian MacArthur, *Eddy Shah: Today and the Newspaper Revolution* (David and

Charles, Newton Abbot, 1988); also Charles Wintour *The Rise and Fall of Fleet Street* (Hutchinson, London, 1989).

335.   State of Fleet Street: Jenkins, *The Market for Glory*, pp. 73–96.

337–40. Start of Wapping: *Financial Times*, 27 January 1986.

341–3. John Cowley's account: author's interview. Also author's interviews with Rupert Murdoch, Lewis Chester, Bruce Matthews.

FLEET STREET

347.   Kelvin MacKenzie and the *Sun*'s newsroom: Melvern, *The End of the Street*, pp. 56–70.

348.   Charlie Wilson and *The Times*' newsroom: Ibid., pp. 80–4; author's interview with Charles Wilson.

350–1. Andrew Neil and the *Sunday Times* newsroom: Melvern, *The End of the Street*, pp. 97–118; author's interviews and correspondence with Don Berry, Lewis Chester, Claire Tomalin, Hugo Young.

351.   Claire Tomalin on Andrew Neil: *Observer*, 2 February 1986.

351–3. First days of Wapping: Melvern, *The End of the Street*, pp. 119–88; Wintour, *The Rise and Fall of Fleet Street*, pp. 215–23.

357.   Auberon Waugh on Wapping: *Spectator*, 3 January 1987.

358.   Murdoch on the *Independent*'s gains from Wapping: Henderson, *Australian Answers*, pp. 249–64

Chapter 11

MELBOURNE

page

Glenda Korporaal provided a long, very useful research memorandum on the story of Murdoch's capture of the Melbourne *Herald*. The story is well told in Paul Chadwick, *Media Mates* (Macmillan, Melbourne, 1989). I have also consulted David Bowman, *The Captive Press* (Penguin Books, Ringwood, Victoria, 1988), pp. 85–106. See also *Time*, Australian edition, 2 February 1987. Amongst those whom the author has interviewed or consulted for this section are Rupert Murdoch, John D'Arcy, Ken Cowley, Keith McDonald, Eric Beecher.

359.   Murdoch "like Father Christmas": *Sydney Morning Herald*, 4 December 1986.

359.   Dame Elisabeth on Murdoch being like his father, and his motives: *Sydney Morning Herald*, 5 December 1986.

360.   Murdoch like Citizen Kane: *Melbourne Age*, 4 December 1986.

361–2. Deirdre O'Connor on Australian cross-ownership rules: author's interview.

362.   Hawke on friendship with Packer: Chadwick, *Media Mates*, pp. 31–2.

362.   Keating as a tiger: Ibid., pp. 35–6.

362.   Hawke on Fairfax as the "Natural enemy" of Labor, and the Melbourne *Herald*: Ibid., p. 36.

364.   Murdoch-Keating dinner: Ibid., p. 19; author's interview with Rupert Murdoch.

364–5. John D'Arcy's arrival and approach at the *Herald*: author's interview.

365.   Keith McDonald's view: author's interview.

365.   Murdoch's approach to the board: author's interviews with Rupert Murdoch, John D'Arcy and Ken Cowley.

366.   Cowley's warning to Murdoch: author's interview.

366.   Murdoch's public announcement: Chadwick, *Media Mates*, pp. 45–6.

366.   Chronology of Murdoch's victory: Ibid., pp. 41–87; *Sydney Morning Herald*, 17 January 1987.

367.   Financial Review complaint: Chadwick, *Media Mates*, p. 45.

367.   Hawke on Murdoch: Ibid., p. 36.
367.   Hawke on *Herald* management: Ibid.
367.   Murdoch's deal with Robert Holmes à Court: Ibid., pp. 67–9; *Sydney Morning Herald*, 17 January 1987.
367–8.   Murdoch and Queensland Press: *Financial Review*, 3 March 1987; author's interview with Keith McDonald.
368–9.   Murdoch and Northern Star: *Sydney Morning Herald*, 30 July 1988.
370.   Murdoch's appointment of Eric Beecher: author's interviews with Murdoch, Beecher and Peter Smark.

THE VILLAGE

371.   News turnover and profits: Paul Johnson, *Spectator*, 28 March 1987.
371.   CBS debts: *Broadcasting*, 26 February 1987.
371.   Sarazen sanguine: *Broadcasting*, 26 February 1987.
372.   Murdoch's plans for *New York Post*: author's interview with Frank Devine; the *Nation*, 13 February 1988.
372.   Murdoch's purchase of *South China Morning Post*: *Business Review Weekly*, Sydney, 5 December 1986; Tuccille, *Rupert Murdoch*, p. 162.
372–3.   Performance of Fox Television stations: *Broadcasting*, 12 February 1987.
373.   Diller on "counter programming": *Broadcasting*, 26 February 1987.
374–6.   Collins history: author's interviews with Ian Chapman, George Craig and Sonia Land.
376.   Harper and Row history: *New York Times*, 5 April 1987.
376.   Murdoch and Chapman takeover bid for Harper and Row: author's interview with Ian Chapman.
377.   Brookes Thomas on Murdoch's bid: *New York Times*, 5 April 1987.
377.   Murdoch's plan in linking Harpers and Collins: Tuccille, *Rupert Murdoch*, p. 175.
377.   Roger Straus on things not pinned to the wall: *New York Times*, 5 April 1987.
377.   Publishing mergers in 1980s: *New York Times*, 5 April 1987.

LONDON

379–81.   Murdoch's takeover of *Today*: Brian MacArthur, *Eddie Shah, Today and the Newspaper Revolution* (David and Charles, Newton Abbot, 1988), pp. 184–93; also, *Sydney Morning Herald*, 2 and 3 July 1987; *Sunday Times*, 5 July 1987; author's interviews with Brian MacArthur and Richard Searby, and correspondence with Lord Young.
383.   Murdoch buys Pearson stake: *Times* and *Financial Times*, 23 September 1987; *New York Times*, 28 September 1987; *Financial Weekly*, 3 March 1988.
383.   Frank Barlow on Murdoch's powerbase: David Kynaston, *The FT: A Centenary History* (Viking, London, 1988), p. 503.
384.   Frank Barlow on Murdoch as honest interferer: author's interview.
384.   Murdoch's vision for *Financial Times*: interview by Raymond Snoddy, *Financial Times*, 1 February 1988; *Forbes*, 22 February 1988.
384.   Sarazen on *Financial Times*: *Observer*, 27 September 1987.
384.   Max Newton on *Financial Times*: Tuccille, *Rupert Murdoch*, p. 181.
384–5.   Murdoch lunch with Blakenham: *Times*, 2 October 1987; *Tatler*, April 1988.
385.   Anthony Lewis in *New York Times*: 5 November 1987.
385.   Andrew Neil's reply to Lewis: *New York Times*, 19 November 1987.
385–6.   Pearson's purchase of *Les Echos*: *Independent*, 23 February, 25 March 1988; *The Times*, 29 March 1988.
386.   Murdoch increases his holdings in Pearson: *Guardian*, 14 January 1988; *Financial Times*, 22 January 1988.
386.   Murdoch on turning into a hostile person: Ray Snoddy, *Financial Times*, 1 February 1988.

386.   Murdoch on not going above 25 per cent: *Financial Times*, 19 January 1988.
386.   News transactions with Pearson shares: *Times*, 11 February 1988; *Financial Times*, 9 February 1989; *Wall Street Journal*, News Cayman/News Corp issue, 9 May 1989.
386.   Murdoch and Blakenham's second meeting: *Forbes*, 22 February 1988.
387.   Murdoch to *Forbes*: 22 February 1988.
387.   Pearson's tactics: author's interview with Frank Barlow; *Financial Times*, 12 January, 15 September 1988, 3 February 1990; *Financial Weekly*, 18 February 1988.

NEW YORK

387.   Murdoch's grief on selling *New York Post*: Tuccille, *Rupert Murdoch*, pp. 187–97; author's interviews with Rupert Murdoch, Frank Devine, Richard Searby.
387.   Max Newton on Kennedy's favour: Tuccille, *Rupert Murdoch*, p. 190.
388.   Steve Dunleavy's style: author's interviews with staff of the *Post*; Marc Fisher, *GQ*, April 1990.
388.   Murdoch on his mistakes with the *Post*: Tuccille, *Rupert Murdoch*, pp. 192–7; interview in *Gannett Center Journal* (Columbia University Press, Winter 1989), pp. 33–41.
389.   Ferraro on *New York Post* attacks on herself and on Murdoch–Reagan connections: *Washington Post*, 20 October 1984; *Wall Street Journal*, 2 November 1984; *Washington Journalism Review*, November 1984.
389.   *Wall Street Journal* on Murdoch's use to administration: 2 November 1984.
389.   Frank Devine on *Post*'s problems: author's interview.
389–90.   FCC and cross-ownership rule: *New York Times*, 11 January 1988; Marc Champion interviews with staff of Senate Commerce Committee.
390.   FCC and waivers: *Boston Globe*, 3 May, 9 and 15 November 1985, 10 January 1988.
390.   Fowler on his best action at FCC: *Boston Globe*, 10 January 1988; *Times on Sunday*, Sydney, 3 June 1988; quoted by senior staff member of Senate Commerce Committee in interview with Marc Champion.
390.   Murdoch on delaying the sale of the *Post*: Tuccille, *Rupert Murdoch*, pp. 195–6; the *Nation*, 13 February 1988; author's interviews with Rupert Murdoch and Frank Devine.
390.   *Wall Street Journal* report: quoted in the *Nation*, 13 February 1988.
390.   *Post* promotion budgets cut: Roger Franklin, the *Bulletin*, Sydney, 29 March 1988.
390–1.   Freedom of Expression suit: the *Nation*, 13 February 1988.
391.   William H. Meyers in *New York Times*, *Business World*: 12 June 1988.
392.   Murdoch papers on Kennedy: the *Bulletin*, Sydney, 29 March 1988.
392.   Howie Carr on Kennedy: quoted in *Time*, 18 January 1988.
392.   *Time* chortling: 18 January 1988.
392.   Marlin Fitzwater on amendment: *New York Times*, 5 January 1988.
392.   Koch on Kennedy's "character flaw" and "in the dead of night": *Time*, 18 January 1988.
392–3.   Kennedy on "signals" etc.: the *Nation*, 13 February 1988.
393.   Lowell Weicker on Murdoch as "number one dirtbag": Senate debate, Congressional Record, 25 January 1988.
393.   Hollings on "unholy alliance": *New York Times*, 2 February 1988.
393–4.   Murdoch's attack on Hollings: *New York Times*, 12 February 1988.
394.   Frank Devine on Murdoch's depression: author's interview.
394.   Murdoch's reluctance to sell the *Post*, and subsequent depression: Tuccille, *Rupert Murdoch*, p. 194; author's interviews with Rupert Murdoch and Frank Devine.

394. Kalikow negotiations: Associated Press, 5 February 1988; *Washington Post*, 5 February 1988.
394. Washington DC Court of Appeal ruling: *New York Times*, 30 March 1988; quoted by Tuccille, *Rupert Murdoch*, p. 190; *Independent*, 30 March 1988.
395. Murdoch on "nightmare": Tuccille, *Rupert Murdoch*, p. 194.

ASPEN
395–8. This account of the Aspen conference is derived principally from interviews with those present, including John Evans, Eric Beecher, Philip Crawley, Simon Jenkins, Stephen Milligan, Paul Kelly, Terry McCrann.
398–9. Newton on "global village": *The Australian*, 29 November 1988.
399. Carolyn Wall to *New York Times*: 14 August 1988.
399–400. John Evans's history: *New York Press*, 24 November 1989; author's interview.
400. John Evans on Murdoch: author's interview.
401. Annenberg's view of Murdoch: author's interview.
401–2. Triangle history: *Financial Times*, 9 August 1988; *New York Times*, 11 August 1988.
402–3. Annenberg on Murdoch being after "whole ball game", and "immense gambler": author's interview.
403. John Veronis's intervention: *New York Times*, 9 August 1988; *Economist*, 13 August 1988; *Advertising Age*, 15 August 1988.
403. Murdoch on being "too keen": author's interview.
403. Warren Buffet's advice to Annenberg: *Wall Street Journal*, 8 November 1991.
403. John Veronis on "natural conversation": *New York Times*, 8 August 1988.
403. Howard J. Rubinstein on "circle of friendship": *New York Times*, 8 August 1988.
404. *Los Angeles Times* on science fiction fantasy: 9 August 1988.
404. Norman Lear's comment: interview with *Time*, 12 August 1988.
404. David Wagenhauser's comment: *Christian Science Monitor*, 10 August 1988.
405. Andrew Jay Schwartzman comment: *New York Times*, 8 August 1988.
405. Murdoch on finances of *TV Guide*: *Newsweek*, 22 August 1988.
405–6. John Evans's doubts: author's interview.
406. *TV Guide* and News's debt: *Wall Street Journal*, 9 August 1988; *Sunday Times*, 14 August 1988.
406. Colin Reader on financing purchase of *TV Guide*: author's interview.
406. News Corp's 20F filing with Securities and Exchange Commission: 19 September 1988.
406. Evans proposal to sell *TV Guide*: author's interview.

Chapter 12

SUN COUNTRY

page

I am grateful to Peter Chippindale and Chris Horrie for permission to quote from their book, *Stick it Up Your Punter*, a comprehensive and amusing account of the history of the *Sun*. I am also grateful to Alan Rusbridger for providing me with all the research notes that he assembled for a book on the *Sun*; to Madeleine Bunting and to Nick LeQuesne for research into different aspects of the *Sun*, and to Lewis Chester for invaluable help in organizing the material.

Other sources include Roslyn Grose's semi-official *The Sun-sation* (Angus and Robertson, London, 1989), and interviews by the author and others with *Sun* journalists, most of whom prefer to remain anonymous.

409. MacKenzie's praise for Murdoch: Chippindale and Horrie, "Punter", p. 8.
409. *Sun* and Press Council: Peter Kellner, *Independent*, 1 February 1988.
410. List of "scum": Ibid., p. 177.
410. MacKenzie on "understanding the reader": Ibid., p. 110.
411. MacKenzie's "True Story Alert": Ibid., p. 211.
411–12. MacKenzie's relations with Murdoch: Chippindale and Horrie, "Punter", pp. 328–9.
412. MacKenzie, *Sun* and Royal Family: Ibid., pp. 352–3; *Sun*, 14 October 1988, 12 December 1989.
413. MacKenzie, *Sun* and French: *Sun*, 12 December 1989, 21 and 22 May 1991; Chippindale and Horrie, "Punter", pp. 169–172.
413. *Sun* on German re-unification: 11 November 1989.
413. *Sun* on Hirohito: 21 September 1988.
413. *Sun* on Spanish Air Controllers: Chippindale and Horrie, "Punter", p. 250.
413. MacKenzie and *Sun* on homosexuals: *Sun*, 13 December 1990; Chippindale and Horrie, "Punter", pp. 181–2.
414. *Sun* on "straight sex and AIDS": 17 November 1989.
414. Press Council condemnation: *UK Press Gazette*, 16 July 1990.
414. *Sun* and "Loony Left": Chippindale and Horrie, "Punter", pp. 219–22.
414. *Marxism Today* on the *Sun*: November 1989.
414. *Sun* on Ken Livingstone: Chippindale and Horrie, "Punter", pp. 130–1.
414. *Sun* on Tony Benn: Ibid., pp. 172–3.
414–5. Michael Foot on debasement of journalism: Ibid., p. 142.
415. *Sun* on Neil Kinnock: Ibid.
415. *Sun*'s "nightmare issue" on Kinnock's election: 8 June 1987.
415. *Sun* and Arthur Scargill: Chippindale and Horrie, "Punter", pp. 175–7.
416. Wendy Henry's priorities: Ibid., pp. 150–2, 240.
416. Ralph Halpern stories: Ibid., pp. 243–4.
417. Wendy Henry's end as editor: Ibid., pp. 332–4.
417. Elton John libel: John Sweeney, *Independent* Magazine, 11 February 1989.
417–18. Murdoch on British "decadence": *Gannett Center Journal* (Columbia University Press, Winter 1989), p. 37.
418–19. David Scarboro death: *Guardian*, 12 June 1989.
419. Alan Bennett on Russell Harty's death: *Guardian*, 17 October 1988, *Listener*, 20 October 1988, and author's correspondence with Alan Bennett.
420. Hillsborough story: *Sun*, 19 April 1989; Chippindale and Horrie, "Punter", pp. 276–94; Press Council ruling, 31 July 1989.
421. David Mellor on "Last Chance Saloon": Chippindale and Horrie, "Punter", p. 306.

SPRINGFIELD, USA

422. The Simpsons and the audience: *Rolling Stone*, 29 June 1990; "Television Business", *Adweek*, 10 September 1990.
423. Barry Diller's background: Huntington Williams, *Beyond Control – ABC and the Fate of the Networks* (Atheneum, New York, 1989); *Playboy* interview, June 1989; *Buzz*, Los Angeles, May–June 1992; Ben Block, *Outfoxed*, pp. 75–8.
423. Murdoch on Diller: *Business Week*, 20 May 1985.
423. Diller on going bananas: *Manhattan Inc*, February 1988.
423. Diller on barbed wire: Ibid.
423. Diller on William Morris background: *Playboy*, June 1989; *Buzz*, Los Angeles, May–June 1992.
424. Diller at Caesar's Palace: *Playboy*, June 1989.
424. Decline of networks after 1977: *Broadcasting*, 17 April 1989; Ken Auletta, "Why ABC Survived Best", *New York Times* Magazine, 28 July 1991.
424–5. Fox reflecting American changes: Nicholas Lemann,"How the Seventies Changed America", *American Heritage*, July–August 1991.

425.   Goldenson's strategy: Ben Block, *Outfoxed*, pp. 122–3.
425–6. Joan Rivers story: Ibid., pp. 140–57.
426.   Murdoch saying "Buy her out": *Business Week*, 1 June 1987.
426.   Rivers' settlement: *Broadcasting*, 8 June 1987.
426.   Fox's losses: *Los Angeles Times* calendar, 12 March 1989; *Forber*, 1 August 1990.
426.   Diller on grafting an alien, and things getting worse before better: author's interview.
426.   Impact of screen writers' strike: J. Max Robbins, *Channels Field Guide*, 1990.
426.   Tracey Ullman success: Jerry Lazar, *New York Times* Magazine, 15 October 1989.
426.   Diller on "cratering" the old company, and grabbing by the throat: author's interview.
427.   "PMS": *Guardian*, 7 April 1989.
427.   Terry Rakolta: *New York Times*, 2 March 1989.
427.   Fox toning down the show: *Wall Street Journal*, 25 May 1989.
427.   *New York Times* editorial: 11 March 1989.
428.   Murdoch on "subversive" Fox: author's interview.
428.   Diller on Republican myths and difference between him and Murdoch: author's interview.
428–9. Povich on Murdoch and his "daredevil squadron": Maury Povich, *Current Affairs, A Life on the Edge* (Putnam, New York, 1991), pp. 51–2 and throughout.
430.   John Walsh and "America's Most Wanted": Monica Collins, "Wanted Captures its Audience", *USA Today*, 2 March 1989, cover story.
430.   Diller on "Most Wanted" success: author's interview.
431.   "Cops" success: Harry F. Waters, "TV's Crime Wave Gets Real", *Newsweek*, 15 May 1989.
431.   "Cops" in Soviet Union: Monica Collins, *USA Today*, 14 July 1989.
432.   Steve Dunleavy story: Marc Fisher, *GQ*, April 1990; Povich, *Current Affairs*, pp. 59–61, 182–7.
433.   Tom Shales in *Washington Post*: Fisher, *GQ*, April 1990.
433.   *New York Times* on "A Current Affair": Ibid.

AUSTRALIA

        The story of the Collins takeover is based on contemporary reports and interviews with the contemporaries, including Rupert Murdoch, Ian Chapman, Sonia Land and George Craig.
433.   Murdoch and phone call from France; Murdoch's synopsis for his autobiography.
433–4. Murdoch and Chapman's relations: author's interviews with Ian Chapman and George Craig.
434.   News International bid for Collins: *Financial Times*, 18 November 1988; *Independent*, 19 November 1988; author interview with Lord Goodman.
434–5. Collins search for "white knight" and News International's "categorical" statement: *Financial Times*, 23 December 1988.
435.   Murdoch's matching bid: *The Times*, 31 December 1988.
435.   Murdoch's statement from Australia: *The Times*, 31 December 1988.
435.   Chapman's reiteration: *The Times*, 31 December 1988.
435.   Presses de la Cité call to Murdoch: Murdoch's synopsis.
435.   Collins with few options: *Financial Times*, 6 January 1989.
436.   Michael Frayn on Murdoch: *Guardian*, 6 January 1989.
436.   Ken Follett on Murdoch: *Independent*, 6 January 1989.
436.   John Harvey-Jones on Murdoch: *Guardian*, 6 January 1989.
436.   Murdoch's response to authors' criticisms: *Daily Telegraph*, 7 January 1989.
436.   Chapman's departure: author's interview.
437.   *Brisbane Sun* and Adelaide *News* arrangements: *Sydney Morning Herald*, 30 July, 1 August 1988.

Source Notes

437. Trade Practices Commission report: "Investigation of Disposal by News International of the *Sun* and *Sunday Sun* in Brisbane and the *News* in Adelaide", August 1989.

437. Murdoch on Warwick Fairfax's courage: *Sydney Morning Herald*, 1 September 1987.

437. Fairfax's demise. There are several authoritative books. The author has used V. J. Carroll, *The Man Who Couldn't Wait* (Heinemann, Melbourne, 1990) and Gavin Souter, *Heralds and Angels* (Melbourne University Press, 1991).

438. Trade Practices Commission stops Murdoch: Carroll, *The Man Who Couldn't Wait*, p. 282.

438. Murdoch's new presses: see for example, Glenda Korporaal, the *Bulletin*, Sydney, 14 February 1989.

438–40. Problems at the Melbourne *Herald*: author's interviews with Rupert Murdoch, Eric Beecher, John D'Arcy, Ken Cowley.

440–1. Beecher on Murdoch: author's interview.

441. Anna Murdoch to *New York Times*: author's interview with William H. Myers, who profiled Murdoch in *New York Times Business World* Magazine, 12 June 1988.

441. Murdoch on Beecher and croissants in South Yarra: author's interview.

441–2. Dame Elisabeth's birthday party: author's interviews with Dame Elisabeth Murdoch, Douglas Brass and Sir James Darling.

443–4. Murdoch's diary: from the synopsis for his autobiography.

Chapter 13

THE CLARKE RING

page

445–8. Background to BSB franchise: *Independent on Sunday*, 25 March 1990; *Financial Times*, 12 August 1989; *The Times*, 25 April 1990; interview by Nick LeQuesne with Brian Champness, *Marketing Week*, 17 June 1988.

448. Background to Sky's development 1983–7: author's interviews with Jim Cruthers, Peter Smith, Brian Haynes and John O'Loan; interview by Nick LeQuesne with Richard Platt.

448–9. Sky launch at BAFTA: author's notes; *The Times, Daily Telegraph, Guardian*, 9 June 1988.

449–50. Branson's withdrawal from BSB; Michael Maconochie, *Sunday Times* magazine, 23 June 1991.

450–1. Building Sky studios; interviews by Nick LeQuesne with Sky personnel; author's interviews with Peter Smith, John O'Loan.

451. Hollywood expenditure and encryption problems: author's interviews with Peter Smith, Jim Cruthers, Jonathan Miller and others.

451. Andrew Neil and Jonathan Miller at Sky: author's interview with Jonathan Miller.

452. John O'Loan on launch: interview with Nick LeQuesne.

452. Lack of dishes: *Observer*, 5 February 1989.

452. Mockery of Sky: *Daily Telegraph*, 4 February 1989; *Independent*, 9 February 1989.

453. Promotion of Sky by News Corp papers: *Independent*, 17 February 1989.

453. BSB dossiers: *Independent*, 28 April and 23 August 1989; "Cross-Media Control in the United Kingdom", Joint Memorandum of Counsel, 4 July 1989.

453. Sky's response to BSB's complaint: "Competition, Diversity and Cross-Media Ownership", News International's response to BSB's Joint Memorandum, August 1989; *Independent*, 23 August 1989.

453.   BSB's delays: "Money Programme", BBC 2, 4 February 1990; *Independent*, 23
       April 1990.
454.   Sky's re-launch: *Television Business International*, February 1990.
454.   Sky's advertising sales problems and Sky's charter advertisers: author's interview
       with Pat Mastandrea of Sky.
455.   Voyager's journey: *Independent*, 28 August 1989.
456.   Murdoch in Edinburgh: *The Times* and *Independent*, 26 August 1989.
457.   Rosie Waterhouse resignation: author's telephone interview.
458.   Murdoch on Britain's "decadent society": *Gannett Center Journal* (Columbia
       University Press, Winter 1989), p. 37.
459.   William Rees-Mogg's response: *Independent*, 29 August 1989.
459.   *Pravda*: Howard Brenton and David Hare (Methuen, London, 1985).

ASPEN

460.   Murdoch saying he was "tapped out": author's interview with News personnel.
460-2.   Story of Media Partners (and Murdoch on failure of): *Wall Street Journal*, 6
         June 1989, 12 April 1990.
462.   Murdoch interest in *Time*: *Financial Times*, 15 June 1989; author's interview
         with John Evans.
463.   Richard Munro on threat of Murdoch: *Wall Street Journal*, 6 March 1989;
         Business Week, 20 March 1989.
463.   Nick Nicholas on global companies: *Wall Street Journal*, 7 March 1989.
463.   Steve Ross on American combinations: *New York Times*, 5 March 1989.
464.   Different characters of the media conglomerates: Smith, *The Age of Behemoths:
         The Globalisation of Mass Media Firms*, pp. 21-39.
465.   Ben Badgdikian, "lords of the global village": the *Nation*, 12 June 1989.
467-70. The account of the Aspen meeting is based on author's interviews with John
         Evans, George Crile, Irwin Stelzer, Eric Beecher and others.
468.   Schwarzenegger and DeVito: *New York Post*, 31 July 1989.
469.   Irwin Stelzer's speech was provided to the author by Rupert Murdoch.

ADELAIDE

471.   Editor of the *Adelaide Review*'s remarks: author's interview.
472.   Original shareholder's bonanza: calculations by Frank Shaw of News Ltd.
472.   Old News journalists at AGM: author's interviews.
472.   News Corp's accountancy methods: the author is grateful to Richard Macdonald,
         Allan Sloan, Glenda Korporaal and Dominic Prince for advice on interpreting
         these figures. He is also grateful to Colin Reader, the treasurer of News Inter-
         national.
473.   "Give me an hour" for *TV Guide* money: Sarazen interview with Ida Picker,
         Institutional Investor, November 1989.
473.   Sarazen's background: *Corporate Finance*, April 1989.
473-4.   Accounting systems: Allan Sloan, *Forbes*, 10 March 1986; also author's inter-
         views with Colin Reader, Allan Sloan and others; *Sydney Morning Herald*, 12
         August 1990.
477-8.   *South China Morning Post* deal: *Far Eastern Economic Review*, 21 and 28 June
         1990.
478.   "Tax Payers or Tax Players?": House of Representatives Standing Committee
         on Finance and Public Administration, Commonwealth Parliament, May 1989.
479-80. Annual General Meeting: author's notes.
480-1.   George Main and Rex Clark remarks: author's interviews.
481.   Murdoch's visit to the *Advertiser*: author's interview with Piers Akerman.
481.   Searby at the Hilton: author's notes.

Source Notes

Chapter 14

THE EVIL EMPIRE

page

482–91.   The story of this journey is based on author's interviews with Rupert and Anna Murdoch, Peter Smith, John Evans, and Rafael Pastore, and Carole Kismaric's interview with Pio Cabanillas.

482–3.   Murdoch's Washington speech: the International Institute of Communications, 1988 annual conference, 15 September 1988. An abridged version was published in *Intermedia*, London, Autumn 1988; Adelaide *Advertiser*, 3 October 1988.

483.   Murdoch on modernization and Americanization: The Wriston lecture, The Manhattan Institute, New York City, 9 November 1989.

485–6.   Murdoch to *Lidove Noviny*: 31 January 1990.

486.   Robert Maxwell and Eastern Europe: Francis Wheen, "Late Show", BBC, 17 January 1990.

487.   Peter Toke and Murdoch: *Spectator*, 13 January 1990.

489.   Murdoch on English-speaking social model: speech at the opening of the Foster's Building, University of Melbourne, Graduate School of Management, 1 October 1991.

489–90.   Berlusconi's background: Smith, *The Age of Behemoths*, pp. 30–4; the *Listener*, 19 July 1990.

LONDON

491.   Australian Ratings on News: *Guardian*, 5 January 1990.

491.   Morgan Stanley on News: research memo by Glenda Korporaal.

491–2.   News Corp's debt: Glenda Korporaal, the *Bulletin*, 5 January 1990; *Wall Street Journal*, 12 April 1990; *The Economist*, 18 August 1990.

492.   Fox and "fin-syn" rules: *Broadcasting*, 5 February 1990: *Independent*, 19 February 1990.

493.   Murdoch on BBC chat show: Terry Wogan, BBC 1, 8 February 1989.

493.   Kelvin MacKenzie's views: *Financial Times, Independent, Guardian*, 19 September 1989.

493.   Murdoch on mustard, and morality: *Washington Post*, 29 October 1989.

494.   Waddington on press: Chippindale and Horrie, "Punter", p. 355.

494.   John Evans on digital world: author's interview.

494–6.   Andrew Knight's appointment and row with Conrad Black: *Financial Times*, 3 January; *Observer*, 7 January; *Daily Telegraph*, 8 January; *Marketing Week*, 12 January 1990; Spectator, 13 and 20 January 1990.

496.   Peregrine Worsthorne's editorial on Andrew Neil and Pamella Bordes; "Playboys and Editors", *Sunday Telegraph*, 19 March 1989.

497.   Andrew Neil and Pamella Bordes: *Independent on Sunday*, 28 January 1989; *Sunday Telegraph*, 28 January 1989; *Sun*, 25 January 1990.

497.   Graham King and *Sunday Times*: author's interview.

498.   Charles Wilson removal: author's interviews; *Independent*, 14 March 1990; *Guardian*, 19 March 1990.

498–9.   Simon Jenkins and *The Times*: author's interviews.

499.   Murdoch and his gamble with Sky: *Financial Times*, 16 October 1989.

499.   *Guardian* on News International's promotion of Sky: 6 January 1990.

499–501.   BSB's problems and launch: *Daily Telegraph*, 23 February 1990; *Independent on Sunday*, 25 March 1990; *Daily Telegraph*, 17 April 1990; *Independent*, 23 April 1990; *Wall Street Journal*, 27 April 1990; *Broadcast*, 4 May 1990.

501–2.   Broadcasting bill debates on Sky and cross-ownership rules: Hansard, House of Lords, 5 June and 11 July 1990; *Sunday Correspondent*, 11 March 1990; *Daily*

Telegraph, 10 May 1990; *The Times*, 10 May 1990; author's interviews with Rupert Murdoch, Jonathan Miller and Edward Bickham of BSB.

502.	Sky-BSB rivalry: *Interspace*, Issue 323; *Financial Times*, 12 August 1990; *Independent*, 23 September 1990; *Financial Times* Survey of British Broadcasting, 16 October 1990.
502.	Banks' warning to BSB: *Sunday Times* magazine, 23 June 1991.
502.	Preliminary talks arranged through John Veronis: Ibid.; author's interview with Frank Barlow, chief executive of Pearson.
502-3.	Max Newton's death: author's interview with Olivia Newton.
503.	Frank Devine on Newton: *The Australian*, 26 July 1990.

THE VILLAGE

The account of News Corp's financial crisis is based on contemporary news accounts and author's interviews with Rupert Murdoch, Ann Lane, Andrew Knight, Dave DeVoe, Colin Reader, William Rhodes and others. Carole Kismaric also conducted extensive interviews with Ann Lane and others.

Excellent published accounts of the crisis on which the author has drawn are "What Murdoch Does Not Want To See", *Business Review Weekly*, 2 November 1990; Stephen Fidler, "Operation Dolphin Rescues Murdoch", *Financial Times*, 4 April 1991; Ida Picker, "Inside the Murdoch Workout", *Institutional Investor*, May 1991.

504.	Murdoch on Kipling: private speech to bank presidents at the International Monetary Conference, Osaka, Japan, 4 June 1991, provided to the author by Rupert Murdoch.
504.	Murdoch on having the year covered: author's interview.
504.	Beginning of News's problems: *Wall Street Journal*, 12 April 1990; *Economist*, 18 August 1990.
505-6.	Murdoch on Standard Chartered Bank: author's interview.
505.	Murdoch on toads and "humble reptilian perspective" and "hopping" on "the risk frontier": speech to bank presidents.
506.	Murdoch merges papers: *Sydney Morning Herald*, 4 October 1990; *Sunday Herald*, Melbourne, 7 October 1990.
507.	Keneally and Beecher on Murdoch: *Sydney Morning Herald*, 19 November 1990, 11 March 1991; *Listener*, 6 December 1990.
507.	Murdoch on Akerman: author's interview.
507-8.	Lane's investigation and prescription: interview with Carole Kismaric.
508-10.	Sky-BSB deal: author's interviews with Rupert Murdoch, Andrew Knight, Frank Barlow, and published accounts, including *Financial Times*, 5 November 1990; *Independent*, 7 November 1990; *Sunday Times* magazine, 23 June 1991.
510.	IBA reaction to BSkyB merger and Lord Thompson's reaction: *Guardian*, 5 November 1990.
511.	*Independent* comment: 14 November 1990.
511-12.	Murdoch on his outstanding achievement: speech to bank presidents.
512.	"Up Yours Delors": *Sun*, 1 November 1990.
512.	News International papers on Mrs Thatcher's fall: 23 November 1990.
513.	Fox's problems: *Business Review Weekly*, Sydney, 2 November 1990; *New York Times*, 20 May 1991.
513-14.	Lane's methods: interviews with Carole Kismaric and author.
515.	Murdoch's "knighthood": *Observer*, 23 and 30 December 1990.
515-16.	"Empire" film: *Variety*, 24 December 1990.
516.	Murdoch criticism of TV film: speech to bankers.
516.	Bill Rhodes interventions: author's interview.
517.	Indian banker hunting: Stephen Fidler, *Financial Times*, 4 April 1991.
517.	End of year crisis: *New York Times*, 20 December 1990.
517.	Andrew Knight on Murdoch and in Aspen: author's interview.
518-21.	January rolls; Stephen Fidler, *Financial Times*, 4 February and 4 April 1991;

author's interviews with Rupert Murdoch, Dave DeVoe, Andrew Knight; Carole Kismaric interview with Ann Lane.

518–19.   Firings at *The Australian*: author's interview with Alastair Diffy.
520.   Sorensen trip to Japan: Carole Kismaric interviews.
522.   Morale at Wapping: author's interviews with News Ltd personnel.
523.   Frank Barlow visit to Arizona: author's interviews with Barlow and Murdoch.
524.   Sale of Murdoch magazines to K3: *New York Times*, 18 March, 26 and 27 April 1991.
524.   Murdoch on being realistic and selling properties: *Forbes*, 2 September 1991.
524–5.   Maxwell and *Daily News*: Allan Sloan and Glen Kessler, *Newsday*, 8 November 1991.
526.   *Super*'s behaviour: *International Herald Tribune*, 21 May 1991; *Newsweek*, 10 June 1991. *Independent*, 6 November 1991; *Wall Street Journal*, 12 November 1991.
526.   Soviet praise for Murdoch; Professor Ya Zassowsky, Dean of Moscow State University, Faculty of Journalism, *Pravda*, 28 May 1990.
527.   Murdoch on Mikhail and Raisa Gorbachev: author's interview; Andrew Knight, *Sunday Times*, 12 May 1991.
527–8.   Murdoch at Kelvin MacKenzie's party: *UK Press Gazette*, 17 June 1991.
528.   Soviet Union joins Intelsat, and "last nail": *Broadcasting Abroad*, October 1991.
528.   Information Revolution and Soviet coup: *Independent*, 24 August 1991.
529.   Murdoch on fall of Soviet Bastille: speech to Melbourne University, 1 October 1991.

Chapter 15

ON THE ROAD

page

531.   News Corp's annual report: *Guardian*, 23 August 1991.
531.   Praise from analysts: *Financial Times*, 5, 6 and 21 October 1991.
532.   Murdoch on News as pin-up boys of banks: *Sunday Telegraph*, 27 October 1991.
532–3.   New refinancing deal: author's interviews with Rupert Murdoch, Ann Lane, Dave DeVoe, Bill Sorensen; *Wall Street Journal*, 22 October 1991.
533–6.   Murdoch's comments on trip to Hartford: author's interview.
537–8.   Diller's comments on plane: author's interview.
538.   December offerings: *Wall Street Journal*, 9 December 1991; author's interview with Dave DeVoe.
540.   Diller's resignation: author's interview; *Wall Street Journal*, 25 February 1992.
541.   World appetite for American films: *Forbes*, 9 December 1991.
542.   Labour threat to Murdoch: *Observer*, 16 February 1992.
542.   *Sun* on immigration: 4 April 1992.
542.   *Sun* and Ghenghis Khan et mob: 8 April 1992.
542.   Murdoch toasting Conservative victory: *Variety*, 13 April 1992.
543.   BSkyB forecasts: *Media Week* 29 May 1992.

Source Notes

Chapter 16

THE VILLAGE

page

544–5. Aspen story: author's interview with attendees at Aspen; *Los Angeles Times*, 23 June 1992.

549. Murdoch on not spending enough time with businesses: author's interview.

549–50. Dame Elisabeth on Murdoch's ultimate aim: *Sydney Morning Herald*, 5 December 1986.

550. Murdoch on his enjoyment, ambition and power: author's interview.

551. Auberon Waugh on Kelvin MacKenzie's power: *Spectator*, 30 May 1992.

552–3. Murdoch on Andrew Neil and republicanism: author's interview.

554–6. Future of the Information Age: Dizard, *The Coming Information Age*, pp. 219–34.

556. Video Empire versus Evil Empire: James Twitchell, *Carnival Culture* (Columbia University Press, New York, 1992), pp. 193–253.

556. Satellites and India: Edward Gargan, *International Herald Tribune*, 31 October 1991.

557. Global appetite for American culture: *Forbes*, 9 December 1991.

557. Murdoch on danger of homogenization: author's interview.

558. Robert Hughes on America: *Time*, 3 February 1992.

558. Video culture and Bill Moyers: Speech to Center for Communications lunch honouring Otis Chandler, 12 March 1992; *International Herald Tribune*, 24 March 1992.

558–9. Murdoch on providing a service: Craig Whitney, *New York Times*, 24 October 1989.

559. John Reith on public broadcasting: Twitchell, *Carnival Culture*, p. 217.

Bibliography

Ashmead-Bartlett, E., *The Uncensored Dardanelles* (Hutchinson, London, 1928)

Baistow, Tom, *Fourth-Rate Estate* (Comedia, London, 1985)

Barber, Lionel and Lawrenson, John, *The Price of Truth: The Story of the Reuters Millions* (Sphere Books, London, 1986)

Bower, Tom, *Maxwell The Outsider* (Mandarin, London, 1991)

Brendon, Piers, *The Life and Death of the Press Barons* (Secker & Warburg, London, 1982)

Cannon, Michael, *The Land Boomers* (Melbourne University Press, Melbourne, 1966)

Carey, John, *The Intellectuals and the Masses* (Faber and Faber, London, 1992)

Carroll, V. J., *The Man Who Couldn't Wait* (Heinemann, Melbourne, 1991)

Chadwick, Paul, *Media Mates* (Macmillan, Melbourne, 1989)

Chippindale, Peter and Horrie, Chris, *Stick it Up Your Punter* (Heinemann, London, 1990)

Cockerell, Michael, Hennessy, Peter and Walker, David, *Sources Close to the Prime Minister* (Macmillan, London, 1984)

Conquest, Robert, *Tyrants and Typewriters* (Hutchinson, London, 1989)

Cooper, William, *Shall We Ever Know? The Trial of the Hosein Brothers for the Murder of Mrs McKay* (Hutchinson, London, 1971)

Coote, Colin R., *Editorial* (Eyre & Spottiswoode, London, 1965)

Cudlipp, Hugh, *Walking on the Water* (Bodley Head, London, 1976)

Curran, James and Seaton, Jean, *Power Without Responsibility – The Press and Broadcasting in Britain* (Routledge, London, 1988)

Dizard Jr, Wilson P., *The Coming Information Age* (Longman, London, 1989)

—— and Swensrud, S. Blake, *Gorbachev's Information Revolution* (Westview Press, Boulder, Colorado, 1987)

Dunkley, Christopher, *Television Today and Tomorrow – Wall to Wall Dallas?* (Penguin Books, Harmondsworth, 1985)

Bibliography

Edgar, Patricia, *The Politics of the Press* (Sun Books, Melbourne, 1979)

Edwards, Robert, *Goodbye Fleet Street* (Jonathan Cape, London, 1988)

Evans, Harold, *Good Times, Bad Times*, (Coronet Books, London, 1984)

Gilder, George, *Microcosm* (Simon & Schuster, New York, 1989)

Giles, Frank, *Sundry Times* (John Murray, London, 1986)

Goodhart, David and Wintour, Patrick, *Eddie Shah and the Newspaper Revolution* (Hodder & Stoughton, London, 1986)

Grose, Roslyn, *The Sun-sation* (Angus & Robertson, London, 1989)

Hall, Richard, *The Secret State: Australia's Spy Industry* (Cassell, Sydney, 1978)

Hamilton, Denis, *Editor-in-Chief* (Hamish Hamilton, London, 1989)

Hammond, Eric, *Maverick* (Weidenfeld & Nicolson, London, 1992)

Harris, Robert, *Gotcha! The Media, The Government and the Falklands Crisis* (Faber and Faber, London, 1983)

— —, *Selling Hitler* (Faber and Faber, London, 1986)

Hearings Before the Committee on Banking, Housing and Urban Affairs, US Senate, 12, 13 May, 1980.

Heren, Louis, *Memories of Times Past* (Hamish Hamilton, London, 1988)

Inglis, K. S., *The Stuart Case* (Melbourne University Press, Melbourne, 1961)

Jacobs, Eric, *Stop Press: The Inside Story of the Times Dispute* (André Deutsch, London, 1980)

Jenkins, Simon, *Newspapers – The Power and the Money*, (Faber and Faber, London, 1979)

— —, *The Market For Glory* (Faber and Faber, London, 1986)

Kiernan, Thomas, *Citizen Murdoch* (Dodd, Mead & Company, New York, 1986)

King, Cecil, *The Cecil King Diary, 1965–70* (Jonathan Cape, London, 1972)

Lamb, Larry, *Sunrise* (Papermac, London, 1989)

Leapman, Michael, *Barefaced Cheek: The Apotheosis of Rupert Murdoch* (Hodder & Stoughton, London, 1983); in the United States as *Arrogant Aussie* (Lyle Stuart Inc, New Jersey, 1985)

— —, *The Last Days of the Beeb* (Allen and Unwin, London, 1986)

MacArthur, Brian, *Eddie Shah, Today and the Newspaper Revolution* (David & Charles, Newton Abbot, 1988)

Melvern, Linda, *The End of the Street* (Methuen, London, 1986)

Munster, George, *Rupert Murdoch: A Paper Prince* (Penguin Books, Ringwood, Victoria, 1987)

Murdoch, Anna, *In Her Own Image* (Collins, London, 1985)

— —, *Family Business* (Collins, London, 1988)

Bibliography

Packer, Clyde, *No Return Ticket* (Angus & Robertson, Sydney, 1984)

Pearl, Cyril, *Wild Men of Sydney* (W. H. Allen, London, 1958)

Pool, Ithiel de Sola, *Technologies of Freedom* (Harvard University Press, 1983)

Porter, Henry, *Lies, Damned Lies and Some Exclusives* (Chatto & Windus, London, 1984)

Postman, Neil, *Amusing Ourselves to Death* (Penguin Books, New York, 1986)

Povich, Maury, *Current Affairs* (G. P. Putnam's Sons, New York, 1991)

Randall, Mike, *The Funny Side of the Street* (Bloomsbury, London, 1988)

Righter, Rosemary, *Whose News Anyway?* (Burnett Books, London, 1978)

Sampson, Anthony, *The Midas Touch* (Hodder & Stoughton, London, 1989)

Seaton, Jean and Curran, James, *Power Without Responsibility – The Press and Broadcasting in Britain* (Routledge, London, 1988)

Smith, Anthony, *Shadows in the Cave* (University of Illinois Press, Champaign, 1973)

— —, *The British Press Since the War – Sources for Contemporary Issues* (David & Charles, Newton Abbot, 1974)

— —, *The Newspaper* (Thames & Hudson, London, 1979)

— —, *The Geopolitics of Information* (Oxford University Press, New York, 1980)

— —, *Goodbye Gutenburg* (Oxford University Press, New York, 1980)

— —, *The Age of Behemoths: The Globalisation of Mass Media Firms* (Twentieth Century Fund, New York, 1991)

Somerfield, S. W., *Banner Headlines* (Scan Books, Shoreham-by-Sea, 1979)

Souter, Gavin, *Company of Heralds* (Melbourne University Press, Melbourne, 1981)

— —, *Heralds and Angels* (Melbourne University Press, Melbourne, 1991)

Stephens, Mitchell, *A History of News* (Viking, New York, 1988)

Stonier, Tom, *The Wealth of Information* (Methuen, London, 1983)

Swanberg, W. A., *Pulitzer* (Charles Scribner's Sons, New York, 1967)

Thompson, Peter and Delano, Anthony, *Maxwell* (Bantam Press, London, 1988)

Thomson, Lord, *After I Was Sixty* (Hamish Hamilton, London, 1975)

Tuccille, Jerome, *Rupert Murdoch* (Donald Fine Inc, New York, 1989)

Twitchell, James B., *Carnival Culture* (Columbia University Press, New York, 1992)

Bibliography

Walker, Mike, *Australia: A History* (Macdonald Optima, London, 1987)

Whitlam, Gough, *The Truth of the Matter* (Penguin Books, Harmondsworth, 1981)

Williams, Valentine, *The World of Action* (Hamish Hamilton, London, 1938)

Wriston, Walter B., *Risk and Other Four-Letter Words* (Harper & Row, New York, 1986)

Zwar, Desmond, *In Search of Keith Murdoch* (Macmillan, Melbourne, 1980)

Acknowledgements

Many people in different countries helped me in the course of the research for this book. Amongst them were John Wilcock in Los Angeles, who also generously provided me with the preliminary research he had done on Murdoch's life; Carole Kismaric in New York; Nick LeQuesne and Alita Naughton in London; Glenda Korporaal, Robert Milliken and Fiona Matthews in Sydney; Marc Champion in Washington and Paul Chadwick in Melbourne. Thomas O'Hanlon in Connecticut sent me a constant, invaluable stream of information and gave me his unpublished manuscript on Murdoch; in London Michael Leapman gave me access to the documents he had collected for his own book on Murdoch, *Barefaced Cheek*.

Within the News Corp empire, Rupert Murdoch was helpful and courteous, as I have noted at the beginning of the book. Amongst his family, so were Anna Murdoch, Dame Elisabeth Murdoch, Helen and Geoff Handbury, and Matt Handbury. Almost everyone at News to whom I asked to give an interview, agreed; some talked on the record, some off. Dorothy Wyndoe, Rupert Murdoch's principal assistant, gave me all possible help.

The idea for the book originally came from Richard E. Snyder and Alice Mayhew, and I am very grateful to them. In London, I was greatly assisted by Carmen Callil and her associates at Chatto and Windus, especially Alison Samuel, who did an extraordinary job of helping me reduce an unwieldy manuscript to a manageable book. Barry Featherstone was unflappable and allowed none of my delays to upset his production process. Lesley Baxter copy-edited with care. In Australia, John Cody of Random House was of great assistance throughout. So were Elaine Greene, Amanda Urban and Lynn Nesbit. Xandra Hardie was generous with suggestions. Lewis Chester gave great help. As usual, John Meakings of American Express arranged my trips with patience and efficiency, and Ken Boys made Qantas very hospitable. Order was kept in my files by Eilean Boniface, and the manuscript was typed and retyped by Coral Pepper.

Amongst those others who either agreed to be interviewed or helped me in different ways, I would like to thank: Piers Akerman, Jonathan Alter, Chris Anderson, Ben Badgdikian, Frank Barlow, Peter Bart, Wendy Beckett, Sally Bedell-Smith, Eric Beecher, Jeff Berg, Don Berry, Christiane Besse, Betty Bienen, Michael Binyon, John Birt, Conrad Black, Ron Boland, Mark Bonham Carter, Tom Bower, David Bowman, Rosie Boycott, John Brademas, Ben Bradlee, Frank Brady, Douglas and Joan Brass, Asa Briggs, Keith Brodie, Patrick Brogan, Les Brown, Gordon Brunton, Kevin and Gail Buckley, John Button, Roderick Carnegie, Vic Caroll, Jean Carr, Sarah Carr, William Carr, Lord Catto, Alexander Chancellor, Ian and Marjorie Chapman, Lewis Chester, Vern Christie, Andrew Clark, Julie Clarke, Michael Cockerell, Barbara Coonole, David Cornwell, John Cowley, Ken Cowley, George Craig, Phillip Crawley, George Crile, Jim Cruthers, Lord Dacre, Blanche d'Alpuget, George Darby, John D'Arcy, Sir James and Lady Darling, Michael Davie, Bill Davies, Richard Davy, Adrian and Gwen Deamer, Marie de Lepervanche, Frank Devine, Dave DeVoe, Alastair Diffy, Barry Diller, Wilson Dizard, Bernard Donoughue, Jessica Douglas-Home, Don Dunstan, Ernie Eban, Fred Emery, Claire Enders, Nora Ephron, Faith Evans, Harold Evans, John Evans, Paul Evans, James Fairfax, Stephen Fay, Helen Feger, Liz Fell, Andrew Fisher, Marc Fisher, Tom Fitzgerald, Douglas Flaherty, Rose Foot, Liz Forgan, Bridget Forster, Glen Frankel, Simon Freeman, Greg Geough, Jim Gerrand, George Gilder, Frank Giles, Anthony Gottlieb, Roy Greenslade, David Greenway, Ros Grose, Phil Gurlach, Richard Hall, Ron Hall, Adrian Hamilton, Christine Hanson, Janet Hawley, Brian Haynes, Gerard Henderson, Seymour Hersh, Ian Hicks, Godfrey Hodgson, Jim Hoge, Anthony Holden, Jeff Hollister, Jonathan Holmes, Anthony Howard, John Howkins, Philip Jacobson, Morton Janklow, Margaret Jay, Peter Jay, the late Peter Jenkins, Simon Jenkins, Andrew Jennings, Roland Joffe, Candace Johnson, Paul Johnson, Paul Kelly,

Acknowledgements

Graham King, Philip Knightley, Donald and Beth Kummerfeld, Ann Lane, Heather Laughton, Roger Laughton, Dominic Lawson, Valerie Lawson, Magnus Linklater, Carol Livingstone, Patty Llosa, Gerald Long, Mike Lynskey, Brian MacArthur, Cal Mac-Crystal, Terry McCrann, Keith McDonald, Ranald and Patricia Macdonald, Richard Macdonald, Doyle MacManus, Michael Marray, Ila Massy Burnside, George Masterman, Melissa Mathis, Linda Melvern, John Menadue, Nelson and Julie Mews, William Meyers, Jonathan Miller, Stephen Milligan, Alex Mitchell, Edward Mortimer, Richard Neville, Olivia Newton, Bruce Page, Bruce Palling, Geneen Parrott, Jeff Penberthy, Ken Phillips, Sir Edward Pickering, Barry Porter, Henry Porter, Maury Povich, Dominic Prince, David Prosser, Robert Pullan, David Puttnam, Sally Quinn, Vera Ranki, Colin Reader, Jane Reed, Richard Reeves, Glen Renfrew, Merv Rich, Elizabeth Riddell, Paul and Marlene Rigby, Rosemary Righter, Nan and Rhyll Rivett, Geoffrey Robertson, Sir Frank Rogers, Lord Roll, George Rosie, Sidney Rubin, Alan Rusbridger, Nigel Ryan, Pierre Salinger, Anthony Sampson, Richard Sarazen, John Scaies, Robert Scheer, Andrew Jay Schwartzman, Richard and Caroline Searby, Richard Sennett, Ross Shackell, David Shaw, Frank Shaw, Brooke Shearer, Stanley Shuman, Victor Shvets, Allan Sloan, Peter and Elizabeth Smark, Peter Smith, Raymond Snoddy, Bob Sorby, Gavin Souter, Jim and Alice Spigelman, Irwin Stelzer, Gerald Stone, Robin Stummer, Max Suich, John Sweeney, Strobe Talbott, Tiziano and Angela Terzani, Daniel Thomas, Peter Thomson, Claire Tomalin, Brian Toohey, Dimity Torbett, Karin Torv, Patricia Tot, Carmel Travis, Neil Travis, Peter Tufo, Malcolm Turnbull, Karel von Wolferin, Brian Walden, Majorie Wallace, Max Walsh, Peter Ward, Chris Warren, Matthew Warren, David Webster, Peter Wilenski, Marion Wilkinson, Donald Wise, Peter Woodward, Walter Wriston, Woodrow Wyatt, Hugo Young, Jules Zanetti.

Above all, I thank Hartley, Conrad and Eleanor Shawcross, and Olga Polizzi for their great patience.

Acknowledgements

PICTURE CREDITS

The author and publishers are grateful to the following for permission to reproduce photographs:
The Herald and Weekly Times, Melbourne (nos. 5 & 23); Ron Boland (nos. 6 & 7); Australian Consolidated Press (no. 8); Hulton Deutsch Collection (nos. 9 & 12); Press Association (nos. 10 & 20); Camera Press/Photo Bill Potter (no. 11); Graham King (no. 13); Olivia Newton (no. 14); Times Newspapers Ltd (nos. 16, 17, 28 & 29); Popperfoto (no. 18); Popperfoto/Reuter (nos. 19 & 21); The Sun (nos. 22a, 22b & 22c); Rex Features/Photo Carrette (no. 24); Tass Photo Library (no. 31); News International (no. 32); TeleFocus/a British Telecom Photograph (back endpaper). Every attempt has been made to trace sources, but in some cases this has proved impossible.

Index

Index

Index

Financial Post, Canada 385–6
Financial Review 117, 367
Financial Times, on Media Partners
461; sought by RM 383–7; and
National Graphical Association
335; on Today negotiations 380
Fininvest 489, 490
Fischer, Gus 522
Fisher, Andrew, Prime Minister 30,
33, 34
Fisher, John 98
Fitzwater, Marlin 393
Flaherty, Doug 107
Fleet Street see Newspaper industry,
Britain
Follett, Ken 436
Foot, Michael 232, 414–15
Football, and BSkyB 543
Forbes magazine 315, 317–18, 387; on
RM 289, 296
Forst, Donald 271–2; on RM 272
Fortune magazine 317; on RM 296–7
Fowler, Mark 325–6, 327, 390, 393;
on RM 326
Fox, William 307–8
Fox Broadcasting 4, 372–3, 492, 536;
RM in charge 540–1, 544
Fox Inc, losses 1988 478, 480; movies
from 517, 536; and Sky 451
Fox Television 317, 421–33; "The
Simpsons" 421–2, 513, 536
Fraser, Malcolm, Prime Minister
169–71
Frayn, Michael 436
Free Church of Scotland 20–1
Freedom of Expression Foundation
389, 390–1
Freeman, John 158
Frost, David 157, 158; interview of
RM 147–8, 158

Gallipoli, and Keith Murdoch 31–6
Gallipoli, film 31
Gambling 202–3; RM liking for 56,
59, 72, 75, 85, 91, 94, 108
Geelong Grammar School, RM at
56–62
Geraghty, Tony 223
Gerbner, George 290
Gibson, Pat 64, 65, 68
Giddy, Harold 77

Gilder, George 292
Giles, Frank 237, 248, 249, 250; and
Falklands War 255; and "Hitler
Diaries" 260–1; on RM 262; sacked
262–3
Gill, Claude, bookshops 434
Gillespie, Bill 341
Glasgow plant, for Sun 334, 357
Glass, John 104
Global village 125, 290, 398–9; and
communist countries 482–3, 529;
and Gulf War 519
Glover, Stephen 356
Godfrey, Arthur 92
Goldenson, Leonard 96, 112, 124, 425
Good Food 402
Gooding, Anthony Simmons 453,
499, 508, 510
Goodman, Lord 179, 277, 376
Gorbachev, Mikhail 293–5, 396, 466,
515, 526–8
Gorbachev, Raisa, memoirs 527
Gorton, John, Prime Minister 128
Gould, Bryan 384
Govett, George 46
Grafton Books 376
Graham, Billy 290, 493
Graham, Katharine 182
Granada Publishing 376
Granada Television 383; and BSB 445,
446; and BSkyB 510, 523
Grant, John 252
Greeley, Horace 175
Greenway, David 273
Greene, Elisabeth see Murdoch,
Elisabeth
Greene, Rupert (grandfather) 20, 46,
54
Greene, Sid, Lord Greene 230
Greene, William Henry (great-
grandfather) 45–6
Groening, Matt 422
Grolier, and Hachette 464
Gross, John 331
Grundy, Bill, on RM 154
Grupo Zeta 455
Guardian, London, comparison with
The Times 337
Guber, Peter 538
Guinness Mahon, and satellite
broadcasting 277

Index

"Information Society" 6–7, 555–6; *see also* Global village
Ingrams, Richard 157
Intelsat 196, 528
Inter-American Satellite Television Inc 274
International Telecommunication Union 197–8
International Thomson Organization 377
Internet, and Russia 528
IPC newspapers 130, 149–50, 151–2
Irvine, Ian 508, 510

Jackson, Professor Derek 131–2, 133, 139, 141–2
James, Clive 179
James, Francis 105
Japanese banks 520
Jenkins, Peter 385
Jenkins, Simon 258–9, 336, 515, 548; editor *The Times* 498–9, 553
John, Elton, *Sun* libel 409, 417
Journalists, *The Australian* 172, 548; and *Chicago Sun-Times* 283–5; and Wapping 345, 346; *see also* National Union of Journalists
Junk bonds 311, 315, 318
Junor, Sir John 212

K3 524
Kalikow, Peter 394
Kaufman, Gerald 72
Kayarem Pty Ltd 479
KDAF, Dallas 317
Keating, Paul 360, 362, 364
Keeler, Christine 145
Kelly, Paul 438, 553
Kempner, Thomas 183
Keneally, Thomas 507
Kennedy, Senator Edward 217–18; criticized by *Boston Herald* 274, 392; and *New York Post* sale 387, 391–3; attacked by RM 391–2, 470
Kennedy, Jack 479
Kerr, Sir John 170–1, 172
Kheel, Ted 183
Kiernan, Thomas 89–90, 297
Kimpton, Miss 53
King, Cecil 73, 130

King, Graham 97–8, 111, 113, 124, 134, 155, 167, 497
Kinnock, Neil, and *Sun* 415, 542
Kinsey Report 80–1
Kipling, Rudyard, quoted by RM 503–4
Kirkpatrick, Jeane 397
Kissinger, Henry 251
Kluge, John Werner 313–17, 326
Knight, Andrew 494–6, 501–2, 509, 510, 517, 522, 523, 554
Koch, Ed 190–1, 268–9, 392
Kommer, Walter 120, 127
Kram, Judge Shirley Wohl 323
Kristol, Irving 545
KRIV, Houston 317
KTTV, Los Angeles 317
Kujau, Konrad 261
Kummerfeld, Donald 267, 283
Kundera, Milan 290
Kupcinet, Irv 284
Kynikos Associates 530

Labor Party, Australian 203–4; *see also* Whitlam, Gough
Labour Party, British 149–50, 382, 384, 511
Lamb, Sir (Albert) Larry 152–3, 166, 210–13, 243; on RM 212
Lambton, Lord 163–4
Lane, Ann 10–12, 14–17, 504, 507–8, 513–14, 517, 520, 524, 532, 539
Lang, Jack 241, 541
Lang, J. T. 48
Lawson, Henry, quoted 28–9
Leapman, Michael 272
Lear, Norman 404
Leasco 150–1, 378
Leist, Jeff 267
Lemann, Nicholas 424–5
Lenin, V. I. 67, 78
Lennon, John, death 230
Levin, Bernard 335, 356
Levin, Gerry 275
Levy, Norma 163–4
Lewis, Anthony 385
Life, sale 524
Lindsay, Joan 55
Linklater, Magnus 233–4, 235, 236, 263
Lippman, Walter 558